PARLIAMENTS AND HUMAN RIGHTS

In many countries today there is a growing and genuinely held concern that the institutional arrangements for the protection of human rights suffer from a 'democratic deficit'. Yet at the same time there appears to be a new consensus that human rights require legal protection and that all branches of the state have a shared responsibility for upholding and realising those legally protected rights. This volume of essays tries to understand this paradox by considering how parliaments have sought to discharge their responsibility to protect human rights. Contributors seek to take stock of the extent to which national and sub-national parliaments have developed legislative review for human rights compatibility, and the effect of international initiatives to increase the role of parliaments in relation to human rights. They also consider the relationship between legislative review and judicial review for human rights compatibility, and whether courts could do more to incentivise better democratic deliberation about human rights. Enhancing the role of parliaments in the protection and realisation of human rights emerges as an idea whose time has come, but the volume makes clear that there is a great deal more to do in all parliaments to develop the institutional structures, processes and mechanisms necessary to put human rights at the centre of their function of making law and holding the government to account. The sense of democratic deficit is unlikely to dissipate unless parliaments empower themselves by exercising the considerable powers and responsibilities they already have to interpret and apply human rights law, and courts in turn pay closer attention to that reasoned consideration.

Volume 5 in the series Hart Studies in Comparative Public Law

Parliaments and Human Rights

Redressing the Democratic Deficit

Edited by

**Murray Hunt
Hayley J Hooper
and
Paul Yowell**

·HART·
PUBLISHING
OXFORD AND PORTLAND, OREGON
2017

Hart Publishing

An imprint of Bloomsbury Publishing Plc

Hart Publishing Ltd
Kemp House
Chawley Park
Cumnor Hill
Oxford OX2 9PH
UK

Bloomsbury Publishing Plc
50 Bedford Square
London
WC1B 3DP
UK

www.hartpub.co.uk
www.bloomsbury.com

Published in North America (US and Canada) by
Hart Publishing
c/o International Specialized Book Services
920 NE 58th Avenue, Suite 300
Portland, OR 97213-3786
USA

www.isbs.com

HART PUBLISHING, the Hart/Stag logo, BLOOMSBURY and the Diana logo are trademarks of Bloomsbury Publishing Plc

First published in hardback, 2015
Paperback edition, 2017

British Library Cataloguing-in-Publication Data
A catalogue record for this book is available from the British Library.

ISBN: PB: 978-1-50991-545-3
HB: 978-1-84946-561-8

Typeset by Compuscript Ltd, Shannon
Printed and bound in Great Britain by
Lightning Source UK Ltd

To find out more about our authors and books visit www.hartpublishing.co.uk. Here you will find extracts, author information, details of forthcoming events and the option to sign up for our newsletters.

For my mother, Jean Hunt and in memory of my father, Bob Hunt, 1935–2013

MH

For my parents, William and Lorna Hooper

HJH

For my parents, Ken and Carol Yowell

PY

Foreword

It is a huge privilege and pleasure to be able to write a few words of appreciation and endorsement for this volume of essays. I believe that this book will be of enormous value to all of those interested in human rights, in modern legislatures, and the relationship between the two. As this is absolutely fundamental to the character and credibility of democracy, academic insight of this sort is especially welcome. This is an area where I expect there to be an ever-expanding community of interest.

It is particularly significant for me to be able to report that the UK Parliament is now far more institutionally attuned to these important issues than it was in the relatively recent past. The creation of the Joint Committee on Human Rights was something of an experiment, consisting as it does of members of both the House of Commons and House of Lords and operating on a distinctly cross-party basis. Since its inception in 2001 it has proved an immensely significant actor in three areas of parliamentary activity. These are: scrutinising laws; undertaking thematic inquiries—deep and long-term studies—into areas of government policy, frequently cutting across Whitehall departments in their scope and, finally, shorter inquiries on urgent matters with evidence sessions.

It seems to me that this agenda is at the very heart of what a modern Parliament should aspire to do. In all of our work we need to engage in serious scrutiny of the executive, we need to show the capacity to think beyond the four or five-year electoral cycle and we need to demonstrate the ability and the agility to deal with matters which have suddenly become a matter of public concern. I am delighted to see from the chapters assembled here that these are international legislative objectives. The cause of human rights is and will be much enhanced by the entrenchment of this trend.

The Rt Hon John Bercow MP
Speaker
House of Commons

Preface and Acknowledgements

This book grew out of a research project on *Parliaments and Human Rights* which was generously funded by the Arts and Humanities Research Council (AHRC) in 2011–12. The project had two broad aims. The first was to assess how, if at all, debate about human rights in the UK Parliament had changed over the 10-year period between the setting up of the UK's first parliamentary human rights committee, the Joint Committee on Human Rights, in 2000 and the end of the 2005–10 Parliament in May 2010. The second was to assess whether and, if so, to what extent courts have considered parliamentary debates about human rights when deciding human rights compatibility issues previously considered by Parliament. The project's findings were published in an AHRC research paper, *Parliaments and Human Rights: Redressing the Democratic Deficit* (AHRC Public Policy Series No 5, April 2012)[1] and were presented at a two-day AHRC conference of the same title held in London on 17 and 18 April 2012.

The research paper was intended to provide the necessary empirical findings to enable participants at the conference to take stock of the role that the UK Parliament already plays in relation to human rights and of the courts' current approach to that role.[2] The purpose of the conference, however, was not merely to disseminate those findings, but to consider their practical implications and identify some concrete practical recommendations which flow from them, in keeping with the AHRC's strategic priority of enhancing the impact of arts and humanities research on the development of public policy and public services. The conference therefore brought together a wide range of practitioners and scholars with relevant expertise, from both the UK and abroad and from a range of professional and academic disciplines, to identify practical ways in which parliaments everywhere can play a more active role in the protection and realisation of human rights, and to consider how courts, in turn, could respond to such an enhanced role for parliaments. The aim was to connect current practice in parliaments and courts with relevant current debates in legal and political theory, in the conviction that the impact of academic research is greatest when practice is informed by theory and vice versa. To that end, the format of the two-day conference was designed with a more theoretical emphasis on the first day and a more practical emphasis on the second day, held in the Palace of Westminster, but with many delegates taking part on both days.

---

[1] Available on the AHRC website http://www.ahrc.ac.uk/News-and-Events/Publications/Documents/Parliaments-and-Human-Rights.pdf.

[2] The research generated a downloadable and searchable database of parliamentary and judicial references to Parliament's Joint Committee on Human Rights which is also available on the AHRC website: http://www.ahrc.ac.uk/What-We-Do/Strengthen-research-impact/Inform-public-policy/Documents/Parliament-Human-Rights-table-of-reference.pdf (parliamentary references) and http://www.ahrc.ac.uk/What-We-Do/Strengthen-research-impact/Inform-public-policy/Documents/Human-Rights-Courts-table.pdf (judicial references).

We were extremely fortunate to attract a very distinguished cast of speakers and an equally distinguished audience, including academics from the fields of law, politics, philosophy and history; members of the House of Commons and the House of Lords; senior civil servants and parliamentary officials; judges; journalists; and practising lawyers. This volume is largely based on papers which were presented for the first time at the conference and subsequently revised for publication. It also includes some other contributions which were not presented at the conference, but which the editors subsequently invited in order to improve the book's coverage of the principal themes which emerged during discussion at the conference. We are grateful to all our contributors for the hard work they put into their contribution and for their good-natured and efficient responses to our editorial queries, and above all for their forbearance in enduring patiently what turned out to be the book's unavoidably long gestation. Invidious as it is to single any out for special mention, Murray would like to acknowledge the debt he has built up over many years to David Dyzenhaus and Andrew Drzemczewski, whose influence on this project will be apparent to all who are familiar with their life's work. He would also like to thank Lois McNay for all the support which made it possible to see the project through.

We would like to thank the AHRC for funding the original research project and the conference at the end of it, and in particular Ben Gibbons for his far-sighted approach to public policy impact; Professor Rick Rylance and Susan Amor; Sam Roythorne for her organisational skills and unflappable nature; Philip Pothen and Jake Gilmore for their shrewd advice on communications; Graham Raikes for opening the conference; and Professor Andrew Thompson for his professional historian's ability to make our research seem much more interesting by connecting it to a fascinating historical canvas.

We are grateful to all those who spoke on different panels at the conference, and in particular Professor Francesca Klug of the London School of Economics; Professor Danny Nicol of the University of Westminster; the Rt Hon Sir Stephen Sedley, former Lord Justice of Appeal and now Visiting Professor at the University of Oxford; Professor Richard Bellamy of University College London (UCL); Dr Hywel Francis MP, Chair of the Joint Committee on Human Rights; the Rt Hon Lord McNally, then Minister of State with responsibility for Human Rights in the Ministry of Justice; Christopher Chope MP, the then Chair of the Committee on Legal Affairs and Human Rights in the Parliamentary Assembly of the Council of Europe (PACE); Almut Wittling-Vogel, Representative of the Federal Government of Germany for Matters Relating to Human Rights; Professor Erik Jurgens, former Member of the Netherlands Parliament and first rapporteur on the implementation of decisions of the European Court of Human Rights for the PACE Committee on Legal Affairs and Human Rights; Marie-Louise Bemelmans-Videc, former member of the PACE Committee on Legal Affairs and Human Rights and former Chair of the Sub-Committee on the Election of Judges and Sub-Committee on Human Rights; Professor Tony Wright, Professor of Government and Public Policy at UCL and former Chair of the Public Administration Select Committee of the House of Commons; the Rt Hon Alan Beith MP, Chair of the House of Commons Justice Committee and the Liaison Committee; Professor Lord Norton of Louth, member and former Chair of the House of Lords Constitution Committee; and Professor

Robert Hazell, Director of the Constitution Unit at UCL. We are also grateful to all those who contributed to the discussion at the conference, and to Julia Lowis, who provided invaluable research assistance during the project and produced a very useful note of the discussions at the conference.

We would like to thank the team at Hart Publishing, Rachel Turner, Mel Hamill, Tom Adams and Jo Ledger, who were all models of patience and efficiency; our scrupulous but anonymous copy editor who saved us from many errors and infelicities; and, last but by no means least, Richard Hart and Jane Parker who moved on from Hart Publishing at the end of April this year, having created, in just 17 years, one of the most successful and principled legal publishers in the world. Had our manuscript been delivered on time, one of us might have earned the unique honour of becoming a pair of Hart bookends, as the author of Richard and Jane's first and last published book. Alas, that was not to be.

Murray Hunt
Hayley J Hooper
Paul Yowell
Oxford, December 2014

Contents

PART VII: A DEMOCRATIC CULTURE OF JUSTIFICATION

List of Contributors

Bruce Adamson is Legal Officer at the Scottish Human Rights Commission.

Thomas Bull is Judge of the Supreme Administrative Court of Sweden and was formerly Professor of Constitutional Law at the University of Uppsala.

Lisa Burton is Research Assistant at the Gilbert + Tobin Centre of Public Law, Faculty of Law, University of New South Wales.

Iain Cameron is Professor of Public International Law at the University of Uppsala.

Colin Caughey is Policy Worker at the Northern Ireland Human Rights Commission.

Alice Donald is Senior Research Fellow at Middlesex University.

Andrew Drzemczewski is a Barrister and is Head of the Legal Affairs and Human Rights Department, Parliamentary Assembly of the Council of Europe, Strasbourg.

David Dyzenhaus is Professor of Law and Philosophy at the University of Toronto.

David Feldman is Rouse Ball Professor of English Law at the University of Cambridge.

Sandra Fredman is Rhodes Professor of the Laws of the British Commonwealth and the United States at the University of Oxford.

Janet Hiebert is Professor of Political Studies at Queen's University.

Hayley J Hooper is Junior Research Fellow at Homerton College, University of Cambridge.

Murray Hunt is a Barrister, Legal Adviser to the Joint Committee on Human Rights of the UK Parliament, and a Visiting Professor of Law at the University of Oxford.

Aileen Kavanagh is Fellow in Law at St Edmund Hall, University of Oxford.

Jeff King is Senior Lecturer in Law at University College London and Attorney at the Bar of New York.

David Kinley is Professor in Human Rights Law, Sydney Law School, University of Sydney and Academic Panel Member, Doughty Street Chambers, London.

Martin Kuijer is senior adviser on human rights law to the Minister of Security and Justice and is Professor of Human Rights at the VU University Amsterdam.

George Kunnath is the former Programme Director of the Westminster Consortium Parliamentary Programme.

Liora Lazarus is Fellow in Law at St Anne's College, University of Oxford.

Philip Leach is Professor of Human Rights Law at Middlesex University.

Julia Lowis is a Barrister and Member of Middle Temple.

Angela Patrick is a Barrister and Director of Human Rights Policy at JUSTICE, the UK branch of the International Commission of Jurists.

Kent Roach is Professor of Law at the University of Toronto.

David Russell is Deputy Director of the Northern Ireland Human Rights Commission and a non-executive director of the Northern Ireland Community Relations Council.

Ingeborg Schwarz is the former Director of the Inter-Parliamentary Union (IPU) Human Rights Programme.

Ann Sherlock is Lecturer in Law at the University of Aberystwyth.

Natasha Simonsen is Lecturer in Law at St Anne's College, University of Oxford.

George Williams is a Barrister and Anthony Mason Professor, Scientia Professor and Foundation Director at Gilbert + Tobin Centre of Public Law, Faculty of Law, University of New South Wales.

Paul Yowell is Fellow in Law at Oriel College, University of Oxford.

1

Introduction

MURRAY HUNT[1]

T HE IDEA THAT human rights suffer from a 'democratic deficit' is now
a commonplace in both popular and political discourse. Arguments about
the proper relationship between human rights and democracy are of course
nothing new, but for some years now the disquiet expressed by some about the
democratic legitimacy of human rights has been rising steadily into a chorus. Today
in the UK there are many voices in the mainstream media and politics that directly
question the democratic pedigree of our institutional arrangements for protecting
and promoting human rights, complaining with growing urgency that the decisions
of democratically elected representatives are being overridden by unelected and
unaccountable judges.

Yet recent years have also seen the emergence of a new consensus about the need
for some form of legal protection for human rights, even in advanced democratic
states, and about the responsibility of all branches of the state for upholding those
rights. Critics of the European Court of Human Rights often defend the European
Convention on Human Rights itself, and critics of the UK's Human Rights Act
advocate in its place a UK Bill of Rights to provide legal protection for indigenous
human rights, with a role for courts as well as parliaments. In academic debates,
the long-running schism within constitutionalism between so-called 'political constitutionalists' on the one hand, who oppose a role for courts in the institutional
arrangements for protecting human rights, and 'legal constitutionalists' on the
other, advocating strong judicial powers to protect human rights against the political branches, has largely given way to a marked convergence around a compromise
position in which each school of thought increasingly accommodates the criticisms of
the other and agrees that there is a shared institutional responsibility for upholding
human rights.

So there is a paradox: just as there emerges a clear consensus that both courts
and parliament have a legitimate role to play in relation to legally protected human
rights, there is also a resurgence of the democratic critique of courts, and not merely
from those who lost the argument against legal protection. Attempting to understand this paradox is the point of departure for this collection. Why is an emerging
consensus about the desirability of legal protection for human rights, and a shared

[1] Thanks to David Dyzenhaus and Dawn Oliver for their invaluable comments on a draft of this Introduction.

institutional responsibility for that protection, accompanied by new levels of dissensus about whether courts or parliaments should have the final say on questions of human rights? Are the two connected? To begin to solve this puzzle, we need to think, first, about whether there really is a 'democratic deficit' in the current institutional arrangements for protecting human rights and, if so, precisely what the nature of any such democratic deficit is. Have courts been given, or arrogated to themselves, too much power or are parliaments failing to empower themselves by exercising the considerable powers and responsibilities that they already have to interpret and apply human rights in the laws they make and when holding the government to account? For debate about that question to be informed by reality rather than determined by preconceived theoretical and political prejudices, we need to take stock of how far legislative review for human rights compatibility has developed in those legal systems where it has taken root and to consider what scope there is for further developing this still relatively novel form of institutional protection for human rights.

To escape the confines of this paradox and to move on from the tired old debate about whether courts or parliament should have the final say on human rights, it may be necessary to revisit some of the received wisdom about the respective roles of our institutions in relation to human rights and to reconceive of our institutional arrangements in terms of a 'democratic culture of justification' rather than a contest between competing claims to supremacy by both the courts and parliament. A democratic culture of justification is a political and legal order based on a shared responsibility for protecting and promoting human rights, in which all action or inaction affecting human rights must be justified by publicly available reasons which are scrutinised in both parliament and the courts for compatibility with society's most fundamental commitments, and in which each of those institutions devises ways of respecting the legitimate role of the other.

Rethinking our institutional arrangements around this powerful idea gives rise to a number of practical questions which demand answers from all parts of our institutional machinery concerned with human rights. Are there steps which governments and parliaments can take to increase the involvement of the democratic branches in deliberation about human rights and in specifying the detailed framework for their protection and realisation? Can and should courts do more to incentivise such increased democratic deliberation about human rights by governments and parliaments? What are the implications for judicial review of legislation for human rights compatibility where both the government and parliament have conducted their own comprehensive and properly advised assessment of a law's compatibility with human rights obligations?

The serious and genuinely held concerns which animate the democratic critique of human rights can then be considered in that context in order to assess the extent to which those concerns can be accommodated within the existing legal and institutional framework for the protection of human rights. What scope is there, in particular, to increase and enhance the role of parliaments, and thereby assuage democratic concerns, within the existing human rights framework including the European Convention on Human Rights (ECHR) and the UN system?

These are some of the most important questions with which the contributions to this volume attempt to grapple. This Introduction does not seek to summarise the wide range of views about those questions on offer in these chapters; it merely seeks to set the scene for the discussion by exploring some of the principal themes. In some of the answers that begin to emerge from that discussion, it is possible to make out the contours of a democratic culture of justification, and the final chapter in this volume will seek to identify some of the questions on which future thinking and research are urgently required in order to accelerate progress towards the full realisation of that emerging paradigm of democratic human rights protection.

I. THE DEMOCRATIC CRITIQUE

In the UK today, decisions of both the European Court of Human Rights and of UK courts under the Human Rights Act are frequently criticised, by both commentators in the media and elected politicians from across the political spectrum, for being profoundly 'undemocratic'. The examples are well known to everyone with an interest in human rights and are too numerous to catalogue, but it is worth reminding ourselves of exactly what has been said in relation to some of the more high-profile cases to try to understand the precise nature of the concerns which lie behind this sustained criticism.

When the European Court ruled that the UK would be in breach of the ECHR if it deported the radical Islamist preacher Abu Qatada to Jordan when there was a real risk that he would be tried there on the basis of evidence obtained by torture,[2] the decision was the subject of the strongest criticism in both the media and Parliament. The Home Secretary, for example, said in Parliament that the Government 'disagree vehemently with Strasbourg's ruling', which was 'simply not acceptable', and the Government was therefore continuing to consider the case for a British Bill of Rights as well as attempting to reform the European Court of Human Rights.[3] When Abu Qatada was finally deported, following the conclusion of a new international treaty between the UK and Jordan specifically addressing the European Court's concerns, the Home Secretary told the House of Commons that one of the lessons to be learned from the case was that:

> We have to do something about the crazy interpretation of our human rights laws ... I have made clear my view that in the end the Human Rights Act must be scrapped. We must also consider our relationship with the European Court very carefully, and I believe that all options—including withdrawing from the Convention altogether—should remain on the table.[4]

---

[2] *Othman v UK* (2012) 55 EHRR 1.

[3] HC Deb 7 February 2012, cols 165–66. In April 2013 the Home Secretary told the House of Commons 'as any sane observer of this case will conclude, it is absurd for the deportation of a suspected foreign terrorist to take so many years and cost the taxpayer so much money. That is why we need to make sense of our human rights laws': HC Deb 24 April 2013, col 888.

[4] Rt Hon Theresa May MP, Home Secretary, HC Deb 8 July 2013, c 24. The proposed reconsideration of the UK's relationship with the European Court of Human Rights should be seen in the wider context of the UK's reconsideration of its relationship with Europe generally: see, eg, Rt Hon Theresa May MP in the Commons debate on the Government's decision to opt out of 130 EU Justice and Home Affairs measures, HC Deb 15 July 2013 c 700 at c 773 (describing it as 'totally unacceptable' that the Court contradicts laws passed by the UK Parliament).

When the European Court of Human Rights decided that, for 'whole life tariffs' to be compatible with the ECHR, there must be a mechanism in UK law which gives the possibility of review,[5] the decision attracted the same charge from Government ministers and others that it was anti-democratic. The Justice Secretary took to the media to denounce the judgment, writing that the 'misguided' ruling 'underlines the need for urgent change. We need to curtail the role of the European Court of Human Rights in the UK. The days when it could interfere with the settled wishes of the British Parliament and people must end'.[6] The Prime Minister said that he 'profoundly disagrees'[7] with the decision and the Home Secretary agreed with the concern expressed by a former Minister for Policing that the decision 'will take away from this House of Commons and our own courts the decision on the crucial matter of whether life should mean life'.[8] Dominic Raab MP described the decision as 'an attack on democracy' which showed the 'warped moral compass' of the Strasbourg Court:[9] 'UK democratic accountability over our criminal justice system is yet again being threatened by the insatiable appetite of the Strasbourg Court. Parliament must rebuff any further mission creep from these unaccountable European judges.'[10] The same criticism echoed across the political spectrum: a former Labour Home Secretary said that his Government had changed the law in 2003 so that life really means life in relation to those who have committed the most heinous crimes and 'it is the right of the British Parliament to determine the sentence of those who have committed such crimes'.[11]

Most famously of all, the decision of the European Court of Human Rights nearly 10 years ago[12] that the UK's ban on convicted prisoners voting is a disproportionate interference with the right to vote in the ECHR[13] has drawn virulently expressed condemnation, again from across the political spectrum, with the Prime Minister, for example, saying that it made him 'physically ill even to contemplate having to give the vote to anyone who is in prison'.[14] Uniquely in the history of the UK's participation in the European Convention system, the judgment has provoked defiance from the Government, with the Prime Minister telling Parliament that prisoners would not be getting the vote under his Government[15] and receiving widespread political and popular support for that position.

---

[5] *Vinter and others v UK* (App Nos 66069/09, 130/10, 3896/10) (9 July 2013) [GC].
[6] 'This Meddling in Our Affairs Must Stop Now, Says Justice Secretary Chris Grayling', *Mail Online* (9 July 2013) www.dailymail.co.uk/news/article-2359065/This-meddling-affairs-stop-says-Justice-Secretary-CHRIS-GRAYLING.html#ixzz2fiv5OKhf.
[7] Downing Street Press Briefing (9 July 2013: Morning), available at: www.gov.uk/government/news/press-briefing-afternoon-9-july-2013.
[8] Rt Hon Theresa May MP, Home Secretary, responding to a question from Nick Herbert MP, HC Deb 9 July 2013, c 187.
[9] Dominic Raab MP, quoted in 'Ministers Angry at European Whole-Life Tariffs Ruling', *BBC News* (9 July 2013) www.bbc.co.uk/news/uk-23245254.
[10] 'Murderer Lodges First "Whole Life" Appeal in Wake of European Human Rights Ruling', *Daily Telegraph* (20 August 2013).
[11] Rt Hon David Blunkett MP, quoted in 'Ministers Angry at European Whole-Life Tariffs Ruling' (n 9).
[12] *Hirst v UK (No 2)* [2005] ECHR 681.
[13] ECHR Article 3, Protocol 1.
[14] HC Deb 3 November 2010, col 921.
[15] David Cameron, speech given on 13 December 2013, Darlington.

Such attacks on court decisions about human rights on democratic grounds cannot be fully explained by concerns about foreign interference with national sovereignty, as they have not been confined to decisions of the European Court of Human Rights. When the UK Supreme Court ruled that the law concerning the Sex Offenders Register was in breach of the right to respect for private life to the extent that it failed to provide an opportunity for independent review of the indefinite requirement to be on the Register,[16] condemnation of the decision came from the highest levels of Government, again on democratic grounds. The Prime Minister said 'how completely offensive it is, once again, to have a ruling by a court that flies in the face of common sense'[17] and the Home Secretary said: 'The Government is appalled by the ruling ... It is time to assert that it is Parliament that makes our laws, not the courts; that the rights of the public come before the rights of criminals; and, above all, that we have a legal framework that brings sanity to cases such as these.'[18] Decisions of UK courts on the deportation of foreign nationals, and in particular foreign national prisoners, have provoked equally impassioned criticisms, with politicians accusing the courts of driving a coach and horses through the system of immigration control by ignoring Parliament and interpreting the right to respect for private and family life in Article 8 ECHR as if it were an absolute right.[19]

Moreover, these criticisms are not confined to the media and politicians—they are also voiced by a number of distinguished legal practitioners, including several members of the Commission on a Bill of Rights, and some (though fewer) academics.[20] While the precise target of the criticism varies (sometimes it is the European Court of Human Rights, sometimes the Court of Justice of the European Union, while sometimes it is courts generally, including our own Supreme Court), the common thread running through this critique is that democracy is being subverted by courts: the democratic will of Parliament is being thwarted by the decisions of unelected and unaccountable judges applying human rights laws.

In one sense, such criticisms of courts by elected politicians for making human rights decisions which are 'undemocratic' are nothing new. It is well known that when the European Court of Human Rights ruled in 1995 that the UK had breached

---

[16] *R (F and Thompson) v Home Secretary* [2010] UKSC 17.

[17] HC Deb 16 February 2011, col 955.

[18] HC Deb 16 February 2011, col 961. The Government complied with the judgment by introducing the Sex Offenders Remedial Order Sexual Offences Act 2003 (Remedial) Order 2012, SI 1883/2012. The Order was improved during its consideration in Parliament by the addition of a right of access to a court, following criticism of the draft Order by the Joint Committee on Human Rights: Nineteenth Report of Session 2010–12, *Proposal for the Sexual Offences Act 2003 (Remedial) Order 2011*, HL Paper 200/HC 1549.

[19] See, eg, the political response to the decisions of the immigration judge and Upper Tribunal (*Secretary of State for the Home Department v Respondent* [2010] UKUT B1) quashing on Article 8 grounds the Home Secretary's decision to deport Aso Mohammed Ibrahim, who had been convicted several years earlier of failing to stop after a traffic accident in which a young girl was killed; the debate on the Government's changes to the Immigration Rules HC Deb 19 June 2012, cols 760–823; and the debate on the Immigration Bill 2013.

[20] See, eg, Michael Pinto-Duschinsky, *Bringing Rights Back Home: Making Human Rights Compatible with Parliamentary Democracy in the UK* (Policy Exchange, 2011) and some contributors to Sceptical Essays (below n 45).

the right to life of the suspected IRA members shot dead in Gibraltar,[21] the then Home Secretary Michael Howard sought to persuade the Cabinet to withdraw from the European Convention in protest at the decision. Examples of similar controversies arising from judicial decisions about human rights could be found for most of the intervening years since then. In recent years, however, they have reached a new intensity and, as will be seen later in this Introduction, such concerns about democratic legitimacy have begun to shape the intergovernmental agenda considering reforms to the international machinery for the protection of human rights, in the Council of Europe, the EU and the United Nations (UN).

What are we to make of this resurgence of the forceful critique from democracy? Some prefer to dismiss it as a cover for hostility towards the very idea of human rights, or for a backward-looking nationalism that rejects all of the many ways in which national sovereignty has been pooled by modern states for their mutual benefit. Such critics would argue that any attempt to engage constructively with the critique is fraught with danger because it lends a spurious respectability to views which conceal their darker motives. But the very essence of a commitment to constitutionalism is to strive to uncover and articulate the potential for agreement about the fundamentals which constitute the arrangements by which societies govern themselves.[22] The critique from democracy cannot simply be dismissed out of hand if we wish to escape the paralysing confines of the paradox identified above. The intuitive appeal of the democratic critique must be acknowledged, the reasons for its appeal identified and rigorously analysed, and its criticisms constructively engaged with. The starting point for doing so, it is suggested, is to situate it firmly in the context of a clearly emerging consensus, at both the national and international levels, about both the necessity of legal protection for human rights and the shared responsibility of all branches of government to protect and promote human rights as an integral part of states' commitment to the rule of law.

II. THE EMERGING CONSENSUS

Until fairly recent times, human rights and democracy were often considered to be in opposition to each other. The legal protection of human rights was considered by many to be undemocratic because of the power it gave to unelected judges to interfere with the laws made by democratic parliaments. Today, however, there is a clear consensus, both nationally and internationally, that human rights have a constitutive role to play in democracies,[23] and that a democratic state's commitment to the

---

[21] *McCann v UK* (1995) 21 EHRR 97.

[22] *Cf* David Feldman's different perspective in *Law in Politics, Politics in Law* (Oxford, Hart Publishing, 2013) 261 that 'democracy and constitutions are not about securing agreement. They are concerned with managing disagreement'.

[23] See, eg, Lord Bingham in the *Belmarsh* case: *A v Home Secretary (No 1) 'Belmarsh'* [2004] UKHL 56 [42]: 'I do not in particular accept the distinction ... between democratic institutions and the courts. It is of course true that the judges in this country are not elected and are not answerable to Parliament. It is also of course true ... that Parliament, the executive and the courts have different functions. But the function of independent judges charged to interpret and apply the law is universally recognised as a cardinal feature of the modern democratic state, a cornerstone of the rule of law itself.'

rule of law necessarily entails an obligation to provide effective legal protection for human rights.[24] While legal theorists may continue to argue over substantive and formal conceptions of the rule of law, the argument is over as far as political actors and international institutions are concerned. A strong preference for the substantive over the formal conception of the rule of law was expressed by Lord Bingham in his influential book *The Rule of Law*, in which he rejected Joseph Raz's formalist conception in favour of a 'thick' definition of the concept, embracing the protection of human rights within its scope.[25] This is a view now shared by the UN General Assembly,[26] the UN Office of the High Commissioner for Human Rights,[27] the European Commission,[28] the Council of Europe[29] and the European Commission for Democracy through Law (the 'Venice Commission').[30] This striking international consensus is also reflected in the framework used by the World Justice Project to measure progress towards achieving the rule of law across the world.[31]

In addition to this clear consensus that legal protection for human rights is an integral part of a state's commitment to the rule of law, there also appears to be an emerging consensus that responsibility for upholding and promoting both the rule of law and human rights is no longer the exclusive preserve of the judiciary, but rather is shared between all the institutions of the state, including parliament and the executive.[32] This international consensus is evident, for example, in the UN General

[24] Australia, however, remains outside this consensus, continuing to prefer an exclusively parliamentary model of rights protection: see Williams and Burton, ch 12 in this volume.

[25] T Bingham, *The Rule of Law* (London, Allen Lane, 2010) 67: 'A state which savagely represses or persecutes sections of its people cannot in my view be regarded as observing the rule of law, even if the transport of the persecuted minority to the concentration camp or the compulsory exposure of female children on the mountain-side is the subject of detailed laws duly enacted and scrupulously observed.'

[26] Declaration of the High-Level Meeting of the General Assembly on the Rule of Law at the National and International Levels, UN General Assembly Resolution A/67/L.1 (19 September 2012), para 5 (reaffirming that 'human rights, the rule of law and democracy are interlinked and mutually reinforcing').

[27] Statement by Ms Navanethem Pillay, High Commissioner for Human Rights, at the High-Level Meeting on the Rule of Law at the National and International Level, (New York, 24 September 2012): the rule of law is 'the backbone of legal protection of human rights'.

[28] Communication from the Commission to the European Parliament and the Council, *A New EU Framework to Strengthen the Rule of Law*, COM (2014) 158 Final (11 March 2014), Annex 1: The Rule of Law as a Foundational Principle of the Union, recognising respect for fundamental rights as being amongst the fully justiciable principles of the European Union with their source in the rule of law.

[29] In 2007 the Parliamentary Assembly of the Council of Europe, concerned by the prevalence of a formalistic conception of the rule of law in some of the emerging democracies in Eastern Europe, passed a resolution making clear that the rule of law is a substantive legal concept: 'The Principle of the Rule of Law' Resolution 1594 (2007).

[30] Report on the Rule of Law adopted by the Venice Commission at its 86th Plenary Session (25–26 March 2011) CDL-AD(2011)003Rev.

[31] *Rule of Law Index 2014*, World Justice Project. One of the four universal principles which make up the notion of the rule of law used by the Project to measure how the rule of law is experienced by ordinary people across the world is that 'the laws ... protect fundamental rights'. 'Under the rule of law, fundamental rights must be effectively guaranteed. A system of positive law that fails to respect core human rights established under international law is at best "rule by law". Rule of law abiding societies should guarantee the rights embodied in the Universal Declaration of Human Rights.'

[32] See eg Dawn Oliver, 'Parliament and the Courts: A Pragmatic (or Principled) Defence of the Sovereignty of Parliament' in A Horne, G Drewry and D Oliver (eds), *Parliament and the Law* (Oxford, Hart Publishing, 2014), referring to 'a pragmatic recognition by politicians and the courts that the functioning of the British system imposes responsibility for the Constitution and the rule of law on every organ of state rather than ... solely or primarily in the hands of a Supreme or Constitutional Court.'

Assembly's recent Declaration on the Rule of Law, in which states recognised 'the essential role of parliaments in the rule of law at the national level'.[33] The journey to that international recognition can be traced through a number of landmark statements, such as the Commonwealth Principles on the Three Branches of Government, which state that 'judiciaries and parliaments should fulfil their respective but critical roles in the promotion of the rule of law in a complementary and constructive manner',[34] and, as will be seen in Part V of this book,[35] in various Council of Europe statements increasingly stressing the importance of the role of parliaments in giving effect to the ECHR.[36] It should come as no surprise, of course, since Parliament, as part of the state, has always shared with all the other organs of the state (including both the executive and the judiciary) the obligations to respect, protect and fulfil the human rights to which the state has bound itself by international treaty to respect and protect. What is significant, however, is the prominence now being given to this fact in international statements and the corresponding increase in international initiatives to increase the role of parliaments in relation to human rights, which is considered in Part V of this book.

As David Dyzenhaus explains in his chapter,[37] this emerging consensus about both the need for legal protection of human rights and the shared institutional responsibility for their protection is also increasingly reflected in the relevant academic debates. Political constitutionalists have traditionally been opposed to the legal protection of human rights because it necessarily accords a role to courts in the interpretation of those rights and, in a democracy, such interpretation should be the exclusive preserve of the democratically elected legislature. Political constitutionalists have therefore tended to be the strongest proponents of parliamentary models of rights protection in which legislatures, rather than courts, carry out a review of legislation for compatibility with human rights. In the US, for example, Jeremy Waldron has consistently argued that legislatures are better than courts at the sort of moral reasoning required by bills of rights,[38] and Mark Tushnet argued for the Constitution to be taken away from the courts;[39] in Canada, Janet Hiebert has argued for recognition of a distinctive parliamentary model of rights protection from a similar starting point;[40] while in Australia, Tom Campbell, Jeffrey Goldsworthy and Adrienne Stone have also argued consistently in favour of the

---

[33] Declaration of the High-Level Meeting of the General Assembly on the Rule of Law (n 26) para 34.

[34] Commonwealth (Latimer House) Principles on the Three Branches of Government, agreed by the Law Ministers and endorsed by the Commonwealth Heads of Government Meeting (Abuja, Nigeria, 2003) 9.

[35] See in particular Drzemczewski and Lowis, ch 15 in this volume.

[36] See, eg, High-Level Conference on the Future of the European Court of Human Rights, the Brighton Declaration (20 April 2012).

[37] See ch 21 in this volume.

[38] J Waldron, *Law and Disagreement* (Oxford, Oxford University Press, 1999) and 'Judges as Moral Reasoners' (2009) 7 *International Journal of Constitutional Studies* 2, in which he contrasts the open-ended moral reasoning in which legislatures are free to engage with the more limited reasoning open to courts, which are constrained by contingent legal frameworks.

[39] M Tushnet, *Taking the Constitution Away from the Courts* (Princeton, Princeton University Press, 1999).

[40] See, eg, J Hiebert, 'New Constitutional Ideas: Can New Parliamentary Models Resist Judicial Dominance When Interpreting Rights?' (2004) 82 *Texas Law Review* 1963.

protection of human rights through the development of institutions and processes not involving courts.[41]

Now, however, advocates of 'political constitutionalism' appear to welcome a role for courts as part of the appropriate institutional machinery for rights protection, at least under certain conditions.[42] In the face of the widespread adoption of bills of rights in recent years, albeit taking a variety of institutional forms, political constitutionalists have softened their traditional resistance to a role for courts and now argue that such institutional arrangements are consistent with political constitutionalism so long as parliaments have the last word in the event of interpretive disagreement about the meaning of the rights and values so protected. Advocates of legal constitutionalism also now, by and large, accept that parliaments too have a legitimate interpretive role in relation to the meaning of the values considered to be fundamental.[43] These are significant developments, because by accepting the legitimacy of a judicial role (and even the desirability of such a role) in the interpretation of human rights, the area of disagreement is significantly reduced to an argument about whether courts or parliaments should have the last word in the interpretation of rights. We return to the implications of that shift below when we consider the idea of a democratic culture of justification as an alternative to the focus on the question of ultimate authority.

Indeed, it is a common theme of a number of the contributions to this volume that it is time to move on from the old battles between legal constitutionalists on the one hand and political constitutionalists on the other.[44] David Kinley, for example, points out that debates about the democratic deficit in the implementation of rights-protecting legislation have tended to focus on the relative merits of the legislature and the judiciary, which is both unhelpful and erroneous. He argues that in modern democracies the different branches of the state should not be seen as antagonists in the protection and promotion of human rights, but considered as a whole, with their respective roles considered in the context of the state's overall responsibilities in relation to human rights. Aileen Kavanagh similarly rejects as false the suggestion that there is a dichotomy between the 'political' and the 'legal' constitution, reminding us that in the UK, under the Human Rights Act, the protection of human rights is and should be a collaborative enterprise between all three branches of government. Kent Roach also agrees that the debate has grown old and tired, and welcomes the search for fresh approaches that promise the possibility of escape from the dead end of polarised positions on the respective roles of courts and legislatures.

---

[41] Tom Campbell, Jeffrey Goldsworthy and Adrienne Stone (eds), *Protecting Human Rights: Instruments and Institutions* (Oxford, Oxford University Press, 2003) and *Protecting Rights Without a Bill of Rights* (Aldershot, Ashgate, 2006).

[42] See, eg, Richard Bellamy, 'Political Constitutionalism and the Human Rights Act' (2011) 9 *International Journal of Constitutional Law* 86; Jeremy Waldron, 'The Core of the Case against Judicial Review' (2006) 115 *Yale Law Journal* 1346.

[43] For a recent analysis of the performance of this interpretive role by a parliamentary committee, see J Simson Caird, R Hazell and D Oliver, *The Constitutional Standards of the House of Lords Select Committee on the Constitution* (The Constitution Unit and The Constitution Society, 2014).

[44] See in particular, in addition to David Dyzenhaus: Kinley, ch 2; Feldman, ch 5; Kavanagh, ch 6; King, ch 8; Bull and Cameron, ch 13; Lazarus and Simonsen, ch 19; Roach, ch 20; and Fredman, ch 22 in this volume.

The dispute within the family of constitutionalists has been over for some time. As the editors of a volume of sceptical essays on the legal protection of human rights significantly said in 2010:

> We have probably now got to the stage of moving beyond a polarized debate in which human rights enthusiasts castigate human rights sceptics for being naive about real world twenty-first century democracy, while human rights sceptics attribute even greater naivety to those who see courts as democratic substitutes.[45]

As with many prolonged civil wars, the terms of the peace are a constant process of iteration and negotiation. There is nothing to be gained from inquiries about who won the war or had the better of the arguments. There is much to be gained, however, from getting on with the difficult work of finding practical but theoretically informed solutions to the many challenges of combining legal protection for human rights with a meaningful role for democratically elected institutions.

III. THE NATURE OF THE DEMOCRATIC DEFICIT

How are we to square the resurgent critique from democracy, outlined above, with the clearly established consensus about the necessity of legal protections for human rights and the emerging consensus about the shared institutional responsibility for upholding them? At one level, the critique from democracy can be understood as a reassertion of traditional scepticism about legal forms of protection for human rights, and therefore as a rejection of the consensus described above. Such sceptics, however, are a dwindling band. Where the critique is articulated by those who accept that there is a legitimate role for courts in the protection of human rights, it must be about more than a mere preference for the decisions of the democratic branches over unelected courts on relative legitimacy grounds. What exactly is the nature of the democratic deficit about which they are genuinely concerned?

One possible explanation for the paradox is that the institutional machinery for the protection of human rights has not caught up with the new consensus about the shared responsibility for protecting legally protected human rights. Democracies throughout the world profess their commitment to human rights as part of their wider commitment to the rule of law, but in most of those democracies the institutional machinery for realising that commitment remains profoundly undemocratic. It still depends, to a very large extent, on unelected judges providing legal remedies for individuals whose rights have been violated, usually by elected legislators or decision-makers. 'Legislative human rights review', in which parliament reviews laws for compatibility with human rights commitments, has proliferated, with a number of jurisdictions having introduced institutional reforms to make it possible,[46] and in a small number of jurisdictions it has taken root in a way which

---

[45] Tom Campbell, Keith Ewing and Adam Tomkins (eds), *The Legal Protection of Human Rights: Sceptical Essays* (Oxford, Oxford University Press, 2010), Introduction, 10.
[46] See S Gardbaum, *The New Commonwealth Model of Constitutionalism* (Cambridge, Cambridge University Press, 2013).

makes it hard to imagine it being reversed. However, we need urgently to take stock of what has been achieved by legislative human rights review, and that is the subject of the contributions in parts I–IV of this book. The picture which emerges is very mixed. While significant progress has undoubtedly been made,[47] the overwhelming sense is of how much more there is to do.[48] If we measure success by the extent to which our institutions and their processes and procedures have developed to encourage democratically elected decision-makers to engage properly with human rights norms and to play a meaningful role in their articulation, interpretation and application, we find that surprisingly little progress has been made, even in those parliaments which are widely considered to be at the forefront of developing institutional means for parliamentary consideration of human rights. Parliamentary human rights committees are now in their second decade of operation and are becoming increasingly widespread, but even as they do so, their limitations in addressing the sense of 'democratic deficit' are becoming increasingly apparent. In most countries, neither the legislative process nor parliamentary means of holding governments to account have changed sufficiently significantly to put consideration of human rights more at the heart of the legislature's role.

Notwithstanding the progress that has been made with the introduction and gradual spread of legislative human rights review, it continues to be the case that 'human rights' are frequently experienced by democratically elected politicians as a disempowering discourse which only constrains and prohibits what democratic governments and parliaments can do. The interpretation of what human rights requires is seen as the exclusive preserve of courts and, therefore, of lawyers, not matters which are the proper subject of interpretive inquiry by political actors in political fora. On this view, decisions about human rights are always something 'done' to politicians by undemocratic courts, a legal stick used to beat elected politicians by less accountable decision-makers, applying norms which themselves are often perceived to suffer from a democratic deficit because they are the product of intergovernmental processes over which democratic legislatures have little effective influence, let alone control.

This sense that democratically elected decision-makers are excluded from decision-making about human rights, sidelined by other institutions making definitive decisions about them, or at least not taken sufficiently seriously by courts even when they do take a view on a human rights issue, could be considered part of a wider malaise affecting parliaments. There appears to be a growing sense that, with globalisation and the trend towards increased decision-making at an intergovernmental level, it is increasingly difficult to hold governments to account through traditional parliamentary channels or to influence intergovernmental or supranational law-making and decision-taking, and a corresponding concern that parliamentary procedures have perhaps not kept up with these developments.[49] In the UK, while

---

[47] See Kavanagh, ch 6, Yowell, ch 7 and King, ch 8 in this volume in particular.
[48] See Kinley, ch 2, Hiebert, ch 3, and Donald and Leach, ch 4 in this volume in particular.
[49] See, eg, Report of the House of Commons European Scrutiny Committee, *Reforming the European Scrutiny System in the House of Commons*, Twenty-Fourth Report of Session 2013-14, HC 109-I; and

recent parliamentary reforms may have done much to reverse Parliament's decline by empowering both select committees and backbenchers,[50] evidence suggests that the public is still not convinced that Parliament holds the Government to account and continues to feel powerless, with little influence over how the country is run.[51] The project of re-empowering Parliament, as the Speaker himself recently acknowledged, is far from complete, and ambitious initiatives are still required in order to restore Parliament's legitimacy and effectiveness in holding the Government to account.[52]

The 'democratic deficit' in the title of this volume therefore has a particular meaning. It is not meant as a reassertion of the traditional rejection of a role for courts in the protection of human rights or as an attack on the legitimacy of judicial decision-making in cases concerning human rights. Rather, it refers to the relative lack of institutional structures, mechanisms and processes for ensuring that human rights are mainstreamed into both Government decision-making and parliamentary processes for legislating and scrutinising the Executive, and holding it to account for its compliance with the requirements of human rights norms. It may be that the failure to develop more imaginative ways in which legislatures can engage with human rights in their day-to-day business has given rise to the strong sense of a 'democratic deficit': a lack of opportunity for politicians to engage in proper debate about what a commitment to human rights norms means in practice, to discuss and argue about, not who has ultimate decision-making authority on a particular issue, but about exactly what our shared commitment to certain fundamental values means in practice when applied to a particular policy problem.

If this is the case, then what is urgently required is a concerted effort to identify such opportunities to engage politicians in these debates. Until elected politicians take ownership of human rights norms and begin to feel that they have a meaningful role to play in discussing and debating what those norms require law and policy to look like, the sense of a democratic deficit will be here to stay. The fact that Parliament in 1998 chose to give courts the powers they now exercise under the Human Rights Act,[53] while obviously significant, can never be a complete answer to the concerns about a democratic deficit in human rights. Each generation of parliamentarians needs to be involved in debates about the meaning and application of human rights in an ongoing way, and the further we get in the UK from the constitutional moment of 1998, the more urgent that need becomes. In this important sense, the force of the democratic critique can be acknowledged in a way which is not inherently at odds with the clear consensus about the importance

references in recent UN General Assembly resolutions to the need to bridge the democratic gap in international relations (considered further in ch 23 below).

[50] See Report of the House of Commons Reform Committee, chaired by Tony Wright MP ('the Wright Committee'), *Rebuilding the House*, First Report of Session 2008-09, HC 1117.
[51] The Hansard Society's 2014 *Audit of Political Engagement*.
[52] Rt Hon John Bercow MP, Speaker, Michael Ryle Memorial Lecture, 30 June 2014.
[53] Often invoked by courts in their judgments when dealing with submissions that they would be usurping the role of the democratically elected branches if they were to find a law to be incompatible with human rights: see, eg, Lord Bingham in the *Belmarsh* case (n 23) and *Nicklinson v Ministry of Justice* [2014] UKSC 38.

of legal protections for human rights and the shared institutional responsibility for upholding them.

The relative absence of such opportunities for parliamentarians to engage meaningfully with human rights results in a disproportionate preoccupation with the question of who has ultimate authority: the 'who decides?' question. It is not surprising that elected decision-makers who feel marginalised by unelected decision-makers should raise questions about who has the more legitimate claim to make the final authoritative decision on an issue. However, to always ask 'who should have the final say on human rights?' can be an unhelpful distraction from the task of devising better institutional mechanisms which reflect the shared responsibility for protecting and promoting human rights. Democratic considerations are extremely important in designing and operating those institutional mechanisms, but approaching every human rights question through the prism of 'who decides' can, paradoxically, prevent proper engagement with those democratic considerations. In the UK, there is universal agreement about the answer to that question at the level of ultimate authority: Parliament can decide, if it wishes, to repeal the Human Rights Act and to withdraw from the ECHR. So long, however, as it remains a signatory to the ECHR, debating the question of who has ultimate authority—Parliament or the European Court of Human Rights—is an obstacle to addressing the much more pressing question of how to devise institutional mechanisms for the effective implementation of human rights which are compatible with the UK's tradition of parliamentary democracy.

This focus on the democratic deficit, so defined, of the institutional arrangements for protecting human rights entails a corresponding focus on legitimacy as the reason why parliaments should be more involved in the promotion and protection of human rights. One of the reasons most frequently given to explain why parliaments should be given an increased role in relation to human rights is the essentially functional reason that it will increase the 'effectiveness' of human rights protection: parliaments, by virtue of their constitutional powers in most states, are well placed to give effect to the human rights obligations which states have undertaken. In particular, parliaments' unique constitutional responsibility for the legal framework of states make them the best-placed institution of the state to realise human rights in the sense of making the necessary adjustments to the legal framework to make sure that human rights are adequately protected and fulfilled. Research studies have been undertaken which suggest that where parliaments are involved, there is a higher rate of implementation of international human rights decisions.[54] A recent King's College research project found that parliaments' effectiveness as human rights actors is not being fully realised and recommended a framework for designing and determining parliament's effectiveness in its oversight of human rights.[55]

[54] See, eg, D Anagnostou and A Mungiu-Pippidi, *Why Do States Implement Differently the European Court of Human Rights Judgments? The Case Law on Civil Liberties and the Rights of Minorities,* JURISTRAS Project (2009).
[55] *Effective Parliamentary Oversight of Human Rights: A Framework for Designing and Determining Effectiveness* (June 2014) www.kcl.ac.uk/law/research/parliamentshr/assets/Outcome-Document---Advance-Copy-5-June-2014.pdf.

Increased effectiveness is an important consideration, but the principal concern of this volume is not functional but normative: it is interested primarily in the role of parliaments in the legitimation of human rights law and discourse. Of course, legitimacy and effectiveness are closely related. The more democratically legitimate human rights norms and decisions are considered to be, the more likely they are to be given effect in national legal orders. The crises of implementation which have confronted the regional and international systems for human rights protection in recent years have tended to be most acute where there is considered to be a deficit of democratic legitimacy. In this sense, then, legitimacy is a precondition of effectiveness. Parliaments are uniquely placed to serve both purposes: as the bodies elected to represent the sovereign people, they are the institutions best placed to confer democratic legitimacy as well as the best placed to create the necessary legal framework for the most effective protection of human rights. The question is whether they are doing enough to fulfil this important role.

One of the purposes of this volume, then, is to stimulate debate about what parliaments can do to empower themselves by placing human rights more at the heart of their function. The book is not another treatise about 'who decides' human rights questions, but about what more can be done to make the role of parliaments in relation to human rights more substantive and meaningful. What reforms to the legislative process would ensure that parliaments always have the opportunity to consider and debate the human rights compatibility of legislation, with the benefit of all relevant information and independent, expert advice about the compatibility of legislation brought forward by governments? How can parliaments make sure that all laws, whether primary or subordinate, are always subjected to such scrutiny for human rights compatibility and that no opportunities for such debate are missed? How can parliaments ensure they have a role in considering the adequacy of important documents which guide the actions of people on the front line in relation to human rights, such as codes of practice and other forms of administrative guidance?[56] How can parliaments make sure that they consider and debate the content of human rights obligations entered into by governments, as well as scrutinise governments' position in intergovernmental fora, or when intervening before international courts, for compatibility with the UK's human rights obligations? How can parliaments ensure that they are involved in considerations of how to respond to courts judgments about human rights? How can they become involved in the international system for monitoring the compliance of governments with their human rights obligations, both by contributing to the monitoring process and by following up on the recommendations which come out of that process? These are the sorts of questions that need to be addressed urgently if there is to be any prospect of redressing the current, very real sense of a democratic deficit in human rights before

---

[56] In a rare public comment, the outgoing Clerk of the Commons, Sir Robert Rogers, told the BBC that he thought Parliament spends too much of its time considering legislation and not enough time scrutinising guidance to front-line staff about how the legal framework is going to be applied and enforced in practice, which is often of more practical significance to people than the legislation itself: *The Westminster Hour* (22 June 2014).

it threatens to reverse the progress which has been made in the legal protection and promotion of human rights through our existing institutional machinery.

IV. A DEMOCRATIC CULTURE OF JUSTIFICATION

One of the purposes of legislative rights review, as noted by some contributors to this volume, is to build 'a human rights culture' or 'a culture of rights'. David Kinley, for example, the scholar with perhaps the most plausible claim to have pioneered legislative rights review for compatibility with the ECHR,[57] says that the dialogue and scrutiny committee-based process in the UK is meant to infiltrate thinking and action in both Whitehall and Westminster, or to inculcate a culture of rights.[58] Cultural change is a necessarily lengthy process of changing deeply ingrained habits, both of mind and of action.[59] It is now becoming apparent, nearly 20 years after the passage of the Human Rights Act, that, in the UK at least, any culture of rights which may have developed is highly precarious because it is vulnerable to the resurgence of the democratic critique. The idea of a 'human rights culture' has started to go the way of the 'health and safety culture': invoked in the mainstream media and politics as a term of abuse, shorthand for the antithesis of common sense and the undermining of democracy.[60] The very label for the cultural change that is sought has become an obstacle to achieving that change because, since courts are considered to be the guardians of rights, it is perceived to be tied to the old polarised debate about whether the courts or Parliament are supreme. To have any prospect of escaping the cul-de-sac in which debate about human rights has become trapped, we need to explore the potential offered by the idea of a democratic culture of justification as a different way of thinking about the institutional arrangements that we have inherited for the protection and promotion of human rights.

The idea of a democratic culture of justification is explored in more depth in Part VII of this book. As David Dyzenhaus reminds us,[61] the idea of a 'culture of justification' was first explored by Etienne Mureinik in the context of South Africa's transition from apartheid to democracy, as a counterpoint to the culture of authority which had gone before.[62] A culture of justification is one built on persuasion, not coercion, a culture in which every exercise of power is expected to be justified by reference to reasons which are publicly available to be independently scrutinised for

---

[57] In his groundbreaking book *The European Convention on Human Rights: Compliance without Incorporation* (Aldershot, Dartmouth Publishing, 1982), which contained the earliest sustained account of a parliamentary model of human rights protection, advocating a system of pre-legislative scrutiny of all legislation for compliance with the rights in the ECHR as an alternative to giving those rights legal effect by incorporating them into the national legal order.

[58] See also Hiebert, ch 3 in this volume to similar effect.

[59] M Hunt, 'The Human Rights Act and Legal Culture: The Judiciary and the Legal Profession' (1999) 26 *Journal of Law and Society* 86.

[60] D Raab, *The Assault on Liberty: What Went Wrong with Rights* (London, Fourth Estate, 2010) chs 5–6.

[61] Chapter 21 in this volume.

[62] Etienne Mureinik, 'A Bridge to Where? Introducing the Interim Bill of Rights' (1994) 10 *South African Journal on Human Rights* 31.

compatibility with society's fundamental commitments. The idea is a powerful one, not only because of its explanatory power in legal orders which have adopted some form of a bill of rights, but also because it is literally empowering of people who are the subject of decisions or omissions by the powerful: it entitles them to demand reasoned justifications for those decisions or omissions in terms of the values which have been considered to be sufficiently fundamental to warrant protection in the bill of rights.

Mureinik's precious legacy of a culture of justification has been carried forward by others, most notably Dyzenhaus himself, who in a series of articles has begun to spell out its far-reaching implications for the way we conceive of constitutionalism, and thereby paved the way for the reduction in hostilities between the warring factions.[63] Dyzenhaus demonstrates why a culture of justification is a democratic advance: it requires the government to offer to both the electorate and parliament justification for their laws and policies in terms of their consistency with the values protected by the constitution, as well as requiring both the government and parliament to offer such justification to the courts. In this way, parliament is empowered against the executive, the courts are empowered against both the executive and parliament, and the electorate is empowered against all three branches of the state, which can more easily be held accountable for their transparent decisions on justification. Approaching difficult and contentious issues of human rights through the prism of a culture of democratic justification shifts the focus away from the distracting question of who has ultimate authority to make a final decision on a particular question and towards the more productive question of how to ensure that the institutional arrangements provide the requisite opportunities for subjecting public justifications to democratic scrutiny.

The question of whether prisoners should have the right to vote has been the crucible in which these debates about the respective roles of courts and legislatures have recently taken place in a number of different jurisdictions, including the UK,[64] and not surprisingly the question therefore looms large in a number of contributions. The issue does provide a particularly telling challenge for traditional advocates of political constitutionalism, involving as it does a limitation on what they regard as 'the right of rights', the right to vote: the pre-requisite of political participation. As Jeremy Waldron said in evidence to the Joint Committee on Human Rights, looking the Commons Members in the eye: 'Parliamentary decision-making and legislation is legitimate because people have the right to vote, not the other way round. Parliament is the guardian of that.'[65]

---

[63] See, eg, 'Proportionality and Deference in a Culture of Justification' in G Huscroft, BW Miller and G Webber (eds), *Proportionality and the Rule of Law—Rights, Justification, Reasoning* (Cambridge, Cambridge University Press, 2014) and 'Dignity in Administrative Law: Judicial Deference in a Culture of Justification' (2012) 17 *Review of Constitutional Studies* 87. See also M Hunt, 'Reshaping Constitutionalism' in J Morison, K McEvoy and G Anthony (eds), *Judges, Transition and Human Rights* (Oxford, Oxford University Press, 2007) and 'Sovereignty's Blight: Why Contemporary Public Law Needs the Concept of "Due Deference"' in N Bamforth and P Leyland (eds), *Public Law in a Multi-layered Constitution* (Oxford, Hart Publishing, 2003) and the literature referred to therein.

[64] Similar debates have also taken place in Canada, New Zealand and South Africa.

[65] Transcript of evidence to the Joint Committee on Human Rights, 15 March 2011, Q53 www.parliament.uk/documents/joint-committees/human-rights/15_March_Oral_Evidence_clickable.pdf.

In Part VII of this book, David Dyzenhaus and Sandra Fredman both use the debate over prisoner voting as a case study demonstrating the normative desirability of a democratic culture of justification. Dyzenhaus argues that the debates on prisoner voting in both Canada and New Zealand show that the issue of whether parliaments or courts should have final authority is a distraction from the more important question of how to achieve an institutional structure in which the justification for laws can be rigorously subjected to scrutiny for compatibility with constitutional commitments. Indeed, he argues persuasively that focusing on the question of ultimate authority is worse than a mere distraction from that task, because by removing the possibility of due deference, it provides no incentive for justification to be offered in a democratically appropriate manner and it therefore diminishes democratic scrutiny.[66] A culture of justification, he argues, is therefore necessary to a democracy, because it facilitates public and transparent debate about the justifications for its laws.[67]

Fredman similarly builds on Mureinik's idea of a culture of justification to develop a 'deliberative model' of human rights adjudication in which courts, far from undermining democratic participation, positively enhance it by demanding that laws are the product of a genuinely deliberative process, in which parliament has properly debated, in a value-oriented way, the justification for laws that limit rights. Like the so-called 'dialogue model' of human rights adjudication, which characterises the institutional relationship between courts and legislatures under human rights laws as being akin to a two-way conversation, Fredman sees the way out of what she describes as the 'democratic dilemma' of human rights adjudication by moving beyond the false dichotomy between courts and legislatures towards a more collaborative approach between the two branches, in which both contribute to a democratic resolution of human rights disputes. Her approach differs from the dialogue model, however. While superficially attractive in the escape it appears to offer from the confines of competing supremacies, she argues that it is unsatisfactory because it is ultimately ambivalent about whether the role of judges is to make authoritative interpretations of the meaning of human rights or to defer to such interpretations by the legislature. Fredman therefore prefers a deliberative model, which goes beyond dialogue by focusing not simply on the final decision but also on the quality of the deliberation preceding that decision (including the parliamentary consideration). The role of courts in such a model is to enhance the democratic accountability of decision-makers, including legislators, by insisting on a deliberative justification for the interpretation of a right or its limitation.

Viewed through the prism of a democratic culture of justification, the litigation and parliamentary debates about prisoner voting in South Africa and the UK provide an interesting comparison. In South Africa, the Constitutional Court, in its

---

[66] *Cf* the discussion below about the use of the doctrines of subsidiarity and the margin of appreciation by the European Court of Human Rights to incentivise democratic deliberation and debate about the justifications for limitations on rights.

[67] See Kuijer, ch 14 in this volume, for an interesting account from the Netherlands of the way in which parliamentary consideration of human rights can shape the Government's approach to the relevance of human rights and in particular the information that the Government routinely provides to Parliament in relation both to proposed legislation and the proposed responses to court judgments.

first consideration of the issue, deliberately left space for democratic deliberation by the legislature, leaving open the possibility that prisoners' right to vote under the South African Constitution could be subject to statutory limitation. However, when the South African Parliament responded by removing the right to vote from all convicted prisoners except those in prison because they were unable to pay a fine, the Constitutional Court declared the law unconstitutional. It did so on the basis that the onus was on the South African Parliament to show that it had addressed the question in a deliberative way and, by the reasons and evidence it relied on to defend the law, it failed to demonstrate that it had done so.

In the UK, the European Court of Human Rights in *Hirst v UK* also left space for democratic deliberation by Parliament as to what limitations on the right of prisoners to vote it considers justifiable: the only option directly precluded by the Court's judgment is the current blanket ban on all convicted prisoners. The Commons debate on a backbench motion, which led to a resolution in favour of keeping the current ban by an overwhelming majority of 224 votes to 22,[68] was therefore not capable of satisfying the Court's requirement that there must be democratic deliberation about the justification for a limitation in the light of modern standards on the treatment of prisoners. As the Court subsequently made clear when rejecting the UK Government's invitation to overturn its decision in *Hirst* in the light of that debate,[69] the mere fact of such a debate is not enough: it is the quality of the deliberation that takes place that matters. A parliamentary committee of both Houses has now conducted a proper deliberative exercise[70] and made a clear recommendation about where the line should be drawn, but Parliament itself has still not been given the opportunity of considering, in the light of contemporary penological standards, the justifications for the possible limitations on the right of prisoners to vote. The episode demonstrates well the desirability of a democratic culture of justification, which encourages democratic debate and scrutiny following an adverse human rights judgment, while a focus on the question of ultimate authority gets in the way of what really matters: proper deliberative debate on the substantive issue.

Parliamentary human rights committees may be one way of seeking to ensure that such democratic deliberation takes place and that it pays close attention to human rights. While some contributors consider that committees such as the Joint Committee on Human Rights in the UK Parliament have generally enhanced democratic deliberation,[71] Hiebert concludes that the hopes many commentators had for legislative rights review—that it would introduce a new norm of rights-based justification into legislative decision-making—have been proved largely misplaced in practice.[72] Based on her extensive interviews with officials in the UK, she finds that it is judicial right-based review under the Human Rights Act, not legislative rights review, that has really influenced government behaviour in the development

---

[68] HC Deb 10 February 2011, cols 493–584. See D Nicol, 'Legitimacy of the Commons Debate on Prisoner Voting' [2011] *Public Law* 681.

[69] *Greens and MT v UK* [2010] ECHR 1826.

[70] See *Report of the Joint Committee on the Draft Voting Eligibility (Prisoners) Bill*, Session 2013–14, HL Paper 103/HC 924 (18 December 2013).

[71] Kavanagh, ch 6 in this volume.

[72] Hiebert, ch 3 in this volume.

of policy and law. For both ministers and civil servants, the risk of an adverse judicial decision under the Human Rights Act counts for far more than the risk of adverse parliamentary comment, for the simple reason that at the end of the day, the Government can nearly always get its way in Parliament because it dominates the House of Commons, which can nearly always be relied upon to overturn amendments to its legislation made as a result of legislative rights review in the House of Lords. A culture of justification has failed to take hold, Hiebert concludes, because the legislative process remains dominated by partisan politics, in which the driving force is the imperative to become the party which dominates the House of Commons. The essential nature of that political process has not changed and she sees no prospect of legislative rights review bringing about any significant behavioural change until the House of Commons itself changes and is prepared to offer more resistance to the dominant executive.

Hiebert's conclusion about the prospects for legislative rights review may be too pessimistic. Far from being abstracted from the political forces that determine how both government and parliament operate in practice, legislative rights review brings human rights into the heart of those processes and seeks to influence and shape them in subtle ways from within. As David Feldman presciently observed in the early days of the UK's experiment, this is necessarily a slow and incremental process.[73] For a culture of justification to take hold does not require the very nature of politics to be utterly transformed. There is much about parliamentary politics that could be changed for the better, but there is also a great deal that is an irreducible part of representative democracy. We do not need an end to antagonistic, partisan politics, or to the system of a parliamentary executive, in order to achieve a culture of justification. It is true that the UK Parliament and politics have not been utterly transformed by legislative rights review, but nor should they be. Progress has demonstrably been made towards a culture in which the Government seeks to justify laws and policies which affect human rights, and Parliament plays its part not only in creating and maintaining the expectation that the Government will do so, but also in occasionally forcing the Government to amend its laws where its justifications for action or inaction fail to satisfy. That is a culture of justification in action. There is a great deal more to do to embed it further and make sure that its future is secure, but we should neither expect it to change the essential nature of democratic politics nor hope that it will do so.

How well legislative rights review is working in each of the devolved legislatures of the UK is the subject of Part III of this book. An issue of general concern which is raised there in relation to all the devolved legislatures is the lack of transparency in their consideration of the human rights issues raised by devolved legislation, and a corresponding lack of information available to the devolved legislatures to inform parliamentary debate. This is partly a consequence of the institutional arrangements for checking the human rights compatibility of such legislation: because, under the devolution settlement, compatibility is a matter of legislative competence, the

---

[73] D Feldman, 'Can and Should Parliament Protect Human Rights?' (2004) 10 *European Public Law* 635–51. And see also ch 5 in this volume.

scrutiny takes place prior to the introduction of the measure, as part of the Presiding Officer's process for ensuring that a measure is within competence. In the absence of any dedicated committee to scrutinise the measure subsequently for human rights compatibility as it progresses, what is lost, as Ann Sherlock puts is, is 'the kind of rigorous public discussion of the potential issues ... the public weighing up of the proportionality of any interferences [and] ... the general awareness of rights issues that can be developed by published reports analysing the issues in full'.[74] There is clearly scope for considerably more political debate about human rights to take place in each of the devolved legislatures.

Theoretical accounts grounded in the powerful idea of a culture of justification may also prove to be more descriptively accurate and therefore more useful than other frameworks such as the 'dialogue theory' referred to above. Some commentators regard the interactions which have taken place in the UK between the courts and Parliament under the Human Rights Act as a dialogue of the deaf, in which the two institutions have paid lip service to the notion of dialogue, but in fact have shown little sign of listening to each other. The fact that Parliament has never sought to defy the courts following a declaration of incompatibility is often cited by such observers as evidence of the lack of meaningful dialogue and as confirmation of the suspicion that the dialogue metaphor is a convenient fig leaf for judicial immodesty.[75] Others consider that the dialogue metaphor captures something of the essence of the institutional interactions that have developed under the Human Rights Act, but regard the dialogue to have been at best 'dysfunctional', lacking the necessary spirit of mutual respect between the courts and the political branches, and resulting in a diminution of legal protection for human rights at the insistence of a legislature which colludes with the Government to suborn an institutionally weak judiciary.[76]

Legal commentators can be quick to despair when elected politicians use political rhetoric to talk about human rights issues or take partisan positions on important human rights questions. We should not be surprised that court judgments on human rights questions often excite political passions and that inflamed comments are often made in the cauldron of political debate conducted under intense media scrutiny. If we take the idea of institutional dialogue literally, it is inevitable that, like all close relationships, it will include disagreements, sometimes flaming rows and maybe even, from time to time, existential crises about the fundamental terms of the relationship. This may be another reason for preferring a democratic culture

---

[74] Sherlock, ch 11 in this volume. In relation to the Scottish Parliament, Bruce Adamson in ch 9 in this volume also raises some concerns about the effectiveness of the procedures for human rights scrutiny, querying whether in relation to some issues, the level of human rights scrutiny provided by the Scottish Parliament and its committees has been adequate. In relation to the Northern Ireland Assembly, Caughey and Russell in ch 10 in this volume express concerns about the limited knowledge of human rights on the part of elected representatives and their willingness to make full use of the procedures at their disposal.

[75] See, eg, J Allan, 'Statutory Bills of Rights: You Read Words in, You Read Words out, You Take Parliament's Clear Intentions and You Shake it All About—Doin' the Sanky Hanky Panky' in Campbell, Ewing and Tomkins (n 45).

[76] Tom Southerden, 'Dysfunctional Dialogue: Lawyers, Politicians and Immigrants' Rights to Private and Family Life' [2014] *EHRLR* 252.

of justification to the dialogue metaphor as the foundational idea to make sense of the subtleties of the relationship between the three branches of government.

The recent interactions between the courts and the political branches on the interpretation and application of the right to respect for private and family life in Article 8 ECHR in the context of deporting foreign national offenders, considered by Hayley J Hooper in her chapter,[77] provide a good example of the culture of justification in action. Not surprisingly, the newspaper headlines have been sensationalist and the political debate has been correspondingly heated. But when viewed in long perspective and considered in the light of all that has been said on the issue by courts, Government ministers, parliamentary committees and now Parliament itself in the Immigration Act 2014, is this really best seen as an episodic event of dysfunctional dialogue which demonstrates the continued vulnerability of the legal protection of human rights to the superior power of politics, as one commentator has suggested?[78] Or is it better viewed as the latest step in the dynamic process by which each branch of government is required by the others to fulfil its proper role in a culture of justification against the background of a shared responsibility for ensuring that the national legal system includes the necessary protection for the right to respect for private and family life?

Looking dispassionately at the outcome, free from rhetorical claims and the heat of partisan politics, it is clear that the courts were not in fact applying Article 8 as if it were an absolute right; the Government did not in fact seek to oust the jurisdiction of the courts to hear Article 8 claims, nor did it or Parliament seek to tie the courts' hands in the determination of individual cases by purporting to provide a conclusive and definitive interpretation of Article 8 in deportation cases. Rather, as the Joint Committee on Human Rights observed in its Report on the Bill,[79] the Government, in response to concerns it had about judicial decisions in deportation cases, invited Parliament to consider a more detailed elaboration of how the right to respect for private and family life in Article 8 ECHR should be interpreted and applied in this particular policy context; Parliament and its committees subjected that legislative scheme to detailed scrutiny,[80] including for compatibility with the underlying human rights standards as applied by the European Court of Human Rights in its case law on Article 8, and debated possible changes to that detailed scheme; , and it is now for the courts to apply the new legal framework in individual cases, ensuring that in doing so, they are themselves acting compatibly with ECHR rights.

This is justification in action: a dynamic, fluid process involving each of the branches of the state interpreting and applying the requirements of human rights norms in a particular regulatory context, and responding to the interpretations of the other branches where it gives rise to disagreement.[81] No branch has the power

---

[77] Chapter 18 in this volume.

[78] As argued by Tom Southerden (n 76).

[79] Report of the Joint Committee on Human Rights, *Legislative Scrutiny: Immigration Bill (Second Report)*, 12th Report of Session 2013–14, HL Paper 142/HC 1120.

[80] See House of Lords Select Committee on the Constitution, 6th Report of Session 2013–14, *Immigration Bill*, HL Paper 148.

[81] It is also subsidiarity in action: see discussion below. See also M Elliott, 'The Immigration Act 2014: A Sequel to the Prisoner Voting Saga?' (Public Law for Everyone Blog, 23 May 2014) http://publiclaw-foreveryone.com/2014/05/23/the-immigration-act-2014-a-sequel-to-the-prisoner-voting-saga.

to stop the debate about how the legal framework should seek to strike the balance between the right to respect for private and family life and competing rights and interests. Changes to the legal framework are settled for now, but, as it should in a democracy,[82] the debate about the justification for the current balance goes on, in light of experience of how the new framework works in practice.

V. THE IMPLICATIONS OF LEGISLATIVE RIGHTS REVIEW FOR COURTS

As a culture of democratic justification begins to take hold and legislative review for human rights compatibility of legislation becomes both more widespread and more sophisticated, what are the implications for courts when they consider legal challenges to the human rights compatibility of legislation which raise the very same compatibility issues as those that have already been considered and decided by Parliament when enacting the legislation? The question arises even more acutely when courts are required to consider the human rights compatibility of a legislative response to an earlier court judgment finding a legislative provision to be incompatible with a right, for example, because it interfered disproportionately with the right.[83] This is the subject of the contributions in Part VI of this book.

The shift in recent years in some jurisdictions towards what we can now conceive of as a democratic culture of justification, outlined in the preceding section, has significant implications for the way in which courts approach the relevance of parliamentary consideration of human rights questions, implications which are only now beginning to be realised. In both Dyzenhaus' culture of justification[84] and Fredman's deliberative model of human rights adjudication,[85] which rest on the same foundation, the quality of the reasoning which lies behind a determination of a human rights issue, whether legislative or judicial, is crucial: it must satisfy the minimum requirements of deliberation, which means, for example, that any limitation of a right must be justified by reference to other fundamental legal values, including the background values that are intrinsic in the right that is being limited. This clearly has important implications for the way in which courts approach legislation interfering with fundamental rights: when scrutinising the justification for the interference, it suggests that the court must consider the quality of parliament's reasoning when passing the law in order to ascertain how well it performed its deliberative role.

In the UK in particular, this raises some delicate constitutional issues on which a range of views are expressed in this collection. Hayley J Hooper considers the use of parliamentary materials by courts in the UK when making judgments about the proportionality of legislative interferences with ECHR rights and in particular the implications of such use for parliamentary privilege.[86] Article 9 of the Bill of Rights

[82] See Lord Mance in *R (Nicklinson) v Ministry of Justice* [2014] UKSC 38 [171].
[83] See Donald and Leach, ch 4 and King, ch 8 in this volume.
[84] Chapter 21 in this volume.
[85] Chapter 22 in this volume.
[86] Chapter 18 in this volume.

of 1689 provides that 'freedom of speech and debates or proceedings in Parliament ought not to be impeached or questioned in any court or place out of Parliament'. Hooper argues that current judicial practice in referring to parliamentary materials in proportionality judgments cannot be easily reconciled with the traditional approach to parliamentary privilege, but points out that the courts have failed to develop a consistent set of rules and principles about the sorts of materials that can be referred to by courts and for what purposes. She does not advocate a complete prohibition on the judicial use of such material in proportionality judgments. However, she does consider there to be dangers inherent in too casual an approach to the use of such material, including the risk of courts dictating the legislative agenda to Parliament. And, conversely, she warns of the risk of the Government and Parliament undermining judicial independence by invoking parliamentary materials to argue that individual human rights cases should be determined in the way that Parliament intended. She calls for caution to be exercised by all constitutional actors, including the courts, to ensure that the purpose behind Article 9 of the Bill of Rights, which is to preserve the independence of both the courts and Parliament, is not unwittingly undermined.

Liora Lazarus and Natasha Simonsen, on the other hand, boldly make the case for courts to consider the quality of democratic deliberation about human rights questions when deciding whether and to what extent they should defer to the legislature's final judgment about the issue, as expressed in legislation.[87] Like Fredman, they argue that such judicial evaluation of the quality of democratic deliberation, far from undermining democracy, will in fact enhance it, because it increases the opportunities for courts to defer to the considered judgment of the legislature and so makes it more likely that deference will be accorded where it is due. Drawing on recent developments in the doctrine of the margin of appreciation as applied by the Strasbourg Court (considered below), they seek to build on Fredman's argument that the quality of the legislature's reasoning on human rights issues must be assessed by courts. They suggest some criteria to guide courts when making that assessment of the quality of the democratic deliberation that has taken place and deciding whether the justifications considered by the legislature are sufficiently cogent to be good enough reasons in a democracy for limiting a right. What on the face of it may appear to be undemocratic, they argue, will in fact place parliaments at the centre of deliberation about human rights and, if they rise to the challenge, make it more likely that courts will defer to their legislative judgments on human rights issues.

Kent Roach adopts something of an intermediate position in this particular debate.[88] He agrees that one way to escape the hackneyed, polarised debate about the respective roles of courts and legislatures is to recognise that they both have important roles to play in rights protection, but he argues that each of them has a variety of roles which need to be separated out in order to have a more meaningful debate about the legitimacy of those roles. He is concerned about the possibility of

[87] Chapter 19 in this volume.
[88] Chapter 20 in this volume.

judicial deference to legislative interpretations of rights, because of the danger of it undermining the important counter-majoritarian role of the courts in a democracy and the threat that this poses in particular to 'truly unpopular' groups such as criminals, asylum-seekers, foreigners and terrorism suspects who are usually unrepresented in the mainstream political process.[89] He therefore argues that courts are the primary decision-makers about the scope of rights and that courts should review legislative interpretations of rights on something close to a correctness standard in recognition of this, with little if any scope for due deference. Legislatures, on the other hand, should be recognised as the primary decision-makers on justifying limitations on rights, and courts should therefore be more prepared to defer to legislative judgments of what is a necessary and proportionate limitation on a right. For Roach, then, the relevance of democratic deliberation about rights to subsequent judicial consideration of the same questions will depend on which aspect of rights protection is being considered. If the issue is the nature and definition of the rights, parliament's consideration of the matter is of little or no relevance to the court's determination. But if the issue is the justification for limitations on rights, the quality of deliberation on the matter in parliament (the primary decision-maker on this aspect) is highly relevant to the court's subsequent assessment of the degree of deference that is due to the legislative decision.

The argument that it will enhance not undermine democracy if courts take into account the extent and nature of democratic deliberation when assessing the human rights compatibility of legislation has recently received some empirical support in an important contribution to the debate by Aileen Kavanagh.[90] After examining exactly how courts have made reference to parliamentary debates in cases where the human rights compatibility of primary legislation has been in issue, Kavanagh has shown that UK courts often take cognisance of parliamentary engagement with human rights in such cases and that, for the most part, this has worked in Parliament's favour. This is because where the parliamentary record shows that Parliament has consciously addressed the human rights implications of a bill and has subjected that issue to careful consideration and extensive debate, courts will treat that consideration with respect and give weight to it when assessing the law's human rights compatibility. In a significant finding, she concludes that the net result of the courts' indirect use of parliamentary material has therefore been an increase in judicial deference paid to Parliament. She goes on to make a normative argument in favour of this emerging practice: the extent and quality of parliamentary engagement with the issue of human rights compatibility *should* have a bearing on the degree of judicial deference to the resulting legislative provision. Giving weight to parliamentary deliberation about human rights provides courts with the opportunity to pay the appropriate amount of respect to Parliament's democratic legitimacy

[89] *Cf* Yowell, ch 7 in this volume, who regards the record of the Joint Committee on Human Rights in the UK Parliament as demonstrating that it is possible to establish within a legislature structures that call attention to and advocate for the interests of minorities, including the truly unpopular.

[90] A Kavanagh, 'Proportionality and Parliamentary Debates: Exploring Some Forbidden Territory' (2014) 34 *Oxford J Legal Studies* 443–79.

and the important role it has, shared with the other branches, in upholding and protecting human rights.

There is of course a further normative justification for courts considering the nature and extent of parliamentary consideration of human rights compatibility: it provides the necessary incentive to both governments and parliaments to conduct their own thorough proportionality assessment of legislation which affects human rights, and to make publicly available all the information on which that assessment rests. Indeed, a version of this incentive argument is made by all the contributors to this volume who advocate a democratic culture of justification in some form.[91] If governments and parliaments want the human rights compatibility of their laws to be upheld by courts, they need to demonstrate a conscientious engagement with all the relevant human rights issues as early as possible in the formulation of a policy, and certainly by the time the measure is introduced into Parliament.[92]

In the UK at least, this particular step on the road to a democratic culture of justification has been established for some time. As explained below and elsewhere, Government departments regularly produce human rights memoranda to accompany Government bills, usually containing a detailed explanation of the Government's reasons for its view that the provisions in the bill are compatible with human rights. Moreover, there are clear signs that the incentive of due deference by courts is beginning to be understood by the Government, which is increasingly willing to encourage detailed debate in Parliament about the human rights implications of its legislative proposals and is occasionally explicit in its acknowledgment that a legislative proposal is more likely to withstand judicial scrutiny for human rights compatibility if Parliament has fully debated the human rights issues that it raises.[93]

[91] Legislatures which ignore the hard questions posed by proportionality analysis do so at the peril of judicial intervention (Roach); judicial consideration of parliamentary deliberation gives Parliament an added incentive to take rights seriously during the legislative process (Kavanagh); courts can steer legislative and executive decision-making away from interest-bargaining and towards deliberation by insisting on a deliberative explanation for the legislature's chosen solution and demanding that sufficient information is available about the necessity and proportionality of the law (Fredman); there is a case for deference to Parliament's interpretation on rights issues only when Parliament takes heed of the rights in an appropriate fashion (Dyzenhaus).

[92] See chs 20 and 23 in this volume for consideration of recent developments in the Strasbourg case law on the margin of appreciation that incentivise parliamentary consideration of human rights.

[93] In the Government's human rights memorandum accompanying the Protection of Freedoms Bill 2012, for example, the Government expressly stated that its proposed legislative solution to the problem of retaining DNA following the adverse judgment of the European Court of Human Rights in *S and Marper v UK* (2009) 48 EHRR 50 would be more likely to withstand subsequent legal challenge if Parliament had fully debated the detail of that particular solution and its human rights implications.

Part I

Legislative Review for Human Rights Compatibility

2

Finding and Filling the Democratic Deficit in Human Rights

DAVID KINLEY

I T HAS BEEN 25 years since I first dabbled in the subject matter of the scrutiny of legislative proposals for human rights compliance.[1] Then it was a somewhat novel proposition, and indeed it was still searching for an adequate or even fitting label to go by. Certainly, I was playing around with titles, including such infelicitous tags as '*ex ante* scrutiny', and 'pre-legislative scrutiny', as well as the utterly abominable 'prophylactic scrutiny'. Like old photos of our tragic fashion statements of previous decades, one's sad and bad published words retain the power to embarrass us for a distressingly long half-life. Middle-aged melancholy aside, legislative scrutiny, or whatever its label, is hardly a novel notion any longer, as the contributions to this volume attest. The invitation to contribute, together with some interesting recent developments on legislative scrutiny in Australia, have prompted me to reflect on the purposes and progress of the whole enterprise during that time, and what might be its prospects for the next quarter-century.[2]

Though the mechanics of the process of such scrutiny are important and intriguing, it is how the process intersects with the engine of government as a whole that really matters, as the title of this volume suggests. The notion of a 'democratic deficit' prompts two threshold questions: (1) whether there is one; and (2) what role legislative scrutiny plays in filling it. Indeed, it is very much on the 'threshold' (via these interconnected two questions) that I dwell in this chapter, leaving the difficult details of practice to be covered by other more skilled and knowledgeable contributors.

---

[1] D Kinley, *European Convention on Human Rights: Compliance without Incorporation* (Aldershot, Dartmouth Publishing, 1993).

[2] In Australia, the Scrutiny of Acts and Regulations Committee (SARC) of the Victorian Parliament is required, under s 17 of the Parliamentary Committees Act 2003 (Vic), to, inter alia, consider any bill introduced into the Victorian Parliament and to report on whether it directly or indirectly trespasses unduly on rights or freedoms or is incompatible with the rights set out in the Charter of Human Rights and Responsibilities Act 2006. A Joint Committee on Human Rights has also been recently established in the Commonwealth Parliament under the Human Rights (Parliamentary Scrutiny) Act 2011 (Cth): see David Kinley and Christine Ernst, 'Exile on Main Street: Progress on an Australian Bill of Rights' (2012) 1 *European Human Rights Law Review* 69–81. See further ch 12 below.

I. IS THERE A DEMOCRATIC DEFICIT IN HUMAN RIGHTS RESPECT, PROTECTION AND PROMOTION?

It is instructive (or at least mildly entertaining) to recall what were the content and tenor of these debates on the very same question some 20-plus years ago, when legislative scrutiny expressly for human rights compliance was but an infant idea, and the instruments by which it might be achieved rudimentary or non-existent, across the common law countries that have come to embrace the notion—the UK, Australia, Canada and New Zealand.

Finding the democratic deficit then, as now, was focused on the interplay between law and politics broadly, and, more specifically, on interactions between the legislative and executive arms of government on the one hand, and the judiciary on the other. The perception of human rights law being a branch of political thought and practice (albeit a highly specialised one), or, at the very least, the view that human rights is inseparable from political endeavours, remains for me as strong an argument as ever. Before, during and after the establishment of the many and various human rights institutions over the past 20 years or so, the evidence of the umbilical attachment between politics and human rights has been abundantly apparent. Thus, bills of rights, scrutiny committees, judicial review on human rights grounds, human rights commissions and the paths beaten to the doors of international human rights tribunals have all engendered political debate, as well as being themselves the objects of political influence in various forms and at differing levels of intensity.

This is, and should be, unsurprising, not just because such is the case with all important issues that are the subject of legal regulation, but because such legal regulation tells only part of the story of human rights, their objects and their mechanics. 'Bills of Rights, written constitutions and judicial decisions on rights are', as Conor Gearty argues, 'merely a means to an end.'[3] Thus, to the extent that public politics in our countries reflect particular versions of democratic governance, the road between human rights laws and human rights politics (as wide as it is) is one that is well travelled.

This situation is not necessarily detrimental to the protection and promotion of human rights, still less their death-knell. Rather, it is more a sincere reflection of their *realpolitik,* and of the means by which social and cultural life is continuously breathed into the inert body of legal interpretation and the enforcement of rights. It is no accident that the vast majority of rights jurisprudence in domestic and international fora is focused on marking the appropriate boundaries of exceptions or limitations to rights rather than on the existence of the rights per se. For it is by way of the permissible, or indeed necessary, limitations to human rights (for reasons of national security, public order or public health, or to protect the rights of others) that our contemporary social mores and (admittedly) political expediencies are channelled and expressed.

Though it certainly took British (and Irish and Australian) judges longer to concede their role as policy-makers than, say, those of the US, India and Canada, their

---

[3] C Gearty, *Can Human Rights Survive?* (Cambridge, Cambridge University Press, 2006) 4.

impact on policy is now undeniably manifest and universally accepted. As long ago as 1972, Lord Reid in the UK was hinting at the policy implications of a 'Judge as Lawmaker',[4] and JAG Griffith was working up to his then iconoclastic, and best-selling, *The Politics of the Judiciary* (1977). And while the sensation that Griffith caused stemmed from his critique of the personal politics of the judiciary (or at least the then predomination of a particular class, education and gender in its ranks), his characterisation of the professional practice of judges was equally profound. In the many and growing numbers of cases involving governmental authorities (that is, especially in administrative law, but also torts, contracts and criminal law), he argued that: 'Judicial decisions in such cases are intimately connected with policy.'[5]

One of the most conceptually articulate representations of the judicial function in this context was—and remains—John Bell's 'interstitial legislator model', in which he observed that:

> [W]hether in making a rule or standards for the future, or basing a decision on an open-ended standard, the judge has to balance a variety of social interests and come to a decision which, within the limits of the discretion available, he considers to be best ... To the extent that these value-judgments are integral to the current operation of the judicial function, and, indeed, would seem to some extent inescapable in any legal system, it is in vital respects qualitatively similar to other governmental functions.[6]

So, nowadays, we accept that judges in the common law world are policy analysts, albeit of a particularly rarefied, adjudicatory and institutionally independent kind. Our concerns regarding 'judges as policy-makers' are today focused not on whether they do it, but on how they do it and, more especially—in the present context—on the democratic legitimacy of how they play the role.

The judiciary's role is not 'Herculean'[7] (or at least no more so than any other part of government), but rather one essential segment in what we might call the cycle of governance comprising the actions of government (executive and bureaucracy), the legislature and the judiciary. The cycle is, at base, a political process in which proposals are aired (and barrows pushed); policies are formulated and adopted; legislation is enacted under pain of coercion and compromise; regulations are interpreted, applied and enforced by bureaucracies both administrative and judicial ... and the outcomes of each of these stages are continuously fed back into the system *ad infinitum*.[8] It is therefore, in truth, more a reticulated process than purely cyclical (and certainly not linear), with the most important point being that the three (or four, if the bureaucracy

---

[4] Lord Reid, 'Judge as Lawmaker' (1972) 12 *Journal of the Society of Public Teachers of Law* 22.
[5] JAG Griffith, 'Judicial Decision-Making in Public Law' [1985] *Public Law* 564, 65.
[6] J Bell, *Policy Arguments in Judicial Decisions* (Oxford, Oxford University Press, 1983) 245.
[7] In reference to Ronald Dworkin's depiction of a quintessential judge in *Law's Empire* (Cambridge, MA, Harvard University Press, 1986), even accepting that Dworkin was constructing 'an imaginary judge of superhuman intellectual power and patience who accepts law as integrity' (at 238), who nonetheless is continuously exercised in resolving the many and various tensions that daily arise in the cases that come before him.
[8] *Cf* my depiction of a 'legal expression and enforcement continuum' in 'Legal Expression of Human Rights' in D Kinley (ed), *Human Rights in Australian Law* (Sydney, Federation Press, 1998) 18–24, an explanation behind which I am still happy to stand, even if, again alas, the same cannot be gladly said of its label.

is counted separately) arms of government are all in it together.[9] Like the motto of the Musketeers,[10] the arms of our governments are 'all for one and one for all', being the inseparable and intersecting constituents of our democratic systems.[11] No one part of the whole, therefore, can lay legitimate proprietary claim to be the, or even the principal, seat of democratic representation, and nor, in this process, can any one branch answer 'We do' to the 'Who decides?' question, as posed in Hunt, Hooper and Yowell's research report, *Parliaments and Human Rights: Redressing the Democratic Deficit*.[12] The strong sinews and tendons of responsible government, the separation of (and balance between) powers, parliamentary sovereignty, the rule of law and judicial independence all bind the skeleton of our constitutions and coordinate the limbs of government in ways of almost infinite variety.

By the same token, it is difficult, if not impossible, to pin responsibility for glitches in governance or deficits in democracy to one particular branch of government or another. We are no more encumbered by 'elective dictatorships' of modern Westminster-style governments than by 'unelected krytocracies' emanating from the jurisprudence of modern superior courts. To the extent, then, that we are badly served by those who govern us, the executive is surely as culpable as the judiciary (or Parliament as the bureaucracy).

In this regard we learn, as ever, from history. In terms of the guardianship of rights, we have swung between preferring judges to elected politicians and back again. In so doing, we are informed not only by what our embedded political prejudices tell us, but also by what we know (or perceive) to be the dominant political persuasions of either group at any given time. Thus, the pre- and post-War Left in Europe tended to see social programme-wielding Big Government as progressive and individual rights-protecting judges as regressive.[13] Today many on the Left argue passionately for courts to be given greater powers to protect human rights against government encroachment. The fact that at any one time the collection of those who support robust rights protection by the judiciary contains sometimes strange bedfellows (ranging across the political, social and economic spectrums—left and right, corporations and non-governmental organisations, wealthy and poor) reflects the fickleness of self-interest. But it also reflects our sensitivities to the shifting dynamics of the politics of, and within, Supreme Courts—now, as much a matter of intense study and debate in the UK and Australia, as has been the case in Canada for at least the last 30 years and in the US since *Marbury v Madison* (1803).

---

[9] A 'shared responsibility', as it is termed in Murray Hunt, Hayley Hooper and Paul Yowell, *Parliaments and Human Rights: Redressing the Democratic Deficit* (Arts & Humanities Research Council, 2012) (at 11).

[10] Also questionably three or four, as D'Artagnan was not, at first, one of the band (the three originals being Athos, Porthos and Aramis) in Alexandre Dumas' eponymous novel (1844), but by altogether dashing and dogged persistence he makes it as the fourth in the end.

[11] *Cf*, in the American context, Aharon Barak, *The Judge in a Democracy* (Princeton, Princeton University Press, 2008).

[12] *The Democratic Deficit Report*: see discussion at 9–12.

[13] See Conor Gearty's candid reflections on his own position regarding just this circumstance in 'The Human Rights Act—An Academic Sceptic Changes His Mind But Not His Heart' (2010) 6 *European Human Rights Law Review* 582.

This exercise in stressing the interconnectedness of arms of government serves an important purpose in the present context. It shifts our focus on where to look for any 'democratic deficit'—that is, away from defining the democratic fitness of governmental institutions according to their form (ie, appointed or elected) and more towards defining their democratic fitness according to their function (ie, what do they do and how do they do it?). So, in our quest to identify and then measure any democratic deficit in our processes for protecting and promoting human rights, we might ask: 'To what extent are "we the people" (or our delegates, representatives, appointees and other fiduciaries) missing from, or misrepresented by, that process?'

This, clearly, is not an easy question to answer, not only because of the conceptual difficulties in determining what precisely constitutes democracy—where is it good or better democracy and when we have enough of it—but also because of the practical problems of measurement. Assessing people's access to ballot boxes is one thing, but gauging how well they are being 'represented' by those that govern them is an entirely different order of complexity. And to ask 'how well do the institutions and processes of democracy serve human rights?' does not make the task any easier.

However, at least one way forward on this first threshold question is presented by addressing my second threshold question.

II. WHAT ROLE CAN OR DOES LEGISLATIVE SCRUTINY PLAY IN FILLING ANY DEMOCRATIC DEFICIT?

The mark of modern government is the preponderance of legislation. Statutes regulate us from well before the cradle to long after the grave. Any issue of any importance—and many of little or none—is invariably governed by legislation. The administrative voice of modern government is expressed through Acts and the rules and regulations they spawn. As such, an obvious place to look for how well that voice reflects the 'will of the people', generally speaking and, specifically, whether the voice respects and complies with established human rights standards is the legislature itself. Or rather, the place to look is in the legislative function, stretching as it does from policy formulation through enactment to enforcement.

Setting aside for one moment the question of whether legislative scrutiny for human rights compliance is effective, there is the antecedent question of whether a scrutiny system set up within the legislature is capable of impacting on the law-making function across its full integrated breadth as described.

Existing legislative scrutiny schemes—at least those with a parliamentary committee at their heart—are designed to engage in what might be called 'border exchanges' with the policy formulating and enforcement arms of government. In the UK, therefore, the dialogue and scrutiny committee-based process is meant to infiltrate thinking and action in Whitehall and Westminster; to inculcate 'a culture of rights',[14] as the Government's 1997 White Paper on the *Human Rights Bill* put it.

---

[14] Which phrase, Janet Hiebert remarks, 'at a minimum ... envisages the expectation that prospective state actions that implicate rights should be subject to scrutiny of their merits and legitimacy before they are passed into law'. See 'Governing under the Human Rights Act' [2012] *Public Law* 29, 31.

And while engagement more broadly[15]—that is, with the 'demos' as a whole—was also championed in those early days, the hyperbolic rhetoric has never really made it into reality.

The success or failure of investing altered attitudes towards rights within and without government is especially crucial for the Westminster model of human rights protection precisely because, unlike orthodox bills of rights regimes, this objective constitutes its main aim. The normal bill of rights regime, which provides the power for courts to strike down non-human rights-compliant legislation, places its emphasis on a censorial relationship between courts and Parliament, and less emphasis on the dialogue between them, or between the Executive and Parliament.[16]

Certainly the opportunities for success are present in the 'dialogue model'—at least in theory. The institution of a parliamentary committee scrutinising all draft legislation for compliance with a set of human rights standards apparently offers a comprehensive and proactive vehicle through which to engage with the executive and bureaucracy before policy crystallises into legislation. This was a wan hope more than an expectation in the early days of thinking about legislative scrutiny. However, it became a fervent aspiration of the Blair administration (with Jack Straw providing much of the fervour) and it has since been the same desire standing behind the scrutiny initiatives introduced into three Australian jurisdictions in more recent years. But, we might ask, can such manufactured institutional apparatus be sufficient to change the organic culture of government?

In fact, as noted by a series of authors and reviews over the past 10 years,[17] the road from potential to practice on this question has been a rocky one, even accepting that the promises were somewhat overdone. To the extent that attitudinal changes within institutions of government can be measured at all,[18] it would seem that the assimilation of a 'human rights culture' by ministers and mandarins has been by way of risk management (a perspective neatly captured in earlier days by the regrettable phrase 'Strasbourg-proofing' (now just 'court-proofing')), rather

---

[15] Jack Straw (the then Home Secretary) 'Building a Human Rights Culture', Address to Civil Service College, 9 December 1999.

[16] Another way to look at it is to say that under a Dialogue Bill of Rights model, the courts play only *permissive* role—namely, at first they interpret imaginatively and when that fails, they fire off a warning flare (that is, a declaration of incompatibility)—as distinct from the constitutional regimes where the courts play a *pre-emptory* role by way of their power to strike down legislation.

[17] Including D Nicol, 'The Human Rights Act and the Politicians' (2004) 24 *Legal Studies* 451; D Feldman, 'The Impact of Human Rights on the UK Legislative Process' (2004) 25(2) *Statute Law Review* 91; J Smookler, 'Making a Difference? The Effectiveness of Pre-Legislative Scrutiny' (2006) 59(3) *Parliamentary Affairs* 522; F Klug and H Wildbore, 'Breaking New Ground: The Joint Committee on Human Rights and the Role of the Parliament in Human Rights Compliance' [2007] *European Human Rights Law Review* 231; M Hunt, 'The Impact of the Human Rights Act on the Legislature: A Diminution of Democracy or a New Voice for Parliament?' [2010] *European Human Rights Law Review* 601; Hiebert (n 14); Equality and Human Rights Commission, *Human Rights Inquiry: Report of the Equality and Human Rights Commission* (June 2009); and Department of Constitutional Affairs, *Review of the Implementation of the Human Rights Act* (July 2006).

[18] The difficulty of which is a point well made by the Department of Constitutional Affairs Review of the UK's Human Rights Act in 2006 (at 19).

than by widespread understanding and active promotion of human rights goals.[19] This is not a bad result, of course, and to be fair it is the stereotypical response of private offices and public bureaucracies everywhere to any new strictures placed on them.

Thus, Janet Hiebert's recent study of the impact of the UK's Human Rights Act 1998 on the behaviour of public officials suggests that the requirement of statements of compatibility, the robustness of the UK's Joint Committee on Human Rights' (JCHR) scrutiny of bills, and the prospect of court sanction (albeit warning rather than annulling) 'has sharpened the focus, regularity and rigour of rights-based vetting across departments'.[20] Similarly—although with the benefit of only four years of hindsight—a 2011 review of the impact of the Victorian *Charter of Human Rights and Responsibilities* (2006) revealed evidence of a number of individual departments (eg, Education, Health and Transport) having policies in place that make explicit reference to the need for policy proposals and draft legislation to comply with the rights provisions in the Charter.[21] The Victorian experience regarding the impact that its scrutiny committee (the Scrutiny of Acts and Regulations Committee (SARC)) has had on parliamentary debates is also encouraging. Data collected by the Victorian Equal Opportunities Human Rights Committee (VEOHRC) noted that of the 90 bills considered by Parliament in 2010, 43 generated active exchanges between the Committee and the MP presenting the bill, and 42 triggered parliamentary comment on human rights issues.[22]

Interestingly, in this specific respect, the experience in the UK was altogether different in its first (five) years, although that has since been conclusively reversed, as noted in Hunt, Hooper and Yowell's research report. So, whereas there were only 23 substantive references to the work of the UK's JCHR between 2001 and 2005, this figure rose to 1,006 between 2005 and 2010.[23]

It can be fairly said, therefore, that the human rights-specific apparatus of legislative scrutiny has helped fill in the democratic deficit, insofar as the above-mentioned outcomes reflect a level of increased engagement on human rights issues across the legislative and executive arms of government. This is the filling of a democratic deficit of a 'representative' or indirect kind.

In terms of legislative scrutiny's more *direct* democratic impact on perceptions of human rights throughout society more broadly, the record is predictably poorer. I say 'predictably' because there is hardly any aspect of Parliament's daily business—with the possible exception of the theatrics of Question Time—that the majority of the wider community is even vaguely familiar with, let alone directly engaging with.

[19] Whitehall has been 'sometimes grumblingly receptive' in this respect, as Conor Gearty puts it: see Gearty (n 13) 582.
[20] Hiebert (n 14) 35 and 41.
[21] Parliament of Victoria, Scrutiny of Acts and Regulations Committee, *Review of the Charter of Human Rights and Responsibilities Act 2006* ('SARC Review (2011)'), ch 4. Interestingly the SARC's somewhat lukewarm finding on this point contrasts with a much more positive interpretation of the situation offered by the VEOHRC's Submission to the SARC Inquiry, *Putting Principle into Practice* (July 2011) 126–41.
[22] ibid 140.
[23] *Parliaments and Human Rights: Addressing the Democratic Deficit* (n 9), (at 7).

So it is unsurprising that legislative scrutiny, even for human rights compliance, attracts so little attention in the broad-based public or media spheres. The very few times that the objects of their scrutiny obtain widespread public attention (such as the UK's identity cards bill or anti-terrorism amendments),[24] it is for reasons other than the revelations of a scrutiny committee's inquiry.

In part, this circumstance can be explained by the very comprehensiveness of coverage of the work of a scrutiny committee itself, for such comprehensiveness is also its curse. The remit of having to scrutinise all (government) legislative proposals before Parliament for their human rights probity makes the work and products of scrutiny committees everyday, humdrum activities, with human rights controversy being the exception rather than the rule. And, indeed, at a fundamental level, that is how it should be: all-inclusive, 'part of the furniture' and finding relatively few skeletons in the cupboards.

There does appear to be evidence of the scrutiny process helping to prompt government departments to consult more thoroughly with relevant community and stakeholder groups on policy proposals (according to the VEOHRC's submission to the 2011 Victorian Review),[25] and certainly the scrutiny process itself, as well as targeted, 'thematic' inquiries on specific and 'pressing' human rights concerns (such as those conducted by the JCHR), do attract wider public interest and participation, albeit mainly from self-selected specialist and stakeholder groups.[26]

Further, the very work of the legislative review inevitably tends towards specialism—not just the specialism of human rights, but also the technicalities of legislation-making and the particularities of the subject matter at hand. As a result, and as a number of commentators have noted,[27] the reports of the UK's JCHR tend toward more heavy analyses of human rights jurisprudence than light-touch briefing notes and action strategies, which parliamentarians have problems understanding, let alone the ordinary voter. That said, it is frankly difficult to see how they could be substantially otherwise; it is nonetheless a valuable and otherwise neglected legislative service; and it is surely fair to expect others (interest groups and activists, the media and those very parliamentarians) to translate the exegeses into policy where required.

---

[24] On which see A Tomkins, 'Parliament, Human Rights, and Counter-Terrorism' in T Campbell et al (eds), *Legal Protection of Human Rights: Sceptical Essays* (Oxford, Oxford University Press, 2011) 21–39.

[25] 'Many departments have advised the Commission that one of the major impacts of the Charter has been a more considered approach to the impact of new laws, which has resulted in better drafting. This approach has included greater community engagement and consultation during the legislative development process': VEOHRC (n 21), (at 128).

[26] For present session publications, see www.parliament.uk/business/committees/committees-a-z/joint-select/human-rights-committee/publications, and for previous sessions' publications (from 2001), see www.parliament.uk/business/committees/committees-a-z/joint-select/human-rights-committee/publications/previous-sessions.

[27] As noted by Klug and Wildbore (n 17) 41; and Heibert (n 14) 43.

CONCLUSION

So, in conclusion, I shall try to bring together my cursory answers to the two threshold questions I posed. First, it would appear that there is something of a common democratic deficit in the understanding, promotion and protection of human rights. Its root lies in the nature of our shared Westminster-based system of government rather than with any one branch of it. And yet the process of legislative scrutiny for human rights compliance—at least in its basic form of establishing a dedicated parliamentary scrutiny committee and instituting a process of departmental self-analysis and regulation—can and does play a meaningful role in combating that deficit, not least by way of engaging the executive/bureaucratic and legislative arms of government in human rights deliberations and analysis. Given this, and to adopt a realistic perspective of what legislative scrutiny might be expected to achieve, it seems to me that it is both worthy and worthwhile, and is making ground. The experience is still young, even for the UK's model, and is positively newborn in respect of the Australian federal model, so more time will fill out the bigger picture.

One might be even bolder and venture that the legislative scrutiny dimension of the various models of bills of rights that are considered in this volume is, in fact, their most subtly successful feature. Certainly, it is the less controversial. For all its limitations and faults, legislative scrutiny has been saved the ignominy of being labelled futile—as Keith Ewing sees the efforts of the courts to protect human rights under the UK's Human Rights Act, or being recommended for excision from the whole process of human rights protection—as was suggested should be the fate of the courts under the Victorian Human Rights and Responsibilities Charter (based on the extraordinary argument that the imprecision of the terms of the Charter were resulting in mixed messages coming from the courts).[28] Whether or not we share these views is not a point I pursue here. Rather, my aim is to stress the fact that legislative scrutiny for human rights compliance is not only a desirable but a necessary feature that enhances democratic governance. And it's here to stay, warts and all.

---

[28] SARC Review, 2011 (n 21), 171–73. To its credit, the Victorian Government's response to this suggestion was to maintain that in its view 'there is an ongoing place for the courts in protecting rights in relation to the Charter', and hinting at the fact that the interpretation of imprecise terms is core function of the courts; see the Victorian Government Response to the SARC Review, 14 March 2012, 23 and 24.

3

Legislative Rights Review: Addressing the Gap between Ideals and Constraints

JANET HIEBERT[1]

B ILLS OF RIGHTS generally operate to invoke 'the machinery of the courts to set binding constraints on political decision-making'[2] and thus combine judicial review with strong judicial remedial power. The UK's Human Rights Act (HRA) departs from this view of how a bill of rights functions. The HRA, which incorporates the European Convention on Human Rights into domestic law, draws a greater distinction between judicial review and judicial remedies than in more conventional models of a bill of rights, and thus does not authorise courts to impose binding remedies such as to invalidate legislation or refuse to enforce laws that are inconsistent with rights. Thus, short of using their interpretive power to render a rights-friendly application of otherwise inconsistent legislation,[3] courts in the UK can only declare legislation to be incompatible with protected rights,[4] at which point redressing judicially identified rights violations is dependent upon a political willingness to implement remedial measures.

The HRA also departs from conventional wisdom in another important way by contemplating regular parliamentary engagement with questions of compatibility with rights. This concept of justifying legislation from a rights-based perspective in parliament can be referred to as legislative rights review. The political decision to introduce legislative rights review can be viewed as an ambitious and optimistic attempt to create a new norm for legislative decision-making, one that emphasises

[1] This chapter borrows from JL Hiebert and JB Kelly, *Parliamentary Bills of Rights. The Experiences of New Zealand and the United Kingdom* (Cambridge, Cambridge University Press, 2015); and JL Hiebert, 'Governing under the Human Rights Act: The Limitations of Wishful Thinking' [2012] *Public Law* 27. I am grateful to Danny Nicol for his critical observations and helpful suggestions. I would also like to acknowledge financial assistance in the form of a grant from the Social Science and Humanities Research Council of Canada.
[2] Sujit Choudhry uses this conception in his discussion of the nation-building function of a bill of rights: S Choudhry, 'Bills of Rights as Instruments of Nation Building in Multinational States: The Canadian Charter and Quebec Nationalism' in JB Kelly and EP Manfredi (eds), *Contested Constitutionalism: Reflections on the Canadian Charter of Rights and Freedoms* (Vancouver, UBC Press, 2009) 239.
[3] Under s 3 HRA.
[4] Under s 4 HRA.

the importance of confronting whether and how proposed legislation implicates rights adversely and engaging in reasoned judgment about whether the initiative should be amended or is nevertheless justified despite its potentially adverse effects for rights. This norm is expected to apply throughout the legislative process, from the early stages of bureaucratic policy development of identifying compatibility issues and advising on more compliant ways to achieve a legislative initiative, through to the Cabinet process of deciding whether to proceed with legislative bills, and ultimately in parliamentary deliberation about whether to approve legislation or put pressure on the government to make amendments. The idea of legislative rights review in the HRA also assumes a political willingness to revisit the merits of legislation and consider remedies in the event of a judicial declaration that legislation is not compatible with protected rights.

The incorporation of legislative rights review into the HRA reflects a highly idealised vision of how rights will be protected. Although it appears modest in terms of assurances that remedies will be forthcoming should courts subsequently rule that legislation is inconsistent with protected rights, the idea of marrying a bill of rights with an expectation for legislative rights review suggests a potentially far-reaching way of guarding against rights infringements because it assumes that all legislation will be subject to some form of rights-based review, and not just that small portion of legislation that will be litigated and subject to judicial review in more conventional bills of rights.[5]

However, before celebrating the transformative potential of legislative rights review in the UK, a strong cautionary warning is appropriate. This chapter raises serious doubts about whether the introduction of legislative rights review will fundamentally reorient political behaviour and legislative decision-making in a manner commensurate with this idealised notion of proactive rights protection—at least any time soon. These doubts are based on reflections on the institutional and political context in which this optimistic idea is situated and on interviews with political officials charged with responsibility for evaluating proposed legislation.[6] Section I

---

[5] This argument was made earlier by the author in JL Hiebert, 'Constitutional Experimentation: Rethinking How a Bill of Rights Functions' in T Ginsberg and R Dixon (eds), *Comparative Constitutional Law* (Cheltenham, Edward Elgar, 2011).

[6] Interviews with public officials were conducted in the UK between 2005 and 2012 for Hiebert and Kelly (n 1). Interviews were conducted on the basis of anonymity, and hereinafter will be referred to as 'Interviews'. Questions asked of public officials and legal advisors included the following. What kind of training was introduced to understand how the bill of rights relates to the department or agency's responsibilities? Was this training adequate? How has the bill of rights altered the process or considerations for assessing legislative proposals? How is the bill of rights interpreted at the departmental or agency level? Are those evaluating policy knowledgeable about the bill of rights? Do policy officials participate in judgment about compatibility? Who determines whether proposed legislation is compatible? Do lawyers dominate determinations of compatibility? Are determinations of compatibility a task that only lawyers can or should perform? How relevant is case law when determining the meaning and scope of rights? How difficult is it to determine whether a legislative initiative is consistent with case law? Does departmental guidance on compatibility change as case law changes? Is there resistance to advice about compatibility? How is resistance expressed? Would the policy process be improved if more departmental officials (non-lawyers in particular) saw their role as requiring assessments about compatibility? How much discretion is there for departments and ministers to proceed with an initiative that is inconsistent with case law? Do ministers resist advice about compatibility? Do ministers place pressure on legal advisers to alter their advice on compatibility so as to permit a positive report? Does political criticism of the

discusses the origins and ideas associated with the concept of legislative rights review. Section II analyses the significance of the institutional context in which this UK experiment with legislative rights review is situated. The chapter argues that although Parliament has the benefit of robust and independent rights-based scrutiny conducted by its specialised rights committee (the Joint Committee on Human Rights (JCHR)), this important resource on its own is insufficient to encourage parliamentarians to focus on the rights-infringing implications of legislation when pursuing amendments or when influencing the vote. Executive dominance of the House of Commons and the centrality of disciplined political parties are the pervasive characteristics of how Westminster parliamentary government operates and together they function in a manner that undermines the capacity of the House of Commons to become an effective venue for legislative rights review.

Legislative rights review in the UK is also undermined by two other factors. One is the nature of the trigger mechanism for disagreeing with adverse judicial rulings and the other is unresolved ambiguity about how the principle of parliamentary sovereignty relates to or affects the mission of a bill of rights that emphasises the importance of confronting and justifying decisions that implicate rights. These factors make non-compliance easier to sustain by weakening political pressure on parliament and government to justify decisions that present serious questions of compatibility.

I. CONSTRUCTING A LEGISLATIVELY ORIENTED BILL OF RIGHTS

The framers of the HRA did not invent the idea of legislative rights review, but they introduced significant modifications to how this practice operates elsewhere (discussed below). The idea originated in 1960 with the introduction of the Canadian Bill of Rights, which envisaged what at the time seemed a novel idea: of marrying the idea of a statutory bill of rights with an expectation that government and parliament consider whether legislation is consistent with rights as a regular part of the policy and legislative processes. Thus, the Canadian federal Justice Minister was required to inform parliament when government bills are inconsistent with rights, which was expected to precipitate pre-legislative rights-based review of proposed legislation within the bureaucracy, create disincentives for ministers to propose legislation that would require an adverse report on consistency, and stimulate increased parliamentary pressure on government to amend bills in the event that government decided to proceed with inconsistent legislation.[7] The introduction of pre-legislative rights review within a Westminster-based parliamentary system was considered by its most ardent defenders as a robust way to protect rights that

---

bill of rights affect policy evaluation or assessments of compatibility? Will ministers claim that a bill is compatible in the face of contrary legal advice? Will a minister proceed to cabinet and sponsor a bill that would require a report of incompatibility? Do departments/ministers shop around for more favourable legal advice on compatibility?

[7] JL Hiebert, *Charter Conflicts: What is Parliament's Role?* (Montreal, McGill-Queen's University Press, 2002) 4–7.

could rival if not surpass the kind of rights protection associated with the US Bill of Rights. As a former Deputy Minister of Justice opined, legislative rights review would enlist all branches of government in this exercise and thus could attain a level of intra-institutional engagement with rights that is not possible in a separated system such as the US:

> All future laws are ... purified before they become laws ... This process is possible only under a parliamentary system of government, where officials are responsible to Ministers, Ministers to the House of Commons, and the House of Commons to the electorate. The whole machinery of government—apart from the courts—is enlisted by the [Canadian] Bill of Rights to ensure that fundamental rights and freedoms are safeguarded ... This kind of control is not possible with a congressional system of government, where there is complete separation between the executive and the legislature and where the executive cannot control the content of bills submitted to the legislature.[8]

Although the concept of legislative rights review in Canada did not evolve as intended,[9] New Zealand subsequently borrowed this idea when developing the New Zealand Bill of Rights Act. The then Prime Minister Geoffrey Palmer (who had earlier visited Canada where he learned about the concept) included it in the Bill of Rights Act in an effort to compensate for a weaker form of judicial power than initially proposed.[10] New Zealand Attorneys-General have not shied away from acknowledging an inability to claim that bills are consistent with the rights and, at the time of writing, have made more than 60 reports of inconsistency.[11] Attorneys-General from different political parties have expressed reservations about the prudence of being constrained by legal perspectives on compatibility. Some have gone so far as to suggest that introducing legislation that would require an acknowledgment of inconsistency can be viewed as a badge of honour, depending on the issue(s) involved.[12]

In explaining his reasons for adopting this concept of legislative rights review for the UK, then Home Secretary Jack Straw emphasised the following two benefits. First, this practice of assessing how proposed legislation implicates rights would help protect rights without undermining the democratic principle of representative self-government. Alongside frequent explanations of how and why the HRA retains the principle of parliamentary sovereignty, the framers praised the HRA for its potential to change the way in which legislative initiatives are assessed before being

---

[8] E Driedger, 'The Meaning and Effect of the Canadian Bill of Rights: A Draftsman's Viewpoint' (1977) 9 *Ottawa Law Review* 316.

[9] Hiebert (n 7) 4–19; JB Kelly, *Governing with the Charter: Legislative and Judicial Activism and Framers' Intent* (Vancouver, UBC Press, 2005) 222–57.

[10] G Palmer, *Unbridled Power? An Interpretation of New Zealand's Constitution and Government* (Wellington, Oxford University Press, 1979) 59–60.

[11] New Zealand, Ministry of Justice, www.justice.govt.nz/policy/constitutional-law-and-human-rights/human-rights/domestic-human-rights-protection/about-the-new-zealand-bill-of-rights-act/advising-the-attorney-general/section-7-reports-published-before-august-2002/section-7-reports-published-before-august-2002.

[12] Interviews were conducted with public officials in New Zealand who assess whether proposed legislation is consistent with the New Zealand Bill of Rights Act. These interviews were conducted between 2006 and 2007 on the basis of anonymity.

passed and also to guide the exercise of power by public authorities.[13] They portrayed the HRA as a way to improve the political process itself, to make governing more sensitive about decisions that implicate rights, and argued that: 'Parliament itself should play a leading role in protecting the rights which are at the heart of a parliamentary democracy.'[14]

Second, legislative rights review was presented as a way to provide more comprehensive rights protection than by relying on a more court-centric bill of rights. In its most idealistic version, political proponents of the HRA boasted that rights would be protected by promoting a culture of rights rather than having to rely solely or predominantly on a litigation culture, because the HRA's prudential design would 'get human rights to run in the bloodstream of each department'.[15] As the then Home Secretary Jack Straw opined, pre-legislative consideration for Convention rights would 'form the anchor for all policy making'—a promise, he insisted, that was not 'mere jargon' because the HRA would change habits of mind, intellectual reflexes and professional sensibilities of public and political authorities.[16] Similarly, Tony Blair echoed this idea that the HRA would facilitate a culture of rights, stating that the HRA 'requires all of us in public service to respect human rights in everything we do'.[17]

Whether or not consciously motivated by perceived shortcomings in how legislative rights review has evolved in Canada and New Zealand, the framers of the HRA made four significant changes to how this practice would function in the UK. First, the reporting requirement was expanded to require a report on all government bills, and not just those that were patently incompatible, which addresses shortcomings that are particularly notable in Canada, where the broad criterion for determining compatibility can produce a misleading assumption that the absence of a report indicates that there is no reason for concern for whether or how a legislative bill implicates rights.[18] Second, responsibility for reporting was vested with whichever minister was introducing a bill, rather than with the Minister of Justice (Canada) or the Attorney-General (New Zealand), to reflect the political intention that the HRA facilitates a culture of rights throughout the government.[19] Third, the reporting requirement recognises the bicameral nature of the UK Parliament by requiring a report both in the House of Commons and in the House of Lords. Fourth, and most significantly, a specialised parliamentary rights committee was created to strengthen Parliament's capacity to question ministerial claims of compatibility and to increase the justificatory burden for proceeding with bills that implicate rights adversely.

---

[13] J Straw, 'Building a Human Rights Culture', Address to Civil Service College Seminar, 9 December 1999, www.nationalarchives.gov.uk/ERORecords/HO/415/1/hract/cscspe.htm.

[14] Home Office, *Rights Brought Home: The Human Rights Bill* (Cm 3782, 1997) para 3.6.

[15] Quotation from unnamed Permanent Secretary, as referred to by J Croft, 'Whitehall and the Human Rights Act' (London, Constitution Unit, 2000), www.ucl.ac.uk/spp/publications/unit-publications/61.pdf.

[16] Straw (n 13).

[17] 'Conventional Behaviour: Questions about the HRA, and Introduction for Aublic Authorities' (Home Office, 1999), as referred to by F Klug, 'The Long Road to Human Rights Compliance' (2006) 57(1) *Northern Ireland Legal Quarterly* 189.

[18] Hiebert (n 7) 13.

[19] Interviews.

II. CONSTRAINTS ON LEGISLATIVE RIGHTS REVIEW

Two institutional reforms were introduced to implement legislative rights review in the UK. One was the introduction of a statutory requirement in section 19 of the HRA that ministers either report to Parliament that a bill is compatible with Convention rights or, alternatively, that they wish to proceed with a bill despite their inability to report that the bill is compatible. This reporting requirement was expected to force ministers to confront how potential legislation implicates rights, to direct departmental and ministerial attention to whether revisions are warranted, and to draw Parliament's attention to the rights dimension of legislation so as to increase the burden on the government to justify legislation that implicates rights adversely. The second reform was the creation of the JCHR to augment Parliament's capacity to review legislation in terms of its compatibility with Convention rights.

An optimistic interpretation of having introduced legislative rights review is that it represents a concerted attempt to create a new norm for legislative decision-making—a norm that emphasises the importance of confronting how legislative initiatives implicate rights and justifying bills in terms of their adverse effects for rights before legislation is passed into law.[20] However, notwithstanding the bold promises made by Jack Straw and Tony Blair of how the union of a bill of rights with legislative rights review would alter political behaviour and practices, they did not explain whether or why the relatively modest changes for facilitating legislative rights review would fundamentally alter the norms for legislative decision-making.

As discussed earlier, executive dominance of the House of Commons and the centrality of disciplined political parties are the driving factors that influence how Westminster parliamentary government operates. Both of these factors shape and constrain political behaviour in a manner that hinders two requirements for effective legislative rights review. One requirement is that ministers explain how bills implicate rights, and what arguments or evidence support a positive report that a bill is compatible with protected rights or justify the government's decision to proceed with a bill where a positive claim of compatibility cannot be made. The second requirement is that parliamentarians assess these explanations and, where unconvinced about their merits, pressure government to redress serious rights-based concerns or provide compelling reasons why a bill is justified, despite its implications for protected rights.

The British House of Commons, like lower houses in other Westminster-based parliamentary systems, operates as an adversarial institution with highly disciplined political parties. Party leaders exert strong control on how members vote, with elected members of the governing party generally supporting the government and members from opposing parties frequently opposing the government, in which case their party leadership tries to establish their party as the best alternative to the government. This orientation has a significant influence on how

---

[20] Hiebert and Kelly (n 1) 1.

bills are evaluated by frequently directing debate to conceive of the resolution of complex issues as often reducible to two viewpoints—in support of the government or in opposition to it.

Assuming that cohesive political parties continue to play a key role organising how the House of Commons functions, robust legislative rights review will require a significant shift in the assumptions and behaviour of how the House of Commons currently operates. More specifically, it will require opposition party leaders to significantly adjust their political strategies so that in addition to their more conventional focus on philosophical and policy differences that distinguish their party from the governing party, the relative merits of leaders' and parties' track records on particular issues, and how to exploit these differences for political and electoral advantage, they also accord more attention to how the HRA appropriately guides or constrains legislative bills and whether proposed legislation is compatible with Convention rights. However, whether due to genuine disagreement about the merits of compatibility-based assessments structuring or influencing the vote, or strategic consideration of what kind of arguments are most useful for political and electoral purposes, party leaders have not yet embraced the idea of incorporating an emphasis on compatibility with Convention rights into their political agendas (this statement was less applicable to the Liberal Democrats before they became part of the Coalition government). To the extent that the Labour and Conservative Parties engage in debates about the HRA, their political strategies do not emphasise HRA compliance, but often take more oppositional and antagonistic positions that exploit public concerns and ambivalence about the merits of the HRA, promote Convention rights and public safety in oppositional terms, and engage in anti-HRA rhetoric so as to gain political traction from the tabloid press' deep hostility towards the HRA.[21]

The Labour government engaged in anti-HRA rhetoric soon after encountering its first serious challenge of legislating under the constraints of protected rights. The then Home Secretary David Blunkett publicly indicated his contempt for judicial review, stating he was 'fed up with having to deal with a situation where Parliament debates issues and the judges overturn them',[22] and characterised the passage of the HRA as the Blair government's 'biggest mistake' in its first term of office.[23] The government's anti-HRA rhetoric intensified significantly a few years later after the London bombings of 2005, when Blair challenged judicial authority on questions involving national security,[24] announced he was prepared to amend the HRA if his government's interpretation of how to protect national security encountered 'legal obstacles'[25] and threatened to renounce aspects of the Convention if the judiciary

---

[21] Hiebert and Kelly (n 1) 398.

[22] F Gibb, 'Blunkett vs. the Bench: The Battle has Begun' *The Times* (4 May 2003), available at: www.business.timesonline.co.uk/tol/business/law/article1115351.ece.

[23] *BBC News* (18 November 2001), available at: www.news.bbc.co.uk/2/hi/programmes/breakfast_with_frost/1662785.stm.

[24] 'The Rules of the Game are Changing' *The Guardian* (5 August 2005), available at: www.guardian.co.uk/attackonlondon/story/0,16132,1543359,00.html.

[25] 'Full Text of Blair Statement on Extremism' *The Times* (5 August 2005), www.timesonline.co.uk/article/0,,22989-1722621,00.html.

blocked deportation decisions.[26] Conservative Prime Minister David Cameron has also been extremely critical of the HRA, not only pledging to repeal it, but going so far as to blame the HRA for the summer 2011 riots that occurred in some metropolitan areas. According to Cameron, human rights laws are having a 'corrosive influence on behaviour and morality'.[27] Cameron has also criticised the idea of having to comply with decisions from the European Court of Human Rights (ECtHR) in his discussions of prisoner voting, in which he has stated publicly that the idea of extending the franchise to prisoners so as to comply with the ECtHR has left him 'physically ill'.[28] In 2013, the Conservatives ramped up their rhetoric against being constrained by judicial review when then Home Secretary Theresa May announced that the Conservative Party would again campaign in the next election on repealing the HRA and that all options, including withdrawing from the European Convention on Human Rights, upon which the HRA is based, should be on the table.[29]

If political leaders continue to ignore compatibility-based assessments in their review of legislative bills, this norm of proactive rights-based justification will only shape parliamentary behaviour in the House of Commons if significant numbers of elected members exert greater independence from their party leadership. Although a substantial number of government backbench members occasionally exert autonomy from party whips, government control over its parliamentary caucus in the House of Commons has been sufficiently robust to minimise the number of defeats the government encounters (particularly when it has a majority). In any event, rebel backbench action is only rarely directed at redressing perceived rights infringements.[30]

The second fundamental characteristic of Westminster parliamentary government is executive dominance of Parliament and, in particular, the House of Commons. Executive dominance and the corresponding decline in Parliament's powers have long been a deep concern in the face of the government's willingness to exploit 'the full scope for untrammelled power latent in the British constitution but obscured by the hesitancy and scruples of previous consensus-based political leaders'.[31] The centrality of disciplined political parties in determining how Westminster operates serves the executive well, particularly when enjoying an electoral majority. For example, the Blair government suffered no legislative defeats in the House of Commons in its first term of office,[32] despite passing

[26] G Jones, 'Blair to Curb Human Rights in War on Terror' *Daily Telegraph* (6 August 2005), available at: www.telegraph.co.uk/news/main.jhtml?xml=/news/2005/08/06/nblair06.xml.
[27] 'Cameron's War on Feckless Families: PM Attacks the Human Rights Laws and Backs National Service' *Daily Mail* (17 August 2011), available at: www.dailymail.co.uk/news/article-2026163/David-Cameron-UK-riots-speech-PM-attacks-human-rights-laws-backs-national-service.html.
[28] 'Prison Votes Will Be Kept to a Minimum' *BBC News* (20 January 2011), available at: www.bbc.co.uk/news/uk-politics-12233938.
[29] S Walters, 'A Great Day for British Justice: Theresa May Vows to Take UK out of the European Court of Human Rights' *Daily Mail*, (4 March 2013), available at: www.dailymail.co.uk/news/article-2287183/A-great-day-British-justice-Theresa-May-vows-UK-European-Court-Human-Rights.html.
[30] Hiebert and Kelly (n 1) 398.
[31] KD Ewing and CA Gearty, *Freedom under Thatcher: Civil Liberties in Modern Britain* (Oxford, Clarendon Press, 1990) 7.
[32] 'Government Defeats on the Floor of the House of Commons', available at: www.election.demon.co.uk/defeats.html.

anti-terrorist measures that were widely criticised for seriously infringing upon rights and were subject to frequent and substantive criticisms by the JCHR and the House of Lords. Although questions of human rights compatibility more often arise in the House of Lords than in the House of Commons, the government's ability to rely on disciplined voting from its party members in the House of Commons has allowed it to frequently overturn rights-inspired amendments passed in the House of Lords. Moreover, if a bill is sufficiently important to the government, party discipline can also be exerted effectively even in the Lords, notwithstanding serious rights-based concerns, as occurred recently with respect to the Justice and Security Bill (discussed below).

A. Assessments of Compatibility

All legislative initiatives are evaluated by departmental legal advisors from the perspective of whether they are compatible with Convention rights. These assessments facilitate consideration about how to make legislative initiatives more HRA-compliant; for example by narrowing or altering the scope of the objective or considering alternative ways to pursue the goal. Legal advisors also provide assessments about the probability that the initiative could be litigated and/or declared incompatible with Convention rights. These risk assessments rely heavily on legal advisors' interpretations of relevant case law. The criterion used is whether a bill has a higher than 50 per cent chance of being declared incompatible with Convention rights. Advisors indicated that they recommend that a minister should not report that the bill is compatible if there is a stronger than 50 per chance that the government would lose if the legislation is subjection to litigation.[33]

This advice plays an important role in helping ministers to fulfil their statutory obligation to report on whether a bill is compatible with Convention rights and, as discussed earlier, is expected to contribute to a new norm for legislative decision-making that ministers and Parliament satisfy themselves that their decision to pass legislation is justified in terms of the potential effects on Convention rights.

In order for a departmental legislative initiative to proceed as a bill before Parliament, the initiative requires Cabinet approval in the Parliamentary Business and Legislation Committee, and the proposed bill must also have been subject to a human rights assessment. Interviews with public officials suggest that although an inability to claim a proposed bill is compatible with Convention rights will not necessarily prevent the initiative from going forward, the government has a strong preference that bills be accompanied by an affirmative report on compatibility.[34] Despite frequent criticisms of the HRA by both Labour and Conservative Party leaders, any government has a strong interest in being fully informed of whether a legislative initiative has a serious chance of being litigated and of ways to reduce that risk before deciding to commit itself politically to introduce the legislative bill.

[33] Interviews.
[34] Interviews.

Litigation can result in the government incurring significant fiscal and policy costs, as well as generating political pressure to revisit the matter, particularly if the ECtHR declares that legislation infringes upon Convention rights.

However, the legal advice about compatibility that ministers or the Cabinet receive is not binding on their decisions of whether to support a legislative initiative.[35] Independent of the idea of developing a new norm of rights-based justification for legislative decisions, whether and how the government acts on this legal advice is ultimately a political judgment about how to manage the risks associated with judicial review and possible political criticism that can be anticipated, particularly from the JCHR and the House of Lords. Once advised about whether an initiative is compatible with Convention rights and the degree of risk it carries of being litigated and subject to judicial censure, the government decides whether and how much risk it is prepared to take.[36] These decisions about how to proceed under the HRA are shaped by a variety of political and electoral considerations that almost certainly include the government's ideological or philosophical views on how Convention rights appropriately guide or constrain the legislative objective in question; the policy and fiscal consequences of having courts rule that legislation is not compatible with Convention rights; calculations about how much time a government might have before legislation is subject to pressure to introduce remedial measures; whether and how the government can utilise a negative judicial ruling in a strategic manner; strategic calculations of how risk-taking or risk-aversion will be interpreted in the broader partisan and political communities that influence the government's political standing and electoral prospects; and, ultimately, a political calculation of whether the political benefits for the government party of passing risky legislation justify any long-term adverse implications.[37]

Interviews with public officials and legal advisors confirm that ministers have claimed compatibility even in circumstances where a relatively high level of risk was identified.[38] Nevertheless, all but two bills introduced into Parliament have been accompanied by an affirmation of compatibility,[39] despite frequent reports by the JCHR that contest ministers' reports of compatibility. This suggests that although the Cabinet is prepared to approve bills where the claim of compatibility is contested, the government is rarely willing to inform Parliament that it cannot be confident that its compatibility assessment will escape successful challenge in court, or explain the reasons for claiming the bill is compatible with Convention rights, despite being advised by its own lawyers that the bill is risky (see below).

---

[35] Interviews.

[36] Interviews.

[37] Hiebert and Kelly (n 1) 288–91.

[38] Interviews.

[39] The Labour government acknowledged an inability to claim compatibility with respect to its Communications Bill in 2002. In 2012, Deputy Prime Minister Nick Clegg in the Conservative-led Coalition government indicated that he was unable to state that the House of Lords Reform Bill 2012–13 was compatible with the HRA (because the provisions dealing with elections for the House of Lords did not extend the franchise to prisoners). In addition, two other negative statements were made following amendments made by the House of Lords to the Civil Partnership Bill and the Local Government Bill.

B. Parliament's Role in Legislative Rights Review

As argued earlier, a key requirement for effective legislative rights review is that Parliament is prepared to critically assess whether bills are compatible with Convention rights and determine if they should be amended, defeated or are justified despite their adverse implications for rights. By implication, this requires scrutinising the reasons a minister has used to conclude that a bill is compatible with Convention rights, or the reasons for deciding to proceed with a bill for which he or she is unable to report as being compatible with Convention rights. This emphasis on substantive explanations for ministerial reports on compatibility should not be interpreted as an expectation that ministers disclose confidential legal advice related to the likelihood of litigation or the specific arguments they anticipate having to make to support their claims of compatibility in any legal proceedings. However, it is difficult to imagine how Parliament can engage in meaningful legislative rights review, and whether amendments are warranted, if Parliament does not require ministers to provide substantial explanations for the assumptions or evidence that support their political judgment that rights have been appropriately considered and that bills are justified in light of their implications for protected rights. This situation is even more problematic if the JCHR has raised serious concerns about compatibility and is not satisfied with the departmental or ministerial responses it has received.

The JCHR plays a significant and supporting role contributing to the norm that legislative decision-making confronts how legislative bills implicate rights and engages in reasoned judgment about whether bills should be amended or are nevertheless justified in light of their implications for protected rights. The JCHR has earned a well-deserved reputation as a principled committee that exercises robust scrutiny of bills, with a particular focus on whether bills are compatible with Convention rights.

One way in which the JCHR contributes to this norm is through its unrelenting questioning of ministers and departments about the reasons for concluding whether a bill is compatible with Convention rights and to explain decisions about the scope of legislative objectives and the means being promoted to achieve these. The JCHR's persistent questioning along these lines has increased officials' interest in avoiding bills being subject to an unnecessary or unintentional critical JCHR report.[40] This admission suggests that the JCHR has encouraged more detailed attention to how proposed legislation implicates rights, and the need for explanations to justify proposed actions, than might otherwise have been the case. A second way in which the JCHR contributes to this norm of justification is through its persistent pressure on ministers to provide adequate safeguards to ensure that policies are implemented in a rights-compatible manner when these are interpreted and implemented by public officials.[41] A third way in which it contributes is through its insistence on evidence-based reasons for implementing new coercive powers, particularly when these implicate rights adversely. A fourth way in which it contributes to this norm is by

[40] Interviews.
[41] Interviews.

reporting its concerns and recommendations in a timely manner, so that Parliament is able to pursue these concerns while the bill is still before at least one House. Finally, it contributes to this norm by maintaining pressure on the government to develop and introduce remedial measures when courts have ruled that legislation is not consistent with Convention rights.[42]

Nevertheless, without discounting the significance of these ongoing contributions, the two essential requirements for effective legislative rights review remain elusive: that ministers explain to Parliament what arguments or evidence support a positive report that a bill is compatible with protected rights (or that justify the government's decision to proceed with a bill where positive claims of compatibility cannot be made) and that parliamentarians exert substantial pressure on the government to redress serious rights-based concerns and/or provide compelling reasons as to why a bill is justified, despite its implications for Convention rights.

Although the JCHR's persistent pressure on departments and ministers to include more substantive explanations to address the human rights implications of bills appears to be having positive effects,[43] the political practice of claiming compatibility to date continues to reflect the position that if the Cabinet concludes that a bill has an acceptable degree of risk and therefore does not warrant acknowledging an inability to claim compatibility, it is not necessary to inform Parliament if interpretations of compatibility are contested, or acknowledge the degree or nature of risk that legislation could result in judicial censure if litigation occurs.

The difficulty for legislative rights review, and its emphasis on rights-based justification, is not that political judgment occurs. It is difficult to imagine how ministerial or Cabinet interpretations of compatibility can escape political judgment of some kind because of the subjective nature of predicting the implications of earlier legal cases for new issues, political and ideological differences between political parties on how protected rights implicate the role of the state, and the subjective dimension of ascertaining whether the relationship between policy objectives and the means chosen to achieve these complies with notions of proportionality. However, the concept of legislative rights review is predicated on a justificatory burden to explain the reasons for pursuing legislation that implicates protected rights in an adverse manner. This burden is not satisfied if the government claims that a bill is compatible with Convention rights and yet is not required to explain its assumptions or conclusions, particularly when serious concerns are raised by the JCHR, the parliamentary body particularly entrusted with responsibility for rights-based review. Nevertheless, the government has been able to avoid meeting this obligation because of insufficient interest or political pressure in the House of Commons to demand such explanations.

The problem is more substantial than a failure to explain how or why the government has concluded that a bill is compatible with Convention rights or why it is justified where compatibility cannot be assured. The government regularly opposes amendments intended to redress possible rights infringements, as suggested by the

---

[42] Hiebert (n 1) 39.
[43] Joint Committee on Human Rights, *Legislative Scrutiny: Protection of Freedoms Bill, 18th Report* (2010–12, HL 195/HC 1490) paras 3–4.

JCHR or proposed by the House of Lords. Public officials interviewed confirm that once a bill has been introduced into Parliament, it is extremely unlikely that the government will agree to substantial changes simply because of a critical JCHR report. Legal advisors explain this refusal in terms of differences of opinion on the legal question of whether a proposed measure is compatible with Convention rights, particularly when the dispute occurs around proportionality criteria.[44] By the time a bill has been approved, it will have been subject to a number of legal analyses, including as high in the chain of expertise as the Attorney-General, and it is highly unlikely that the government will change its assessment that the bill is justified simply because the JCHR has reached a different opinion on the question of compatibility. In 2006, Harriet Harman, then Minister of State for Constitutional Affairs, advised the JCHR that its focus on compatibility was not influential precisely for this reason.[45]

A political explanation for the government's reluctance to amend bills in response to JCHR queries or House of Lords concerns is that the government only amends bills when it fears losing a key vote.[46] It rarely has this fear from the House of Commons, where the government party members rarely rebel against the government in sufficient numbers to defeat a bill, and where both ministerial section 19 claims of compatibility and JCHR reports have a negligible impact on parliamentary deliberations. In those rare instances where JCHR reports are raised, these are usually at the instigation of a member of the JCHR[47] and have little traction in the broader Commons debate about the bill in question.

The House of Commons' reluctance to hold the government to account for bills that raise serious concerns of compatibility with Convention rights does not mean that rights-inspired considerations never arise in political debates. However, when rights-based concerns are raised, these tend to be framed in the more general and abstract language of civil liberties and draw little from the language of Convention rights or from the JCHR's emphasis on compatibility.[48] Thus, on those occasions when rights talk occurs in any significant manner, the JCHR and the House of Commons frame their arguments and concerns differently, and are in essence talking past each other. However, it is not simply the lack of a common focus that helps explain why JCHR reports have had relatively little influence on the House of Commons. At times, rights-oriented debates in the House of Commons are framed as if to suggest a serious conflict exists between the idea of protecting civil liberties, which parliamentarians appear comfortable defending, and the idea of complying with Convention rights (the emphasis in JCHR reports), which members frequently

---

[44] Interviews.

[45] Joint Committee on Human Rights, *Oral Evidence and Memoranda Given by Rt Hon Harriet Harman QC MP, Minister of State, Mr Edward Adams, Head of Human Rights Division, and Ms Vina Shukla, Legal Division, Department for Constitutional Affairs*, (2005–06, HL 143/HC 830-i).

[46] Interviews.

[47] M Hunt, HJ Hooper and P Yowell, 'Parliaments and Human Rights: Redressing the Democratic Deficit', AHRC Public Policy Series (No 5) 24, available at: www.ahrc.ac.uk/News-and-Events/Publications/Documents/Parliaments-and-Human-Rights.pdf.

[48] Hiebert and Kelly (n 1), 398.

portray in pejorative terms by implying that the HRA interferes with Parliament's historic role of safeguarding British civil liberties.[49]

As long as MPs demand little from the government with respect to persuasive arguments or evidence to justify not redressing concerns raised by the JCHR, it is unlikely that the government will willingly accept rights-improving amendments, particularly if these are viewed as undermining or significantly delaying passage of its legislative agenda. Once the government has decided on a course of action, has consulted with the various stakeholders, has addressed internal disagreements and has publicised its commitment in the form of a legislative bill, it is generally reluctant to agree to amendments that could renew internal conflicts, require more time in an often crowded parliamentary calendar, and could be interpreted politically and in the media as a sign of the government's weakness in the highly partisan environment of Westminster parliamentary politics.

It is precisely this problem that motivated Andrew Dismore, former Chair of the JCHR, to consider how the Committee could become involved earlier in the policy process, for example, by reviewing government White or Green Papers. The assumption was that if rights-based scrutiny could occur before the government had high political stakes associated with a particular legislative bill, the government would be more amenable to changes because agreeing to rights-inspired amendments would not carry the same political liabilities.[50] Nevertheless, most of the JCHR's work is directed at existing bills and therefore its opinions on compatibility usually appear too late in the process to exert more substantial influence on the government, because these reports are presented after the government has committed itself to a bill.[51]

To the extent that the government fears a realistic chance that a bill will be defeated, and thus is willing to consider rights-inspired amendments, this fear is almost entirely associated with opposition from the House of Lords.[52] However, the government is frequently able to subsequently defeat these amendments, particularly when it is in a strong majority position or it is in a relatively stable coalition partnership and can rely on party discipline to control its parliamentary caucus in the House of Commons. A good example of this was debate about the government's controversial Anti-terrorism, Crime and Security Bill. The government encountered serious concerns raised by the JCHR,[53] but was able to get the bill passed in the House of Commons without amendment. Although the government had a considerably more difficult time in the House of Lords, which called for significant rights-protecting amendments, many of these amendments were subsequently defeated when the bill returned to the House of Commons;[54] a pattern that has been all too common in the House of Commons. A more recent example is the Justice and Security Bill, which is discussed below.

---

[49] D Nicol, 'The Human Rights Act and the Politicians' (2004) 24 *Legal Studies* 464–65.
[50] Interviews.
[51] Hiebert (n 1) 40.
[52] Interviews.
[53] JCHR, Second Report, 2001–02, paras 17–68.
[54] HM Fenwick and GP Phillipson, 'Legislative Over-Breadth, Democratic Failure and the Judicial Response: Fundamental Rights and the UK's Anti-terrorist Legal Policy' in V Ramraj, H Hor and K Roach (eds), *Global Anti-Terrorism Law and Policy* (Cambridge, Cambridge University Press, 2005) 458.

C. The JCHR's Influence on the Justice and Security Bill[55]

A good example of the difficulty of compelling the government to accept rights-improving amendments was the Justice and Security Bill, which was passed in March 2013. What distinguished the Justice and Security Bill was that the seriousness of the critique of the government's initiative in and beyond Parliament, and the JCHR's stature for principled and hard-hitting analysis of the legislation, combined in a manner rarely seen so that JCHR reports framed debate in both the House of Commons and in the House of Lords, and also shaped how the government responded to critics.

The bill authorised the use of closed material procedures (CMP) in civil proceedings that involve discussion of sensitive materials relating to national security or intelligence.[56] The government's stated motivation was to provide a way to proceed with civil cases in which government agencies could not otherwise defend themselves, resulting in taxpayers being responsible for costly settlements.[57]

The JCHR conducted its own hearings on the implications and potential justification for the legislation,[58] as it has done in other situations where government claims of requiring new rights-abridging powers are presented without evidence to justify them. The JCHR reported that it was not persuaded by the evidence available of the justification for measures that represented such a 'radical departure from the United Kingdom's constitutional tradition of open justice and fairness'.[59] The JCHR contested the government's claim that the bill was compatible with protected rights, arguing that the government had not given due consideration to the impact that closed proceedings would have on the common law's protection for the right to a fair hearing, which includes 'the right to an open and adversarial trial on equal terms and reasons for the court's decisions'.[60] The JCHR proposed substantial amendments to the bill and urged that Parliament's assessment of the bill be guided by consideration for whether the government 'has persuasively demonstrated, by reference to sufficiently compelling evidence, the necessity for such a serious departure from the fundamental principles of open justice and fairness; values that are central both to our common law tradition and to the international human rights obligations that have been so influenced by that tradition'.[61]

The House of Lords took up this plea and made substantial amendments that addressed the majority of the JCHR's concerns,[62] only to have these defeated at report stage in the House of Commons and replaced by changes that the government

---

[55] Hiebert and Kelly (n 1) 336–42.
[56] HM Government, *Justice and Security Green Paper* (Cm 8194, 2011).
[57] ibid.
[58] JCHR, *The Justice and Security Green Paper, Oral Evidence*, HC 1777-i-v (24 January 2012).
[59] JCHR, *Legislative Scrutiny: Justice and Security Bill, 4th Report* (2012–13, HL Paper 59/HC 370) para 15.
[60] ibid para 16.
[61] ibid para 18.
[62] HL Deb 21 November 2012, vol 740, cols 1852, 1855–56, 1859, 1862–64. Amendments included provisions to ensure that judges would decide whether a CMP should be used in any a given case (in contrast to the original draft, which would have required a judge to order a CMP when materials impact on national security); that a CMP would only be available as a procedure of last resort and if fairness could

claimed were consistent with the spirit of the JCHR's concerns, but which the JCHR strongly disputed.[63] The most contentious of the government's amendments altered the conditions that must be met by non-government parties when applying for a CMP declaration, diminished the requirement of full judicial balancing of the competing public interests in play when deciding whether to order a CMP, and replaced the requirement that CMP be used only as a last resort with the less onerous requirement of being in the interests of the fair and effective administration of justice.[64]

Critics of the bill in the House of Commons questioned the legitimacy of closed proceedings and characterised the debate as one in which Parliament should defend the rule of law and the traditional rights that have been established in the common law.[65] Opposing MPs also questioned why the government was so willing to dismiss the concerns of the JCHR and so many others who were critical of this change.[66] Conservative members supporting the bill argued that critics' rights-based concerns were misplaced because the changes influenced civil and not criminal proceedings,[67] reinforcing the claim made earlier by Kenneth Clarke, the minister responsible for the bill, that 'nothing in the Bill will affect the criminal law' and that 'No one will be prosecuted on the basis of secret evidence'.[68] However, shortly before the bill's final consideration in the House of Lords, a media story accused Clarke of having 'misled' Parliament on this issue of whether the use of CMPs would be confined to civil proceedings, and revealed that a Cabinet Office spokesperson had confirmed that CMPs could be used in habeas corpus claims where a 'judge has found that their use would be in the interests of the fair and effective administrative of justice'.[69]

Although the House of Lords has more autonomy from partisan pressures, the government's determination to pass the legislation was strong enough to compel Liberal Democrat peers to support the bill, despite the fact that their party membership had earlier rejected the validity of the government's objective.[70] Thus, when the bill returned to the Lords for final consideration, the government was able to defeat new rights-inspired amendments, including a Labour-sponsored change that would have allowed the use of CMPs only if a judge determined that it would not be impossible to reach a fair verdict 'by any other means', by imposing an effective three-line whip on Liberal Democrat peers to defeat new amendments.[71]

---

not be otherwise achieved; and that when deciding whether to agree to the use of a CMP, courts would be required to balance the interests of national security against the interests of fairness and open justice.

[63] JCHR, *Legislative Scrutiny: Justice and Security Bill (2nd Report), 8th Report* (2012–13, HL 128/HC 101) paras 14, 33–99.
[64] ibid paras 36–87.
[65] HC Deb 7 March 2013, vol 559, col 1221 (D Winnick); HC Deb 7 March 2013, vol 559, cols 1225–26 (J Corbyn).
[66] ibid, D Winnick.
[67] HC Deb 7 March 2013, vol 559, col 1223 (G Howarth).
[68] HC Deb 18 December 2012, vol 685, col 717 (K Clarke).
[69] M Townsend, 'Ken Clarke "Misled" Parliament over Secret Courts Bill' *The Guardian* (24 March 2013).
[70] R Syal, 'Secret Courts Plan Receives Blow at Lib Dem Conference' *The Guardian* (12 September 2012), available at: www.theguardian.com/law/2012/sep/25/secret-courts-lib-dem-conference.
[71] N Watt, 'Last-Ditch Bid to Dilute Secret Courts Plan Fails' *The Guardian* (27 March 2013).

This bill emphasises the difficulty of compelling the government to amend bills to redress serious adverse implications for rights, even when Parliament has access to the necessary resources for reasoned judgment on these issues. The UK Parliament's resources for engaging in rights-based scrutiny far exceed those available to other parliaments in countries like Canada and New Zealand, which have similarly adopted statutory obligations for the government to report on whether bills are compatible with protected rights. The UK Parliament has access to the expertise of a specialised rights committee, whose assessments are highly respected and are not discounted because of perceptions of partisan bias or government domination of committee decisions. The JCHR offers critical analyses of how bills implicate rights while the bill is before at least one House of Parliament, thus giving parliament an opportunity to demand amendments, and conducts evidence-based hearings when government claims of new coercive powers are not substantiated. Finally, the transparent nature of the JCHR's proceedings allows parliament to be privy to correspondence between the JCHR and ministers and department officials about the reasons for and potential consequences of the legislative initiative and possible amendments. If one's mission were to identify the kinds of resources required for effective parliamentary rights scrutiny, it would be difficult to conclude that those offered to the UK Parliament fall seriously short.[72] As Stephen Gardbaum characterises the JCHR, it represents a gold standard which other jurisdictions interested in legislative rights review seek to emulate.[73]

Nevertheless, access to essential resources does not inevitably alter political behaviour. Although the House of Lords frequently utilises JCHR reports to justify amendments, the House of Commons is generally far less interested in addressing JCHR concerns or focusing on whether proposed legislation is compatible with protected rights. Moreover, the government is often confident in its dominance of the House of Commons, and party whips' ability to control members' votes in order to defeat rights-improving amendments passed in the Lords.

D. Other Factors Undermining the Norm of Rights-Based Justification

Effective legislative rights review in the UK is also undermined by two other factors: a weaker incentive for compliance with adverse judicial rulings than in more conventional bills of rights, and unresolved ambiguity about how the principle of parliamentary sovereignty relates to or affects the mission of a bill of rights that is predicated on confronting and justifying decisions that implicate rights. These factors make non-compliance easier to sustain by weakening the pressure parliament and the government incur to justify decisions where serious questions of compatibility arise.

---

[72] This doesn't mean one cannot quibble with the reporting style of the JCHR, whose assessments are often fairly dense and legalistic and thus require considerable energy time for the reader (a potential problem for busy elected members and their overworked staff).

[73] S Gardbaum, *The New Commonwealth Model of Constitutionalism: Theory and Practice* (Cambridge, Cambridge University Press, 2013) 224.

One of the concerns expressed with bills of rights that constrain judicial remedies is that rights are more vulnerable where judicial remedial powers are weak. This view clearly influenced the advice given to a pre-HRA British audience by then Associate Justice William J Brennan Jr of the US, when he opined on the merits of adopting a bill of rights so that judges could serve as a 'constant guardian of individual liberty' while also warning against emulating Canada's decision to include a notwithstanding clause, which he said would allow for the 'suspension of a bill of rights when a legislative majority deems it expedient'.[74] It is reasonable to speculate that the UK's decision to retain the principle of parliamentary sovereignty would have been viewed sceptically by Brennan Jr for denying courts the authority to authorise remedies (other than through their general interpretive power).

Those who disagree with the idea that courts have the only compelling or reasonable interpretations of rights (including the author) will dispute the idea that rights are at risk unless courts can play the above-mentioned guardian role. In any event, and without engaging in this particular debate about whether rights are more vulnerable if courts lack the remedial authority to veto inconsistent legislation, it is misleading to assume that the question of political compliance with rights-based norms is settled entirely by how a bill of rights conceives the scope of judicial remedial power.

It is both obvious yet important to recognise that bills of rights are not self-enforcing. Regardless of where responsibility resides for authorising remedial measures, the extent to which political actors are willing to act in a manner that is profoundly inconsistent with relevant judicial rulings will be influenced by several factors, such as the level of political support for the impugned policy objective, the perceived political ease or difficulty of passing or sustaining legislation that contradicts judicial rulings, and institutional and political assumptions about whether the courts have exceeded their authority when declaring legislation invalid or inoperative.

Compliance will occur regularly under bills of rights that constrain the scope of judicial remedies if political behaviour assumes that compliance with judicial rulings is an important norm,[75] just as non-compliance can occur under a bill of rights that gives courts strong remedial powers (such as invalidating inconsistent legislation) particularly if judicial rulings are controversial, as demonstrated by Martin Sweet's assessments of how American legislatures have ignored, evaded or overridden negative judicial rulings on a range of controversial issues such as affirmative action, flag burning, hate speech and school prayer.[76] Non-compliance can also occur in both weak and strong form systems when legislatures genuinely misinterpret whether new legislation is compatible with a previous ruling.[77]

---

[74] WJ Brennan Jr, 'Why Have a Bill of Rights? (1989) 9(4) *Oxford Journal of Legal Studies* 425.

[75] M Tushnet, *Weak Courts, Strong Rights: Judicial Review and Social Welfare Rights in Comparative Constitutional Law* (Princeton, Princeton University Press, 2008) 43–76.

[76] MJ Sweet, *Merely Judgment: Ignoring, Evading, and Trumping the Supreme Court* (Charlottesville, University of Virginia Press, 2010).

[77] M Tushnet, 'Policy Distortion and Democratic Debilitation: Comparative Illumination of the Countermajoritarian Difficulty' (1995) 94(2) *Michigan Law Review* 270.

However, while it is unhelpful to treat compliance and remedies as flowing automatically from whether a bill of rights authorises a judicial veto of inconsistent legislation, what is significant is how the institutional mechanism for disagreeing with a judicial ruling is conceived. The nature of the trigger mechanism for acting in a non-compliant manner is relevant because how a parliament is required to act to give effect to its disagreement can influence the pressure that politicians incur for decisions to dissent from courts. In systems with strong remedial powers, intentional non-compliant behaviour will generally require legislative action to ignore or contradict the very judicial objection that led to earlier constitutional censor. It is this burden of having to act in a deliberately defiant manner, by passing legislation that conveys the message that parliament intends to deliberately contradict a judicial interpretation of a protected right, which is expected to dissuade political actors from regularly embarking on this path. In contrast, the UK's triggering mechanism for disagreeing with a judicial interpretation of a right is less confrontational and, more importantly, does not invite the same criticism for being inconsistent with constitutional principles because the HRA denies courts the power to veto inconsistent legislation (although parliament's capacity to disagree is more difficult to sustain when the dispute involves a decision of the ECtHR because of the treaty character of its decisions). Thus, the UK Parliament can dissent from a domestic court decision by simply maintaining the status quo, but must act affirmatively to provide a remedy for a ruling that legislation is not compatible with the HRA.[78]

E. Ambiguity about Parliamentary Sovereignty

A second reason why the incentive for compliance in the UK is weaker than in some other systems is lingering ambiguity about whether and how the principle of parliamentary sovereignty constrains expectations of compliance with judicial interpretations of the HRA. This ambiguity is a logical consequence of a political attempt to construct a bill of rights that emphasises a juridical approach for interpreting liberal constitutional values and yet also relies on a political willingness to enact remedies. Thus, on the one hand, the HRA is said to have created an expectation of compliance with judicial interpretations of liberal constitutional norms,[79] while on the other hand, many equate the retention of parliamentary sovereignty with the democratic principle that parliament retains the final say on the validity of legislation.[80] Lacking in political debates is a recognition of how these principles should be reconciled, how the concept of legislative rights review should direct this reconciliation and what criteria or processes might distinguish reasonable from unreasonable judgments about rights. As Murray Hunt argues, tension between these potentially

---

[78] The government will encounter its highest pressure to comply with a judicial ruling when the ruling comes from the ECtHR because of the treaty implications of these judicial decisions. However, political officials and constitutional scholars disagree on the question of whether defiance in this context is a political act, with political implications for the country's international reputation and the future of its treaty agreement, or is mandated by respect for the rule of law.

[79] Interviews.

[80] AL Young, *Parliamentary Sovereignty and the Human Rights Act* (Oxford, Hart Publishing, 2009).

competing principles of liberal constitutional values and parliamentary sovereignty has resulted in a willingness to invoke whichever one perspective best serves the argument at hand.[81]

III. CONCLUSION

The HRA's introduction of judicial rights-based review has influenced bureaucratic processes for developing legislative initiatives. It has also impacted on government behaviour by encouraging the government to undertake strategic decisions about whether and how much risk it is willing to take when pursuing legislation that raises questions about compatibility, because of the prospect of litigation and judicial censure (whether by altering the scope or effects of legislation to render a more rights-compliant effect or by declaring legislation incompatible with Convention rights). However, these political calculations have little to do with the normative or idealistic assumptions connected to the idea of legislative rights review. Instead, they are a logical and political consequence of managing the risks associated with judicial review that can be expected in any political system with a bill of rights, particularly where the government exerts substantial control over the legislative agenda.

Despite the optimistic assumption that legislative rights review will alter the norms of legislative decision-making, this concept is unlikely to significantly change the norms of legislative decision-making in the UK—at least any time soon. The reason for the failure for this norm of rights-based justification to take a stronger hold is that this ambitious idea is abstracted from the political forces that shape and constrain how the government and parliament operate. The driving force for assessing legislation in Westminster parliamentary government is not predicated on an ideal of how to improve legislation from a rights perspective, but instead operates as an opportunity for rival parties to demonstrate why they are the better choice for the next government, where highly disciplined political parties organise and give meaning to the vote, and where the government generally dominates the House of Commons. Although it is premature to dismiss the potential of legislative rights review out of hand, this concept cannot be expected to facilitate significant behavioural changes, at least in the way its proponents implied it would, until the government incurs stronger political consequences for failing to acknowledge the extent to which its claims of compatibility are based on discretionary judgment that can cloak high levels of risk, and the House of Commons is willing and powerful enough to compel the government to justify or amend bills that pose serious rights concerns as a condition for approving legislation.

[81] M Hunt, 'Reshaping Constitutionalism' in J Morison (ed), *Judges, Transition, and Human Rights* (Oxford, Oxford University Press, 2007) 468–69.

4

The Role of Parliaments Following Judgments of the European Court of Human Rights

ALICE DONALD AND PHILIP LEACH

THE NEED FOR more effective national implementation[1] of European Court of Human Rights (ECtHR) judgments has become the principal focus of the human rights work of the Council of Europe (CoE). The statistics explain why. In March 2014, the Court had a backlog of 96,050 applications,[2] more than 40,000 of which concerned repetitive cases arising from systemic or structural violations of the European Convention on Human Rights (ECHR).[3] At the end of 2013, more than 11,000 non-executed judgments were pending before the Committee of Ministers, the political branch of the CoE and the main body charged with supervising the execution of judgments—more than four times the number a decade earlier.[4] Moreover, 2013 saw an increase in the number of non-executed 'leading'

---

[1] The terms 'implementation' and 'execution' are sometimes used interchangeably, but, although they overlap, they are not identical. Execution refers to the steps taken by a state to remedy violation/s of the European Convention on Human Rights (ECHR) identified by the European Court of Human Rights (ECtHR) in judgments against it. Implementation is a broader term which includes execution in the above sense, but also encompasses steps taken by a state in response to an adverse judgment against another state, where the same problem of principle exists within its own legal or administrative system. In so doing, that state respects the interpretative authority of the Court, established under Articles 1 and 19 of the ECHR. Implementation might also be understood to include a more proactive approach to ECtHR decisions generally, including consideration of judgments in policy-making and in the process of designing, drafting and scrutinising legislation. This chapter uses the broader term implementation except when referring to the formal process of supervision of the execution of judgments by Council of Europe (CoE) bodies.

[2] www.echr.coe.int/Documents/Stats_pending_month_2014_BIL.pdf. This was, however, a substantial reduction on the peak of more than 160,000 pending cases in September 2011; see 'President Spielmann Highlights the Court's Very Good Results in 2013', ECHR 030 (2014), 30 January 2014.

[3] Dean Spielmann, President of the ECtHR, 'Le succès et les défis posés à la Cour, perçus de l'intérieur' (Conference on the Long-Term Future of the European Court of Human Rights, Oslo, 7–8 April 2014) 1.

[4] Council of Europe Committee of Ministers, *Supervision of the Execution of Judgments and Decisions of the European Court of Human Rights: 7th Annual Report of the Committee of Ministers 2013* (Strasbourg, Council of Europe, 2014) 36. Under Article 46(2) ECHR, the Committee of Ministers is responsible for supervising the execution of ECtHR judgments, namely: payment of just satisfaction; implementation of individual measures to remedy the violation for the individual/s concerned; and general measures aimed at preventing similar violations in the future. This chapter is principally concerned with general measures.

cases; that is, cases revealing structural problems requiring legal, administrative or policy reform to remedy the violation/s.[5] These figures attest to the 'implementation crisis' identified by the Open Society Justice Institute (OSJI) as afflicting not only the European human rights system but also other regional and international human rights mechanisms.[6]

The Strasbourg Court is also under political strain, notably from a strident discourse by some politicians, jurists and commentators in the UK who have raised the possibility of withdrawal from the jurisdiction of the ECtHR,[7] or from the Convention itself,[8] steps which no democracy has ever taken. Particular controversy surrounds the appropriate response to the ECtHR's decisions on the disenfranchisement of convicted prisoners,[9] which has led the UK Government to contemplate breaking treaty obligations.[10] This argument is sometimes couched in terms of a 'democratic override' of ECtHR judgments to which a majority in Parliament is opposed.[11]

At the ministerial conference in Brighton in 2012, States Parties to the ECHR affirmed their strong commitment 'to fulfil their primary responsibility to implement the Convention at national level'.[12] The Brighton Declaration encouraged states to 'facilitate the important role of national parliaments in scrutinising the effectiveness of implementation measures taken'[13] and welcomed the role of the Parliamentary Assembly of the Council of Europe (PACE) in monitoring the execution of judgments.[14] In 2010, PACE's Committee on Legal Affairs and Human

---

[5] ibid 10. This statistic masks more positive trends, such as the more rapid execution and closure of new judgments which became final after 2011, compared to older judgments.

[6] Open Society Justice Initiative, *From Rights to Remedies: Structures and Strategies for Implementing International Human Rights Decisions* (New York, Open Society Foundations, 2013) 23.

[7] See, eg, M Pinto-Duschinsky, *Bringing Rights Back Home: Making Human Rights Compatible with Parliamentary Democracy in the UK* (London, Policy Exchange, 2011); N Herbert MP, 'On Prisoner Voting, We Shouldn't Defy the [European Court of Human Rights], We Should Resile from it Altogether' *Conservative Home* (22 November 2012).

[8] On 24 April 2013, the Home Secretary, Theresa May, stated that temporary withdrawal from the ECHR was one option being considered by the UK government in its efforts to deport the Islamic cleric Omar Mohammed Othman (also known as Abu Qatada); Hansard HC 24 April 2013, col 887. Two members of the Commission tasked with investigating the creation of a UK Bill of Rights advocated withdrawal from the ECHR unless the Court ceased its 'judicially activist approach': J Fisher QC and Lord Faulks QC, 'Unfinished Business' in Commission on a Bill of Rights, *A UK Bill of Rights?: The Choice Before Us*, Vol 1 (London, Commission on a Bill of Rights, 2012) 182. See also R Broadhurst, *Human Rights: Making Them Work for the People of the UK* (London, European Research Group, 2011); D Hannan MEP, 'Britain Should Withdraw from the European Convention on Human Rights' *Daily Telegraph* (12 February 2011).

[9] *Hirst v UK (No 2)* No 74025/01 [GC] 6 October 2005; *Greens and MT v UK* Nos 60041/08 and 60054/08, 23 November 2010.

[10] One of the three options proposed in the Voting Eligibility (Prisoners) Draft Bill, CM 8499, November 2012 is a re-statement of the existing ban on the right of all prisoners to vote, which would be a straightforward breach by the UK of its undertaking in Article 46(1) ECHR to abide by the final judgment of the Court in any case to which it is a party.

[11] Jack Straw MP, Hansard HC 10 February 2011, col 503.

[12] High Level Conference on the Future of the European Court of Human Rights, Brighton Declaration, 20 April 2012, para 9(a).

[13] ibid para 29(a)(iii).

[14] ibid para 29(e).

Rights (CLAHR) went so far as to say that unless national parliaments assumed a more active role in this respect:

> [T]he key role of the Convention, its supervisory mechanism and the Council of Europe as a whole, in guaranteeing the effective protection of human rights in Europe, is likely to be put in jeopardy.[15]

PACE identifies various reasons why parliaments are critical to the implementation of ECtHR judgments and ECHR standards.[16] It ventures that parliamentary involvement confers democratic legitimacy on the process where this is perceived to be lacking, as well as helping to promote a culture of respect for human rights.[17] Moreover, parliaments may help prevent human rights violations by identifying remedies for structural problems that lead to repetitive cases. Drzemczewski and Gaughan argue that:

> [N]ational parliaments may be able in specific instances more effectively than the Committee of Ministers, to identify the social or political problems underlying a violation and understand the measures required to prevent the recurrence of similar infringements.[18]

The JURISTRAS study of nine CoE states suggests that a strong parliamentary role is a significant factor in the effective implementation of ECtHR judgments.[19] However, in seven of the nine states, parliaments 'do not have an active or decisive role' in this regard.[20] PACE laments that most national parliaments are 'far from exploiting their full potential' to provide effective oversight of human rights implementation.[21]

In 2012–13, the authors undertook a comparative study to elucidate and analyse models of parliamentary engagement in the implementation of Strasbourg judgments.[22] The study focuses on five states: Ukraine, Romania, the UK, Germany and the Netherlands. They include civil and common law countries, monist, dualist and hybrid systems, and presidential, semi-presidential and parliamentary systems. They also differ greatly in terms of the number and severity of human rights violations

---

[15] Parliamentary Assembly of the Council of Europe, Committee on Legal Affairs and Human Rights, *Implementation of Judgments of the European Court of Human Rights*, 7th report, AS/Jur (2010) 36, 9 November 2010.

[16] See also Open Society Justice Initiative (n 6) 56–59.

[17] See especially Parliamentary Assembly of the Council of Europe, Committee on Legal Affairs and Human Rights, *National Parliaments—Guarantors of Human Rights in Europe*, Doc 12636, 6 June 2011 (Rapporteur Mr Christos Pourgourides).

[18] A Drzemczewski and J Gaughan, 'Implementing Strasbourg Court Judgments: The Parliamentary Dimension' in W Benedek, W Karl and A Mihr (eds), *European Yearbook on Human Rights 2010*, vol II (Antwerp, European Academic Press, 2010) 247–58.

[19] D Anagnostou and A Mungiu-Pippidi, *Why Do States Implement Differently the European Court of Human Rights Judgments? The Case Law on Civil Liberties and the Rights of Minorities*, JURISTRAS Project (2009) 23. However, JURISTRAS considers parliamentary involvement within the context of overall 'government effectiveness' rather than as a factor in its own right.

[20] ibid; the states found lacking were Austria, Bulgaria, France, Greece, Italy, Romania and Turkey; the exceptions were Germany and the UK.

[21] See Parliamentary Assembly of the Council of Europe, Committee on Legal Affairs and Human Rights (n 17) at para 91.

[22] The authors are grateful to the Nuffield Foundation for funding this research. The findings will be incorporated into a book to be published in 2015 by Oxford University Press.

giving rise to applications and judgments at the ECtHR[23] and the number of non-executed judgments.[24] Within each state, the authors examined the structures and processes used by, and the capacity of, parliamentary bodies in responding to adverse judgments. Using a qualitative methodology,[25] the authors also explored the *political* dimensions of legislative deliberation about human rights judgments, given the inherent contestability of human rights in the political sphere.

This chapter selectively summarises themes arising from the research. First, we outline the structures and processes for parliamentary involvement in the implementation of judgments, including those against other states. Second, we examine the relationship between national parliaments and CoE bodies. Third, we discuss the nature of implementation as a political as well as a legal process. This leads us, in conclusion, to explore the normative value of parliamentary engagement: to what extent does the (perceived) legitimacy of ECtHR judgments depend upon the engagement of parliaments?

I. STRUCTURES AND PROCESSES FOR PARLIAMENTARY INVOLVEMENT

This section considers the main ways in which parliaments can become systematically involved in the implementation of ECtHR judgments.[26] This includes consideration of parliaments' relationship with other actors, such as the executive, courts and national human rights institutions. For reasons of space, we focus primarily on the relationship between parliaments and executive bodies.

A. National Legislation on the Implementation of Judgments

States may enact legislation which enshrines the authorities and duties of Parliament and other actors in responding to judgments; however, such instances are rare.[27] Within Europe, the pre-eminent example is Ukraine, which in 2006 introduced a law imposing specific obligations on state actors after a judgment of the ECtHR

---

[23] European Court of Human Rights, *Annual Report 2013* (Strasbourg, Council of Europe, 2014). On 31 December 2013, there were 13,284 applications pending against Ukraine and 6,173 against Romania, the second and sixth highest totals in the CoE. There were 2,519 applications pending against the UK, 502 against Germany and 453 against the Netherlands (see 192). In 2013, there were 65 ECtHR judgments finding at least one violation of the ECHR against Ukraine; for Romania there were 83 adverse judgments; for the UK eight; for Germany three; and for the Netherlands five (see 200–01).

[24] See Council of Europe Committee of Ministers (n 4) 39–41. As a snapshot of the states' respective records, on 31 December 2013, the number of leading cases pending execution was as follows: Ukraine 127; Romania 84; the UK 19; Germany 17; and the Netherlands 13.

[25] The authors conducted around 75 semi-structured interviews with: current or former Members of Parliament; government and parliamentary officials; judges and practising lawyers; national human rights institutions; civil society organisations and academics. Interviews were also conducted with judges of the ECtHR and officials in Council of Europe bodies.

[26] See Open Society Justice Initiative (n 6) ch III.

[27] ibid 47–49.

against Ukraine has become final.[28] Among other provisions, within 10 days, the Government Agent[29] is required to summarise the judgment for publication in an official newspaper.[30] The Agent must also disseminate translated summaries of judgments against Ukraine to the Ombudsman (the Parliamentary Commissioner for Human Rights) and to state bodies, officials and others directly affected.[31] The Agent must send a quarterly 'motion on general measures' to the Cabinet of Ministers.[32] The 2006 Law requires administrative acts to be adopted and relevant draft laws to be submitted by the Cabinet of Ministers to Ukraine's unicameral Parliament, the Verkhovna Rada, within three months of the Prime Minister's instruction to the relevant ministries.[33] In May 2012, proposals to amend the 2006 law so as to strengthen parliamentary oversight of the implementation of judgments were passed at first reading by the Verkhovna Rada.[34] However, MPs rejected an accompanying parliamentary resolution and, at the time of writing, the amendments to the 2006 law have not been finally adopted.[35]

In spite of the unusual specificity of the 2006 Law, interviewees concurred that it is not in fact effectively applied in relation to general measures.[36] Moreover, scepticism exists about the *need* for a specific law on implementation. For Pavlo Pushkar, senior lawyer in the Registry at the ECtHR, the law is emblematic of Ukraine's overly positivistic legislative culture: 'When things are not working they think a new law will help—but it's not the law that's the problem, it's the practical implementation.'[37] The MP who tabled the amendments to the 2006 Law, Serhiy

---

[28] Law on the Enforcement of Judgments and the Application of the Case-Law of the European Court of Human Rights Judgments 2006, Law No 3477-IV of 23 February 2006. Certain, largely technical amendments were made under Law No 3135-VI (2011). For an unofficial English translation of the 2006 law, see Open Society Justice Initiative (n 6) Appendix II, 171–79. Similar laws have been passed in Italy, Colombia and Peru, and proposed in Argentina and Brazil. In Romania, under Law No 29/2011, which amends and supplements Law No 24/2000 regarding the norms of legislative technique for drafting enactments, the government is required to submit to Parliament within three months of an adverse ECtHR judgment against Romania a draft law for amending and supplementing or repealing the enactment (or part thereof) that contravenes ECtHR case law.

[29] The Government Agent is the executive body designated to represent states before an international or regional human rights body. Commonly, as in Ukraine, the Government Agent also coordinates the implementation of adverse judgments.

[30] Article 4 of the 2006 Law, as amended.

[31] Articles 5 and 6 of the 2006 Law, as amended.

[32] Article 14 of the 2006 Law, as amended.

[33] Article 15 of the 2006 Law.

[34] The amendments would have required the Government Agent to submit the motion on general measures to Parliament at the same time as to the Cabinet of Ministers. They would also have stated that the Verkhovna Rada shall 'carry out parliamentary control in the area of implementation of judgments and application of the case law' of the ECtHR and that the Government Agent shall submit to the Verkhovna Rada an annual report about the implementation of judgments and application of ECtHR case law. We are grateful to Dmytro Kotliar, former Deputy Justice Minister of Ukraine, for providing an unofficial translation of the amendments.

[35] The resolution 'On the Parliamentary Control of Implementation of the European Court of Human Rights Judgments' would have required the parliamentary Justice Committee to conduct regular scrutiny of the implementation of judgments not only against Ukraine but also against others states, including hearings at least every six months. Unofficial translation provided by Dmytro Kotliar.

[36] Telephone interview with Elina Shyshkina, member of Verkhovna Rada (BYuT ('Motherland')), 5 July 2012.

[37] Interview with Pavlo Pushkar, Lawyer, Registry of the European Court of Human Rights, Strasbourg, 26 June 2012.

Holovaty, was himself sceptical about their likely effectiveness in the absence of political will.[38]

Despite the ineffectiveness of the Ukrainian law, and the still uncertain impact of similar laws elsewhere, some commentators argue that providing a legal basis for the implementation of decisions of international courts is inherently beneficial, since there is less potential for such legislative measures to be 'undone by executive fiat'.[39] Such laws may provide a foundation for more effective national systems of implementation—for example, by increasing the status of the Government Agent within the state apparatus, stipulating timeframes for implementation; simplifying complex administrative procedures and ensuring systematic reporting by the executive to Parliament. Nevertheless, as Ukraine's experience demonstrates, the mere existence of such legislation is not a sufficient condition for effective implementation.

B. The Structure and Remit of Parliamentary Committees

There are two main models for organising parliamentary committees with respect to human rights. One is a specialised, standing committee with a remit covering human rights, which may be interpreted to include specific matters such as the implementation of judgments. The other is a cross-cutting or 'mainstreamed' model in which human rights are considered by different parliamentary committees as they arise within their specific mandates. There are also hybrids in which committee/s with an express human rights mandate exist, but do not play the principal role in screening legislation for human rights compliance or scrutinising government responses to judgments. This section will consider whether there are inherent merits to any particular institutional arrangement.

i. Ukraine

In Ukraine, the Verkhovna Rada has various committees whose remits could be relevant to human rights implementation. These include the Committees on the Rule of Law and Justice ('the Justice Committee'); Human Rights, National Minorities and International Relations ('the Human Rights Committee'); European Integration; and Legislative Support of Law Enforcement. However, none is in fact routinely involved in the implementation of ECtHR judgments. The Justice Committee is particularly influential, partly because it is involved in politically sensitive areas such as the appointment of judges. The Human Rights Committee has a lower status; as one government official observed, speaking anonymously: 'The Human Rights Committee doesn't matter in this parliament and it won't matter in the next parliament.'

The Committee does not routinely screen laws for human rights compliance and nor does it have any formal responsibility in relation to ECtHR judgments.[40]

---

[38] Interview with Serhiy Holovaty, former Minister of Justice of Ukraine, Strasbourg, 28 June 2012.

[39] See Open Society Justice Initiative (n 6) 61.

[40] For example, Ukraine's new Criminal Procedure Code, which came into force in November 2012, was scrutinised by the Justice and Law Enforcement Committees, but not the Human Rights Committee. Information supplied by Pavlo Pushkar.

Interviewees ascribed its weak status to several factors, including: its lack of budgetary powers; intellectual incoherence about the notion of human rights in the domestic context (for example, whether economic and social rights or civil and political rights are accorded greater priority); and ineffective leadership. Instability is created by the fact that the structure and remit of parliamentary committees has no permanent basis, but is determined by a resolution in each parliament.

ii. Romania

Romania, with its bicameral Parliament, presents a different model. Both the lower house (the Chamber of Deputies) and the upper house (the Senate) have Committees on Human Rights, Cults and National Minorities[41] ('the Human Rights Committee') and Legal Matters, Discipline and Immunities ('the Legal Committee'). In addition, in 2009, the Legal Committee in the lower house created a sub-committee to monitor the execution of Strasbourg judgments. According to its website, the sub-committee discussed only one issue: the delayed implementation of the pilot judgment of 2010 in the case of *Maria Atanasiu and others v Romania*.[42] This judgment requires general measures to resolve shortcomings in the system of restitution or compensation in respect of properties nationalised or confiscated by the state before 1989.[43] Strikingly, almost none of the Romanian interviewees knew of the sub-committee's existence, and those who did regarded it as largely ineffective. A member of the sub-committee in the 2008–12 Parliament, speaking anonymously, acknowledged that its advisory staff and most of its members lacked detailed knowledge of the Convention. It was also a weakness that no equivalent sub-committee existed in the Senate. Nevertheless, the sub-committee had been instrumental in drafting a law which seeks to ensure the compatibility of national legislation with the ECHR and requires the Government to inform Parliament of its response following an adverse ECtHR judgment.[44] Since parliamentary sub-committees (unlike full committees) have no permanent status, their remit is vulnerable to change between elections. The sub-committee continues to exist in the Parliament elected in December 2012.

---

[41] This committee's purview includes 'human rights and citizens' rights, the problems of minorities, freedom of conscience, the problem of religious cults, and freedom of expression other than press freedom', according to the Romanian Parliament's website at: www.ipu.org/parline/reports/instance/2_45. htm.

[42] Nos 30767/05 and 33800/06, 12 October 2010. See www.cdep.ro/co/sedinte.lista?tip=111&an=2011.

[43] On 20 May 2013, after the deadline for execution had twice been extended, a new law reforming the restitution/compensation mechanism came into force in Romania. The Committee of Ministers described the law as 'an important step in the execution process' of the *Atanasiu* group of cases. See Memorandum CM/Inf/DH(2013)24. At its meeting on 4–6 June 2013, the Committee of Ministers encouraged the Romanian authorities to continue to cooperate with the Department for the Execution of Judgments with a view to clarifying various outstanding issues, including the absence from the new law of provisions for a system of indexation to take account of inflation of the value of nationalised properties. It also underlined the importance of a 'close and constant monitoring' of the application of the new law at the domestic level so that the authorities can intervene rapidly if necessary, including by legislative measures, with a view to ensuring the effective operation of the newly established mechanism. Progress towards full execution is to be reviewed by the Committee of Ministers at its meeting in December 2014 at the latest.

[44] See n 28.

Its chair reports that it meets weekly and is better resourced than in the previous Parliament, having gained three experienced legal advisers.[45]

As in Ukraine—and for similar reasons—the Human Rights Committees in both houses were viewed by interviewees as lower status than the more powerful Legal Committees. The Human Rights Committee in the lower house was regarded as lacking in credibility; for example, its President since 2000, Nicolae Păun, had introduced (unsuccessfully) a draft law to ban begging[46] and proposed legislation to outlaw fortune-telling and witchcraft.[47] Interviewees suggested that such measures indicated, at best, an idiosyncratic approach to the Committee's remit. Similar disquiet was expressed about the attempt by a former member of the Legal Committee in the Senate, Iulian Urban, to introduce the death penalty for certain paedophiles, in defiance of both the ECHR and the Romanian Constitution.[48]

iii. The UK

The parliamentary model of human rights implementation adopted in the UK has been widely studied, especially in relation to its systematic scrutiny of government legislation for compatibility with all the UK's human rights obligations.[49] The Joint Committee on Human Rights (JCHR) began work in 2001, with its 12 members drawn equally from the House of Commons and House of Lords. The JCHR exemplifies the 'specialised' committee model and has been lauded by the CoE as a model of good practice.[50] Its formal remit is broad, covering 'matters relating to human rights' in the UK, excluding consideration of individual cases.[51] According to David Feldman, the JCHR's first legal adviser, the monitoring of the implementation of ECtHR judgments was a 'relatively late acquisition' to the Committee's activity after some two years of operation.[52] It grew out of the Committee's formal role in considering remedial orders—a form of delegated legislation amending primary legislation following a declaration by a UK court that it is incompatible with the ECHR or a Strasbourg judgment in a case concerning the UK. The JCHR is required by its terms of reference under its Standing Orders to scrutinise and report on remedial orders, according to a strict timetable.

In its early years, where ECtHR judgments raised issues of general implementation, the Committee wrote to the relevant minister to request information about the

---

[45] Interview with Daniel Florea, member of the Chamber of Deputies (Social Democrat Party), London, 14 October 2013.

[46] 'Propunere legislativa pentru reglementarea unor masuri privind cer etoria' ('Legislative Proposal to Regulate Measures on Begging'), No 306/2012.

[47] See 'Two "Witches" Detained in Romania on Extortion Charges' *The Guardian* (14 December 2011).

[48] Interview with Diana Hatneanu, Executive Director, Association for the Defence of Human Rights in Romania (Helsinki Committee), Bucharest, 24 May 2012.

[49] See Part II of this volume; this chapter focuses on the JCHR's role in monitoring the implementation of ECtHR judgments.

[50] See Parliamentary Assembly of the Council of Europe, Committee on Legal Affairs and Human Rights (n 17) 13–14.

[51] See www.parliament.uk/business/committees/committees-a-z/joint-select/human-rights-committee.

[52] Interview with David Feldman, former Legal Adviser to the JCHR, Cambridge, 25 April 2012.

proposed response.[53] Uniquely among the parliamentary committees we have examined, the JCHR began in 2006 to publish regular progress reports on its monitoring of the implementation of Strasbourg judgments.[54] This was followed in 2007 by its first report bringing together its monitoring of ECtHR judgments and declarations of incompatibility with the Human Rights Act (HRA) 1998 made by domestic courts.[55] This report also recommended improvements to the way in which the UK Government responded to judgments, including a central coordinating role for the Ministry of Justice.[56] In addition, the JCHR committed itself to 'a more coherent approach to our scrutiny work in this area'.[57] This included writing to the Ministry of Justice and lead government department within three months of a final adverse judgment, recommending general measures where necessary and querying the reasons for any delay. In its 2008 report, the JCHR lamented the Government's failure to provide a substantive response to the Committee's recommendations, which were expanded to include, among other steps, an annual report by the Government on the implementation of judgments.[58]

The JCHR's latest monitoring report was published in 2010 and recommended further improvements to the Government's implementation system in order to facilitate timely and effective parliamentary scrutiny.[59] These included the systematic provision to the JCHR of action plans (and any subsequent significant submissions) detailing the Government's response to adverse judgments at the same time as they are sent to the Committee of Ministers.[60] The Committee also produced guidance for Government departments on responding to human rights judgments, given what it viewed as inconsistent and opaque practice across departments. These included a requirement for the Government to notify the JCHR of ECtHR judgments against the UK within 14 days, provide detailed plans as to its response within four months and make a final decision as to how the incompatibility will be remedied within six months.[61]

At the beginning of the 2010–15 Parliament, the Committee adopted its predecessor's Guidance for Government Departments and announced that it would be

---

[53] Joint Committee on Human Rights, Nineteenth Report of Session 2004–05, *The Work of the Committee in the 2001–2005 Parliament*, HL Paper 112, HC 552 (London, The Stationery Office, 2005).

[54] Joint Committee on Human Rights, Thirteenth Report of Session 2005–06, *Implementation of Strasbourg Judgments: First Progress Report*, HL Paper 133, HC 954 (London, The Stationery Office, 2006).

[55] Joint Committee on Human Rights, Sixteenth Report of Session 2006–07, *Monitoring the Government's Response to Court Judgments Finding Breaches of Human Rights*, HL Paper 128, HC 728 (London, The Stationery Office, 2007).

[56] ibid paras 151–63.

[57] ibid para 162.

[58] Joint Committee on Human Rights, Thirty-First Report of Session 2007–08, *Monitoring the Government's Response to Human Rights Judgements* [sic]: *Annual Report 2008*, HL Paper 173, HC 1078 (London, The Stationery Office, 2008).

[59] Joint Committee on Human Rights, Fifteenth Report of Session 2009–10, *Enhancing Parliament's Role in Relation to Human Rights Judgments*, HL Paper 85, HC 455 (London, The Stationery Office, 2010).

[60] ibid para 175.

[61] ibid pp 69–76 ('Annex: Guidance for Departments on Responding to Court Judgments on Human Rights').

continuing its practice of scrutinising the Government's responses to adverse court judgments concerning human rights and periodically reporting to Parliament on the adequacy of those responses.[62] Since 2010, however, the JCHR has produced no further monitoring reports, an omission ascribed by its legal adviser, Murray Hunt, principally to a reduction in the number of legal advisers to the Committee.[63] Hunt observed that the lower priority accorded to this function in the current Parliament illustrates the vulnerability of such systems to changes in resources, personnel and appetite within the Committee. He added that the *need* for routine scrutiny of implementation had diminished, thanks to improvements made by the Government. These include—as requested by the JCHR—an annual report on responding to human rights judgments initiated in 2011.[64] Implementation has also become more efficient thanks to measures introduced by the Ministry of Justice, which assumed more of a coordinating role in 2010 (again, as requested by the JCHR).[65] These measures include a standardised form to elicit from the relevant Government department/s within a set timeframe what action they intend to take in response to a judgment.[66] This information forms the basis of the Government's action plan, which the Ministry of Justice has committed in principle to providing to the JCHR at the same time as sending it to the Committee of Ministers.

The Committee has continued to monitor the implementation of ECtHR judgments selectively and in July 2013 issued a call for evidence from civil society organisations on the UK's implementation of adverse human rights judgments, signalling a return to more systematic scrutiny of the Government's response to such court judgments.[67] In addition, it has argued for domestic parliamentary and other national scrutiny of Government responses to be reported routinely within Government action plans in accordance with the principle of subsidiarity. An example is the case of *Gillan and Quinton v UK*,[68] which concerned the stop and search under section 44 of the Terrorism Act 2000 of two individuals near an armaments fair. The ECtHR had found that the law under which the stop and search powers were used was too broadly defined and contained insufficient safeguards to act as a curb on the wide powers afforded to the executive, amounting to a violation of the right to respect for private and family life (Article 8 ECHR). The Government's response was to issue an urgent remedial order to repeal and replace

[62] See JCHR Press Notice 10 September 2010, 'JCHR to Review Government's Response to Judgments Identifying Breaches of Human Rights in the UK', www.parliament.uk/business/committees/committees-a-z/joint-select/human-rights-committee/news/human-rights-judgments-call-for-evidence.
[63] Interview with Murray Hunt, Legal Adviser to the JCHR, London, 10 July 2012.
[64] Ministry of Justice, *Responding to Human Rights Judgments: Report to the Joint Committee on Human Rights on the Government's Response to Human Rights Judgments 2010–11*, CM 1862 (London, The Stationery Office, 2011); Ministry of Justice, *Responding to Human Rights Judgments: Report to the Joint Committee on Human Rights on the Government Response to Human Rights Judgments 2011–12*, CM 8432 (London, The Stationery Office, 2012); Ministry of Justice, *Responding to Human Rights Judgments: Report to the Joint Committee on Human Rights on the Government Response to Human Rights Judgments 2012–13*, CM 8727 (London, The Stationery Office, 2013).
[65] The role had previously been held by the deputy head of the UK mission in Strasbourg.
[66] Ministry of Justice, CM 1862, 27.
[67] See www.parliament.uk/business/committees/committees-a-z/joint-select/human-rights-committee/news/human-rights-judgments-call-for-evidence1.
[68] No 4158/05, 12 January 2010.

the offending provisions with new, more circumscribed powers.[69] Both the JCHR and the Independent Reviewer of Terrorism Legislation reported to Parliament, welcoming the Government's willingness to change the law, but criticising the remedial order and the accompanying Code of Practice and recommending amendments, since the discretion conferred on officers remained too broad to remove the risk of arbitrariness identified by the ECtHR.[70] Further, the JCHR deplored the fact that the Government's action plan, submitted to the Committee of Ministers, made no mention of the scrutiny conducted by both the Committee and the Independent Reviewer of Terrorism Legislation. The JCHR noted that:

> [T]he principle of subsidiarity ... requires the Government to keep the Committee of Ministers fully informed of any relevant parliamentary consideration of the measures proposed by it in response to a Court judgment.[71]

The UK Government subsequently produced an updated action plan which did refer to the proposed amendments, but rejected them as unnecessary.[72] However, following public consultation in 2012 on the revised draft Code of Practice, changes were made to satisfy some of the concerns raised by the JCHR and the Independent Reviewer.[73] Thus, their combined scrutiny achieved tangible results, illustrating the benefits of Parliament acting in tandem with other domestic actors concerned with human rights implementation.

There is continuing debate about how the JCHR might achieve the optimum balance between, on the one hand, systematic scrutiny of bills and compliance with ECtHR decisions and, on the other hand, a more thematic and less legalistic approach which may be more likely to stimulate democratic exchange between Parliament, the executive and the public.[74] Notwithstanding this uncertainty, the Committee is widely respected both within and outside the UK. Interviewees acknowledged the symbolic value of 'keeping human rights alive' within the parliamentary culture and of having a specialised committee which applies a human rights 'lens' to all areas of law and policy.[75] The dedicated nature of the Committee had helped it to attract high-quality legal staff with human rights expertise. Its joint nature was also praised, since it ensures that the Committee combines the (generally

---

[69] Ministry of Justice, CM 1862, 15–17.

[70] Joint Committee on Human Rights, Fourteenth Report of Session 2010–12, *The Terrorism Act 2000 (Remedial) Order 2011: Stop and Search without Reasonable Suspicion*, HL Paper 155, HC 1141; Joint Committee on Human Rights, Seventeenth Report of Session 2010–12, *The Terrorism Act 2000 (Remedial) Order 2011: Stop and Search without Reasonable Suspicion (Second Report)*, HL Paper 192, HC 1483 (London, The Stationery Office, 2011); D Anderson (Independent Reviewer of Terrorism Legislation), *Report on the Operation in 2010 of the Terrorism Act 2000 and of Part 1 of the Terrorism Act 2006* (London, The Stationery Office, 2011).

[71] JCHR, HL Paper 192, HC 1483, para 10.

[72] *Gillan & Quinton v the United Kingdom (Application No 4158/05): Updated Information Submitted by the United Kingdom Government on 10 October 2011*, DH—DD(2011)851E.

[73] D Anderson (Independent Reviewer of Terrorism Legislation), *The Terrorism Acts in 2011: Report of the Independent Reviewer on the Operation of the Terrorism Act 2000 and Part 1 of the Terrorism Act 2006* (London: The Stationery Office, 2012) para 8.19.

[74] See especially Joint Committee on Human Rights, Twenty-Third Report of Session 2005–06, *The Committee's Future Working Practices*, HL Paper 239, HC 1575 (London, The Stationery Office, 2006).

[75] Interview with David Feldman, former Legal Adviser to the JCHR, Cambridge, 25 April 2012.

acknowledged) greater expertise and capacity for reflection of the Lords with the political muscle of the Commons. However, even admirers of the JCHR recognise its greater relevance to Westminster-style parliaments. Germany and the Netherlands present contrasting constitutional models.

iv. Germany

The German Parliament has two chambers: the Bundestag (lower house), whose members are directly elected, and the smaller Bundesrat (upper house), whose members are delegated by the Länder governments. Of the 22 committees within the Bundestag, the two which primarily deal with human rights questions are the Committee on Human Rights and Humanitarian Aid (hereinafter 'the Human Rights Committee') and the Committee on Legal Affairs (hereinafter 'the Legal Committee').

The Human Rights Committee was originally established as a sub-committee of the Committee on Foreign Affairs. However, it has subsequently been established as a full committee and has shifted its focus to also consider domestic matters. Petra Follmar-Otto of the German Institute for Human Rights (the country's national human rights institution) views the remit of the Human Rights Committee as 'ambiguous and unclear', since individual members and party groups interpret the balance to be struck between domestic and international concerns differently.[76] She advocates a stronger human rights monitoring system in which the Human Rights Committee would act as the 'entry point' for decisions or recommendations from both the regional and UN human rights systems, 'diffuse' them to thematic committees and monitor subsequent implementation.

Neither the Human Rights Committee nor the Legal Committee has an explicit mandate to consider the implementation of ECtHR judgments; their involvement depends on the particular topic and questions of timing.[77] Depending on the judgment, more than one parliamentary committee may be involved in considering how to respond. Where new or revised legislation is required to implement a judgment, the issue will also be considered by the Legal Committee. In those circumstances it is common for the Legal Committee to summon representatives of the Ministry of Justice to explain and justify its response.

v. The Netherlands

The bicameral Parliament of the Netherlands has a fully 'mainstreamed' committee structure, with no committee in either the House of Representatives (lower house) or the Senate (upper house) having an express human rights mandate or remit to monitor ECtHR judgments. Each house has a permanent Justice Committee; human rights judgments may also be taken up by other thematic committees. The monist

---

[76] Interview with Petra Follmar-Otto, Head of Department of Human Rights Policies (Germany/ Europe), German Institute for Human Rights, Berlin, 20 March 2012.

[77] Interview with Marina Schuster, member of the Bundestag (Free Democratic Party), Berlin, 21 March 2012.

system in the Netherlands provides for the direct application of international norms, meaning that the judiciary and executive are the central 'pillars' of the process of implementation.[78] In practice, there are so few ECtHR judgments against the Netherlands (one in 2013[79] and five in 2012)[80] that systematic parliamentary review of judgments has not been developed. Rather, parliamentarians submit questions to the executive as judgments arise.[81]

Interviewees had mixed views about the desirability of establishing a committee with a human rights remit or adding human rights to the remit of an existing committee. Some favoured such an idea as a way of concentrating expertise and encouraging 'ownership' of domestic human rights among MPs.[82] Others expressed concern that such a committee could become either swamped or overly specialised. A further anxiety was that, at present, the parliamentary committee structure mirrors that of government ministries; therefore, a human rights committee would lack influence and might be used by other committees to offload responsibility for contentious issues. In any event, reform aimed at strengthening human rights monitoring was generally agreed to be unfeasible in a climate in which human rights and the ECtHR have become politically controversial in the Netherlands.[83]

vi. Specialised or Mainstream?

The former PACE rapporteur on the implementation of judgments has said that:

> National parliaments should establish appropriate parliamentary structures to ensure rigorous and regular monitoring of compliance with and supervision of international human rights obligations, *where possible through dedicated human rights committees* whose remits should be clearly defined and enshrined in law.[84]

Similarly, the 'Draft Principles and Guidelines on the Role of Parliaments in the Protection and Realisation of Human Rights'—one of the products of the 'Parliaments and Human Rights' research project funded by the Arts & Humanities Research Council—recommend that parliaments should ideally identify or establish a specialised parliamentary human rights committee 'dedicated solely to human rights'.[85] However, the document states that parliaments could, alternatively, identify or establish a relevant parliamentary committee which includes human rights within a broader remit. Either is referred to as a 'human rights committee'.

---

[78] Telephone interview with Barbara Oomen, Dean, Roosevelt Academy, 12 June 2012.

[79] See European Court of Human Rights (n 23) 201.

[80] European Court of Human Rights, *Annual Report 2012* (Strasbourg, Council of Europe, 2013) 155.

[81] Interview with Martin Kuijer, Senior Legal Adviser, Ministry of Justice, The Hague, 23 March 2012.

[82] See also E Rieter, 'Het EHRM ontlasten: de rol van de nationale parlementen bij het toezicht op de naleving van het EVRM' ('Unburdening the ECtHR: The Role of National Parliaments in Monitoring Compliance with the ECHR') in AB Terlouw and JH Gerards (eds), *Amici Curiae* (Oisterwijk, Wolf Productions, 2012) 1–11.

[83] See Kuijer, ch 14 in this volume.

[84] See Parliamentary Assembly of the Council of Europe, Committee on Legal Affairs and Human Rights (n 17) 1, emphasis added.

[85] See M Hunt, H Hooper and P Yowell, *Parliaments and Human Rights: Redressing the Democratic Deficit* (London, Arts & Humanities Research Council, 2012) 3. See also Hunt, ch 1 in this volume.

This non-prescriptive approach to the structure of parliamentary human rights committees correctly recognises that different systems may require different models. For example, the OSJI ventures that in a weak parliamentary system characterised by strong party discipline and dominance by a single party, 'mainstreaming human rights might have little effect'.[86] Murray Hunt rejects the binary choice between specialisation and mainstreaming, preferring to view a dedicated human rights committee as an 'engine of mainstreaming'.[87] Addressing the UK context, Hunt sees the need for a more proactive approach to human rights among legal advisers to committees other than the JCHR. Such an approach would require the parliamentary legal service to draw the attention of other committee/s to particular judgments (or the human rights implications of particular draft legislation) as appropriate to their thematic remit. However, Hunt acknowledges that this balance is not presently achieved: 'the tendency is that if you've got a functioning human rights committee, then other [committees] leave it to that committee, and so it becomes more and more of a silo'.

vii. Principles and Functions

At the CoE level, the development of parliamentary models of human rights scrutiny is embryonic and context-dependent; there is no ideal model. However, we may identify some principles and functions that are essential to this role. One is for human rights committees to have a clear and broadly defined remit which expressly reflects the imperative for parliaments to protect and realise human rights in the state concerned. This is a pre-requisite for the development of an intellectually coherent view of human rights within the domestic context. Such committees should be independent of the executive and have a permanent status in order to protect them from instability between elections. In addition, in bicameral parliaments, there are merits to having a joint human rights committee in order to maximise the potential for both detailed scrutiny and political influence. Scrutiny of the executive's response to human rights judgments should be established as a core function of human rights committees, and they should report regularly to their respective parliaments on the promptness and adequacy of the executive's response (as the JCHR did from 2006 to 2010). Since legislation may be needed to give effect to judgments by domestic or international courts, it is also desirable for human rights committees to have the power to propose amendments to legislation and introduce bills to parliament as appropriate to their remit.

Even in systems with such features, human rights committees may struggle substantively to influence executive responses to adverse judgments. This is due partly to their reliance on the executive as the gatekeeper of information and the often short timeframes involved, as well as the availability of independent and expert legal advice—factors examined in the following sections.

---

[86] See Open Society Justice Initiative (n 6) at 68.
[87] Interview with Murray Hunt, Legal Adviser to the JCHR, London, 10 July 2012.

C. Reporting Procedures

This section examines the various reporting procedures that seek to ensure a timely flow of the necessary information from executive bodies to parliaments about the implementation of human rights judgments.

i. Annual Reports

In three of the states under review—the Netherlands, the UK and Germany—the executive reports annually to parliament on the implementation of human rights judgments.[88] In the Netherlands, a report on adverse judgments was initiated in 1996 at the request of the House of Representatives. Since 2006, it has included information on implementation and since 2009, it has included information about judgments against third countries which have immediate implications for Dutch law or policy. Since 2010, it has included updates about reasoned inadmissibility decisions by the ECtHR in Dutch cases. The reports themselves have not, however, been debated in the Dutch Parliament.

In the UK, the Ministry of Justice has since 2011 published an annual report on responding to human rights judgments in advance of the JCHR's annual evidence session with the Human Rights Minister.[89] Previously, the government responded to the JCHR's monitoring report. A government interviewee, speaking anonymously, noted that the reports had created a 'public, ongoing dialogue' between the JCHR and the government; the fact that the Ministry provided information proactively for scrutiny was a 'big step forward' and had encouraged a less defensive governmental stance. Again, however, the reports have not been debated in Parliament.

The German Ministry of Justice has reported on ECtHR judgments annually since 2004 to both the Human Rights Committee and the Legal Affairs Committee.[90] Initially, the report simply covered judgments and decisions against Germany. Since 2007, it has covered the implementation of judgments. Since 2010, a separate annual report has also been produced covering judgments against other states which have potential implications for Germany.[91] There is no formalised procedure to

---

[88] Annual reports are also produced in Bulgaria, Hungary, Italy and Moldova; see Round-table on Recommendation 2008(2) of the Committee of Ministers to Member States on efficient domestic capacity for rapid execution of judgments of the European Court of Human Rights (15–16 December 2011, Tirana, Albania), 'Synthesis of the Replies by Member States to the Questionnaire on the Domestic Mechanisms for Rapid Execution of the Court's Judgments', www.coe.int/t/dghl/monitoring/execution/Source/Documents/HRTF/TR%2012.11/Overview_questionnaire.pdf, 7. An annual report is also now provided in Poland: see n 95 below.

[89] See n 64.

[90] The report is also sent to the Petitions Committee, which examines requests or complaints made by citizens to the Bundestag.

[91] For the latest report, see H Sauer, 'Bericht über die Rechtsprechung des Europäischen Gerichtshofs für Menschenrechte in Fällen gegen andere Staaten als Deutschland im Jahr 2012' ('Report on the Case Law of the European Court of Human Rights in Cases against States Other than Germany in 2012') (2013). Available at: www.bmj.de/SharedDocs/Downloads/DE/pdfs/Bericht_ueber_die_Rechtsprechung_des_EGMR_2012_andere_Staaten.pdf?__blob=publicationFile.

respond to these reports.[92] Parliamentary committees may put it onto their agenda for discussion (although this is not done routinely) and they may summon government representatives for questioning.

It is difficult to identify tangible impacts resulting from annual reports in relation to the implementation of specific judgments, especially where parliament has access to timelier sources of information such as states' action plans and action reports on the Committee of Ministers' website.[93] As the OSJI notes, there is a risk that annual reports are 'more ceremonial than substantive' where they are not followed up or debated in parliament.[94] However, they may have longer-term impacts, such as encouraging both executives and parliaments to systematise their approach and creating an accessible public account of a state's implementation record. Certainly, it would be a retrograde step to abandon such mechanisms where they exist, since that would discourage moves to strengthen accountability for human rights implementation in newer CoE states. In Poland, the Ministry of Foreign Affairs published its first annual report on the execution of ECtHR judgments in 2013. The report had been requested by the Committee of Justice and Human Rights in the lower house to inform the public and 'raise the rank of the problem of enforcement of judgments and acknowledge it to MPs and ministers'.[95] Unlike the reports in Germany, the Netherlands and the UK, the Polish report has already been debated in Parliament.

ii. Action Plans

The Committee of Ministers has placed increasing emphasis on the provision of 'action plans' (or 'action reports') setting out the measures that the respondent state intends to take (or has taken) to implement a judgment.[96] Action plans were introduced in 2004 and the practice became more embedded in the supervision process in 2009, when the Committee of Ministers formally invited states to provide, within six months of a judgment or decision becoming final, an action plan or action report.[97]

Aside from any formal correspondence, action plans are often the first point in the implementation process at which a government must give a reasoned, public explanation for the action it proposes to take in response to a judgment. Nevertheless, of the parliamentary bodies under review, only one—the JCHR in the UK—has

---

[92] Interview with Christoph Strässer, member of the Bundestag (Social Democratic Party), Berlin, 21 March 2012.

[93] See, however, the caveat noted below n 98.

[94] See Open Society Justice Initiative (n 6) 70.

[95] Europe of Human Rights, 'MFA on the Report on Implementation of ECHR Judgments', 18 October 2012. Available at: www.europapraw.org/en/news/msz-o-raporcie-nt-wykonywania-wyrokow-etpcz.

[96] Recommendation CM/Rec(2008)2 of the Committee of Ministers to Member States on Efficient Domestic Capacity for Rapid Execution of Judgments of the European Court of Human Rights, para 6.

[97] *Action Plans—Action Reports: Definitions and Objectives*, Memorandum prepared by the Department for the Execution of Judgments of the European Court of Human Rights, CM/Inf/DH(2009)29rev, 3 June 2009. Action plans set out the state's intended response to the judgment, while action reports invite the Committee of Ministers to close their supervision of the case in light of the action that has already been taken.

attached importance to regular scrutiny at the earliest possible stage of action plans and subsequent significant updates. As noted above, the JCHR has secured a commitment in principle from the Ministry of Justice to send it action plans at the same time as they are sent to the Committee of Ministers (although we understand that compliance with this commitment is a matter of continuing discussion).[98] No other state we reviewed has such an arrangement. Nor did we find proactive parliamentary scrutiny of analogous documents, such as the motion on general measures which the Ukrainian Government Agent submits to the Cabinet of Ministers; according to a government official, speaking anonymously: 'Parliament has the power to demand any information it wishes from any state authority ... but they never asked [for a copy of a motion] and I have never provided it.'

Parliamentarians outside the UK explained that action plans are regarded as technical documents of limited interest. It was suggested that parliaments have other mechanisms to acquire the same information; for example, annual reports, written or oral questions to ministers or government agents, or, where legislation is required, draft bills or advance frameworks of draft bills. However, given the increasing centrality of action plans to the formal process of supervision and the importance of avoiding unnecessary delay in the implementation of judgments, routine provision of these documents to parliamentary human rights committees has the potential to strengthen implementation. This is especially so where parliamentarians have the capacity to scrutinise the government's response and engage in public dialogue as to its adequacy and timeliness. Indeed, human rights committees might in some instances correspond with the executive *before* the action plan is published, suggesting options for remedy; for example, to encourage full implementation rather than minimal compliance with a judgment and thus minimise the risk of repeat litigation. The JCHR did so in the case of *S and Marper v UK*[99] concerning the systematic and indefinite retention of DNA profiles and cellular samples of people who have not been convicted of any crime, in violation of Article 8 of the ECHR. The Committee wrote to the government within five days of the judgment, asking questions about its proposed response and reminding it of the timetable by which the Committee expected it to propose general measures to remedy the violation.[100] The Committee has also written very soon after the judgment if the remedial action appears to require a straightforward statutory amendment and there is already a bill before Parliament which would be an appropriate legislative vehicle for such an amendment.[101]

---

[98] Although action plans are published on the Committee of Ministers' website in advance of the meeting at which they are considered, this does not always happen as soon as they are received, a delay which might in some cases impede effective scrutiny of the government's response in the national parliament.

[99] Nos 30562/04 and 30566/04 [GC] 4 December 2008.

[100] Joint Committee on Human Rights, Twenty-Seventh Report of Session 2008–09, *Retention, Use and Destruction of Biometric Data: Correspondence with Government*, HL Paper 182, HC 1113 (London, The Stationery Office, 2009).

[101] As happened, eg, following *Connors v UK* No 66746/01, 27 May 2004.

D. Independent and Expert Legal Advice on Human Rights

National parliaments employ various approaches to providing human rights advice to members. No parliament we have reviewed provides human rights training to MPs; however, training may be offered to MPs or legal staff by non-governmental organisations (NGOs) or national human rights institutions. In the UK, MPs receive impartial research briefings from the House of Commons Library, which may be provided proactively or upon request, but these do not constitute legal advice. They may also seek ad hoc advice from lawyers in the Scrutiny Unit.[102] The German Parliament has a scientific service, which provides independent expert advice to parliamentarians, including on matters of international law.[103] The Ukrainian Parliament has a legal department and a separate scientific expert department, which prepares opinions on all draft laws submitted to Parliament. The remit of the scientific expert department is not strictly defined, but in essence it analyses draft laws for compliance with the Constitution, relevant international treaties and other legal acts. It also occasionally makes reference to human rights, but there is no formal system for it to verify compliance with the ECHR or ECtHR judgments, and its opinion is often ignored if it is politically inexpedient.[104] Legal services departments also exist within each house in the Romanian Parliament.

The JCHR is one of a small number of committees in the UK Parliament which is serviced by its own permanent, specialised legal advisers (in recent years, the number has fluctuated between one and three). In relation to ECtHR judgments, the legal advisers selectively provide Committee members with: a summary of the judgment; analysis as to its significance; advice about the options for implementation, where relevant; draft correspondence that the Committee may send to the executive; and advice about the adequacy of the government's response.[105]

We found widespread endorsement of the practice of having permanent, specialist advisers who are both politically independent and recognised human rights experts. This ensures the independence (and the *appearance* of independence) of the Committee as it conducts its scrutiny roles. One former adviser to the JCHR explained the importance of politically neutrality:

> The minute [parliamentarians] think the advice reflects [the adviser's] own take on politically important questions, they start to distrust [it]. If you can give them consistent legal advice it at least gives them some cover if they are moving away from their particular party line.[106]

It was noted that the development of a professional parliamentary staff provides continuity between parliaments and ensures the creation of an institutional memory attached to a human right committee, both in relation to substantive issues and

---

[102] The Scrutiny Unit is part of the Committee Office in the House of Commons and exists to strengthen the scrutiny function of the House.

[103] Interview with Marina Schuster, member of the Bundestag (Free Democratic Party), Berlin, 21 March 2012.

[104] Interview with Dmytro Kotliar, former Deputy Justice Minister of Ukraine, Kiev, 21 May 2012.

[105] Interview with Angela Patrick, Head of Policy, JUSTICE, London, 8 March 2012.

[106] ibid.

working methods. This is much less likely to occur where advisers are transient political appointees of either individual MPs or party groups.

E. Monitoring the Implications of Judgments against Other States

The ECtHR provides final, authoritative interpretation of the rights and freedoms defined in the ECHR. The interpretative authority of Court judgments imposes a duty on national authorities, including legislators, to take into account the Convention as interpreted by the Court even in judgments concerning violations that have occurred in other states—an imperative reinforced by the Interlaken Process of reform of the Court.[107] In the UK, the JCHR has expressed concern that the binding effect of Strasbourg judgments is limited in practice by states taking an 'essentially passive approach' to compliance with the ECHR.[108]

Monitoring ECtHR case law is no easy task: in 2013, the Court delivered 916 judgments.[109] Moreover, transposing judgments from one national context to another is complicated by several factors. Among these are: the discretion or 'margin of appreciation' that the Court affords to states in determining the necessity of the restriction of a right; the extent to which judgments are fact- and context-specific; and the need to determine in each case the true source of a violation.

In practice, where monitoring of ECtHR case law occurs, it is initiated by the executive. Since 2010, the German Ministry of Justice has commissioned annually an analysis of judgments against other CoE states which have implications for the German legal order.[110] The reports are compiled by academics and analyse some 25 judgments each year.[111] They commonly identify trends in Strasbourg jurisprudence which may require Parliament to monitor particular areas of law or policy rather than immediate reform; for example, cases concerning access to fertility treatment.[112] There is no evidence that the reports have led to any specific changes in German law or policy and nor have the academics concerned been invited to speak to Parliament. Holger Haibach states that during his time as a member of the Bundestag (2002–11), ECtHR judgments against states other than Germany were

---

[107] High-Level Conference on the Future of the European Court of Human Rights, Interlaken Declaration, 19 February 2010, para 4(c).

[108] See Joint Committee on Human Rights (n 59) para 188.

[109] European Court of Human Rights (n 23) 197.

[110] For the latest report, see H Sauer, 'Bericht über die Rechtsprechung des Europäischen Gerichtshofs für Menschenrechte in Fällen gegen andere Staaten als Deutschland im Jahr 2012' ('Report on the Case Law of the European Court of Human Rights in Cases against States Other than Germany in 2012') (2013). Available at: www.bmj.de/SharedDocs/Downloads/DE/pdfs/Bericht_ueber_die_Rechtsprechung_des_EGMR_2012_andere_Staaten.pdf?__blob=publicationFile.

[111] Telephone interview with Professor Marten Breuer, Konstanz University, 4 May 2012; Professor Breuer compiled the reports covering judgments in 2009–11.

[112] Professor Breuer highlighted the case *SH and others v Austria*, No 57813/00 [GC] 3 November 2011, concerning two Austrian couples wishing to conceive a child through in vitro fertilisation, in which the Grand Chamber underlined (at [118]) the importance of states (which includes their legislatures) keeping legal and scientific developments in the field of artificial procreation under review.

not considered by MPs, primarily because of their heavy workloads—an account confirmed by current members.[113]

In the Netherlands, civil servants responsible for human rights affairs within the Ministries of Justice and Foreign Affairs monitor Strasbourg case law for decisions that have implications for the Dutch legal order. Such cases are drawn to the attention of the relevant government departments and are included in the annual report to Parliament. Parliamentarians may also ask questions about non-Dutch cases, as happened, for example, in cases concerning the deportation of failed asylum seekers to Somalia[114] and the transfer of asylum seekers within the EU,[115] which led to policy changes in the Netherlands despite their politically contentious nature.[116] In some instances, the government response to judgments against other states has been exceptionally rapid: in the case of *Salduz*, the Dutch government announced within a day that the law would be changed to bring it into compliance.[117]

In the UK, the JCHR has recommended that the Ministry of Justice, working with the Foreign Office, should give systematic consideration to whether ECtHR judgments against other countries have implications for the UK and to inform Parliament accordingly.[118] The government rejected this approach, saying that primary responsibility for identifying significant cases lies with individual government departments.[119] The role of the Ministry of Justice is supplementary to, and supports, the work of other departments. It produces a confidential cross-departmental *Human Rights Information Bulletin* to highlight significant cases (domestic and international), which is not shared with Parliament.[120] The interviewee added that specialised staff in the Ministry of Justice monitor systematically all Grand Chamber judgments; a non-UK judgment would only be drawn to the JCHR's attention if it had 'direct, immediate and obvious' implications for national policy or practice—as with *Salduz*, which had led to legislative change in Scotland.[121]

---

[113] Telephone interview with Holger Haibach, former member of the Bundestag (Christian Democratic Union), 15 June 2012; interview with Christoph Strässer, member of the Bundestag (Social Democratic Party), Berlin, 21 March 2012.

[114] *Sufi and Elmi v UK* Nos 8319/07 and 11449/07, 28 June 2011.

[115] *MSS v Belgium and Greece* No 30696/09, 21 January 2011.

[116] See Kuijer, ch 14 in this volume.

[117] On 1 April 2010, the new policy rules of the Dutch Legal Aid Board concerning the provision of legal assistance at police interrogations entered into force. These rules, together with an instruction from the Ministry of the Public Prosecutor, were intended to ensure compliance with *Salduz* in the period before legislation could be introduced. A Draft Bill on Legal Assistance and Police Interrogation (*Conceptwetsvoorstel rechtsbijstand en politieverhoor*) was submitted to Parliament on 15 April 2011. However, it has been criticised for failing to include provisions that would implement *Salduz* fully; for example, the Bill allows exceptions to be made if the 'interest of the investigation' prohibits the presence of a lawyer. Before implementing the Bill, the Dutch Government has awaited the outcome of negotiations on a 'Proposal for a Directive of the European Parliament and of the Council on the Right of Access to a Lawyer in Criminal Proceedings and on the Right to Communicate upon Arrest' COM(2011) 326 final, 8 June 2011. See also C Brants, 'The Reluctant Dutch Response to Salduz' (2011) 15(2) *Edinburgh Law Review* 298–305.

[118] See Joint Committee on Human Rights (n 59) paras 187–93.

[119] The Government's Human Rights Policy and Human Rights Judgments, Oral Evidence HC 1726-I, Rt Hon Kenneth Clarke MP, Oral Evidence, 20 December 2011, Q23. See also Ministry of Justice, CM 8432, 10.

[120] Ministry of Justice, CM 8432, 10.

[121] Criminal Procedure (Legal Assistance, Detention and Appeals) (Scotland) Act 2010.

We found no evidence in Ukraine of a system for monitoring judgments against other states, or of parliamentary scrutiny of executive action in this area. An anonymous government interviewee acknowledged that there is resistance in the executive to implementing non-Ukrainian judgments that have financial implications, since it may be cheaper to wait for a possible case against Ukraine and pay compensation. Moreover, as Ukrainian ECtHR Judge Ganna Yudkivska explains, there remains judicial resistance to viewing Strasbourg case law as a source of law: the legal provision to this effect was 'dead', since judges—especially those in the lower courts—viewed it as alien to Ukraine's civil law tradition.[122] Nevertheless, in rare instances, Ukrainian law or policy has been reformed as a result of judgments against other states, albeit with substantial delay. These include laws or amendments concerning the right to correspondence of people in detention or imprisonment and the placing of children in juvenile reception centres.[123]

There were mixed accounts of the extent to which the Romanian government monitors non-Romanian cases. The Government Co-agent, Irina Cambrea, states that all ECtHR case law is 'monitored constantly'; the agent then informs the appropriate government department and relevant judgments are translated and made available on the website of the Superior Council of Magistracy.[124] However, former Justice Minister Monica Macovei observed that there is 'no office or person to systematically look at [non-Romanian] judgments', although this might happen sporadically depending on individuals' initiative.[125] We found no evidence of parliamentary scrutiny of the implementation of non-Romanian judgments.

In the states under review, both executive and parliamentary attention to judgments against other states is variable. On the parliamentary side, this is unsurprising; judgments against other states are rarely politically compelling, with cases such as *Salduz* being exceptional.[126] Moreover, determining the implications of judgments against one state for the legal order of another is a complex and unavoidably exploratory exercise—one in which hard-pressed parliamentarians may be unwilling to invest. However, we suggest that, at a minimum, governments and parliaments should expressly *recognise* the ECtHR's interpretative authority and parliamentary human rights committees should scrutinise executive systems (or lack thereof) for monitoring Strasbourg judgments against other states.

---

[122] Interview with Judge Ganna Yudkivska, Strasbourg, 27 June 2012.

[123] Committee on Legal Affairs and Human Rights, 'Contribution to the Conference on the Principle of Subsidiarity', Skopje, 1–2 October 2010, AS/Jur/Inf (2010) 04, 25 November 2010, 37.

[124] Written response from Irina Cambrea, Romanian Government Co-agent, 25 June 2012. In 2012, 14 non-Romanian judgments (and 67 Romanian judgments) were translated on the Superior Council of Magistracy website; the reasoning behind the selection, and the implications for Romanian law, are not explained on the website. See www.csm1909.ro/csm/index.php?cmd=950301.

[125] Interview with Monica Macovei MEP, Strasbourg, 12 June 2012.

[126] See, for example, the 'Salduz Watch' website maintained by the Legal Aid Reformers' Network: www.legalaidreform.org/police-station-legal-advice/salduz-watch.

F. Structures and Processes: Conclusions

There is no blueprint for the involvement of national parliaments in the implementation of ECtHR judgments; rather, it is the function of the various structures and actors that matters, as well as the principles that underlie the chosen institutional arrangement—for example, the impartiality of legal advice. The clarity and permanence of a human rights committee's remit are also of critical importance.

Both the precise form and extent of parliamentary involvement are significantly determined by the wider political context. A parliament that is little more than a rubber stamp for an over-mighty executive is unlikely to engage in effective scrutiny of the implementation of judgments regardless of the legal or institutional arrangements. As the OSJI notes, the mere existence of implementation structures does not imply that a state's commitment to implementation is genuine or will be effective: 'mechanisms can risk creating the illusion of compliance'.[127]

Implementation at the national level involves disparate actors who operate under different—often competing—institutional pressures and timetables. In this section, we have considered primarily the relationship between executives and parliaments, especially with regard to the provision of information at multiple points in the implementation process. At issue are both the quality and timeliness of this information: a purely retrospective reporting mechanism will not permit parliaments to influence or scrutinise the executive response to adverse judgments in 'real time'. There is potential to improve parliamentary scrutiny of implementation by placing greater emphasis on the sharing of action plans. National systems should also incorporate structural guarantees of reporting mechanisms to ensure that they become entrenched and survive between elections.

II. THE RELATIONSHIP BETWEEN NATIONAL PARLIAMENTS AND THE COE

In what ways can CoE bodies encourage greater engagement by national parliaments in the implementation of ECtHR judgments? We consider this question in relation to PACE and the ECtHR.

A. The Role of PACE[128]

PACE emphasises the 'double mandate' of its members, who are members of both the Assembly and their respective national parliaments.[129] PACE delegates can only realistically fulfil this duty if they belong to a relevant parliamentary committee at the domestic level and, ideally, to the equivalent committee within PACE, the

---

[127] See Open Society Justice Initiative (n 6) 16.
[128] See Drzemczewski and Lewis, ch 15 in this volume.
[129] Parliamentary Assembly of the Council of Europe, *National Parliaments: Guarantors of Human Rights in Europe*, Resolution 1823 (2011), para 3.

CLAHR. In some states, like Germany, such overlap exists.[130] In others, there is no crossover: for example, no member of the JCHR has ever been an active member of the equivalent committee of PACE, a situation lamented by the JCHR, which sees 'considerable merit' in having both overlapping membership and closer official links.[131] However, UK MP Christopher Chope, who at the time of writing chairs the CLAHR, offered a contrary view, in part because of the logistical challenges of dual membership. Chope adds that:

> The contribution that people like me can make [at PACE] ... is to spread good practice among other countries rather than trying to bring the UK government to book because the JCHR does that perfectly well already ... There is no need for us to double up.[132]

This opinion is debatable: the UK was one of 10 states whose parliamentary delegations were called to innovative hearings held by CLAHR in 2012–13 to account for structural problems that have led to repeat violations and/or delays in the full implementation of judgments.[133] Moreover, it is surely incumbent on members of PACE to engage in domestic political discussion about human rights protection. At a minimum, PACE members should view it as part of their role to rectify factual inaccuracies and misperceptions about the Strasbourg system.[134] Further, they are uniquely well-placed to champion the principle underpinning the system of the collective guarantee of human rights. Open defiance to implementing a Court judgment—as has happened in the UK—is an affront to this principle.[135]

B. Parliamentary Scrutiny as a Factor in ECtHR Judgments

The appropriate degree of judicial deference to the elected branches of government is a matter of continuing debate. Kavanagh distinguishes between 'minimal' and 'substantial' judicial deference.[136] Minimal deference is *always* due and simply requires that judges 'cannot make light of, or be sceptical about, attempts by Parliament to solve a social problem in legislation'. Substantial deference has to be 'earned' by the elected branches and is justified only where a court considers itself to suffer from

---

[130] At the time of interview in 2012, two members of the 18-strong German PACE delegation were members of the Bundestag Human Rights Committee (including Marina Schuster); one was a member of the Legal Committee and one (Christoph Strässer) was a member of both. Christoph Strässer and Marina Schuster belonged to the PACE Committee on Legal Affairs and Human Rights. In addition, Ms Schuster was a member of the CLAHR Sub-committee on Human Rights.

[131] See Joint Committee on Human Rights (n 59) paras 195–96.

[132] Interview with Christopher Chope MP (Conservative), Strasbourg, 27 June 2012.

[133] Committee on Legal Affairs and Human Rights, 'Implementation of Judgments of the European Court of Human Rights', Extracts from the Minutes of Hearings, Organised by the Committee, Held in Strasbourg in April 2012, in June 2012, in October 2012 and in January 2013, AS/Jur (2013) 13, 28 March 2013.

[134] Such as the assertion that ECtHR judges are unelected; see, for example, 'Unelected Euro Judges are Bringing Terror to the Streets of Britain' *Daily Mail* (18 January 2012).

[135] For example, Prime Minister David Cameron told Parliament that 'no one should be in any doubt: prisoners are not getting the vote under this Government': Hansard HC 24 October 2012, vol 551, col 923.

[136] A Kavanagh, 'Nature and Grounds of Judicial Deference' in A Kavanagh (ed), *Constitutional Review under the Human Rights Act* (Cambridge, Cambridge University Press, 2009) 181.

particular institutional shortcomings with regard to a particular matter. These are cases in which a court judges a parliament or executive to have more institutional competence, more expertise and/or greater legitimacy to assess a particular issue.[137]

While the debate about deference has commonly been addressed to constitutional arrangements within a state, it is also relevant to the ECtHR. The extent to which there has been parliamentary scrutiny of questions arising in human rights cases may be an important factor in the Court's adjudications,[138] which has frequently reiterated that:

> [B]y reason of their direct and continuous contact with the vital forces in the society, national authorities—and particularly national legislatures—are in principle better placed than an international court to evaluate the local needs and conditions and to decide on the nature and scope of the measures necessary to meet those needs.[139]

The extent of domestic parliamentary scrutiny was highly relevant, for example, to the Court's judgment in the case of *Animal Defenders International v UK*, in which the Grand Chamber upheld by a narrow majority (9:8) the UK's ban on political advertising on television and radio as a necessary interference with the right to free expression.[140] The majority reaffirmed that:

> [I]n order to determine the proportionality of a general measure, the Court must primarily assess the legislative choices underlying it ... The quality of the parliamentary and judicial review of the necessity of the measure is of particular importance in this respect, including to the operation of the relevant margin of appreciation.[141]

In this case, the ban on political advertising in the broadcast media had been enacted by Parliament with cross-party support and without any dissenting vote: it was 'the culmination of an exceptional examination by parliamentary bodies of the cultural, political and legal aspects of the prohibition'.[142] It was this particular competence of Parliament—and the extensive pre-legislative consultation on the Convention compatibility of the prohibition—which explained the degree of deference shown by the domestic courts to Parliament's decision to adopt the ban.[143] For its part, the ECtHR attached 'considerable weight to these exacting and pertinent reviews, by both parliamentary and judicial bodies'.[144] Thus, the Court effectively endorsed 'a

---

[137] ibid 182.

[138] See Lazarus and Simonsen, ch 19 in this volume.

[139] *Animal Defenders International v UK* No 48876/08, 22 April 2013 (concurring opinion of Judge Bratza at [11]).

[140] ibid; the decision was a departure from previous case law in *VgT Verein gegen Tierfabrik v Switzerland* No 32772/02, 30 June 2009, in which the authorities' refusal to broadcast a commercial concerning animal welfare was found to be a violation of Article 10.

[141] ibid [108].

[142] ibid [114]. The judgment also notes (at [44]) that the JCHR 'acknowledged that the prohibition could well be found incompatible with Article 10 having regard to *VgT*. However, it urged caution in reversing the prohibition given the important rationale of the prohibition and the difficulty of devising a more circumscribed solution'.

[143] ibid [115].

[144] See also *SH and others v Austria* No 57813/00 [GC] 3 November 2011, concerning restrictions on in vitro fertilisation, in which the Court alluded (at [114]) to 'the careful and cautious approach adopted by the Austrian legislature in seeking to reconcile social realities with its approach of principle in this field'.

notion of judicial restraint in deference to the substance and process by which the decisions were undertaken in this situation'.[145]

At the opposite end of the spectrum is *Greens and MT v UK*,[146] concerning the disenfranchisement of convicted prisoners, in which the ECtHR indicated that there had not been adequate parliamentary scrutiny and debate on the matter since the Grand Chamber judgment on the same issue in *Hirst v UK (No 2)* in 2005.[147] In applying its pilot judgment procedure in *Greens*, the Court stipulated an obligation of parliamentary involvement by requiring that the UK government must 'bring forward ... legislative proposals' to render the law Convention-compliant.[148] Arguably, the Court could have gone further to bring about substantive parliamentary consideration of the issue by being more prescriptive as to timescales. Subsequent to *Greens*, it granted the UK government an extension of the six-month time limit for introducing legislative proposals, which was due to expire on 11 October 2011. This was as a result of the Grand Chamber hearing of *Scoppola v Italy (No 3)* in November 2011,[149] which raised analogous issues to those in the UK cases. The UK government intervened in the hearing and was granted an extension of six months from the date of the *Scoppola* judgment. An alternative approach would have been for the Court to refuse the UK government's request for an extension, thereby obliging it to introduce (at least) a draft bill by the original deadline. This would, in turn, have required there to be parliamentary consideration of the proposed legislation. Murray Hunt of the JCHR describes this as a 'missed opportunity' since 'the longer Parliament can be ... engaging with the substantive issues at stake before they actually have to legislate the better'.[150] In the event, the UK government introduced a draft bill in November 2012 that was scrutinised by an ad hoc committee of both parliamentary houses.[151] At the time of writing, it is highly doubtful whether legislation will be passed before the general election due in 2015 to remedy the violation first identified in the Chamber judgment in *Hirst* in 2004.

In relation to other cases, the UK government has shown itself aware of the benefits of ensuring parliamentary deliberation on human rights matters. In the course of its response to the *S and Marper* judgment, the government suggested that

---

[145] J King, 'Deference, Dialogue and Animal Defenders International', *UK Constitutional Law Blog* (25 April 2013); http://ukconstitutionallaw.org/2013/04/25/jeff-king-deference-dialogue-and-animal-defenders-international/#_ftn1.

[146] *Greens and MT v UK* Nos 60041/08 and 60054/08, 23 November 2010.

[147] *Hirst v UK (No 2)*, (n 9). In *Greens* (n 146), the ECtHR cited (at [41]) the JCHR's statement that the UK Government's delay in bringing forward proposals for consideration by Parliament was 'unacceptable'. The *Greens* judgment also cites (at [44]) the Committee of Ministers Interim Resolution CM/ResDH(2009)160, 3 December 2009, which recalled that the Court (in *Hirst v UK (No 2)*) had found 'no evidence that Parliament has ever sought to weigh the competing interests or to assess the proportionality of a blanket ban on the right of a convicted prisoner to vote'.

[148] *Greens* (n 146) operative [6(a)].

[149] *Scoppola v Italy (No 3)* No 126/05, 22 May 2012.

[150] Interview with Murray Hunt, Legal Adviser to the JCHR, London, 10 July 2012.

[151] For details of the Bill, see n 10. See also Joint Committee on the Draft Voting Eligibility (Prisoners) Bill, Session 2013–14, *Draft Voting Eligibility (Prisoners) Bill: Report*, HL Paper 103, HC 924 (London: The Stationery Office, 2013), which stated that the UK was under a binding international law obligation to comply with ECtHR judgments and recommended that the Government bring forward a bill at the start of the 2014–15 parliamentary session giving the vote to all prisoners serving sentences of 12 months or less and those who are within six months of their scheduled release date.

'where a complex issue has been subjected to Parliamentary scrutiny, there is an argument that a wide margin of appreciation should be applied'.[152] Similarly, Dutch officials confirmed that, when defending a case, the government routinely refers to parliamentary scrutiny and debate: where Parliament has expressly considered the proportionality of the restriction of a qualified right, it 'helps a great deal'.[153]

These contrasting examples illustrate the potential impact at domestic level of the Court demonstrating explicitly in its judgments that both the extent of parliamentary scrutiny and debate on a human rights matter, and the quality of reasoning in those debates, are factors that inform its application of the margin of appreciation. Such an approach provides an opportunity both to the executive and parliament to 'earn' deference from the Court through the quality of the legislative process.

Some caveats are necessary. Even if we start with the assumption (disputed by some in the UK) that judicial assessment of the quality of democratic deliberation is an inherently valid exercise, it is not necessarily a straightforward one. For example, the quality of the debate in the UK Parliament on prisoners' voting rights in February 2011 has been differently assessed by different authors, principally in respect of whether MPs engaged with the substantive human rights issue (the scope of the right at stake and the proportionality of options for restricting it) as opposed to merely the question of whether the ECtHR had exceeded its authority.[154] Further, the strong notion of parliamentary sovereignty that pertains in the UK does not apply in other European states where, for example, the will of the people is expressed through a written constitution and the legislature has only qualified democratic standing. The ECtHR thus faces the challenge of developing an approach that is consistent across the CoE in respect of the deference it pays to parliamentary deliberation. Further, the Court must be aware of the risk that executives or parliaments may orchestrate proceedings to create the appearance of democratic deliberation in order to seek to earn judicial deference which is not, in fact, warranted. These observations vindicate the Court's position of attaching no special or automatic weight to parliamentary deliberation, but demonstrating in its judgments when it has examined parliamentary materials and found cause to defer to the reasoned arguments advanced therein.

C. The Extent to Which the Court is Directive or Prescriptive in its Judgments

Article 46 of the ECHR obliges states to comply with the final judgment of the ECtHR in any case to which they are a party. States are required to stop the breach, provide a remedy for the individual concerned and prevent new or similar breaches. The Court has traditionally left considerable discretion to states as to precisely

---

[152] Home Office Memorandum on the Protection of Freedoms Bill, February 2011, para 13.
[153] Interview with Martin Kuijer, Senior Legal Advisor, Ministry of Security and Justice, The Hague, 23 March 2012.
[154] Contrast J King, 'Should Prisoners Have the Right to Vote?' *UK Constitutional Law Group Blog* (8 May 2011) with D Nicol, 'Legitimacy of the Commons Debate on Prisoner Voting' [2011] *Public Law* 681.

how they amend their law, policy or practice to meet these obligations. However, in earlier research, one of us traced a shift in the Court's practice from a previously limited, declaratory approach to redress to one which is more directive and sometimes prescriptive.[155] This more expansive approach has been applied both to cases concerning individuals (especially those involving property restitution, unfair trials and unlawful detention) and to situations where there have been large-scale, endemic human rights violations. In relation to the latter, the most significant innovation is the 'pilot judgment' procedure, in which the Court identifies a systemic violation of the Convention and stipulates general measures in the operative part of the judgment in order that the state should resolve the systemic issue.[156] It may also impose binding time limits for such measures to be enacted, varying from six to 18 months.[157] Allied to the pilot judgment procedure is the increasing use of Article 46 of the Convention, together with Article 41, in which the Court uses directive wording in judgments concerning systemic breaches of Convention rights (typically requiring legislative reform, the elements of which may be specified), but this wording is not included in the operative provisions.

Our research participants almost unanimously endorsed the pilot judgment procedure. The *Rumpf* pilot judgment against Germany in 2010 (the first directed at a Western European state) accelerated the resolution of the problem of overly lengthy domestic legal proceedings, which had remained unresolved since the Grand Chamber judgment in *Surmeli* on the same issue in 2006 (and, indeed, since *Kudla v Poland* in 2000,[158] which had first convinced the German Foreign Ministry that reform was necessary).[159] According to one academic interviewee, the pilot judgment was 'like a red line—if you have one, parliamentarians realise they have to do something'.[160] However, interviewees ventured that pilot judgments are less likely to be effective when there is no pre-existing political will to resolve the problem. A case in point is the 2009 pilot judgment in *Yuriy Nikolayevich Ivanov v Ukraine*,[161] concerning systemic non-enforcement of domestic court decisions—a problem first highlighted by the Court in 2004.[162] After several resolutions by the Committee of Ministers,[163] a law was finally passed in response to the judgment in June 2012, which only partially resolved the issue.[164] Similarly, the lack of political will in the

[155] P Leach, 'No Longer Offering Fine Mantras to a Parched Child? The European Court's Developing Approach to Remedies' in A Follesdal, B Peters and G Ulfstein (eds), *Constituting Europe: The European Court of Human Rights in a National, European and Global Context* (Cambridge, Cambridge University Press, 2013).
[156] P Leach, H Hardman, S Stephenson and BK Blitz, *Responding to Systemic Human Rights Violations—An Analysis of 'Pilot Judgments' at the European Court of Human Rights and their Impact at National Level* (Antwerp, Intersentia, 2010).
[157] See Leach (n 155) 163–64.
[158] *Kudla v Poland* No 30210/96, 26 October 2000.
[159] Interview with Almut Wittling-Vogel, Representative of the Federal Government for Matters Relating to Human Rights, Berlin, 20 March 2012.
[160] Interview with Sebastian Müller, Bielefeld University (formerly), Berlin, 20 March 2012.
[161] *Yuriy Nikolayevich Ivanov v Ukraine* No 40450/04, 15 October 2009.
[162] *Zhovner v Ukraine* No 56948/00, 29 September 2004.
[163] CM/ResDH(2008)1, CM/ResDH(2009)159, CM/ResDH(2010)222, CM/ResDH(2011)184.
[164] The law does not provide for its retroactive application and therefore does not resolve the problem of the older, repetitive applications pending before the Court; see Interim Resolution CM/ResDH (2012)234.

UK to implement the *Hirst* judgment on prisoner voting has meant that the pilot judgment in *Greens and MT v UK*, which for the first time in a UK case prescribed a timetable for the introduction of a law, remains unimplemented.

The Court's more expansive approach to the identification of general measures will increasingly require parliamentary engagement in the implementation of judgments. As one of us has suggested elsewhere, this is a welcome development since it gives the respondent state—including its parliament—clarity and certainty as to what is required by way of implementation and makes it easier for the Committee of Ministers to monitor whether or not compliance has been achieved.[165]

Outside of the pilot judgment procedure, the concept of subsidiarity is interpreted by some as meaning that the Court should not interfere unduly with issues that are properly the domain of national authorities.[166] The former Romanian judge at the ECtHR, Corneliu Birsan, observed that judgments must be 'clear, educative and specific' as to the nature and cause of the violation, but that it is the role of politicians to resolve the general problems that underlie individual complaints.[167] The Romanian Government Co-agent, Irina Cambrea, ventured that an overly prescriptive approach 'carries the risk of generating solutions which could be less adapted to domestic realities'.[168]

There was less anxiety about the Court being prescriptive as to timescales, since this does not intrude as starkly on the policy competence of national authorities; however, interviewees observed that unfeasibly short deadlines risk bringing the process into disrepute. For example, the one-year deadline for a legislative solution in the case of *Rumpf* was only met because the government had already begun to draft legislation.[169]

III. IMPLEMENTATION AS A POLITICAL PROCESS

As the JCHR observes, given the discretion inherent in the supervision mechanism, the process of implementing a Strasbourg judgment is an 'unavoidably political process', albeit one constrained by legal obligations.[170] Once a judgment is open to political consideration, there may be calls for more *radical* implementation, more *restrictive* implementation or, exceptionally, *non*-implementation.

Some research participants, including government officials and civil society groups, were sceptical about the merits and feasibility of fostering a greater role for parliaments in the implementation of judgments in their states. For some, this was a pragmatic assessment based on their view that parliamentarians lacked human rights expertise or were opportunistically prone to manipulate the issues raised in

---

[165] See Leach (n 155) 160.
[166] See Hunt, ch 1 in this volume.
[167] Interview with (former) Judge Corneliu Birsan, Strasbourg, 25 June 2012.
[168] Written response from Irina Cambrea, Romanian Government Co-agent, 25 June 2012.
[169] Interview with Almut Wittling-Vogel, Representative of the Federal Government for Matters Relating to Human Rights, Berlin, 20 March 2012.
[170] See Joint Committee on Human Rights (n 59) para 15.

judgments.[171] In Ukraine and Romania, corruption and the relative weakness of Parliament vis-a-vis the executive were also cited as factors. Certainly, it cannot be assumed that parliamentarians will invariably urge the executive towards full or swift compliance with a judgment; sometimes, the opposite is the case. Interviewees in Ukraine and at the CoE observed that the delay in implementing the *Ivanov* pilot judgment was partly due to an unwillingness to lift a moratorium on enforcing judgments against entities that were partly state-owned and partly privately owned—including by Members of Parliament. As a government official noted (speaking anonymously), implementing *Ivanov* had direct 'negative economic consequences' for some deputies.

As PACE has recognised, in any national implementation system, an intricate relationship exists between the executive, parliament and the judiciary.[172] Judgments necessitating complex reform may require action from all three and it may not always be immediately evident whether legislation is required or the violation can be remedied via the judicial route alone. Where judgments are politically contentious, the process of responding to a judgment can be exceptionally challenging for the coordinating authority within a state.

This complexity is illustrated by the case of *M v Germany*,[173] concerning the retrospective and effectively indefinite prolongation of preventive detention of prisoners (mainly sex offenders) considered to be dangerous to the public. The Court found this regime to be a breach of the right to liberty and security (Article 5 of the ECHR) and of the prohibition of retroactivity (Article 7(1)). The German government representative for human rights, Almut Wittling-Vogel, recalls that, even before the judgment, legislative proposals on preventive detention were being drafted as part of the coalition's programme; these intended to abolish the retrospective nature of preventive detention in the future.[174] German parliamentarians interviewed for this research explained that, following the judgment, there was a political consensus that it must be implemented, but prolonged debate—amid considerable public disquiet—about how to do so. Christoph Strässer confirmed that the Legal Committee made several attempts to fashion a solution that would comply with the

---

[171] For example, ECtHR case law is cited in the preamble to a controversial draft law introduced in Romania which would have restricted women's access to abortion by making 'counselling' mandatory and imposing a 'reflection' period before services could be accessed. The preamble cites the judgment in *Vo v France* No 53924/00, 8 July 2004 to support the statement that 'embryos and foetuses are not excluded' from protection under Article 2 ECHR, the right to life ('Legislative proposal on the establishment, operation and organisation of Centres for Pregnancy Crisis Counselling', 10). In fact, the Vo judgment notes (at [84]) that within the CoE, 'there is no consensus on the nature and status of the embryo and/or foetus' and (at [85]) that it is 'neither desirable, nor even possible as matters stand, to answer in the abstract the question whether the unborn child is a person for the purposes of Article 2 of the Convention'. The draft law—co-sponsored by Marius Dugulescu, who was at the time Vice Chair of the Human Rights Committee in the Chamber of Deputies—was rejected.

[172] 'The execution of a Strasbourg judgment is often a complex legal and political process, requiring cumulative and complementary measures implemented by several state organs': Progress Report of the Rapporteur of the Committee on Legal Affairs and Human Rights, Implementation of Judgments of the European Court of Human Rights, AS/Jur (2009) 36, para 14 (Mr Christos Pourgourides), September 2009.

[173] *M v Germany* No 19359/04, 17 December 2009.

[174] Interview with Almut Wittling-Vogel, Representative of the Federal Government for Matters Relating to Human Rights, Berlin, 20 March 2012.

judgment, but the issues were technically difficult and consensus was elusive.[175] In the event, the ECtHR judgment was reinforced by a subsequent ruling of the Federal Constitutional Court (FCC), which declared unconstitutional all existing provisions on preventive detention insofar as they had retrospective effect or allowed treatment of persons in preventive detention which was substantially similar to that of ordinary prisoners.[176] The FCC imposed on the government and Parliament the 'duty to develop a new overall conception for a preventive detention regime oriented towards liberty and therapy', with certain minimum requirements, to be adopted by the end of May 2013.[177] It made transitional arrangements until the entry into force of this new legislation. Almut Wittling-Vogel recalls the acute sensitivity of the case:

> There aren't many politicians who are ready to say that, even if there is a risk to children ... you must set these people free ... The political problems remained, but the day of the FCC judgment was the day that it was clear to everyone, not just the experts, that we had to do something.[178]

Dr Wittling-Vogel added that much of the ensuing detailed discussion took place informally, within and between the pro-government parties, rather than on the floor of Parliament. The governments of the Länder, which are responsible for running prisons, were also extensively involved in preparing the necessary legal and organisational steps.[179] Thus, *M v Germany* demonstrates the multiple actors whose involvement may be required to implement a judgment—and the pressures that elected politicians face when judgments are contentious.

Similarly, the Grand Chamber judgment in *Gäfgen v Germany*[180] aroused strong public interest. This case concerned inhuman treatment on account of the fact that the applicant, a man suspected of child abduction, was threatened by the police with torture in order to make him disclose the child's whereabouts (in violation of Article 3 of the ECHR). The formal execution of *Gäfgen* lay with the executive, via translation of the judgment and its dissemination to the entire judicial apparatus, the police, the Interior Ministry and the Länder.[181] No legislation was required. However, former Bundestag member Holger Haibach recalls that *Gäfgen*—and the domestic proceedings which preceded it—'broke the ice' on public debate about domestic human rights issues.[182] There was parliamentary discussion about the

---

[175] Interview with Christoph Strässer, member of the Bundestag (Social Democratic Party), Berlin, 21 March 2012.

[176] No 2 BvR 2365/09, May 4, 2011. See M Andenas and E Bjorge, '"Preventive Detention": No 2 BvR 2365/09—Federal Constitutional Court of Germany Ruling on the Compatibility of Preventive Detention Legislation with the European Convention on Human Rights' (2011) 105 *American Journal of International Law* 768.

[177] DH—DD(2011)652E, revised action plan/action report (communication from Germany concerning the case of M against Germany (Application No 19359/04)) 4.

[178] Interview with Almut Wittling-Vogel, Representative of the Federal Government for Matters Relating to Human Rights, Berlin, 20 March 2012.

[179] Committee of Ministers 1136th meeting (6–8 March 2012).

[180] *Gäfgen v Germany* No 22978/05 [GC], 1 June 2010.

[181] DH—DD(2011)647E, updated action plan/action report (communication from Germany concerning the case of Gäfgen against Germany (Application No 22978/05)) 2.

[182] Telephone interview with Holger Haibach, former member of the Bundestag (Christian Democratic Union), 15 June 2012.

ethical dimension of the case (the 'ticking bomb' scenario) and the Human Rights Committee questioned the responsible minister:

> The committee came up with a [parliamentary] resolution ... saying that we condemn every kind of torture. We got some fire for that and I always responded that, if I were the parent of that child, I would beat the hell out of that man, but as a politician and lawmaker I cannot allow it because if you give in on one point, where do you stop?

The impact of political discussion of *Gäfgen* is hard to evaluate, since the execution of the judgment demanded no formal parliamentary involvement. However, there may have been less tangible benefits. As the JCHR has noted, parliamentary involvement:

> [R]aises the political visibility of the issues at stake and provides an opportunity for public scrutiny of the justifications offered by the Government for its proposed response to the judgment or for its delay in bringing such a response forward.[183]

The JCHR adds that:

> In so doing it helps both to ensure a genuine democratic input into legal changes following Court judgments and to address the perception that changes in law or policy as a result of Court judgments lack democratic legitimacy.[184]

It is to this question of legitimacy that we turn in conclusion.

IV. CONCLUSION: THE ISSUE OF (DEMOCRATIC) LEGITIMACY

Discussion of the legitimacy of judicial review first emerged in relation to the normatively appropriate division of authority between the branches of national governments. Similar arguments have since extended to courts and tribunals beyond the state. As Harlow notes, the term 'legitimacy' is 'capable of bearing variant meanings, both contingent and contestable'.[185] Some accounts of the legitimacy of international judicial review are rooted in legal discourse and establish criteria such as the determinacy of judicial decisions, and their coherence both with precedent and the decisions of other international courts.[186] Other authors emphasise the procedural aspects of international judicial review. By this account, the legitimacy of such courts depends upon the structure and operation of the procedure by which judgments are reached, as well as the sound reasoning and consistency of those judgments.[187]

---

[183] See Joint Committee on Human Rights (n 59) para 15.

[184] ibid, para 17.

[185] C Harlow, *The Concepts and Methods of Reasoning of New Public Law: Legitimacy*, LSE Law, Society and Economy Working Papers 19/2010.

[186] See especially the legitimacy indicators developed by Thomas Franck, discussed in T Treves, 'Aspects of Legitimacy of Decisions of International Courts and Tribunals' in R Wolfrum and V Röben (eds), *Legitimacy in International Law* (Dordrecht, Springer, 2008).

[187] T Barkhuysen and M van Emmerik, 'Legitimacy of European Court of Human Rights Judgments: Procedural Aspects' in N Huls, M Adams and J Bomhoff (eds), *The Legitimacy of Highest Courts' Rulings: Judicial Deliberations and Beyond* (The Hague, TMC Asser Press, 2009); J Goldstone, 'Achievements and Challenges—Insights from the Strasbourg Experience for Other International Courts' (2009) 5 *European Human Rights Law Review* 603.

These approaches are not necessarily preoccupied with the *democratic* legitimacy of regional or international courts, except insofar as aspects of their institutional design and operation may affect their democratic credentials; for example, the manner in which judges are appointed or (as in the ECtHR) elected, the transparency and openness of the court, and the opportunities provided for third-party interventions and the participation of civil society.[188] Other accounts are more expressly concerned with democratic legitimacy, in the sense of the appropriate separation of powers between an international court and democratic decision-making at the national level—an approach which captures the normative as well as efficiency-related imperatives of subsidiarity.[189] Von Staden argues that the ECtHR achieves a normatively sensitive separation of powers through its doctrine of the margin of appreciation, which grants national decision-makers a degree of discretion, subject to supervision of the Court, when it takes legislative, administrative or judicial action in the area of a Convention right.[190] Democratically based defences of international judicial review are also underpinned by the notion that human rights are constitutive of and strengthen democracy rather than constraining it.[191] In the case of the ECtHR, judicial review:

> [D]oes not *replace* political, democratic domestic contestation ... Rather, the role of the ECtHR is to ensure that such contestation remains respectful of the equal dignity of all citizens—including those whose views are in permanent minority in legislatures.[192]

Moreover, the Court draws legitimacy from the will of democratic states and their voluntary acceptance of the jurisdiction of the Court and the right of individual application—an argument that weighed heavily with our research participants.

A. Challenges to the Legitimacy of the ECtHR

As noted earlier, there have been sustained attacks by some UK government politicians, jurists and commentators on the legitimacy of the ECtHR, causing disquiet among senior figures in the Court.[193] These challenges have been based on various grounds, relating both to the perceived quality of the Court's procedures and its purported wish to interfere unduly with national decision-making.[194]

---

[188] A von Bogdandy and I Venzke, 'In Whose Name? An Investigation of International Courts' Public Authority and its Democratic Justification' (2012) 23(1) *European Journal of International Law* 7.

[189] A von Staden, 'The Democratic Legitimacy of Judicial Review Beyond the State: Normative Subsidiarity and Judicial Standards of Review' (2012) 10(4) *International Journal of Constitutional Law* 1023.

[190] ibid.

[191] J Mayerfield, 'The Democratic Legitimacy of International Human Rights Law' (2009) 19(1) *Indiana International & Comparative Law Review* 49.

[192] A Føllesdal, 'The Legitimacy of International Human Rights Review: The Case of the European Court of Human Rights' (2009) 40(4) *Journal of Social Philosophy* 595, 603, emphasis in original.

[193] N Bratza, 'The Relationship between the UK Courts and Strasbourg' (2011) 5 *European Human Rights Law Review* 505; M O'Boyle, 'The Future of the European Court of Human Rights' (2011) 12 *German Law Journal* 1862.

[194] A Donald, J Gordon and P Leach, *The UK and the European Court of Human Rights*, Research Report 83 (Manchester, Equality and Human Rights Commission, 2012) 162–64.

In the Netherlands too, the role of the ECtHR became highly contentious in 2011 and 2012, prompting a strong counter-reaction, particularly in the Senate, to criticisms of the Court from various quarters.[195] The conservative-liberal People's Party for Freedom and Democracy (VVD) sought to change Article 94 of the Dutch Constitution (which prescribes that international treaties have direct effect) and thereby give Parliament a greater role in the interpretation of international treaties.[196] In 2011, the Ministry for Foreign Affairs issued a policy document stating, *inter alia*, that the ECtHR should refrain from getting involved in 'peripheral' cases and that in order to sustain its credibility, it should leave more space for the margin of appreciation.[197] In response to this and other developments, a motion was tabled in the Senate and adopted almost unanimously, calling upon the government to continue its efforts to promote human rights in accordance with its obligations under the Convention and the jurisprudence of the Court.[198] In April 2012, ahead of the Brighton Conference on reform of the Court, all parties in the Senate—with the exception of the right-wing Party for Freedom (PVV)—passed a motion endorsing 'with complete conviction' the work of the ECtHR.[199]

It must be emphasised that attacks on the legitimacy or putative 'activism' of the ECtHR are the exception rather than the norm across the Council of Europe's 47 Member States.[200] While particular judgments sometimes provoke negative reactions, such responses tend to diminish over time.[201] The central finding of a 2011 study of the perceived legitimacy of the Court among domestic politicians, judges and lawyers in five states was that: 'There is strong constitutive support for a human rights court above and beyond the state in actively intervening in states' domestic decisions in rights protections.'[202] Of 107 respondents, only one thought that the ECtHR did not enjoy 'constitutive' legitimacy.[203] Moreover, elected politicians across the five states supported the Court as an 'external corrective' more than lawyers and judges did.[204]

The notion that there should be 'democratic override' of ECtHR judgments was strongly resisted by the majority of our research participants. Interviewees

---

[195] See also AB Terlouw and JH Gerards (eds), *Amici Curiae* (Oisterwijk, Wolf Productions, 2012); Kuijer, ch 14 in this volume.

[196] S Blok, K Dijkhoff and J Taverne, 'Verdragen mogen niet langer rechtstreeks werken' ('Treaties Can No Longer Have Direct Effect') *NRC Handelsblad* (23 February 2012).

[197] Ministry of Foreign Affairs, 'Verantwoordelijk voor Vrijheid: Mensenrechten in het Buitenlands Beleid' ('Responsibility for Freedom: Human Rights in Foreign Policy'), 5 April 2011.

[198] See the motion tabled by Marie-Louise Bemelmans-Videc (CDA/Christian Democrat) on 10 May 2011: EK 32.502/32.500 V, B.

[199] SP International, 'Government and Senate Reach Agreement on Independent European Court of Human Rights', 14 March 2012, available at: http://international.sp.nl/bericht/84181/120314-government_and_senate_reach_agreement_on_independent_european_court_of_human_rights.html.

[200] See Donald, Gordon and Leach (n 194) 175.

[201] J-P Costa, 'On the Legitimacy of the European Court of Human Rights' Judgments' (2011) 7 *European Constitutional Law Review* 173, 174.

[202] B Çali, A Koch and N Bruch, *The Legitimacy of the European Court of Human Rights: The View from the Ground* (London, Department of Political Science, University College London, 2011) 35. The research covered the UK, Ireland, Germany, Turkey and Bulgaria.

[203] ibid. Constitutive legitimacy relates to 'whether there are good reasons for an institution to exist' and 'whether those reasons demand deference to that institution's decisions'.

[204] ibid 36.

in Ukraine and Romania noted that although the implementation of judgments is variable, open defiance of Court judgments by elected politicians is extremely rare. Christoph Strässer notes that in Germany:

> In nearly every case, implementation is rapid … There is no … fundamental difference between the political parties on this … We say, 'we have to respect [judgments], whether we like it or not'.[205]

Nevertheless, the tenor of public discussion in the UK highlights the risk that, as the profile of the Court and the reach of its judgments grow, it may face increasing challenges to its legitimacy. As one UK interviewee observed (anonymously): 'It only takes one nasty judgment … I don't think that pre-*Hirst*—or even later—you could have predicted that Parliament would turn round and vote to say it would not implement a judgment.'

It is here that both the practical and the normative arguments for greater parliamentary engagement in human rights implementation coincide. Structures which embed parliamentary consideration of judgments (and promotion of Convention standards) may help to pre-empt opportunistic attacks on the European system of human rights protection by *obliging* parliamentarians to engage with reasoned, justificatory arguments and the often finely balanced arguments as to the scope of rights and the necessity and proportionality of restrictions upon them. As Friederycke Haijer, President of the Dutch Section of the International Commission of Jurists, ventures in relation to the Dutch lower house:

> One problem is the lack of ownership [of human rights] by parliamentarians … There's a sense in parliament that [the ECHR] is not their treaty. They can shoot at it without shooting themselves. If they had been more involved, they wouldn't be so critical.[206]

This approach is congruent with the conceptual framework elaborated elsewhere in this volume that views human rights as contributing to a 'culture of justification' within a democratic legal order. Such an approach would also have the effect of building knowledge and understanding of the Convention system among both parliamentarians and those whom they represent. Notwithstanding the concerns of those sceptical about the efficacy of parliamentary engagement, it is neither feasible nor desirable to seek to shield human rights questions from political debate. The imperative is to equip parliamentarians to hold governments to account for their action, or inaction, in responding to human rights judgments.

---

[205] Interview with Christoph Strässer, member of the Bundestag (Social Democratic Party), Berlin, 21 March 2012.
[206] Interview with Friederycke Haijer, President, Nederlands Juristen Comité voor de Mensenrechten, Leiden, 22 March 2012.

Part II

Legislative Human Rights Review in the UK Parliament

5

Democracy, Law, and Human Rights: Politics as Challenge and Opportunity

DAVID FELDMAN*

IN ONE WAY, this can be seen as the age of human rights. These international standards have strongly influenced the drafting of constitutional and statutory provisions in many countries. Examples include the Canadian Charter of Fundamental Rights, which became part of the Constitution in 1982, the New Zealand Bill of Rights Act 1990 and numerous constitutions in transitional states such as South Africa in 1993 and 1996, Bosnia and Herzegovina in 1995, and more recently still Afghanistan and Iraq. Other well-established parliamentary democracies are now following the lead, with the UK's Human Rights Act 1998, the Australian Capital Territory's Human Rights Act 2004, and Victoria's Charter of Human Rights and Responsibilities Act 2006.[1]

Yet from another perspective human rights are fragile growths in modern political systems. In the UK, which enacted a Human Rights Act in 1998, the government and opposition currently profess to see human rights as threats to democratic politics and constraints on their ability to advance the public interest through policies and legislation, especially in relation to combating terrorism and crime, and controlling immigration. The Act made a number of the rights which bind the UK in international law under the European Convention on Human Rights (ECHR) part of municipal law in the UK. It does not allow courts to strike down legislation, but there is an obligation to read and give effect to legislation so far as possible in a manner compatible with Convention rights. When not protected by primary legislation, action by public authorities is unlawful to the extent of any incompatibility with a Convention right.

This is a weak protection for rights, yet the Labour Prime Minister who oversaw its enactment, Tony Blair, came to regard the Act as problematic for government (though after leaving office he said that his worst mistake had been to legislate for

---

* This is a lightly revised and updated version of a lecture delivered at the opening of the conference on *Parliamentary Protection of Human Rights* organised by the Centre for Comparative Constitutional Studies and held on 20–22 July 2006 at the University of Melbourne, where I was a Miegunyah Distinguished Visiting Fellow.

[1] It testifies to the prescience of the organisers of the lecture and the conference that the legislation completed its parliamentary stages on the afternoon of 20 July 2006, about two hours before this lecture was given.

freedom of information). The Act has become a subject of party-political controversy. At the General Election in 2010, the Conservative Party's manifesto included a commitment to repealing the Act with a view to replacing it with a home-grown British Bill of Rights. Although the Conservatives became the largest single party in the House of Commons, and their leader David Cameron became Prime Minister, they lacked an overall majority in the Commons. They were forced into a coalition with the Liberal Democrats, who had always keenly supported the enactment of human rights. As part of the Coalition Agreement, the future of the Act and the possibility of a UK Bill of Rights was referred to a Commission, which was established in March 2011 and reported in December 2012. The membership of the Commission and the inconclusiveness of its report reflected the fact that there was no consensus among the political elite as to the desirability or otherwise of giving domestic legal effect to the ECHR.[2] Parties are likely to be similarly divided at the 2015 General Election.

The reasons for this controversy are varied. First and foremost, one has to bear in mind that politics are irreducibly political. Politicians typically go into politics mainly in order to change things. They share a desire to improve society. Few people enter politics in order to keep things as they are, even (some would say particularly) if they call themselves Conservatives. Human rights can improve society, but in a fairly diffuse and often unquantifiable way. Politicians like to introduce programmes that aim to deal directly with an identified problem. This is both more satisfying and more likely to gain the support of constituents than aiming to maintain a set of background values, although values may be important. The 800th anniversary of Magna Carta in 2015 is likely to affect the symbolism and rhetoric of the debate.

Even more awkward is the perception, and sometimes the reality, that legally enforceable human rights restrict the freedom of elected politicians to pursue particular objectives or to pursue objectives in certain ways. Politicians and the media frequently present human rights to the public as anti-democratic, and highlight examples of what they see as daft or anti-social assertions of rights to flout common sense and good administration. They also inveigh against individual judges who make decisions they dislike. Concerns are reinforced by the structure of the Human Rights Act 1998, which requires UK judges to take into account case law of the European Court of Human Rights (ECtHR), and that Court's dynamic interpretation of the Convention, which can sometimes frustrate government policies or individual decisions.[3] When countries face threats from war, terrorism, natural disasters or economic globalisation, the public may be all too ready to accept the need for human rights to be marginalised or excluded altogether.

Human rights face another problem. Many people see them as the preserve of lawyers and judges, to be protected mainly through legal rather than political processes. This can exacerbate tensions between the judiciary and the executive or legislature,

---

[2] Ministry of Justice, *Commission on a Bill of Rights: A UK Bill of Rights? The Choice Before Us* (London, The Stationery Office, 2012); Mark Elliott, 'A Damp Squib in the Long Grass: The Report of the Commission on a Bill of Rights' [2013] *European Human Rights Law Review* 137.

[3] On the reasons for this, see David Howarth, 'The politics of public law' in Mark Elliott and David Feldman (eds), *Cambridge Companion to Public Law* (Cambridge, Cambridge University Press, 2015) ch 4.

which are inevitable when the judiciary takes seriously its role in giving effect to the rule of law over and sometimes against other public institutions. Politicians tend to be distracted from the merits of a rights-based development and become focused instead on who should decide on the merits. When judges reach conclusions that some politicians dislike, politicians respond not by seriously debating the issue, but by criticising the judges' role in making such decisions on grounds such as lack of democratic legitimacy or political accountability. When the judges in question form part of an external legal order, such as those of the ECtHR, politicians' deprecation of judges is reinforced by suspicion of external limits on national legislatures. In such circumstances it can be easy to forget why it is important to protect rights, and to do so through (as well as outside) political and parliamentary processes.

This chapter seeks to redress the balance by advancing four propositions.

First, judges and their work are not to be criticised for lack of democratic legitimacy or for adversely affecting national sovereignty. There are many ways in which institutions may be more or less legitimate. They include input measures, such as the method by which their officials are selected (by election or for professional or personal qualities), or the effectiveness of their working methods to foster well-informed decision-making. They also include output measures, such as the legal and moral justifications for their decisions, and the quality and transparency of the reasoning supporting them. It will be immediately obvious that judges in common law systems and in the ECtHR are likely to score more highly than politicians on most of these criteria. I have explored these issues (some would say ad nauseam) elsewhere, so will say no more about them here.[4]

Second, human rights are part of the standards of public decency and private freedom to which any worthwhile democracy aspires. By making human rights standards an integral part of political discussion, we improve the quality of that discussion and of decisions emerging from it, safeguard the values which make society worth protecting, and foster proper accountability and transparency in public decision-making.

Third, to improve the quality of political discourse in that way, politicians and all of us must address questions about a number of matters, including: the part played by human rights obligations in defining the place of the state in the world; the roles of parliaments and governments in respect of human rights obligations within the state; and the nature of our conception of human rights. Merely by focusing attention on these matters, human rights standards contribute to transparent and accountable public decision-making.

Fourth, the beneficial effect of human rights on public decision-making does not depend on judges. Using human rights is something that politicians, parliaments and public servants can and should do for themselves, for their own benefit and that of

---

[4] If interested, my views can be found in David Feldman, 'The Left, Judicial Review and Theories of the Constitution' in William Watts Miller (ed), *Socialism and the Law* (1992) 49 *Archiv für Rechts- und Sozialphilosophie* 71; David Feldman, 'Establishing the Legitimacy of Judicial Procedures for Protecting Human Rights' (2001) 13 *European Review of Public Law* 139; David Feldman, 'Human Rights, Terrorism and Risk: The Roles of Politicians and Judges' [2006] *Public Law* 364; David Feldman, 'Sovereignties in Strasbourg' in Peter Leyland and Richard Rawlings (eds), *Sovereignty in Transition? National, European and Global Perspectives* (Oxford, Oxford University Press, 2013).

the democratic process, regardless of anything the judges may be doing in parallel to them.

In other words, making human rights important in political discourse serves to improve the legitimacy of that discourse in terms of both input and output measures of legitimacy. The remainder of this chapter concentrates on the second to fourth of these matters.

I. USING HUMAN RIGHTS TO IMPROVE THE QUALITY OF THE PUBLIC SPHERE AND PARTICULARLY THE WORK OF PARLIAMENTS

Let us start by thinking about the roles of parliaments. Parliaments legislate, scrutinise governments and conduct inquiries. By asking questions of ministers and their departments, parliaments can probe the reasons for decisions, bring them before the public by publishing governmental responses, and concentrate the minds of ministers and their advisers on important but perhaps under-appreciated matters. This can improve the quality of policy-making and implementation, bolster responsibility to Parliament and enhance the transparency of governmental decision-making, thus strengthening representative democracy and, where human rights standards are used, helping to create the conditions for protecting those rights.

On the other hand, parliaments cannot take practical steps that directly help people whose rights are threatened. Parliaments as institutions cannot give advice to individuals, although many individual parliamentarians do important work in taking up grievances on behalf of their constituents and others as part of their case-work function. Perhaps the most important protective work of parliaments as institutions is tied up with scrutiny, either of government policy-making and implementation or of governments' legislative proposals.

It is often difficult for parliaments to perform their scrutiny role especially robustly, in view of the way that most government parties in parliamentary systems dominate the institution that has to scrutinise government. Government ministers value the freedom to make policy and to use their party's majority in the Parliament to give legislative force to it. They do not welcome scrutiny. Much of politics in a healthy democracy is therefore dominated by continuous, low-grade, endemic tensions: both a tension between ministers (who call in aid their public servants) and Parliament over the extent to which each should control information and respond to the demands of the other, and a tension between members of the Parliament acting as such and the machines of the parties of which they are members (especially the whips). This is healthy, because these conflicts show that they all take their roles in the public interest seriously. Conflict cannot be allowed to become too disruptive too often because (apart from anything else) politics has to be made to work, and each side depends on the other's cooperation in order to achieve anything. But tension is ever present and is not pathological. As an eminent English parliamentarian, Lord Cormack, once said in my presence, Parliament is never as dangerous as when everyone agrees.

Members of parliaments have to use whatever levers they have at their disposal to extract as much information as possible from governments and to encourage ministers to make themselves accountable to the parliaments as often as possible on as wide a range of matters as possible.

Human rights can be a useful lever because (unlike most political values, which are party-specific and subject to negotiation between the parties) human rights (at least in one sense) are objective standards existing independently of any party, but carrying considerable moral weight. If members of parliaments can draw on them, they can use them to apply pressure on government ministers by demanding that they show, as a minimum standard, that their acts and decisions are justifiable by reference to them.

But here we might seem to encounter a problem. Why should politicians use, or ministers acknowledge, human rights existing outside the political system as standards with moral weight within it? Are human rights in this sense not a restriction of the freedom of democratically elected and accountable governments to advance their policies?

This suggestion is, in my view, misconceived. The idea that electoral democracy is all that is needed for a system of policy-making and law-making to be legitimate is seductive. It is espoused, for example, by Professor Jeremy Waldron, who writes of 'the dignity of legislation' as stemming from the potential of the legislative process to foster reflection on values with results shaped by democratic choices rather than from the substantive values embodied in the legislation or from the compatibility of the legislation with external standards.[5] In reality, as anyone who has had anything to do with the legislative process in a modern parliamentary democracy will be only too aware, legislation is far from dignified. It is typically framed in secret and pushed through parliaments at the highest possible speed using all the disciplinary powers at the governing party's disposal to whip its members into line behind it. Important parts of the legislation are often not debated at all within the parliament because of timetabling (or 'guillotine') arrangements to streamline the business of the parliament. Only rarely is the dignity of which Waldron speaks manifested in the practice of parliaments, at least those operating on a Westminster model.

Policy-making is even more secretive; its justifications are frequently obscure and its implementation is rarely properly overseen. The more urgent or vital a problem is thought to be, the less likely it is that the government and its parliamentary business managers will ensure that the parliament has enough time and information to consult and deliberate seriously about proposals. Debate on both policy and legislation is usually dominated by party-political interests rather than an assessment of the merits of the proposal by reference to clearly articulated moral standards.

That is not to say that there are no objective standards that can be, and in some places are, brought to bear on proposed legislation in the course of the legislative process. There are committees of parliaments which subject bills to scrutiny for compliance with formal standards, such as clarity of drafting, prospective rather than retrospective effect, interference with civil liberties, and conferral of legislative power on subordinate bodies. The Australian Senate Scrutiny of Bills Committee is a good example of this kind of exercise, as are the equivalent committees in

---

[5] Jeremy Waldron, *The Dignity of Legislation* (Cambridge, Cambridge University Press, 1999).

Australian state legislatures. Select committees sometimes subject policy initiatives to similar scrutiny, together with an element of review of the merits of the policy. However, in most parliaments, this kind of review has three different kinds of limitation. First, it is often unsystematic: scrutiny of legislation may be continuous and equally applicable to all legislation (as in the case of the Scrutiny of Bills Committee already mentioned), but scrutiny of policy is more ad hoc and, being concerned with the merits of policies rather than formal standards, tends to become politicised in ways that make recommendations more controversial than those concerned with formal matters. Second, the standards applied are typically not moral or substantive, although some of them (such as generality and prospectiveness) are important elements of the rule of law, which in turn is a significant part of liberal constitutional systems. Third, the review often goes no further than flagging up possible matters of concern. It does not usually go so far as to offer a fully reasoned assessment of the degree of risk that a given policy or bill will violate a particular principle, let alone to give a view as to the proper response to the risk.[6]

Review for compatibility with human rights is rather different. Human rights are (or can be) objective, legal standards independent of the merits of a policy or bill. It is sometimes said that rights are too vague and indeterminate, but even relatively amorphous standards can generate useful standards for concrete legal and political judgements. Anyone who doubts this should think about the hollowness of the test for negligence in common law jurisdictions, combining reasonable foreseeability of harm to a reasonably foreseeable class of people causing reasonably foreseeable damage, in circumstances where (in England and Wales at any rate) it is fair, just and reasonable to impose a duty of care.[7] Despite the lack of substance in the standards, they are used regularly and apparently successfully to determine a huge range of claims in tort.

It would therefore be wrong to deny that human rights standards can help scrutineers in a parliament to offer an indication both of the extent of the risk of violating rights and of the steps that might limit the risk. As compliance with these standards provides a foundation for the legitimacy of legislation and policies (or, at any rate, incompatibility may be a ground for criticising the legislation or policies), human rights can be the basis for rational discussion of a particular form of merit-based legitimacy independent of party-political controversy. Human rights thus offer standards that can be used to ameliorate (although never remove) the problem of the lack of dignity in the political process by allowing members of parliaments to ask governments to explain and justify their proposals systematically by reference to objective standards with clear moral weight, and then to debate proposals rationally.

It is appropriate to use these standards for this political purpose because (as will be discussed in the next section) the state will normally have accepted the standards as binding on it by signing and ratifying relevant human rights treaties, or

---

[6] This is less of a problem where, as in New Zealand, fairly detailed information about the Government's own assessment of compatibility with rights is published for use by parliamentarians and the general public.

[7] See eg *Caparo Industries Plc v Dickman* [1990] 2 AC 605, HL.

the standards will be regarded by all civilised states as obligatory on all sovereign states as a matter of customary international law. It is entirely legitimate for a state institution scrutinising government to ask it how its acts, decisions and legislative or policy proposals affect the capacity of the government to secure compliance with obligations into which the state has voluntarily entered on the international plane and which bind the state in public international law.

II. THE STATE AND HUMAN RIGHTS

We can now turn to the issue of the relationship between the state's international human rights obligations and its national political system.

A. The Place of the State in the World

A sovereign state is permitted, as an aspect of its sovereignty, to enter into agreements with other sovereign states. These agreements are both an expression of the sovereignty of the state and a limitation on its freedom to exercise it in an unconstrained way. Human rights treaties are of this kind. If the state wishes to be seen as a full member of the community of nations, it must be prepared to honour the treaties it has concluded. Governments and legislatures are regularly prepared to extend their powers to give effect under municipal law to international treaties: some important cases in Australia, where the High Court held that the legislative competence of the Commonwealth Parliament extended to legislating to override states' laws and interests where necessary to implement obligations under international treaties, provide examples of this.[8] A federal government or legislature may also be willing to limit the freedom of the governments or legislatures of subordinate entities within the state in order to secure compliance with international obligations, as when Tasmanian legislation was overridden by the Commonwealth in order to give effect to the decision of the Human Rights Committee of the UN under the International Covenant on Civil and Political Rights that the prohibition on homosexual acts in Tasmania violated the International Covenant on Civil and Political Rights.[9]

On the other hand, national (including federal-level) governments and parliaments rarely accept that they should limit their own powers in order to respect obligations on the state under treaties in international law. Yet national institutions in their domestic activities must accept the burdens as well as the benefits of being regarded as having international personality. If a state's institutions fail to respect

---

[8] See, eg, *Koowarta v Bjelke-Petersen* (1982) 153 CLR 168 (racial discrimination); *Commonwealth v Tasmania (The Tasmanian Dam Case)* (1983) 158 CLR 1 and *Richardson v Forestry Commission* (1988) 164 CLR 261 (World Heritage Sites); *Victoria v Commonwealth (The Industrial Relations Act Case)* (1996) 187 CLR 416 (relating to the ILO Convention concerning Equal Opportunities and Equal Treatment for Men and Women Workers: Workers with Family Responsibilities).

[9] Human Rights (Sexual Conduct) Act 1994 (Cth), on which see *Croome v Tasmania* (1997) 191 CLR 119.

those burdens, it leaves the state in breach of its obligations in international law and also makes it hard for the state to justify exercising its domestic power in situations where such exercise is necessary purely in order to give effect to international obligations on the state. One need not go as far for our purposes as the High Court of Australia did in *Teoh*,[10] where it held that individuals have a legitimate expectation that a government will comply with the state's international treaty obligations in its dealings with them, to accept that the state has a duty in that direction to other states, and that failing to respect that duty can undermine the authority of the state at home and abroad. In other words, if the state is to be regarded as a full member of the community of nations, it must shoulder the restrictions as well as the benefits that go along with that status in municipal law and politics as well as on the international plane.

B. The Roles of Parliaments and Governments within the State

The state, then, has obligations under international law which may have implications for domestic policy and law. It is reasonable to expect state institutions, including governments and parliaments, to be aware of those implications when making policy, drafting legislation, and scrutinising both legislation and policy. Of course, what is reasonable is not always practical. Governments may have the resources to keep track of their international legal obligations, although often this function reposes with the department responsible for foreign affairs, and domestic departments may have no means of systematically monitoring the relationship between their domestic activities and the international obligations of the state. But whatever their difficulties, governments are likely to be far more aware of the international implications of their policies, and of the implications for domestic policy of international obligations, than parliaments.

There are several reasons for this. Three are particularly significant; the first two arise from constitutional theory and the third from resource limitations.

First, in Westminster-style parliamentary systems, treaty-making is usually a prerogative of the executive. Parliaments normally have relatively little control over it and may not even be aware of treaties being negotiated or recently concluded in the name of the state.[11]

Second, in Westminster-style systems, treaties normally have no direct effect in domestic law, although (as noted earlier) they may have an indirect effect by

---

[10] *Minister for Immigration and Ethnic Affairs v Teoh* (1995) 183 CLR 273.

[11] In the UK, there used to be a convention (the 'Ponsonby rule') that the Government would not ratify certain treaties unless they had been laid before Parliament for 21 days. This was replaced by statutory provisions in Constitutional Reform and Governance Act 2010: ss 20–25, though these provisions merely give Parliament a right to receive information, not a right to block ratification. There are specific provisions in relation to EU treaties and other EU provisions in European Union Act 2011: ss 2–4 and 6 provide that a Minister may not ratify a treaty or confirm approval of (or, in some cases, vote in favour of) a European Council decision increasing the competences of the EU in specified respects without an Act of Parliament or, in certain cases, holding a referendum. On the effect of this, see *Wheeler v Office of the Prime Minister and Secretary of State for the Home Department* [2014] EWHC 3815 (Admin).

bringing within the competence of (for example) a federal legislature a matter not normally within its competence, such as environmental protection. Where treaties have no direct effect domestically, parliaments typically see no reason to worry about them: as a matter of formal constitutional law, they pose no threat to the parliament's domestic legislative sovereignty or competence. Parliamentarians may even regard it as unconstitutional to consider them (although that view is misconceived).

Third, parliaments typically lack a sufficient number of lawyers with expertise in international law to keep up to date with even a small part of the state's international obligations and analyse their implications for domestic law-making and policy-making. They can sometimes ask government departments for help, but that makes the parliament's assessment dependent on the government, weakening the parliament's role as an independent scrutineer and critic of government, and compromising the conditions necessary for making the government accountable to the parliament. There is often no spare capacity to provide continuous advice on the implications of international law for domestic law, except in the fields of EU law (which is not really international law at all) and human rights law. As other contributions to this volume demonstrate, availability of high-quality advice to legislative bodies is variable between parliaments and from time to time.

This affects the way that parliaments can be expected to approach the task of scrutinising policies and legislation for their compatibility with a state's human rights obligations. So far as those obligations arise from law (whether international or municipal, including constitutional law), scrutiny is likely to be either focused on particular topics or lacking in depth and rigour.

For example, in the UK Parliament, the Joint Select Committee on Human Rights (JCHR) has a very wide remit: essentially to consider and report on matters relating to human rights in the UK, excluding individual cases. The Committee's first task was to sort out its priorities within this vast field. It decided to examine the human rights implications of all bills and draft bills, but did not generally scrutinise subordinate legislation unless it was either intended to remedy a human rights violation or was referred to the Committee by members of either House, by another Committee or by the Government, or (as in the case of annual orders to renew certain anti-terrorism powers) followed on from earlier legislative scrutiny where the Committee had identified a significant risk of incompatibility with rights.

Scrutiny of policy, as distinct from legislation, was usually limited to selected areas in which the Committee felt it had something special to offer, such as an examination of the case for a Human Rights Commission and the human rights implications of deaths in custody.[12]

Even this attenuated level of human rights scrutiny in respect of policy and subordinate legislation, alongside the blanket coverage of bills and draft bills, imposed a significant burden on the staff of the Committee and its members, a burden spread unevenly across the parliamentary year. When I worked for the Committee (2000–04), it was (and I believe still is) fortunate to have the services of outstanding

---

[12] See, eg, David Feldman, 'The Impact of Human Rights on the Legislative Process' (2004) 25 *Statute Law Review* 91.

Clerks from both Houses, joined after a short period by a Committee Specialist who happened to be a very good human rights lawyer and increasingly shouldered the burden of advising on policy issues. They were assisted by an enthusiastic, very efficient and highly conscientious Committee Assistant, who provided a good deal of help with research, and by a number of part-time specialist advisers brought in to assist with particular inquiries. Without their expertise and energy, the Committee could not have kept up with its self-imposed workload.

The point is that human rights scrutiny is a labour-intensive business requiring appropriate expertise to be on call when needed. Not all of this support takes the form of legal advice and advisers, or human rights experts. Human rights expertise is necessary but not sufficient. Advisers must have a sufficient understanding of the domestic policy and legal background to be able to spot the points at which domestic law and policy may collide with human rights. Members of the parliaments must then be willing to spend time on potential problems in those areas and must have the administrative support that is needed if they are to be able to do so effectively.

How much legal expertise in the field of human rights is needed? That depends on the answers to two other questions. First, how does the political system visualise human rights? And, second, what does the parliament see as its role in relation to human rights?

C. Conceptions of Human Rights in the Political Process

A parliament establishing a human rights role for itself must decide what human rights are to be for its purposes. The term 'human rights' signifies different things to different people. For human rights lawyers, it refers to a body of positive law, usually originating in international law (typically in a treaty with 'rights' or 'prevention of discrimination' or the like in its title) imposing obligations on States Parties to respect various rights of individuals or groups within their respective jurisdictions, or to take steps towards the progressive realisation of rights.

For politicians, including parliamentarians, there may be persuasive reasons for adopting a different conception of human rights. On one side are arguments for a more restrictive model. On this view, parliaments should adopt as standards for scrutiny only rights arising under treaties which the parliament in question has itself approved or, better still, transformed into municipal law by way of an Act. It would be inappropriate, in the sense of being inconsistent with its dignity and sovereignty, for a parliament to concern itself with standards that have been imposed on it from outside without its consent. A bill of rights can be a useful aid in structuring scrutiny, but is it essential? I think not, for two reasons.

First, parliaments have as their main function the role of scrutinising government. It does not compromise the dignity of a parliament to check a government's activities by reference to criteria that the parliament has not previously sanctioned. They do that all the time, using standards of financial efficiency or ethical propriety originating in normative systems over which the parliament has no control. Having access to those standards strengthens a parliament's armoury for scrutinising government departments, and that can only be good for the parliament. Using the standards for that purpose does not commit the parliament to legislating for the standards or to censuring government for failing to abide by them. They merely form a basis for asking questions of government, to see whether governments consider that they are acting in accordance with the standards, whether their view is tenable and, if they are acting inconsistently with the standards, whether the action can be justified by reference to other criteria.

The second reason why a restrictive approach would be disappointing is that it deprives the parliament of a marvellous opportunity to strengthen its capacity to scrutinise a government's activities in the realm of foreign affairs. In federal systems, this is particularly relevant to federal-level parliaments. In Westminster-style constitutions, at least, legislatures often have little control over foreign affairs, including treaty-making. They have difficulty in opening up foreign relations to effective review. Human rights compatibility in a broad sense provides one instrument by which to open up foreign relations in general to scrutiny, as well as a critical framework for evaluating domestic law and policy. In the UK Parliament, the JCHR has established a practice of examining the UK's compliance with a wide range of treaties. It follows up the review by various treaty bodies (such as the Committee on Economic, Social and Cultural Rights and the Committee for the Prevention of Torture) of the UK's mandatory periodic reports on progress of compliance. When the relevant treaty body has published its concluding observations, the JCHR pursues any recommendations and criticisms with the relevant government department, asking what the Government proposes to do about them. The JCHR then follows up the Government's response, asking from time to time what progress has been made with any steps that the Government said it was proposing to take. This allows Parliament to assert some authority over one aspect of the field of foreign policy—treaty-making and treaty compliance—which has in the past been notoriously difficult for it to police.

It therefore makes sense for parliaments to adopt an expansive view of human rights for scrutiny purposes. They could include rights under any treaty binding the state in international law, whether or not it was approved or transformed into municipal law by the legislature. This reinforces the parliament's armoury in its constant battle with the government for control over information and relative authority. In the UK, it allows parliamentarians to extract answers from the Government about such matters as why the Government does not intend to ratify Protocol No 12 to the ECHR (relating to discrimination in relation to guarantees of other legal rights and obligations) or to legislate for social and economic rights in municipal law, and why it refuses to withdraw certain reservations to the Convention on the Rights of the Child. In this way it contributes to open government and accountability to Parliament. They should be seen as sources of reasonably hard-edged, legally binding obligations, in order to limit the scope of political controversy as to the content of the standards. However, there are other views.

The first argues that human rights should be seen as values rather than sources of rules. This view seems to me to entail the notion that parliamentarians should not seek to establish whether a policy or bill complies with human rights, but should instead try to educate and encourage government ministers, officials and other public bodies to make use of the values as one of a range of relevant considerations in developing and implementing policy and drafting legislation. This approach seems to me to give rise to a problem. By severing the idea of human rights from objective, legal standards, it makes it far more difficult to prevent party-political controversy over the meaning and effect of the values from dominating proceedings. A scrutiny body operates most effectively when it applies relatively cut-and-dried, objective criteria. Uncertainty about the content of values tends to undermine unanimity and lay the scrutineers open to a charge that they are conducting a disguised party-political campaign. This reduces the moral weight of any conclusions with both government and the public.

Another view is that human rights, or some human rights, are mere aspirations of a more or less attainable kind. On this view, one cannot criticise a government or official for acting incompatibly with human rights, because there is no reason to expect that it will be possible now (or, perhaps, ever) to realise the right. This is more convincing in relation to some rights than others. For example, the rights under the ECHR are mainly civil and political rights, and the ECtHR has repeatedly stressed that they are realisable here and now, and that it is the obligation of states (not least under Article 1 ECHR) to make the rights real and effective, not merely theoretical or illusory. On the other hand, the International Covenant on Economic, Social and Cultural Rights (ICESCR) expressly recognises that the realisation of some economic, social and cultural rights must be progressive, and the obligation of governments is to develop programmes to facilitate the progressive realisation of the substance of the rights consistently with available resources and competing demands. Nevertheless, even here the obligation can be formulated with enough precision to allow parliaments to question governments about their plans for progressively realising the rights, and to evaluate the effectiveness of the programmes. Even as a legal matter, the Indian courts have held that their constitutional Directive Principles of State Policy, while not directly enforceable, are relevant considerations whenever they apply to all governmental and legislative decision-making. The courts will invalidate policies and legislation in fields such as health or environmental protection if they appear to conflict with the Directive Principles and it is not shown how they were taken properly into account in the decision-making process.[13] The Constitutional Court of South Africa adopts a somewhat similar approach to social rights.[14] If courts in India and South Africa can take that approach, how much more can and should parliaments elsewhere in the world make similar demands of governments through the political process?

---

[13] See eg *Centre for Environmental Law WWF-1 v Union of India* (1999) 1 SCC 263.
[14] See eg *Minister of Health v Treatment Action Campaign* (2002) 1 SA 721.

D. What Parliament Can Expect of Itself and What We Can Expect from Parliament in Terms of Protection of Human Rights

We can now summarise what we can expect of parliaments as protectors of human rights. The nature of parliamentary bodies gives them considerable authority and power, but there are inherent limits to what we can expect of them.

First, parliaments provide a forum for asking questions and (sometimes) getting answers. It can legislate, criticise, inquire and make recommendations. These activities can help to make government ministers and officials conscious of the requirements of human rights, and they can contribute directly to maintaining a robust, effective system of political democracy. But they cannot directly achieve many of the other things we want human rights to do: delivering dignified treatment to people in hospitals and homes for the elderly; protecting children against mistreatment; helping people with disabilities to live fulfilling and worthwhile lives; and ensuring that people are free from arbitrary and excessive interference with their freedom and well-being. For that to be achieved, we need ordinary people doing ordinary jobs—people like us—to make human rights standards part of the day-to-day, hour-by-hour thought processes by which we make decisions affecting other people. Legislation can help that process, but does not achieve anything in itself.

Second, parliaments are unavoidably political and usually party-political. This is often a good thing. Almost all the politicians I have met have seriously and sincerely wanted to improve society, although they have very different views as to how to do that and some of their views seem to other politicians to be plain silly. In a democracy, they offer us visions of a good life or a good society and we try to choose between them. This can be valuable, especially when the visions are consistent with human rights.

However, it is unreasonable to expect politicians to have human rights as their primary focus. For most politicians, human rights (and the rule of law) operate as constraints. Occasionally they seek to prevent a government or parliament from pursuing a particular goal at all. More often, they restrict the ways in which a government or parliament can legitimately pursue the goal. There can be no doubt that combating crime, including terrorist crime, is a legitimate goal, but equally there can be no doubt that pursuing this objective by way of torture, indefinite detention without conviction of any offence and indiscriminate killing violates human rights standards that are absolute and cannot be justifiably infringed. For example, the House of Lords has held that information shown to have been obtained by torture abroad cannot be used in the UK for the purpose of supporting a decision to detain someone or restrict his or her movement or activities.[15] Also in the context of anti-terrorism measures, the House of Lords held in *Secretary of State for the Home Department v AF (No 3)*[16] that the regime of 'control orders' introduced by the Prevention of Terrorism Act 2005 to replace the detention measures of the Anti-terrorism, Crime and Security Act 2001, restricting movement and activities of

---

[15] *A v Secretary of State for the Home Department (No 2)* [2005] UKHL 71, [2006] 2 AC 221, HL.
[16] *Secretary of State for the Home Department v AF (No 3)* [2009] UKHL 28, [2010] 2 AC 269, HL.

suspected terrorists in and around their own homes, violated the right to a fair hearing under Article 6.1 ECHR unless the legislation was interpreted as incorporating a right to a fair hearing, including, particularly, disclosure by the state of enough information about the evidence justifying the restrictions to allow the person subject to an order to challenge the order effectively. Even less intrusive and damaging measures may infringe human rights standards, but they do so in ways which are potentially justifiable. In relation to these measures, human rights standards require politicians and officials to justify their decisions and actions by reference to previously established and publicly articulated criteria set out in relevant human rights instruments. Is the interference prescribed by law? Does it pursue a legitimate goal? Is there a pressing social need to interfere with the right in order to achieve the goal? Does the measure interfere with the right more than is necessary to achieve the goal? Does it interfere in an illegitimately discriminatory manner? Is the impact on the person affected excessive, having regard to the significance of the objective, the strength of the arguments for giving effect to the measure in question in this case and the extent to which the person can still exercise the right?

The answers to these last questions are context-dependent and call for judgments about how best to pursue public interests while respecting individual rights. Parliament ought to be well-placed to consider them. There is no reason for them not to do so. In the UK, ministers who introduce legislation to either House of Parliament are required by section 19(1) of the Human Rights Act 1998 to make a written statement that either the minister considers that the bill is compatible with Convention rights or the minister is unable to say that it is compatible, but nevertheless wishes the House to consider the bill. The implication is that the two Houses are expected to consider the merits of the statement, or in other words to evaluate the implications of the bill for Convention rights. This is, or should be, an important part of the process of legislative scrutiny in a system that values human rights, and the JCHR has always regarded it as an important part of its role to contribute to that.

However, in the UK, the government does not always make it easy for Parliament to obtain the information it needs in order to exercise this function. The explanatory memoranda to bills are now more informative than they were previously about the rights that may be affected by particular provisions of a bill, and about the government's reasons for thinking that the provisions are compatible with the rights. But information about the extent and seriousness of the problem that a provision seeks to address can often be obtained only by way of clear and careful questioning of the minister or his or her department, and this requires continuing action by a committee with a clear human rights focus.

The difficulty faced by parliamentary bodies in obtaining worthwhile information on which to assess the compatibility of measures with human rights is most obvious in fields relating to national security, terrorism and crime. For operational reasons, governments and their various agencies are understandably reluctant to reveal details of their anti-terrorism plans and sources of their information about threats to security. As a member of the JCHR once remarked to me, 'Would you reveal sensitive information to people like us?' Nevertheless, the government's coyness often makes it impossible for a parliament and its committees to say whether a measure affecting human rights is justified. For example, in relation to the deten-tion provisions of the Anti-terrorism, Crime and Security Bill that became the Act of 2001, the JCHR said initially, and again when the Government tabled periodic orders for renewal of the powers, that it had received no information about the nature and seriousness of the terrorist threat, and so could not be satisfied that the measures were strictly required by the exigencies of the situation or proportionate to it. Eventually in 2004, the JCHR said that it was not satisfied that the threat justified the measures.[17]

A similar reluctance to explain proposals was evident in relation to the Bill which became the Terrorism Act 2006. It originally included a measure which would have allowed the police to hold for up to 90 days without charge individuals arrested on suspicion of various offences of terrorism. This compared with the then-current limit of 14 days. When pressed by its own supporters to explain the need for this huge increase, the Government released a briefing paper from the Metropolitan Police listing a number of reasons for extending the time limit. However, only one of the reasons related specifically to terrorism investigations, and none could be said to be particularly compelling. The Government's own supporters in the House of Commons rejected the proposal. A compromise was eventually agreed, increasing the time limit to 28 days (itself excessively long in some people's view). The House of Commons Select Committee on Home Affairs then published a report criticis-ing the Government for having failed to subject the request by the police for more power to rigorous examination before putting the proposal before Parliament.[18]

This illustrates one of the practical, political limits to the ability of parliaments to evaluate the human rights implications of government policies and proposals. It remains important that parliaments should seek to do so, and should enhance their powers whenever possible to get relevant information and make rigorous assessments of the rationality and balance of claims made by governments and law-enforcement agencies.

The fact that parliaments ought to address such matters does not entail an exclu-sive competence to do so. The executive must also equip itself to deal rigorously and fairly with them. The courts, too, have a role in this field when they are required by law to decide whether legislation or executive action is compatible with human rights, even if (as in the UK) the effect of a declaration of incompatibility will not be to invalidate primary legislation. The principles of the rule of law require that courts should properly evaluate the justifications advanced for interfering with rights. In the context of anti-terrorism measures, the House of Lords in *A v Secretary of State for the Home Department*[19] in December 2004 had to examine in its judicial capacity provisions in the Anti-terrorism, Crime and Security Act 2001 allow-ing the Home Secretary to authorise potentially indefinite detention of suspected

---

[17] JCHR, Second Report of 2001–02, HL Paper 37, HC 372, paras 29–30; JCHR, Fifth Report of 2001–02, HL Paper 51, HC 420, para 4; JCHR, Fifth Report of 2002–03, HL Paper 59, HC 462, para 27; JCHR, Sixth Report of 2003–04, HL Paper 38, HC 381, para 34.
[18] House of Commons Select Committee on Home Affairs, Fourth Report of 2005–06, HC 910-I, paras 29–31.
[19] *A v Secretary of State for the Home Department* [2004] UKHL 56, [2005] 2 AC 68, HL.

foreign (but not British) terrorists who were potentially subject to removal from the country, but could not be removed either for practical reasons or because there no country to which they could be sent where they would be free from a significant risk of being tortured or killed. The Government had accepted that these measures might violate the right to liberty under Article 5 ECHR and had purported to derogate from that article pursuant to Article 15 ECHR on account of a public emergency threatening the life of the nation. The House decided that the derogation was unlawful because the measures were not 'strictly required by the exigencies of the situation' as required by Article 15: this implied a proportionality test, and the measures failed this test because there was no rational connection between the threat from terrorism and the introduction of measures affecting only foreigners, and after removal left the suspected foreigners free on foreign soil to pursue their terrorist goals. In addition, the measures violated the right to be free from discrimination under Article 14, because they applied only to foreign nationals and the differential treatment could not be objectively and rationally justified for the same reasons. The decision of the House of Lords was undoubtedly correct as a matter of law, and as a matter of practical judgment was borne out by the terrorist attacks in London in July 2005, which all appear to have been carried out by UK nationals.

It is important to bring out the limited nature of the impact of human rights standards in these cases. Only rarely do human rights prevent a government or parliament from taking action. Normally they make it illegitimate for the action to take certain forms, and require the measures and their impact to be justified publicly on the basis of information and arguments that can be rationally assessed.

One sometimes hears people say that judges should not be making such assessments; they are political, not legal, and should be made by politicians. Once politicians have made their assessments, judges should simply respect and accept them. It is understandable that government ministers should want to advance this sort of argument, but it is more surprising to find that respectable lawyers, including human rights lawyers, have not only accepted it but have also constructed a theory (sometimes described as the notion of deference) to dignify it and give it a sheen of conceptual respectability. It was refreshing, therefore, to see that the Senior Law Lord, Lord Bingham of Cornhill, in *A v Secretary of State for the Home Department* politely but firmly insisted that the judiciary must make all assessments necessary to give effect to rights under the ECHR, pointing out that (apart from other arguments) the Westminster Parliament had itself required the courts to do so by enacting the Human Rights Act 1998. Judges must not surrender their responsibility for upholding the rule of law merely because rights involve considerations that are also relevant to other bodies. Politicians and judges each have separate and legitimate authority to consider questions of proportionality.[20]

When politicians shoulder this burden, the experience of the UK Parliament since 2001 shows, I think, that the process of questioning ministers and their departments, publishing information and arguments, and making rational assessments can help to make human rights into important standards, although not usually

[20] I have expanded on this theme in Feldman, 'Human Rights, Terrorism and Risk' (n 4).

dominant ones, in the political process. It does not always lead to policies and bills being compatible with human rights, but it forces departments to give more careful thought to the human rights implications of their proposals than they might other-wise have done, thus raising the profile of human rights in government as well as in Parliament. Most importantly, perhaps, the process of questioning and assessment can serve to strengthen Parliament and the accountability of the executive to it, and so can bolster the general health of parliamentary democracy.

These are modest gains, but important ones. They will be achievable only if the conditions are favourable. What are those conditions?

III. THE CONDITIONS NECESSARY FOR PARLIAMENTARY SCRUTINY ON HUMAN RIGHTS GROUNDS TO WORK

The first condition is that parliaments should take human rights seriously. This means that they should have a conception of what they mean by human rights (as discussed earlier). Parliaments should recognise that they, like other public institu-tions, have a responsibility for making sure that policies and legislation are as far as possible compatible with human rights. They should also understand how scrutiny of a government on human rights principles can contribute to the authority of the parliament, the perceived legitimacy of government and the state, the quality and transparency of decision-making within the state, and the standing of the state on the international plane.

Second, parliaments should recognise their own limitations in the pursuit of human rights. Some limitations are purely practical—as already mentioned, parlia-ments can do very little to produce practical effects in the world—and others stem from the political nature of parliaments. This last point means that human rights can never be the sole or even dominant engine of policy-making and legislation. They will usually take the form of side-constraints.

Third, parliaments should recognise the corresponding strengths of other institu-tions. Organisations and individuals that deliver services to people to protect rights need to be respected and encouraged, not subjected to abuse or unreasoned and excessive criticism. Parliaments should understand that other institutions have their own important constitutional and institutional roles, and may have to take a dif-ferent line from that of any parliament. In particular, courts have as their primary function the maintenance of the rule of law. That is a socially valuable function. Where human rights form part of the legal order, the courts must enforce them alongside other sources of law. In a Rechtstaat, only courts usually have authority to pronounce finally and authoritatively on the meaning and effect of constitutions, legislation and rights. Their independence from the political arena gives them special authority in times of risk and danger. As Aharon Barak, President of the Supreme Court of Israel, has written,[21] the courts can, unlike politicians, stand back from the maelstrom of fear and loathing and the demands for action and revenge which too

---

[21] Aharon Barak, 'A Judge on Judging: The Role of a Supreme Court in a Democracy' (2002) 116 *Harvard Law Review* 16, 150.

often dominate the political arena in difficult times; this lack of engagement with the political realm, and lack of accountability to it, makes judges' decisions at such moments particularly important and authoritative. Politicians should respect such decisions even when they dislike them. When politicians attack judges for their decisions, it undermines the rule of law as well as human rights, and ultimately weakens the authority of the state as a whole. At the same time, as Lord Steyn has said, it undermines the judicial role if judges begin to see themselves as being on the same side as governments or parliaments in combating crime or terrorism and become too cosy with the government. Judges must consciously avoid that sort of thinking, which can too easily lead to a failure to subject the activities of governments and parliaments to proper, legal analysis and evaluation.

Fourth, at a more pragmatic level, parliaments must equip themselves to deal seriously with human rights. The responsibility lies with the whole of a parliament and should not be sidelined through delegation to a small group of members. Nevertheless, there is a need for some specialised advice and information to be available to the parliament as a whole. That can best be provided by a committee with special and continuing responsibility for advising and informing the parliament on human rights, reporting regularly to the parliament on human rights issues generally and on the impact of specific policies or measures on particular rights. In the UK Parliament, this has been the role of the JCHR since early in 2001. As already mentioned, the Committee has a very wide remit and it established its focus and working methods in such a way that, as a result of its self-discipline and commitment, it has been able to report on every bill before either House, on nearly every draft bill published by the government for consultation, and on a significant number of other legislative measures. It has also been able to inquire into and report on a number of policy areas with extensive human rights implications, and its reports have been generally influential in subsequent policy formation. This wide remit, coupled with a capacity to set priorities and stick to them, is an important strength of the Committee.

Fifth, a committee established to do this sort of thing needs to foster the right working conditions. I regard a number of factors as significant to the work of the JCHR. They include:

— an independently minded chair who was determined to keep party politics out of the Committee's work and was skilled in constructing consensus;
— absence of government ministers and whips from the membership of the Committee;
— members who were interested in aspects of human rights, willing to work by consensus and able to put their commitment to human rights ahead of their party-political ambitions;
— a willingness of the Committee to put difficult questions to the Government and to analyse the answers critically;
— a programme of regular reporting;
— an enthusiastic and expert secretariat; and
— independent and expert legal advice.

It also helped (although was perhaps not essential) that the Government's party had no majority of members on the Committee. The Committee was fortunate in its first Chair, Jean Corston MP (now Baroness Corston). From the inception of the Committee until the General Election in May 2005, she steered the Committee with independence, clarity of vision, good humour and a business-like approach to the work. Divisions in the Committee's deliberations were very rare, and the Committee quickly acquired respect: the late Hugo Young, doyen of English political commentators, said of the Committee's reports on the Anti-terrorism, Crime and Security Bill in 2001 that they took apart the Government's case for the detention measures with 'devastating sobriety'. This was the tone at which the Committee aimed, avoiding emotive language, giving clear reasoning and basing everything possible on standards firmly rooted in human rights law.

Finally, members of parliaments must be prepared to read, reflect on and use the reports of their committees when deliberating in the chamber and when voting.

To sum up, it is not easy to make human rights an effective part of the parliamentary process, and the capacity of parliaments to protect rights out in the real world is limited by the nature of parliaments and political processes generally. I have tried to outline some of the problems and needs involved in bringing human rights into politics. If it can be done successfully, both human rights and parliaments gain in effectiveness, legitimacy and authority.

People are vital to this process. Any system is only as good as the strong-minded and conscientious people who work within it. Human rights norms do not implement themselves and will not always be popular. Sometimes they will even be portrayed by some politicians as the problem rather than part of the solution to it. This is a phase we are in at the moment in the UK, where some very muddled and unproductive thinking and speech-making has resulted. However, human rights are always important. They are the bedrock of dignity and democracy, which make our societies worth protecting. The ability and willingness of a political and parliamentary system to accommodate them and internalise them in their deliberations and decision-making will determine the extent to which parliaments can contribute to human rights, and to which human rights can achieve their potential to enhance parliamentary processes, executive decision-making, the quality of legislation, and the authority of institutions within and beyond the state.

6

The Joint Committee on Human Rights: A Hybrid Breed of Constitutional Watchdog

AILEEN KAVANAGH*

I. THE COLLABORATIVE ENTERPRISE OF PROTECTING RIGHTS

U NDER THE HUMAN Rights Act 1998 (HRA), the protection of human rights is, and should be, a collaborative enterprise between all three branches of government.[1] When reflecting on his time as the first legal adviser to the parliamentary Joint Committee on Human Rights (JCHR), David Feldman observed that:

> Systematic engagement with human rights in a democratic political process can come about only when it is seen as a goal of all institutions, executive, legislative and judicial, working towards a common goal when exercising their different but complementary functions.[2]

This insight is built into the scheme of the HRA.[3] Indeed, it is widely believed that one of the central purposes of the HRA was to strengthen the ability of the courts to protect rights, whilst at the same time encouraging greater parliamentary sensitivity to, and engagement with, human rights concerns.[4] The HRA embodies a multi-institutional approach to upholding and protecting rights, which seems to envisage a significant role for Parliament in upholding and promoting human rights.[5]

I would like to thank Janet Hiebert, Murray Hunt and David Feldman for their extremely helpful comments on this chapter.

[1] For further exploration of this theme of human rights protection as a collaborative enterprise, see A Kavanagh, *Constitutional Review under the UK Human Rights Act* (Cambridge, Cambridge University Press, 2009) 406–11; J King, 'Institutional Approaches to Judicial Restraint' (2008) 28 *OJLS* 409, 427–28. For the related idea that human rights protection is a shared responsibility between all the institutions of the state, see M Hunt, 'The Joint Committee on Human Rights' in G Drewry, A Horne and D Oliver (eds), *Parliament and the Law* (Oxford, Hart Publishing, 2013) 226.

[2] D Feldman, 'The Impact of Human Rights on the UK Legislative Process' (2004) 25(2) *Statute Law Review* 91, 92; M Hunt, 'The Impact of the Human Rights Act on the Legislature: A Diminution of Democracy or a New Voice for Parliament' [2010] *European Human Rights Law Review* 601, 602.

[3] F Klug and H Wildbore, 'Breaking New Ground: The Joint Committee on Human Rights and the Role of Parliament in Human Rights Compliance' [2007] *European Human Rights Law Review* 231, 233–34.

[4] B Galligan and E Larking, 'Human Rights Protection—Comparative Perspectives' [2009] *Australian Journal of Political Science* 1, 7.

[5] Klug and Wildbore (n 3) 232.

As the Government White Paper preceding the enactment of the HRA outlined: 'Parliament itself should play a leading role in protecting the rights which are at the heart of a parliamentary democracy.'[6]

To this end, the HRA put in place some institutional mechanisms to try to ensure that Parliament takes rights seriously during the legislative process. One such mechanism (but by no means the only one) is the statutory obligation on a government minister under section 19 HRA to make a statement of the compatibility or otherwise of proposed legislation. Section 19 has meant that the issue of human rights compliance is formally placed on the legislative agenda.[7] But it was the setting up of the JCHR which gave this provision real potency.[8] After persistent pressure, the JCHR managed to convince the Government to supplement the bald statement of compatibility under section 19 with a more detailed human rights memorandum where the Government's views on human rights compliance are set out in more detail.[9] These mechanisms matter. They show that human rights in the UK are not the exclusive dominion of the courts, and that is exactly how it ought to be.[10]

The focus of this chapter is on the specific role of the JCHR in the parliamentary machinery for protecting rights. Whilst acknowledging the notorious difficulty of eliciting the full empirical evidence on the extent and effectiveness of legislative human rights scrutiny,[11] the argument of this chapter will be that the JCHR plays a significant role as part of the wider collaborative enterprise of human rights protection in the UK. It strengthens the parliamentary machinery for protecting human rights in two main ways: first, by improving the quality of legislative scrutiny for human rights compliance (at least to some degree); and, second, by providing an important accountability mechanism for the Government within Parliament with reference to human rights issues.

The argument presented in this chapter is divided into four parts. The first explains why the JCHR should be viewed as a hybrid breed of constitutional watchdog.[12] The second examines the functions and working practices of the JCHR, highlighting the reactive, proactive and interactive dimensions of its work. The third discusses the audiences to which JCHR reports must be addressed and the role

---

[6] Home Office, *Rights Brought Home: The Human Rights Bill 1997* (Cm 3782, 1997), para 1.16.

[7] See generally Klug and Wildbore (n 3).

[8] A Lester, 'The Magnetism of the Human Rights Act 1998' [2002] *Victoria University of Wellington Law Review* 53, 76.

[9] Hunt (n 2) 607; Lester (n 8) 78.

[10] See generally Hunt (n 2) 602, 608; D Feldman, 'Parliamentary Scrutiny of Legislation and Human Rights' [2002] *Public Law* 323, 324; J Hiebert, 'Parliament and the Human Rights Act: Can the JCHR Help to Facilitate a Culture of Rights?' (2006) 4 *International Journal of Constitutional Law* 1, 13.

[11] M Russell and M Benton, 'Assessing the Policy Impact of Parliament: Methodological Challenges and Possible Future Approaches' (Paper for PSA Legislative Studies Specialist Group Conference, 24 June 2009, UCL), available at www.ucl.ac.uk/constitution-unit/research/parliament/policy-impact; A Brazier and R Fox, 'Reviewing Select Committee Tasks and Modes of Operation' [2011] *Parliamentary Affairs* 354, 364; S Evans and C Evans, 'Evaluating the Performance of Legislatures' [2006] *Human Rights Law Review* 545.

[12] Robert Hazell observed that the JCHR, together with the Delegated Powers and Regulatory Reform Committee and the Constitution Committee in the House of Lords, formed the 'three new pillars of the constitution', acting as 'internal guardians [within Parliament] of values customarily regarded as integral to the legal order'; see R Hazell, 'Who is the Guardian of Legal Values in the Legislative Process: Parliament or the Executive?' [2004] *Public Law* 495, 499.

of legal expertise in carrying out the Committee's functions. I argue that since the JCHR is a hybrid body, it defies the compartmentalised and polarised thinking which sometimes accompanies the suggestion that there is a dichotomy between the 'political' and 'legal' constitution. That dichotomy is false. The JCHR has to communicate and collaborate with a wide array of people and groups, including ministers, parliamentarians, government lawyers, judges, academics, the media, non-governmental organisations (NGOs) and wider civil society. The legal element in this multi-faceted set of interactions should not be overlooked.

The final section grapples with the thorny issue of impact and influence. It will be argued that whilst the impact of the JCHR in terms of securing amendments to legislation does not yet seem substantial, we should not judge it purely in these terms. When we consider the broader aims of the Committee, namely, to enhance the quality of deliberation about human rights issues and achieve greater parliamentary and democratic accountability for legislative decisions, we can see some of the more subtle forms of influence the Committee can and does exert both inside and outside Parliament.

II. THE JCHR AS A HYBRID BREED OF PARLIAMENTARY OVERSIGHT COMMITTEE

The work of the JCHR has become a familiar and settled part of the UK human rights landscape and has earned an excellent reputation for the quality of its reports within the legal community and beyond.[13] However, it is worth reflecting on the JCHR's composition and characteristics in order to evaluate critically the role it currently plays (and could play in the future) as part of the machinery for legislative human rights protection. Let us start with the basics.

The JCHR is a parliamentary joint select committee which came into being in January 2001. It has 12 members, six from the Lords and six from the Commons. It has a permanent legal adviser. The party-political composition of the Committee mirrors broadly the party-political composition of each House, but the Chair of the Committee does not have to be a member of the governing party.[14] In fact, given that the Commons and Lords membership broadly reflects the composition of each respective House, this has generally meant that there is no Government majority on the Committee. This explains, in part, why the JCHR tends to act in a consensual

---

[13] See Klug and Wildbore (n 3); M Tolley, 'Parliamentary Scrutiny of Rights in the United Kingdom: Assessing the Work of the Joint Committee on Human Rights' (2009) 44 *Australian Journal of Political Science* 41, 45, 47; J Rozenberg, 'Damning Verdict on Ill-Thought-Out Secret Justice Proposals' *The Guardian* (4 April 2012), available at: www.guardian.co.uk/law/2012/apr/04/justice-security-green-paper-verdict.

[14] C Evans and S Evans, 'Legislative Scrutiny Committees and Parliamentary Conceptions on Human Rights' [2006] *Public Law* 785, 788. The Committee of Selection (which allocates positions on select committees) is dominated by the party whips and this sometimes gives rise to the fear that the Government can try to control appointments to these key positions; see A Bradley and K Ewing, *Constitutional and Administrative Law* (Harlow, Pearson, 2011) 210; Liaison Committee, *Shifting the Balance: Select Committees and the Executive* (1999–2000, HC 300).

and relatively non-partisan manner.[15] Certainly, its reports display little or no signs of overt partisanship and even though some of its members will necessarily come from the majority party, those members seem to remain relatively 'independent-minded'[16] when working on the Committee. This is a characteristic which the JCHR shares with other select committees, namely, that they tend to function with a relatively high degree of cross-party consensus and cooperation.[17] As David Feldman explained:

> [T]his is partly because ministers, whips and opposition spokesmen are excluded from select committees, and partly because the specialised focus of a select committee attracts people whose interest in the subject-matter of its inquiries can override, for particular purposes, the party allegiance which is more usually dominant.[18]

In fact, this consensual and non-partisan feature of the operation of select committees may be more pronounced on the JCHR, since the composition of select committees tends to reflect the composition of the House of Commons alone, thus creating a Government majority on most Select Committees.[19] This, together with the fact that the JCHR directly employs independent legal advice, gives it a reputation for being more independent than most Commons committees.

Even from this cursory account of its composition and characteristics, we can see that the JCHR is a *hybrid* breed of parliamentary oversight committee. Its hybrid nature is evidenced in the following four ways. The first is the one just mentioned: although the JCHR has a partly party-political composition, it operates in a relatively non-partisan and consensual manner.[20] Second, it is a hybrid breed in the sense that it is a *joint* committee of both the House of Commons and the House of Lords. Half of its members are democratically elected, whilst the other half are unelected peers. The partly unelected membership contributes to its ability to operate in a relatively non-partisan fashion and to maintain a large degree of independence from the Government. At the very least, it prevents Government domination of the Committee. Indeed, some commentators have observed that the functions of the Committee sit well with the functions of the House of Lords more generally. Thus, Francesca Klug and Helen Wildbore argue that the priority given by the Committee to bill scrutiny is 'complementary to the role and expertise of the House of Lords as a revising chamber'.[21]

Third, although the JCHR is composed of politicians and peers from both Houses of Parliament, it has an independent expert legal adviser who plays a key

---

[15] Evans and Evans (n 14) 788; Feldman (n 10) 327.
[16] Hiebert (n 10) 15.
[17] M Russell, 'Parliament: Emasculated or Emancipated?' in R Hazell (ed), *Constitutional Futures Revisited: Britain's Constitution to 2020* (Basingstoke, Palgrave Macmillan, 2010) 1. The Hansard Society opined that Joint Committees of both Houses tend to operate with a lower degree of partisanship than other select committees; see F Klug, 'The Klug Report: Report on the Working Practices of the JCHR', published in Joint Committee on Human Rights, *The Committee's Future Working Practices, Twenty-Third Report* (2005–06, HL 239/HC 1575), para 5.8, note 123.
[18] Feldman (n 10) 327.
[19] Hunt (n 1) 243.
[20] See generally Hiebert (n 10) 16–17.
[21] Klug and Wildbore (n 3) 242.

role in writing JCHR reports, as well as deciding which bills will receive detailed JCHR scrutiny.[22] Therefore, it has both political acumen and independent legal expertise, and can bring both these perspectives to bear on the work it undertakes.[23] Finally, it is a hybrid breed in that it combines two distinct but related roles, namely, legislative scrutiny and executive oversight. Traditionally, the British House of Commons splits the functions of legislative scrutiny and executive oversight between two separate sets of committees. The committee stage of legislation is taken in non-specialist, temporary and inexpert 'public bill committees', whilst executive oversight is carried out by a set of specialist 'select committees' which shadow government departments.[24] The JCHR is a hybrid combining both of these roles.

III. THE FUNCTIONS OF THE JCHR

As set out on its website, the 'formal remit'[25] of the JCHR is to consider:

(a) matters relating to human rights in the United Kingdom (but excluding consideration of individual cases);
(b) proposals for remedial orders, draft remedial orders and remedial orders made under the Human Rights Act 1998; and
(c) in respect of draft remedial orders and remedial orders, whether the special attention of the House should be drawn to them on any of the grounds specified in HC Standing Order No. 151 (Statutory Instruments (Joint Committee)).

The open and general wording of its terms of reference (especially the first one) has left a great deal of discretion to the JCHR in the interpretation of its mandate and in carving out various roles for itself.[26] It has taken an expansive approach to the phrase 'matters relating to human rights'. Rather than confining itself to rights contained in the European Convention on Human Rights (ECHR), it has regard to the provisions of other international human rights instruments to which the UK is signatory[27] and has also sought to raise awareness of the importance of economic and social rights.[28]

---

[22] For a more detailed account of the 'sifting' process, see Hunt (n 1) 227–28; Hazell (n 12) 497.

[23] Other select committees that have their own specialist legal advisers are the House of Lords European Union Committee, the House of Lords Constitution Committee, the Joint Committee on Statutory Instruments and the Delegated Powers and Regulatory Reform Committee.

[24] M Benton and M Russell, 'Assessing the Impact of Parliamentary Oversight Committees: The Select Committees in the British House of Commons' [2012] *Parliamentary Affairs* 1. For this reason, David Kinley describes the JCHR as 'an eclectic beast: part standing committee; part select committee; part Royal Commission'; 'Human Rights Scrutiny in Parliament: Westminster Set to Leap Ahead' (1999) 10 *Public Law Review* 252.

[25] This the term used on the JCHR's website, available at: www.parliament.uk/business/committees/committees-archive/joint-committee-on-human-rights.

[26] Evans and Evans (n 14) 792.

[27] See, eg, JCHR, *Fifteenth Report, Legislative Scrutiny: Seventh Progress Report* (2005–06, HL 144/HC 989, 20 March 2006) 3; Hunt (n 2) 605; Evans and Evans (n 14) 797.

[28] M Hunt, 'Enhancing Parliament's Role in relation to Economic and Social Rights' [2010] *European Human Rights Law Review* 242.

In only a decade, the JCHR has established itself as an important constitutional watchdog for the protection of human rights in the UK.[29] It has three overarching and interrelated aims in this regard:

1.   to enhance the protection of human rights within the parliamentary process and in the UK generally;
2.   to increase the accountability of the Executive to Parliament for human rights issues; and
3.   to improve the quality of deliberation about human rights issues during the legislative process.

These three aims (enhancing rights-protection, increasing Government accountability and improving legislative deliberation) permeate all the functions carried out by the JCHR and are inextricably linked.

How does the JCHR seek to realise these aims? From its inception, legislative scrutiny has been a central part of the JCHR's work.[30] Its legal adviser examines all bills going through Parliament to see if they raise significant human rights issues that may require scrutiny.[31] If they raise such concerns, the JCHR publishes a report on the bill and recommends amendments to bills to give effect to its reports on bills before the Report stage in the House of Commons.[32] This legislative scrutiny function engages all three of the JCHR's aims.

As is well-known, for legislative scrutiny to be meaningful and effective, timing is of the essence. The earlier that the Committee can scrutinise legislation or legislative proposals, the more likely it is to influence policy.[33] As an Australian parliamentarian put it, 'once a Bill hits the floor, you can do nips and tucks at best'.[34] For this reason, the JCHR now engages in probing pre-legislative scrutiny.[35] It does so by corresponding with the relevant department about a policy proposal in a Green or White Paper before the policy has been finalised, and then feeds that pre-legislative scrutiny work into its scrutiny of the subsequent bill.[36] Pre-legislative

---

[29] Hazell (n 12) 497–99; Bradley and Ewing (n 14) 211–12; D Oliver, 'The Modernisation of the United Kingdom Parliament', in J Jowell and D Oliver, *The Changing Constitution* (6th edn, Oxford, Oxford University Press, 2007) 177.

[30] A Lester, 'Parliamentary Scrutiny of legislation under the Human Rights Act 1998' [2002] *European Human Rights Law Review* 432, 438; see also JCHR, *Fourteenth Report* (2001–02, HL 93, HC 674) [1], which described legislative scrutiny as the 'first priority' of the Committee.

[31] The Committee has published criteria by which it assesses 'significance'; see Joint Committee on Human Rights, *The Committee's Future Working Practices, Twenty Third Report* (2005–06, HL 239/ HC 1575) [27].

[32] Hunt (n 2) 603.

[33] Klug and Wildbore (n 3) 239–40; Lester (n 30) 441.

[34] C Evans and S Evans, 'Messages from the Front Line: Parliamentarians' Perspectives on Rights Protection' in T Campbell, K Ewing and A Tomkins (eds), *The Legal Protection of Human Rights: Sceptical Essays* (Oxford, Oxford University Press, 2011) 339.

[35] Klug and Wildbore (n 3).

[36] Hunt (n 2) 603. For a good recent example of this phenomenon, see the JCHR Report on the Justice and Security Green Paper, which framed some of the parliamentary debate when the Justice and Security Bill was debated in both Houses of Parliament. For links to the JCHR report on the Green Paper, as well as transcripts of its oral evidence sessions on this issue and all the communications between the Chair of the Committee and the Government, see www.parliament.uk/business/committees/committees-a-z/ joint-select/human-rights-committee/inquiries/parliament-2010/justice-and-security-green-paper.

scrutiny gives MPs advance warning of problems before the bill hits the floor of the House of Commons, thus enabling them to consider tabling amendments or initiating a debate on the human rights issue raised by the Committee's report in the Chamber.[37]

The JCHR also engages in post-legislative scrutiny by seeking to monitor how legislation is working in practice and whether its ongoing application raises further human rights problems. For example, it reported annually on the renewal of the control orders regime[38] and carried out a similar review of Terrorism, Prevention and Investigation Measures (TPIMs) introduced in 2001.[39] It also reported on the power to detain terrorist suspects for up to 28 days before charge.[40] This kind of follow-up work is hugely important in terms of fulfilling its watchdog function.

Another instance of this 'follow-up' work is provided by the JCHR's active monitoring of Government responses to court judgments finding a violation of human rights.[41] Given that the courts are neither institutionally suited nor equipped to carry out this kind of monitoring, the JCHR performs an invaluable role in this regard—engaging in an iterative process of pressing the Government to reveal how it plans to respond to judgments and alerting Parliament (and the public) to the fact that there may be scope to respond to such judgments in different ways. This is but one example of the various institutional collaborations in the joint enterprise of protecting rights in the UK. When monitoring the implementation of court judgments, the JCHR also collaborates with a range of other bodies such as the Committee on Legal Affairs and Human Rights of the Parliamentary Assembly of the Council of Europe, as well as with the work of the Committee of Ministers supervising the implementation of judgments by states. As part of this endeavour, the JCHR has sought to embed the good practice which followed from this monitoring work by issuing *Guidance for Departments on Responding to Court Judgments on Human Rights*.[42] Murray Hunt has observed that the Government:

> [N]ow routinely keeps Parliament, through the Committee, informed of relevant judgments and publishes an annual report to the Committee, in advance of the Human Rights Minister's annual appearance before it, setting out the Government's response to all judgments of the European Court of Human Rights against the UK and all declarations of incompatibility by UK courts in the preceding year.[43]

---

[37] Hunt (n 2) 603.

[38] Joint Committee on Human Rights, *Renewal of the Control Orders Legislation 2011* (Eighth Report of Session 2010–11, March 2011, HL 106/HC 838); see further Hunt (n 1) 235ff.

[39] www.parliament.uk/business/committees/committees-a-z/joint-select/human-rights-committee/news/evidence-session-160713---tpims.

[40] Joint Committee on Human Rights, *Counter-terrorism Policy and Human Rights: Bringing Human Rights Back, 17th Report* (2009–10, HL 86/HC 111).

[41] Hunt (n 2) 604.

[42] Joint Committee on Human Rights, *Enhancing Parlament's Role in Relation to Human Rights Judgments, 15th Report* (2009–10, HL 85/HC 455).

[43] Hunt (n 1) 237. See, eg, Ministry of Justice, *Responding to Human Rights Judgments: Report to the Joint Committee on Human Rights on the Government Response to Human Rights Judgments 2011–12* (September 2012, Cm 8432).

This suggests that the JCHR guidelines are taking root at least in some departments and that the relevant actors within departments engage in a dialogue with the JCHR on implementation issues.[44]

From this brief overview, we can see that the legislative scrutiny work carried out by the JCHR certainly has a *reactive* dimension—the JCHR must respond to the legislative agenda set by the Government and scrutinise bills as they come through Parliament. But the JCHR also adopts *proactive* and *interactive* modes of engagement with human rights issues. The *proactive* dimension of the JCHR's work is evidenced in a number of ways. For example, in the post-legislative scrutiny outlined above, the JCHR actively contributes to the 'mainstreaming' of human rights standards within Government departments. Moreover, alongside its ongoing scrutiny of bills which come before Parliament, the JCHR carries out broader thematic inquiries that are similar to the policy-orientated inquiries on which most select committees focus.[45] It has carried out such inquiries in areas such as deaths in custody, human trafficking and its long-running inquiry into counter-terrorism policy and human rights.[46] As the current legal adviser to the JCHR observed, these enquiries enable the JCHR to 'gain a deeper understanding of recurring themes in Government policy'[47] as well as to anticipate, and hopefully influence, the direction in which that policy is going. Moreover, they enable the Government (and, crucially, Government lawyers) to anticipate some of the Committee's concerns and reservations about a particular policy in advance of publishing a bill.[48]

The JCHR's legislative scrutiny work goes hand in hand with these broader inquiries. When it needs to respond quickly and effectively to new legislative proposals, the JCHR can draw on its deep knowledge base from its broader inquiries, which are often based on first-hand information that has been gathered in its oral evidence sessions. This has certainly been true for its ongoing inquiries into counter-terrorist legislation post-9/11, where its numerous reports have gained a strong reputation for authoritative and informed analysis of this type of legislation.[49] Thus, when the Government proposed to introduce the Justice and Security Bill, the JCHR was able to report on this policy proposal when it was still at a formative stage. It could then engage in in-depth pre-legislative scrutiny combined with repeated timely reports at early stages of the legislative passage of the Bill through Parliament.[50] No doubt, this contributed to the fact that the JCHR's proposals for amendments to the legislation

---

[44] The former Attorney General, Dominic Grieve commented that 'human rights issues are never far from [the Attorney General's] mind or that of government lawyers more generally'; see D Grieve, 'The Role of Human Rights in a Law Officer's Work: Challenges Facing the HRA and the ECHR' [2012] *Judicial Review* 101, 102.

[45] Klug and Wildbore (n 3) 237–38; Hunt (n 1) 240ff.

[46] Hunt (n 2) 605; Klug and Wildbore have described these broader inquiries into counter-terrorism policy and human rights as 'scrutiny inquiries', since they combine bill scrutiny with analysis of the wider policy context, thus being a hybrid of legislative scrutiny and thematic inquiries; see Klug and Wildbore (n 3) 238, 247.

[47] Hunt (n 2) 605.

[48] See Hiebert (n 10) 21.

[49] For the JCHR's most recent report on the Justice and Security Bill, see www.publications.parliament .uk/pa/jt201012/jtselect/jtrights/286/28602.htm.

[50] Hunt (n 1) 235.

received sustained consideration and debate in both Houses of Parliament.[51] This is just one example of how the JCHR can help to influence the legislative agenda in a proactive way rather than resting content with a more reactive role.

The broader thematic inquiries also highlight the *interactive* dimension of the JCHR's work.[52] When formulating a position on the human rights implications of legislation, the JCHR actively seeks representations from interested parties, including submissions from individuals who are affected by a bill, specialised charities working in the field, academic experts and NGOs with expertise in human rights.[53] By taking evidence in this way, the JCHR interacts with a broad range of individuals and civil society groups. It fulfils a participatory function by giving 'human rights specialists and NGOs, and members of society more generally, an additional, more systematic channel for involving themselves in the political engagement with human rights'.[54] It can offer a voice to those who may otherwise be overlooked in policy debates and provides them with a chance to engage directly with parliamentarians and Government ministers.[55]

Crucially, the JCHR also interacts with the relevant Government department or responsible minister. After a bill is published, there is usually a meeting between the 'bill team' (comprising the civil servants and departmental lawyer responsible for advising ministers on the details of a bill) on the one hand and the JCHR's legal advisers on the other. These meetings allow the JCHR's legal advisers to raise possible human rights concerns with regard to the bill and to identify any additional information which has not been provided by the department, but which might assist the Committee in the scrutiny of the bill. As Murray Hunt observed:

> [T]he meetings are intended both to facilitate scrutiny by the Committee and to help the Department. They are informal and off the record, but are conducted on the explicit and mutual understanding that there will be formal, on the record correspondence between the Chair of the Committee and the Minister in due course.[56]

As part of the formal process, the Chair of the Committee writes to the minister asking for an explanation and clarification of the department's reasons for thinking that the form and content of the provision in question are appropriate. This explanation, together with the Committee's comments and own analysis of the compatibility issue, can then be reported to each House to inform debate on the measure, and is published for all to see.[57]

This is an interactive and iterative process designed to keep the Government on its toes regarding human rights protection. By publishing this correspondence

---

[51] See Joint Committee on Human Rights, *Legislative Scrutiny: Justice and Security Green Paper, 24th Report* (2010–12, HL 286/HC 1777) and the Government's response to the Report (Cm 8365, 2012).

[52] Feldman (n 10) 333.

[53] ibid. Note that there is also some civil society involvement in the selection of inquiry subjects by the JCHR; see further Hunt (n 1) 241–42.

[54] Feldman (n 2) 114.

[55] Murray Hunt noted that the JCHR facilitates discussion between these interested parties on the one hand and parliamentarians and Government ministers on the other at the Committee's 'mini-conferences', or roundtables to discuss possible inquiry topics; Hunt (n 2) 42; see also Benton and Russell (n 24) 18.

[56] Hunt (n 1) 229.

[57] Feldman (n 10) 333.

with the relevant minister or Government department, the JCHR furthers its aim of enhancing executive accountability which, in turn, may have an impact on legislative formation.[58] It does so, in part, by getting the Government to be more transparent about its thinking on important human rights issues, but also by putting pressure on the Government to consider its human rights arguments more deeply and engage with counter-arguments presented by the JCHR.[59] This is a key aspect of the JCHR's work. It shows the JCHR in its role as a reason-demanding body,[60] assisting Parliament in performing its role of holding the Executive to account.

Before going on to examine how the JCHR carries out this accountability function in more detail, it is worth pausing to reflect on two related aims which are often attributed to it in this context. These are that it should help to create both a 'culture of rights'[61] and a 'culture of justification'.[62] These aims sound lofty and grandiose. What do they mean? The basic idea at work in a 'culture of rights' is simply that the JCHR should help to create a climate of respect for rights within Parliament. In such a climate, human rights would be treated as important considerations to bear in mind when formulating policy and enacting legislation. Robert Blackburn characterises the culture of rights as an expectation that 'human rights should form part of the "rules of the game" under which the system of politics and government is conducted'.[63] What about the culture of justification? This is the allied idea that ministers and governments ought to give reasons for their policies and legislative proposals and, in particular, be willing to justify them in terms of rights.[64] It is the requirement that the Government should demonstrate its 'human rights reasoning'.[65] Both of these aims are instrumental to the ultimate aim of enhancing the protection of human rights within the UK parliamentary process, and the JCHR strives to foster both.

The idea of the 'culture of justification' is one lens through which we can view the JCHR's role in securing greater executive accountability within Parliament. Murray Hunt argues that the HRA commits the UK to a culture of democratic justification since it 'sets up mechanisms for the transparent scrutiny of the adequacy of public

[58] In the Working Practices Report, Francesca Klug thought that this iterative process had some impact on legislative formation (at para 8.3).

[59] See generally C Murray, 'What Next for the UK Parliament Joint Committee on Human Rights?' *The Guardian* (5 July 2010), available at: www.guardian.co.uk/law/2010/jul/05/human-rights-human-rights-act.

[60] For the view that Parliament as a whole is a reason-demanding institution, see D Dyzenhaus, 'Deference, Security and Human Rights' in B Gould and L Lazarus (eds), *Security and Human Rights* (Oxford, Hart Publishing, 2007) 143.

[61] For further elaboration of this idea, see Hiebert (n 10) 4; J Hiebert, 'Governing under the Human Rights Act: The Limitations of Wishful Thinking' [2012] *Public Law* 28ff; Jack Straw, 'Building a Human Rights Culture' (Address to Civil Service College Seminar, 9 December 1999), available at: www.nationalarchives.gov.uk/ERORecords/HO/421/2/hract/cscspe.htm; D Nicol, 'The Human Rights Act and the Politicians' (2004) 24 *Legal Studies* 453ff.

[62] Dyzenhaus (n 60) 152; Hunt (n 2) 603.

[63] R Blackburn, 'Towards a Constitutional Bill of Rights for the United Kingdom' in D Oliver and G Drewry (eds), *The Law and Parliament* (Toronto, Butterworths Canada, 1999) 175–80.

[64] Feldman (n 10) 347.

[65] Grieve (n 44) 102.

justifications for interferences with, or failures to protect, human rights'.[66] Here, the focus is not exclusively on trying to ensure that Parliament reaches a good outcome on a particular human rights issue (though this is obviously extremely important)— it is also that Parliament engages with the human rights concern in a considered, conscientious and informed manner which takes account of all the available legal and political arguments concerning human rights.

The JCHR carries out its accountability function in a variety of ways—some direct and others indirect. It engages directly with the Government and government departments by demanding explanations and reasons from them, publishing reports on the bills going through Parliament and monitoring the human rights impact of legislation once it is on the statute books. More indirectly, though no less importantly, it also seeks to engage parliamentarians with human rights concerns, prompting them to strengthen their own role in holding the Executive to account.[67] In order for parliamentarians to carry out informed and meaningful scrutiny of Government proposals, it is essential that MPs have enough information on which to base that scrutiny so that they can ask probing questions during parliamentary debate. JCHR reports are a valuable resource for parliamentarians in this regard because they place a wealth of information in the public domain and contain well-argued reservations about—indeed often forthright and robust criticisms of— Government policies. This material can be used in rigorous parliamentary scrutiny of the legislative proposal.

The reason-demanding strand of the JCHR's role can clearly be seen in its persistent pressure it placed on the Government to provide more detailed statements of its reasons for believing a bill to be Convention-compatible under section 19 HRA. As is well-known, section 19 requires that when introducing legislation to Parliament, a minister must 'make a statement to the effect that in his view the provisions of the Bill are compatible with the Convention, or alternatively, if he or she feels unable to make such a statement of compatibility, the Minister can announce that the Government wishes to proceed with the legislation nonetheless'. In the first few years of the operation of the HRA, the Government rested content with making a bald statement of compatibility, without providing any reasons for this conclusion. It steadfastly refused to give any further explanation of its position on human rights compliance, despite the fact that the Cabinet Committee on Parliamentary Business and Legislation required all departments to produce a memorandum containing what a former Attorney General described as a 'full and frank legal analysis of the strengths and weaknesses of the human rights issues raised in the Bill and an indication of whether the minister in charge of the Bill can make a statement that in his or her view the provisions of the Bill are compatible with the Convention rights as required by s 19 of the Human Rights Act'.[68]

After persistent pressure from the JCHR, the Government accepted in 2002 that it would include an outline of its views on compatibility with Convention rights

[66] Hunt (n 2) 603.
[67] See Hunt (n 2) 603–05; Feldman (n 2) 91.
[68] Grieve (n 44) 102; Feldman (n 10) 339.

in the Explanatory Notes published with every Government bill.[69] This was an improvement on a bald statement of compatibility, but the Notes were of variable quality and the JCHR therefore continued to press the Government for more information, with the result that it is now increasingly common for departments to supplement the information provided in the Explanatory Notes to a bill with a much more detailed human rights memorandum.[70] These memoranda enhance the transparency of the Government's thinking behind the bill in question and places a greater onus on ministers to explain to Parliament the human rights implications of Government policies.[71] They also contribute to the 'mainstreaming' of human rights reasoning in Government departments. Not only does it force ministers and Government lawyers to take rights seriously when drafting bills, it has also led to a number of other institutional interactions to further the goal of ensuring compliance with rights. It is now common for the human rights unit within the Ministry of Justice 'to assist Government departments with the human rights information accompanying a Bill and advising on the expectations of the Joint Committee'.[72] Moreover, Cabinet Office Guidelines have now changed to instruct departments to provide an explanation for their position on compatibility in the explanatory notes to a bill.[73] These guidelines alert departments to the fact that the JCHR will 'examine closely the arguments put forward by the department justifying interference with a Convention rights' and note that it 'clearly advantageous if the JCHR reports favourably early in the Bill's passage'. This gives departments a motivation to 'identify areas likely to concern the Committee and prepare briefing ahead of time'.[74]

In terms of fulfilling its role as an accountability mechanism within Parliament (and indeed helping Parliament to fulfil its own role in this regard), getting the information in these human rights memoranda into the public domain is one of the great achievements of the JCHR. By eliciting such information, which governments are sometimes reluctant to give, the JCHR is both watchdog and bloodhound.[75] The bloodhound sniffs out the information and the watchdog barks as necessary to warn the Government, Parliament and the public at large of possible incursions into human rights. The importance of improving the quality and consistency of the information which the Government provides to Parliament on the human rights implications of bills has been a constant theme in the JCHR reports, as well as in the broader thematic inquiries.[76] As Murray Hunt has observed, 'the steady increase in the quality of the relevant information provided to Parliament has made possible more focused human rights scrutiny of legislation'.[77]

---

[69] Lester (n 30) 448; Hiebert (n 10) 25.
[70] For a detailed account of the JCHR's attempts to secure the publication of such memoranda, see further Hunt (n 1) 229ff.
[71] For examples of practice developing in departments in this regard, see Hunt (n 1) 231–32.
[72] Hunt (n 1) 230.
[73] Cabinet Office, *Guide to Making Legislation* (June 2012), available at: www.cabinetoffice.gov.uk/making-legislation-guide/echr.aspx.
[74] ibid, para 12.30.
[75] Lester (n 30) 434.
[76] See Report on The Committee's Working Practices, para 41.
[77] Hunt (n 1) 232.

IV. VOICE, AUDIENCE AND EXPERTISE

One of the most controversial issues surrounding the working practices of the JCHR (at least in the academic literature) has been whether it should assess Convention-compatibility in a way which second-guesses how the courts might decide the issue. In its early reports, the JCHR assessed Convention-compatibility by applying the existing case law on Convention rights to the issue and, if the existing jurisprudence was unclear, anticipating future court rulings. This gave rise to the criticism that by relying on a 'quasi-judicial'[78] or 'court-centred'[79] approach, parliamentarians were given the false impression that human rights issues were the preserve of expert legal opinion rather than issues on which everyone should have a considered view.[80] Francesca Klug and others made the point that the HRA envisaged a multi-institutional approach to human rights protection, whereby Parliament would play a central and active role.[81] For Klug, the role of the JCHR was to 'help Parliament to develop its "voice" on human rights'[82]—a role which would be diminished if the JCHR simply mimicked the judgments of the courts and pressed Parliament to accept them and no more.

In recent years, the JCHR has decided to express its own views about compatibility rather than merely attempt to predict what courts might say about the compatibility of a measure.[83] Of course, it does so after receiving legal advice about the relevant legal framework, including what the courts will or might say where this is sufficiently clear. However, the Committee is not bound to share the same stance as the courts and, in those cases where it disagrees with a judicial interpretation of the Convention or takes a different view about its application, it explains the difference of view with explicit reasons within its report. This seems like a sensible approach. After all, the courts and the JCHR perform different functions and have different institutional responsibilities. The courts are constrained by precedent, both domestically and from Strasbourg, and they are often under a duty to show deference to Parliament or the Government. Courts can make decisions on human rights questions which have legal force, whereas the JCHR only has the power to influence, advise and recommend. The JCHR has no power to compel the Government to accept any of its findings. As a result, it has more freedom to criticise the case law where appropriate and to press the Government for greater levels of human rights protection than the courts may demand in the context of an individual case. Of course, it probably has more chance of getting the Government to change its mind if it can cite Supreme Court rulings in support of its argument. But on a few occasions, the JCHR has decided to reject a decision of the court and has used its freedom to criticise a particular ruling, arguing that it does not go far enough to

---

[78] Klug and Wildbore (n 3) 245.
[79] T Campbell, 'Parliamentary Review with a Democratic Charter of Rights' in Campbell, Ewing and Tomkins (n 34) 458.
[80] Klug and Wildbore (n 3) 245; J Tham, 'Parliamentary Deliberation and the National Security Executive: The Case of Control Orders' [2010] *Public Law* 79, 101–02.
[81] Klug and Wildbore (n 3) 249–50.
[82] ibid 250.
[83] Hunt (n 2) 603.

protect rights fully. It has also criticised the Government for misrepresenting court decisions or hiding behind them in order to justify a position which is at odds with human rights values.[84] It seems right that the JCHR should feel free to make these calls as it sees fit.

However, it is nonetheless important not to lose sight of the significant and valuable role of legal expertise in the work done by the JCHR. One of the central tasks of the JCHR is to scrutinise legislation for compliance with the HRA and other human rights instruments. Like it or not, these are legal documents which have a body of jurisprudence built up around them. Whilst it is of course necessary and valuable for MPs to have meaningful discussions about the values underpinning human rights and the broad issues of principle which flow from them, including the justification of the broader policy objectives it wishes to pursue, when the Government proposes legislation which impinge on rights, there may also be issues where detailed legal expertise is required or at the very least desirable.[85]

Recent research into the impact of the JCHR on parliamentary and judicial deliberations on rights reveals that the subject areas where JCHR reports are most widely cited (both in parliamentary debates and in the courts) are counter-terrorism and criminal justice.[86] There may be many reasons for this, including the fact that the topic of counter-terrorism has been the subject of broader thematic inquiries by the JCHR and intensive pre-legislative scrutiny.[87] However, one reason often overlooked for the influence of its reports in the areas of counter-terrorism and criminal justice is that these are areas where legal expertise is valuable in understanding the detailed and often complex human rights implications of the legislation proposed by the Government. In these areas, questions arise such as whether the employment of so-called 'Special Advocates' are sufficient to mitigate the potential unfairness of closed material proceedings and the attendant non-disclosure of information in assessments of the legality of control orders;[88] or whether closed material proceedings are themselves preferable to a public interest immunity (PII) exercise.[89] The relative advantages or disadvantages of these types of proceedings require (or at least benefit from) detailed legal knowledge.[90] This is not to say that these complex issues cannot be explained to parliamentarians without any legal training, but simply that in order to engage in effective and probing scrutiny, MPs would be at a disadvantage if they did not have access to expert legal advice to help them understand the issues at some level.

[84] See generally A Kavanagh, 'Special Advocates, Control Orders and the Right to a Fair Trial' (2010) 73 *MLR* 836, 849–50.
[85] See Feldman (n 10) 334, 337.
[86] M Hunt, HJ Hooper and P Yowell, *Parliament and Human Rights: Redressing the Democratic Deficit* (Swindon, Arts and Humanities Research Council, 2012).
[87] See Hunt (n 1) 233ff.
[88] Kavanagh (n 84).
[89] The JCHR Report on the Justice and Security Green Paper as well as the JCHR reports on the Justice and Security Bill; see also Justice Report on Secret Evidence (2009), available at: www.justice.org.uk.
[90] See further J Ip, 'Al Rawi, Tariq, and the Future of Closed Material Procedures and Special Advocates' (2012) 75 *MLR* 606, 608.

The importance of legal expertise to the effectiveness of legislative human rights review is borne out by a recent empirical study into the performance of the Australian Parliament in protecting rights.[91] A recurrent theme in the findings of this study was that Australian parliamentarians without any legal training doubted their ability to even identify human rights concerns, let alone evaluate the possible consequences or implications of certain forms of legislation for human rights.[92] Some parliamentarians were 'frank in their own admission that they did not always have the relevant skills to [carry out these tasks]'.[93] As a consequence, the independent and expert advice of the parliamentary committee's adviser was 'identified by many as critical for their success in issue identification'.[94] When analysing the findings of their study, the authors concluded that a lack of legal expertise in evaluating human rights problems was a major limitation on the capacity of parliamentarians to scrutinise legislation for compliance with human rights. They concluded that 'effective scrutiny is more tied to legal expertise than is usually acknowledged'.[95]

Parliamentary committees like the JCHR can perform an important accountability function by providing parliamentarians with legal advice and expertise which is independent of the Government. If the JCHR reports are written in an accessible style, they can be a good way of improving parliamentarians' 'human rights literacy'[96] and can enable MPs to engage with detailed arguments about the human rights implications of complex legislation. In this way, legal expertise can *serve* legislative deliberation across the board and strengthen the ability of parliamentarians to probe legislation in a meaningful and effective way.

However, although non-specialist parliamentarians are a key audience for JCHR reports, they also have to be pitched to a highly specialist legal audience as well. It is well-known that when the Government is preparing legislation, it relies heavily on its own legal advice when coming to a view about the human rights implications of a bill.[97] Therefore, in an effort to maximize its influence and impact, the JCHR must try to persuade Government lawyers that they may have overlooked or underestimated the importance of some legal issue and, where justified, provide strong legal counter-arguments to the Government's legal advice.

In the Cabinet Office guidelines for departments on securing compliance with Convention rights, ministers are advised that in order to make a section 19 statement of compatibility, they should establish that 'at a minimum, the balance of legal argument supports the view that the provisions are compatible'.[98] In this situation,

---

[91] Evans and Evans (n 34) 329.

[92] ibid 338.

[93] ibid.

[94] ibid.

[95] ibid 346. Dawn Oliver has also made the point that parliamentarians have neither the skill nor the time to engage in detailed scrutiny of bills and, when they do so, they tend to rely heavily on expert assistance from the clerks of select committees or legal and other advisers; Oliver (n 29) 170. In her Working Practices Report, Francesca Klug observed that some non-legal members of the JCHR felt that they were 'left in a passive role with the committee driven by its staff and legal experts': para 11.6(viii).

[96] Hunt (n 2) 607.

[97] See Hiebert (n 10); Hiebert (n 61) 34; Grieve (n 44) 101–02.

[98] Cabinet Office Constitution Secretariat, *The Human Rights Act 1998 Guidelines for Departments* (2nd edn, Department for Constitutional Affairs, 2000) para 35, available at: www.dca.gov.uk/hract/

where there are plausible legal arguments both ways, there is room for persuasion and it is not inconceivable that the JCHR might provide the tipping point on at least some issues. Clearly, the quality and persuasiveness of the legal argumentation contained in the JCHR reports is vital if the Committee is to have influence in this way.[99] Rather than detracting from it, the specialist legal dimension of the JCHR enhances Parliament's ability to hold the Executive to account by raising awareness of human rights concerns and providing detailed information and advice on how those concerns play out in practice. In this way, the legal expertise of the Committee can be used as a tool of political influence.

In some of the existing literature on the JCHR, commentators have seized upon the fact that the JCHR is a *parliamentary* committee and therefore part of the *political* machinery which helps Parliament to uphold rights. The work of the JCHR is often celebrated by those who wish to defend the so-called 'political constitution'.[100] These scholars tend to argue that the JCHR is better at protecting rights than the courts and that this shows that political methods of rights-enforcement are more effective than legal ones. Ironically, this type of analysis tends to be overly court-centric, since it assesses the performance of the JCHR primarily with reference to the courts. There are a number of problems with this approach. First, since the JCHR and the courts perform different functions, have different institutional structures and pursue different (though complementary) aims, it is difficult to measure the relative success of these institutions against single criteria. I have argued elsewhere that when judging any political institution, we should use standards of assessment which are sensitive to the nature, limits and functions of that institution.[101] This may mean that we should use different criteria for success when assessing the JCHR on the one hand and the courts on the other. Second, and more importantly, we do not need to choose between political and legal forms of rights-enforcement. It is more helpful to explore the various ways in which they interact, as well as how they discharge their own distinctive roles whilst discharging what is ultimately a shared responsibility to protect rights.

There is a third problem with presenting the JCHR as the mascot of the political constitution, namely, that it may lead commentators to downplay the legal dimensions of the Committee's work and concentrate exclusively on the its parliamentary and political credentials. It may also lead them to under-estimate the important role of the Committee's legal advisers (who are of course unelected expert lawyers), who play a pivotal role in the working practices of the JCHR. This is just one of

guidance.htm. Janet Hiebert argues that the emphasis on legal compatibility and prediction of what would succeed before the courts has 'softened' since 2000, leaving room for more personal assessment by the relevant minister. However, her interviews with legal officials suggested that they thought it extremely unlikely that a minister would contradict clear legal advice given to them; see Hiebert (n 61) 35.

[99] David Feldman commented that the influence of the Committee depends largely on the esteem in which the Committee is held 'since committees have no power to force their views on an unwilling executive'; Feldman (n 10) 347; see also Hiebert (n 10) 15.
[100] See, eg, A Tomkins, 'Parliament, Human Rights and Counter-terrorism' in Campbell, Ewing and Tomkins (n 34).
[101] A Kavanagh, 'Judging the Judges under the Human Rights Act 1998: Deference, Disillusionment and the "War on Terror"' [2009] *Public Law* 287, 303.

many issues which is not illuminated (and in fact is distorted) by viewing it through the false dichotomous lens of the legal versus political constitution. The JCHR is a hybrid body which combines legal and political dimensions in various ways and therefore defies the compartmentalised thinking which often goes hand in hand with the view that the political and legal constitution are polar opposites. Legal and political methods of human rights enforcement are not binary opposites—they can be complementary. As the JCHR itself shows, both methods can be combined within one institution.

V. IMPACT, INFLUENCE AND THE STANDARD OF SUCCESS

At the beginning of this chapter, I argued that the JCHR has three aims that are inextricably linked: enhancing rights protection, increasing Government account-ability and improving legislative deliberation about rights. The obvious question then arises: how successful has the JCHR been in advancing these aims? Is it mak-ing a real difference to rights protection in the UK? Is it securing greater Executive accountability on issues concerning human rights? Has it succeeded in improving the quality (or indeed quantity) of legislative deliberation about human rights issues?

These questions are easier to ask than to answer, in part because of the dif-ficulty of eliciting the relevant empirical information on which to base reliable answers. In their work assessing the policy impact of the British Parliament, Meg Russell and Meghan Benton have documented the enormous methodological and other challenges facing scholars who wish to gather systematic information of this kind. As they observe, 'much of Parliament's influence is subtle, largely invisible, and frequently even immeasurable'.[102] Similar problems beset any assessment of the impact and influence of parliamentary oversight committees such as the JCHR.[103]

Whilst acknowledging these difficulties, it is still possible to make some tentative assessments of the performance and effectiveness of the JCHR, judging it against the three aims outlined above. Let us take the issue of Government accountability first. It is certainly the case that thanks partly to the work of the JCHR (and partly to the existence of section 19 HRA itself), governments are now under a greater onus to provide information on their 'human rights reasoning' when proposing legisla-tion in Parliament. The persistent pressure brought to bear by the JCHR urging the Government to provide a human rights memorandum alongside the section 19 state-ment of compatibility has made a great stride in this direction. The gradual bedding-in of the JCHR's *Guidance for Departments on Responding to Court Judgments on Human Rights* could be considered another potential achievement in this regard. It is a step on the road to mainstreaming human rights thinking in departmental business. Even the fact of the iterative process of requesting information from

---

[102] See n 11, above.
[103] Benton and Russell (n 24) 2.

Government ministers on the human rights implications of particular pieces of legislation and then publishing the ensuing correspondence puts more information about the Government's position in the public domain and increases Executive accountability.

What about Parliament? Is Parliament performing its own role of holding the Executive to account for potential human rights violations and, if so, is the JCHR assisting Parliament to do so? This is a more difficult question to answer. One way of testing it would be to see if JCHR reports are cited in parliamentary debate. This shades into the third aim of the JCHR, namely, to ensure that human rights issues are given serious consideration in Parliament and are subjected to high-quality, well-informed and properly advised deliberation.

The most recent and systematic empirical information on this question is provided by the AHRC-funded project carried out by Murray Hunt, Hayley Hooper and Paul Yowell.[104] One of the aims of this study was to assess how, if at all, debate about human rights in Parliament changed between 2000 and 2010. The research revealed that whilst there were only 23 references to the JCHR in parliamentary debates in the period 2000–05, there were 1,006 entries for the 2005–10 Parliament. This huge increase suggests that parliamentarians are finding JCHR reports useful as a basis for interventions in parliamentary debate. It is an indicator of the success of the JCHR in raising awareness of human rights issues and stimulating debate about them in Parliament. But why was there such a dramatic increase after 2005? One reason is that the JCHR produced more reports in the second half of the decade.[105] Another reason may be that after 2005, the JCHR adopted a deliberate strategy of recommending amendments to bills to give effect to its recommendations and encouraging its members to table amendments to this effect on the floor of both Houses of Parliament.[106]

When we look at who made the references to the JCHR, some interesting facts emerge. A total of 35 per cent of all references were made by just seven parliamentarians, six of whom were JCHR members and five of whom were members of the House of Lords. As the authors of the report observe, 'the relatively small number of members who are responsible for most of the references to JCHR reports is striking, as is the obvious importance of active members [of the Committee] to force debates about the Committee's work in the chamber'.[107] Clearly, getting members of the Committee to table amendments in Parliament is a good way of raising awareness of the JCHR's work amongst parliamentarians as a whole, though it seems that the members of the JCHR drawn from the House of Lords are much more active on this front than their counterparts in the House of Commons. Overall, citations of JCHR reports were twice as likely in the House of Lords as they were in the House of Commons.[108] The authors of the report suggested that there was a 'distinctive kind

---

[104] AHRC Report (n 86).
[105] ibid 22.
[106] ibid 22; Hunt (n 2) 603.
[107] AHRC Report (n 86) 25.
[108] Citations in the House of Lords account for 66 per cent of the total number: ibid 7, 24.

of engagement with JCHR reports and debate about human rights' in the House of Lords.[109] In the House of Lords, references to the reports were:

> [G]enerally longer and more detailed than references in the House of Commons ... Debates in the House of Lords often involved two, three or more members successively making a number of points based on JCHR reports and entering into dialogue with Government representatives and other members about human rights issues.[110]

So both the quantity and possibly also the quality of engagement with JCHR reports is far greater in the unelected House of Lords than in the democratically elected House of Commons.[111] This may be because of the affinity between the scrutinising functions of the JCHR and the role of the House of Lords as a revising, scrutinising chamber,[112] or it may be due to the expertise available in the House of Lords. When Francesca Klug and Helen Wildbore conducted interviews with backbench MPs as part of their research into the JCHR's working practices in 2005: 'Peers affirmed the authority and high esteem with which JCHR reports are generally received in the House of Lords.'[113] Some backbenchers interviewed for the Klug Report suggested that the reports were not taken as seriously in the House of Commons.[114] There was also a perception amongst members of the JCHR that 'the culture of the "expert peer"'[115] dominated the proceedings of the JCHR. That was in 2005 and the situation may be different now. The AHRC-funded research did not explore this issue. Clearly, if one of the tasks of the JCHR is to infuse human rights thinking into parliamentary deliberations, then enhancing the quality and indeed quantity of debate on such issues amongst the democratically elected members of the House of Commons is a major challenge. The increase in the number of references to JCHR reports in the Commons in the 2005–10 Parliament seems to suggest that the JCHR is making inroads into this daunting task, but there is clearly some way to go.

However, when we come to the issue of whether the JCHR is making a difference in terms of securing amendments to legislation, the results are less heartening. Out of these 1,006 citations, there were only 16 where the Government offered amendments to a bill or agreed to do so apparently in response to a JCHR report.[116] There were a further seven further instances in which the Government issued guidance on the basis of recommendation in JCHR reports to administrative and law enforcement officials on how certain terms in the law should be understood.[117] Moreover, these figures do not include various recommendations by the JCHR which the Government has accepted when making remedial orders under the HRA.[118] So

---

[109] ibid 26; see also Nicol (n 61) 466–67, 472.
[110] AHRC Report (n 86) 26.
[111] See also Klug (n 17) paras 9.5, 13.3. Janet Hiebert also suggests that both the HRA and the JCHR 'are considerably more prominent' in the House of Lords than they are in the deliberations of the House of Commons; see Hiebert (n 61) 42.
[112] Klug and Wildbore (n 3) 242.
[113] ibid 241–42.
[114] ibid 242.
[115] 'The Klug Report', above n 17, para 11.6(ix).
[116] Hunt, Hooper and Yowell (n 86) 43.
[117] ibid 44.
[118] For multiple examples of this, see Hunt (n 1) 238. See also King, ch 8 in this volume.

there may well be successes in terms of outcomes which are not picked up by this study. Nonetheless, given that the JCHR has written over 200 detailed reports, alongside many broader thematic studies, not to mention the wealth of oral and written evidence that it has collected and published on issues of immense importance for human rights, the result in terms of actual changes to legislation seems underwhelming.

Janet Hiebert has arrived at similar downbeat conclusions following her comparative empirical study in Canada, the UK and New Zealand on the question of whether parliamentary bills of rights augment the capacity of parliaments to hold governments to account for legislation that implicates human rights adversely.[119] Based on 150 expert interviews with public and political figures in these countries, Hiebert concluded that parliamentary scrutiny for compliance with human rights does not tend to augment Parliament's ability to protect rights:

> Research in all three jurisdictions suggests that legal costs [associated with failing to comply with judicial rulings on human rights] are more persuasive than parliamentary criticism when encouraging government to take rights seriously or guiding or constraining decisions. Unless parliamentary pressure is sufficient to threaten defeat of a bill, governments have generally been unwilling to amend bills.[120]

Despite commending the UK's JCHR as 'extremely impressive by all measures of what can be expected from a parliamentary scrutiny committee',[121] Hiebert nonetheless draws the following conclusion, which is worth quoting in full:

> [T]he existence of a specialised parliamentary committee, even one which performs its role robustly, does not alter substantially the fact that Parliament remains weak relative to the executive and, as a general matter, is not able to regularly compel government to amend bills ... Although the JCHR has had some success pressuring government to provide more complete explanations for claims of compatibility, and in securing some amendments (particularly the anti-terrorist measures), it has not been particularly effective at getting the government to revisit claims of compatibility for which it contests. Those public officials interviewed indicated that a negative report by the JCHR does not generally result in the government changing its decision about whether to proceed with a bill. Although departments anticipate the JCHR's review, and where possible make adjustments to avoid a negative report, their primary focus is on whether proposed legislation satisfied the government's legal advisers' assessment of compatibility in the complex pre-legislative review process that can include review by the Attorney General. Thus, the government is unlikely to change its mind on the basis of a single but contrary parliamentary committee report.[122]

It is of course true that under the Westminster model, it is the Executive (not Parliament) that is in the driving seat of the legislative process. It is also true that the existence of one single committee (such as the JCHR) is not going to alter that fact substantially. However, there are a number of points which must be borne in mind in order to contextualise Hiebert's analysis. First, we need to view the JCHR against the broader backdrop of the select committee system as a whole. Since their

---

[119] J Hiebert, 'Governing Like Judges?' in Campbell, Ewing and Tomkins (n 34) 40.
[120] ibid 61.
[121] ibid 63; see also Hiebert (n 61) 38.
[122] ibid 63.

establishment in 1979, select committees in the House of Commons have been perceived to be 'one of Parliament's great success stories'.[123] It is widely believed that they provide a valuable oversight and accountability mechanism within the Westminster Parliament and can have both a direct and indirect influence on the content of legislation.[124] True, if we judge the effectiveness of these committees purely in terms of securing amendments to bills as they pass through Parliament, or indeed the even stronger criterion used by Hiebert of 'getting the Government to change its decision about whether to proceed with a Bill' at all, then the success rate of these committees may look disappointing to say the least.

However, many recent empirical studies on the impact and performance of select committees warn against assuming that success in terms of securing amendments to legislation should be the only or even the most important criterion by which to judge the effectiveness of such committees.[125] In a recent study of the impact of parliamentary select committees, political scientists Meghan Benton and Meg Russell argue that take-up by government of recommendations by committees 'is only one form of committee influence and arguably not even the most important'.[126] Other forms include: influencing policy debate (both in Parliament and in the media); spotlighting issues and altering policy priorities, 'raising them up the departmental and ministerial agenda';[127] brokering in policy disputes and aiding communication and transparency within and between government departments;[128] providing expert evidence; holding government to account by subjecting government proposals to close examination and sustained questioning;[129] exposure of poor decision making by using the power of publicity;[130] and generating fear so that governments might amend a legislative proposal before it becomes a bill in order to make it 'as committee-proof as possible'.[131]

As outlined above, the power of publicity is an extremely important form of influence which the JCHR brings to bear when it publicises its correspondence with Government ministers and departments. Some of the important work of the JCHR

---

[123] Brazier and Fox (n 11) 354; Bradley and Ewing (n 14) 208–212. Dawn Oliver is sceptical of the capacity and willingness of select committees to hold the Government to account or even to engage in detailed legislative scrutiny (see Oliver (n 29) 169–72), although she seems to consider the JCHR to be one of the more important and influential select committees (at 177).

[124] S Kalitowski, 'Rubber Stamp or Cockpit? The Impact of Parliament on Government Legislation' (2008) 61 *Parliamentary Affairs* 694, 705; Brazier and Fox (n 11) 356; Feldman (n 10) 328; Benton and Russell (n 24) 2.

[125] Benton and Russell (n 24) 26; Evans and Evans (n 11) 551–52; Kalitowski (n 124) 705. In Louise Thompson's study of the impact of bill committees in the House of Commons, she also notes that formal changes made to Government bills in committee 'paints only a partial picture of the work being undertaken in committee' and that bill committees can have 'a more extensive impact on government legislation' through securing informal assurances and undertakings from ministers; see L Thompson, 'More of the Same or a Period of Change? The Impact of Bill Committees in the Twenty-First Century House of Commons' (2013) 66 *Parliamentary Affairs* 459, 469–70.

[126] Benton and Russell (n 24) 26.

[127] ibid 19.

[128] ibid.

[129] ibid 20.

[130] ibid; M Ryle, 'Pre-legislative Scrutiny: A Prophylactic Approach to Protection of Human Rights' [1994] *Public Law* 192, 195.

[131] ibid 21.

takes place in off-the-record meetings with the teams of officials working on bills either before or after they are introduced into Parliament. Most of the meetings with bill teams take place after the bill has been introduced. Clearly, beforehand would be better, but there is very rarely the time to do so, unless a bill has been preceded by a draft bill or other pre-legislative documents which have been scrutinised by the JCHR, such as the Justice and Security Green Paper.[132]

In their study of legislative scrutiny in the Australian Parliament, Evans and Evans also observed the importance of 'having a "quiet word" outside the official committee report to persuade the government to change legislation in order to avoid a negative committee report'.[133] Other forms of subtle influence behind the scenes were often perceived to be more effective than the formal processes.[134] These forms of influence are, by their nature, less tangible and less measurable than straightforward take-up by government of committee recommendations.[135] In fact, the more integrated and effective the committees become in the policy-making process, the more difficult it is to isolate their influence from other actors. Nonetheless, Benton and Russell conclude that 'overall, oversight committees strengthen the policy-making process inside and outside government by exposing decision-making to rigorous tests, and by encouraging more careful consideration'.[136] Though the challenges of quantifying such impact are great indeed, they conclude that the views of select committees are taken relatively seriously and have a significant influence on policy formation at Westminster. It seems clear that the JCHR actively seeks exactly the kinds of influence that Benton and Russell outline in their study and it seems as if it is having some measure of success when judged against this broader set of criteria.

Third, we need to bear in mind that even with reference to the Government's take-up of JCHR recommendations, it is not always easy to ascertain whether there is a direct causal connection between a Government amendment and a JCHR report. As Francesca Klug commented in her Working Practices Report:

> It is very difficult to assess the extent to which JCHR reports have been directly responsible for amendments to Bills. Even where there is a connection between what the JCHR suggests and an amendment, it is not always possible to assess how crucial the Committee's proposals have been or whether there were other more significant sources or reasons for an amendment.[137]

Moreover, when the Government frames its legislative proposals in anticipation of the adverse reaction of a committee, this influence can be 'relatively hidden, or even wholly invisible'.[138] In fact, Hiebert's research reveals that the JCHR reports have this anticipatory influence at least some of the time: Government departments anticipate adverse comments from the JCHR and 'where possible make adjustments

---

[132] HM Government, *Justice and Security Green Paper* (Cm 8194, 2011); see further Hunt (n 1) 233ff.
[133] Evans and Evans (n 34) 338.
[134] ibid.
[135] ibid 22; see also M Russell, M Benton, D Gover and K Wollter, 'A Parliament that Bows and Scrapes?: The Westminster Parliament's Impact on Government Legislation 2005–2010' (Paper to the PSA, Belfast, 3–5 April 2012, on file with Meg Russell) 2.
[136] Above n 24, 22.
[137] Klug and Wildbore (n 3) 241.
[138] Russell et al, above n 135, 2.

to avoid a negative report'.[139] As Hiebert observes in this volume, the JCHR's persistent demand for reasons and justifications for the Government's position on human rights compatibility has 'increased officials' interest in avoiding bills being subject to an unnecessary or unintentional critical JCHR report'.[140] This anticipatory influence is confirmed by interviews conducted as part of the Klug Working Practices Report in 2005. There, Klug discovered that when considering human rights compatibility, departmental legal advisers were likely to ask themselves 'How would this run by the JCHR?'[141] This anticipatory influence is by its very nature difficult to measure, but is nonetheless potentially very important for the enterprise of enhancing rights-protection in the UK.

It may also be that committees such as the JCHR have more success in securing relatively minor changes to legislation than in securing large changes or even a complete withdrawal of the legislation.[142] This suggestion is borne out by the findings of the first detailed cross-departmental investigation of the impact of select committees on government policy for many years. There, the researchers concluded that 'recommendations calling for medium or large changes to policy were less likely to be accepted or implemented. Recommendations relating to flagship policies were also significantly less likely to be accepted'. However, 'recommendations calling for disclosure and guidance had a higher chance of success'.[143] These findings need to be tested empirically with specific reference to the JCHR, but they seem plausible on the available evidence about the 16 amendments to Government bills which are said to be a direct result of JCHR activity according to the AHRC report. In the context of counter-terrorism, the JCHR has been more successful in getting governments to accept safeguards such as annual renewals, sunset clauses and judicial supervision than it has with recommendations concerning the core substantive proposals in the legislation. Since Hiebert's analysis seems to focus on large-scale changes or complete withdrawals, it may under-estimate the impact of these more subtle changes.

Hiebert acknowledges that the JCHR has been successful in securing some amendments to legislation and the scale of this achievement should not be under-estimated, precisely because of the Executive dominance of Parliament in the Westminster system. As with all our political institutions, the standard of assessment for the JCHR has to be 'success in some measure, not absolute success'.[144] The Committee has only been in existence for a decade. It cannot create a culture of rights overnight. Hiebert is absolutely right that we need to ask whether the JCHR has made a real difference in terms of securing amendments to bills. Outcomes matter and their importance should not be downplayed. Hiebert is also right that, as far

---

[139] Hiebert, above n 119, 63; Hiebert (n 61) 39; Kalitowski (n 124) 706–07.

[140] Hiebert, ch 3 in this volume, text accompanying n 32.

[141] Klug (n 17) para 8.4.

[142] Benton and Russell (n 24) 11, 14; Kalitowski (n 124) 707. In an empirical study of the relative influence of the JCHR, the Independent Reviewer and the courts on counter-terrorist legislation, Jessie Blackbourn concluded that the Government was always much more likely to accept smaller changes which preserve the status quo, no matter which actor proposed the change; see J Blackbourn, 'Evaluating the Independent Reviewer of Terrorism Legislation' [2012] *Parliamentary Affairs* 1, 10.

[143] Benton and Russell (n 24) 14.

[144] A Kavanagh, 'Constitutional Review, the Courts and Democratic Scepticism' (2009) 62 *Current Legal Problems* 102, 122, 123.

as we can tell, direct impact in terms of securing legislative amendment is relatively low. She strikes a note of caution which stems from 'the frank and often repeated acknowledgement by officials interviewed that a critical JCHR report, by itself, will not likely lead to substantial changes to a bill'.[145] This acknowledgement should not be swept aside and is a healthy counterpoint to a possible tendency amongst human rights lawyers to assume that since the JCHR reports provide excellent, well-argued and well-respected legal analysis of the relevant human rights issues, this will necessarily translate into legislative impact in the form of amendment or withdrawal of the offending legislative provision. This assumption is not warranted, as Hiebert's analysis shows.

Nonetheless, the JCHR is engaging in invaluable legislative scrutiny and is holding the Executive to account in multiple ways. Far from relying on a purely reactive role, the JCHR approaches its tasks in proactive and interactive ways. Sometimes the causal connection between its activities and resulting legislation is hard to establish definitively. The hope is that better scrutiny and better deliberation will lead ultimately to better legislation and that the efforts of the JCHR to enhance accountability and improve the quality of legislative deliberation will be instrumental to the ultimate goal of protecting rights. The JCHR seeks to achieve the ultimate daunting aim of enhancing rights-protection by fighting on a number of different fronts. A study which focuses exclusively or even primarily on securing Government amendments will not reveal various gains in accountability, scrutiny and deliberation, which, though instrumental to the ultimate aim, are also valuable in themselves. Nor will it pick up on, or give adequate credit for, the value of the post-legislative scrutiny carried out by the JCHR and its important follow-up work in pressing the Government to implement court judgments on human rights.

CONCLUSION

When the HRA was about to come into force, there was a lively discussion amongst legal scholars as to whether it would be one more nail in the coffin of the political constitution. Some commentators feared that 'institutions such as Parliament, the Ombudsman and others are likely to find it more difficult to make their scrutineering voices fully heard in the post-Human Rights Act legal order'.[146] The worry was that by 'locating the task of enforcing rights in the courts',[147] other more political methods of rights protection would be 'suffocated'.[148]

Fifteen years on, these predictions seem exaggerated at best. Much of the empirical evidence points in the opposite direction. Since 1998, the various Ombudsman offices have multiplied and strengthened.[149] Within government, section 19 HRA

---

[145] Hiebert (n 61) 40.
[146] A Tomkins, 'Introduction' in Campbell, Ewing and Tomkins (n 34) 9.
[147] ibid 9.
[148] ibid.
[149] See generally Kavanagh (n 1) 396–400; A Abraham, 'The Ombudsman and "Paths to Justice": A Just Alternative or Just an Alternative?' [2008] *Public Law* 1; A Abraham, 'The Ombudsman and Individual Rights' (2008) 61 *Parliamentary Affairs* 370.

has institutionalised a formal consideration of compatibility with Convention rights. In Parliament, the assiduous work of the JCHR has ensured that the Government now provides Parliament with more detailed information on its human rights reasoning than ever before. JCHR reports are now more widely cited and discussed in parliamentary debate than in the first years of its existence. Its reports and views are cited in the media and are often presented in a favourable light. JCHR guidance on implementing court judgments is being gradually mainstreamed into standard departmental business. At the very least, it seems that the JCHR is raising the political costs for governments that may wish to pass legislation with rights problems.

Many legal commentators believe that the quality of parliamentary engagement with human rights issues has improved to some degree in the last decade.[150] In fact, some of those who initially feared parliamentary emasculation post-HRA now argue that thanks to the 'persistent, challenging, and informed input from the United Kingdom's parliamentary Joint Committee on Human Rights', we are now experiencing 'more rigorous and evidence-based parliamentary debate than used to be the case'.[151] No doubt, there is still a long way to go in terms of enhancing parliamentary scrutiny and still a longer way to go in terms of getting governments to accept amendments to bills as they go through Parliament. The JCHR is neither complacent nor sanguine about the enormity of this task, but it deserves credit for helping Parliament to take steps in the right direction.

---

[150] Kavanagh (n 1) 382–85; C Gearty, 'Rethinking Civil Liberties in a Counterterrorism World' [2007] *European Human Rights Law Review* 115; C Gearty, '11 September 2001, Counter-Terrorism and the Human Rights Act' (2005) 32 *Journal of Law & Society* 18, 21; Feldman (n 2) 91ff; Feldman (n 10) 348.

[151] Tomkins (n 146) 6; KD Ewing, *Bonfire of the Liberties: New Labour, Human Rights and the Rule of Law* (Oxford, Oxford University Press, 2010) 275. From his study of parliamentary deliberation relating to control orders in the UK and Australia, Joo-Cheong Tham concludes that 'the contribution made by parliamentary committees is significantly enhancing the quality of parliamentary deliberation', Tham (n 80) 97.

7

The Impact of the Joint Committee on Human Rights on Legislative Deliberation

PAUL YOWELL

INTRODUCTION

THE MAIN AIM of this chapter is to provide an empirical analysis of how reports of the UK's Joint Committee on Human Rights (JCHR) were used in parliamentary debate from 2001 to 2010 and what impact they had on deliberative processes in Parliament. The analysis is based on a comprehensive study of references to JCHR reports by a research team.[1] Our analysis of impact on legislative deliberation includes several instances in which ministers have stated that, in response to JCHR proposals, the Government had adopted amendments to proposed bills or would issue guidance regarding the interpretation of legislation. Aside from collecting such concrete statements, however, our research did not attempt to make an overall assessment of the causal influence of the JCHR on legislative outcomes. The focus of our research was instead on debate and deliberation within Parliament. We began with quantitative questions such as these: how many times were JCHR reports discussed, by whom and in what context? Are JCHR reports used more frequently by the House of Commons or the House of Lords? Is there a correlation between use of JCHR reports and political party membership? More importantly, we considered qualitative questions concerning the purpose for which JCHR reports were cited, the ways in which JCHR reports affected the nature or quality of parliamentary debate about human rights, and the use of JCHR reports to identify concerns related to minority or marginalised groups. Our findings include the following:

— There was a dramatic increase in the use of JCHR reports in the 2005–10 Parliament (reports were cited 1,006 times in total and over 200 times in each of the first four years) in comparison to the 2001–05 Parliament (reports were cited fewer than 10 times per year).

---

[1] The research team was composed of Murray Hunt, Hayley J Hooper and Paul Yowell.

— JCHR reports were discussed more frequently and in greater depth in the House of Lords than in the House of Commons.
— On about 150 occasions, an MP referring to a JCHR report also cited specific empirical evidence contained in the report or that had been generated or collected by JCHR investigative processes.
— Over 60 per cent of all references to JCHR reports (about 600 in total) have to do with the interests of minority or marginalised groups. The range of such groups whose interests were represented in this way is wide; it includes immigrants, asylum-seekers, criminal and terrorist suspects, elderly people in care homes and many others.
— References to JCHR reports were distributed fairly evenly among Labour and Conservative MPs. Liberal Democrat MPs made significantly more references on average than Labour or Conservative MPs, mainly due to 11 high- and medium-frequency users who together accounted for about 25 per cent of all references to JCHR reports.
— References to JCHR reports helped to provoke robust, evidence-based deliberation and debate over human rights concerns. Most of the JCHR's 129 reports during the 2005–10 Parliament were cited at some point, and several were cited frequently and discussed in depth, particularly in the House of Lords.

I. METHODOLOGY

Our research sought to identify all the instances in which a Member of Parliament (MP) relied on a JCHR report in parliamentary proceedings or otherwise specifically represented or discussed the views or work of the JCHR. I call such instances 'substantive references to JCHR reports' (or in short form 'JCHR references').[2] Using a global search of an electronic database[3] and selection criteria to differentiate between substantive references to JCHR reports and instances in which the JCHR was mentioned in a non-substantive way,[4] we identified a total of 1,029 JCHR

---

[2] In a large majority of 'substantive references', a JCHR report is either cited or informs the content of the discussion; however, I also use the term for discussions of the work or views of the JCHR outside the context of a particular report.

[3] To find mentions of the JCHR, we searched the JUSTIS Parliament database maintained by Justis Publishing Ltd, London, with the following terms using Boolean logic: 'joint committee on human rights' or jchr or ('joint committee' within 1 'human rights').

[4] We define substantive references to JCHR reports as the subset of total mentions of the JCHR that meet one or more of the following relevance criteria:

— specific reference to the content of a JCHR report;
— reference to specific views or positions of the JCHR on particular issues, including members of the committee speaking explicitly or implicitly on behalf of the JCHR;
— commendation of a JCHR report;
— discussion of particular influence of JCHR on an issue;
— discussion of oral evidence given to the JCHR or written evidence gathered by the JCHR;
— reference to the JCHR's conclusion that a particular bill is or is not compatible with human rights, as well as references to the JCHR's silence on a bill to support an inference that the JCHR considers the bill to be compatible with human rights;
— discussion of amendments moved by or directly influenced by the JCHR or JCHR members' substantive Government responses to JCHR proposals, including discussion of action taken or that will be taken and promises to scrutinise a bill in the light of JCHR analysis.

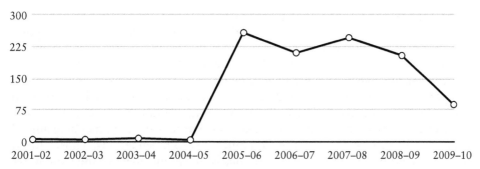

Figure 7.1: JCHR substantive references 2001–10

references in the 2001–05 and 2005–10 Parliaments. The mentions of the JCHR that do not count as substantive references by our criteria are not entirely irrelevant to understanding the role of the JCHR in Parliament during this period, but their relevance is marginal to this project.[5] The total number of substantive references to JCHR reports by parliamentary session is represented in Figure 7.1.

II. THE INCREASE IN SUBSTANTIVE REFERENCES IN THE 2005–10 PARLIAMENT

Figure 7.1 illustrates a dramatic increase in substantive references to JCHR reports in the 2005–10 Parliament over the 2001–05 Parliament. The number of references remained in single digits during each session of the 2001–05 Parliament, for a total of 23, but increased to over 200 references per session for the first four sessions of the 2005–10 Parliament, for a total of 1,006.[6] (The parliamentary sessions of 2004–05 and 2009–10 were short sessions compared to the others, with only about half the number of days in session, which explains why they curve in Figure 7.1 tails off in 2009–10.)

---

[5] According to our selection criteria, a substantive reference to a JCHR report did not include the following:

— mere acknowledgment of someone as a member of the JCHR, including a declaration of interest arising from such membership (however, identification of someone as a member of the JCHR that contextually implies a claim to speak on behalf or with the authority of the JCHR is counted as a substantive reference);
— general praise for or commendation of the work of the JCHR as a whole or of someone's participation in the JCHR (as opposed to discussion of the particular influence of the JCHR);
— indications that scrutiny of a bill by the JCHR will occur in the future;
— mere acknowledgment by the Government that a JCHR report will be considered as part of routine parliamentary procedure (however, specific promises of serious scrutiny in response to particular JCHR claims are counted as substantive references);
— mention of the JCHR as only one of a number of committees or other organisations that support a claim or conclusion or hold a view (however, if the JCHR is providing leadership among other groups, this is counted as a substantive reference).

[6] The number of references by term is given here in brackets following the year: 2001–02 (6); 2002–03 (5); 2003–04 (8); 2004–05 (4); 2005–06 (258); 2006–07 (210); 2007–08 (246); 2008–09 (204); 2009–10 (88).

There are a number of possible explanations for this significant increase. The Committee produced more reports in the 2005–10 Parliament (129 reports) than in 2001–05 (90 reports). However, since the number of reports was already high in 2001–05, this seems unlikely to account for much of the large disparity between the two terms. Of likely greater importance is that the Committee changed its working practices in 2006, partly in an attempt to make its work of more relevance to debate in Parliament, and in the Commons in particular.[7] One of the changes was the adoption of a deliberate strategy of recommending amendments to bills to give effect to the Committee's recommendations. Those amendments were often moved by some particularly active members of the Committee, resulting in more debate of the Committee's reports on the floor of both Houses. Furthermore, the bombings to the London transport system in July 2005 led to an increase in counter-terrorism legislation, which in turn led to an increase in debate over the human rights implications of such legislation. The JCHR produced several reports on these issues, and this raised its public profile and brought increased attention to its work. Whatever the cause of the increase, the relative abundance of JCHR references in 2005–10 compared to the paucity in 2001–05 led us to a decision to focus our further quantitative and qualitative analysis on the 2005–10 Parliament.

III. HOW ARE JCHR REPORTS USED IN PARLIAMENT?

A. Types of Reference

We classified the 1,006 substantive references to JCHR reports in 2005–10 according to seven types of use indicated in Figure 7.2. The primary activity of the JCHR is legislative scrutiny. Every Government bill is reviewed by the JCHR for compatibility with human rights,[8] and the JCHR produced 129 reports in the 2005–10 session, most of them involving detailed review of bills. About 60 per cent of substantive references to JCHR reports involve legislative scrutiny of various kinds, including proposing: (i) amendments to bills or existing law; (ii) the rejection of provisions in bills (in the absence of revision); and, occasionally, (iii) the repeal of existing law.

---

[7] See 23rd Report of 2005/06, The Committee's Future Working Practices, HL 239/HC 1575.
[8] Statement of Andrew Dismore, 7 December 2006.

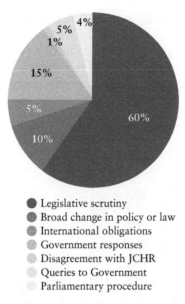

● Legislative scrutiny
● Broad change in policy or law
◐ International obligations
◔ Government responses
◌ Disagreement with JCHR
○ Queries to Government
○ Parliamentary procedure

Figure 7.2: Types of reference

In addition to legislative scrutiny, the JCHR conducts general studies of areas where there are concerns about human rights abuses, as reflected, for example, in reports on deaths in custody,[9] human trafficking[10] and the human rights of older people in care homes.[11] These and similar reports include recommendations regarding broad changes in policy and law, or the adoption of new policies or laws. About 10 per cent of references to JCHR reports are in this category. Another five per cent of references concern the international dimension of human rights obligations, such as an argument that the UK should do more to implement a human rights treaty or ratify a treaty. About 15 per cent of references involve responses by ministers or other Government representatives to JCHR concerns, and another five per cent involve queries to Government representatives in which a JCHR report or concerns are mentioned (often using the procedural form of a written or oral question).

In about five per cent of cases, someone discusses disagreement with the JCHR. Most of these instances are in Government responses (disagreement with the JCHR accounts for roughly one-third of Government responses), and when this occurs the two categories overlap. Only about one per cent of JCHR references concern disagreement expressed outside of a Government response.[12] Finally, about four per cent of references involve points about the nature and function of parliamentary scrutiny for human rights compatibility, including matters such as the time available for debating bills, the role and aims of the JCHR, and the general institutional framework in which scrutiny occurs.

---

[9] 3rd Report of 2004/05, Deaths in Custody, HL 15-I/HC 137-I, HL 15-II/HC 137-II.
[10] 26th Report of 2005/06, Human Trafficking, HL 245/HC 1127-I, II.
[11] 18th Report of 2006/07, The Human Rights of Older People in Healthcare, HL 156-I, II/HC 378-I, II.
[12] The 'Disagreement with JCHR' component in Figure 7.2 (one per cent) depicts disagreement only when it occurs outside a Government response.

B. In Which Contexts are JCHR Reports Referred to?

Figure 7.3 below provides a count of the contexts in which JCHR reports are most frequently referred to. (The total count of references in the table is greater than the actual number of references because some involve more than one context.)

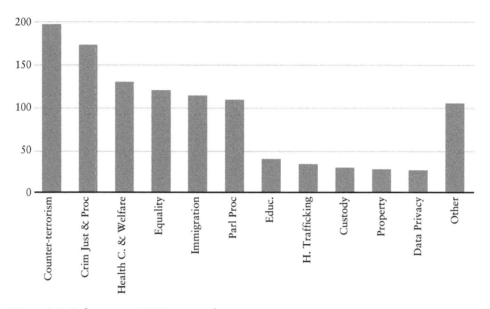

Figure 7.3: References to JCHR reports by topic

The most common contexts are: (1) counter-terrorism; and (2) criminal justice and procedure. Other common subject areas are: (3) health care and welfare; (4) equality and discrimination; (5) immigration, deportation and asylum; and (6) the institutional framework of human rights scrutiny. Each of these is involved in more than 100 references. Other subject areas in which JCHR references occur with some frequency are: (7) education and schools; (8) human trafficking; (9) treatment in custody; (10) property and housing rights; and (11) data privacy. The 'Other' entry in the table includes the following: identity cards; labour and employment; protests and free speech; financial regulation; local government; prohibition of smoking; elections and voting; family law; charities and trusts; business, commerce and licensing; euthanasia and assisted suicide; planning and environment; tax and revenue.

C. Positive and Negative Rights

The JCHR embraces the idea that human rights entail both negative and positive obligations on the state. A majority of JCHR references could be classified in the first category, particularly in the areas of counter-terrorism and criminal justice and procedure, because they concern arguments on such matter as limitations on the legitimate sphere of state action and the procedures that must be followed before depriving someone of liberty or imposing punishment or liability in the context of criminal or civil justice.

A large minority of references, however, make claims regarding the state's positive duties. It is difficult to provide an exact quantification of this, both because the boundary between a positive and negative duty is not always clear, and because some human rights span both categories. The right to equality, for example, can involve both negative duties on the state not to discriminate and positive duties to improve access to services and opportunities for disadvantaged groups. The JCHR's commitment to this positive dimension of human rights is seen not only in the hundreds of substantive references to JCHR reports in areas such as health care and welfare, equality, education and schools, human trafficking, and housing and property rights (see Figure 7.3), but also in several statements by JCHR representatives and in reports that overtly reflect this understanding of rights. For example, the JCHR's report on corporate manslaughter and homicide[13] notes the wording of Article 2(1) of the European Convention on Human Rights (ECHR), which provides that 'Everyone's right to life shall be protected by law' and endorses the European Court of Human Rights' interpretation of this as laying down a 'positive obligation on states to take appropriate steps to safeguard the lives of those within its jurisdiction'.[14] This positive obligation is emphasised in several places in the report and, in the JCHR's view, it includes a duty 'to secure the right to life by putting in place effective criminal law provisions to deter the commission of offences against the person', which should be backed up by effective law enforcement.[15] The positive obligation includes an obligation to protect individuals against threats to their life not only from the state, but from the actions of other private individuals.[16] In the context of scrutiny of counter-terrorism legislation, Andrew Dismore frequently framed his contributions to the debates by stating that the starting point was the state's positive obligation to protect its citizens and the whole community arising from the right to life.[17] He stated that the JCHR's 10 reports on counter-terrorism policy in the 2007–08 Parliament 'all start from the same basic premise in human rights law: the state's positive obligation to protect us all from terrorism and violence, and the state's duty to prosecute those who are guilty and to make that prosecution more effective.'[18] References to JCHR reports have also addressed the state's positive human rights obligations in a variety of other contexts, such as human trafficking[19] and protection of children in immigration.[20]

---

[13] 27th Report of 2005/06, Legislative Scrutiny: Corporate Manslaughter and Corporate Homicide Bill, HL 246/HC 1625.

[14] ibid 7 (citing *LCB v UK* (1998) 27 EHRR 212 [36]; *Paul and Audrey Edwards v UK* (2002) 35 EHRR 19).

[15] 27th Report of 2005/06 (n 13).

[16] ibid.

[17] Eg, Statements of Andrew Dismore on 21 February 2008, 11 June 2008 and 1 March 2010.

[18] Statement of Andrew Dismore, 1 April 2008. His statement on 11 June 2008 makes the same point.

[19] Statement of the Earl of Onslow, 1 July 2009.

[20] Statement of Damian Green, 1 July 2009, which quotes reference to the state's positive obligations to children in the JCHR's 19th Report of 2003/04, Children Bill, HL 161/HC 537.

D. Modes of Argumentation in JCHR References

There are a number of modes of argumentation when JCHR reports are referred to in parliamentary debates. Often the JCHR report is used to identify the main human rights issue raised by a particular bill. Some arguments engage directly with the justifications for a provision in a bill, offering critical analysis of its substance and potential effects, in a way that resembles legislative scrutiny in other contexts. Many references cite the ECHR or other human rights sources, and many others refer to individual rights without citing any specific textual sources. Only a few references employ argumentation based explicitly on case law. In a significant proportion of references, an MP discusses evidence that was received by the JCHR during committee meetings or investigation. Many references employ elements of the standard proportionality inquiry either explicitly or implicitly as part of the critical analysis of a bill, sometimes discussing the extent of a bill's interference with a right, analysing the Government's justifications for the legislation and considering whether there are less restrictive alternatives. The role played by the JCHR report is often to frame this debate and also to inform it by not only identifying the appropriate questions to ask from a human rights perspective, but analysing the adequacy of the Government's response to those questions.

The extent to which JCHR reports are referred to in such debates ranges widely from brief, general references to extensive, detailed discussion of proposed amendments and the reasons for those amendments. In section V below I consider the use of legal sources and other modes of argumentation in more detail, as part of a more general evaluative assessment of references to JCHR reports and the contextual parliamentary debate.

E. Representation of Marginal Groups and Vulnerable People

About 60 per cent of JCHR references involve speaking on behalf of members of minority or marginalised groups in society, or people who are vulnerable, weak or less well-off. The Chair of the JCHR during the 2005–10 Parliament, Andrew Dismore MP, drew a distinction between: (1) 'unpopular minority groups' or 'people on the fringes of society for whom public sympathy is low or non-existent'; and (2) 'vulnerable persons in the mainstream'.[21] This was in the context of introducing the JCHR's report on the human rights of older people in health care,[22] which he gave as an example of the second category. These distinctions should not be taken as mutually exclusive. Nonetheless, the two categories can be used to classify a range of JCHR references, and they provide some insight into how the JCHR understood its role between 2001 and 2010 and how it was perceived in Parliament. Baroness Stern, for example, describes concern for the 'vulnerable and powerless' as a motivation for the JCHR.[23] Ivan Lewis, a Government minister at the time, spoke of the

---

[21] HC Deb 13 March 2008, vol 472, col 115.
[22] 18th Report of 2006/07 (n 11).
[23] HL Deb 29 April 2008, vol 701, col 36.

need for 'championing unfashionable causes',[24] and Andrew Dismore has stated that the JCHR 'embraces the universality of human rights by examining and reporting on popular and unpopular causes alike'.[25]

The 'vulnerable people in the mainstream' on whose behalf the JCHR has spoken include the elderly, residents of care homes and public housing, children, welfare recipients, teenage mothers, young offenders and those with addictions. The minority and marginal groups for whom the JCHR has provided representation include asylum-seekers, immigrants and people in various stages of immigration proceedings (including deportation), the gypsy and traveller communities, refugees, victims of human trafficking, criminal suspects and criminals, suspected terrorists, suspected members of youth gangs, HIV/AIDS sufferers, members of minority religions, and various national and ethnic minorities.

The characteristic that seems to be most distinctive of the use of JCHR reports in Parliament is providing representation for a wide range of minorities, marginal groups and vulnerable persons. Hanna Pitkin has distinguished 'standing for' representation, wherein a representative shares characteristics of the represented group (such as ethnicity, class, gender, religion and age), from 'acting for' representation, wherein a representative speaks and acts on behalf of the interests of the represented group.[26] In this latter sense of representation, the JCHR provided an active voice in the 2005–10 Parliament for many kinds of minority groups, as shown in the description above. The wide range bears out Andrew Dismore's description of the JCHR as being 'prepared to stand up for less popular, often demonised, groups who do not have the ear of the media or general public sympathy',[27] and the extensive use made of such reports shows that Parliament as a whole was receptive to being informed in this way.

There were around 600 total references that involved discussion of the interests of minorities and vulnerable persons. This finding—and the debates in which these references occur—should be of interest to scholars of legislative activity as well as to those who study political institutions more generally, judicial review of legislation and the theory of democracy. Further study will need to be done to gauge the overall impact and effectiveness of the activity of the JCHR and the use of its reports in Parliament in the area of minority interests, but, as shown below, the present study concludes that this activity achieved a number of discrete results in the 2005–10 Parliament in terms of amendment of legislation. Aside from measurable impact, the fact that the JCHR was able to provide representation for many different minority and marginal groups, and to make substantial contributions to parliamentary debate, challenges the assumptions and conclusions of some theorists about the nature of legislative decision-making and of democratically elected bodies.

A longstanding concern in constitutional and political theory is that electoral systems and legislatures are structured to give effect to preferences or interests of

---

[24] HC Deb 13 March 2008, vol 472, col 140.
[25] HC Deb 13 March 2008, vol 472, col 115. See also Andrew Dismore, HC Deb 1 July 2009, vol 495, cols 316–18 ('It is often said that human rights are all about unpopular causes').
[26] H Pitkin, *The Concept of Representation* (Berkeley, University of California Press, 1967) 144.
[27] HC Deb 19 February 2007, vol 457, cols 82–83.

the majority, to the neglect of minority groups. Ronald Dworkin has argued that legislatures are systematically biased against minority interests because representatives must, in order to be re-elected, side with the majority 'in any serious argument about the rights of a minority against it'.[28] Dworkin argues that courts should have power to review—and strike down—legislation because judges do not face electoral pressures and are thus better situated to protect minority interests.[29] Some have gone further, claiming that due to the political incentives facing legislatures, they are not well-positioned institutionally to engage in principled decision-making or to make disinterested judgments,[30] or to give reasons for their decisions.[31] Others have come to the defence of legislatures with regard to their capacity for reasoned debate and ability to give due regard to minority interests, and the legitimacy of majority voting as a way to resolve disagreement.[32] The debate has carried on, with one recent entrant arguing that the problem with legislatures is not so much one of systematic bias against minorities as one of oversight, which may be due to lack of time and rushed decisions.[33] A common thread to many criticisms of the legislature is to assume that its perceived failures need to be remedied by an outside force, with the most eligible institution being that of courts. The JCHR's demonstrated capacity to bring issues about minority rights to the attention of Parliament and the time that members of the House of Lords in particular have been able to devote to sustained, detailed scrutiny of bills suggest that if there are deficiencies in the legislative process, there are means of addressing them by internal measures and structures. Moreover, as mentioned above and discussed in more detail below, the JCHR's arguments regarding minority rights (and other issues) often draw the Government into dialogue in which both sides give reasons for their decisions. This does not entail that judicial power to review legislation for human rights compatibility is not needed, but it does suggest that some criticisms of the legislative process as intrinsically ill-suited for principled debate and consideration of minority interests are exaggerated.

[28] R Dworkin, *Law's Empire* (Cambridge, MA, Harvard University Press, 1986) 375.
[29] ibid.
[30] Eg, D Otter, *Judicial Review in an Age of Moral Pluralism* (Cambridge, Cambridge University Press, 2011) 19–20, 310–11; O Fiss, 'Between Supremacy and Exclusivity' in R Bauman and T Kahana (eds), *The Least Examined Branch* (Cambridge, Cambridge University Press, 2006) 452, 464. Fiss states the legislatures are charged either with enacting the will of electors or 'promoting some public policy', using policy in the sense that Dworkin did when he distinguished it from principle. Dworkin states that judicial review of legislation is needed to ensure that 'the most fundamental issues of political morality will finally be set out and debated as issues of principle and not political power alone, a transformation that cannot succeed, in any case not fully, within the legislature itself': *A Matter of Principle* (Cambridge, MA, Harvard University Press, 1985) 70.
[31] See Otter (n 30) 310.
[32] J Waldron, *Law and Disagreement* (Oxford, Oxford University Press 1999); 'A Rights-based Critique of Constitutional Rights' (1993) 13 *OJLS* 18;'The Core of the Case against Judicial Review' (2006) 115 *Yale LJ* 1346; R Bellamy, *Political Constitutionalism* (Cambridge, Cambridge University Press 2007) 241 ('most legislation is not the product of a homogeneous majority imposing its will upon a constituent minority, but of a series of compromises brokered by winning coalitions of different minorities').
[33] See R Dixon, 'A Democratic Theory of Constitutional Comparison' (2008) 56 *American Journal of Comparative Law* 947, 967.

IV. WHO USES JCHR REPORTS?

Our research found that use of JCHR reports among MPs was widely distributed, but that many references were narrowly concentrated among a set of *high-frequency* and *medium-frequency* users. High-frequency users are those with 30 or more references. Medium-frequency users are those with 5–29 substantive references. (The abbreviations HF and MF are used in the tables below to indicate high- and medium-frequency users respectively.) Responses by Government representatives to the JCHR were counted in our research as substantive references. Such responses include indications that the Government has amended a bill or plans to amend a bill or issue interpretative guidance; promises by the Government to scrutinise a bill in the light of specific JCHR concerns; and, occasionally, statements disagreeing with the JCHR. The great majority of substantive references supported or reflected the position of the JCHR, but, not surprisingly, some references were opposed to the position of the JCHR. In either case it is clear that the work of the JCHR has provoked debate in Parliament about human rights. From the total of 1,006 substantive JCHR references

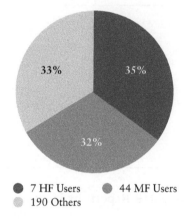

Figure 7.4: References of category by user

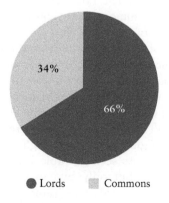

Figure 7.5: Total references in each House

in the 2005–10 Parliament, 241 MPs made at least one reference. There were seven high-frequency users. Two are members of the House of Commons: Andrew Dismore, MP for Hendon and Chair of the JCHR for the 2005–10 Parliament; and Dr Evan Harris, MP for Oxford West and Abingdon and member of the JCHR from 2005 to 2010. The remaining five were members of the House of Lords: Lord Lester of Herne Hill; Lord Judd; Baroness Stern; Lord Avebury; and the Earl of Onslow.

Of the seven high-frequency users, six were members of the JCHR: only Lord Avebury was not. There is a low correlation, however, between JCHR membership and being a medium-frequency user. There were 36 medium-frequency users, only two of whom served on the Committee (Lord Dubs and Lord Morris). High-frequency users contributed 352 references and medium-frequency users contributed 317 (see Table 7.1 and Figure 7.4). Together high-frequency and medium-frequency users accounted for 669 of the 1006 total references to JCHR reports, or 66 per cent.

Table 7.1: High-frequency users

Member	Refs.
Andrew Dismore	80
Lord Lester of Herne Hill	66
Lord Judd	48
Evan Harris	47
Baroness Stern	45
Lord Avebury	36
Earl of Onslow	30
Total	352

A. Comparison of Users of JCHR Reports by House

References to JCHR reports were significantly more frequent in the House of Lords than in the House of Commons. The Lords contributed 667 references or 66 per cent of the total, while the Commons contributed 339 references or 34 per cent (see Figure 7.5). Of the total of 241 MPs who made at least one reference, 133 of these were from the House of Lords and 108 from the House of Commons.

Of the interventions in the Commons, 128 interventions (38 per cent of the total) were by the two high-frequency users, Andrew Dismore MP (with 80) and Dr Evan Harris MP (with 48). There were eight medium-frequency users in the Commons contributing another 14 per cent of the total; together, the 10 high- and medium-frequency users accounted for about half (51 per cent) of all references in the Commons.

The House of Lords had significantly more high- and medium-frequency users than the House of Commons. As seen in Table 7.1 above, there were five high-frequency users in the Lords, but only two in the Commons. There were 28 medium-frequency users in the Lords (see Table 7.2 below), but only eight in the Commons. Combined, the high- and medium-frequency users in the Lords contributed 74 per cent of the total references in that chamber. In the Commons JCHR references were more widely distributed; the high- and medium-frequency users contributed only 51 per cent of references in that chamber.

The sizeable contingent of 33 high- and medium-frequency users in the House of Lords contributed to a distinctive kind of engagement with JCHR reports and debate about human rights. The substantive references involving these users were generally longer and more detailed than references in the House of Commons (except for the references by the two high-frequency users there). Debates in the House of Lords often involved two, three or more members successively making a number of points based on JCHR reports and entering into dialogue with Government representatives and other members about human rights issues. This kind of sustained debate on human rights occurred less frequently in the House of Commons.

B. Comparison of Use of JCHR Reports by Political Party

Table 7.2 below provides information on numbers of references to JCHR reports by party affiliation of MPs. To calculate a party's strength within Parliament, we took the sum of (1) seats that parties took in the 2005 election and (2) number of seats the parties hold in the House of Lords in January 2012. The latter is used as a proxy for party strength in the House of Lords from 2005–10, which would be difficult to quantify exactly due to the changing membership of the House of Lords. Accounting for party strength in this way allowed us to calculate, in addition to gross totals of substantive references, what percentage of members of a given party made use of JCHR reports and how frequently that occurred relative to the party's number of seats in Parliament. The distribution of references across the three major parties and cross-benchers in Lords is as follows: Labour 413, Liberal Democrats 296, Conservatives 183 and cross-benchers 101.

Table 7.2: Use of JCHR reports by political party

Party	No of seats	Refs	Party members making refs	Members making refs as percentage of party	No of refs per party seat
Labour	594	413	103	17 per cent	0.70
Conservative	416	183	63	15 per cent	0.44
Liberal Democrat	153	296	46	30 per cent	1.93
Cross-Bench	186	101	23	12 per cent	0.54
Bishop	25	9	4	16 per cent	0.36
Plaid Cymru	4	3	1	25 per cent	0.75
Independent	1	1	1	100 per cent	1.00

154   *Paul Yowell*

The Liberal Democrats had substantially more members who made references as a percentage of the party (30 per cent) than Labour (17 per cent) or the Conservatives (15 per cent). The Liberal Democrats also had substantially more references per party seat (1.93) than Labour (0.70) or the Conservatives (0.44). However, 50 per cent of all Liberal Democrat references were by just three members: Dr Evan Harris, Lord Lester and Lord Avebury. And 80 per cent of all Liberal Democrat references were by their three high-frequency and eight medium-frequency users. The distribution of references is broader for Labour (64 per cent of party's references by high- and medium-frequency users) and the Conservatives (52 per cent of party's references by high- and medium-frequency users). Figures 7.6 and 7.7 below depict total references by party—and the distribution within the party of high- and medium-frequency users and others—for the House of Commons (Figure 7.6) and House of Lords (Figure 7.7).

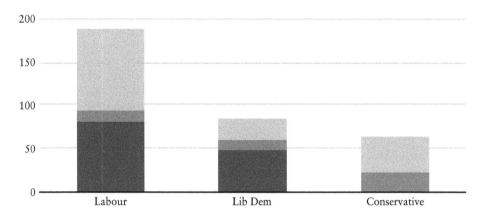

Figure 7.6: Refs by party, showing MF and HF users (House of Commons)

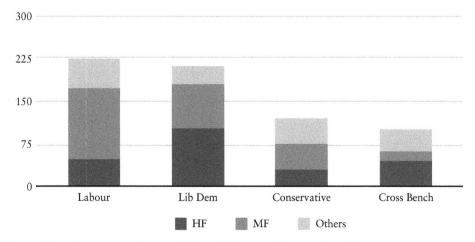

Figure 7.7: Refs by party, showing MF and HF users (House of Lords)

Table 7.3: Use of JCHR reports by chamber and political party

Party	Refs	No. of HF users	Refs by HF users	HF users as percentage of party	No of MF users	Refs by MF users	MF users as percentage of party	HF+MF users as percentage of party
Labour	413	2	128	31 per cent	16	138	33 per cent	64 per cent
Conservative	183	1	30	16 per cent	8	66	36 per cent	52 per cent
Liberal Democrat	296	3	149	50 per cent	8	90	30 per cent	81 per cent
Cross Bench	101	1	45	45 per cent	3	17	17 per cent	61 per cent
Bishop	9	—	—	—	1	6	5 per cent	67 per cent

Table 7.3 provides the figures reflected in Figures 7.6 and 7.7, but combined for both the House of Lords and the House of Commons.

In comparing interventions by the Labour Party to other parties, it should be noted that Labour's total was increased by the fact that responses to the JCHR, which we have counted as substantive references, were by Labour Government representatives. Such responses amount to about 15 per cent of the Labour total. If Labour's total references are reduced by 15 per cent to 350, then Labour interventions are 0.59 per party seat as compared to 0.44 for Conservatives. This suggests that Labour and the Conservatives are approaching parity in terms of references per party seat when accounting for references specifically owing to the fact that there was a Labour Government in 2005–10; moreover, as indicated above, Labour and the Conservatives are also near parity in the percentage of party members making use of JCHR reports. The Liberal Democrats substantially exceed the two larger parties on these measures, owing primarily to the activity of their three high-frequency and eight medium-frequency users.

V. EVALUATING THE EFFECT OF JCHR REPORTS ON LEGISLATIVE DELIBERATION

A principal aim of our research project was to evaluate parliamentary deliberation with respect to arguments referring to JCHR reports and the effect of the work of the JCHR on debate about human rights. We relied on an evaluative framework comprising five main considerations:

1. What use was made, explicitly or implicitly, of human rights sources in the debate?
2. What use was made, explicitly or implicitly, of the concept of proportionality?
3. Has the work of the JCHR led the Government to provide more detailed justification for laws and policies affecting human rights?

4. Has the work of the JCHR framed, stimulated or influenced debate in Parliament?
5. Has the work of the JCHR led to more informed debate in Parliament?

A. Use of Human Rights Sources

The use of legal sources relates in particular to the JCHR's task of advising Parliament regarding its obligations to comply with human rights instruments both in domestic and international law, as well as with judgments of the European Court of Human Rights. Beyond this, the JCHR has sought to draw attention to human rights as providing a general framework for legislative and governmental activity and of promoting certain values and interests that might otherwise be overlooked. The Universal Declaration of Human Rights states that every organ of society should strive 'to promote respect for these rights and freedoms and by progressive measures, national and international, to secure their universal and effective recognition and observance'.[34] In keeping with this, several MPs have referred to concepts such as a 'human rights culture', a 'human rights ethos'[35] or a 'human rights-based approach',[36] and Baroness Stern has said that the 'human rights framework has considerable importance in structuring the ethos of public life in this country'.[37] Baroness Wilkins echoed these views, adding that the core principles of human rights are autonomy, dignity and equality.[38]

About 20 per cent of parliamentary references to JCHR reports include express citation of at least one human rights instrument, with several citing more than one. The great majority of these citations are to the ECHR or the Human Rights Act 1998. There were 17 citations to the UN Convention on the Rights of the Child and nine to the UN Convention against Torture—relatively low numbers compared to references to the ECHR. Beyond these, the frequency of citation of other instruments tails off, but several other human rights sources are cited on occasion, including the Universal Declaration on Human Rights 1948, the UN Convention on the Rights of Persons with Disabilities, the UN Convention and Protocol Relating to the Status of Refugees, the European Convention on Action against Trafficking in Human Beings, the European Convention for the Prevention of Torture, and the International Convention on the Protection of the Rights of All Migrant Workers and Members of Their Families.

Citation of these sources is generally used to frame a debate or to indicate a particular value or values at stake, in many cases preliminary to evidence-based argument or application of the principle of proportionality. Human rights instruments

---

[34] United Nations Universal Declaration of Human Rights, Preamble.
[35] Lord Darzi, HL Deb 21 April 2008, vol 700, col 246.
[36] Sandra Gidley, HC Deb 18 February 2008, vol 472, col 52.
[37] HL Deb 29 April 2008, vol 701, cols 47–49.
[38] HL Deb 29 April 2008, vol 701, col 51.

are not typically used in rule-like fashion to contend directly for a particular conclusion without further argument based in law, policy or evidence.

About 100 of the JCHR references included citation to a court judgment. In a number of these, the JCHR proposed amendments to bills or existing law to comply with rulings against the UK in the European Court of Human Rights or declarations of incompatibility by a UK court under section 4 of the Human Rights Act. Parliamentary debates on counter-terrorism measures frequently included JCHR references, and several of these cited the 2004 *Belmarsh* decision in the House of Lords and other cases on the compatibility of such measures with human rights.[39] Citations to judgments by the Strasbourg Court in cases involving the UK covered a range of topics.[40] In another category, JCHR references cited cases as authority for a general position regarding how a right should be interpreted or a conclusion on a particular issue regarding human rights.[41] Finally, some references involved citation of a case where the JCHR disagreed with the court's interpretation of the law on an issue related to human rights protection and sought legislative reform in order to counter the effect of the judgment in question.[42]

Some have questioned the effectiveness and propriety of legalistic argument in parliamentary debate. One author has criticised the JCHR's contributions to the debate over control orders, for example, as being too legalistic, and contends that such arguments bring about 'democratic debilitation' by limiting access to debates about human rights to those who have legal expertise.[43] Bridget Prentice MP took a different view of the effect of JCHR contributions. She observed that 'Human rights matters are sometimes perceived as arguments that are best left to lawyers and judges' and are dealt with more commonly in the House of Lords, but added that amendments proposed by JCHR members in the Commons 'put human rights on the agenda of the elected House—where they belong, at the heart of our democratic process'.[44]

JCHR reports generally combine legal argumentation with other kinds of argument, and on the whole were well received by both Houses of Parliament. Many

---

[39] *A v Home Secretary (Belmarsh)* [2004] UKHL 56; *Home Secretary v AF (No 3)* [2009] UKHL 28; *A v UK* [2009] ECHR 301.

[40] *S and Marper v UK* (2009) 48 EHRR 50 (retention of DNA samples); *Aslef v UK* App No 11002/05 (27 May 2007) (the power of labour unions to expel members); *Connors v UK* (2005) 40 EHRR 9 (rights of gypsy and traveller communities); *Grieves v UK* (2004) 39 EHRR 8 (court martial). A debate in the House of Lords on the Government's response to adverse human rights judgments in general included references to *Hirst v UK* (2006) 42 EHRR 41 (blanket prohibition on prisoner voting ruled inconsistent with the principle of free elections) and *Dickson v UK* (2006) 46 EHRR 419 (right of a prisoner and his spouse to artificial insemination facilities).

[41] Eg, *DH and others v Czech Republic* (2008) 47 EHRR 3, cited for the proposition that the need for the state to take positive action is a necessary element in the right to equality. See Lord Lester, HL Deb 9 February 2010, vol 717, col 650–53.

[42] An example of such a case is *YL v Birmingham City Council* [2007] UKHL 27. The JCHR sought to broaden the definition of public authority beyond the interpretation adopted by the House of Lords in that case.

[43] Joo-Cheong Tham, 'Parliamentary Deliberation and the National Security Executive: The Case of Control Orders' [2010] *Public Law* 79, 101.

[44] HC Deb 3 July 2009, vol 495, cols 657–58.

of the references to JCHR reports show that what the report has done is to provide
a framework within which parliamentary debate about human rights can take
place, advising, for example, about the evidential questions that it is necessary to
settle, rather than purporting to prescribe particular outcomes or rule out particular
options. Many references included commendation of and appreciation for JCHR
reports by non-JCHR members, and there were only isolated expressions of criticism
of the JCHR.

B. Use of Proportionality

The proportionality inquiry is often associated with adjudication in human
rights cases in the UK, but proportionality can also be taken into account in the
process of law and policy-making.[45] Evaluating Government bills by reference
to proportionality standards has been regarded as a continual responsibility of
the JCHR according to Andrew Dismore.[46] In the references to JCHR reports,
there are numerous explicit mentions of proportionality, as well as to 'necessity'
and 'balancing' as components of the proportionality inquiry. Apart from such
explicit mentions, there are many implicit uses of proportionality-style reasoning,
for example, when members probe Government ministers about alternatives to
proposed measures that would have a lesser burden on the right in question, or
when members engage in evaluative argument that involves weighing the value of
legislative proposals against their effects on rights-protected interests. Examples
of proposed measures that were objected to in debate on grounds of their disproportionality include provisions in the Identity Cards Bill 2005 that could result in
disclosure of private information in a way that disproportionately interferes with
the right to private life,[47] a strict liability offence for paying for a prostitute in the
Policing and Crime Bill 2009[48] and the crime of glorification of terrorism in the
Terrorism Bill 2005.[49]

C. Has the Work of the JCHR Framed, Stimulated or
   Influenced Debate in Parliament?

The extent to which the work of the JCHR has stimulated debate in Parliament can
be gauged partly by the number of substantive references to JCHR reports (1,006)
identified by our study. It seemed clear to us that on the whole, these references,
and the arguments based on them, are taken seriously in Parliament. There are

---

[45] R Ekins, 'Legislating Proportionately' in G Huscroft, B Miller and G Webber (eds), *Proportionality and the Rule of Law: Rights, Justification, Reasoning* (Cambridge, Cambridge University Press 2014).
[46] HC Deb 7 December 2006, vol 454, cols 159–61.
[47] Earl of Northesk, HL Deb 14 December 2005, vol 676, cols 1350–52.
[48] Evan Harris, HC Deb 19 May 2009, vol 492, cols 1423–6.
[49] Lord Lester, HL Deb 5 December 2005, vol 676, cols 439–40.

many instances in which Government ministers and non-members of the JCHR commend JCHR reports for their quality and for making important contributions to the debate. In many references, non-members of the JCHR urge others to read a particular report.

There were several debates in the 2005–10 Parliament that included extensive discussion of a JCHR report. These include most prominently debates over various bills relating to counter-terrorism measures, touching on topics including the period of pre-charge detention for terrorism suspects, control orders, deportation that could result in torture of the suspect, and the use of evidence obtained by torture. Other bills in which JCHR reports figured prominently in debate are the Identity Cards Bill, the Criminal Justice and Immigration Bill, the UK Borders Bill and the Health and Social Bill. JCHR reports were also used extensively in discussions and debates in Parliament outside of proposed bills, for example, on human trafficking, the treatment of the elderly and others in nursing and care homes, and the problems facing adults with learning disabilities. Table 7.4 is a list of 10 frequently cited JCHR reports.

Table 7.4: Frequently cited JCHR reports

10 frequently cited JCHR reports
3rd Report of 2004/05, Deaths in Custody
5th Report of 2004/05, Identity Cards Bill
3rd Report of 2005/06, Counter-Terrorism Policy and Human Rights: Terrorism Bill and Related Matters
26th Report of 2005/2006, Human Trafficking
10th Report of 2006/07, The Treatment of Asylum Seekers
13th Report of 2006/07, Legislative Scrutiny: Sixth Progress Report
18th Report of 2006/07, The Human Rights of Older People in Healthcare
5th Report of 2007/08, Legislative Scrutiny: Criminal Justice and Immigration Bill
7th Report of 2007/08, A Life Like Any Other? Human Rights of Adults with Learning Disabilities
26th Report of 2008/2009, Legislative Scrutiny: Equality Bill

The selection above is just some of the more prominent cases. Over 100 different JCHR reports were referred to in the 2005–10 Parliament, which includes most of the 129 reports the JCHR produced in 2005–10 (and includes some reports produced during the prior Parliament).

D. Has the Work of the JCHR Led to More Informed Debate in Parliament?

The JCHR receives a great deal of evidence on human rights issues from government officials, law-makers, academics and others, and gathers other evidence of various kinds. The JCHR makes much of this information publicly available by publishing oral and written evidence on its website, as well as by including highlights and summaries of evidence in its reports. About 150 of the JCHR references identified in the study discuss evidence generated by the JCHR, and around half of these references are by non-members of the JCHR, suggesting that the efforts of the JCHR in this area are having some influence on parliamentarians who are not members of the Committee. Most of the discussions of evidence generated by the JCHR occur in references we have classified as legislative scrutiny or proposals for broad change in law or policy, or concerning the UK's international human rights obligations. About 20 per cent of all such references involve argument based on evidence produced through the efforts of the JCHR.

E. Has the Work of the JCHR Led the Government to Provide More Detailed Justification for Laws and Policies Affecting Human Rights?

When arguments based on JCHR reports are made in Parliament, this very frequently results in a Government minister or representative providing a substantive response. Indeed, about 15 per cent of all JCHR references identified in our study involve the Government responding to an issue raised by the JCHR. Another five per cent of references are those in which use has been made of the procedural mechanism of oral or written questions to elicit a response from the Government involving a point raised by the JCHR. The debate is often carried out in a way that suggests that both sides are taking seriously the potential consequences of legislation and the way in which it will affect human rights. When Government ministers express disagreement with the JCHR, which occurs in roughly one-third of its references, they often explain their reasons in detail and provide information to support their conclusion. This kind of exchange, however, occurs more frequently in the House of Lords than in the House of Commons.

The Government often agrees with points raised by the JCHR, at least in part. The next section discusses those instances in which references indicate that the Government has agreed to amend a bill or to issue guidance regarding interpretation or application of the law as a result of a JCHR recommendation. In some cases the Government indicates a measure of agreement with a JCHR point, but explains why it does not agree with a proposed amendment.[50] In other cases the Government promises to consider a JCHR recommendation or criticism and give further scrutiny to a bill. It can sometimes be difficult to distinguish between a serious promise and

---

[50] Eg, Baroness Scotland, HL Deb, 13 July 2005, vol 673, cols 1145–46. Here Baroness Scotland expressed agreement with the JCHR that the wording in a section of the Equality Bill was too wide, but said that the Government did not agree with the JCHR's amendment. She added that 'we will continue to give thought to the matter [and] try to come back with something that meets our joint purpose'.

mere politeness, but there are several instances which suggest that the Government gives weight to JCHR reports. Lord West, in a statement representative of several others, promises scrutiny related to a JCHR report on counter-terrorism policy:

> The first thing that I should say on the Joint Committee on Human Rights is how welcome is the huge amount of very valuable work that it does. I am not saying that the Government agree with every single thing in the report, but it raises the right sort of issues that we need to look at. We will look in detail at a number of those and come back when we have done so with a response to the various points.[51]

As Baroness Ashton put it, the JCHR gives advice which is not always welcome to the Government, but is nonetheless important.[52]

F. Amendments and Related Impact

Apart from the JCHR's effect on shaping deliberation as described in the last section, our study identified more discrete impacts of the JCHR's legislative scrutiny. With respect to at least 16 of the JCHR references identified in our study, the Government offered amendments, or indicated its agreement to amend a bill, based on recommendations in JCHR reports. (On most of these occasions, the JCHR recommendation is described as the sole influence, but on a few, the JCHR recommendation is described prominently among other influences.) The Government's response on some of these occasions included more than one amendment. It is likely that the total number of amendments influenced by the JCHR during the 2005–10 Parliament is significantly higher than what we found explicitly referenced in debates, because the scope of our study did not include identifying all amendments proposed in any stage of parliamentary proceeding as the result of JCHR recommendations—nor did we attempt to trace what eventually transpired with regard to all of the hundreds of amendments proposed in JCHR references (which would involve the difficult task of analysing, among other things, the causal effect of JCHR recommendations in relation to other influences on the legislative process). The scope of our study on this point of impact was limited to the JCHR references found in our search methodology and to oral evidence of a Member of Parliament that an amendment resulted from JCHR recommendations.

In 15 out of these 16 occasions, the Government's response is indicated in proceedings in the House of Lords. The bills amended include: the Charities Bill 2005, to ensure there is no discrimination between religious and non-religious charities;[53] the Terrorism Bill 2005, to remove terrorism against property from the offence of glorification of terrorism;[54] the Police and Justice Bill, to ensure conformity with

---

[51] Lord West, HL Deb 27 February 2008, vol 699, cols 734–5 (referring to JCHR, 10th Report of 2007/08, Counter-Terrorism Policy and Human Rights (Eighth Report): Counter-Terrorism Bill, HL 50/HC 199).

[52] HL Oral Questions, 18 February 2008, vol 699, col 8.

[53] Baroness Whitaker, HL Deb 12 October 2005, vol 674, col 292.

[54] Lord Goodhart, HL Deb 7 December 2005, vol 676, cols 641–2 and 660–61.

UN Convention on the Rights of the Child;[55] the Education and Inspections Bill;[56] the Safeguarding Vulnerable Groups Bill;[57] the Criminal Justice and Immigration Bill;[58] the Financial Services Bill;[59] the Digital Economy Bill;[60] and the Equality Bill.[61]

In addition to amendments to bills, there are at least seven instances in which the references show that the Government issued guidance on the basis of recommendations in JCHR reports (or agreed to do so) to administrative and law enforcement officials on how certain terms in the law should be interpreted and on criteria for applying laws and other kinds of decision-making. As with amendment, the actual number of instances of guidance issued in 2005–10 could be significantly higher due to the same methodological issue mentioned above.

In some of the above cases the Government took up part but not all of the JCHR's recommendations in agreeing to amendments or issuing guidance. Some of the JCHR references criticise the Government for not doing enough and continue the debate over what is required to comply with the requirements of human rights law.

CONCLUSION

The work of the JCHR did not receive much notice in the first years of its operation, but attention to its reports increased dramatically beginning in 2005. In the 2001–05 Parliament there were 23 references to JCHR reports; this number increased to 1,006 in the 2005–10 Parliament. This study focused on the 2005–10 Parliament, determining which MPs cite JCHR reports, with what frequency, and for what purposes. More importantly, the study assessed the impact the JCHR's activity had on parliamentary deliberations.

The use of JCHR reports was wide—241 MPs cite a report at least once—though somewhat narrowly concentrated. About one-third of references to JCHR reports were by seven high-frequency users who made more than 30 citations, and another third was by the next 36 medium-frequency users who made between 5 and 29 citations. The House of Lords discussed several JCHR reports extensively and in depth. The House of Commons discussed reports with less frequency and depth, and use was more concentrated: the two most frequent users of reports (including the chair of the JCHR) contributed almost 40 per cent of references, and only eight other members in the Commons fell into the medium-use category, compared to 28 in the Lords.

One of the most significant findings of our research is that there were about 600 references—60 per cent of the total—in which the interests of various minority or

[55] Baroness Stern, HL Deb 6 July 2006, vol 684, cols 418–19.
[56] Lord Avebury, HL Deb 17 October 2006, vol 685, cols 724–26.
[57] Lord Adonis, HL Deb 1 November 2006, vol 686, cols 380–82.
[58] Lord West, HL Deb 23 April 2008, vol 700, cols 1556–57.
[59] Ian Pearson, HC Deb 25 January 2010, vol 504, cols 641–43.
[60] Lord Young, HL Deb 1 March 2010, vol 717, cols 1310–11.
[61] Baroness Scotland, HL Deb 19 October 2005, vol 673, cols 1145–46; Lord Lester, HL Deb 13 February 2006, vol 678, cols 1007–08.

marginal groups were discussed. This tallies with the fact that the most frequent subject areas for discussing JCHR reports were counter-terrorism and criminal justice, followed by health care and welfare, equality and immigration. The capacity to represent minority interests is a prominent characteristic of the JCHR and is an important part of its mission as understood by its members. This finding deserves consideration in theoretical analyses of democracy and majoritarianism. Many scholars argue that democracy has an inherent bias toward majoritarian interests, and some have argued that the only hope for countering that bias is through the courts and judicial review. Our research shows that it is possible to set up internal structures and groups within a legislature that draw attention to and advocate for the interests of minorities. Further research needs to be done on how effective such representation is with regard to influencing legislative outcomes. We found 23 occasions where Government ministers stated explicitly that legislation was amended or that interpretative guidance would be issued in response to proposals by the JCHR. The effect of the JCHR on legislative outcomes is by no means exhausted by such explicit statements in Hansard. Much of the legislative process in the British Parliament takes place behind the scenes and off the record, in preparatory discussions leading to the production of White Papers and Green Papers, and there is evidence that the shape of bills is affected by anticipation of scrutiny by the JCHR.[62]

In any event, the main aim of our research was not to assess the concrete effect of JCHR reports on particular legislative outcomes, but on the general quality of deliberation regarding bills in parliamentary sessions. The study shows that JCHR reports became an important touchstone for debate in Parliament around the time of the counter-terrorism legislation following the 2005 bombings in London. The work of the JCHR continued to be used frequently throughout the 2005–10 Parliament; several reports were discussed extensively and in depth, and evidence generated by the JCHR on various topics was cited by a wide range of MPs. As a result, it became common to discuss legislation within a human rights framework, which made reference not only to judgments of the European Court of Human Rights and other sources of human rights law, but also to proportionality as a method of determining compatibility with human rights. Such debate, however, was not narrowly legalistic. The work of the JCHR has led to vigorous, evidence-based debate that assesses policy on many subjects in light of a wide range of values recognised in human rights law.

---

[62] See Hiebert, ch 3 in this volume, p 49.

8

Parliament's Role Following Declarations of Incompatibility under the Human Rights Act

JEFF KING*

THE HUMAN RIGHTS Act 1998 (HRA) has been called 'the cornerstone of the New Constitution'[1] and even 'one of the most important pieces of legislation to be enacted in the twentieth century'.[2] As is well known, however, UK courts have no power to strike down a statute on account of it violating the European Convention on Human Rights (hereinafter the 'Convention'), which the HRA effectively makes the UK's bill of rights. Rather, if a UK court cannot 'so far as possible' read a UK statute consistently with Convention rights under section 3, it repairs to section 4(2): 'If the court is satisfied that the provision is incompatible with a Convention right, it may make a declaration of that incompatibility.' Furthermore, section 4(6) of the HRA confirms that any such declaration 'does not affect the validity, continuing operation or enforcement of the provision in respect of which it is given; and ... is not binding on the parties to the proceedings in which it is made'.

Thus far, UK courts have issued 20 such section 4 declarations that were not overturned on appeal,[3] and the purpose of this chapter is to explore the practice of

---

* The author would like to thank Alison Young, Murray Hunt, Paul Yowell, Nicholas Bamforth, Aileen Kavanagh, Nick Barber, James Melton, Aileen McHarg, Hayley Hooper, Cheryl Thomas, Richard Ekins, George Letsas, Tom Hickman and Gordon Anthony for helpful substantive guidance at various points. For research assistance, I would like to thank Cosimo Montagu, Nick Bamber, Stefan Theil, Quentin Montpetit and William Achorn. I thank in particular the UCL Faculty of Laws and the UCL Constitution Unit for making extensive resources available to me, both human and financial. I wish to record a particularly outstanding debt to Nick Bamber and Cosimo Montagu. Their extensive work in collecting judicial data and finding and organising Hansard was critical to the project and was conducted with the very highest degree of academic excellence.

[1] V Bogdanor, *The New British Constitution* (Oxford, Hart Publishing, 2009) ch 3.

[2] J Stanton, 'Review: Parliamentary Sovereignty and the Human Rights Act—By Alison L Young' (2010) 30 *Legal Studies* 689, 689.

[3] Note that hereinafter, these judicial decisions will be referred to by party name only and not with constant citation in the text. As of June 2014, the cases include (with numbering added for convenience): (1) *R(H) v Mental Health Review Tribunal for the North and East of London Region, and the Secretary of State for Health* [2001] EWCA Civ 415; (2) *McR's Application for Judicial Review* [2002] NIQB 58; (3) *International Transport Roth GmBH v SSHD* [2002] EWCA Civ 158; (4) *R (on the application*

the UK courts under this system, how that compares with some experiences abroad, how Parliament has responded to such declarations, and what it all says about the nature and constitutional role of the remedial scheme for the judicial review of legislation set out in the HRA. More particularly, I will shed preliminary light on the answers to the following set of questions:

— What form have parliamentary and governmental responses to section 4 declarations taken, how promptly and what kind of policies were enacted in response?
— Does the HRA promote or hinder democratic deliberation about rights in Parliament?
— Is there an emerging constitutional convention that the Government and Parliament[4] are constitutionally obligated to respond to section 4 declarations by amending the offending legislation?

The preliminary answers to such questions do not all fit into a simple conceptual scheme bearing a headline message. The evidence is mixed. We must also be mindful, furthermore, of the methodological issue that such legal remedies have only been available for 14 years at the time of writing (10 of them under the Labour Party that enacted the HRA). On the other hand, this brief period enables a more or less exhaustive examination of the record in Parliament. The findings presented here are based on scrutiny of all parliamentary debates on every remedial response to a section 4 declaration, on the floor of each House, in Committees, at Report and 'Ping Pong' (consideration of amendments) stages, and in consideration of the relevant scrutiny reports of the Joint Committee on Human Rights (JCHR) on each

---

of *Anderson) v SSHD* [2002] UKHL 46; (5) *R(D) v SSHD* [2002] EWHC 2805 (Admin); (6) *Blood and Tarbuck v SS for Health* (3 March 2003, unreported); (7) *Bellinger v Bellinger* [2003] UKHL 21; (8) *R(M) v Secretary of State for Health* [2003] EWHC 1094; (9) *R (Wilkinson) v Inland Revenue Commissioners* [2003] EWCA Civ 814; (10) *R (Hooper) v SSWP* [2003] EWCA Civ 875; however, see [2005] UKHL 29; (11) *A and others; X and others v SSHD* [2004] UKHL 56; (12) *R (Morris) v Westminster CC and the First Secretary of State* [2005] EWCA Civ 1184; (13) *R (Gabaj) v First Secretary of State* (unreported); (15) *R (Clift) v SSHD* [2006] UKHL 54; (16) *Smith v Scott* [2007] CSIH 9 (Scotland); (17) *R (Baiai) v SSHD* [2008] UKHL 53; (18) *R (Thompson) v SSHD* [2010] UKSC 17; (19) *R (Royal College of Nursing) v SSHD* [2010] EWHC 2761 (Admin); (20) *R(T) v Chief Constable of Greater Manchester* [2014] UKHL 35. This mirrors the findings in the Ministry of Justice's *Responding to Human Rights Judgments* (2012, Cm 8432) Annex A, apart from the last, which was decided in June 2014. Note: *Hooper* is inaccurately represented in the official list. The decision reported at [2003] EWCA Civ 875 was final, but did not involve the issuance of a declaration of incompatibility. The correct citation for the *Hooper* appeal case addressing the substantive issue was [2003] EWCA 813. However, this case was overruled in [2005] UKHL 29. The House of Lords acknowledged the incompatibility and confirmed the analysis of Moses J at first instance (which issued a declaration of incompatibility), but felt that due to the repeal of the statute, a new declaration was no longer needed (see [52], [79]). Despite the tortuous path of litigation and unclear message, I have elected to keep *Hooper* on the list.

⁴ Although private members are entitled to put forward bills in Parliament, it remains the case that 'private members' bills which arouse any substantial degree of opposition are unlikely to pass into law' (M Jack (ed), *Erskine May: Parliamentary Practice* (24th edn, London, LexisNexis, 2011) 526) and hence those that succeed typically have cross-party support. In practice, therefore, the role of Parliament is dictated by the choices of the Government on how to proceed in remedying the incompatibility. Even so, the Human Fertilisation and Embryology (Deceased Fathers) Act 2003 is one example of a private member's bill remedying a section 4 declaration of incompatibility. The Bill passed without division in both Houses of Parliament: HC Deb 13 June 2003, vol 406, col 996; HL Deb 18 September 2003, vol 652, col 1057.

remedial response.[5] Thus, while the period is too brief for sweeping generalisations about the definitive constitutional role of section 4 declarations, the completeness of the record allows some interesting insights to emerge. The general picture is of a remedial regime that differs in important ways from some other weak and strong form systems of constitutional judicial review. The parliamentary record displays an attitude that has been predominantly accepting of and collaborative with the courts' role, though also minimalist in some responses and on the whole manifesting delays by the Government that have no principled defence. Lastly, it appears that there is, indeed, evidence of an emerging constitutional convention of response by the Government and Parliament to section 4 declarations of incompatibility.

I. THE LANDSCAPE OF SECTION 4 DECLARATIONS OF INCOMPATIBILITY

A. The Types of Legislative and Government Response

The Government may respond to a declaration of incompatibility in various ways. First, it legally can choose to do nothing at all. Where this has occurred, however, it was because Parliament had already amended the offending legislation prior to the declaration (as noted in Figure 8.1 below). On the other hand, despite some lengthy delays and the possible exception of prisoner voting (as discussed further below), there has been no case to date where the Government or Parliament affirmatively chose not to remedy incompatible legislation. Second, the Government can ask Parliament to repeal the offending provision by way of an Act of Parliament. In doing so, it can either introduce an act among whose central purposes is the intention to address the incompatibility (which I will call 'whole act responses') or it can add a provision to an existing bill that may be related to the issue, but that primarily concerns other matters (which I will call 'tacking responses'). Third and finally, the Government can amend and replace the offending provision by way of a remedial order under section 10 of the HRA. This section empowers a minister to use subordinate legislation (an executive order) to amend the act to remove the incompatibility. As specified in Schedule 2 to the HRA, the remedial order must be laid before Parliament for an affirmative resolution, either before it comes into force or, in urgent cases where it is necessary to give it immediate effect, by way of affirmative resolution after it has come into force. The remedial orders are also subject to scrutiny by the JCHR, which has also given guidance in relation to when the use of remedial orders is appropriate.[6] Indeed, the JCHR's role in the parliamentary process is absolutely crucial, though it is explained in detail elsewhere in this volume. The broader landscape of the response to declarations of incompatibility under the HRA is set out in Figure 8.1.

---

[5] I have not examined any remedial responses to findings of rights violations by the European Court of Human Rights.
[6] Joint Committee on Human Rights, *Making of Remedial Orders* (2001–02, HL 58, HC 473); see also the Committee's *Enhancing Parliament's Role in Relation to Human Rights Judgments* (2009–10, HL 85, HC 455) [22]–[24]. See also Guidance to Departments at back of this Report.

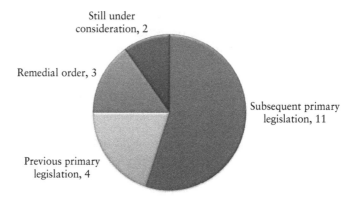

Figure 8.1: Parliamentary responses to section 4 declarations[7]

The chart in Figure 8.1 discloses an unmistakable preference for acting through the ordinary legislative procedure. This may explain some of the delays I will shortly detail. I return to this issue below.

B. Promptness of Response

One of the most important differences between the HRA and some foreign systems is the fact that the Government is capable of delaying its response to a section 4 declaration by a considerable amount of time. Only political pressure—usually from the JCHR and civil society—can accelerate the response. As Figure 8.2 shows, the delay between the court judgment and the remedial provision coming into force is fairly substantial.

The two outliers in Figure 8.2 are the *R(M)* and *Smith v Scott* cases. The former case involved a defect in the mental health regime, which for the relevant mental health patients automatically appointed as guardian the 'nearest relative' without the possibility of the patient applying for variation. In *M*'s case, the patient's 'nearest relative' was her adoptive father, whom she accused of having sexually abused her. The case thus involved a classic legislative oversight. The incompatibility was conceded in the *M* case, as shown through the exhaustive analysis by Alison Young of the passage of the remedial legislation through Parliament, which demonstrates that the process was exemplary of dialogue working rather than of stubborn foot-dragging.[8] Whether the delay was justifiable is another story. The *Smith v Scott* case applied the Strasbourg Court's *Hirst* decision,[9] which found a blanket ban preventing convicted prisoners from voting to be a disproportionate interference with their (constructive) right to vote under Article 3 of the First Protocol to the Convention.

---

[7] Please consult the methodological appendix at the end of this chapter for information on all other figures in this chapter.

[8] AL Young, 'Is Dialogue Working under the Human Rights Act 1998?' [2011] *Public Law* 773, 783–84.

[9] *Hirst v UK (No 2)* [2005] ECHR 681.

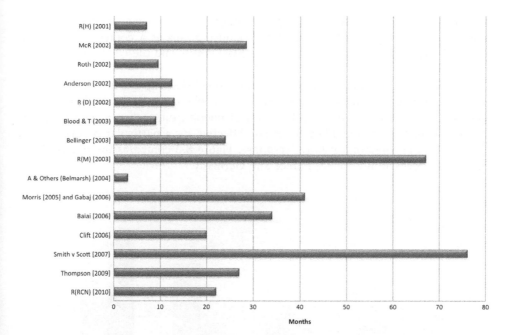

Figure 8.2: The delay between the section 4 declaration and the remedy coming into force

The Government has published a draft bill in response, which presents three mutually exclusive options: (1) a voting ban on prisoners sentenced to four years or more;
(2) one for those sentenced to more than six months; and (3) maintenance of the
current blanket ban in outright defiance of the Strasbourg judgment.[10] The draft bill
has now been scrutinised by a joint committee.[11] The Government has sent mixed
messages about its plans for the draft bill. On the one hand, the Prime Minister
declared unequivocally in response to a parliamentary question that 'prisoners are
not getting the vote under this government'.[12] On the other hand, there is a repeated
affirmation that the Government's policy is to comply with its international obligations, including the decision of the Strasbourg Court, but that the ultimate decision
rests with Parliament.[13] The constitutional significance of this delay for the role of
the HRA is further complicated by the fact that UK courts flatly denied to award a

---

[10] I White, *Prisoners' Voting Rights* (SN/PC/01764) (London, Parliament and Constitution Centre,
House of Commons Library, 15 May 2013).
[11] See *Report of the Joint Committee on the Draft Voting Eligibility (Prisoners) Bill*, Session 2013–14,
HL Paper 103/HC 924 (18 December 2013).
[12] HC Deb 24 October 2012, vol 551, col 923.
[13] HC Deb 22 November 2012, vol 553, col 745 (Chris Grayling MP): 'The Prime Minister has made
clear, on the record, his personal views on this subject, and I have done the same. Those views have not
changed. However, the Government are under an international law obligation to implement the Court
judgment. As Lord Chancellor, as well as Secretary of State for Justice, I take my obligation to uphold
the rule of law seriously. Equally, it remains the case that Parliament is sovereign, and the Human Rights
Act 1998 explicitly recognises that fact.' The Ministry of Justice's explanatory memorandum for the draft
Bill (Cm 8499) makes the same point at [2].

declaration of incompatibility in the pre-Strasbourg UK challenge under the HRA,[14] and the matter is generally viewed by parliamentarians as a contest between the UK and Strasbourg, instead of between the UK courts and the UK Parliament and Government.

Quite apart from these cases, the delays are nonetheless significant. This is evident even if we compare the UK with jurisdictions where courts have a practice of suspending the effect of their declarations of unconstitutionality, a remedy which allows the unconstitutional law to remain effective for a particular period of time pending an appropriate legislative response. Figure 8.3 compares the rate of delay with that observed in Canada, France and Germany.

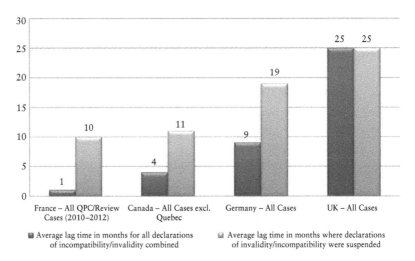

Figure 8.3: Remedial lag time averages for rights cases: 2000–12

Thus, even where the constitutional remedy of delaying or suspending the operation of the declaration of unconstitutionality exists in other systems, the overall period of delay under the HRA is significantly higher. There may or may not be aspects of the legislative process that are partly responsible for this delay. Yet it is reasonable to conclude that a major cause of this difference is the binding effect of the period stipulated by the foreign courts and, more importantly, because suspended declarations only account for a subset of overall cases. At first it appears that once we exclude the *R(M)* (mental health) and *Smith v Scott* (prisoner voting) cases, the differences between the UK, Canada and Germany are not particularly strong. If we exclude them, for instance, the average lag time for the UK is approximately 17 rather than 25 months. However, if we look at the figures for delay regarding *all* declarations of unconstitutionality in the Canadian and German courts rather than the subset of those where the declaration was suspended, we see that

---

[14] *R (on the application of Pearson and Feal-Martinez) v SSHD*; *Hirst v HM Attorney General* [2001] EWHC Admin 239; HC Deb 10 February 2011, vol 523, cols 493–586.

the overall average delay is still much greater in the UK. Furthermore, if we exclude only *R(M)* and continue to include the prisoner voting case, which is highly pertinent to the enquiry here and arguably not a case of good faith dialogic engagement, the average delay remains 22 months. On any accounting, therefore, the delays are substantially greater in the UK.

C. General Impact on the Legislative Process

We can consider the question of impact by looking at the number of judgments and extent of the impact of such judgments. As to the first, data compiled for this study shows that the number of statutes declared unconstitutional or subject to declarations of incompatibility is rather low in international comparison with Canada, France or Germany.

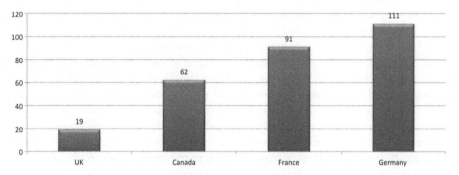

Figure 8.4: Number of statures declared unconstitutional/incompatible on rights-based grounds by all courts 2000–12

Admittedly, the number of declarations of incompatibility is only one (albeit important) aspect of the judiciary's impact on legislation under the HRA. Some writers treat the particularly muscular power of legislative interpretation available under section 3 of the HRA (allowing reading in and reading down) as a form of judicial supremacy tantamount to a strike down power.[15] Although to date no systematic analysis of how often section 3(1) is used in this fashion has been undertaken (nor to my knowledge of its analogues in the Canadian and German systems),[16] it appears to be relatively infrequent in the UK. At any rate, the low number of declarations of incompatibility under the HRA means that the law-makers' business is disrupted somewhat infrequently by rights review under the HRA. This may help explain why they have what Sathanapally calls a 'low profile'[17] in Parliament.

---

[15] S Gardbaum, *The New Commonwealth Model of Constitutionalism* (Cambridge, Cambridge University Press, 2013) 171, 185.

[16] Both of which are explained in the Methodological Appendix at the end of this chapter.

[17] A Sathanapally, *Beyond Disagreement: Open Remedies in Human Rights Adjudication* (Oxford, Oxford University Press, 2012) 138–39.

Another potential reason for the low profile relates to the extent of impact generated by the particular decisions. Impact can be judged along a number of lines.[18] It can have direct and indirect effects. It may involve symbolic or expressive impact (such as non-pecuniary satisfaction, strengthening constitutional values, exposing unlawful behaviour in the media or by eroding public support for human rights values by providing opportunities for media spin). It may involve the provision or loss of certain benefits, services or other rights for individuals. It may consist of new allocative costs and other disruptions to administration or result in a response that eliminates a discretion that was previously used to benefit a number of persons. Alternatively, it may be a form of political backlash in which opposition to the judgment sets back the overall enjoyment of the right even further.[19] On the whole, impact concerns not only the number of persons affected by the decision, but also the nature of the impact on particular individuals.

These are difficult dimensions in the study law and politics, and they caution against making sweeping generalisations about impact in particular regimes. Subject to that caveat, it is important to have a look at the most immediate political impact judged by the policies enacted in response to the various judgments, responses which have been endorsed as compliant with the judgments by the independent JCHR. Table 8.1 sets out a representative sample of such responses.[20] It shows that the immediate discernible impact of the HRA, while in my view very worthwhile, has also been relatively modest in respect of the number of people affected and the extent of intrusion into controversial legislative territory. A number of such cases concern procedural rights or matters regarded as legislative oversight, and relatively few extended expensive or controversial benefits. Even the most significant cases tended to affect thousands of persons (at least in the initial years following the judgment), contrary to what is often the case in America and Germany.

---

[18] See S Halliday and M Hertogh (eds), *Judicial Review and Bureaucratic Impact* (Cambridge, Cambridge University Press, 2004).

[19] I have explored a number of these areas and the phenomenon of backlash in *Judging Social Rights* (Cambridge, Cambridge University Press, 2012) 63–85.

[20] The sample contains most and is definitely representative. I have omitted cases where the legislation was in place before the declaration. I also omitted the much-debated impact of the *Belmarsh* case, which led to the Prevention of Terrorism Act 2005 and with it the new control order regime. In numbers, between 2005 and 2011, there were a total of 52 control orders issued, all related to suspected Islamic terrorists, primarily in later years against UK nationals (not permitted under the pre-Prevention of Terrorism Act regime). See D Anderson, *Control Orders in 2011: Final Report of the Independent Reviewer on the Prevention of Terrorism Act 2005* (London, The Stationery Office, 2012). As a matter of sheer numbers, then, the impact appears modest and perhaps even facilitated the expansion of executive detention without charge through a rushed parliamentary process: see pp 178–81 below. However, since the case and its successors have concerned deprivations of liberty without ordinary due process, it took on a symbolic importance among writers that is far greater than these numbers suggest.

Table 8.1: Impact of section 4 declarations: a representative sample

Impact	Case	Outcome
Minimal	*McR*	Repeal of rarely enforced anti-sodomy statute.
	Anderson	Replacement of Home Secretary's discretion to increase duration of term of imprisonment (the tariff) served without parole with a legislative scheme of proposed 'starting point' minimum sentences, dubbed 'Blunkett's revenge' by a peer.[21]
	Blood and Tarbuck	Amendment to scheme to allow deceased father's name to be added to a child's birth certificate.
Moderate	*Morris and Gabaj*	Challenged scheme for fighting 'benefits tourism' required local authorities assessing priority need for homelessness assistance to disregard non-nationals who required leave to remain in the country. New scheme extended rights to British, EU and certain Commonwealth citizens to be given an offer of accommodation (no more) in the private rented sector for a duration of one year.[22]
	Royal College of Nurses	Challenged scheme allowing persons barred from working with children or vulnerable adults due to past criminal convictions the right to make representations only *after* the barring decision. Revised scheme permits representations before the barring decision.[23]
	Thompson	'The remedial order only provides a mechanism by which a sex offender can apply for a police review of whether they should cease to be on the [Sex Offenders] register.'[24] It also provided a right of appeal to the magistrates' court on any such administrative determination.

(continued)

[21] HL Deb 16 June 2003, vol 649, col 588 (Lord Ackner); see also cols 575–77 (Lord Woolf). The new sentencing guidelines in effect provided a legislative framework of sentencing that not only replaced the guidelines developed by the judges earlier, but also departed substantially from them in substance. The case may therefore be considered an instance of political backlash and in that respect its impact, seen as cutting against the spirit of the judgment to which it responded, may have been more than moderate.
[22] HC Deb 21 July 2008, vol 673, cols 610–13.
[23] Protection of Freedoms Act 2012, s 67.
[24] HL Deb 5 July 2012, vol 738, cols 875, 876 (Baronness Stowell of Beeston, introducing the order in the Lords). See Joint Committee on Human Rights, *Draft Sexual Offences Act 2003 (Remedial) Order 2012 (Second Report)* (2012–13, HL 8, HC 166) [14]–[17] (discussing the dialogue between the JCHR which convinced the Government to add the appeal to the magistrates' court, but not to the High Court or Crown Court. The case serves as a good example of the benefits of intra-parliamentary dialogue on rights review).

Table 8.1: (continued)

Impact	Case	Outcome
Significant	*Bellinger*	The Gender Recognition Act 2005 clarified the legal consequences of gender recognition and established the Gender Recognition Tribunal, which by 2012 had issued 3,108 full Gender Recognition Certificates.[25]
	Roth	Replacement of mandatory heavy penalty scheme applicable to hauliers carrying clandestine entrants to the UK with a new executive power to reduce fines coupled with new rights of appeal.
	Baiai	Abolition of a discriminatory scheme that, in an effort to prevent 'sham marriages' prohibited people subject to immigration control from marrying without authorisation, *except* in a Church of England (CoE) religious ceremony. The Government did not level down, but extended to all such persons the rights enjoyed by those marrying in a CoE religious ceremony.

II. DO DECLARATIONS OF INCOMPATIBILITY PROMOTE GREATER DEMOCRATIC DELIBERATION?

There has been a significant amount written about the idea of constitutional judicial review as 'democratic dialogue' between courts and legislatures, notably in Canada,[26] in respect of the HRA,[27] and in at times unfairly neglected earlier work on this theme by Barry Friedman in the US.[28] The basic idea as outlined in the seminal article by Hogg and Bushell (now Thornton) is as follows: 'Where a judicial decision is open to legislative reversal, modification, or avoidance, then it is meaningful to regard the relationship between the Court and the competent legislative

[25] Ministry of Justice, *Statistics Bulletin: Gender Recognition Statistics: October to December 2012* (4 April 2012).
[26] See (2007) 45 *Osgoode Hall Law Journal* 1 for an issue dedicated entirely to the metaphor of dialogue and reply by the principal authors of the idea in Canadian law to their critics. Kent Roach has expounded and defended the idea in a range of publications: see, eg, 'Dialogic Judicial Review and its Critics' (2004) 23 *Supreme Court Law Review* 49 and 'Sharpening the Dialogue Debate: The Next Decade of Scholarship' [2007] 45 *Osgoode Hall Law Journal* 169. For a fresh perspective, see R Dixon, 'The Supreme Court of Canada, Charter Dialogue, and Deference' [2009] 47 *Osgoode Hall Law Journal* 235 (exploring in particular the role of courts in 'second-look' cases where legislation enacted in response to previous judgments is challenged again).
[27] T Hickman, 'Constitutional Dialogue, Constitutional Theories and the Human Rights Act 1998' [2005] *Public Law* 306; AL Young, *Parliamentary Sovereignty and the Human Rights Act* (Oxford, Hart Publishing, 2009) esp ch 5; AL Young, 'Deference, Dialogue and the Search for Legitimacy' (2010) 30 *OJLS* 815; Sathanapally (n 17).
[28] B Friedman, 'Dialogue and Judicial Review' (1993) 91 *Michigan Law Review* 577. At 653, for instance, he states: 'The Constitution is not interpreted by aloof judges imposing their will on the people. Rather, constitutional interpretation is an elaborate discussion between judges and the body politic.'

body as a dialogue.'[29] The authors argue that where dialogue occurs, 'any concern about the legitimacy of judicial review is greatly diminished'.[30] However, they later appear to back down from this normative claim.[31]

It is important not to be distracted by the metaphor of dialogue and the debates about its accuracy and significance.[32] The more focused question is whether there is something about the scheme in the HRA that promotes improved democratic deliberation,[33] not whether it leads to exchanges that are iterative in the egalitarian sense implied by the dialogue metaphor. So some pertinent questions include the following: are Members of Parliament welcoming of judicial decisions under the HRA thus far or do they feel dominated by them? Do they exercise their own normative capacities when scrutinising remedial legislation or do they merely ratify what the judges say? Are they considering issues that may have been neglected or are they being forced to backtrack grudgingly from earlier legislative commitments?

Two excellent studies have examined a few of these questions in some detail, though for reasons of space they cannot be reviewed fully here.[34] In her important article, Alison Young examines whether dialogue is working under the HRA by looking at Hansard relating to a range of legislative responses for important select cases.[35] Young both reviews the experience under the HRA and also presents an analytical framework detailing normative guidance for legal interpretation that will enhance democratic dialogue under the HRA. My concern here is with the former aspect. Young examines, in this respect, legislative debates that involved interpretation of the rights that extended well beyond the judicial interpretations, particularly in the cases of *R(M)*, *Bellinger*, *Roth* and *Morris*.[36] She regards the debates surrounding *R(M)* and *Bellinger* as showing extensive debates regarding the appropriate remedy, rather than definition of the right, and that *Morris* involved debates about both. *Roth*, by contrast, was an instance of where the legislature largely accepted the Court of Appeal's analysis and did not engage with the balancing exercise presented by the issue. Young concludes that judicial deference on questions of rights is preventing the proper functioning of democratic dialogue, because the judges have pre-empted discussion in Parliament by showing a priori deference in their judgments. The judges should rather avoid withholding their views, so that parliamentarians can take them well into account when devising their response.

---

[29] PW Hogg and AA Bushell, 'The Charter Dialogue between Courts and Legislatures (or Perhaps the Charter of Rights isn't Such a Bad Thing after All)' (1997) 35 *Osgoode Hall Law Journal* 75, 79.

[30] ibid 80.

[31] PW Hogg, AAB Thornton and WK Wright, 'Charter Dialogue Revisited—or Much Ado about Metaphors' (2007) 45 *Osgoode Hall Law Journal* 1, 30: 'Dialogue theory does not provide a justification for judicial review.'

[32] For sceptical views about the relevance of the debate and metaphor, see A Kavanagh, *Constitutional Review under the UK Human Rights Act* (Cambridge, Cambridge University Press, 2009) 408–11; Gardbaum (n 15) 15–16 and ch 5.

[33] For the view that judicial review can play this role more generally, see S Fredman, *Human Rights Transformed: Positive Rights and Positive Duties* (Oxford, Oxford University Press, 2008).

[34] The research in this chapter was completed shortly before the publication of Sathanapally's *Beyond Disagreement* (n 17), precluding any extensive consideration. I have nonetheless referred to parts of the analysis throughout this chapter.

[35] Young (n 8).

[36] ibid 782–91.

Sathanapally's book examines dialogue and deliberative democratic theory before exploring in detail the use of section 4 declarations and, in particular, illuminating case studies of the *Bellinger* and *Belmarsh* cases.

My own analysis examining all instances of Hansard (debates in the Commons and the Lords, inclusive of Committee, Report and Ping Pong stages), as well as relevant committee reports, is at present still underway. However, some pictures are emerging that complement and to some extent confirm and extend the analyses by Young and Sathanapally. As to the idea that the courts may be 'dominating' Parliament in some fashion, there is almost no evidence of this occurring if we are to take expressions of protest in Parliament as the key indicator. My analysis on this point accords with Sathanapally's, which finds that: 'The nature of interaction has generally been cooperative rather than conflictual.'[37] The case of *Thompson* (concerning the Sex Offenders Register), on which see section III below, was the exception to this general rule, but a bit of chafing does not undo the norm. The overall trend is one of simple workaday acceptance of the domestic court's judgment and the need to respond to it, *sin ire et studio*, or 'without passion or hatred'.[38] However, the superficial calm towards particular judgments should not necessarily be equated with political satisfaction with the substantive legal regime in place under the HRA. The acceptance of domestic court judgments may reflect a certain respect for judicial independence in British constitutional arrangements. The Conservative Party made a manifesto commitment prior to the 2010 election to repeal the HRA and replace it with a British bill of rights, though the commitment to repeal was abandoned in the Coalition Agreement (with the Liberal Democrats) that followed the election.[39]

One might, on the other hand, believe that the impact upon Parliament has been more insidious, with parliamentarians laconically accepting the policies implicitly mandated by the courts in section 4 declarations. On this point, there is clear evidence, in my view, that parliamentarians *do* view the role for courts as being one of interpreting the rights at first instance, and the role of Parliament to fashion the remedy as well as to undertake any balancing exercise not implicitly foreclosed by the judgment. As statements reproduced in section III below affirm, parliamentarians tend to view themselves as accepting and working with the judgments of the courts and not ordinarily being in a position to offer a contrary interpretation of the right once the court has ruled definitively on the issue. This is not necessarily insidious domination or subtle policy distortion, though it is arguably so. It may equally or perhaps better be regarded as evidence of parliamentarians accepting the constitutional division of responsibilities implied by the HRA and accession to the European Convention. As just observed, it is furthermore impossible to say that these latter grander constitutional questions have been in any way 'passive' in

[37] Sathanapally (n 17) 224.

[38] The expression is borrowed from M Weber, *Theory of Economic and Social Organization* (trans AR Henderson and T Parsons, New York, Free Press, 1947) 340.

[39] *An Invitation to Join the Government of Britain: The Conservative Manifesto 2010* (available at: www.conservatives.com) at 79 (proposing to replace the Act with a UK bill of rights that would 'encourage greater social responsibility'). The Coalition Agreement committed both parties to the investigation of the possibility of a bill of rights that would 'ensure' the Convention 'continues to be enshrined in British law'. See *The Coalition: Our Programme for Government* (London: Cabinet Office, May 2010) 11.

British politics since 2010. The UK's constitutional moment is as much right now as it was in 1998.

The phenomenon of 'passive acceptance' may, on the other hand, undercut any strong argument that under the HRA, Parliament plays an equal, revisory or final role in defining the rights themselves and assessing limitations to them, a point regarded as quite important by some writers.[40] On the whole, however, there is perhaps too much emphasis on the point of 'normative finality' in discussions on this issue. Judges, under the HRA, hardly try to provide expansive or exhaustive definitions of the rights. Rather, they give case-by-case indications of how particular policies fail to comply with abstract rights, leaving much undecided both at the normative stage and in particular at the constructive remedial stage.[41] And, furthermore, there is much room for parliamentary analysis of human rights obligations by the JCHR in particular when assessing bills for compatibility, an exercise that is routine and wide-ranging in each session rather than limited to the few cases a year considered by the courts. So the 'normative finality' accepted by Parliament in the cases examined here is in fact a small part of normative scope of the right and balancing exercise associated with it. It is a norm relating to the avoidance of conflict and accepting the court's ultimate interpretive supremacy rather than a reluctance to carry out its own assessments.

More broadly, it is not a widely shared tenet in modern constitutionalism that only legislatures can speak with the authority of a democratic institution. If our view of a contemporary democracy comprises not only respect for rights, but also the practice of rights-based constitutional review, then judicial review can itself claim a non-legislative variety of democratic pedigree.[42] On that view, which is also held by some prominent deliberative democrats, the question is whether the practice does contribute defensibly to outcomes best described as democratic or democracy-promoting.[43] There are features of practice under the HRA that would count favourably in such an analysis.

One such feature is the extent to which courts can assist legislatures to overcome what Rosalind Dixon calls blind spots and burdens of inertia in the legislative process, or what I have elsewhere called an absence of legislative focus on rights issues.[44] By absence of legislative focus, I mean either that the legislature has not considered the point at all or that the act was adopted at a time when the concept of rights was

---

[40] See below, nn 69 and 70 and accompanying text.

[41] They largely fit, in other words, the model outlined and endorsed in C Sunstein, *One Case at a Time: Judicial Minimalism on the Supreme Court* (Cambridge, MA, Harvard University Press, 2001).

[42] See R Dworkin, 'Introduction: The Moral Reading and the Majoritarian Premise' in his *Freedom's Law: The Moral Reading of the American Constitution* (Cambridge, MA, Harvard University Press, 1996) 1.

[43] J Habermas, (W Rehg (trans)) *Between Facts and Norms* (Cambridge, Polity Press, 1996), 280: '[A] rather bold constitutional adjudication is even required in cases that concern the implementation of democratic procedure and the deliberative form of political opinion and will-formation.'

[44] R Dixon, 'Creating Dialogue about Socioeconomic Rights: Strong-Form versus Weak-Form Judicial Review Revisited' (2007) 5 *International Journal of Constitutional Law* 391, 402ff; J King, *Judging Social Rights* (Cambridge, Cambridge University Press, 2012) 164–65, 169–73. For an in-depth study of this issue in UK constitutionalism, see A Kavanagh, 'Proportionality and Parliamentary Debates: Exploring Some Forbidden Territory' (2014) 32 *OJLS* 443.

substantially different from that which the society has presently legally embraced through its constitution or ratification of international instruments. Figure 8.5 demonstrates that approximately 37 per cent of section 4 cases thus far concerned statutes where in my estimation there was an absence of legislative focus.

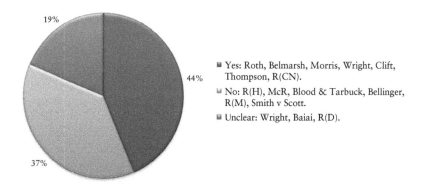

Figure 8.5: Of the incompatibilities remedied by post-decision legislative response, did the challenged act manifest legislative focus on the rights issue?[45]

Furthermore, Table 8.2 below demonstrates that a substantial majority of successful claimants are from marginalised groups that do not enjoy favourable representation in Parliament. It also shows that most of the remaining claimant groups were, though not in any way particularly vulnerable, still in most cases reasonably discrete and unlikely to register on any political agenda (and hence face what Dixon calls the 'burdens of inertia'). On this view, then, the practice of judicial review has arguably promoted the interests and raised the profile of vulnerable groups, a significant number of whom could not or did not vote at all.

Other features of the practice under the HRA are less favourable from the perspective of deliberative democracy. One such feature is the consistent strategy by the Government of aiming only for 'minimal compliance', one that has provoked 'recurring criticism' by the JCHR.[46] Another is the time given in Parliament for deliberation. One early concern was whether responses to section 4 declarations might in any way overburden Parliament. Quite to the contrary, the paucity of time spent on floor debates and even in committee proceedings can be quite remarkable, all the more so in view of the delays involved in providing remedies. The response to the *Roth* case was an interesting example, also noted by Young and Sathanapally.[47] In *Roth*, the Court of Appeal found a penalty regime for hauliers who knowingly

[45] This concerns those declarations where the legislative response occurred post-decision, except for *Wright*, which was nearly simultaneous. In *Chester v Secretary of State for Justice* [2013] UKSC 63 [136], Lord Sumption rejected the contention that there was no substantive legislative debate supporting the legislative ban on prisoner voting in the UK Parliament supporting the Representation of the People Act 2000.

[46] Joint Committee on Human Rights (n 6) [168]–[170].

[47] Young (n 8) 787–88; Sathanapally (n 17) 145–46.

Table 8.2: Claimant groups and section 4 declarations of incompatibility

Marginalised groups		Non-marginalised groups	
Case	Claimant group	Case	Claimant group
R(H)	Mental health patients	*Roth*	Hauliers, lorry drivers
McR	Homosexual men	*Blood and Tarbuck*	Children of deceased fathers, conceived by fertility treatment
Anderson	Prisoners	*Wilkinson*	Widowers
R(D)	Prisoners	*Hooper*	Widowers
Bellinger	Transgender persons	*Wright*	Care workers
R(M)	Mental health patients	*R (Royal College of Nursing)*	Care workers
Belmarsh	Foreign suspected terrorists		
Morris/Gabaj	Poor non-citizens		
Baiai	Foreigners having non-CoE marriages		
Clift	Prisoners		
Smith v Scott	Prisoners		
Thompson	Convicted sex offenders		
R(T)	Persons subject to police cautions		

or unknowingly transport clandestine entrants into the UK to be an unfair violation of the Article 6 right to a fair trial and disproportionate interference with the right to property under Article 1 of the First Protocol. By way of response, however, the Government introduced the legislative amendment at Report stage in the Commons, and debate on it was severely curtailed by the use of timetabling or 'guillotine' motions, to the dismay of a number of MPs and even peers.[48] The evidence showed that many parliamentarians wanted much more time, not less, spent on responding to the judgment. Even so, the JCHR praised the resulting Schedule 8 to the Nationality, Immigration and Asylum Act 2002, finding it to be a 'measured and proportionate response to the decision of the Court of Appeal in *Roth*'.[49]

The process leading to the Prevention of Terrorism Act 2005 has been identified as another example of inadequate time for debate.[50] The Government announced

[48] See in particular the protest of Baroness Anelay HL Deb, 24 June 2002, vol 636, col 109.

[49] Joint Committee on Human Rights, *Immigration, Nationality and Asylum Bill* (2001–02, HL 132, HC 961) [110].

[50] Sathanapally's (n 17, 196–204) analysis is particularly thorough.

at first reading of the Bill that one of its central purposes was to comply in good faith with the *Belmarsh* decision,[51] which found powers permitting indefinite detention of foreign suspected terrorists incompatible with Articles 5 and 14 of the Convention. The Government decided to introduce new legislation rather than prolong the incompatible scheme, which was due to expire within three months of the judgment. As is well known, the Bill's proposed invasions of personal liberty were profound,[52] and so the first question asked by David Davis MP, the Shadow Home Secretary (Conservative), was: 'What is the immediate emergency that demands that draconian powers against British subjects be rushed through these Houses of Parliament without proper consideration, scrutiny or debate?'[53] Davis suggested that the Lords' judgment, which he agreed with and supported,[54] was being used opportunistically to ram through an invasive piece of post-9/11 legislation in short order. The JCHR also protested loudly and clearly:

> [T]here can be no justification for including such wide and unprecedented powers of executive detention in legislation which is being rushed through Parliament at a speed which prevents proper scrutiny, in order to be on the statute book in time to deal with those detained under provisions which are shortly to expire. Legislation passed at such speed should be confined to that which is essential to deal with the problem about to arise ... which means that all of the provisions concerning derogating control orders should be taken out of the Bill, if necessary to be returned to when there is more opportunity for careful parliamentary scrutiny.[55]

Although it is easy (and right) to focus on the parliamentary dismay about the rushed timetable, in actual fact, the legislative response to the *Belmarsh* decision evidenced by far the most legally and constitutionally sophisticated, highly principled and certainly the most drawn-out parliamentary discussion about the key rights issue identified by the courts under the HRA. The only other bill generating anywhere near the depth, scope and sophistication of response was the post-*Bellinger* passage of the the Gender Recognition Bill. In both cases, the responses were whole act responses, so we can compare them very crudely by noting the overall volume of discussion to the entire bill in floor debates. If we look to the overall number of words spoken during the floor debates for responses to both decisions, the Commons debate responding to *Belmarsh* was roughly twice the length of that

---

[51] HC Deb 22 February 2005, vol 431, cols 151–55 (Charles Clarke MP). Such a debate on first reading is exceptional in the legislative process, and ostensibly was due to the high profile of the judgment and the Government's decision to characterise the situation as exceptionally urgent.

[52] The Bill introduced a new scheme of 'control orders', which applied to British nationals as well as foreigners and allowed, among other things, pervasive control of the lives of the controlees through a combination of house arrest, electronic tagging, mobility restrictions and control on communications. The orders, furthermore, could be imposed as a civil measure without the controlee ever seeing the evidence in support of the orders or even being able to communicate with the special advocate who represented him after the advocate had seen closed evidence.

[53] HC Deb 22 February 2005, vol 431, col 156.

[54] ibid (quoting from the judgment in his response to the Home Secretary).

[55] Joint Committee on Human Rights, *Prevention of Terrorism Bill: Preliminary Report* (2004–05, HL 61, HC 389) [8]. See also Joint Committee on Human Rights, *Prevention of Terrorism Bill* (2004–05, HL 68, HC 334) para 1.

responding to *Bellinger*, and the Lords debate was approximately a third longer.[56] Of course, this comparison does not confirm *adequacy* of discussion, for the issues were arguably more complex and disagreements far more heated.

If we pan out from these interesting but distinctive examples, a fairly clear theme regarding timing and deliberation emerges from the evidence on the whole. In most cases apart from those mentioned above, there is very little, if any, direct engagement with the rights issues raised in the courts' judgments and almost no engagement with the judicial reasoning itself. In a number of instances, the judgments are not mentioned by name and the issue gets only fleeting mention in the general debates of either House. A more interesting factor, relating more to the legislative process itself, is that the quality of deliberation in Parliament tends to be correlated with the type of response, and specifically whether it is a whole act, remedial order or tacking response. Figure 8.6 gives the present distribution of responses along these lines.

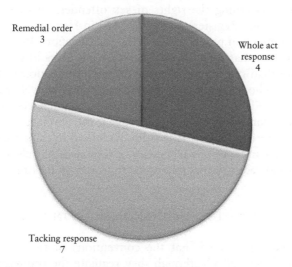

Figure 8.6: Legislative responses to DOIs under the HRA

Notwithstanding a clear preference for tacking responses, the evidence suggests that there is much clearer engagement with the rights issue and remedial options in cases of both whole act responses and, though to a much lesser extent, parliamentary scrutiny of remedial orders. There are a few reasons for this. The first is that the rights issue is likely to figure more prominently among the key issues during the second reading of the bill, where its key principles are debated and views of the House can not only be formed but also fed into the subsequent amendments at

---

[56] And both such debates were indeed massive: the Commons Hansard for the Prevention of Terrorism Act 2005 amounts to approximately 150,000 words (according to an MS Word count), whereas the Lords Hansard amounted to approximately 144,000 words. Furthermore, Commons Committee Hansard adds about 75,000 words to that figure, whereas the Lords Committee adds 109,000 words to its own. The Ping Pong stage adds another 125,000 words. In all cases, roll call votes for divisions have been included in the word count, so real figures are somewhat lower.

committee stage before executive views become ossified. Another is that tacking amend-ments are often inserted into extremely important and wide-ranging bills that will affect millions of people.[57] MPs and peers are thus likely to face issue exhaustion, and compat-ibility issues will be subordinated to the more important battles. Furthermore, tacking responses tend to get introduced late in the legislative process and sometimes quite late in the day (or evening), compounding issue exhaustion with physical exhaustion.

The debates concerning remedial order responses, on the other hand, are focused precisely on the rights issue, and the dossier available to parliamentarians will make the JCHR reports central to the issue before them,[58] and the JCHR has been no less vigilant in its review of proposed remedial orders (as well as of the use of the reme-dial order procedure). The possible flaw with them, however, is that since they are executive orders approved by resolution rather than primary legislation, they may enjoy an even lower profile in Parliament than have some of the other amendments. For instance, the debate in the Lords concerning the remedial order following the *Thompson* case (concerning the rights of sex offenders to request their removal from the Sex Offenders Register) reads very well in Hansard. It is focused, careful and engaged with material points raised in the JCHR report. What Hansard did not report, however, was that there were fewer than 10 peers in the room during the debate and more than one was evidently not paying attention to the discussion.[59] Indeed, a debate an hour earlier on a motion regarding the welfare and transporta-tion of horses in the EU was much more lively and well attended. Even so, the JCHR has urged the Government to make more frequent use of remedial orders to 'remedy incompatibilities more swiftly'.[60] And were one asked to rank the quality of delib-eration and scrutiny in types of parliamentary responses, the clear order appears to be whole acts, followed by remedial orders, followed by tacking responses.

III. A CONSTITUTIONAL CONVENTION OF RESPONSE?

Albert Venn Dicey considered that the conventions of the constitution 'consist of maxims or practices which, though they regulate the ordinary conduct of the Crown, of Ministers, and of other persons under the constitution, are not in strict-ness laws at all'.[61] The hallmark of a constitutional convention in this tradition is that it is regarded as *constitutionally* binding, but not legally binding. Some authors, Aileen Kavanagh prominent among them, have speculated there may be an emerg-ing constitutional convention in favour of legislative amendment following a section

---

[57] Some examples include the Criminal Justice Act 2003 (response to *Anderson*); the Mental Health Act 2007 (much delayed response to *R(M)*); the Housing and Regeneration Act 2008 (delayed response to *Morris* and *Gabaj*); and the Sexual Offences Act 2003 (response to *McR*).

[58] Remedial orders followed *R(H)*, *Baiai* and *Thompson*, the details for which are available in the Ministry of Justice's *Responding to Human Rights Judgments* (2012, Cm 8432) Annex A.

[59] These are based on the author's observations from the gallery during the debate, which is reported in HL Deb 5 July 2012, vol 436, cols 876ff. There are (remarkably) no official attendance records.

[60] Joint Committee on Human Rights (n 6) para 22.

[61] AV Dicey, *Introduction to the Study of the Law of the Constitution* (10th edn, London, Macmillan, 1959) 23–24.

4 declaration.[62] This section presents evidence that supports that view, though it is not conclusive.

In an influential[63] analysis, Ivor Jennings identified three key questions in any inquiry about the existence of a constitutional convention: 'First, what are the precedents; secondly, did the actors in the precedents believe that they were bound by a rule; and thirdly, is there a reason for the rule?'[64] Starting with the first of these for our present subject, the precedents suggest an almost uniform practice of legislative amendment by way of response. The arguable exception has been the *Smith v Scott* decision on prisoners' rights to vote (which accepts and applies the decision of the European Court of Human Rights in *Hirst*), yet there too, as discussed above, a response is awaited.[65] At any rate, this one instance of either extreme delay or non-compliance is not conclusive. Some commentators do not believe that complete uniformity of action is required to establish a constitutional convention,[66] and in international law it is not necessary that a practice manifest 'absolutely rigorous conformity with the rule' in order to determine the existence of *legally* binding international custom.[67] And, as previously noted, the distinctive aspect of that case is that anger has been directed at Strasbourg rather than at UK courts, the latter tending (with some variation) to agree with the Government that the issue is a matter for Parliament.[68]

Passing over the second question momentarily, we can consider the third, which is whether there is a reason for the rule. Different answers are plausible. The sceptical view, which we may associate with Francesca Klug and Danny Nicol,[69] would maintain that it was precisely both the legal and policy aim of the HRA to reserve legal and political sovereignty for the UK Parliament, as supplemented by the well-informed activity of the JCHR. Gardbaum also argues that a legislative response should not follow automatically, but rather that Parliament should have the political

[62] Kavanagh (n 32) 289. See also 488.
[63] See, eg, *Reference re Questions Concerning Amendment of Constitution of Canada* [1981] 1 SCR 753, 888 (the 'Patriation Reference').
[64] I Jennings, *The Law and the Constitution* (5th edn, London, University of London Press, 1959) 136. See also J Jaconelli, 'Do Constitutional Conventions Bind?' (1999) 64 *CLJ* 149; N Barber, 'Laws and Constitutional Conventions' [2009] *LQR* 194.
[65] See White (n 10).
[66] Jaconelli (n 64) 153, but see also 165–66.
[67] *Military and Paramilitary Activities in and against Nicaragua Case (Nicaragua v United States of America) (Merits)* [1986] ICJ Rep 14 [186].
[68] This was the approach taken in the judgment of Laws LJ in *Chester v Secretary of State for Justice* [2010] EWCA Civ 1439, which ruled not only that a second declaration of incompatibility was inappropriate, but also, at [32]–[35], that the question of prisoner enfranchisement was *in principle* not a matter suitable for resolution in UK courts. In the Supreme Court decision on this case ([2013] UKSC 63), the leading judgment of Lord Mance concentrated almost entirely on the obligation to give effect to Strasbourg jurisprudence on the topic and touched very briefly upon the genuine rights issue at issue: compare [35] with the remainder of his judgment. Lady Hale and Lord Clarke did discuss the substantive issues briefly ([86]–[98]; [109]–[111]), while Lord Sumption discussed the substantive matter at the greatest length and concluded at [137] that he would not have found UK arrangements incompatible with the Convention absent the clear view of the Strasbourg Court on the matter. See also *Pearson and Feal-Martinez* (n 14) for similar statements.
[69] F Klug, 'Judicial Deference under the Human Rights Act 1998' [2003] *European Human Rights Law Review* 125, 131; D Nicol, 'Law and Politics after the Human Rights Act' [2006] *Public Law* 722, 744.

discretion to reasonably disagree with the court's assessment.[70] The more supportive view of a constitutional convention could offer the following reasons for the rule: to not do so would: (a) likely put the UK in breach of its binding international obligations; (b) disrupt the scheme of the HRA, which seeks to give real rather than illusory remedies in UK courts for violations of Convention rights; and (c) undermine the constitutional position of the judiciary and thus strain relations of comity between it and the other branches of government. And by way of rebuttal of the sceptical view, critics could point to the widely held view that the HRA *was* intended to function in a scheme that would generate considerable if not overwhelming political pressure to amend the laws to ensure conformity. On this view, the parliamentary sovereigntist's proper mode of disagreement would be to repeal or amend the HRA, or take an exceptional legislative stand on particular issues when they arise.

If we turn to the second of Jennings' questions—whether the actors felt bound to obey—then we can see that parliamentary views have been uneven, but when matters have come to a head, most have sided more with the view that there is some sort of obligation. Although this is not the place for an exhaustive survey, some examples corroborate this view. The first can be found in a pertinent statement in the White Paper setting out the case for the Human Rights Bill: '2.10 A declaration that legislation is incompatible with the Convention rights will not of itself have the effect of changing the law, which will continue to apply. But it will almost certainly prompt the Government and Parliament to change the law.'[71] This is consistent with views later stated in Parliament during some responses to declarations of incompatibility. For example, after the decision in *A and others v Secretary of State for the Home Department*, the then Home Secretary, Charles Clarke, engaged in the following exchange during the second reading for what became the Prevention of Terrorism Act 2005:

> **Mr. Clarke (Home Secretary):** The third motivating principle [for the bill] is the need to meet the Law Lords' judgment. In general, I do not regard it as a successful and positive state of affairs when the senior judiciary of this country, the Law Lords, and the Executive are in rather different places, and certainly not in terms of measures of this type. Their criticism of the regime in place was that it was disproportionate in character and discriminatory, and we should take that criticism extremely seriously. The measures that I am putting to the House in the Bill would address that question directly.
>
> ...
>
> **Mr. Cash (Con):** ... It is not a question of whether or not he is complying with the Law Lords' judgment. The problem arises because the Government have got themselves into a complete mess with regard to the human rights legislation. Surely the point is simply that, to ensure that the House can legislate on its own terms, it must legislate notwithstanding the Human Rights Act 1998, and then he is in the clear. Does he not see that?
>
> **Mr. Clarke:** I do not accept any of that. I simply do not accept the argument. I do not think that it is correct. What I do think is that when the Law Lords of this country make a set of

---

[70] Gardbaum (n 15) 27, 36, 123, 201–02. For my critique of this proposal, see J King, 'Rights and the Rule of Law in Third Way Constitutionalism' (2014) 30 *Constitutional Commentary* 101.
[71] *Rights Brought Home: The Human Rights Bill 1997* (Cm 3782, 1997) para 2.10.

criticisms about the way that we are operating that is well founded, by a vote of eight to one, it is incumbent on the Government—and, I would argue, on Parliament—to respond to that and decide how to deal with it.[72]

In an earlier part of the debate, as well, Mr Clarke observed that: 'If the Law Lords say that we have discriminatory and disproportionate legislation, I believe that there is an obligation on the whole House, not simply on the Government, to address that, and that is what we are doing.'[73]

In almost all legislative responses, there have been no direct calls by frontbenchers to disregard a declaration of incompatibility by UK courts. Indeed, one must look with diligence to find *any* reference to the judicial decision in most parliamentary debates, and in a few cases there is none at all. There have been occasional references to the 'non-binding' nature of the declarations, however. For instance, the JCHR in its report in the 2002–03 session commented that, unlike after an adverse decision of the European Court of Human Rights, the Government is not 'obliged' to respond to a declaration of incompatibility.[74] And while in the response to the *Roth* decision of the Court of Appeal, the Home Secretary, David Blunkett, at one point said 'We must also take account of the *Roth* judgment ... and we shall table an amendment', another minister (Rosie Winterton) later tabled the amendment itself declaring that at least part of it 'addresses a non-binding concern of the Court of Appeal in *Roth*'.[75] However, both these statements appear to refer to a legal notion of bindingness rather than anything material to a constitutional convention.

Until quite recently, and apart from the distinctive issue of prisoner voting that I have addressed above, nearly all cases have not been about *whether* to amend the legislation, but rather *how*. However, the response to the *Thompson* case broke new ground in ways that both support and detract from the view that there is a constitutional convention of response by amendment. In *Thompson*, the Supreme Court held incompatible a legislative scheme that prevented convicted sex offenders from having any possibility of having their names removed from the Sex Offenders Register. Both the Prime Minister, David Cameron,[76] and the Home Secretary, Theresa May,[77] declared themselves 'appalled' by the Court's decision, a sentiment echoed by the Labour Shadow Home Secretary, Yvette Cooper, when the matter came before Parliament.[78] Indeed, even Jack Straw, a former Labour Lord Chancellor and Secretary of State for Justice, had the following to say in support of his political adversary:

> I support the Home Secretary's views on the merits of the existing sex offenders register and her concern about the Court's decision, but will she confirm that under section 4 of the Human Rights Act 1998 there is absolutely no obligation on her or the House to change

---

[72] HC Deb, 23 February 2005, vol 431, cols 345–46.
[73] HC Deb 22 February 2005, vol 431, col 158.
[74] Joint Committee on Human Rights, *Draft Gender Recognition Bill (Nineteenth Report)* (2002–03, HL Paper 188-I, HC 1276-I) para 17.
[75] HC Deb 12 July 2002, vol 386, col 928.
[76] R Ford, 'Sex Register Ruling Provokes an Outrage' *The Times* (London, 17 February 2011) 5.
[77] HC Deb 16 February 2011, vol 523, col 959.
[78] HC Deb 16 February 2011, vol 523, cols 959–69.

the law one bit? All the Court did was to issue a declaration of incompatibility and section 4 makes it absolutely clear that any decision following that is a matter for the sovereign Parliament. It would be entirely lawful for the House and her to say that the existing regime will continue without any amendment.[79]

This statement flatly contradicts the idea of a constitutional convention, from a senior parliamentarian. By way of reply, the Home Secretary noted his statement, but continued with her overarching message that 'we are appalled by the decision ... but we do have to make a change. We will do so in the most minimal way possible'.[80] Furthermore, the Government delivered a mixed message in its subsequent parliamentary introduction of the remedial order. It arose for consideration first in a delegated legislation committee, where the Parliamentary Under-Secretary of State, Lynne Featherstone, a Liberal Democrat member of the Coalition Government, introduced and discussed the remedial order. Her view of the Court's decision was more upbeat:

> We clearly believe that it was a correct judgment and, as the Government, we comply with Supreme Court judgments ... We do not believe that a public review is needed—the ruling was quite clear and unequivocal, and we have responded.[81]

The language of compliance here, also found in other relevant portions of Hansard, implies the existence of an obligation. Furthermore, when the remedial order was introduced in the Lords a month later by Baroness Stowell of Beeston, a Conservative peer, she stated the following:

> Our constitutional arrangements are such that when the highest court of the land identifies an incompatibility with the European Convention on Human Rights, the Government of the day, whoever is in power, take remedial action. This is for various reasons, not the least of which is to ensure that the Government are not left vulnerable to further legal proceedings, potentially involving millions of pounds of taxpayers' money ... The Government were disappointed with the UK Supreme Court's ruling, but we take our responsibility to uphold the law seriously, and that includes human rights law.[82]

This is presently where matters lie. It is not possible to conclude that there is a constitutional convention that there should be a legislative amendment as a reply to a declaration of incompatibility; however, evidence is mounting that one is perceived by the Government and some legislators to exist. Of course, conventions can change and there are furthermore the deeper questions of whether any purported convention would require legislative amendment or only good faith engagement with the issue, and whether the convention only applies to declarations of incompatibility made by the Supreme Court or to any final declaration of incompatibility decision (recalling that 14 out of 20 final declarations have issued from lower courts). Proper discussion of such matters must be addressed on another day.

---

[79] HC Deb 16 February 2011, vol 523, col 963.
[80] HC Deb 16 February 2011, vol 523, col 961.
[81] HC Deb 19 June 2012, vol 546, col 10 (Eight Delegated Legislation Committee, Draft Sexual Offences Act 2003 (Notification Requirements) (England and Wales) Regulations 2012).
[82] HL Deb 5 July 2012, vol 738, cols 875, 886.

CONCLUSION

The HRA is a key constitutional statute in the UK and has created a new and excit-ing period in law and politics. This chapter has explored the feature of that system that is most novel in comparative perspective, namely, the ability to declare primary legislation incompatible with human rights without legally affecting its validity or continuing operation. I examined the practice of issuing such declarations and the nature of the responses thus far, and compared it with the experience of constitu-tional judicial review in some similar nations. I found the UK model distinct in that the delay between the declaration of incompatibility and the legislative response tended to be substantially greater than the one in foreign countries where the delay period (where available) for legislative response was set by the courts. Furthermore, the fact that declarations of incompatibility had declaratory rather than invalidat-ing force did not lead the UK courts to be any more assertive. They tended to be less assertive in finding statutes incompatible/invalid, and, though no comparative analysis of direct impact was conducted, even the casual comparativist can tell from the data that UK constitutional judicial review has had rather modest impact when either considered alone or in comparison with other nations. The portrait on the whole suggests a non-activist judiciary, though nothing there supports the view that they have not done their job under the HRA. These are not akin to statistics regard-ing convictions for rape, where the numbers alone give cause to shudder.

As to the question of whether the experience under the HRA has promoted delib-erative democracy, I noted that there is little evidence that the Government and Parliament feel dominated by judges under the HRA, and section 4 declarations have not been a significant issue for them. The evidence instead supports a view of collaboration and divided responsibilities, with courts adjudicating cases and setting out findings on narrow issues, while the Government and Parliament work from these conclusions to refashion policy accordingly. Where there has been serious ten-sion (eg, after the *Anderson* case and the *Thompson* case), the Government fought back by presenting to Parliament a policy that was different in only small ways from the original policy. Indeed, the responses to *Anderson* and *Belmarsh* may well have been regressive if we consider the matter in utilitarian terms.

At the same time, most of the cases raised issues that Parliament had not con-sidered in great depth (where there was an absence of legislative focus) and about which it often had no strong feelings. Since most cases were taken by marginalised groups, there is evidence of enhanced deliberative input, in the sense of ensuring that the needs of people who have less voice are properly taken into account in public decision-making. I further found that whole act responses and remedial orders were better than tacking responses, which make scant room for proper scrutiny of the implications of remedial measures. I lastly presented evidence that tends to support the view, though is ultimately inconclusive, that there exists a constitutional convention of responding to section 4 declarations of incompat-ibility. The Government and many parliamentarians do appear to feel obligated to respond to a section 4 declaration, at least so long as the HRA is in force. This appears to be proper constitutional policy, though there is room for considerable further analysis of this point.

One final point has not yet been given sufficient emphasis: the quality of much of these parliamentary debates is extremely impressive and not just (or even primarily) in the Lords. The popular picture of parliamentarians as crude rent-seekers is belied by the record here. The following comment by Mr Christopher Leslie (Labour), concluding the debate prior to the vote on the second reading of the Gender Recognition Bill, is more characteristic of the UK Parliament:

> I believe that the test of a civilised society is its approach to minorities and the respect that we have for their rights. Transsexual people face obstacles and legal problems on a day-to-day basis, quite unnecessarily. They have human rights that need defending, and freedoms that deserve respect. The Bill will right a wrong that currently exists, and I commend it to the House.[83]

The vote that followed immediately was 336 in favour, with 26 against. While there is important room for improvement, the record tends on the whole to demonstrate in no small way the virtues of a parliament that takes rights seriously, working for the most part in constitutional harmony with its colleagues on the bench.

---

[83] HC Deb 23 February 2004, vol 418, col 105.

Methodological Appendix

The breadth of data gathered for this study is too voluminous for ordinary legal citation in this book. The data is held in analytical summaries with complete citation and case-history (or 'sheppard') data in the possession of the book's editors and are publicly available on request from the author at jeff.king@ucl.ac.uk. The methodology for aggregating statistics is outlined below.

Figure	Comment
Figure 8.2 Delays	This table excludes declarations of incompatibility from three cases in which the declaration of incompatibility was issued *after* the remedial amendment came into force: *R (Wright) v (1) Secretary of State for Health (2) Secretary of State for Education & Skills* [2009] UKHL 3; *R (on the application of Hooper and others) v Secretary of State for Work and Pensions* [2003] EWCA Civ 813; and *R (on the application of Wilkinson) v Inland Revenue Commissioners* [2003] EWCA Civ 814. See the remedial provisions set out in Ministry of Justice, *Responding to Human Rights Judgments* (2012, Cm 8432) Annex A.
Figure 8.3 Remedial lag time averages	The method of aggregating Canadian, French and German data is described in the notes to Figure 8.4 below.
	The lag time for responses to UK declarations of incompatibility are calculated up to the date on which the remedial provision came into force. The lag time averages for Canada, France and Germany are calculated based on the times stipulated in the court decisions. There may be a gap between when remedial legislation entered into force and the date stipulated by the judicial decision, but the working assumption is that typically the remedial legislation will enter into force before the expiry of the date stipulated by the court.
	Notably, two German cases did not specify a timeline for implementation, and in some Canadian cases, the claimants returned to court for further extensions. Where the latter occurred, the total sum was calculated on the basis of the entirety of the period obtained.
Figure 8.4 Comparative declarations of unconstitutionality	To facilitate cross-national comparison (especially with the UK) and to respond to theoretical concerns of rights-based review in particular, certain filters were applied. Generally, the subset of cases considered here include those declarations in which: (1) the court assessed the constitutionality of a primary statute, including those of federal, provincial/state/Land/devolved assembly (thus excluding regulations and other subordinate legislation); and (2) the grounds for decision were based wholly or partly on the primary national constitutional bill of rights.

(continued)

Figure	Comment
	The United States was reluctantly excluded from the comparison because neither do US courts suspend declarations of invalidity nor is there any database counting both state and federal court strike downs in the periods of comparison used in this chapter. The author holds the data for the US Supreme Court, US federal courts, and for all states in particular years.
	Canadian data was compiled by manually examining all law reports for the SCC, Federal Courts and 9 of the 10 provinces. There was reliance on the analytical indices provided in these reports (examining them for 'Charter', 'Civil Rights', and 'Constitution Act'), and a measure of human error is possible both in the law reports themselves as well as in our review of them. This is, however, unlikely, given the importance of such cases and frequency of appeals. The results were cross-checked against partial lists compiled in the publications of Hogg, Bushell/Thornton, Roach and Choudhry, and the methodology and sample of results was cross-checked by different readers. The Canadian data focused on review by higher courts (not tribunals, which may also review legislation for constitutionality) of legislation for compliance with the Canadian Charter. Furthermore, we excluded a significant number of cases whose remedies could conceivably have been available under the interpretive presumption under section 3 HRA (which arguably includes remedies called reading in, reading down and severance in Canada (under *Schachter v Canada* [1992] 2 SCR 679): cf *Ghaidan v Godin Mendoza* [2004] 3 WLR 113 (HL) and A Kavanagh, *Constitutional Review under the UK Human Rights Act* (Cambridge, Cambridge University Press, 2009), chs 3 and 4), even though the interference with the legislative scheme was unmistakable. Only the case of *Skolski v Quebec* [2005] 1 SCR 2001 was excluded from the SCC batch on such grounds. The rest are available in the analytical summaries noted above. Due to lack of accessible law reports, it was not possible to include Quebec for the entire period or Alberta cases after 2010.
	All case histories were followed up or 'sheppardised'. No declaration within the same proceedings was double-counted, and thus any lower court decision which proceeded to the higher courts and was affirmed or reversed was counted once or struck from the list. In one case, a declaration of a lower court that was approved in principle by the Supreme Court of Canada, but in different proceedings, was counted: see *Canada (AG) v Several Clients and Several Solicitors* (2000) 189 NSR (2d) 313; (2001) 197 NSR (2d) 42 (affirmed, NS Court of Appeal), and cf *Lavallee (et al) v Canada (AG)* [2002] 3 SCR 209.
	Constitutional judicial review is available outside the Canadian Charter for rights cases, eg, under the Canadian Bill of Rights and under certain provincial charters of rights (eg, Quebec). However, the invalidation of statutes on such grounds is relatively uncommon, despite notable exceptions (eg, *Chaoulli v Quebec (AG)* [2005] 1 SCR 759).

Figure	Comment
	Constitutional review under the Basic Law in Germany and under the Constitution of the Fifth Republic in France are centralised through the German Constitutional Court and the French Constitutional Council. In each case, a list of all declarations was obtained via the detailed statistics provided by the German Constitutional Court and elaborate search-engine for researchers provided on the website of the French Constitutional Council. In the case of Germany, all decisions issued since 2000 were individually examined to determine the subset of cases concerning rights-based review of primary statutes (in Germany's case, both federal and Land). The cases were selected from instances where the statutes were declared unconstitutional, and not where they were interpreted under a strong presumption of conformity with the Basic Law. This latter interpretive remedy is known as *Verfassungskonformeauslegung* (ie, 'Constitutionally compatible interpretation') and these were not included in the sample.
	In the case of France, a subset of declarations of unconstitutionality was obtained through the Conseil's online database and all examined individually to determine the subset pertaining to rights-based review. In each case, the exercise was carried out by native speakers of German (Stefan Theil) and French (Quentin Montpetit) respectively.
	The precise grounds for decision in French cases are not always clear. The author and researcher decided that where the recitals indicated an incompatibility with the rights provisions of the 1958 Constitution (as amended), it was counted for our purposes regardless of whether other grounds proved more preponderant in the analysis. Some borderline cases were excluded. Furthermore, non-compliance with the Charter of the Environment (2004), which is incorporated into the Constitution, was also counted.
	In France, the traditional jurisdiction of the Constitutional Council was invoked only by the procedure under Article 61 of the Constitution, which triggered at the request of the President, Prime Minister, presidents of the national assembly or senate, or 60 senators or deputies, a constitutional *preview* procedure for certain bills prior to their being enacted as law. An amendment in 2008 introduced Article 61-1, and with it a procedure whereby references could be made from the Court of Cassation and the Council of State (Conseil d'Etat) where constitutional rights and liberties are in question. Thus, France has had rights-based constitutional *review* since this amendment came into force on 1 March 2010. Questions referred to the Council under this procedure are known as *Questions Prioritaires de Constitutionnalité (QPC)*. Despite their short lifespan, QPC cases account for 51 of the total of 91 rights-based declarations of unconstitutionality between 2000 and 2012.

(continued)

Figure	Comment
Figure 8.5 Absence of legislative focus	In this case the author made a qualitative assessment of whether it was reasonable to infer that the point at issue in the case was among the moral and policy considerations considered during the legislative process. It was *not* a condition of finding legislative focus that any use or consideration of rights rhetoric occurred. Nor was the assessment based on an extensive forensic search of Hansard. Where there was doubt, the category of 'unknown' was applied.
Figure 8.6 Tacking, whole act and remedial order responses	The only close call in this section was Part V of the Protection of Freedoms Act 2012. I included it as a whole act response given the nature of that particular Act.

Part III

Legislative Human Rights Review in the UK's Devolved Jurisdictions

9

The Protection of Human Rights in the Legislative Process of Scotland

BRUCE ADAMSON

The Scottish parliament is one of the newest parliaments in the world. It opened in 1999 with great hope and celebration:

> 'There shall be a Scottish Parliament.' Through long years, those words were first a hope, then a belief, then a promise. Now they are a reality.[1]

The Scotland Act 1998 which created the Scottish Parliament placed the European Convention of Human Rights (ECHR) at the heart of the Parliament by linking legislative competence to Convention rights drawn from the ECHR. The Parliament developed its processes and procedures around this competence and has prided itself on the fact that its grounding in human rights principles and its strongly represen-tative and participative committee system ensured that legislation received robust scrutiny. However, there has been some criticism that the lofty ideals have not been met in practice.[2]

Since it began, the Scottish Parliament has passed over 200 Acts and thousands of pieces of subordinate legislation. This chapter will consider the role that protec-tion of human rights has played in the process of Scottish parliamentary legislative scrutiny and look at examples of where Scottish parliamentary legislation has been challenged or may be challenged as beyond competence on the basis of a breach of Convention rights.

The processes for legislative scrutiny in Scotland reflect the integral importance of human rights protections to the Parliament's competence. Before a bill can be introduced, its competence must be considered by both the member in charge of the bill[3] and the Parliament's Presiding Officer. Once the bill is introduced, it must pass a three-stage process of consideration involving both the full chamber of the Parliament and a number of representative committees.

---

[1] Donald Dewer MSP, First Minister of Scotland, at the official opening of the Scottish Parliament, 1 July 1999.

[2] A O'Neill, 'Human Rights and People and Society' in EE Sutherland, KE Goodall, GFM Little and FP Davidson (eds), *Law Making and the Scottish Parliament: The Early Years* (Edinburgh, Edinburgh University Press, 2011).

[3] Under the Scotland Act 1998, this only applied to Scottish Executive Bills, but was extended to Members' Bills via s 6 of the Scotland Act 2012.

To date, there have been few challenges to the competence of Scottish legislation on the basis of breach of Convention rights, although this is now beginning to increase. We can only speculate as to why there have been so few, but we can learn lessons from those that have been taken. There are some issues that have not yet been challenged, but where the level of scrutiny provided by the Parliament and its committees may have been inadequate.

The case studies set out in this chapter cover a number of issues where the Parliament's procedures have been tested or where scope for challenge has arisen. They cover a range of issues from the detention of patients under mental health legislation, to the introduction of time-bar for claims for breaches of Convention rights, to the retention of DNA for minor offences and the provision of legal representation to ensure a fair hearing. Each case examines the scrutiny provided in an attempt to illustrate the strengths and weakness of the Scottish system for scrutinising legislation.

I. HISTORY

Scots law has a complicated history that draws its roots from Celtic and Roman times. Unlike England, Scotland maintained a strong Roman law system of 'rights' and 'obligations', although it also developed common law in line with England.

While the crowns of the two countries were joined in 1603, the union of the countries themselves did not take place until 1707, when the two Parliaments asked the Queen to appoint commissioners on their behalf to draft a treaty of union. The task was completed in nine weeks. It was controversial at the time, and remains so. The Treaty of Union did not create the United Kingdom (UK) as a federal state with governmental responsibilities formally divided between London and Edinburgh; instead, it created the conditions under which London-based institutions could govern across an expanded territory.[4]

Scotland maintained its own legal system under the Treaty. The Treaty enabled the UK Parliament to make laws for Scotland; it did not amend existing Scots law, nor did it create a united legal system. In fact, Article XIX of the Treaty provided for the continued existence and jurisdiction of the Court of Session and the High Court of Justiciary, and ensured that no cause in Scotland be cognoscible by the Courts of Chancery, Queen's Bench, Common Pleas or any other court in Westminster Hall.[5]

The move towards self-determination for Scotland gained momentum during the twentieth century, resulting in the Scotland Act 1978, which would have created a devolved Scottish Assembly. The Act was subject to approval via a post-legislative referendum in 1979. While the referendum passed on popular majority (51 per cent), it failed the condition that 40 per cent of the entire electorate needed to vote

---

[4] C Himsworth and C O'Neill, *Scotland's Constitution Law and Practice* (2nd edn, London, Bloomsbury Professional, 2009) 39.
[5] Although a route of appeal to the House of Lords from the Court of Session developed and following the creation of the UK Supreme Court, both civil matters and those criminal matters which raise devolution issues can be appealed to the Supreme Court in London.

in favour of the Act. The Scotland Act 1978 was therefore repealed and devolution was delayed.

Devolution eventually came when the incoming Labour Government of 1997 fulfilled its manifesto commitment to a programme of constitutional reform, including devolution in Scotland and the incorporation of the ECHR into UK law.

Following a pre-legislative referendum in September 1997, which received 74 per cent support, the UK Government introduced the Scotland Act 1998.

The White Paper on the Human Rights Bill published in October 1997 set out how devolution and human rights would be combined in Scotland:

> The Government has decided that the Scottish Parliament will have no power to legislate in any way which is incompatible with the Convention; and similarly that the Scottish Executive will have no power to make subordinate legislation or to take executive action which is incompatible with the Convention. It will accordingly be possible to challenge such legislation and actions on the grounds that the Scottish Parliament or Executive has incorrectly applied its powers. If the challenge is successful then the legislation or action would be held to be unlawful.[6]

The Scottish Parliament was created by the Scotland Act 1998 and met for the first time on 12 May 1999. It was opened[7] by Dr Winnie Ewing, as the Oldest Qualified Member, with the inspiring, but not entirely accurate, words:

> The Scottish Parliament which adjourned on 25 March in the year 1707 is hereby reconvened.[8]

The modern Scottish Parliament elected under a proportional representation system bears very little resemblance to its ancient ancestor, the Estates of Parliament, but there was significant importance in Scotland having its own Parliament once again. Dr Ewing closed her opening remarks by calling for a consensual style of politics:

> It was said that 1707 was the end of an auld sang. All of us here can begin to write together a new Scottish song, and I urge all of you to sing it in harmony—fortissimo.[9]

Fifteen years on, the devolution journey is not yet over. In September 2014 Scotland held a referendum on independence. The referendum was accompanied by significant public engagement and the turnout of 84.6 per cent was the highest recorded for an election or referendum in the UK since the introduction of universal suffrage. While a majority of 55.3 per cent voted against independence, the membership of the pro-independence parties rose dramatically following the result, and there are still active campaigns for independence. The UK Government has undertaken to give additional powers to Scotland following the general election in 2015.

---

[6] *Rights Brought Home: The Human Rights Bill* (Presented to Parliament by the Secretary of State for the Home Department by Command of Her Majesty, October 1997, Cm 3782) 2.21.
[7] Following the formal swearing in of Members of the Scottish Parliament.
[8] Dr Winnie Ewing MSP (Official Report of the Scottish Parliament 12 May 1999).
[9] ibid.

II. NATIONAL HUMAN RIGHTS FRAMEWORK

The dualist nature of the UK system means that generally speaking the rules of international law that bind the UK in its international dealings do not create rights and obligations that are enforceable domestically. Prior to the coming into force of the Human Rights Act 1998 in October 2000, individuals could not directly enforce the rights protected by the ECHR in Scottish courts and instead had to take a case to the European Court of Human Rights in Strasbourg.

Traditionally the Scottish courts took the view that they were not entitled to have regard to the ECHR even as an aid to interpretation.[10] This changed over time, and around the point that the movement for a Human Rights Act gained momentum in the 1990s, the Lord President of the Court of Session described the Scottish approach as outdated and expressed the view that the Scottish Courts could use the ECHR as an aid to interpretation.[11]

The Human Right Act 1998 was introduced with the intention of giving people in the UK opportunities to enforce their rights under the ECHR in UK courts rather than having to incur the cost and delay of taking a case to Strasbourg.[12] It provides four key obligations:

So far as it is possible to do so, primary legislation and subordinate legislation must be read and given effect in a way which is compatible with the Convention Rights.[13] If the court is satisfied that a provision of primary legislation is incompatible with a Convention right it may make a declaration of incompatibility.[14]

In that event, a Minister of the Crown may by order make such amendments to the legislation as he considers necessary to remove the incompatibility.[15]

It is unlawful for a public authority (including a court or tribunal) to act in a way which is incompatible with a Convention right.[16]

A Minister of the Crown in charge of a Bill in either House of Parliament must, before the Second Reading of the Bill make a statement about the compatibility of the Bill with Convention Rights.[17]

Convention Rights are defined as the rights and fundamental freedoms set out in Articles 2–12 and 14 of ECHR; Articles 1 to 3 of Protocol 1, Articles 1 and 3 of Protocol 6, and Article 1 of Protocol 13, as read with Articles 16–18 of the ECHR.[18]

The Human Rights Act 1998 applies across the UK and the Scotland Act 1998 provides additional protection in relation to powers of the Scottish Parliament and Scottish Ministers by linking their competence to Convention rights. The

---

[10] *Kaur v Singh* (1980) SC 319.
[11] *T Petitioner* 1997 SLT 724.
[12] *Rights Brought Home* (n 6).
[13] Human Rights Act 1998, s 3.
[14] ibid, s 4.
[15] ibid, s 10.
[16] ibid, s 6.
[17] ibid, s 19.
[18] ibid, s 1.

Scotland Act also transfers devolved functions to Scottish Ministers, including the implementation of other international obligations within the devolved context.

There were very few cases relying on the Scotland Act 1998 in the early years; however, there have been some interesting developments over recent years as a result of the case of *AXA General Insurance Ltd and others v Lord Advocate and others*.[19] *AXA* was a challenge by a number of insurance companies to legislation which had negated the effect of a decision by the House of Lords. In *Rothwell v Chemical & Insulating Co Ltd*[20] the House of Lords held that, as pleural plaques caused no symptoms, did not increase susceptibility to other asbestos-related diseases or shorten life expectancy, their mere presence in the claimants' lungs did not constitute an injury which was capable of giving rise to a claim for damages. Prior to *Rothwell*, such claimants had been able to claim compensation and there had been a large number of compensation payments over a 20-year period. Anticipating that while the decision in *Rothwell* was not binding on the Scottish courts, it would be highly persuasive,[21] the Scottish Parliament passed the Damages (Asbestos-related Conditions) (Scotland) Act 2009 to negate the effect of the decision and 'to defend and confirm the right of access to justice for those who have been negligently exposed to asbestos and have sustained injury as a result'.[22] The legislation left AXA and other insurance companies open to significant claims for compensation and so they sought judicial review. The case contained a number of important elements relating to the powers of the Scottish Parliament, its relationship with Westminster and the other devolved jurisdictions, the human rights of insurance companies and the extent of 'standing' in Scots law to bring applications for judicial review. One of the grounds of challenge was that the legislation was an irrational exercise of legislative authority and thus was unlawful at common law. This argument had failed in *Adams v Scottish Ministers*,[23] but had not been considered on appeal. At first instance in *AXA,* it was held that, like any statutory body, the Scottish Parliament could be reviewed on common law grounds. The Supreme Court held that while there did remain, over and above the Scotland Act 1998 Act, common law powers that would allow the court to interfere with an Act of the Scottish Parliament, those powers would be available only in exceptional circumstances, where the Parliament attempted to abrogate fundamental rights or to violate the rule of law. Thus, the primary means for challenging an Act of the Scottish Parliament is upon the grounds laid down in section 29 of the Scotland Act 1998.

---

[19] *AXA General Insurance Ltd and others v Lord Advocate and others* [2011] UKSC 46.

[20] *Rothwell v Chemical & Insulating Co Ltd* [2007] UKHL 39.

[21] Scottish Courts gave early indications that they would follow *Rothwell* in *Wright v Stoddard International plc (No 2)* [2007] CSOH 173.

[22] Scottish Parliament Official Report, Wednesday 11 March 2009, Minister for Community Safety Fergus Ewing MSP, col 15653.

[23] *Adams v Scottish Ministers* 2003 SLT 366.

III. DEVOLUTION AND DEVOLVED COMPETENCE

The mode of devolution adopted by the Scotland Act 1998 is a 'reserved' model. The Scotland Act confers a general power to make laws, but this power is subject to a number of reserved areas set out in Schedule 5 to the Act.[24]

There is a perception that the reserved model allows the Scottish Parliament more power, but it will depend on how restrictively the reservations are construed and how often Westminster seeks to legislate on devolved issues.[25]

Section 29 of the Scotland Act provides for the legislative competence of the Scottish Parliament. It sets out that an Act is not law if it is outside legislative competence[26] and a provision is outwith competence insofar as it is incompatible with Convention rights.[27] Section 57(2) places a similar restriction and corresponding obligations on the competence of Scottish Ministers.

Section 126 of the Scotland Act defines Convention rights by reference to the Human Rights Act, namely the rights and fundamental freedoms set out in Articles 2–12 and 14 of ECHR; Articles 1 to 3 of Protocol 1, Articles 1 and 3 of Protocol 6, and Article 1 of Protocol 13, as read with Articles 16–18 of the ECHR.

The Scotland Act also links the competence of the Scottish Government and the Scottish Parliament to EU law. This is particularly relevant with the growing importance of the Charter of Fundamental Rights of the European Union and the jurisprudence of the Court of Justice of the European Union.

While foreign affairs and international relations are reserved to the UK Parliament, the Scotland Act creates an exemption to ensure that Scottish Ministers understand their responsibility for observing and implementing international obligations.[28] It is important to appreciate that this is defined not simply by reference to the specific Convention rights defined in the Human Rights Act, but applies to all international obligations. If Scottish Ministers fail to meet these obligations they may be subject to enforcement action against them on the part of the Secretary of State by virtue of section 58 of the Scotland Act. This has led to the understanding that Scottish Ministers are bound to respect the whole range of international treaty obligations, even where they have not been incorporated into the domestic law of the UK.[29] It may be argued that while not making international obligations directly part of the domestic Scots law,[30] the Scotland Act embodies a legitimate expectation that the actions of the Scottish devolved institutions will be compatible with all of the UK's international obligations.[31]

---

[24] This can be contrasted with the scheme of devolution, which was considered by the Scotland Act 1978, which had transferred listed powers.

[25] R Reed and J Murdoch, *A Guide to Human Rights in Scotland*, (2nd edn, Edinburgh, Tottel Publishing, 2008) 13.

[26] Scotland Act 1998, s 29(1).

[27] ibid, s 29(2)(d).

[28] Ibid, para 7(2) of sched 5.

[29] *T Petitioner* (n 11).

[30] *Whaley v Lord Advocate* 2008 SC (HL) 107, Lord Hope at 110–11.

[31] A O'Neill, 'The European Court and the Duty to Investigate Deaths' (October 2009) *Journal of the Law Society of Scotland*.

Schedule 4 to the Scotland Act gives additional protection by providing that certain provisions are protected from modification. These include both the Human Rights Act and the legislative competence established by section 29 of the Scotland Act itself.

The Scotland Act also provides guidance in relation to the interpretation of legislative provisions. Section 101 of the Scotland Act requires Acts of the Scottish Parliament to be interpreted as narrowly as required to bring them within legislative competence. This contrasts with the obligation under section 3 of the Human Rights Act, which requires all legislation to be interpreted as far as possible to be Convention-compliant. This was considered by the Judicial Committee of the Privy Council in *DS v HM Advocate*,[32] a case concerning the disclosure of previous sexual offences and the right to a fair hearing guaranteed by Article 6. Lord Hope (with whom Lord Rodger and the rest of the Court agreed) commented:

> The word 'narrowly' ... looks awkward in a case where the question is whether a provision in an Act of the Scottish Parliament is incompatible with Convention rights. Where incompatibility with the Convention rights is in issue, the obligation in section 3(1) of the Human Rights Act is to construe the provision in a way that is compatible with them ... The explanation for the choice of language in section 101(2) is to be found in the way the limits of the legislative competence of the Scottish Parliament are defined in section 29(2). The matters listed there extend well beyond incompatibility with the Convention rights. An attempt by the Scottish Parliament to widen the scope of its legislative competence will be met by the requirement that any provision which could be read in such a way as to be outside competence must be read as narrowly as is required for it to be within competence. It is otherwise in the case of the Convention rights. The proper starting point is to construe the legislation as directed by section 3(1) of the Human Rights Act. If it passes this test, so far as the Convention rights are concerned it will be within competence. The obligation to construe a provision in an Act of the Scottish Parliament so far as it is possible to do so in a way that is compatible with the Convention rights is a strong one. The court must prefer compatibility to incompatibility. This enables it to look closely at the legislation to see if it can be explained and operated in a way that is compatible and, if it is not, how it can be construed so as to make it so.

Baroness Hale of Richmond emphasises the high threshold for any attempt to challenge on ECHR grounds legislation which had been passed by an elected legislature such as the Scottish Parliament. She notes in paragraph 92:

> The legislature can get ahead of Strasbourg if it wishes and so can the courts in developing the common law. But it is not for us to challenge the legislature unless satisfied that the Convention rights, as internationally agreed and interpreted in Strasbourg, require us to do so.

---

[32] *DS v HM Advocate* [2007] UKPC D1, 2007 SCCR 222.

IV. LEGISLATIVE SCRUTINY

> Now, it is of great moment that well-drawn laws should themselves define all the points they possibly can and leave as few as may be to the decision of the judges (Aristotle, *Rhetoric*)

Those drafting the Scotland Act 1998 understood the importance in creating a parliament of limited competence of including a variety of mechanisms by which the competence of an Act of the Scottish Parliament could be tested. In an effort to avoid the potentially serious consequences of an Act being found to have breached the Parliament's legislative competence, a number of provisions are included in the Scotland Act which allow testing of legislative competence.

A. Pre-legislative Scrutiny

i. Statement of Competence by the Presiding Officer[33]

Section 31(2) of the Scotland Act provides:

> The Presiding Officer shall, on or before the introduction of a Bill in the Parliament, decide whether or not in his view the provisions of the Bill would be within the legislative competence of the Parliament and state his decision.

This is reflected in Rule 9.3.1 of the Standing Orders of the Scottish Parliament, which provides:

> A Bill shall on introduction be accompanied by a written statement signed by the Presiding Officer which shall—
> (a) indicate whether or not in his or her view the provisions of the Bill would be within the legislative competence of the Parliament; and
> (b) if in his or her view any of the provisions would not be within legislative competence, indicate which those provisions are and the reasons for that view.

The Presiding Officer is not obliged to seek any advice before making the statement, but in practice parliamentary lawyers provide advice, seeking counsel's opinion when necessary. The legal advice informing the statement is never disclosed and is protected under the exemption for legal advice under Freedom of Information legislation.[34]

The statement is simply that the Presiding Officer is of the view that the bill is within the competence of the Parliament. Section 31(2) requires the statement, but there is no restriction on the Parliament passing a bill in a situation where the Presiding Officer is of the view that it is not compliant. Equally, there is no guarantee that a bill that receives a statement of competence will not be challenged and perhaps be found to be outwith the competence of the Parliament. However, the

---

[33] The Presiding Officer is the speaker of the Parliament, elected by secret ballot and maintaining no party allegiance.
[34] Freedom of Information (Scotland) Act 2002, s 30.

Presiding Officer's statement does sometimes prove to be an essential check on the exercise of power by the Government and there have been examples where, following an indication that competence may be at question, that the Government has amended a bill prior to introduction.[35]

While the Presiding Officer's statement is useful, there may be a risk that it offers a false sense of security to Members of the Scottish Parliament (MSPs) who may rely on the statement of competence, without having the benefit of seeing the legal advice which will have identified potential risks. There is also an issue in that there is no procedural mechanism which permits or requires the Presiding Officer to re-evaluate the decision on competence at later stages of the bill. There is no procedure whereby the Presiding Officer could consider the competence of an amendment to a bill.

ii. Statement of Competence by the Person in Charge of the Bill

The person in charge of the bill must make a statement that he or she considers the bill to be within the competence of the Parliament, but as with the statement of the Presiding Officer, the legal advice supporting the statement does not need to be disclosed and similar statements are not required for amendments. Originally only Executive Bills required such a statement, but this was extended to Members' Bills by the Scotland Act 2012. The Scotland Act 1998 as amended provides at section 31:

> 31(1) A person in charge of a Bill shall, on or before introduction of the Bill in the Parliament, state that in his view the provisions of the Bill would be within the legislative competence of the Parliament.

The Standing Orders of the Parliament reflect this at Rule 9.3, providing that a person in charge of a bill must provide not only a statement of compliance, but also a policy memorandum which includes an assessment of the effects, if any, of the bill on human rights and other matters.[36] This policy memorandum may be significant in assessing the compatibility of legislation with Convention rights, particularly in applying the test of proportionality.[37]

There is also a power provided under section 33 of the Scotland Act for Scotland's law officers to make a pre-assent reference to the Supreme Court. Section 35 provides a similar power to the UK Secretaries of State.

B. The Legislative Process

The Scotland Act provides minimum requirements for the process to be followed by the Parliament in passing bills. Section 36(1) requires there to be at least three distinct stages of scrutiny for bills: a stage when members can debate and vote on the

---

[35] See Case Study 2 below.

[36] This is compulsory for Government and Members' Bills, but optional for Committee Bills.

[37] *A v Scottish Ministers* 2002 SC (PC) 63 at 66, 2001 SLT 1331 at 1334m, per Lord Hope of Craighead.

general principles of the bill; a stage when they can consider and vote on its details; and a final stage when the bill can be passed or rejected.[38]

Given the short amount of time available for plenary consideration, the vast bulk of scrutiny takes place in committees. There are mandatory and subject committees, along with committees to consider particular issues or pieces of legislation. Mandatory committees are established at the beginning of each session and their remits are determined by parliamentary rules. Those established in session four in June 2011 were: Equal Opportunities; European and External Relations; Finance; Public Audit; Public Petitions; Standards, Procedures and Public Appointments; and Subordinate Legislation (which became the Delegated Powers and Law Reform Committee in June 2013). Subject committees are usually established at the beginning of each session. Those established at the start of session four were: Economy, Energy and Tourism; Education and Culture; Health and Sport; Infrastructure and Capital Investment; Justice; Local Government and Regeneration; and Rural Affairs, Climate Change and Environment. Additional committees to consider Welfare Reform and the Independence Referendum were established in 2012.

The Commission on Scottish Devolution which was supported by both the UK and Scottish Parliaments and reported in 2009 found that the Scottish Parliament Committees worked well, but that they were overloaded with legislation and this meant that the time available for legislative scrutiny was often limited by tight time-frames.[39] The Commission noted that there had originally been concerns about the possibility of executive dominance in the context of the unicameral nature of the Parliament, but it considered that this was addressed through the counterweight of the powerful committee system. In evidence to the Commission, the Auditor General for Scotland said that 'the situation has been completely transformed ... the level of scrutiny is much more extensive and robust than that which existed before devolution'.[40]

However, the Commission did raise some concerns, in particular, that despite the focus early on in the process on consultation and an evidence-based approach, the later amending stages are often rushed, giving outside interests insufficient opportunity to make representations. A related concern is that new provisions are sometimes introduced late in the process, shortly before the legislation is passed, thereby bypassing detailed scrutiny in committee.[41]

There is no specialist human rights committee, although the committees do make use of specialist advisers/researchers and external consultants. A number of groups in Scotland have been campaigning for the establishment of a specialist human rights committee.

In 2011 Aiden O'Neill QC contrasted the role of the Joint Committee on Human Rights at the UK Parliament with the lack of a specialist committee in Scotland:

> The failure by the Scottish Parliament to establish any Scottish Human Rights Parliamentary Committee with the resources and expertise to be able and willing to test the Convention

---

[38] Scottish Parliament Guidance on Public Bills, available at www.scottish.parliament.uk.
[39] *Serving Scotland Better: Scotland and the United Kingdom in the 21st Century* (Final Report, June 2009, Commission on Scottish Devolution) 6.22.
[40] ibid 6.23.
[41] ibid 6.44.

compatibility of the administrative and legislative action and inaction of the Scottish Government casts grave doubt on the extent to which a human rights culture has indeed taken root at the heart of the Scottish institutions of government.[42]

In 2012 the Scottish Parliament's Cross-Party Group on Human Rights commissioned a short-term piece of evidence gathering research on the need for a human rights committee in the Scottish Parliament. The research, carried out by the Glasgow Human Rights Network, based at the University of Glasgow, looked at the Official Report for a single calendar month (November 2011) and considered the way in which a number of committees operated. The report concluded:

> Although we are limited by the terms of reference to a single calendar month, the evidence for the period reveals a widespread disregard of the normative and institutional framework for conceptualising and analysing human rights issues. Although there is no evidence to suggest that this is deliberate, most Committees did not seize the opportunity to imbue human rights in their respective field of activities.

> More concerning is the perspective of the Justice Committee on human rights. As the only committee with the sole competence over general human rights issues, the Committee should have insisted and pushed Government departments to take into account the human rights framework in their proposed legislation and in the implementation of their policies. Whenever the Committee scrutinizes legislations for issues that are of equal importance for human rights and the administration of criminal justice, the logic that informs and inspires its particular action or inaction seems to be rooted, more often than not, in the discourses of criminal justice than human rights.

> ...

> Given the depth and breadth of the remit of the Justice Committee, if the current arrangement is not changed, we think there is a serious risk that human rights might be trapped in the penumbra of justice, reduced to the narrower terrain of criminal justice, and lose their vibrant, transformative and dynamic normative force.[43]

The report was criticised by the Convener of the Justice Committee and others for only looking at a short period of time rather than considering the wider work of the Committee:

> This is a skewed snapshot of public evidence taken over one month and in no way reflects the achievements of the committee in scrutinising human rights issues. It is very much regretted such cursory attention was paid to our work.[44]

One of the reasons for the tension between external critics, who only have access to the public sessions of committees and their final reports, and the committees themselves, who take pride in their human rights record, may be the lack of information in terms of what the committee is actually doing. As with the legal advice that is provided in relation to pre-legislative statements of legislative competence,

---

[42] O'Neill (n 2) 44.

[43] A Allo, C MacLellan, S Nash, B Pearson, L Reid, R Woodford and J Young, *Scottish Parliament Committees' Perspective on Human Rights* (Glasgow, Glasgow Human Rights Network, 2012).

[44] www.heraldscotland.com/politics/political-news/record-on-human-rights-slammed.17546688.

the advice to committees and the private committee sessions where reports are discussed are kept confidential.

In July 2013 Professor Alan Miller, the Chair of the Scottish Human Rights Commission, called for human rights to be better integrated into the Scottish Parliament's committee system and suggested that if a separate human rights committee was not established, then a member of each current committee should be responsible for making sure that sufficient steps are taken. The importance of such integration and of role of parliaments and national human rights institutions was reflected in the Belgrade Principles on the Relationship between National Human Rights Institutions and Parliaments.

In evidence to the Justice Committee on 18 February 2014, Professor Miller suggested the creation of a rapporteur to have an ongoing dialogue with the process delivering Scotland's National Action Plan which is the roadmap for the realisation of all internationally recognised human rights in Scotland. It is based on evidence and broad participation. It has been developed by a Drafting Group from across the public and voluntary sectors and overseen by an Advisory Council whose members reflect the diversity of Scottish civic life. It is not a traditional action plan, but a transformative programme of action including agreed outcomes, priorities and a process for working together from 2013 to 2017 to progressively realise the potential of human rights in all areas of life. Professor Miller argued that a rapporteur would be able to ensure the exchange and free flow of information.[45] The Justice Committee accepted this recommendation and has now appointed John Finnie MSP as its first Human Rights Rapporteur.

C. Post-legislative Scrutiny

It is possible to challenge the validity of an Act of the Scottish Parliament after Royal Assent. The scope for such devolution issues and the process for taking a challenge is set out in paragraph 1 of Schedule 6 to the Scotland Act 1998 and specifically includes the issues of whether an Act is within legislative competence,[46] whether the actions of a member of the Scottish Government are incompatible with Convention rights,[47] or a failure to act.[48] Under the Scotland Act 2012, there is now a specific statutory right of appeal to the Supreme Court in Scottish criminal cases where a 'compatibility issue' arises.

A challenge to an Act of Parliament is not raised against the Parliament itself, but rather against the top law officer in Scotland, the Lord Advocate, as representative of the public interest. In *Adams v Scottish Ministers*, Lord Nimmo held that

---

[45] Scottish Parliament Official Report, 18 February 2014, col 4215.
[46] Scotland Act 1998, para (1)(a) of Sched 6.
[47] ibid, para (1)(d) of Sched 6.
[48] ibid, para (1)(e) of Sched 6.

following Royal Assent, an Act passes out of the hands of the Parliament, which, thereafter, has no legal responsibility to defend its validity.[49]

Challenges are most likely to arise in relation to litigation on the validity of a decision made by a member of the Scottish Government exercising powers established by an Act of the Scottish Parliament or in the context of a criminal prosecution where a person seeks to establish that a provision under which he is charged was itself beyond the Parliament's competence.

One of the difficulties in relation to post-legislative scrutiny has been the narrow approach to standing in judicial review in Scotland. The Scottish courts have applied a test of 'title and interest', which has, in practice, required petitioners for judicial review to demonstrate a strong relationship between themselves and the decision being impugned. Often this has led the courts to look for a financial, property or other interest to be impacted by the decision—with the effect that representative parties, such as pressure groups or informal associations, have been unable to pursue actions for judicial review in Scotland. In *AXA*, the Supreme Court fundamentally changed the Scottish approach, recognising that there is a 'public interest involved in judicial review proceedings, whether or not private rights may also be affected' and that 'a public authority can violate the rule of law without infringing the rights of any individual'. That being the case, a purely rights-based approach to standing was incompatible with the courts' duties to protect the rule of law. Instead, the test should be whether those seeking judicial review had a 'sufficient interest' in the decision in question. This change may allow for a significant improvement in terms of access to justice.

Even where the court does find legislation to be incompatible with Convention rights and that the relevant provision could not be read as being compliant, it is hesitant to sever the unlawful provision, instead choosing to use the powers under section 102 of the Scotland Act 1998 to suspend the effect of the decision to allow Parliament to cure the defect.[50]

The Supreme Court has provided additional guidance in relation to its approach in *Imperial Tobacco Ltd v Lord Advocate* (Scotland),[51] which was the first challenge on the ground that provisions of an Act related to matters reserved to the Westminster Parliament. The provisions in question prohibited the display of tobacco products in shops and banned vending machines selling tobacco products. Lord Hope began by making some general points which should be considered when deciding if an Act is outside the Scottish Parliament's competence. He stated that the task was essentially one of statutory construction. Rather than relying on arguments as to the constitutional status of the Scotland Act, he set out three principles which he held should be followed: first, the rules in the 1998 Act should be followed, as these had been set down by the legislature for that purpose; second, these rules should be interpreted in the same way as any rules in a UK statute, namely, according to the ordinary meaning of the words used; third, the fact that the 1998 Act was constitutional was not a guide to interpretation in itself. Lord Hope also held

---

[49] *Adams v Scottish Ministers* 2004 SC 665.
[50] See *Salvesen v Riddell* [2013] UKSC 22.
[51] *Imperial Tobacco Ltd v Lord Advocate (Scotland)* [2012] UKSC 61.

that the headings and sidenotes in the schedule to the 1998 Act, which contained the list of reserved matters, were part of the context of the Act and accordingly should be taken into account when interpreting the meaning of the reserved matters. Finally, he found that the Explanatory Notes which accompanied the Scotland Bill should be considered when interpreting the provisions of the Scotland Act, but that Explanatory Notes which were published in 2004 were useful as guidance only when interpreting its provisions and had no more weight than any other post-enactment commentary, as they did not form part of the context of the Act.

D. Retrospective Effect

In the event that a provision is found to be beyond competence, this would have retrospective effect, which could impact a large number of people, particularly if the provision had been in place for a long time. Along with allowing for the court to suspend its decision, the Scotland Act 1998 provides at section 102 for the court to make an order removing or limiting the retrospective effect of the decision for any period, subject to the conditions that the court sees as appropriate. The ability to suspend a decision for the Parliament to remedy the defect and to remove or limit the retrospective effect can work hand in hand. In coming to its decision, the court must consider the extent to which persons who are not directly involved would be adversely affected by the decision not to make such an order. This provision was discussed during the passage of the Scotland Act 1998, where it was said that the discretion is intended to be exercised only exceptionally in criminal proceedings.[52]

i. *Case Study 1:* Anderson v Scottish Ministers[53]

This was the first challenge under the Scotland Act and provided a useful example of the way in which the court would consider devolution issues. It was an action against the Mental Health (Public Safety and Appeals) (Scotland) Act 1999. Considering the legislative process for scrutiny outlined above, it was perhaps a worrying omen that the first Act of the Scottish Parliament was passed on an emergency basis using truncated procedures. This followed a decision in the Sheriff Court in the case of *Noel Ruddle*,[54] which established that the law then in force did not permit the continued detention of a patient who, it was argued, presented a serious risk to public safety, but whose mental disorder was not 'treatable'.

The Bill received statements of compliance from the relevant Minister and the Presiding Officer. Neither statement nor the accompanying documents addressed any human rights concerns. However, following concerns raised by a number

---

[52] 593 HL Official Report (5th series), cols 595–606.
[53] *Anderson v Scottish Ministers* 2000 SLT 873.
[54] *Noel Ruddle v Secretary of State for Scotland*, Decision in Summary Application, Sheriff Court, Lanark, 2 August 1999.

of opposition MSPs and organisations, such as the Law Society of Scotland, the Scottish Executive amended the Bill and issued a media statement which stated:

> We had to ensure that the legislation would be compatible with the European Convention on Human Rights. The Scotland Act does not allow Ministers to bring forward legislation that is incompatible. I am now confident that we have a robust and effective piece of legislation that will stand up to challenge in the courts.[55]

The Parliament agreed to consider the Bill under emergency procedure and the total amount of parliamentary consideration was less than five hours.

During the debate at Stage 1, opposition MSPs raised a number of concerns:

> My concerns, however, are whether the bill actually tackles the key issue of availability of treatment, because it seems to be absent, and whether therefore it is compliant with the European Convention on Human Rights. There is no mention in the bill of any measures that would ensure that patients have access or the right to access treatment where that treatment exists.

> Section 1 also raises serious human rights questions. Article 7 of the European Convention on Human Rights specifically guards against retrospective criminal legislation. Yet the bill is changing the goalposts for those who were convicted before 1 September this year. The rules governing appeals and discharge will be much tighter following the new legislation than they would have been at the time of such a person's conviction. I seek the reassurance of the minister that that aspect of section 1 does not amount to a breach of article 7.[56]

The Deputy Minister for Community Care, Iain Gray MSP, responded:

> I recap some of the essential points of the emergency bill. First, it is a short bill with a clearly defined purpose—public safety. Secondly, it will introduce practical and immediate steps to close the loophole exposed by the *Ruddle* case. Thirdly, the protections that are essential to an approach based on the European Convention on Human Rights are there; I am happy to assure members who have asked that the legislation has been fully considered against the convention, including articles 7 and 5. Our view is that the legislation meets the requirements of the convention.[57]

The Act was challenged by three detained patients who, but for the new Act, would have been entitled to seek release from the State Hospital at Carstairs[58] on the basis of the Sheriff's earlier ruling in *Ruddle*. In *Anderson v Scottish Ministers*, the detained patients argued that the Act was outside legislative competence because it breached their right to liberty under Article 5 ECHR.[59]

The Inner House of the Court of Session noted that the right to liberty under Article 5 ECHR was not absolute and had to be balanced against the duty imposed

---

[55] Scottish Government News release SE0438/99.

[56] Scottish Parliament Official Report, 2 September 1999, Roseanna Cunningham MSP, cols 108–09.

[57] Scottish Parliament Official Report, 2 September 1999, Deputy Minister for Community Care Iain Grey MSP, col 125.

[58] It is interesting to note that soon after this case, the State Hospital at Carstairs was the first public authority in Scotland to adopt a human rights-based approach to its work, an evaluation of which can be found at: www.scottishhumanrights.com.

[59] *Anderson v. Scottish Ministers* 2001 SC 1, 2002 SC (PC) 63, [2003] 2 AC 602.

on governments under Article 2 ECHR to protect life and health. As long as the court was satisfied under the original legislation that there was a risk of serious harm to the public, continued detention was justified and did not contravene the detainee's human rights, and retrospective application of the 1999 Act amendment was legitimate. The validity of the 1999 Act was upheld on appeal by the Judicial Committee of the Privy Council, though not on the basis of the weighing of rights approach taken by the Inner House.

Lord President Roger emphasised the needs of the wider community for protection. He also noted the importance of giving due deference to the assessments which the democratically elected legislature had made of the policy issues involved in considering whether section 1 of the 1999 Act violates the applicants' rights under Article 5 of the Convention:

> We require to bear in mind that 'inherent in the whole of the Convention is a search for a fair balance between the demands of the general interest of the community and the requirements of the protection of the individual's fundamental rights'.[60]

This approach lies behind the observations of Lord Hope of Craighead in *R v DPP ex parte Kebilene*.[61] Speaking of the application of the Convention, he said (at 994 A–E):

> In this area [the application of the Convention] difficult choices may have to be made by the executive or the legislature between the rights of the individual and the needs of society. In some circumstances it will be appropriate for the courts to recognise that there is an area of judgment within which the judiciary will defer, on democratic grounds, to the considered opinion of the elected body or person whose act or decision is said to be incompatible with the Convention. This point is well made in Human Rights Law and Practice (1999) p 74, par 3.21, of which Lord Lester of Herne Hill QC and Mr David Pannick QC are the general editors, where the area in which these choices may arise is conveniently and appropriately described as the 'discretionary area of judgment'. It will be easier for such an area of judgment to be recognised where the convention itself requires a balance to be struck, much less so where the right is stated in terms which are unqualified. It will be easier for it to be recognised where the issues involve questions of social or economic policy, much less so where the rights are of high constitutional importance or are of a kind where the courts are especially well placed to assess the need for protection.

ii. Case Study 2: The Convention Rights Proceedings (Amendment) (Scotland) Bill

This cases study relates to the decision of the UK and Scottish Governments to introduce a time bar for actions on the basis of breach of Convention rights under the Scotland Act.

This issue came to light following a series of cases taken by prisoners claiming ill-treatment, particularly in relation to the practice of slopping out, where no toilet facilities were provided in shared cells.

---

[60] *Soering v UK* Series A No 161 (1989) 35 at [89].
[61] *R v DPP ex p Kebilene* [1999] 3 WLR 972.

One such case, *Somerville and others v Scottish Ministers*,[62] focused on the issue of whether a time bar existed in relation to claims taken under the Scotland Act. A time bar was set in section 7(5)(a) of the Human Rights Act imposing a one-year time limit from the date of the act or omission complained of within which court proceedings must be brought. There was no time bar on the face of the Scotland Act. Scottish ministers argued that the Human Rights Act time bar applied to all actions for claims of breach of Convention rights, including those brought under the Scotland Act.

In October 2007 the House of Lords reversed the decision from the Court of Session and held that there existed no statutory time limit applicable to court actions brought against the devolved institution in Scotland in respect of 'acts' which were beyond their competence.[63]

This confirmed previous cases on the effect of the Scotland Act. As Lord Rodger of Earlsferry had earlier observed *R v HM Advocate*:

[W]henever a member of the Scottish Executive does an act which is incompatible with Convention rights, the result produced by all the relevant legislation is not just that his act is unlawful under section 6(1) of the Human Rights Act. That would be the position if the Scotland Act did not apply. When section 57(2) [Scotland Act] is taken into account, however, the result is that, so far as his act is incompatible with Convention rights, the member of the Executive is doing something which he has no power to do: his act is, to that extent, merely a purported act and is invalid, a nullity. In this respect Parliament has quite deliberately treated the acts of members of the Scottish Executive differently from the acts of Ministers of the Crown.[64]

Scottish Ministers were unhappy with this decision and issued a briefing note for journalists on the implications of the decision setting out their concerns:

The House of Lords ruled that no one-year time-bar applies to Scottish Ministers because of the wording of the Scotland Act. The practical effect is that the Scottish Government is exposed to tens of thousands of potential claims from prisoners for compensation for being held in slopping-out conditions. By contrast, every other public authority in Scotland, and virtually every public authority in the UK, including the UK Government, can rely on the one-year time bar when faced with human rights based claims.[65]

While the UK Government was initially unwilling to amend the Scotland Act, it finally agreed and on 19 March 2009 the Scottish and UK Governments introduced a joint statement:

Following intensive discussions between officials, we have reached agreement in principle to a quick and practical solution to the anomaly exposed by the House of Lords judgment in *Somerville*.

[62] *Somerville and others v Scottish Ministers* 2007 SC 140, 2008 SC (HL) 45.
[63] ibid.
[64] *R v HM Advocate* 2003 SC (PC) 21, 64.
[65] Scottish Government Briefing Note (11 March 2009) Somerville: time bar on human rights actions against Scottish Ministers, at para 7. (Following the 2007 Scottish parliamentary election, the Scottish National Party formed a minority administration, which was renamed the 'Scottish Government' instead of the 'Scottish Executive'; this change was reflected in law in the Scotland Act 2012.)

> We will work together to deliver a one-year time-bar in Scotland by the summer.
>
> Our joint aim is to restore the situation to what it was before this anomaly became apparent, and to protect the public interest in Scotland.

The process for change was to produce an Order in Council which allowed the Scottish Parliament to amend section 100 of the Scotland Act 1998. The Scotland Act 1998 (Modification of Schedule 4) Order 2009[66] was laid before both the UK and Scottish Parliaments on 1 April 2009. Once it had received the approval of both Parliaments, fast-tracked legislation at the Scottish Parliament was to be laid to introduce a time bar of one year for any cases brought on the ground that an act was incompatible with Convention rights. The time bar was to be introduced immediately, so that cases older than one year would instantly be time-barred.

It was clear that the time bar would go much further than a cap on the bringing of historical claims by prisoners for damages in respect of their slopping out. Instead, it would impose a time bar in relation to all and any Convention rights claims against the administrative action or inaction of Scottish ministers, regardless of whether damages were sought by the Convention rights victims in these actions, and regardless of whether these actions are brought by or on behalf of the apparently deserving as contrasted with the allegedly undeserving.[67]

The Bill was prepared for introduction, along with a motion to use emergency procedures and was submitted to the Presiding Officer for a statement of competence. The statement from the Minister responsible for the Bill focused on Articles 6 and 13 of the Convention and argued that the Bill was compliant with these rights. However, the statement of legislative competence sought from the Presiding Officer under section 31 was not forthcoming.

After a short period, the Bill was amended and received a statement of legislative competence in its amended form. While the legal advice provided to both the Scottish Ministers and to the Presiding Officer is confidential, it is possible to ascertain the legal issue by looking to the changes made to the Bill. The amended Bill still introduced a time bar, but delayed the commencement date.

Limitation periods are not incompatible with the Convention.[68] As Lord Rodger of Earlsferry has noted in *Robertson v Higson*:

> A time-limit for taking proceedings is not incompatible with the Convention. Under Article 35(1) an application to the European Court of Human Rights must be made within six months from the date when the final domestic decision was taken. Similarly, under section 7(5) of the Human Rights Act 1998 proceedings against a public authority for an alleged violation of Convention rights must be brought within the period of one year beginning with the date when the act complained of took place, or such longer period as the court or tribunal considers equitable having regard to all the circumstances. This is subject to any rule imposing a stricter time-limit in relation to the procedure in question.[69]

This issue was that Scottish Ministers had originally intended that the time bar would be introduced immediately in July 2009, therefore stopping any claim for

---

[66] SI 2009/draft.
[67] O'Neill (n 31).
[68] *Stubbings v UK* (1996) 23 EHRR 213.
[69] *Robertson v Higson* 2006 SC (PC) 22 [28].

injury prior to July 2008 and from that point onwards any claim older than a year. This was modified to put the commencement date back until November 2008.

It can be inferred that the change in date reflected concerns over the interference with the property rights protected by Article 1 of Protocol 1 to the Convention. Property was defined to include a legitimate expectation of a claim succeeding based on its clear recognition at domestic law being considered property.[70]

It is well established in decisions of the European Court of Human Rights, beginning with *Sporrong and Lönnroth v Sweden* decided in 1982, that Article 1 of Protocol 1 comprises three distinct parts:

— the overarching right to the peaceful enjoyment of possessions;
— the principle that a deprivation of possessions must be in the public interest and subject to the conditions provided for by law and by the general principles of international law;
— the principle that states are entitled to control the use of property in accordance with the general interest and to secure the payment of taxes and other charges and penalties.

What constitutes property, or 'possessions', in Article 1 of Protocol 1, is defined widely and includes a range of economic interests, including movable or immovable property, and tangible or intangible interests.

The three parts set out above are connected as the interferences allowed under the second and third parts must be construed and applied in light of the general principle in the first sentence. Any interference, even those which are specifically allowed for, must be justified, and such an interference can only be justified if it is shown to represent a fair balance between the rights of the individual and the general interest of the community.[71]

The introduction of a time bar would be construed as a deprivation of the legitimate exception of a claim for those who had current claims dating prior to 31 July 2008. This could not be justified on the basis of arguments that claims under the Scotland Act should be brought into line with those under the Human Rights Act, or on the political justification that those who have committed serious criminal offences should not be paid compensation even if they had their rights breached by Scottish ministers.

While the state has a wide margin of appreciation in implementing social and economic policies that have the effect of interfering with the right to property, the courts have a role to play in assessing the legitimacy of such interference. As the European Court of Human Rights observed in *James v UK*:[72]

> [A]lthough the Court cannot substitute its own assessment for that of the national authorities, it is bound to review the contested measure under Article 1 of Protocol 1 and, in so doing, to make an inquiry into the facts with reference to which the national authorities acted.[73]

---

[70] *Pressos Compania Naviera SA and others v Belgium* (1996) 21 EHRR 301; *Kopecky v Slovenia* (Grand Chamber) 2004.
[71] *Broniowski v Poland* (2005) 40 EHRR 21 [147]–[151].
[72] *James v UK* A98 (1986).
[73] ibid [46].

In order to be justified, any interference with the right to property must serve a legitimate objective in the public, or general, interest. It must also be proportionate. In *Sporrong and Lönnroth v Sweden*, the Court made the following statement of principle concerning the justification of an interference:

> [T]he Court must determine whether a fair balance was struck between the demands of the general interests of the community and the requirements of the protection of the individual's fundamental rights ... The search for this balance is inherent in the whole of the Convention and is also reflected in the structure of Article1 [of Protocol 1].[74]

While Scottish Ministers had initially considered that immediate commencement was justifiable on balance with the general interest of the community, the amended Bill shows that during the period that the Presiding Officer was considering whether to issue a statement of legislative compliance, ministers conceded this point. They amended the commencement date to allow for anyone with a legitimate expectation to have enough time to take an action before the time bar was introduced and to thereby satisfy the proportionality test.

It is important to note that the original proposal had unanimous parliamentary support and the Parliament had agreed to pass the Bill under emergency procedures that allowed it to go through the whole process of legislative scrutiny in a single day. It was the check provided by the statement of the Presiding Officer that forced the change.

During the debate on the amended Bill, there were minimal references to human rights implications and there was very little attention given to the change in the commencement date or the reason for it.

The Bill could have proceeded without the Presiding Officer's statement of legislative compliance. The fact that it was not given forced the Scottish Government to reconsider, or to press forward with a statement of non-compliance drawing attention to possible deficiencies.

While some senior constitutional lawyers have called for the removal of the requirement for a statement from the Presiding Officer as 'serving no useful purpose',[75] this example shows that there are times when the power has been a useful one. However, the fact that the advice provided to the Presiding Office is never released means that it cannot be used to inform debate and a statement of legislative competence may give members a false sense of security as to the compliance with Convention rights. Ultimately the Act passed, under truncated procedures, with very little scrutiny. The short debate in Parliament focused almost exclusively on limiting prisoners' rights and under this guise, the Parliament significant reduced the level of judicial protection afforded to people whose human rights were breached. The time bar has now been affirmed through the Scotland Act 2012. A requirement to provide reasons along with the statement might go some way to ensuring better transparency and more informed debate.

---

[74] *Sporrong and Lönnroth v Sweden,*(1983) 5 EHRR 35, para 69.
[75] *Serving Scotland Better* (n 39) 6.88.

iii. Case Study 3: The Criminal Justice and Licensing (Scotland) Bill

While the previous case study highlighted the benefits of the Presiding Officer's statement of legislative competence, this case study considers a deficiency in that process. The statement of legislative competence is only given in relation to a bill as it is introduced. There is no such scrutiny of amendments to a bill after introduction.

The Criminal Justice and Licensing Bill was passed on 30 June 2010. It was introduced with 148 sections and five schedules, but there were approximately 900 amendments over the course of the passage of the Bill. The vast majority of the amendments were minor or technical amendments, but some were significant.

One particular example was the introduction of a power to retain the DNA of those who had accepted a fixed penalty notice for minor offences. This had been considered during the policy consultation, but rejected by the Scottish Government due to concerns over compliance with the Convention. The Association of Chief Police Officers in Scotland and the Scottish Police Services Authority argued that such DNA retention was necessary for the prevention of crime.

In its Stage 1 Report, the Justice Committee noted a degree of uncertainty about whether the provisions in the Bill should be extended to allow the retention of forensic data taken from people who are dealt with by way of alternatives to prosecution. It did, however, indicate that it would 'look forward to a stage 2 amendment that would allow for the retention of data in such circumstances'.[76]

In its written response to the Stage 1 Report, the Scottish Government stated that:

> When we published our retention proposals for DNA and fingerprints in February 2009, we undertook to consider further the issue of retention in relation to fiscal disposals and police Fixed Penalty Notices (FPNs) issued under the Antisocial Behaviour (Scotland) Act 2004. Since then Stewart Maxwell [the responsible Minister] has made public his intention to lodge a stage 2 amendment that would allow for the retention of data in relation to police FPNs. We understand that he also intends to lodge a similar amendment to ensure that DNA and fingerprints can also be retained in relation to disposals issued by Procurators Fiscal.

These Stage 2 amendments sought to allow the retention of fingerprint and DNA data in cases dealt with by alternatives to prosecution, including cases where a person accepts a prosecution offer of certain alternatives to prosecution (eg, a fiscal fine) or cases where a person pays a fixed penalty notice issued by the police under the Antisocial Behaviour etc (Scotland) Act 2004. These include offences such as urinating in a public place, being drunk in a public place, persisting in playing musical instruments, singing etc after being required to stop, and vandalism.

In support of his amendments, the Minister said:

> It is clear that the quite correct move to the greater use of non-court disposals has meant that DNA and so on that would have been retained is not being retained because of that administrative change. I believe that the amendments will plug a loophole in the current law.[77]

---

[76] Scottish Parliament Justice Committee, *Stage 1 Report on the Criminal Justice and Licensing (Scotland)* Bill (18th Report, SP Paper 334 2009 (Session 3)) 372.
[77] Scottish Parliament Justice Committee 2010, col 3009.

Some Justice Committee members sought reassurance that the approach put forward in the amendments was a proportionate response given the nature of the offences involved. For example, Bill Aitken MSP noted that:

> I recognise that there is an anomaly and he is right to bring it to the committee's attention, but I am not yet entirely convinced that the amendments are proportionate. The committee has some unfinished business involving summary justice reforms and the way in which the Procurator Fiscal Service is dealing with them. Although some concerns have arisen, no case has been brought to my attention in which a conditional offer, fiscal fine or fixed penalty has been made in respect of a sexual or serious violent offence. If that had happened, there would have been considerable concern on the part of all members.

> I would have thought that a case in which there is an argument for DNA retention should be a matter for prosecution so that the court can apply a realistic disposal.[78]

However, following debate, all members of the Committee supported the amendments. The issue was not debated at Stage 3 and the provisions passed into law without further consideration.

Article 8 ECHR requires respect for private and family life, home and correspondence. These concepts are sometimes indistinguishable as the area of focus is on the protection of the moral and physical integrity of the individual. This concept can therefore encompass a wide range of issues. DNA samples contain a significant amount of sensitive information about an individual's identity, including information about health, and a unique genetic code. In the context of forensic data, privacy rights are crucial, in particular the need to balance the right to private life with the right of the general public to be protected from crime.

While the acquisition and retention of forensic information could play a role in criminal justice policy and practice, such practices raise serious human rights concerns, particularly privacy issues. The Council of Europe recommends that the introduction and use of these techniques should take full account of and not contravene such fundamental principles as the inherent dignity of the individual and the respect for the human body, the rights of the defence and the principle of proportionality in the carrying out of criminal justice.[79]

In *S and Marper v UK*, the European Court of Human Rights noted that:

> The protection afforded by Article 8 of the Convention would be unacceptably weakened if the use of modern scientific techniques in the criminal justice system were allowed at any cost and without carefully balancing the potential benefits of the extensive use of such techniques against important private life interests.[80]

Article 8 of the Convention is a qualified right, which requires the state to justify any interference by reference to its legality, necessity and proportionality. This should be the starting point and basis for assessing risk and harm. Human rights are rights

---

[78] ibid, col 3010.
[79] Council of Europe Committee of Ministers Recommendation R(92)1 on the Use of Analysis of Deoxyribonucleic Acid (DNA) within the Framework of the Criminal Justice System (Adopted by the Committee of Ministers on 10 February 1992 at the 470th Meeting of the Ministers' Deputies).
[80] *S and Marper v UK* App Nos 30562/04 and 30566/04.

of individuals and groups, and their limitation must be assessed according to the harm that it will cause to the rights of the individual (or group) and whether that is:

> [I]n accordance with the law: 'requires the impugned measure both to have some basis in domestic law and to be compatible with the rule of law, which is expressly mentioned in the preamble to the Convention and inherent in the object and purpose of Article 8. The law must thus be adequately accessible and foreseeable, that is, formulated with sufficient precision to enable the individual—if need be with appropriate advice—to regulate his conduct'.[81]

> [I]n pursuit of a legitimate aim: a public authority which intends to interfere with a person's rights under Article 8 must be able to demonstrate that such interference is based on one of the legitimate aims set out in Article 8(2), including 'the prevention of disorder or crime' and 'the protection of the rights and freedoms of others'.[82]

> [N]ecessary in a democratic society: 'an interference will be considered "necessary in a democratic society" for a legitimate aim if it answers a "pressing social need" and, in particular, if it is proportionate to the legitimate aim pursued and if the reasons adduced by the national authorities to justify it are relevant and sufficient'.[83]

The Court in *S and Marper v UK* also commented:

> A margin of appreciation must be left to the competent national authorities in this assessment. The breadth of this margin varies and depends on a number of factors including the nature of the Convention right in issue, its importance for the individual, the nature of the interference and the object pursued by the interference. The margin will tend to be narrower where the right at stake is crucial to the individual's effective enjoyment of intimate or key rights. Where a particularly important facet of an individual's existence or identity is at stake, the margin allowed to the State will be restricted.[84] Where, however, there is no consensus within the Member States of the Council of Europe, either as to the relative importance of the interest at stake or as to how best to protect it, the margin will be wider.[85]

While the retention of DNA data in itself is not a breach, the retention of DNA data for minor offences dealt with by fines is disproportionate. Council of Europe Recommendation R(92)1 requires that retention should only take place 'where the individual concerned has been convicted of serious offences against the life, integrity or security of persons'.[86]

The lack of scrutiny of provisions introduced by amendment and passed by committees consisting of small numbers of MSPs raises concerns over the robustness of the legislative scrutiny in relation to Convention rights.

---

[81] ibid.
[82] *Khan v UK* App No35394/97 (ECHR).
[83] *S and Marper v UK* (n 80).
[84] *Evans v UK* App No 6339/05 (ECHR)
[85] *Dickson v UK* App No 44362/04 (ECHR)
[86] Council of Europe Committee of Ministers Recommendation R(92)1 (n 79).

iv. Case Study 4: The Children's Hearings (Legal Representation) (Scotland) Rules 2002

This case study concerns Scotland's Children's Hearing system and considers the situation where cases taken on the basis of the failure to act by Scottish ministers were in breach of Convention rights.

The Children's Hearing system was introduced in 1971 following the Kilbrandon Report of 1964 and the Social Work (Scotland) Act 1968. Kilbrandon recommended a welfare-based system to provide an integrated approach to children who had committed offences and children in need of care and protection. Cases are heard by a lay tribunal who make decisions based on the best interest of the child.

The legislation that currently underpins the Children's Hearing system, the Children's Hearings (Scotland) Act 2011 and its predecessor the Children (Scotland) Act 1995, was designed to incorporate the principles set out in the United Nations Convention on the Rights of the Child and the ECHR.

Children and relevant persons[87] have always had the right to legal representation. However, state-funded legal aid only extended to advice prior to a hearing or representation at an appeal, not representation at the hearing itself.

In 2001 the Court of Session considered the case of *S v Miller*,[88] where a child was placed under compulsory measures of supervision with authorisation to be held in a secure unit. The child had not received legal representation. The Court confirmed that:

> Children's hearing proceedings and the related proceedings before the sheriff … have always been regarded as civil in character, even where they concern a ground of referral under offence grounds.
>
> …
>
> While Article 6 does not require that a state funded lawyer is provided in every case.[89]
>
> … the lack of free legal representation before the hearing might well significantly impair the child's ability to affect the outcome of the hearing. In any event, the child would not receive a fair hearing within the meaning of Article 6(1) before the children's hearing. It is not sufficient that legal aid would be available on appeal to the sheriff.

As a consequence, the Children's Hearings (Legal Representation) (Scotland) Rules 2002[90] were introduced to provide a system of free legal advice and representation where necessary. They were subject to the negative procedure of Parliament, which means that they pass into law unless the Parliament passes a motion to annul them. Subordinate legislation does not require a statement of legislative competence, but is considered by the Delegated Powers and Law Reform Committee, which is tasked with ensuring that it is within the legislative competence of the Scottish Parliament

---

[87] This includes anyone with parental responsibilities and rights in relation to the child, and any other person who has significant involvement in the child's upbringing (although the definition has changed over time).

[88] *S v Miller* 2001 SLT 531.

[89] ibid [35], citing *Airey v Ireland* Series A No 32 (1979).

[90] SSI 2002/63.

and within the scope of the empowering legislation. The Parliament's Education Culture and Sport Committee considered the Rules on 12 March 2002 and welcomed them without debate. No MSP brought forward a motion to annul.

In 2009 a mother whose baby was placed in foster care brought a case on the basis that she did not have access to state-funded legal representation. As the mother had the cognitive abilities of a child under 10 years of age, she argued that without legal representation, she would not be able to participate effectively in the hearing.

Prior to the Court of Session case being decided, the Scottish Government brought forward interim measures to bring relevant persons into the same position as children, allowing for state-funded legal representation to be appointed. The Children's Hearings (Legal Representation) (Scotland) Amendment Rules 2009 were drafted on the same basis as the 2002 Rules, but they received very different treatment from the Scottish Parliament.

On 8 September 2009, the Education, Lifelong Learning and Culture Committee refused to support the new Rules. A majority of the Committee was concerned that the introduction of additional lawyers into the Children's Hearing system might undermine the welfare-based nature of the hearing and considered that the Scottish Government should have waited until the Court of Session had issued its judgment and a motion was lodged to annul the Rules. The Convener of the Committee commented:

> Governments lose court cases on a fairly regular basis, and it is right that law and public policy are tested in that manner. However, the Scottish Government has not yet lost the case. We have not even heard a judicial decision—if, indeed, we ever will.

> The introduction of this will undoubtedly lead to the whole complexion of the children's hearings system changing from child friendly to legalisation and the focus on the child will be lost in the ensuing legalese. Any changes to the system must ensure that we get it right for every child.

> Protecting the rights of parents—some of whom will have placed a child in a position of neglect or harm—should not impact negatively on the right of the child to be protected from harm. I agree with that. That is why I firmly believe that we must get the legislation right and that changes to legal representation should be considered in the context of primary legislation. I do not believe that ECHR compliance should supersede that.[91]

A minority of members of the Committee dissented and supported the Rules:

> One of the issues that have been playing on my mind since questions were raised at last week's meeting is that it is the wrong approach to legislate only after something has happened, when a case has been lost that may involve something as fundamental as somebody's human rights. The approach that we should take is to pre-empt some of this and legislate to protect people before a case is tested in court. That is the course of action that should be taken in a serious human rights-based system. From my experience, I think that that would provide better outcomes for everybody who is involved in the children's hearings system.[92]

---

[91] Scottish Parliament Official Report, Education, Lifelong Learning And Culture Committee, 8 September 2009, Col 2639.
[92] ibid, Col 2646.

The matter was referred for a debate of the whole Parliament, and the challenge to the Rules was rejected by 65 votes to 60, with one abstention. The fact that a Parliamentary Committee and almost half of the members of the Parliament took the view that the Government should only act when required to do so by the courts raises significant concern.

When the Court did issue its judgment in *SK v Julie Paterson*,[93] it followed the reasoning of the *Miller* judgment and held that the absence of any state-funded legal representation for relevant persons was 'an inbuilt systematic flaw in the system' and was incompatible with Articles 6, 8 and 14. While the Court did not comment on the efficacy of the new Rules, it did comment that the Scottish ministers had been correct to act to rectify the incompatibility.

V. CONCLUSION

Scotland has always been a country proud of its human rights heritage, but it has been slow to bring international norms into its domestic legal system. The changing attitudes of the judiciary and the creation of a Scottish legislature which has human rights built into its fabric have created an environment where a new attitude towards human rights in policy-making and legislative development can emerge.

The protections built into the Scotland Act, both in terms of the legislative competence of the Parliament and the checks and balances provided by the Parliament's procedures, mean that a high level of legislative scrutiny is possible in terms of human rights standards. However, there remain concerns over how effective these procedures are in practice and how transparent the process is.

The fact that there have been so few challenges to legislation since the introduction of the Scotland Act may attest to the effectiveness of the protections instituted through the Scotland Act, or it may point to the challenges of accessing justice. It will be interesting to see whether the liberalisation of rules relating to standing may lead to increased challenges in future.

The Scottish courts clearly have confidence in the Scottish Parliament and acknowledge that it is for the Parliament to determine the balance between rights. They have been hesitant to strike down legislation, but they are increasingly sending strong messages to the Parliament. Conversely, the Scottish Parliament has at times been reticent to legislate without a court judgment compelling it to do so.

The link between legislative competence and the requirement of statements of Convention compliance at the introduction of a bill mean that human rights issues are at least considered in relation to primary legislation. However, the fact that the legal advice given to Scottish Ministers and to the Presiding Officer is not released and that the statements do not generally set out the reasoning for the decision mean that there is a lack of transparency in this scrutiny and it is not able to inform parliamentary debate. The fact that subordinate legislation and amendments to bills

---

[93] *SK v Julie Paterson* [2009] CSIH 76.

do not require statements of competence means that provisions introduced by these methods do not have the benefit of this scrutiny at all.

While the committee system is constructed to provide robust scrutiny and committees benefit from being representative of the Parliament as a whole, the broad remits of the committees and the very busy legislative programme mean that it can prove difficult for them to find the time to consider all of the issues. The decision not to have a specialist human rights committee or to have human rights rapporteurs within every committee raise questions as to the level of institutional expertise that can be developed. The power that committees have to pass amendments at Stage 2 and the lack of scrutiny of those provisions by the Parliament at Stage 3 can create situations of potential incompatibility.

Each of these mechanisms provides a valuable addition to the human rights scrutiny of legislation in Scotland and, taken as a whole, they provide a framework for ensuring human rights protection. The further development of better practice and expertise will be essential to ensuring that the system functions effectively.

The development of Scotland's National Action Plan,[94] which provides a process for the realisation of all internationally recognised human rights, and the commitments made by Government and the Parliament, can give a great deal of hope that there is a commitment to improve, but these commitments must be turned into action.

---

[94] www.scottishhumanrights.com/actionplan.

10

The Devolution of Human Rights and the Northern Ireland Assembly

COLIN CAUGHEY AND DAVID RUSSELL[*]

D EVOLUTION HAS TRANSFORMED the UK into a quasi-federal state. This has significant consequences for human rights.[1] In a reconfigured democracy, the maintenance of human rights standards continues to reside, as a matter of international law, with the sovereign parliament. But as a matter of practice, the situation is much more complex. Since the powers to make many laws and policies have been transferred to regional governments, as a consequence, there is a responsibility to adhere to the United Nations (UN) and Council of Europe treaties ratified by the UK when exercising those powers.

In this chapter we illustrate the relationship between devolution and human rights by examining the case of Northern Ireland. We consider how human rights protections have been interwoven into the legal framework that transferred legislative competencies from the Westminster Parliament to the regional Northern Ireland Executive and legislative Assembly. We also examine how the obligations resulting from international treaties have been contextualised by those who established a new constitutional settlement, and how in doing so an attempt has been made to give universal principles a local currency.

This chapter sets out in detail how the Belfast (Good Friday) Agreement (hereinafter referred to as 'the Agreement') and the Northern Ireland Act 1998 recognise human rights as a central tenet of the institutions of devolved government, thereby placing limits on the exercise of political powers. It also assesses the experience of the legislature and the performance of Assembly members in using human rights to inform political discourse and decision-making. The mechanisms and procedures designed to engage human rights within Northern Ireland are significant, but we argue that the knowledge of elected representatives, and their willingness to make full use of the procedures at their disposal, has been limited.

[*] The authors would like to make clear that this chapter is written in a personal capacity and does not reflect the opinion of any organisations to which they are affiliated. The authors would also like to thank Hugh Widdis and Ian O'Flynn who provided comments on the draft and Laura Curran who provided research assistance.
    [1] See, for example, V Bogdanor, *The New British Constitution* (Oxford, Hart Publishing, 2009) 115.

I. COMPETENCIES AND CONTROLS ON POLITICAL POWER

Discussing devolution and human rights requires us to consider how universal laws are, paradoxically, justified on the basis of a cultural particularity. The moral force of human rights may derive from fundamental concepts such as inherent dignity and intrinsic equality, but to operate effectively, it is also necessary for them to reflect the values and norms of the societies within which they are applied. Human rights in practice are, as Jürgen Habermas suggests, ethically permeated, by which he means:

> [T]he process of setting normative rules for modes of behaviour is open to influence by the society's political goals. For this reason every legal system is also the expression of a particular form of life and not merely a reflection of the universal content of basic rights.[2]

Following Habermas, we can see how a commitment to human rights standards set down in international treaties will also most appropriately represent an agreed understanding of what those standards mean in a particular social or political setting. At the same time, a critical distance must be maintained so that an external 'universal' perspective can be offered on the internal democratic and legal processes within a given jurisdiction.

In Northern Ireland the correlation of human rights to the experience of the people living there is perhaps most clearly set out in the declaration of support for the Agreement, which states:

> The tragedies of the past have left a deep and profoundly regrettable legacy of suffering. We must never forget those who have died or been injured, and their families. But we can best honour them through a fresh start, in which we firmly dedicate ourselves to the achievement of reconciliation, tolerance, and mutual trust, and to the protection and vindication of the human rights of all.[3]

The parties that negotiated the Agreement in 1998 affirmed their collective commitment to the mutual respect, the civil rights and the religious liberties of everyone. Against a background of violent inter-communal conflict, they affirmed, in particular:

> [T]he right of free political thought; the right to freedom and expression of religion; the right to pursue democratically national and political aspirations; the right to seek constitutional change by peaceful and legitimate means; the right to freely choose one's place of residence; the right to equal opportunity in all social and economic activity, regardless of class, creed, disability, gender or ethnicity; the right to freedom from sectarian harassment; and the right of women to full and equal political participation.[4]

In Northern Ireland the recognition of human rights as an essential component of the peace process was also necessarily reflected in the system of governance envisaged by the Agreement and subsequently established through the Northern Ireland Act 1998. This system is a complicated power-sharing arrangement underpinned by

---

[2] J Habermas, 'Struggles for Recognition in the Democratic Constitutional State' in A Gutmann (ed), *Multiculturalism* (Princeton, Princeton University Press, 1994) 124.

[3] *The Agreement: Agreement Reached in the Multi-party Negotiations* (1998), Declaration of Support, para. 2.

[4] ibid, Rights, Safeguards and Equality of Opportunity, para. 1.

an inclusive coalition government, proportional representation and mutual vetoes in legislative decision-making. The mechanisms and procedures that engage human rights are numerous and have been designed to act, in part, as a check on the exercising of political powers. Indeed, the mainstreaming of human rights and equality duties within the framework for governance often supersedes the standard catalogue of anti-discrimination measures found in most Western-liberal democracies.[5]

In Northern Ireland equality duties have been mainstreamed within the governance framework, most notably through the application of section 75 of the Northern Ireland Act 1998. Section 75 places a positive duty on designated public authorities to have due regard to the need to promote equality of opportunity. The inclusion of such safeguarding measures is unsurprising given the history of Northern Ireland and the violations and abuses that took place during the conflict.

As observed by Christine Bell, most contemporary peace accords tend to give rise to legal guarantees of equality and protections for human rights. Political settlements in such contexts will routinely include 'measures such as bills of rights, constitutional courts, human rights commissions or other national institutions for protecting rights'.[6] However, these protections are not unique to transitional societies. Most constitutional democracies contain institutions and procedural guarantees designed to uphold fundamental rights and freedoms. But it is the central role that such mechanisms play in helping to prevent future conflicts and a recurrence of inter-community violence that is of particular note in a society like Northern Ireland. In essence, the centrality of human rights in Northern Ireland is underpinned, as explained by Michelle Pavliet, by a recognition that a deprivation of needs through the sustained denial of rights was a structural cause of violent conflict and divisions, so 'sustained protection of rights is essential for dealing with conflict constructively'.[7]

II. LEGISLATIVE COMPETENCY

The Northern Ireland Act 1998 sets parameters for the legislative competencies of the regional Executive and Assembly. These competencies are circumscribed in a number of ways; for example, the Assembly can never legislate in a manner that is inconsistent with EU law, nor can it legislate on certain matters that remain the sole responsibility of the UK Government, such as national security and immigration. These matters are essential functions of an independent state and are necessary to ensure its independence. Hence, they cannot be devolved, since decisions on the affected policy areas would have a significant impact on the entire sovereign

---

[5] C McCrudden, 'Equality' in Colin Harvey (ed), *Human Rights, Equality and Democratic Renewal in Northern Ireland* (Oxford, Hart Publishing, 2001) 109.

[6] C Bell, 'Human Rights and Minority Protection' in J Darby and R MacGinty (eds), *Contemporary Peacemaking: Conflict, Violence and Peace Processes* (Basingstoke, Palgrave Macmillan, 2003) 162; For a detailed account, see C Bell, *Human Rights and Peace Agreements* (Oxford, Oxford University Press, 2000).

[7] Michelle Parleviet, 'Bridging the Divide: Exploring the Relationship between Human Rights and Conflict Management' (2002) 1 *Track Two* 11, 18.

territory. The 1998 Act separates competencies into three categories; transferred matters; reserved matters; and excepted matters. The Northern Ireland Assembly can legislate on transferred matters. It can also legislate on reserved matters, with the permission of the Secretary of State. It cannot, however, legislate on excepted matters unless they are 'ancillary to other provisions ... dealing with reserved or transferred' matters.[8]

There is a procedure provided for by the 1998 Act that enables matters designated as reserved to be re-designated and transferred to the legislative competency of the Assembly. The Secretary of State may lay before the Westminster Parliament, in accordance with section 4(2), the draft of an Order in Council proposing that a matter ceases to be or, as the case may be, becomes a reserved matter. By way of example, the Northern Ireland Act 1998 (Devolution of Policing and Justice Functions) Order 2010 made a provision of this sort to devolve policing and justice powers.

The Westminster Parliament's ability to propose the transfer of, or recall, an area of competency is a necessary qualification required so as to maintain the constitutional modus operandi of the UK. The authority to remove competencies from the Assembly is a mechanism for ensuring the preservation of the doctrine of parliamentary sovereignty, which, according to the classic reading provided by Albert Venn Dicey:

> [M]eans neither more nor less than this, namely, that Parliament ... has ... the right to make or unmake any law whatever; and, further, that no person or body is recognised by the law ... as having a right to override or set aside the legislation of Parliament.[9]

International relations, which include the ratification of human rights treaties, are excepted matters for which the UK Government retains exclusive responsibility.[10] Only sovereign states are recognised and have the power to ratify treaties at the UN or the Council of Europe. Devolved institutions cannot carry out this function, but this does not mean they have no responsibilities. On the contrary, a failure by the Northern Ireland administration to abide by the provisions of a human rights treaty is just as likely to be subject to scrutiny as a failure by the UK Government. There is also an expectation that the devolved government, represented by the Office of the First Minister and the Deputy First Minister, will play its part in reporting to relevant UN committees. This includes the provision of information for state reports and appearing before the committees as part of the delegation when the UK is periodically examined.

However, the experience of cooperation between the Northern Ireland Executive and the UK Government in reporting to the UN and Council of Europe on human rights issues has been rather disappointing. For example, in the final stage of the examination by the Human Rights Council as part of the Universal Periodic Review in 2012, the representative of the UK Government, Lord McNally, reported that he was unable to provide any information with respect to Northern Ireland. It later emerged that the Northern Ireland Executive had failed to agree how to address

---

[8] Northern Ireland Act 1998, s 8 and scheds 2 and 3.
[9] AV Dicey, *An Introduction to the Study of the Law of the Constitution* (London, Macmillan, 1959) 39–40.
[10] Northern Ireland Act 1998, sched 2(3).

two issues for which the Human Rights Council had sought information—namely, access to abortion within the regional jurisdiction and investigations into conflict-related deaths.[11] As a consequence of an internal political dispute, a decision was taken to withdraw the entire Northern Ireland input, thereby significantly impacting the UK report. Unfortunately, this was not an isolated incident. Similar problems with regard to reporting have been evident during the Council of Europe examinations on the Charter for Regional and Minority Languages and the UN examination on the International Covenant on Civil and Political Rights.[12]

Despite these difficulties, the role of regional governments when it comes to protecting and preserving human rights should not be overlooked. The UN monitoring committees have recognised the important role of devolved administrations in ensuring respect for and fulfilment of treaty obligations. The Committee on the Rights of the Child in its General Comment No 5 has stipulated that:

> [I]n all circumstances, the State which ratified or acceded to the Convention remains responsible for ensuring the full implementation of the Convention throughout the jurisdiction. In any process of devolution, States Parties have to make sure that the devolved authorities do have the necessary financial, human and other resources effectively to discharge responsibilities for the implementation of the Convention. The governments of States Parties must retain powers to require full compliance with the Convention by devolved administrations … and must establish permanent monitoring mechanisms to ensure that the Convention is respected and applied for all children throughout its jurisdiction without discrimination. Further, there must be safeguards to ensure that decentralisation or devolution does not lead to discrimination in the enjoyment of rights by children in different regions.[13]

Similarly, the Committee on Economic, Social and Cultural Rights has stated that:

> [W]here responsibility for the implementation of the right to social security has been delegated to regional or local authorities or is under the constitutional authority of a federal body, the State party retains the obligation to comply with the Covenant, and therefore should ensure that these regional or local authorities effectively monitor the necessary social security services and facilities, as well as the effective implementation of the system. The States parties must further ensure that such authorities do not deny access to benefits and services on a discriminatory basis, whether directly or indirectly.[14]

III. THE HUMAN RIGHTS ACT 1998

The framework governing the legislative competencies of the Northern Ireland Assembly is directly circumscribed only by those international human rights law commitments which have been introduced to the UK by way of domestic legislation. The Northern Ireland Act 1998 declares that the Assembly does not have competency to legislate in a

---

[11] Human Rights Council Report of the Working Group on the Universal Periodic Review United Kingdom of Great Britain and Northern Ireland, 6 July 2012, A/HRC/21/9, paras 110.77 and 110.92.

[12] UN Human Rights Committee List of issues in relation to the seventh periodic report of the United Kingdom of Great Britain and NI, the British Overseas Territories and Crown Dependencies October 2014, para 4.

[13] General Measures of Implementation for the Convention on the Rights of the Child, General Comment, No 5 (Committee on the Rights of the Child, 2003).

[14] The right to social security (Article 9) General Comment No 19 (Committee on Economic, Social and Cultural Rights, 2008).

manner that is inconsistent with the European Convention on Human Rights (ECHR), which in practice means those ECHR rights incorporated into domestic law by way of the Human Rights Act 1998 (HRA).[15] Under section 6(1) of the Northern Ireland Act 1998, a provision of an act of the Assembly is not law if it is in breach of ECHR rights.[16]

If the Assembly were to attempt to pass legislation which appeared to contravene the ECHR, then the Attorney-General for Northern Ireland may, before the bill receives Royal Assent, refer the relevant provisions of the proposed law to the Supreme Court for it to decide whether the matter is, or is not, ultra vires.[17] In this way the Attorney-General acts as a final gatekeeper charged with ensuring that legislation is not enacted by the devolved administration in contravention of the ECHR.

However, it must be recognised that, despite the best efforts of the Assembly, international human rights law, including the ECHR, is constantly evolving. The Convention rights are developed by way of jurisprudence from both the domestic courts and from the European Court of Human Rights (ECtHR). It is therefore possible that legislation enacted by the Assembly which is in compliance with the ECHR when it comes into force could at some future point become incompatible as a result of emerging case law. In such unforeseen circumstances, amending legislation may be introduced to the Assembly or, alternatively, where legal proceedings are brought, the higher courts can use their powers under the HRA to interpret the relevant provisions in a manner that is compliant with the relevant Convention rights.

Acts of the Northern Ireland Assembly are considered subordinate legislation for the purposes of the HRA. The implication is that the domestic courts have a broad discretion to read and give effect to Assembly legislation in a way which is deemed compliant with the ECHR. For example, in 2012 the Northern Ireland High Court ruled that Articles 14 and 15 of the Adoption (Northern Ireland) Order 1987 were in breach of the right to private and family life as protected by Article 8 ECHR. These legislative provisions had restricted the eligibility to adopt in the jurisdiction to married couples only. In finding a breach, the court read down the Articles to provide that they do not prevent couples who are not married, or in a civil partnership, from applying to adopt a child.[18]

By way of contrast, Acts of the Westminster Parliament for the purposes of the HRA are designated as primary legislation and hence the interpretive creativity of the domestic courts is subject to much greater limitations than is the case with Acts of the Northern Ireland Assembly. Whereas the Belfast High Court in the aforementioned case regarding adoption law was able to interpret the relevant Articles in a manner that was inconsistent with the plain English interpretation of the wording of the provisions, this would not have been permissible if the relevant legislation had been generated by the Westminster Parliament. As Lord Hope has explained:

> [C]ompatibility is to be achieved only so far as this is possible. Plainly this will not be possible if the legislation contains provisions which expressly contradict the meaning which the enactment would have to be given to make it compatible.[19]

---

[15] ibid, Northern Ireland Act 1998, s 6(2)(c).
[16] ibid, s 6(1).
[17] ibid, s 11(1).
[18] *The Northern Ireland Human Rights Commission's Application* [2012] NIQB 77 (Postscript).
[19] *R v Lambert* [2002] 1 AC 45, 67–68.

In circumstances where a plain English interpretation of the relevant provision cannot be taken to be compatible, the courts may issue a declaration of incompatibility in accordance with section 4(3) of the HRA.[20] This declaration does not impact on the legal status of the Act; rather, it provides Parliament with a written notice that there is a problem. Once a declaration of incompatibility has been issued, a minister may bring forward a remedial order which requires the approval of both Houses of Parliament.[21] Here is a demonstration of the hierarchy of legislative instruments and the operational difference between sovereign government and a devolved administration. On the one hand, Acts by the devolved Assembly are demonstrably subordinate to the human rights protections that have been incorporated into domestic law by an Act of the Westminster Parliament. On the other hand, Acts by the Parliament itself are of much greater constitutional standing and have a degree of equivalence to incorporated human rights standards. As explained by Vernon Bogdanor with respect to primary legislation:

> [Human rights] still depend upon the discretion of Parliament. There is no legal obligation upon either the Parliament or the government to amend a legislative provision that has been found to be incompatible with the Convention [ECHR].[22]

Bogdanor has further stated that the process of a declaration of incompatibility is a part of a process of democratic dialogue between Parliament and the judiciary. With respect to the Northern Ireland Assembly, there is, however, no equivalent dialogue necessary since the courts have extensive powers of interpretation and may use them as they see fit.[23]

IV. INTERNATIONAL HUMAN RIGHTS LAWS

The UK is a dualist state, meaning that the ratified international human rights treaties must be incorporated into domestic law by an Act of Parliament before a member of the public within the jurisdiction can rely directly on the protections they provide in a court of law. But the treaties may impact nonetheless upon the actions of the Northern Ireland Executive or on the legislative timetable of the Assembly in circumstances where the Secretary of State feels that an action or inaction may jeopardise compliance with an international human rights obligation. In particular, under section 26 of the 1998 Act, the Secretary of State may, by order, direct that an action be taken on a matter within the legislative competency of the Assembly as required for the purpose of giving effect to international obligations. Such action can include the introduction of a bill into the Assembly.[24] It is important to note that the Secretary of State has a power to introduce, but not to enact legislation.

---

[20] Human Rights Act 1998, s 4(3).
[21] ibid, sch 2.
[22] Bogdanor (n 1) 60. There is, though, a clear legal obligation on the UK under Art 46 ECHR to abide by a judgment of the ECtHR in a case to which it is a party.
[23] For further discussion on the dialogical nature of relations between the judiciary and legislature, see AL Young, *Parliamentary Sovereignty and the Human Rights Act* (Oxford, Hart Publishing, 2009).
[24] Northern Ireland Act 1998, s 26(3).

Moreover, if this power were to be exercised, then the Northern Ireland Assembly, its committees and members would retain the ability to amend the relevant bill as introduced.

When making a decision with respect to international obligations, the Secretary of State must recite the reasons for making the order and may make a provision having retrospective effect.[25] In theory the impact of this power should be that ministers in the Northern Ireland Executive and Assembly ensure due diligence with regard to the treaties, being mindful that the Secretary of State can override any proposed action by a devolved government department that is determined to be incompatible with human rights treaties.[26]

Section 26 of the 1998 Act has not been engaged since the advent of devolution. However, it remains an option open to the UK Government should there be an identified need to bring the law of Northern Ireland into line with a treaty obligation. It also assumes that, first, the Assembly itself would continue to refuse or be unable to deal with the matter when faced with the reality of an intervention by the Secretary of State, and, second, that the Secretary of State would maintain the resolve to forcibly introduce the necessary changes in the area of dispute. No doubt such an issue would be of significant controversy and political discord. The exercise of this power would therefore most likely be as a measure of last resort, as such an action would undoubtedly strain the relationship between the UK Government and the devolved administration.

V. THE NATIONAL HUMAN RIGHTS INSTITUTION

To provide a source of advice for the devolved government and another control on the exercise of political power, the Agreement mandated the creation of a human rights commission. The inaugural Northern Ireland Human Rights Commission was appointed in 1999 with duties that include keeping under review the adequacy and effectiveness in Northern Ireland of law and practice relating to the protection of human rights. It is empowered to advise both the Secretary of State and the Executive of legislative and other measures that ought to be taken to protect human rights 'as soon as reasonably practicable after receipt of a general or specific request for advice; and on such other occasions as the Commission think appropriate'.[27] The Commission also has a duty to advise the Assembly.[28] Section 69(4) of the 1998 Act states that: 'The Commission shall advise the Assembly whether a Bill is compatible with human rights.'[29]

The Commission operates in full accordance with the 'Principles Relating to the Status of National Institutions' (the Paris Principles) and has 'A' status accreditation

---

[25] ibid, s 26(5).
[26] ibid, s 26(1) and (4).
[27] ibid, s 69(3).
[28] ibid, s 69(4).
[29] ibid.

at the UN as a National Human Rights Institution (NHRI).[30] It is one of three NHRIs in the UK. The Scottish Human Rights Commission has similar responsibilities for reviewing the laws of Scotland and the policies or practices of any Scottish public authorities,[31] and the Equality and Human Rights Commission has responsibility for reviewing all law and policies in England and Wales, and matters relating to Scotland that are reserved to the Westminster Parliament.[32]

The Northern Ireland Human Rights Commission is a resource upon which the Northern Ireland Assembly may draw to ensure that proposed laws adhere to international human rights obligations committed to by the UK Government. It may operate as a similar source of advice to the Secretary of State. If the Commission so wished, it could advise the Secretary of State of measures required to be taken, or measures which must cease, in Northern Ireland to ensure compliance with international human rights law obligations. The Commission may therefore perform a role in informing the Secretary of State on the potential exercise of the power to take actions in areas that are within the competency of the Executive and Assembly, but upon which the devolved administration is refusing to act.

As an NHRI, the Commission also engages with the bodies established to monitor compliance with various international human rights treaties. In this role the Commission can highlight issues of compliance with respect to Northern Ireland which have not received the attention of either the regional Assembly or the Westminster Parliament. In doing so, the Commission may seek the support of the international human rights system to encourage actions by the Northern Ireland Assembly and Executive in areas of transferred responsibility, or by the UK Government and Westminster Parliament regarding excepted matters.

As a measure of last resort, the Commission can impact the workings of the Assembly and Executive through legal action. The Commission has standing to bring court proceedings involving law or practice relating to the protection of human rights.[33] This is not restricted to the assistance of victims of perceived violations, since the Commission may engage on the basis that 'there is or would be one or more victims of the unlawful act'.[34] In light of the subordinate status of the legislation of the Northern Ireland Assembly, the exercise of this power can lead to significant changes in law, policies and practices within the jurisdiction.

---

[30] Principles Relating to the Status of National Institutions (the Paris Principles) (annexed to General Assembly resolution 48/134), 1993, s 3(a). Further information on the relationship between human rights commissions and parliaments is provided in Office of the UN High Commissioner of Human Rights, *National Human Rights Institutions: History, Principles, Roles, Responsibilities* (New York and Geneva, OHCHR, 2010). See also the Belgrade Principles (2012) on the relationship between national human rights institutions and parliaments.

[31] Scottish Commission for Human Rights Act 2006.

[32] Equality Act 2006, s 11.

[33] Northern Ireland Act 1998, s 69(5).

[34] ibid, s 71(2B).

VI. LEGISLATIVE SCRUTINY

Executive ministers are the principal sources of legislative bills introduced into the Northern Ireland Assembly.[35] Such bills are typically drafted by one of 12 Northern Ireland government departments, each of which has responsibility for a number of specified matters that are within the competency of the Assembly. 'The Practical Guide to Policy Making in Northern Ireland', published by the Office of the First Minister and Deputy First Minister, provides direction to civil servants on the procedures to be followed when developing policies or legislation.[36] This guidance recalls the need to consider human rights implications, but it is limited to the application of the ECHR and, more specifically, to those articles that have been given further domestic effect through the HRA.[37]

A government department in Northern Ireland may complete a degree of human rights screening of a proposed bill during its development. However, this will usually be integrated into a process that is chiefly focused upon domestic equality and non-discrimination laws set out in sections 75 and 76 of the 1998 Act rather than any detailed scrutiny of compliance with human rights obligations set out in the relevant international treaties. Nonetheless, where a problem is identified, advice may be sought from the Departmental Solicitor's Office, and also from the Human Rights Commission if civil servants or the minister are so minded. For example, in 2012 officials within the Department of Education sought advice from the Commission on the compatibility of proposed reforms of the special educational needs system and the provisions governing redress.[38] The minister, in this instance, referred to the Commission's advice in his briefing statement to the Assembly.[39] Typically, where the Commission is engaged, its advice will be wide-ranging within the limits of those human rights treaties that have been ratified by the UK Government.

Once a department has completed an initial screening exercise, any proposed legislation will then be subject to a public consultation over a period of 12 weeks, during which time comments will be made by interested community and voluntary sector organisations or members of the general public.[40] The extent to which human rights compliance is analysed within a consultation paper will depend on the subject matter and the thoroughness of those charged with directing the process. In some cases, a department will simply record that human rights obligations have been considered and that no issues have been identified for particular scrutiny.[41] On other occasions, human rights issues will be identified and a preliminary assessment

---

[35] For a list of bills currently before the Northern Ireland Assembly, available at: www.niassembly.gov.uk/Assembly-Business/Legislation/Primary-Legislation-Current-Bills.

[36] *A Practical Guide to Policy Making in Northern Ireland* (OFMdFM, 2003).

[37] ibid, 41.

[38] *Redress within the Special Educational Needs System and the Requirements of International Human Rights Law* (NIHRC, 12 June 2012), available at: http://www.nihrc.org/Publication/detail/redress-within-the-sen-system-and-ihrl.

[39] *Special Educational Needs Review: Ministerial Briefing* (NIA, 13 June 2012), available at: www.niassembly.gov.uk/Assembly-Business/Official-Report/Committee-Minutes-of-Evidence/Session-2011-2012/June-2012/Special-Educational-Needs-Review-Ministerial-Briefing.

[40] *Code of Practice on Public Consultations* (HMSO, July 2008).

[41] *Speeding up Justice: Reform of Committal Proceedings* (DoJNI, January 2012) para 33.

made regarding compliance and how the department intends to address the matters raised.[42] Again, this will usually be limited to the ECHR rather than any substantive consideration of the full body of human rights treaties engaged. Following the consultation process, a department will routinely produce a report setting out how the views of respondents have been taken into account and any amendments that have been made.[43]

During the pre-legislative development process, there is the greatest opportunity for a department to amend its proposals. At this point, the minister and civil servants would ideally adopt a human rights-based approach in which those rights-holders most likely to be affected by any subsequent decisions would be encouraged to participate in the development of the legislation. Guidance on how to formulate a human rights-based approach has been published by the Office of the High Commissioner for Human Rights[44] and the right to participate, in particular, is recognised in a number of the UN and Council of Europe treaties. Article 12 of the Convention on the Rights of the Child, for example, requires an assurance that children who are capable of forming their own views are able to 'express those views freely in all matters affecting the child, the views being given due weight in accordance with the age and maturity of the child'.[45] The Convention on the Rights of Persons with Disabilities similarly states 'that persons with disabilities should have the opportunity to be actively involved in decision-making processes about policies and programmes, including those directly concerning them'.[46]

There are a number of positive examples of where Northern Ireland departments and Executive Ministers have sought to involve rights-holders in the development of policies and legislation, such as the regional strategy to improve the lives of disabled people published in 2012.[47] However, the Guide to Policy Making does not oblige departments to take proactive measures to ensure that those affected by a set of proposals are able to exercise their right to participate. Moreover, there is little evidence to suggest that the devolved administration is either conscious of or has a general understanding of what it actually means to take a human rights-based approach. A fair assessment would be that there is a willingness to engage, but there is no evidence of a systematic method to ensure that right-holders directly affected by a set of proposals are involved in the associated development process.

---

[42] ibid.

[43] See, for example, *Transforming Your Care Vision to Action a Post Consultation Report* (DHSSPS, March 2013).

[44] Office of the High Commissioner for Human Rights, 'Technical Guidance on the Application of a Human Rights Based Approach to the Implementation of Policies and Programmes to Reduce Preventable Maternal Morbidity and Mortality', A/HRC/21/22, 2 July 2012.

[45] www.ohchr.org/EN/ProfessionalInterest/Pages/CRC.aspx.

[46] www.ohchr.org/EN/HRBodies/CRPD/Pages/ConventionRightsPersonsWithDisabilities.aspx#preamble.

[47] See, for example, *A Strategy to Improve the Lives of Disabled People 2012–2015* (OFMdFM, March 2012).

VII. INTRODUCTION OF A BILL TO THE NORTHERN IRELAND ASSEMBLY

Before, or on the occasion of a bill being introduced into the Assembly, the responsible Executive Minister in Northern Ireland is required to make a statement to the Speaker indicating that in his or her opinion, the proposal is within the competency of the legislature.[48] In making this determination, a minister must assure himself or herself that the bill complies with the ECHR.[49] This is not a case of simply adhering to a procedural obligation, but rather is a vitally important check which will determine if the bill can proceed. The Assembly Standing Orders state:

> [N]o Bill shall be introduced in the Assembly if the Speaker decides that any provision of it would not be within the legislative competence of the Assembly.[50]

Therefore, the Speaker will refuse to allow introduction of a bill where he or she considers that it is incompatible with the ECHR. To assist the process of scrutiny, the Assembly Standing Orders require that a bill:

> [S]hall be accompanied by an explanatory and financial memorandum detailing as appropriate—(a) the nature of the issue the Bill is intended to address; (b) the consultative process undertaken; (c) the main options considered; (d) the option selected and why; (e) the cost implications of the proposal/s.[51]

There is no express requirement for a memorandum to include information regarding human rights compliance. Nonetheless, it is common practice in Northern Ireland for comments of this sort to be made, albeit very few of them. Of the 149 bills introduced into the Assembly between 1999 and April 2013, only 25 addressed the question of human rights obligations in more than a single sentence. Furthermore, even on those occasions in which human rights received attention, the depth of analysis provided was minimal, with the accompanying memorandum failing to identify the substantive rights engaged or to cite relevant standards beyond the ECHR.

In general, draft legislation in Northern Ireland has acknowledged the relevance of universal standards, but there has been a notable absence of any consideration to determine how those standards might be given best effect in the circumstances of the jurisdiction. A typical example of this minimalist approach to human rights analysis is the memorandum to the Pollution, Prevention and Control Bill (2001–02), which stated in totality that the:

> [P]rovisions of the Bill are considered to be compatible with obligations in relation to human rights on grounds that the fundamental purpose of the Bill is to reduce emissions in the air, land and water to achieve a high level of protection of the environment.[52]

[48] Northern Ireland Act 1998, s 9(1).
[49] ibid, ss 24 and 26.
[50] Standing Orders as amended 16 October 2012, 30, available at: www.niassembly.gov.uk/Assembly-Business/Standing-Orders/Standing-Orders/#30.
[51] Standing Orders as amended 16 October 2012, 41, available at: www.niassembly.gov.uk/Assembly-Business/Standing-Orders/Standing-Orders/#41.
[52] Pollution Prevention and Control Bill Explanatory and Financial Memorandum, NIA Bill 19/01.

This Bill gave powers to officials to inspect certain buildings and to fine individuals for polluting the environment,[53] thus engaging the right to a fair hearing, the right to property and the right to respect for private life protected by both the International Covenant on Civil and Political Rights and the ECHR. Yet the memorandum provided no information to members of the Assembly suggesting that relevant international standards or ECHR and HRA jurisprudence had been considered by the Department prior to the Bill being introduced.

Experience demonstrates that when an explanatory memorandum provides significant human rights analysis or when the Human Rights Commission is engaged, the subsequent debates at the Second Stage of passage in the Assembly are more informed and the level of political discourse is enhanced.[54] It is important to note that the individual Assembly members charged with legislative scrutiny do not have access to the policy and legal advisers of the departments which generate bills. The principal opportunity for a detailed consideration of human rights is during the Committee stage, at which point a clause-by-clause analysis is undertaken.[55] Committees have access to the Assembly research and legal staff. In addition, they hold evidence sessions with interested stakeholders and experts. The Human Rights Commission also makes its expertise available and will provide both written and oral submissions to committees either on its own motion or upon request in accordance with its statutory function set out in the 1998 Act and in accordance with the Paris Principles.[56]

The utility of the Committee stage is, in large part, dependent upon the willingness of the individual members to engage with and analyse the issues at stake from a human rights perspective. Or, to be more precise, the committee members must be minded to use the resources at their disposal in order to raise the level of political debate and to interrogate the provisions of the bill for compliance with the relevant international standards. The difficulty is that at times there is an apparent aversion on behalf of some Assembly members to accept that the limits which human rights law places on the exercise of political powers serve a useful democratic function. It also appears that there is little understanding that this is a necessary constraint intended by Westminster, in part, to maintain the concept of parliamentary sovereignty in the context of devolution.

One illustration of this attitude was the Criminal Justice Bill 2012, which amended, amongst other things, the framework governing the circumstances in which an individual arrested, charged or convicted of a criminal offence could have his or her DNA retained.[57] The Bill included provisions that responded to a judgment of the ECtHR[58]—or, as one member stated, the:

> [R]eason why we are in this predicament is because of the so-called European Court of Human Rights … In a test case, those individuals have ruled that, as a society, we have to

---

[53] Pollution Prevention and Control Bill, NIA Bill 19/01.

[54] See, eg, Official Report (Hansard) 25 September 2012, vol 77, No 6, Private Members' Business Civil Service (Special Advisers) Bill: Second Stage.

[55] Northern Ireland Act 1998, s 13(2).

[56] Northern Ireland Act 1998, s 69(4).

[57] Criminal Justice Bill, clauses 10/11–15.

[58] *S and Marper v UK* (2008) ECHR 1581.

restrict the opportunities to retain DNA, fingerprints and photographs. We are bound by that, and I am not happy that we are bound by it.[59]

The Human Rights Commission appeared before the Assembly Justice Committee providing advice on this subject and recommended that a number of amendments could be brought to ensure compliance with emerging ECtHR jurisprudence.[60] Still, a number of Committee members made clear that they preferred a minimalist approach and that they had no desire to be 'exemplars in human rights'.[61] The Committee did not include the Commission's recommendations in its final report,[62] but a number of Assembly members did subsequently introduce amendments at the Consideration and Further Consideration Stages, which to some degree addressed the issues at hand.[63] However, the adoption of such a partisan approach to human rights is unlikely to lead to universal standards having meaning to rights-holders throughout Northern Ireland.

VIII. SPECIAL PROCEDURES

The Assembly Standing Orders provide for two mechanisms that can be engaged to enhance scrutiny of the human rights implications of a bill. Standing Order 34 provides that an Assembly member may propose a motion that:

[T]he Northern Ireland Human Rights Commission be asked to advise whether the ... Bill (or draft Bill or proposal for legislation) is compatible with human rights.[64]

Standing Order 35(5) provides that a member of the Executive Committee or chairperson of an appropriate committee may propose a motion that:

[T]he ... Bill (or draft Bill or proposal for legislation) be referred to an Ad Hoc Committee on Conformity with Equality Requirements [and human rights observations].[65]

It is of interest to note that neither Standing Order 34 nor 35 is restricted to the substantive rights protected by the ECHR, but may also extend to international obligations derived from treaties ratified by the UK Government. It is also worth noting that a motion under either Standing Order may be proposed prior to the introduction of a bill. This means that both mechanisms could be engaged to perform an educative function for the members of the legislature if they so desired.

---

[59] Northern Ireland Assembly Plenary Debate, sched 2 (Arts 63B–63O of the Police and Criminal Evidence (Northern Ireland) Order 1989, as inserted, 19 February 2013).
[60] *Criminal Justice Bill: DNA/Fingerprint Retention Clauses* (Official Report, Hansard, 4 October 2012).
[61] ibid, 8.
[62] *Report on the Criminal Justice Bill*, NIA10/11-15 (Committee for Justice), 13 December 2012.
[63] See, for example, *Criminal Justice Bill Marshalled List of Amendments Consideration Stage* (NIA, 19 February 2013), available at: www.niassembly.gov.uk/Assembly-Business/Legislation/Primary-Legislation-Current-Bills/Criminal-Justice-Bill/Criminal-Justice-Bill-Marshalled-List-of-Amendments-Consideration-Stage-Tuesday-19-February-2013.
[64] Standing Orders as amended 16 October 2012, 34.
[65] ibid, r 35(5).

In 2012, pursuant to a motion passed under Standing Order 35, an Ad Hoc Committee was established to report on the conformity of the Welfare Reform Bill with equality and human rights requirements. This was the first time such a motion had been passed since devolution. It was introduced during the Committee stage of the Bill's passage. The Report of the Ad Hoc Committee was of value to the scrutiny process on the Welfare Reform Bill as it afforded a further opportunity to raise human rights concerns and allowed for more detailed consideration of obligations emerging from international human rights laws beyond the ECHR. The focus in this instance included, amongst others, the application of the Convention on the Rights of Persons with Disabilities, the Convention on the Rights of the Child, the Convention on the Elimination of Discrimination against Women and the European Union Charter of Fundamental Rights.[66]

Unfortunately, the Ad Hoc Committee's Report on the Welfare Reform Bill was not accepted by the Assembly.[67] A review of the Hansard report of the plenary session indicates that those who voted against accepting the report felt that it was unacceptable as it failed to identify any breaches of human rights law.[68] However, the contributors to the debate did not set out the particular rights they considered would be violated, nor did they identify the relevant standards engaged. The report in fact identified a number of issues that could potentially result in breaches of human rights in the absence of mitigating measures, but these were not considered in any detail. Thus, the value of the Ad Hoc Committee was substantive in raising the level of understanding amongst Committee members, but it appears that little was achieved in terms of generating serious political considerations as to how the Assembly could ensure that international human rights standards were reflected in the Welfare Reform Bill in light of the particular circumstances of Northern Ireland.[69]

Since 2012 was the first occasion on which the mechanism of an Ad Hoc Committee was used, it is not possible to conclude whether this particular process would or would not have a significant impact on political discourse within the devolved legislature if it were to be engaged on a more regular basis. The obvious comparison, however, is with the Joint Committee on Human Rights in Westminster, the value of which as a source of specialist advice has been acknowledged within Parliament.[70] Nevertheless, in this regard, there can be no doubt that there is a significant opportunity for the Assembly, both the secretariat and the members, to learn from the experience of other legislatures in the UK.

---

[66] *Report on Whether the Provisions of the Welfare Reform Bill are in Conformity with the Requirements for Equality and Observance of Human Rights*, NIA 92/11-15 (NIA, 21 January 2013).

[67] *Welfare Reform Bill: Report of the Ad Hoc Committee on Conformity with Equality Requirements* (Official Report, Hansard, 29 January 2013) vol 81, No 4.

[68] ibid, 5–6.

[69] ibid.

[70] For further information on the work of the JCHR, see www.parliament.uk/business/committees/committees-a-z/joint-select/human-rights-committee. See, for example, Joint Committee on Human Rights, *Counter-Terrorism Policy and Human Rights: Bringing Human Rights Back In (16th Report)* (2009–10, HL Paper 86/HC 111).

CONCLUSION

In this chapter we have examined the prominence afforded to human rights within the constitutional settlement of the UK and, in particular, have considered how this has impacted the institutions of devolved government in Northern Ireland. To our mind, an appropriate balance has been struck. The obligation of the Westminster Parliament to maintain the standards required by ratified international treaties has been written into the devolution statute. At the same time, responsibility to adhere to human rights laws has in a substantive sense been passed to the Northern Ireland Executive and legislative Assembly.

For practical purposes, it appears to us that human rights have been devolved. There is no reason why this should not be the case. The UN, as we have demonstrated, recognises the ability to devolve the obligations derived from the international treaties. Indeed, it encourages states to ensure that all relevant authorities are made aware of their duties. However, in doing so, the state must maintain its oversight and continue to acknowledge the primacy of central government as the sovereign authority. The established concept of parliamentary sovereignty in UK, reinforced within the provisions of the 1998 Act, is in this regard an important continuing check on the exercise of political power in Northern Ireland.

Beyond the institutions of government, we have also considered in this chapter the practices of the Executive and the Assembly when making domestic laws and policies. In summary, it appears that there has been at best a selective approach to human rights, with declarations of unreserved support met with declarations of unswerving opposition, both of which have been generally informed by a limited appreciation for the practical implications. Political discourse concerning human rights which recites the content of treaties or ECHR and HRA jurisprudence has been limited in the official records of debates in the devolved legislature.

In principle, the mechanics are in place in Northern Ireland to make human rights a driver for legislation. The fact that one of the human rights scrutiny mechanisms provided for by the Assembly's Standing Orders, the establishment of an Ad Hoc Committee on the Welfare Reform Bill 2012, has been used is a positive step. In addition, the statutory committees of the Assembly are routinely seeking the views of the Northern Ireland Human Rights Commission regarding the implications of bills and Executive policies. We do see evidence, on a few occasions, of green shoots of constructive dialogue emerging, with an increasing use of the mechanisms that enable elected politicians to scrutinise legislation for human rights compliance. This needs to be encouraged in order for devolution to reach its full potential in providing a local currency for universal human rights standards.

11

Human Rights in the National Assembly for Wales

ANN SHERLOCK

G IVEN THE LIMITED powers accorded to the National Assembly for Wales (hereinafter 'the Assembly') until relatively recently, it might be thought that there would be little to say about the Assembly's involvement in human rights issues. It was only in 2007 that the Assembly acquired primary legislative powers, and even then on only a limited range of subjects until further changes took place in 2011. Nonetheless, despite the limited powers, or indeed perhaps *because* of the limited powers, there has been a distinct direction in the development of rights in Wales which has placed a stronger emphasis on the broad *promotion* of inclusion, citizenship and equality than on the more specific issue of *avoiding breaches* of civil and political rights. The work of the Assembly has exemplified a cross-party consensus on adopting a rights-based approach to developing policy and a clear willingness to embrace social and economic rights.

This chapter discusses the context in which the Assembly operates and the factors which have provided an impetus for the direction in which rights have developed in post-devolution Wales.[1]

I. THE DEVOLUTION ARRANGEMENTS FOR WALES

The Government of Wales Act 1998 (GWA 1998) created a devolution settlement of limited powers and institutions for Wales. Given the impact that the powers and structures had on the development of the new Assembly's priorities, including those relating to human rights, it is worth outlining the terms of the devolution settlement at the outset.

In terms of institutions, unlike the legislation for Northern Ireland and Scotland, which established legislative and executive bodies, the GWA 1998 established a single corporate body, the National Assembly for Wales, which would exercise all the functions, executive or legislative, which were provided for. In practice, however, from the start, the system worked with an executive (which eventually adopted the title of the Welsh Assembly Government) and a parliamentary side, but this was a de

---

[1] The chapter presents the position existing at the time of writing in summer 2013.

facto arrangement and one which was not enshrined in law until the Government of
Wales Act 2006 (GWA 2006) entered into force. This Act replaced the single body
corporate with a legislative body, the National Assembly for Wales, and an executive body, the Welsh Assembly Government (hereinafter the 'Welsh Government').[2]

In terms of powers, it is notable that the GWA 1998 referred to the exercise of
'functions' rather than powers. The 1998 Act made provision for functions to be
transferred to the Assembly by Order in Council,[3] and, of course, functions could
be transferred by Act of Parliament. The functions which were transferred in the
first major transfer Order[4] were powers previously exercised by the Secretary of
State for Wales. The GWA 1998 made no provision for the allocation of primary
legislative powers: the only legislative powers were powers to make subordinate
legislation. It had been considered that the fact that the powers would be exercised
by a democratically elected body, and not an individual minister, might lead to the
delegation of wide framework powers, but in the event this did not emerge as a
consistent practice. Not only were the powers limited in status, but the functions
allocated to the Assembly amounted to a somewhat haphazard collection of powers
previously exercised by the Secretary of State and made it difficult for the development of coherent policy where legislative authority was needed.[5] This led to a tendency to focus on the areas in which more significant powers had been devolved,
as for example in relation to children. To execute policy which required primary
legislation depended upon the agreement in principle of the UK Government and
Parliament and sufficient time in the UK legislative timetable for the proposal to
have a chance of success in practice. In the context of this chapter, it is of interest to
note that the first provisions thus secured in UK legislation were those in the Care
Standards Act 2000, which established the Children's Commissioner for Wales.

Changes to the legislative powers of the Assembly came in two stages. Part 3
of the GWA 2006 provided for the Assembly to have primary legislative powers.
However, the areas in which the Assembly could legislate were to be added to the
Act on an incremental basis in a process which required the Assembly's request for
additional powers to be agreed to by the UK Government and then approved by
both Houses of Parliament.[6] A cumbersome process, it involved a high proportion
of the Assembly's time being spent seeking, rather than exercising, legislative powers. Nonetheless, during the four-year period when Part 3 was in force, it is notable
that one of the Measures enacted was the groundbreaking Rights of Children and
Young Persons (Wales) Measure 2011, which is discussed later. A number of the
other Measures[7] very clearly pursued inclusion and equality goals: for example,

[2] Although the GWA 2006 uses the term 'Welsh Assembly Government', since 2011, the term 'Welsh Government' has been used in practice.
[3] GWA 1998, ss 21 and 22.
[4] National Assembly for Wales (Transfer of Functions) Order 1999 (SI 1999/672).
[5] For an account of the early powers of the Assembly, see David Lambert, 'The Government of Wales Act—An Act for the Laws to be Ministered in Wales in Like Form as it is in this Realm?' (1999) 30 *Cambrian Law Review* 60.
[6] GWA 2006, s 95.
[7] Primary Assembly legislative enactments under Part 3 of the GWA 2006 were called Measures. Since Part 4 of the GWA 2006 entered into force, the term 'Acts' is used for the Assembly's primary legislation.

the Education (Wales) Measure 2009 gave children (rather than parents only) a right to appeal to the Special Educational Needs Tribunal for Wales; the Children and Families (Wales) Measure 2010 made statutory provision for the Welsh Government's commitment to eradicate child poverty; and the Welsh Language (Wales) Measure 2011 aimed to modernise provision for the use of Welsh in the delivery of public services.

Part 3 of the GWA 2006 was replaced by Part 4 in 2011 following a positive vote in a referendum on this question. Under this part of the Act, powers were transferred en bloc to the Assembly. Despite the greater range of areas of competence than under Part 3, the arrangement remains different from that in Scotland and Northern Ireland in being a 'conferred powers' model rather than a 'reserved powers' model: only those issues specifically listed in Schedule 7 to the GWA 2006, and not subject to exceptions, come within the Assembly's competence.

As with any division of powers, 'boundary disputes' will arise. One such rights-related competence issue which arose during the third Assembly[8] concerned whether the Assembly could legislate to prohibit the smacking of children. If the legislation was regarded primarily as a matter of criminal law, the Assembly lacked competence, whereas if it was considered primarily to relate to protecting the well-being of children, then it was a devolved matter. The issue continues to be discussed, but at the time of writing[9] no legislation on the issue has been enacted or proposed. However, it is very likely that some Assembly Members will propose an amendment to the Social Services and Well-being (Wales) Bill, currently before the Assembly, which would effectively prohibit the physical punishment of children in all circumstances. At the time of writing, the stage for proposing amendments has not yet been reached, but when the Health and Social Care Committee took evidence from the Deputy Minister for Social Services in relation to the general principles of the Bill, the issue was raised. The Deputy Minister's view was that if such a provision were included, there would be a challenge to the competence of the Bill from the UK Government: she described the question of whether the matter was a welfare issue or a criminal justice issue as one 'that would not be easily resolved, with firm views here in the Assembly and equally firm views in the Government at Westminster'.[10] While competence disputes may arise under any model of dividing powers, evidence to the current Silk Commission[11] indicates that there is a growing consensus that these disputes are more likely to arise under the conferred-powers model. A specific rights-related example was provided in the Welsh Government's evidence to the Silk Commission, which expressed the need for greater clarity as to which powers in relation to equal opportunities actually had been devolved.

---

[8] The Assembly elected in 2007.

[9] Summer 2013.

[10] Transcript of Evidence Session No 1, Health and Social Care Committee, 18 April 2013, paras 45–49, available at: www.senedd.assemblywales.org/documents/s16600/18%20April%202013%20-%20DRAFT.html?CT=2#ybi.

[11] The Commission on Devolution in Wales, chaired by Paul Silk, was established in 2011 by the UK Government to review the powers of the Assembly and the model of devolution for Wales. The relevant documents, including the evidence presented to the Commission, are available at: http://commissionondevolutioninwales.independent.gov.uk.

The nature of the areas of competence is relevant to the human rights agenda in a number of ways: the fact that there is no competence in relation to criminal justice may explain the absence of cases challenging Assembly legislation on human rights grounds, there being fewer opportunities in which rights might be breached. However, the limits on competence may also mean that the ability to promote human rights is hampered, as may be seen in relation to the area of equalities. A number of submissions to the Silk Commission have urged that the Assembly be given primary legislative competence in relation to the Public Sector Equality Duty under the Equality Act 2010.[12] As it stands, while the Welsh ministers (but not the Assembly) were given the power to introduce specific duties for Wales, these specific duties would fall if the UK Parliament were ever to repeal the general duty. In addition, a number of submissions to the inquiry by the Assembly's Communities, Equality and Local Government Committee on the future of equality and human rights in Wales have expressed concerns about the fragmented nature of the accountability structures in this area.[13] More generally, the fact that there is no general competence to promote human rights leads to a greater focus on the areas in which the Assembly or the Welsh Government has specific duties to promote certain outcomes.

II. OBLIGATIONS TO COMPLY WITH OR PROMOTE HUMAN RIGHTS

Although the devolution model for Wales is one of conferred powers in contrast to the reserved powers model which exists in relation to Scotland and Northern Ireland, the Assembly shares with the other devolved legislatures the quality of being a body with limits on its powers. Legislation which goes beyond the limits on competence will be ultra vires and can be challenged before the courts. In addition to the requirement that legislation may be enacted only on subjects falling within the terms of Schedule 7 to the GWA 2006, it is also a requirement that it must not be incompatible with the 'Convention rights' (as defined in the Human Rights Act 1998) or with EU law.[14] Accordingly, the rights under these two systems represent a constitutional and legal constraint for the Assembly. Under Schedule 9, the question of whether legislation is within the Assembly's legislative competence is classified as a 'devolution issue' and, if raised in the courts, is subject to a system of references to higher courts which is reminiscent of the EU preliminary rulings system. It is also possible for legislation to be referred by one of the law officers, pre-enactment, to the Supreme Court for a ruling on whether it exceeds the Assembly's competence.[15] In addition, there is the power of the Secretary of State[16] to prohibit the submission of a bill for Royal Assent if he or she considers that the bill contains provisions

---

[12] Including those of the Welsh Government, the Equalities and Human Rights Commission, and the joint submission by the Children's Commissioner for Wales and the Older People's Commissioner for Wales.

[13] Details of this inquiry, including evidence presented to the Committee, are available on the Committee's website: www.senedd.assemblywales.org/mgIssueHistoryHome.aspx?IId=6256.

[14] GWA 2006, s 108(7).

[15] ibid, s 99.

[16] ibid, s 114(1)(d) and (2).

which are incompatible with an international obligation; this could therefore cover instances of non-compliance with rights other than those protected in accordance with the Human Rights Act 1998 or under EU law. This would cover, for example, issues concerning rights in other international treaties which bind the UK, such as the International Covenant on Civil and Political Rights or the International Covenant on Economic, Social and Cultural Rights. However, this operates as a negative constraint rather than a positive competence to promote rights: legislation must be rights-compliant to be valid, but this does not confer a competence to create processes and machinery for the protection of rights where such competence has not already been conferred. Indeed, in 2002, when the question was raised as to whether the remit of the then Equality of Opportunity Committee should be extended to cover human rights issues, one of the reasons given by the Committee for rejecting the suggestion focused on the difference in the statutory obligations in the two areas: 'the Assembly's equal opportunity obligation carries a positive duty to promote the equality of opportunity for all people while its human rights obligation is the negative duty to not infringe Convention rights'.[17] The reference to the equal opportunity obligation by the Committee refers to one of a number of positive duties in the GWA 2006 which, although not necessarily expressed in the language of rights, have significant implications in relation to the development of rights in relation to language, equality and environment.

In terms of the Assembly's own proceedings, these are to be 'conducted with due regard to the principle that there should be equality of opportunity for all people' and, as far as is appropriate and practicable, in accordance with the principle that the Welsh and English languages are 'treated on a basis of equality'.[18]

The GWA 2006 places obligations on the Welsh ministers to arrange that their functions are carried out with due regard to equality of opportunity for all people: the requirement to publish, and lay before the Assembly, an annual report assessing the effectiveness of these arrangements provides the Assembly with an opportunity to scrutinise the Welsh Government on this.[19] There is a similar obligation to report annually to the Assembly on the arrangements made for the promotion of the use of the Welsh language and of the requirements for the use of Welsh by those providing services to the public in Wales.[20] Finally there is the obligation to report to the Assembly on the implementation of the Welsh ministers' duty to promote sustainable development.[21] While the requirements to be proactive in promoting these different goals are placed on the Welsh ministers, the requirement in all cases for the ministers' reports to be laid before the Assembly provides an opportunity for Assembly scrutiny and input. In addition, Assembly legislation has created obligations to consider certain human rights obligations, most notably in relation

[17] Equality of Opportunity Committee, Minutes of Meeting of 26 June 2002.
[18] GWA 2006, s 35(1) and (2).
[19] ibid, s 77.
[20] ibid, s 78.
[21] ibid, s 79.

to having regard to children's rights as guaranteed by the UN Convention on the Rights of the Child (UNCRC).[22]

The requirement to *promote* certain issues, coupled with the duty *not to breach* the Convention rights or other international obligations, has been responsible to some extent for the profile of human rights in the Assembly's work. Unless the Assembly has specific competence to promote rights under a particular subject heading, as it does for example in relation to children, the explicit positive duties have received more attention than the topic of human rights per se. In many ways, human rights have tended to be treated as a subset of equality of opportunity rather than the other way round. This is evident in the way in which the Welsh Government assesses its proposals for legislation: a consideration of compliance with human rights requirements forms part of the equality impact assessments which accompany legislation.[23] This is not to suggest that there is a failure to ensure that there is compliance with the Human Rights Act, but merely to observe the much greater prominence of the consideration of equality rights than of other rights.

III. THE LEGISLATIVE PROCESS IN THE ASSEMBLY

As a body with limits on its competence, the Assembly's legislative process builds in a number of points at which it is a legal requirement that issues of competence, including those relating to human rights, must be considered. The person in charge of the bill[24] must provide a statement that the provisions of the bill are within the Assembly's competence.[25] In addition, the Presiding Officer must state whether or not the provisions of the bill are within the Assembly's competence,[26] although there is no equivalent of the provision in the Northern Ireland Act 1998 which bars the introduction of a bill into the Northern Ireland Assembly, which is regarded by that Assembly's Presiding Officer as falling outside competence.[27]

The Presiding Officer's statement is a short statement that, in his or her view, the provisions of the bill, as introduced, are within the Assembly's competence. Thus far, there has been no legislation which has failed to be declared to be within competence by the Presiding Officer. However, there has been once instance, in relation to the Recovery of Medical Costs for Asbestos Diseases (Wales) Bill, where the Presiding Officer found the issue to be very finely balanced and chose to write to the relevant committees to alert them to the fact that, while declaring the Bill to be within competence, she was aware that there were arguments to the contrary which

---

[22] The relevant Measure is discussed in section V below.

[23] These impact assessments are part of the explanatory memorandum which accompanies each bill introduced. See for example, the assessment on the Social Services and Well-being (Wales) Bill, available at: www.senedd.assemblywales.org/mgIssueHistoryHome.aspx?IId=5664 and on the Human Transplantation (Wales) Bill, available at: www.senedd.assemblywales.org/mgIssueHistoryHome .aspx?IId=5178.

[24] As defined in Assembly Standing Order 24; it is usually a minister.

[25] GWA 2006, s 110(2).

[26] ibid, s 110(3).

[27] Northern Ireland Act 1998, s 10(1).

the committees might wish to consider further in their scrutiny of the Bill.[28] The issues of competence were not set out on the face of the Presiding Officer's letter, but, as summarised by the Chair of the Health and Social Care Committee, they appear to be 'subject-matter' competence issues.[29] On the other hand, later correspondence to the Presiding Officer from an interested party opposed to the legislation did make reference to an alleged lack of compliance with the requirements of Article 1 of Protocol No 1 to the ECHR regarding the right to property.[30] It is interesting and encouraging that the Presiding Officer chose to take this step in order to encourage the relevant committees scrutinising the legislation to ensure that relevant issues were aired in their consultation on, and consideration of, the proposed Bill.[31]

Following the introduction of a bill, the GWA 2006 requires at least three stages for the scrutiny of legislation.[32] At the first stage, there must be a general debate on the bill with the opportunity for Assembly members to vote on its general principles; under Standing Orders, the Business Committee decides whether to remit the bill to a committee for consideration of its general principles prior to the Assembly voting on it.[33] The second stage mandated by the GWA requires the consideration of the details of the bill and, again, there must be an opportunity for Assembly members to vote on these. Under Standing Orders, the Business Committee must remit the bill to a committee for consideration unless it secures a vote in plenary for the bill to be considered by a committee of the whole Assembly. The bill may be amended at this stage. The third stage provided for in Standing Orders sees the bill return to the Assembly in plenary, where it can be amended. A fourth stage, the Report Stage, is provided for in Standing Orders: at this stage, the member in charge of the bill may move that amendments be considered during the Report Stage. The final stage required by the Act is one at which the bill may be passed or rejected. Unless covered by an exception in Standing Orders, no bill may be passed unless the text is in both English and Welsh.[34]

The final check on competence in the legislative process which is required by the GWA 2006 is the power of the Counsel General[35] or the Attorney-General (for England and Wales) to refer to the Supreme Court the question of whether a bill, or any of its provisions, is within the Assembly's competence.[36] Thus far, one bill, the Local Government Byelaws (Wales) Bill, has been referred to the Supreme Court by the Attorney-General: the issue was unrelated to human rights.[37]

---

[28] The letter from the Presiding Officer was sent to the Constitutional and Legislative Affairs Committee and the Health and Social Care Committee. It is available at: www.senedd.assemblywales. org/documents/s12317/HSC4-01-13p7-e-PO%20Letter%20Asbestos%20Bill.pdf. Documents concerning the Bill are available at: www.senedd.assemblywales.org/mgIssueHistoryHome.aspx?IId=4837.

[29] Transcript of the meeting of the Health and Social Care Committee of 5 December 2012.

[30] www.senedd.assemblywales.org/documents/s17152/Correspondence%20between%20the%20 Association%20of%20British%20Insurers%20and%20the%20Presiding%20Officer.pdf.

[31] The responses of the relevant committees are noted in section IV, text accompanying n 52 below.

[32] GWA 2006, s 111.

[33] Standing Order 26.

[34] GWA 2006, s 111(5).

[35] The Welsh law officer is a member of the Welsh Government: ibid, s 49.

[36] ibid, s 112.

[37] *Local Government Byelaws (Wales) Bill 2012—Reference by the Attorney General for England and Wales*, [2012] UKSC 53. The Bill was held to be within the Assembly's competence.

IV. STRUCTURES FOR SCRUTINY IN THE ASSEMBLY

The specific requirements for scrutiny in the legislative process are set out in the GWA 2006. As discussed, the Presiding Officer has a specific role in policing matters of competence in relation to the legislative process. In general terms, the main structures for scrutiny of the development of legislation and policy are the committees and the Assembly in plenary.

At the outset, however, attention must be focused on the very small size of the Assembly, which has only 60 members. When the 12 ministerial offices and the Presiding Officer are deducted from this number, this leaves 47 members to hold the Welsh Government to account and to scrutinise legislation. While the Richard Commission[38] recommended a rise to 80 members, this was not accepted by the UK Government. Indeed, even within the Assembly itself, while there is awareness of the small size, there is a resignation that it would be inadvisable politically to attempt to convince the public of the need for additional representatives in a time of economic recession and public scepticism regarding the value of politicians.[39] However, it remains the case that the size, which may have been appropriate for the Assembly under the 1998 legislation, becomes increasingly untenable for a body with primary legislative powers. Its effect on the committee system is obvious, with the Assembly opting to decrease the number of committees as time has passed. Even so, while members are spread over fewer committees, the same level of work remains, and indeed increases with the volume of legislation proposed.[40]

One of the initial aims of the Assembly structure had been to foster inclusive politics and cross-party working. An element of this was the provision under the GWA 1998 that Assembly committees would combine policy-making and scrutiny roles, and ministers would be members of the committees that shadowed their portfolios, the 'subject committees'. This combination of policy-making and scrutiny roles was not always an easy one for the committees and involved two different relationships with the relevant ministers: one opposition Assembly member commented that it was 'difficult to scrutinise the Minster while he or she sits as a Member of the Committee'.[41] The requirement for ministers to be members of the relevant Assembly committees was ended by the 2006 Act, thus removing one impediment to effective scrutiny. However, on a positive note, research on the working of the Assembly's committee system has found that the initial corporate status of the Assembly has left a 'cultural legacy' whereby there is a high level of ministerial

[38] Report of the Richard Commission (2004). Available at: http://image.guardian.co.uk/sys-files/Politics/documents/2004/03/31/richard_commission.pdf.

[39] Michael Cole, Laura McAllister and Diana Stirbu, 'The Capacity of the National Assembly: UK Changing Union Project' (2013), available at: www.ukchangingunion.org.uk/en/wp-content/uploads/2013/03/Chapter-1-The-Capacity-of-the-National-Assembly.pdf.

[40] ibid.

[41] *The Record* (14 February 2002) 70 (Cynog Dafis): http://www.assembly.wales/record%20of%20proceedings%20documents/the%20record-14022002-9396/bus-chamber-3c6cfa3a000d18cc0000162b00000000-english.pdf.

cooperation with the committee system and a willingness to engage with a high level of committee scrutiny.[42]

The GWA 1998 was very prescriptive as to the Assembly committees which had to be established, and the Assembly's first set of Standing Orders committed it to establishing certain other committees. The 60-member Assembly had 10 subject committees, four regional advisory committees and seven standing committees. It is not surprising that there has since been a move towards reducing the number of committees. To some extent, this is made easier by the GWA 2006, which is far less prescriptive than its predecessor statute and requires the establishment only of an Audit Committee. However, the workload of the Assembly is increasing (and could increase further if the current Silk Commission results in any additional powers being given to the Assembly). Clearly the committee system needs to be designed as strategically as possible. One change in 2011 was to abandon the practice of having a number of permanent legislation committees devoted solely to the scrutiny of bills (although other relevant committees might have some input too).[43] Now, the cross-party Business Committee determines whether a bill is to be referred to a committee and, if so, to which of the subject committees. While this arrangement allows for committee members to develop expertise on a subject area, as has been observed elsewhere, the danger is that the scrutiny of legislation may dominate committee time and leave less time for policy scrutiny.[44]

The absence of a committee dedicated to the examination of human rights issues, the equivalent of the UK Parliament's Joint Committee on Human Rights (JCHR), must therefore, at least partly, be seen in the light of the Assembly's stretched resources. However, there are also issues relating to the perception of human rights and the prioritisation of certain issues. The first Assembly, with the limited powers accorded under the GWA 1998, had a Committee on Equality of Opportunity: this committee continued in that form until 2011, when the topic of equality of opportunity became combined in the remit of the Communities, Equality and Local Government Committee. However, suggestions in the first Assembly that a committee on human rights was needed came to nothing.[45] As noted earlier, a proposal that the Committee on Equality of Opportunity could have human rights added to its title and remit was rejected by that committee, which considered the issue on two occasions.[46] While one may appreciate the Committee's concerns about an increased workload, the argument that human rights, as a 'cross-cutting issue', did not require its own committee is less than convincing in that the same could be said of equality of opportunity.[47] As already observed, the Committee saw the equality

---

[42] Cole, McAllister and Stirbu (n 39) 8.

[43] For example, three committees were involved with the Rights of Children and Young Persons (Wales) Measure 2011.

[44] Cole, McAllister and Stirbu (n 39) 9, 12–13.

[45] Evidence to the Assembly Review of Procedure by Cardiff Charter 88 and by Professor R Rawlings: *Final Report of the Assembly Review of Procedure* (2002). See also R Rawlings, *Delineating Wales— Constitutional, Legal and Administrative Aspects of National Devolution* (Cardiff, University of Wales Press, 2003) 483–85.

[46] See minutes of the meeting of 26 June 2002, Committee on Equality of Opportunity.

[47] See further Rawlings, *Delineating Wales* (n 45) 484.

of opportunity duty under the GWA 1998 as a positive duty and the human rights obligation as a negative duty. It considered that there was a value in 'joining human rights to the equality agenda in the context of informing the work of the committee rather than driving it'. The Committee did consider that it was necessary to have 'an effective mechanism' for scrutinising compliance with human rights legislation, but did not consider that it was the appropriate forum. It remains the case, over a decade later, that there is no committee with the specific remit of scrutinising for such human rights compliance. Of course, in contrast to the UK Parliament, which has the JCHR, the Assembly does have the check built in by the Presiding Officer's scrutiny of the competence issues. What that scrutiny does not provide, however, is the kind of rigorous public discussion of the potential issues and the public weighing up of the proportionality of any interferences; of course, one assumes that this is the process which the Presiding Officer and her legal advisors go through, but what is lost is the general awareness of rights issues that can be developed by published reports analysing the issues in full.

One committee with a general remit that could in principle embody the human rights remit is the Constitutional and Legislative Affairs Committee. Under Standing Orders, it is required to consider subordinate legislation with regard to vires and other features which should be drawn to the attention of the Assembly, and to consider the appropriateness in Assembly bills and UK bills of provisions which grant powers to make subordinate legislation to the Welsh Government.[48] Under the remit establishing the Committee, it may also consider any other legislative matter referred to it by the Business Committee. In some ways, this might be an obvious committee to have an explicit remit concerning compliance with human rights, but this is not provided for in Standing Orders. Even the issue of reviewing the Assembly's general competence in relation to the legislation is not explicitly stated (although the reports of the Committee on Assembly bills do refer briefly to the issue of competence), but the primary focus of the reports is on the extent to which the bills allow for the making of subordinate legislation.[49]

More generally, it is not clear to what extent the committees see an examination of competence generally, and of compliance with human rights in particular, as part of their functions. For the most part, human rights issues have not been contentious in the legislation proposed thus far and, on the whole, proposed legislation has also had general support across the parties. But there is very little legislation on which to make this assessment. When Part 3 of the GWA 2006 was in force, Measures could be enacted only after the particular powers had been added to Schedule 5 to the Act in order to give the Assembly competence. The examination of the requests for powers at the UK level tended, controversially, to attempt to examine the way in which the powers would be exercised by the Assembly.[50] Accordingly, issues of competence, whether general or human rights-related, were not very likely to occur. Since the entry into force of Part 4 of the Act, only four Acts have entered into

---

[48] Standing Order 21.
[49] Its reports are available at: www.senedd.assemblywales.org/mgCommitteeDetails.aspx?ID=219.
[50] See further Ann Sherlock, 'Devolution in Transition in Wales' (2011) 17 *European Public Law* 25, 26–27.

force. None of them was controversial in terms of human rights issues, although the first of them was referred to the Supreme Court for pre-enactment scrutiny regarding subject-matter competence issues. It was found to be within the Assembly's competence.[51]

As observed earlier, the Presiding Officer wrote to the Constitutional and Legislative Affairs Committee and the Health and Social Care Committee in order to alert them to the existence of 'credible' arguments which could be made against the Assembly's competence to enact the Recovery of Medical Costs for Asbestos Diseases (Wales) Bill. This was a bill proposed by an Assembly member,[52] and the member explained that discussions on the Bill with Welsh Government officials had not led to any negative feedback regarding competence to enact the Bill. The Bill had been sent to the Secretary of State for Wales and no issue had been raised by that Office. As a private member, discussions between him and the UK Government would not be expected, but Government to Government contact was more likely. The member considered that the function was clearly within competence and any questions related more to the incidental consequences of the main function. In its report, the Constitutional and Legislative Affairs Committee observed that the issues raised by the Presiding Officer (principally as to whether the Bill sought to bind the Crown) were potentially contentious, but, given that the issues had been raised at any early stage and prior to the amending stages, it expected that any potential difficulties could be addressed by Government to Government contact during the legislative process.[53] The Committee's discussion indicated that committee members found it helpful that the Presiding Officer was willing to take this transparent approach and the Committee had indeed raised the issue with the member in charge of the Bill.[54]

A cautious note was sounded by the Health and Social Care Committee in its discussion which considered whether it was within the remit of the Committee to discuss an issue of competence. The Committee was keen to ensure that it was not putting itself in the position of reviewing the decision of the Presiding Officer, ultimately justifying its role in pursuing the issues as 'compiling a body of evidence to help [the Presiding Officer] in her job' and at her invitation.[55] The issue was taken on board in relation to the questions which would be put to those providing evidence. Having rehearsed the arguments made about competence, including referring to the evidence given in relation to the right to property, the Committee concluded in its report: 'Ultimately, whether the Bill is within the Assembly's legislative competence is a matter for judicial rather than legislative decision.'[56] It noted the existence

---

[51] See above n 37.

[52] The equivalent of a UK private member's bill.

[53] Constitutional and Legislative Affairs Committee, *Report on the Recovery of Medical Costs for Asbestos Diseases (Wales) Bill* (March 2013), available at: www.senedd.assemblywales.org/mgCommitteeDetails.aspx?ID=219.

[54] ibid, transcript of meeting of 7 January 2013.

[55] Transcript of meeting of Health and Social Care Committee of 5 December 2012, available at: www.senedd.assemblywales.org/mgCommitteeDetails.aspx?ID=227.

[56] Report of Health and Social Care Committee on the Bill of March 2013, , para 19, available at: http://www.assembly.wales/Laid%20Documents/CR-LD9245%20-%20Health%20and%20Social%20Care%20Committee%20Stage%201%20Committee%20Report,%20Recovery%20of%20Medical%20Costs%20for%20Asbestos%20D-07032013-243799/cr-ld9245-e-English.pdf.

of a mechanism for the Bill to be referred to the Supreme Court to resolve such a question and it noted that the Presiding Officer had found the Bill to be within competence. It is clear that the Committee had no wish to substitute its own view for that of the Presiding Officer on this legal issue and was happy to rely on her earlier scrutiny and on the subsequent availability of judicial scrutiny of the provisions. It is evident, however, that the Presiding Officer's letter of alert did ensure that the issues were raised in the Committee discussions and also in plenary,[57] and will be pursued in the Bill's later stages.

In addition to the scrutiny of legislation and development of new policy, it is important that the implementation of agreed policy is scrutinised. In its Legacy Report in 2011, the Children and Young People Committee, in reflecting on its four-year term at the end of the third Assembly, noted concerns that Wales is 'policy rich but implementation poor'.[58] This point highlights that a crucial element in securing the *actual* protection of human rights is scrutiny which aims to ensure that the Welsh Government is delivering the agreed policies. It is both interesting and realistic that the Children and Young People Committee's recommendations for future inquiries by any successor committee were largely regarding the delivery of, and implementation of, existing policies and strategies.[59] Accordingly, opportunities for Assembly committees and the Assembly in plenary to scrutinise and debate reports on progress are important, as for example with the annual reports of the Children's Commissioner and the Commissioner for Older People. While the legislative requirement is that these reports are submitted to the Welsh Government rather than the Assembly, they have nonetheless provided useful opportunities for relevant committees and the Assembly in plenary to hold the Welsh Government to account for its development and delivery of policy.

V. CHILDREN'S RIGHTS IN WALES

The protection and promotion of children's rights in Wales is a useful case study on Welsh approaches and values, and on the role of the Assembly in the process. It is an area in which there has been a significantly distinctive approach in Wales post-devolution. Various reasons have been suggested for the attention paid to children's rights in the new Assembly.[60] Among the Assembly members elected to the first Assembly were a significant number, including the First Minister, who had previously worked in youth and children's services. It has also been suggested that the unusually high number (in UK terms) of women in the first Assembly (25 out

---

[57] National Assembly for Wales, *Official Record*, 19 March 2013.
[58] *Legacy Report of the Children and Young People Committee*, 2011, para 179. Available at: www.assemblywales.org/bus-home/bus-third-assembly/bus-guide-docs-pub/bus-business-documents/bus-business-documents-doc-laid.htm?act=dis&id=213805&ds=3/2011.
[59] ibid.
[60] For a useful overview, see Ian Butler and Mark Drakeford, 'Children's Rights as a Policy Framework in Wales' in Jane Williams (ed), *The United Nations Convention on the Rights of the Child in Wales* (Cardiff, University of Wales Press, 2013).

of 60) and the first Cabinet (four of nine ministers) helped to prioritise the case of children's rights as a topic for action.[61]

The restricted power of the Assembly was also an influential factor. The powers given to the Assembly under the 1998 Act were limited and disparate: policy requiring primary legislation meant acquiring the legislation or the legislative powers from the UK level. The Assembly as first elected produced a minority government and therefore any attempts to acquire additional powers needed cross-party support. Such cross-party consensus existed in relation to children's rights in general and in relation to the creation of a Children's Commissioner in particular. When the Assembly was established, the report from the Waterhouse Inquiry[62] into abuse in children's homes in North Wales had recently been issued: Waterhouse had recommended the creation of a commissioner on children's rights, but it has been observed that this idea had been raised even before then.[63]

That cross-party consensus was successful in securing the inclusion in the Care Standards Act 2000 of provisions to establish the Children's Commissioner for Wales.[64] The commitment to a rights-based approach was evident in the subsequent Regulations on the Commissioner enacted by the Assembly, with the Regulations requiring the Commissioner to have regard to the UNCRC in carrying out his functions—the first requirement in legislation in the UK to have regard to that international treaty. Of particular significance in terms of the commitment to a rights-based approach, and to the UNCRC in particular, was the resolution adopted by the Assembly in plenary committing itself to using the UNCRC as the benchmark for all policy developed by it in relation to children.[65] The Welsh Government's paper *Children and Young People: Rights to Action* then translated the rights from the UNCRC into seven core aims for children and young people with explicit acknowledgement regarding their UNCRC foundations. The Assembly, while having limited powers, had committed itself strongly to a rights-based approach for children.

In 2009 the Welsh Government published *Getting it Right*,[66] a rolling action plan to respond to the 2008 Concluding Observations of the UN Committee on the Rights of the Child in its periodic review of the UK. During the four-year period in which Part 3 of the Act was in force, among the matters of competence added to Schedule 5 to the GWA 2006 included a number which made it possible to pursue the children's rights agenda further. In the social welfare field, the Legislative Competence Order successfully proposed by the Assembly included a definition of 'well-being' in relation to individuals as, inter alia, relating to 'securing their

---

[61] N Thomas and A Crowley, 'Children's Rights and Well-being in Wales in 2006' (2007) 19 *Contemporary Wales* 161, 162.

[62] R Waterhouse, *Lost in Care: Report of the Tribunal of Inquiry into the Abuse of Children in Care in the Former County Council Areas of Gwynedd and Clwyd since 1974* (1999–2000, HC 201).

[63] O Rees, 'Devolution and the Children's Commissioner for Wales: Challenges and Opportunities' (2010) 23 *Contemporary Wales* 52, 55.

[64] The powers were subsequently extended by the Children's Commissioner for Wales Act 2001 (UK).

[65] National Assembly for Wales, *Official Record*, 14 January 2004.

[66] Welsh Government, *Getting it Right* (2009).

rights'.[67] This period also saw the adoption of a groundbreaking (at least in UK terms) piece of legislation regarding the further implementation of the UNCRC in Wales, the Rights of Children and Young Persons (Wales) Measure 2011 (hereinafter 'the 2011 Measure'). This Measure also provides an interesting example of the Assembly scrutiny system having a significant impact on the content of legislation.

The origins of the 2011 Measure lay in a proposal by the then First Minister, Rhodri Morgan, in July 2009 for legislation on the protection of children's rights involving a general duty on ministers to have regard to the UNCRC when exercising their functions. However, opposition within the civil service, combined with a change in the ministerial team, led to a rather watered-down version of the proposed Measure being presented in September 2009, followed by a number of variations which, instead of placing a duty on the Welsh ministers which was pervasive across all their functions, restricted the duty in some way.[68] One version would have applied the duty to functions determined by the ministers themselves to be 'relevant functions', whereas a subsequent version would have made the duty pervasive as to the range of areas covered, but would have restricted the duty to decisions 'of a strategic nature'. That the Measure ultimately emerged with a pervasive duty on ministers to have due regard to the UNCRC when exercising *any* of their functions was the result of a combination of circumstances: the existence of a coalition government in which the smaller party was unwilling to countenance the adoption of the weaker versions of the Measure, sustained lobbying by the children's rights non-governmental organisation (NGO) community which was strongly against the weaker measures, and the work of three Assembly Committees which were involved with the consideration of the Measure.

The main scrutiny was undertaken by Legislation Committee No 5, but two other committees were involved—the Constitutional Affairs Committee and the Children and Young People Committee. The latter committee conducted a brief pre-legislative evidence-gathering exercise on the Welsh Government proposal, the result of which was to underline the consensus in favour of a pervasive Measure biting on all ministerial functions rather than only on the proposed 'relevant' functions. By the time the Measure was introduced into the Assembly, the 'relevant functions' approach had been abandoned in favour of the duty applying to all ministerial decisions of a strategic nature. The questioning by, and evidence to, the Legislation Committee on this showed the lack of support for this limited duty.[69]

In the end, the Measure was amended and as enacted contains a duty on the Welsh ministers to have due regard to the requirements of the UNCRC when exercising any of their functions. The entry into force of the duty has been split into two stages with the duty applying to all ministerial functions from May 2014.[70] The ultimate agreement of the Welsh Government to return to the original idea for the Measure has

---

[67] The National Assembly for Wales (Legislative Competence) (Social Welfare and Other Fields) Order 2008 (SI 2008/3122).

[68] For a more detailed account of the making of the Measure, see Michael Sullivan and Helen Mary Jones, 'Made to Measure: Cooperation and Conflict in the Making of a Policy' in Williams (n 60).

[69] See also the questioning of the Deputy Minister on this issue by the Constitutional Affairs Committee in June 2010.

[70] Rights of Children and Young Persons (Wales) Measure 2011, s 1.

been hailed as a success for the 'coalition of forces [that] emerged from both within the Assembly and from wider civil society'.[71] The willingness of the relevant committees to seek and hear evidence from the NGO community and others with expertise in relation to the subject matter clearly enhanced the ability of the committees to engage in robust scrutiny of the Government proposal. Indeed, this illustrates a potentially more general feature: with an Assembly of only 60 members, the ability of external stakeholders to influence and inform may be a particularly strong feature of the Welsh policy development and scrutiny process. It must be remembered in this particular case that the existence of a coalition government in which the smaller party was willing to withhold support for the weaker version of the Measure was also significant. In addition, there was perhaps an unusual degree of agreement among the NGO community regarding the need for a pervasive duty which was supported by academic and practising lawyers. The policy community mobilised quickly and effectively on this issue and found a receptive audience in the relevant committees and among other Assembly members. This combination of factors may not be easy to replicate on many other issues. Nonetheless, this instance shows the potential for well-informed Assembly committees, backed up by cross-party support, to act as agents for change.

The Measure breaks new ground in the UK in making the UNCRC a reference point which must be given due consideration in the exercise of all of the Welsh Government's functions. A Children's Scheme must be adopted with a view to securing compliance with the main 'due regard' duty.[72] There is also a duty to raise awareness and understanding of the Convention in Wales.[73]

The challenge is now for this commitment in legislation to be turned into practical changes and the role of the Assembly in scrutinising the Measure's implementation will be important. The Measure requires the Welsh Government to report to the Assembly on a five-yearly basis on its compliance with the due regard duty.[74] While this is a lengthy interval between reports, it provides a minimum legislative requirement for scrutiny. In any case, this does not prevent more regular scrutiny of the Welsh Government on its performance in this area. The Children and Young People Committee clearly sees the scrutiny of the delivery of the Measure to be a significant part of its remit and has already held hearings to review the Children's Scheme which has been in place for just over one year and to consider the Welsh Government's national action plan on children's rights.[75] Part of the Children's Scheme requires proposals for legislation and policy changes to undergo a children's rights impact assessment (CRIA). This is a very positive development in principle although, because so far these CRIAs are not generally publicly available, it is difficult to evaluate quite how the issues are being assessed in practice. The greater the level of transparency in how these issues are assessed, the more effective the scrutiny which can be exercised by the Assembly as well as by external bodies.

[71] Sullivan and Jones (n 68) 33.
[72] Rights of Children and Young Persons (Wales) Measure 2011, s 2.
[73] ibid, s 5.
[74] ibid, s 4.
[75] Meeting of Children and Young People Committee, 9 May 2013. Transcript available at: www.senedd.assemblywales.org/documents/s17544/9%20May%202013.pdf.

CONCLUSION

A number of themes emerge regarding the Assembly's role in relation to human rights. The nature of the Assembly, its initial composition and its powers, and the political and economic context in which it was established have led to a focus on inclusion, equality and citizenship. Political traditions in Wales seem to have also led to a greater willingness to view individuals as citizens and rights-holders.[76] This common ground has proved to be a fertile culture in which rights can be developed. There has been general cross-party support for the adoption of a rights-based approach towards policy.

There is perhaps a psychological benefit for the Assembly in being a body constrained by a founding constitutive Act. Whereas the UK Parliament has had to grapple with new challenges to its traditional sovereignty, described elsewhere by Hunt as the 'greatest obstacle to any reshaping of [British] notions of constitutionalism',[77] the Assembly is a young institution created from the outset as a body with limits on its powers: compliance with human rights is the norm rather than a new development. The Assembly also operates in an environment in which the Commission on a Bill of Rights[78] found much less public antipathy or hostility towards the European Court of Human Rights and the ECHR in Wales than in England. However, while there has been no question of the Assembly failing to adhere to the requirements of the ECHR, there has been less emphasis on civil and political rights than on the promotion of social and economic rights, with particular emphasis on increasing equality of opportunity for previously marginalised groups. To some extent this is a result of economic and political values in Wales and to some extent it is the result of the nature of the legal obligations within which the Assembly works. Both the GWA 1998 and the GWA 2006 have placed a good deal of emphasis on duties to promote rights by having 'due regard' to certain values. The Assembly itself has adopted this approach in its 2011 Measure on the Rights of Children and Young Persons. It is an approach which aims to be proactive rather than reactive in seeking to provide individual remedies after a breach. Although the failure to have 'due regard' could be litigated by way of judicial review, the primary aim of the Measure, and of the scheme which implements it, is to ensure that the UNCRC is duly considered when any decisions are being made. It is an approach in which parliamentary scrutiny is vital and is emphasised over individual judicial remedies.

It remains to be seen whether issues concerning the powers of the Assembly in relation to equality and human rights are addressed in a way which enhances the ability of the Assembly to play a significant role more generally. It also remains to be seen whether there will be the political courage to grapple with the issue of the size of the Assembly in order to ensure that its capacity to scrutinise is maintained.

---

[76] See Butler and Drakeford (n 60) 12 and 18; Sullivan and Jones (n 68) 22–26.

[77] Murray Hunt, 'Reshaping Constitutionalism' in J Morison, K McEvoy and G Anthony (eds), *Judges, Transition and Human Rights* (Oxford, Oxford University Press, 2007) 467.

[78] Commission on a Bill of Rights, *A UK Bill of Rights? The Choice Before Us* (2012), available at: www.justice.gov.uk/about/cbr.

Part IV

Legislative Human Rights Review in Other National Parliaments

12

Australia's Parliamentary Scrutiny Act: An Exclusive Parliamentary Model of Rights Protection

GEORGE WILLIAMS AND LISA BURTON*

A USTRALIA IS THE only remaining democratic nation without some form of national Human Rights Act or Bill of Rights.[1] Instead, Australia relies on the common law, a handful of provisions in its Constitution and the democratic process to protect human rights.[2] In 2008, a federal inquiry was initiated to determine whether change was required. This inquiry recommended the enactment of a Human Rights Act similar to the Human Rights Act 1998 (UK). However, Australia's federal government rejected this recommendation and instead established a new national human rights framework focusing on the pre-enactment scrutiny of new legislation. As a result, the Human Rights (Parliamentary Scrutiny) Act 2011 (Cth) (hereinafter the 'Parliamentary Scrutiny Act') now requires bills and legislative instruments to be accompanied by a statement of their compatibility with human rights. These statements can be examined, and other human rights matters investigated, by a new parliamentary Joint Committee on Human Rights.

This system is unique in that it provides no role for the courts. If the UK Human Rights Act can be described as a 'parliamentary rights model',[3] the Parliamentary Scrutiny Act must be described as an 'exclusive parliamentary rights model'. It establishes a scheme of rights protection in which Parliament has an exclusive role. This system is self-regulating and, to a large extent, voluntary. Statements of compatibility produce no legal consequences and cannot be reviewed by the courts. The way that rights are 'defined' in the Parliamentary Scrutiny Act is also unusual. No human rights are spelt out in the legislation; rather, the Parliamentary Scrutiny Act incorporates the (many) rights contained in several international treaties to which Australia is a signatory.

---

* This chapter is developed from an article published in the *Statute Law Review*.
[1] Human Rights Acts have been passed in two sub-national jurisdictions: the Human Rights Act 2004 (ACT); and the Charter of Human Rights and Responsibilities Act 2006 (Vic).
[2] See generally G Williams and D Hume, *Human Rights Under the Australian Constitution* (2nd edn, Melbourne, Oxford University Press, 2013).
[3] J Hiebert, 'New Constitutional Ideas: Can New Parliamentary Models Resist Judicial Dominance When Interpreting Rights?'(2004) 82 *Texas Law Review* 1963, 1963.

This novel means of recognising and protecting human rights warrants analysis and assessment.[4] This chapter examines the design of the Parliamentary Scrutiny Act in detail and its first six months of operation. From this, we draw conclusions about the impact and effectiveness of the new regime and consider whether a system which relies entirely on Parliament to protect human rights will be effective.

I. THE ORIGINS OF THE PARLIAMENTARY SCRUTINY ACT

In December 2008, the federal government established a National Human Rights Consultation chaired by Father Frank Brennan to examine and report on human rights protection in Australia. The Brennan Committee undertook an exhaustive process of consultation and discussion with the community, travelling 'the length and breadth of the country'.[5] It received 35,014 written submissions—then the largest number ever for a national consultation in Australia. At the end of this process, 'the Committee was left in no doubt that the protection and promotion of human rights is a matter of national importance'.[6]

The Brennan Committee report of September 2009 concluded that 'Australia measures well against many other countries in terms of its human rights protection' and that: 'Many Australians enjoy a standard of living that is at least equal to that in other First World countries and rarely would need to reflect on human rights or whether they are adequately protected.' However, it also found that '[Australia's] record is not perfect' and that some groups of people continued to need 'greater protection (or at least assistance in exercising their rights)': for example, children, people with a mental illness, people with disabilities and Indigenous Australians.[7]

The Brennan Committee made a raft of recommendations, including that the federal Parliament enact a national Human Rights Act in a similar form to the UK Human Rights Act; that is, a law providing protection for a wide range of predominately civil and political rights through enhanced parliamentary scrutiny, judicial interpretation of legislation and non-binding declarations of incompatibility issued by courts. This recommendation reflected the finding that the federal Parliament is incapable of effectively protecting human rights alone.

For example, the Committee concluded that Parliament may abrogate human rights in times of emergency. Hence, in 2007 the federal Parliament enacted a

---

[4] For initial treatments of the new Act, see J Stellios and M Palfrey, 'A New Federal Scheme for the Protection of Human Rights' (2012) 69 *Australian Institute of Administrative Law Forum* 13; D Kinley and C Ernst, 'Exile on Main Street: Australia's Legislative Agenda for Human Rights' (2012) 1 *European Human Rights Law Review* 58; R Dixon, 'A New (Inter)National Human Rights Experiment for Australia' (2012) 23 *Public Law Review* 69; D Meagher, 'The Significance of the Human Rights (Parliamentary Scrutiny) Act 2011 (Cth)' (Paper Presented at Australian Association of Constitutional Law Victorian Seminar Series 2012, Melbourne, 7 June 2012); H Mannreitz, 'Commonwealth Statements of Compatibility—Small Steps, Early Days' (2012) 71 *Human Rights Law Centre Bulletin* 8.

[5] Brennan Committee, 'Summary', National Human Rights Consultation Report (2009), xiii, available at http://www.ag.gov.au/RightsAndProtections/HumanRights/TreatyBodyReporting/Pages/HumanRightsconsultationreport.aspx.

[6] ibid, xiii.

[7] ibid, 99.

package of legislation known as the 'Northern Territory Intervention' to address shocking allegations of child sexual abuse in indigenous communities in the Northern Territory. The Bills—running to 604 pages—were introduced in the House of Representatives on 7 August 2007; the first at 12.32 pm and the last at 1.47 pm. All five Bills were passed by the House at 9.34 pm that same day. Among other things, the Bills suspended the operation of the Racial Discrimination Act 1975 (Cth).

Similarly, the federal Parliament entered a phase of 'hyper-legislation' after the 9/11 terrorist attacks,[8] enacting 48 new anti-terrorism laws between September 2001 and 2007—one every 6.7 weeks.[9] Much of this legislation had significant human rights implications. For example, the Anti-Terrorism Act (No 2) 2005 (Cth) created a controversial new system of control orders and preventative detention orders. These orders can be made against individuals who are believed to have engaged in some terrorist activity, but have not necessarily been convicted or charged with any crime. These orders are made via a civil process not attenuated by the safeguards of the criminal justice system. In the wake of the London bombings and aided by the fact it held a majority in both Houses of Parliament, the Howard government was able to have this legislation enacted after just six hours and 24 minutes of parliamentary debate.[10]

These examples are reflective of a broader problem about the time constraints facing federal parliamentarians. In 2011, 238 bills were introduced into the House of Representatives, totalling 7368 pages. 190 bills were enacted. In addition, Parliament was required to scrutinise 286 legislative instruments running to many thousands more pages.[11] As the Brennan Committee concluded, it is simply impossible for parliamentarians to rigorously scrutinise the rights implications of so much legislation, particularly if there is political pressure to pass the legislation quickly.[12] Even if parliamentarians try to do so, they may lack the expertise needed to effectively assess the human rights implications of some laws.[13] Further, the strong party culture, which constrains Australian politics may prevent parliamentarians from speaking out against certain laws.

The Brennan Committee also concluded that Parliament may ignore the rights of minorities or those who lack political power. For example, a blanket prisoner voting

---

[8] K Roach, *The 9/11 Effect: Comparative Counter-terrorism* (New York, Cambridge University Press, 2011) 309.

[9] G Williams, 'A Decade of Australian Anti-Terror Laws' (2011) 35 *Melbourne University Law Review* 1136, 1145.

[10] See generally A Lynch, 'Control Orders in Australia: A Further Case Study in the Migration of British Counter-terrorism Law' (2008) 8 *Oxford University Commonwealth Law Journal* 159.

[11] Department of the House of Representatives, Work of the Session: 43rd Parliament: 1st Session (2011), 1, 4. An equivalent statistic is not provided for the Senate, but some information is provided at Parliament of Australia Chamber Research Office, House of Representatives—Legislation Statistics Since 1901 (2011) 3; Parliament of Australia, Senate StatsNet, www.aph.gov.au/Parliamentary_Business/Statistics/Senate_StatsNet.

[12] Brennan Committee (n 5) 106.

[13] C Evans and S Evans, 'The Effectiveness of Australian Parliaments in the Protection of Rights' (Paper Presented at the Conference on Legislatures and the Protection of Human Rights, University of Melbourne Law School, 20–21 July 2006) 3; C Evans and S Evans, 'Messages from the Front Line: Parliamentarians' Perspectives on Rights Protection' in T Campbell, K Ewing and A Tomkins (eds), *The Legal Protection of Human Rights: Sceptical Essays* (New York, Oxford University Press, 2011) 338.

ban and 'electoral integrity measure', which had the practical effect of disenfranchising thousands of young people, were enacted in 2006. Both measures were found to be an unnecessary and disproportionate limitation on the right to vote by the High Court.[14] If there is sufficient political impetus, Parliament may also override rights safeguards which are not constitutionally entrenched. Thus, in 1998, the federal Parliament suspended the Racial Discrimination Act in order to establish a new Native Title regime, which was enacted to 'pour bucket-loads on extinguishment' on the native title rights of Indigenous Australians.[15]

The Brennan Committee recognised that the electoral process may not be enough to guard against these dynamics. Federal politicians only face re-election every three years, and so human rights violations may be forgotten by the time that they are held to account, or may simply be irrelevant to the voting intentions of the majority of the population. Something more was needed. However, the federal government rejected many of the Brennan Committee's recommendations. In particular, it decided not to support a Human Rights Act on the basis that it would be 'divisive'.[16] The government did, however, announce that it would implement some of the Committee's recommendations in the form of a new 'human rights framework',[17] the centrepoint of which is the new Parliamentary Scrutiny Act.

II. THE PARLIAMENTARY SCRUTINY ACT

The Parliamentary Scrutiny Act was enacted in 2011. The Act defines 'human rights' for the purposes of the Act, requires that a statement of compatibility (SOC) be prepared for all bills and legislative instruments subject to disallowance, and establishes the Parliamentary Joint Committee on Human Rights (PJCHR).

A. Definition of Human Rights

'Human rights' are defined in section 3 of the Parliamentary Scrutiny Act as 'the rights and freedoms recognised or declared by the following seven international instruments':

— the International Convention on the Elimination of All Forms of Racial Discrimination;[18]
— the International Covenant on Economic, Social and Cultural Rights (ICESCR);[19]

---

[14] *Roach v Electoral Commissioner* (2007) 233 CLR 162; *Rowe v Electoral Commissioner* (2010) 243 CLR 1.
[15] R Manne, 'The Howard Years: A Political Interpretation' in R Manne (ed), *The Howard Years* (Melbourne, Black Inc Agenda, 2004), 18.
[16] R McClelland (former Attorney-General), 'Address to the National Press Club of Australia— Launch of Australia's Human Rights Framework' (Speech delivered at the National Press Club of Australia, Canberra, 21 April 2010).
[17] Australian Government Attorney-General's Department, Australia's Human Rights Framework, http://www.ag.gov.au/Consultations/Documents/Publicsubmissionsonthedraftbaselinestudy/AustraliasHumanRightsFramework.pdf.
[18] Signed 7 March 1966 [1975] ATS 40 (entered into force 4 January 1969).
[19] Signed 16 December 1966 [1976] ATS 5 (entered into force 3 January 1976).

— the International Covenant on Civil and Political Rights (ICCPR);[20]
— the Convention on the Elimination of All Forms of Discrimination against Women;[21]
— the Convention against Torture and Other Cruel, Inhuman or Degrading Treatment or Punishment;[22]
— the Convention on the Rights of the Child;[23] and
— the Convention on the Rights of Persons with Disabilities.[24]

This reflects the recommendation of the Brennan Committee that Australia's domestic human rights laws should be brought into line with its international obligations.[25] Importantly, it means that no rights are expressly set out in the Parliamentary Scrutiny Act. This is a different model from the Charters of Rights in place in the Australian Capital Territory (ACT) and the State of Victoria, and the Bills of Rights of other nations. Such instruments usually list rights which are modelled on—but not necessarily the same as or coextensive with—the rights recognised in international treaties. As a result, the Parliamentary Scrutiny Act recognises 'well over 100 rights and freedoms',[26] a larger set of rights than the ACT and Victorian laws or the Bill of Rights of any other democratic nation.[27]

The fact that the Parliamentary Scrutiny Act defines human rights is necessary and valuable. The Brennan Committee concluded that the enactment of a definitive list of human rights would fill an important gap in Australian law and 'serve as an important symbolic statement of Australian values'.[28] Such a list of rights may lend clarity to parliamentary debate and invest those rights with democratic legitimacy. Without a clear definition of human rights, concerns about new legislation may fail to gain traction and 'fizzle out'.[29] Without legislative recognition of human rights, it may be easy for parliamentarians to dismiss them.

However, the unusual way in which rights are defined may thwart some of this potential. The incorporation of so many rights means that the Parliamentary Scrutiny Act has enormous breadth—but likely at the cost of depth. Many of the rights contained in the treaties are broad, aspirational standards, in the way that treaty provisions often are. Few have been implemented in domestic Australian law and so there is no pre-existing material setting out what they comprise of and what they require. Nor has there been any attempt to adapt the rights to the Australian setting. This may be less of an issue for civil and political rights, which can be found in Bills of Rights and Human Rights Acts in Australia and elsewhere, than for economic, social and cultural rights, which raise a new set of conceptual and legal challenges.

---

[20] Signed 16 December 1966 [1980] ATS 23 (entered into force 23 March 1976.).
[21] Signed 18 December 1979 [1983] ATS 9 (entered into force 3 September 1981).
[22] Signed 10 December 1984 [1989] ATS 21 (entered into force 26 June 1987).
[23] Signed 20 November 1989 [1991] ATS 4 (entered into force 2 September 1990).
[24] Signed 13 December 2006 [2008] ATS 12 (entered into force 3 May 2008).
[25] Brennan Committee (n 5) 347.
[26] Kinley and Ernst (n 4) 62.
[27] See Dixon (n 4) 75; Kinley and Ernst (n 4) 61.
[28] Brennan Committee (n 5) Summary.
[29] Evans and Evans (n 13, 'Messages from the Front Line: Parliamentarians' Perspectives on Rights Protection') 344.

The federal Attorney-General's Department has published fact sheets and analytical 'tools' to assist in understanding the protected rights. However, the task of understanding and synthesising the broad list of international human rights with Australian law remains a Herculean one.[30] As a result, SOCs (which will probably be prepared by departmental employees with no expertise in international law or even legal training) may be broad-brush and simplistic. The Parliamentary Scrutiny Act also does not make clear whether these rights should be interpreted by reference to the text of the treaties alone or whether parliamentarians should 'attempt to engage with various international and comparative sources, such as United Nations committee decision and overseas court judgments, as potential guides to the meaning of the text'.[31]

Further, the rights listed in the Act are not a carefully defined list of rights which the Australian public has been found to recognise or accept. In fact, there are sound reasons to believe that many Australians would not accept a set of international human rights norms.

International law has always struggled for acceptance in Australia. Australia has ratified the major international human rights treaties, but 'treaties do not have the force of law [in Australia] unless they are given that effect by statute'.[32] Sometimes, a finding that Australia has breached its international human rights obligations can prompt legislative change. For example, the UN Human Rights Committee's condemnation of Tasmanian legislation which criminalised homosexual sex prompted the federal Parliament to pass its own legislation overriding the Tasmanian law.[33]

Other problems identified by the UN have not been rectified.[34] For example, in 1997 the UN Committee on the Elimination of Racial Discrimination found that harsh mandatory sentencing laws in place in the Northern Territory breached Australia's international treaty obligations because they targeted crimes more likely to be committed by Indigenous Australians and punished them disproportionately. These concerns were dismissed. The Chief Minister of the Northern Territory said that the UN's intervention was 'designed' to cause embarrassment: 'This is designed to shame Australians. And to my mind [this is] an opportunity for Australians to tell them to bugger off.'[35] Prime Minister John Howard also rejected any international pressure, saying that 'we are mature enough to make decisions on these matters ourselves, full stop'.[36]

---

[30] See Kinley and Ernst (n 4) 61.

[31] Dixon (n 4) 76.

[32] *Kioa v West* (1985) 159 CLR 550, 570 (Gibbs CJ). See generally H Charlesworth, M Chiam, D Hovell and G Williams, 'Deep Anxieties: Australia and the International Legal Order' (2003) 25 Sydney Law Review 423.

[33] Views of the Human Rights Committee under Article 5, Paragraph 4, of the Optional Protocol to the International Covenant on Civil and Political Rights, Communication No 488/1992, UN Doc CCPR/C/50/D/488/1992 (8 April 1994).

[34] D Hovell, 'The Sovereignty Strategem: Australia's Response to UN Human Rights Treaty Bodies' (2003) 28 *Alternative Law Journal* 6.

[35] Australian Broadcasting Corporation, 'NT under Fire Again for Mandatory Sentencing' PM (21 July 2000), www.abc.net.au/7.30/stories/s168960.htm.

[36] Australian Broadcasting Corporation, 'PM Holds Line on Mandatory Sentencing' The World Today (25 February 2000), www.abc.net.au/worldtoday/stories/s103292.htm.

This suggests that international human rights standards cannot be presumed to have the support of the Australian community. Thus, critics could argue that the Parliamentary Scrutiny Act incorporates an illegitimate list of international standards, not an Australian set of rights. Australian 'legislators are politicians and respond to the issues that their constituents regard as important'.[37] If the rights listed in the Parliamentary Scrutiny Act are not important to the wider community (or can be portrayed that way), they may be readily dismissed.

B. Statements of Compatibility

Part 3 of the Parliamentary Scrutiny Act sets out the requirements of SOCs. The same requirements apply to SOCs for both bills and legislative instruments.[38] A member who introduces a bill into either House of Parliament 'must cause a statement of compatibility to be prepared' and 'presented' to Parliament.[39]

The Act does not specify when the SOC should be presented.[40] The Explanatory Memorandum accompanying the Parliamentary Scrutiny Act states that an SOC 'will ordinarily form part of the explanatory memorandum for the Bill'. However, there is nothing to prevent a statement being introduced after debate has begun or even after the bill has been passed.[41] In fact, there are no legal consequences for failing to table an SOC at all.

The Parliamentary Scrutiny Act provides little guidance for the preparation of an SOC. The Act specifies only that the SOC must include an assessment of whether the Bill is compatible with human rights.[42] The Explanatory Memorandum states that SOCs 'are intended to be succinct assessments aimed at informing Parliamentary debate and containing a level of analysis that is proportionate to the impact of the proposed legislation on human rights'.[43] However, the nature of this 'assessment' is unclear. The Act does not stipulate how parliamentarians are to make this judgment. It does not prescribe any criteria or tests (such as the proportionality test typically used in other jurisdictions) to determine when a right has been infringed. There is also no requirement to explain the reasons for finding that a bill is compatible or incompatible.[44]

The Attorney-General's Department has published information to guide this process.[45] A 'policy triggers' document sets out the kind of laws which may impact

---

[37] Evans and Evans (n 13, 'The Effectiveness of Australian Parliaments in the Protection of Rights') 10.
[38] Parliamentary Scrutiny Act, ss 8 and 9.
[39] ibid, s 8(1) and (2).
[40] ibid, ss 8 and 9.
[41] *Cf* Charter of Human Rights and Responsibilities Act, s 28(2).
[42] Parliamentary Scrutiny Act, s 8(3).
[43] Explanatory Memorandum, Human Rights (Parliamentary Scrutiny) Bill 2011 (Cth) 4.
[44] *Cf* Charter of Human Rights and Responsibilities Act, s 28(3). See also Stellios and Palfrey (n 4) 15.
[45] Australian Government Attorney-General's Department, *Tools for Assessing Human Rights Compatibility* http://www.ag.gov.au/RightsAndProtections/HumanRights/PublicSector/Pages/Toolforassessinghumanrightscompatibility.aspx, The PJCHR has indicated that it will publish more guidance material: Harry Jenkins (Chair of the PJCHR), Statement to the Commonwealth House of Representatives, 20 June 2012, 3.

on human rights so as to alert government decision-makers to potential rights issues.[46] For example, it suggests in basic terms that a law which affects the delivery of medical treatment to patients may impact on the right to life. A flowchart published by the Attorney-General's Department states that any limitations on rights must be justified on the basis of a standard proportionality analysis; that is, the limitation must be 'reasonable, necessary and proportionate' to achieving 'a legitimate aim'. Thus, it should be considered whether:

— the limitation is 'sufficiently precise to ensure that it only addresses those matters it is intended to capture';
— there are other 'less restrictive' ways in which the purpose could be achieved;
— the limitation has a disproportionate impact on particular individuals or groups;
— the limitation destroys 'the very essence' of the right; and
— the bill/legislative instrument includes appropriate, practical human rights safeguards.[47]

This clearly goes further than the requirements of the Parliamentary Scrutiny Act. It also establishes a traditional legal methodology which departmental officers without legal training may struggle to perform.

The human rights listed in the relevant international conventions are afforded different levels of protection by those conventions. The Parliamentary Scrutiny Act and the Explanatory Memorandum are silent on whether these categorisations are imported into the Australian regime. Information published by the Attorney-General's Department suggests that they are.[48] Thus, if the relevant convention states that a right is absolute, a bill which limits that right in any way should be incompatible with the right for the purposes of the Parliamentary Scrutiny Act.[49] Similarly, if the convention states that a right can be limited (typically subject to certain conditions), then a bill will not be incompatible if the limitation complies with those conditions.[50] On this reasoning, the Parliamentary Scrutiny Act also imports the distinction between derogable and non-derogable rights in the ICCPR.[51]

No consequences flow from failing to present an SOC. The Parliamentary Scrutiny Act states that: 'A failure to comply with this section in relation to a Bill that becomes an Act does not affect the validity, operation or enforcement of the Act or any other provision of a law of the Commonwealth.'[52] In effect, the 'requirement'

---

[46] Australian Government Attorney-General's Department, *Policy Triggers*, 1, available at http://www.ag.gov.au/RightsAndProtections/HumanRights/PublicSector/Pages/Toolforassessinghumanrightscompatibility.aspx#4policy.

[47] Australian Government Attorney-General's Department, Flowchart for Assessing the Human Rights Compatibility of Bills and Legislative Instruments, 1, available at http://www.ag.gov.au/RightsAndProtections/HumanRights/PublicSector/Pages/Toolforassessinghumanrightscompatibility.aspx#3flowchart.

[48] Australian Government Attorney-General's Department, *Absolute Rights*, available at http://www.ag.gov.au/RightsAndProtections/HumanRights/PublicSectorGuidanceSheets/Pages/Absoluterights.aspx. *cf* Human Rights Act 2004 (ACT) and Charter of Human Rights and Responsibilities Act (Vic).

[49] Eg, ICCPR, arts 7, 8(1) and (2).

[50] Eg, ibid, art 12.

[51] ibid, art 4.

[52] Parliamentary Scrutiny Act, s 8(5).

to table an SOC is optional. If a bill is found to be incompatible or no SOC is ever tabled, the bill can still be passed.[53]

If an SOC is tabled, it has limited legal effect. The SOC 'is not binding on any court or tribunal'.[54] The SOC does not create legal rights or entitlements, and administrative decision-makers need not act compatibly with the listed rights or take the rights or an SOC into account when making a decision. However an SOC may be used to interpret the legislation to which it was attached.[55] David Kinley and Christine Ernst suggest that an SOC that concludes a bill is compatible with human rights 'is an invitation (if not a direction) to courts to interpret legislation consistently with [human rights]'.[56] This would be a significant departure from the approach that the courts usually take to extrinsic materials. Other commentators have emphasised that extrinsic material, including SOCs, cannot trump the literal meaning of the text.[57] The approach that the courts will take remains uncertain.

In any event, SOCs have a very limited role. Their potential benefit lies in enhancing parliamentary debate about proposed legislation by making the rights implications of that legislation clear, thereby enabling parliamentarians to make a more informed decision about whether to amend or pass it. This may increase political pressure to legislate compatibly with rights. While not creating a dialogue between the Parliament and the courts, the regime may create a dialogue between the Executive, the Parliament and ultimately the people by requiring Parliament to reveal and justify rights infringements.[58] In turn, this may cause departments and drafters to be mindful of human rights in developing laws and ultimately to draft legislation which is compatible with human rights.

These benefits will only accrue if the non-binding requirement to table SOCs is respected by Parliament in substance and not just form. The obvious danger is that the procedure will be treated as a mere 'box to be ticked' and SOCs will be hastily compiled without rigorous analysis of the implications of the legislation. This is unfortunately what has occurred in relation to a similar mechanism for the treaty-making process. In 1995, a Senate inquiry found that the treaty-making process suffered from a significant democratic deficit, as treaties were ratified by the Executive without the need for any parliamentary or public involvement.[59] Treaties must now be tabled in Parliament before they are signed, with an accompanying National Interest Analysis (NIA) outlining the obligations imposed by the treaty and the benefits for Australia of entering into the treaty.[60] These requirements have been complied with in form. However, NIAs are typically brief and general with little in-depth

---

[53] ibid.

[54] ibid, s 8(4).

[55] Acts Interpretation Act 1901 (Cth), s 15AB.

[56] Kinley and Ernst (n 4) 68.

[57] ibid, 17–18; Meagher (n 4) 6. See also Dixon (n 4) 77–78.

[58] See also Stellios and Palfrey (n 4) 16; Dixon (n 4) 79; Kinley and Ernst (n 4) 69.

[59] Senate Legal and Constitutional References Committee, *Parliament of Australia, Trick or Treaty?: Commonwealth Power to Make and Implement Treaties* (1995).

[60] See generally H Charlesworth, M Chiam, D Hovell and G Williams, *No Country is an Island: Australia and International Law* (Sydney, University of New South Wales Press, 2006) ch 2.

analysis, often simply summarising the treaty and the reasons why Australia intends to ratify. Therefore, these reforms have been described as mere 'window dressing'.[61]

C. The PJCHR

Part 2 of the Parliamentary Scrutiny Act provides for the PJCHR. The Committee must consist of 10 members—five members each from the Senate and the House of Representatives.[62] Members of Parliament who hold certain positions, such as ministers, are disqualified.[63] The PJCHR's role is:

(a)   to examine Bills for Acts, and legislative instruments, that come before either House of the Parliament for compatibility with human rights, and to report to both Houses of the Parliament on that issue;

(b)   to examine Acts for compatibility with human rights, and to report to both Houses of the Parliament on that issue; and

(c)   to inquire into any matter relating to human rights which is referred to it by the Attorney-General, and to report to both Houses of the Parliament on that matter.[64]

In order to enable it to fulfil these functions, Parliament has resolved that the Committee has a range of powers, including the capacity to hold public hearings and examine witnesses.[65]

The PJCHR acts as a double-check upon SOCs. It also has a broader jurisdiction—to examine existing Acts (but not legislative instruments) on its own motion or to inquire into other human rights issues when directed to do so by the Attorney-General. Thus, the PJCHR is not limited to scrutinising proposed legislation.

In theory, the PJCHR has the jurisdiction and powers to rigorously scrutinise the human rights implications of new and existing legislation, and thereby encourage compliance with the Parliamentary Scrutiny Act. In practice, it is highly unlikely that the Committee will act quite so robustly. As explained above, the international human rights enshrined in the Parliamentary Scrutiny Act are not widely viewed as legitimate standards. There is also no requirement that the PJCHR be given time to examine a bill before it is passed, so it may have little or no impact on parliamentary debate.

More fundamentally, parliamentary committees dominated by members from the governing party are unlikely to speak out against government policy. The self-interest of these members, and their hopes for promotion, tend to deter them from making life difficult for the government, producing a generally 'tepid' and modest approach.[66] Parliamentary committees dominated by non-government members are often more willing to oppose government policy, but the government may be more

---

[61]   ibid, 43.

[62]   Parliamentary Scrutiny Act, s 5(1).

[63]   ibid, s 5(2).

[64]   ibid, s 7.

[65]   Resolution to Establish the Australian Parliamentary Joint Committee on Human Rights, 13 March 2012.

[66]   Evans and Evans (n 13, 'The Effectiveness of Australian Parliaments in the Protection of Rights') 7.

willing to ignore their recommendations. In the end, the impact of parliamentary committees is significantly dampened by the reality of party politics.

A similar committee to the PJCHR, the Joint Standing Committee on Treaties (JSCOT), bears out these concerns. The JSCOT was created as part of the 1995 reforms designed to remedy the democratic deficit in the treaty-making process. The JSCOT scrutinises proposed treaties and reports on their potential benefits and detriments. Like the PJCHR, the JSCOT's powers are advisory only. It has tended to take a cautious approach by making recommendations that the government is likely to accept; as such, it has not enhanced the treaty-making process to any significant extent.[67]

D. The Parliamentary Scrutiny Act in Operation

The Parliamentary Scrutiny Act came into effect on 4 January 2012. In this section we examine its impact on bills over the autumn and winter sessions of that year, a period of six months to the end of June 2012. The following table summarises the results:

Total number of bills	134
Bills accompanied by an SOC	129
SOCs identifying rights engaged	57
SOCs identifying rights limitation	35
SOCs identifying incompatibility	0

The vast majority of bills were accompanied by an SOC. There were some omissions when the Parliamentary Scrutiny Act first came into operation, but only one bill passed since 14 February has lacked an accompanying SOC. SOCs are usually contained in a specific section in the Explanatory Memorandum accompanying the bill, or very occasionally provided in a separate document.

Of the SOCs tabled, just under half identified that the bill did not affect human rights. This statistic has remained quite constant across the months since the Parliamentary Scrutiny Act was introduced. In many cases this was appropriate; for example, in respect of bills that proposed technical and consequential amendments or 'stocktake' bills which proposed to repeal out-of-date laws.

In others, this was surprising. For example, the Poker Machine Harm Reduction ($1 Bets and Other Measures) Bill 2012 (Cth) proposed implementing gambling harm minimisation regulations on the use of 'pokie machines' by stipulating that such machines could not accept more than $20 or bets of more than $1 at a time. This Bill was said not to engage any human rights, despite having clear implications for the personal freedoms of persons who use pokie machines and the economic

---

[67] See generally Charlesworth et al (n 60).

rights and interests of the people who operate them. Interestingly, bills which engage the human rights of non-Australian citizens have also been identified as not engaging human rights.[68]

Most problematically, most SOCs are brief and many display a disturbing lack of analytical rigour. The explanation of the bill which appears in the SOC is often brief and opaque. Typically, the reader will have to read the entirety of the Explanatory Memorandum or indeed the bill to understand it, and even then may not succeed. For example, the SOC accompanying the Social Security Legislation Amendment (Fair Incentives to Work) Bill 2012 (Cth) (hereinafter the 'Fair Incentives Bill') states:

> The Bill amends the Social Security Act 1991 to implement income support measures announced as a part of the 2012–13 Budget. The Bill will enact changes to the eligibility rules for 'grandfathered' Parenting Payment recipients that will effectively close those grandfathered conditions. The Bill will increase the Liquid Assets Waiting Period to double the maximum reserve threshold for liquid assets to $5,000 for singles without dependants or $10,000 for others. The Bill will broaden the definition of termination payment for the purposes of the Income Maintenance Period to also allow it to also include any payments connected with the termination of a person's employment.

This dense explanation provides very little insight into the proposed amendments. This was despite the Bill, inter alia, amending the Social Security Act 1991 (Cth) so that a welfare payment to single parents would cease when their child turned eight, rather than 16 as previously. Parents affected by the change have held public protests, claiming that the changes will force them poverty and are incompatible to the right to social security in Article 9 of the ICESCR.[69]

SOCs which state that a bill does not engage any rights tend to do so in just a few words. SOCs which identify that a bill does engage and limit rights tend to assert that those limitations are justified without engaging in any proportionality or other analysis. A common formula is to: (a) acknowledge that a right can be limited if this is necessary to serve certain purposes; and (b) assert that the limitation in question was a proportionate measure to serve such a purpose, without explaining why.

For example, the SOC accompanying the Classification (Publications, Films and Computer Games) Amendment (R 18+ Computer Games) Bill 2012 (Cth) identified that the Bill engaged the right to freedom of expression in Article 19 of the ICCPR.[70] It then stated:

> The right to freedom of expression ... may be restricted on several grounds including the classification of material where this is necessary on a limited number of grounds including

---

[68] Eg, the SOC accompanying the Migration (Visa Evidence) Charge (Consequential Amendments) Bill 2012 (Cth) states that as the impact of the Bill 'will be mostly, if not wholly, on persons outside Australia's jurisdiction, to whom Australia does not owe obligations under the ICCPR', it is compatible with human rights.

[69] 'Single Mums to Rally over Payment Cuts' The Australian (7 October 2012) www.theaustralian.com.au/news/breaking-news/single-mums-to-rally-over-payment-cuts/story-fn3dxiwe-1226489025709; National Council of Single Mothers and their Children, 'Child Poverty is No Way to Fund a Surplus' (Press Release, 5 October 2012).

[70] The SOC initially asserted that the Bill did not engage any human rights. A correction was later issued.

where this is necessary to protect public health and morals, or the rights of others, including protecting children and young people against the harm caused by age-inappropriate material.

Without further analysis or explanation, the SOC concluded that the Bill was compatible with human rights 'because it advances the protection of human rights and to the extent that it may also limit human rights, those limitations are reasonable and proportionate'.

Very occasionally, no justification for a limitation is provided at all. For example, the Family Assistance and Other Legislation Amendment Bill 2012 (Cth) made several changes to the social security entitlements of families. Broadly speaking, these amendments either raised the threshold of eligibility for these entitlements (for example, by requiring parents to immunise their children in order to receive the family tax benefit) or provided that the value of the entitlements would be paused at the current amount without further indexation. The SOC acknowledged that these amendments engaged Article 9 of the ICESCR and Article 26 of the Convention on the Rights of the Child. The SOC concluded that the Bill was compatible with those rights, stating only that:

> Australia has one of the most generous family payment systems in the world. The most recent analysis shows that spending on cash family benefits by Australia was 1.80 per cent of GDP in 2007, well above the OECD average of 1.22 per cent. These changes will make the family payment system sustainable for the long term.

There was no analysis of the impact that the measures would have on individuals (or children) or whether they were a proportionate response to a legitimate aim.

Some SOCs have gone into far more detail, though again without rigorous proportionality analysis of the kind proposed by the federal Attorney-General's Department. For example, the Aviation Transport Security Amendment (Screening) Bill 2012 (Cth) sought to enable the introduction of body scanners at Australian international airports in order to prevent aviation terrorism. The SOC clearly set out the reasons why the new measures were thought necessary and how they were intended to assist in preventing terrorism. The SOC also noted several ways in which the government had attempted to minimise the impact of the new measures on human rights.

There are also other positive indications. Some SOCs have demonstrated a willingness to look to international materials to determine the meaning and content of the protected rights, such as the manner in which the UN has interpreted certain rights and applied the proportionality test. Several SOCs also make reference to the guidance material which has been published by the Attorney-General.[71] This suggests that some parliamentarians are attempting to prepare detailed and considered SOCs. Many SOCs have noted that a bill engages rights in a positive way. For example, the Military Court of Tribunal Bill 2012 (Cth) proposes establishing a new military court satisfying the requirements of independence and security of tenure of a constitutional court. This was identified as enhancing the right to a fair

---

[71] See, eg, Commonwealth Government Securities Legislation Amendment (Retail Trading) Bill 2012 (Cth).

trial. Interestingly, SOCs which identify a positive impact on rights often tend to be clearer and longer than SOCs that identify a rights limitation.

The fact that SOCs have varied to such a great extent suggests that different departments have different levels of expertise and interest in compliance, and that the level of scrutiny that the system provides will be patchy. The PJCHR has recognised this, stating that 'not all statements of compatibility' have been up to standard, though it is 'early days' and 'the overall quality of statements appears to be improving'.[72] It is unclear whether this is true; some recent SOCs are quite good, but others are very poor. The PJCHR has indicated that more time is needed. Most of the SOCs tabled to date have accompanied legislation which was formulated before the introduction of the Parliamentary Scrutiny Act, meaning that the SOCs were something of an afterthought. Ideally, SOCs will come to be 'the culmination of a process that commences early in the development of policy'.[73] The PJCHR has also said that it will aim to improve the quality of SOCs 'by seeking to foster an effective dialogue with the Executive and Departments' and 'working with Ministers and Departments to effectively meet the requirements'.[74]

At the time of writing, SOCs had not had an impact on parliamentary debate. Many of the bills tabled had not yet been debated at length. Some had been both debated and passed without any meaningful reference to SOCs.

i. The PJCHR

At the time of writing, the PJCHR had tabled two general reports.[75] These provide a brief overview of each bill and the respective SOC, and provide the PJCHR's independent assessment of the compatibility of the bill with human rights. The PJCHR's assessment is usually longer and more detailed than the SOCs tabled in Parliament. The PJCHR does not just reproduce the SOC; it often provides additional analysis (for example, by making more use of the way in which the UN has interpreted the relevant right than is typically seen in SOCs).[76] The PJCHR frequently reported that it had 'sought clarification' of or more information about the rights-compatibility of bills, indicating that the SOC was inadequate.[77] The PJCHR did not report a final conclusion on these bills. Otherwise, the PJCHR agreed with the assessment of the rights-compatibility of each bill. Though the PJCHR's assessments were of a higher standard than that seen in most SOCs, they still tended to lack rigorous proportionality analysis.

The PJCHR had also begun two inquiries. First, the Australian Council of Social Service (ACOSS) requested the PJCHR to examine the Fair Incentives Bill.[78]

---

[72] Jenkins (n 45) 2.
[73] PJCHR, Examination of Legislation in Accordance with the Human Rights (Parliamentary Scrutiny) Act 2011: Bills Introduced 18–29 June 2012—First Report of 2012 (August 2012) 4.
[74] ibid.
[75] ibid; PJCHR, Examination of Legislation in Accordance with the Human Rights (Parliamentary Scrutiny) Act 2011: Bills Introduced 14–23 August 2012—Second Report of 2012 (September 2012).
[76] See, eg, PJCHR (n 73) 11, 14-15.
[77] See, eg, ibid, 2.
[78] ACOSS, Letter to the PJCHR, 15 June 2012 https://www.vinnies.org.au/icms_docs/182594_Request_for_inquiry_by_the_Parliamentary_Joint_Committee_on_Human_Rights_into_the_Social_Security_Legislation_Amendment_Fair_Incentives_to_Work_Bill_2012.pdf.

As discussed above, this Bill was controversial and was accompanied by a particularly brief and vague SOC asserting that it was compatible with human rights. The PJCHR invited representatives of ACOSS, the Department of Education, Employment and Workplace Relations (DEEWR) and other special interest groups to a hearing.[79] The PJCHR heard numerous concerns about the breadth and depth of the SOC, and described the SOC as 'very bland' and 'selective' in addressing human rights concerns.[80] The representatives of DEEWR who attended the hearing were not involved in the drafting of the legislation or the SOC and so were unable or 'unprepared' to answer most of the PJCHR's questions.[81] DEEWR later submitted a written response to the PJCHR. This summarised the changes that the Bill proposed to make more clearly. However, DEEWR declined to provide additional advice about the compatibility of the Bill with human rights. It asserted that the SOC 'contains a level of detail and adopts an approach that is consistent with guidance from the [Commonwealth Attorney General]'. It noted that SOCs are 'intended to be 'succinct assessments', 'should describe in general terms' and need not 'list every human rights point which could be raised'.[82]

The PJCHR filed an interim report on the Fair Incentives Bill in September 2012.[83] It again stated that the SOC was inadequate. The Committee acknowledged that some further information had since been provided, but stated that 'the provision of a more comprehensive statement at the introduction of the Bill would have greatly assisted the committee in its scrutiny of [the Bill] and would have improved the parliament's understanding of the precise impacts of these changes in a more timely way'.[84]

More substantively, the PJCHR expressed considerable doubt about the rights compatibility of the Bill. It accepted that the proposed changes had legitimate objectives; namely, encouraging parents to re-enter the workforce and enhancing the equity and consistency of welfare entitlements. However, it stated that 'it does not necessarily follow that the measures ... are justified'. Rather, it had to be shown that the changes were a proportionate response to those objectives. The Committee noted that 'it is not apparent ... that the government has considered any alternative' ways of achieving its stated aims. These criticisms were squarely aimed at the lack of proportionality analysis in the SOC. The Committee indicated that the emerging formula—this Bill is intended to serve a legitimate purpose and therefore is compatible with human rights—is inadequate.[85]

---

[79] The transcript of this hearing is available at: http://parlinfo.aph.gov.au/parlInfo/search/display/display.w3p;query%3DId%3A%22committees%2Fcommjnt%2F9ae0f94c-616c-4170-a780-a0ce7c56f700%2F0000%22.

[80] PJCHR, Parliament of Australia, Canberra, 21 June 2012, 11 (Ursula Stephens).

[81] PJCHR, Parliament of Australia, Canberra, 21 June 2012, 11 (Deputy Secretary DEEWR, Jennifer Taylor)

[82] DEEWR, Submission to PJCHR, Submission by DEEWR on the Social Security Legislation Amendment (Fair Incentives to Work) Bill 2012 to the PJCHR, 25 June 2012, 7.

[83] PJCHR, Interim Report—Social Security Legislation Amendment (Fair Incentives to Work) Bill 2012 (September 2012).

[84] ibid, 2.

[85] ibid.

The Committee concluded that the government had not shown that the Bill was compatible with Article 9 of the ICESCR and more evidence was needed about the position in which single parents would be left following the changes.[86] Ultimately, the PJCHR recommended that the government defer the changes until the Senate Education, Employment and Workplace Relations Reference Committee completed a specific inquiry on the adequacy of the alternative welfare payments.[87] This Committee has yet to file a report.

The New South Wales subsidiary of ACOSS described this is as 'an historic finding in Australia', as it was the PJCHR's 'first ever recommendation' and 'recognises the human right to social security and an adequate standard of living', which has never been formerly protected by any other means.[88] However, this 'historic finding' was ignored, with the government refusing to accede to the PJCHR's recommendation to defer the passage of the Bill.[89]

The PJCHR was also asked by the National Congress of Australia's First People to examine the bills introduced in 2011 to continue the Northern Territory Intervention.[90] These were introduced into Parliament before the Parliamentary Scrutiny Act came into force, but the PJCHR is empowered to examine existing Acts. The PJCHR invited the Minister for Families, Community Services and Indigenous Affairs to provide advice on the rights compatibility of the relevant bills. In a 23-page response, the Minister explained the bills in some detail and their impact on human rights. In particular, she explained her reasons for concluding that the bills did not discriminate against Indigenous Australians.[91]

More time is needed to draw definitive conclusions about the operation of the PJCHR. However, these two examples suggest that parliamentarians' responses to the PJCHR will vary. The Minister for Families, Community Services and Indigenous Affairs provided lengthy and detailed responses to the PJCHR in relation to the Stronger Futures Legislation, but the Minister for the DEEWR's response in relation to the Fair Incentives Bill was brief and displayed a reluctance to provide more information than already given in the SOC—even though the PJCHR advised that the SOC was inadequate. The government was also willing to ignore the recommendations made by the PJCHR in respect of the Fair Incentives Bill.

The Committee's reports have also been equivocal. The PJCHR's first and second reports demonstrate that the PJCHR will independently assess each bill and will require further information if the initial SOC is inadequate. However, the reports

---

[86] ibid, 2–3.

[87] ibid, 3. The Senate Education, Employment and Workplace Relations Legislation Committee made the same recommendation: Social Security Legislation Amendment (Fair Incentives to Work) Bill 2012 [Provisions] (August 2012).

[88] Council of Social Service of New South Wales, 'Stop Cuts to Sole Parent Payments', www.ncoss.org .au/index.php?option=com_content&task=view&id=7450&Itemid=100.

[89] Press Conference with Hon Peter Garrett MP, Minister for School Education, 21 September 2012.

[90] Stronger Futures in the Northern Territory Act 2011 (Cth) and two related bills.

[91] J Macklin, Minister for Families, Community Services and Indigenous Affairs, Letter to the Chair of the PJCHR, 27 June 2012, http://www.aph.gov.au/Parliamentary_Business/Committees/ Joint/Human_Rights/Committee_Inquiries/strongerfutures/background/~/media/Committees/Senate/ committee/humanrights_ctte/activity/stronger_futures/correspondence/mfcsia_chair_280612.ashx.

are generally expressed in cautious terms. They were also published long after the bills in question were introduced into Parliament. The PJCHR has therefore emphasised the importance of getting SOCs right in the first place.[92]

In the hearing and report into the Fair Incentives Bill, the PJCHR demonstrated a willingness to criticise SOCs, but did not push the matter. The PJCHR expressed significant concerns about the compatibility of the Bill with Article 9 of the ICESCR, but ultimately made a rather modest recommendation, advising only that the Bill should be deferred until another committee completed its inquiry. The fact even this modest recommendation was rejected outright suggests that the PJCHR currently lacks any political bite.

Further, the PJCHR has recognised that it is not immune to the pressures that diminish Parliament's ability to effectively scrutinise legislation for compatibility with human rights. The PJCHR has said that, like Parliament, it 'cannot possibly consider every bill and every instrument in detail'.[93] Therefore, the PJCHR 'is developing a triage process to assist it in this regard'. It has expressed hope 'that in due course, the Parliament will take account of the work of the committee by factoring time for the committee's deliberations into the legislative program'.[94]

III. WILL AN EXCLUSIVE PARLIAMENTARY RIGHTS MODEL WORK?

The Parliamentary Scrutiny Act has several strengths. First, it defines human rights for the purposes of making legislation in the federal Parliament. This may lend greater clarity to parliamentary debate. This, along with the requirement to table SOCs and the work of the PJCHR, may increase the profile and legitimacy of human rights, and create political pressure to legislate compatibly with human rights. However, the way in which the Act defines rights is problematic and likely to thwart some of this potential.

Even if these problems are remedied, there remains a significant question about the basic design of the regime. The Parliamentary Scrutiny Act is an 'exclusive parliamentary rights' model that places sole responsibility for the recognition and protection of human rights on Parliament and creates no scope for judicial supervision. Will such a model work?

A. A Self-regulating System

There is one obvious reason an exclusive parliamentary rights model might fail. The model is entirely self-regulating. Parliamentarians can ignore the requirements in the Parliamentary Scrutiny Act altogether (for example, by not tabling an SOC) or give

---

[92] H Jenkins, 'The PJCHR's Role in Enhancing Respect for Human Rights' (Address to the 2012 Australian Government and Non-government Organisations Forum on Human Rights, Canberra, 14 August 2012) 3.
[93] Jenkins (n 45) 2.
[94] ibid.

them mere lip service (for example, by tabling a brief and vague SOC or asserting that a bill does not engage rights when it clearly does). The PJCHR may grow into a respected parliamentary institution, but Parliament can still ignore or reject the Committee's recommendations, as it often does with regard to the recommendations of other committees.

There is also no legal impediment to passing a law which is incompatible with human rights. A finding of incompatibility in an SOC or report by the PJCHR does not prevent a bill being passed, nor can it be used to challenge the legality of the law once enacted. Ideally, the requirement to table an SOC and the reports of the PJCHR will increase political pressure to comply compatibly with rights. However, this too is entirely self-regulated. There is thus no legal cost for failing to comply with the Parliamentary Scrutiny Act, merely the potential of a political one. This means the Parliamentary Scrutiny Act will only work if it fosters a genuine, increased respect for rights in Parliament that makes non-compliance politically damaging.

The problematic aspects of the Parliamentary Scrutiny Act's design make it unlikely that this will occur. Rather than setting down an achievable task, the use of over 100 often aspirational human rights standards makes it very difficult for parliamentarians to effectively scrutinise legislation for compatibility with human rights. Further, the international human rights enshrined in the Parliamentary Scrutiny Act may be unrepresentative of the views of the broader community, and so able to be limited without incurring political damage. And if there is no legal or political cost for non-compliance, why would Parliament comply? The fact that parliamentarians are politically accountable (and in Australia at the federal level must face re-election around every three years) is not likely to foster compliance.

It is too early to reach a definitive conclusion on the basis of the SOCs produced so far, but some early observations can be made. First, the vast majority of new bills are accompanied by an SOC, and so the requirement is being complied with in form. Second, these SOCs are typically terse and do not engage in rigorous proportionality or other analysis. This suggests that SOCs are perceived as a mere procedural hurdle; something they will try to get out of the way as quickly and painlessly as possible, just like NIAs in the treaty context. Third, the example of the Fair Incentives Bill suggests that it is not unreasonable to fear the SOC procedure and the PJCHR will not be taken seriously.

B. No Judicial Scrutiny of Assessments of Compatibility

Parliament has many strengths as a deliberative chamber.[95] As the elected arm of government, it has an inherent degree of democratic legitimacy which the other arms lack. It can act proactively and develop generally applicable policies and laws, rather than responding to problems on an ad hoc basis. In this way, Parliament may have the potential to foster genuine and lasting protections for human rights.

---

[95] See generally J Waldron, *Law and Disagreement* (New York, Oxford University Press, 1999).

However, Parliament also has weaknesses. Parliamentarians may lack the rationality and analytical capacity that judges, especially judges of appeal, can bring to questions of law and human rights. Judges also have the advantage of looking at problems sometime after the fact rather than in the heat of the moment. They can therefore analyse the concrete impact of a law at a very specific level. Judges are also more insulated from the political pressures facing elected parliamentarians.

This does not mean that a court should replace Parliament in determining questions of human rights. A system dominated by the courts may prove self-defeating if people feel that the power to make important decisions about their lives has been taken out of their (and their representatives') hands.[96] However, it does mean that courts have something to offer that Parliaments do not. Even if Parliament were to perform as hoped, the regime would still benefit from judicial involvement.[97] As Lynch argues, judicial controls and political controls are not diametrically opposed, but can coexist and complement each other: 'The very existence of legal controls, regardless of whether they are ever resorted to ... necessarily informs and shapes the contours of ... political debate.'[98]

Parliamentarians are pragmatic. They may prioritise issues that are pressing or will lead to practical consequences. Most importantly, governments do not want to see legislation that they support challenged in the courts or struck down. This was clearly evident in debate about the anti-terrorism legislation enacted in Australia in 2003, where claims that the process for issuing a warrant would breach the separation of powers (and would therefore be unconstitutional) prompted some of the most rigorous debate about the structure of the regime.[99] The possibility of external scrutiny—and criticism—encourages logical, rigorous and defensible decision-making. In this system, the prospect of the courts reviewing the compatibility of a bill with human rights is likely to encourage Parliament to prepare SOCs of a far higher standard—and, eventually, to legislate in a way that is compatible with human rights in the first place.

C. An Exclusive Parliamentary Rights Model is Unlikely to Ameliorate the Federal Parliament's Weaknesses

While Australia's Parliament is generally effective at protecting human rights, it has systemic weaknesses which become particularly prominent in certain circumstances. For example, Parliament may be willing or able to enact legislation with

---

[96] See also Murray Hunt, Hayley Hooper and Paul Yowell, *Parliaments and Human Rights: Redressing the Democratic Deficit* (London, Arts & Humanities Research Council, 2012) 9-11.

[97] See also ibid, 11, 16.

[98] A Lynch, 'Exceptionalism, Politics and Liberty: A Response to Professor Tushnet from the Antipodes' (2008) 3 *International Journal of Law in Context* 305, 307. See also 308–09. See generally Andrew Lynch, 'The Impact of Post-enactment Review on Anti-terrorism Laws: Four Jurisdictions Compared' (2012) 18(1) *Journal of Legislative Studies* 63, especially at 76.

[99] For the impact of the European Convention on Human Rights and the Human Rights Act 1998 (UK), see Lynch, 'Exceptionalism' (n 97) 308; D Bonner, 'Responding to Crisis: Legislating against Terrorism' (2006) 122 *Law Quarterly Review* 602, 627–29.

negative human rights implications in actual or perceived emergencies. When the community is in fear—for example, of a terrorist attack—governments face intense political pressure to act (to do something!) to respond to the threat. The responses favoured may be drastic and novel. In such circumstances, Parliament can muster sufficient impetus to override non-entrenched rights protections (such as the Racial Discrimination Act) and restrict fundamental human rights (such as the right to liberty).

In theory, the Parliamentary Scrutiny Act will temper these dynamics. The requirement to table an SOC will create a procedural hurdle which slows the process and forces Parliament to analyse the potential impact of the proposed law. In practice, the regime may be equally vulnerable to the same dynamics. The requirement to table an SOC may be ignored altogether, legislation may be vaguely asserted to be compatible with human rights because it is necessary to meet an urgent threat, or an obvious incompatibility with rights may be excused because of the political imperative to act. An entirely self-regulating model may be incapable of ameliorating the systemic weaknesses which led the Brennan Committee to conclude that greater human rights protections were needed in the first place.

The same could be said of circumstances in which the government holds a majority in both Houses of the federal Parliament, or when the rights in question are those of an unpopular minority. In such circumstances, the ability of Parliament to resist or force amendments to government-sponsored legislation is limited. There is no reason to believe that the Parliamentary Scrutiny Act will alter those dynamics.

A model which incorporates some form of independent, judicial supervision would be more effective in these circumstances. Though we must be careful not to overstate the capacity of the courts to resist the dynamics of emergency, courts are by their very nature less concerned with party politics or what would gain favour with the majority of voters. Even if it is not appropriate to give the courts ultimate power to determine contentious rights, there are sound reasons to give them a role in the rights protection process.

CONCLUSION

Australia's human rights record is generally good. However, as the Brennan Committee found, there is still significant room for improvement. The Parliamentary Scrutiny Act seeks to enhance Parliament's protection of human rights in a way that is democratically legitimate, leaving the ultimate power to make contentious rights decisions to the elected arm of government. The very existence of this Act may raise the profile and legitimacy of human rights in parliamentary and public debate, and increase political pressure to legislate in a manner which is compatible with those rights.

However, the system is entirely self-regulating. It will only be effective if Parliament respects the (essentially voluntary) requirements imposed by the Act and complies with them in substance rather than mere form. Unfortunately, there is good reason to suspect that the regime will have a minimal impact on legislative process. This is due in part to the design of the Parliamentary Scrutiny Act—particularly the unusual and derivative way in which rights are defined, and the fact that bills may be debated and passed without the tabling of an SOC or report of the PJCHR. Most importantly, this 'exclusive parliamentary rights model' does not provide any independent, external check to encourage compliance. This removes one of the most important incentives for Parliament to comply with the regime, as well as the complementary benefits that flow from judicial involvement.

While it is too soon to draw final conclusions, the operation of the Parliamentary Scrutiny Act in the months since its enactment suggests that the new regime will be complied with in form, but that SOCs will lack rigorous proportionality analysis, SOCs will do little to influence parliamentary debate and the PJCHR will lack political clout. This suggests that the Parliamentary Scrutiny Act may do little to improve the protection of human rights in Australia.

13

Legislative Review for Human Rights Compatibility: A View from Sweden

THOMAS BULL AND IAIN CAMERON

T HE SWEDISH SYSTEM for protection of constitutional rights is likely to be of considerable interest to British public lawyers. In the UK, the guiding constitutional principle has been that of parliamentary sovereignty. Following the incorporation of the European Convention on Human Rights (ECHR), there has been considerable recent debate about the 'democratic deficit' of a system which gives, or is seen as giving, considerable powers to judges to control legislation. There has also been discussion as to whether the UK should have its own, national catalogue of human rights. Sweden incorporated the ECHR in 1995, a few years before the UK did. However, Sweden also has separate catalogues of constitutional rights going beyond the rights set out in the ECHR. These are to be found, first, in chapter 2 of *Regeringsformen*,[1] the Instrument of Government (IG), second, in the Freedom of the Press Act (*Tryckfrihetsförordningen* (TF))[2] and, third, in the Freedom of Expression Act (*Yttrandefrihetsgrundlag* (YGL)).[3] The general rights catalogue is in the IG; the Freedom of the Press and the Freedom of Expression Acts are lex specialis and deal, respectively, with the printed and electronic media.[4] Like the UK, Sweden has traditionally had a strong attachment to parliamentary democracy: the party which dominated government in Sweden for most of the period between 1932 and 2006—the Social Democratic Party—stressed the 'self-vaccinating' function of periodic elections as regards risks of abuse of power and downplayed the role of judicial protection. The main mechanism for protecting constitutional rights has been not the judiciary, but the legislative process. However, as we shall show, the legislative pre-control and judicial post hoc

---

[1] SFS 1974:152. References to the Swedish statute book (Svensk *författningssamling* (SFS)) are given by year, followed by the relevant number. References to a constitutional provision are by chapter and article number.

[2] SFS 1949:105.

[3] SFS 1991:1469.

[4] They regulate the fields in detail (the TF has 122 sections, divided into 14 chapters; the YGL has 65 sections, divided into 11 chapters) providing inter alia for a special system of criminal responsibility for offences committed by means of the printed or electronic medias (defamation, breaches of the Secrecy Act etc) and for the right to jury trial for those accused of committing such offences. They prohibit censorship and lay down the right to receive official information and (for civil servants) to communicate information, even secret information, to the press for publication, subject to certain narrowly defined exceptions.

control cannot be easily separated from one another; they form part of a complicated, integrated whole. Moreover, while the main part of the system is undoubtedly
the legislative process, this is not the same thing as calling it 'parliamentary': the role
of Parliament in the process of protecting human rights is, in reality, not as large as
might first appear.

I. A BRIEF NOTE ON SWEDISH LEGAL AND POLITICAL CULTURE

Any system of protection of human rights is to large degree dependent upon the
culture of a given society.[5] Of specific interest is, of course, the legal culture within
which the rights are to operate and the political culture that determines what rights
are to be respected and to what extent. A brief overview of the Swedish political
and legal culture is thus necessary in order to set the scene for the Swedish system
of legislative review of constitutional rights works in practice. In addition, saying
something about this reduces the ever-present dangers of comparative enterprises—
finding parallels where there are none and not seeing similarities because they are
hidden. Beginning with the legal system of Sweden, it is to a large extent a civil law
system, based mainly on statutory law. The legislative tradition is one of relatively
abstract formulation of legal norms combined with detailed discussions in the
travaux préparatoires of how these norms could be applied. These include comments on the general purposes of the law, more specific comment on every section,
including the reasons why it has been formulated the way it has, and recommendations on how to interpret in concrete cases that may arise. The legislative history
and comments on the draft proposal together with the changes that the government
may have made are also included before presenting the bill before Parliament. The
Swedish courts (unlike the tradition in the UK courts) show great loyalty vis-a-vis
the will of the legislator as it is expressed in the *travaux préparatoires*. Even if
European law has brought changes to the material content as well as the legal status
of this kind of material (see further below), the *travaux préparatoires* remain the
most important interpretative tool within the Swedish legal system.

As for the political system and culture, two factors should be mentioned here. The
first is that the electoral system of Sweden is highly proportional, and the threshold
of representation is set at four per cent. The combined effect of this is that it is possible for a relatively large number of parties to achieve representation in Parliament
(at present eight parties). With such a system, it is difficult for one party to obtain
a majority of seats, and for most of the last 50 years of Swedish political history,
the government has not had a clear majority in Parliament, but rather has been
dependent upon cutting deals with one or more small parties for support. This situation is now so established that it seems to be the natural order of Swedish politics.

---

[5] Jurgen Habermas talks about three building blocks of any democratic society: a legal sphere of individual and equal rights, an organisational aspect in which administrative power make collective actions
possible and a sense of social solidarity that is necessary for the political formation of public opinion.
J Habermas, *The Crises of the European Union–A Response*, trans C Cronin (Cambridge, Polity Press,
2012) 19 ff. These factors can be roughly translated into issues of rights, institutions and culture.

There is a debate among political scientists as to whether the Swedish political system can be described, following Liphart's taxonomy,[6] as 'majoritarian' with consensus elements, or as 'consensus' with majoritarian elements,[7] but it is clear that a consequence of the party system has been that negotiations and political solutions that cross party lines are common in political life in Sweden. This fits well with a political culture that is also very consensus-oriented in other aspects, such as labour market relations and economic policy. The building of consensus rather than conflict is a trademark of much of Swedish politics and is something that is at times a strength and at other times a weakness.[8]

The second point is that Sweden does not have ministerial government. Government decisions are collective (IG 7:3). The Swedish system separates the administration from the government. Only a relatively small number of people (around 1,800) are employed in government departments. The bulk of the central public administration is performed by administrative agencies. There is relatively strong local government in Sweden, and most public services are at the local level, albeit largely funded (and supervised) by central government. Central administrative agencies have a duty to obey government directives. They can be steered by government in a number of different ways; however, they have the constitutionally protected freedom to interpret and apply the law in individual cases (IG 12:2). This means inter alia that there is not the same need for the courts to intervene to prevent the government from steering the administrative system (and the distribution of benefits) for party political reasons.

II. THE LEGISLATIVE PROCESS AS A MEANS OF PROTECTING HUMAN RIGHTS

A. Introduction

The system of commissions of inquiry is the foundation of the Swedish legislative process. It is a longstanding tradition to have any issue of upcoming legislation examined by such a commission. The constitutional basis for this is the requirement in IG 7:2 that all governmental business should be well prepared before the government takes any decision.

To give a brief summary, the Swedish system has these basic features: commissions are composed of either MPs from all parties represented in Parliament or an expert on legislative matters (typically a serving or former Supreme Court judge with experience from the law department of the government or a professor

---

[6] A Lijphart, *Patterns of Democracy*, (New Haven, Yale University Press, 1999).

[7] M Isberg, 'Is Sweden Going Majoritarian?' in T Persson and M Wiberg (eds), *Parliamentary Government in the Nordic Countries at a Crossroads: Coping with Challenges from Europeanisation and Presidentialisation* (Stockholm, Santerius, 2011).

[8] The system has produced stable governments until very recently: the September 2014 general election resulted in a centre/right and a social democratic/green/left block of more or less equal size, with a populist far-right wing party holding the balance of power. When the minority social democratic/green government failed to get its budget approved by parliament, it threatened to hold an extra general election. The threat led to a six-party 'gentleman's agreement', valid until 2022, making it (even) easier for a minority government to rule the country.

of law/political science). As a rule, the commission also consists of experts from governmental agencies working in the field to be regulated and other experts (most often professors). The need to bring in 'outside' expertise is because government departments are rather small, a byproduct of the separation between government and administration. The commission will be given a directive (which can be broad or narrow) and a time limit in which to make its report containing any proposals deemed necessary for new legislation. A general directive to all commissions is to report on the constitutional (and financial) implications of their proposal. Every year about 100 such reports are published in the series *Statens offentliga utredningar* (SOU), some of which attract a lot of media coverage. An alternative to the commission is a departmental inquiry, which is normally used for more technical issues of law reform. This can be a one-person inquiry or a group. If it is a group, it usually consists of only civil servants from the departments and relevant administrative agencies, but external experts can also be appointed. Departmental inquiries are also published in *Departementserien* (Ds).[9]

The report is then—once again in accordance with IG 7:2—sent for comments (*remiss*) to a wide range of institutions and organisations. This includes governmental agencies, courts, and universities, but will also include unions and non-governmental organisations (NGOs). These bodies will be given the chance (usually within a three month period) to make written comments on the proposal. These comments can be of any kind, but often end up approving the proposal (in whole or in part) or in recommending the government not to base any bills on the commission's proposal. As there is a constitutional right to petition the government at any time, anyone, and also any organisation, can comment on a commission report, but of course the government tends to pay more attention to comments from some institutions or organisations than others. These comments are also public, and the media can pick up on them, particularly critical comments. In this respect, mention should also be made of the wide-ranging right of access to official documents under the Freedom of Press Act; only limited exceptions are permitted under the Openness and Secrecy Act 2009. Relatively little latitude is given to public officials to refuse access, and their judgment is subject to appeal to an administrative court of appeal.[10]

Strong and unified criticism from influential institutions and organisations can lead to changes being made in the bill or even, though more rarely, a proposal being quietly dropped. If the proposal is not dropped, the relevant ministry prepares a

---

[9] The published reports for the last seven years are: 2006: 24 Ds, 124 SOU, 2007: 53 Ds, 114 SOU, 2008: 53 Ds, 138 SOU, 2009: 69 Ds, 101 SOU, 2010: 46 Ds, 107 SOU, 2011: 49 Ds, 90 SOU, 2012: 56 Ds, 95 SOU, 2013: 78 Ds, 97 SOU. Not all of these inquiries were to investigate the need for new legislation.

[10] This decision can in turn be appealed in the Supreme Administrative Court and these appeals are free of charge. See, eg, RÅ (*Regeringsrättens Årsbok, Yearbook of the Supreme Administrative Court*) 1998 ref 47, where a governmental agency denied access to a document (the so-called 'Scientology Bible') on the basis that continued access was causing tension with the US, which considered it to be covered by intellectual property law. It is possible to declare a document secret if its disclosure would seriously affect Swedish international relations. However, the court found that this provision could not be interpreted as to justify secrecy merely because irritation was being caused in international relations. The court accordingly struck down the agency's decision on secrecy.

draft bill which is sent to the Law Council (*lagrådet*).[11] The Law Council normally consists of six people, of whom four should be acting judges of the Supreme Courts.[12] The remaining two can be retired judges from the same courts. The courts, not the government, choose who to send to the Law Council, and this is usually done so that each judge will take his or her 'turn' in serving two years on the Council. The Law Council normally works in two sections with three members in each. The government is never bound by the opinion of the Law Council. Moreover, although the Law Council should be heard; if for some reason it has not been heard,[13] then this in itself is no reason for not enacting the law. The Law Council is thus only an advisory body, and its opinions have no formal legal effect.

In accordance with IG 8:19, the Law Council's scrutiny of draft bills is focused on five specific issues: the effect on the Constitution, the coherence of the proposal with the existing system of legal regulation, the likely impact on the principle of legal certainty, whether the law is constructed in a way that will make it possible to achieve its underlying objectives and, finally, to detect issues that may become problematic in practice.

The Law Council can thus be said to fulfil two very different tasks. The first is quite technical, concerning the logic of law and its effects; ensuring that terms and concepts are consistent with existing law, proposing new wording of individual provisions if they are imprecise or unintelligible, etc. Here one might say that the Law Council works as a highly qualified proofreader. The second task is quite different; the Law Council should check any upcoming legislation against constitutional law and the principle of legal certainty. This involves the constitutional rules on the delegation of legislative powers to the government and local authorities, the protection of constitutional rights and the general principle that legislation should be introduced in a foreseeable way.[14] This kind of scrutiny—especially when the principle of proportionality is taken into account—comes much closer to the sensitive boundary between law and politics. Here we can talk about the Law Council as a form of judicial preview.

As is clear from the above discussion, the Law Council gives a form of expert legal advice that all governments receive one way or another from institutions within the government. In that way, there is nothing special about the Law Council. Where it differs from most other institutions that provide legal advice is that its advice carries special weight both as being independent and as coming from the highest judges in the country. Furthermore, this advice is given in full view of the public and is open to all to peruse and discuss, facilitating informed public debate on complicated

---

[11] For more detail, see T Bull, 'Judges without a Court: Judicial Preview in Sweden' in T Campbell, KD Ewing, and A Tomkins (eds), *The Legal Protection of Human Rights: Sceptical Essays* (Oxford, Oxford University Press, 2011).

[12] The Supreme Courts, of course, do not let members who have commented upon draft legislation as members of the Law Council later on take part in a judgment on the constitutionality of that same law.

[13] IG 8:19 provides that there is no need to send a draft bill to the Law Council if the change in the law in question is of minor importance (ie, it is a minor technical issue) or if submitting the draft bill would delay the legislation such that major negative consequences would follow. The latter exception is occasionally invoked regarding taxation legislation.

[14] See C Sampford et al, *Retrospectivity and the Rule of Law* (Oxford, Oxford University Press, 2006) for a general discussion of such issues with a focus on common law jurisdictions.

legal/constitutional issues.[15] This means that the expert legal opinion from the Law Council has a much wider impact and function than similar legal advice that takes place solely within the government.

Lastly, it should be mentioned that in its bill to Parliament, the government will comment on the opinion of the Law Council. This will sometimes be done in order to draw attention to the fact that the Law Council has nothing to say, which is quite usual. On the other hand, in cases of criticism, the government will want either to let it be known that it has changed the proposal since the Law Council made its comments or it will argue for its own position in a bit more detail.

In conclusion on the Law Council, the government in general—and particularly the public officials that in practice draft the laws—takes the Law Council's arguments seriously and the system contributes to higher quality in the legislation than would otherwise be the case.[16]

The bill is then drafted and submitted to Parliament. All bills are sent to the permanent select committee which deals with the relevant subject matter, tracking government departments. The composition of the committees is in general in proportion to the seats that the party has won in the election. A member of the opposition chairs the committee. The fact that an MP sits as an ordinary or substitute member in a given committee for the whole mandate period (four years) allows a degree of specialisation in the areas in question. Having said this, who gets to sit in which committee is decided by the party leadership.[17] In the event that a bill raises constitutional issues (institutional or individual rights), it will be reviewed by the Constitutional Committee of Parliament and the Committee will produce a written statement to Parliament on those issues. Committees can ask for each other's opinion on a bill which has implications for several policy areas. In the written report to the plenary, comments from the earlier stages of the procedure can reappear, as politicians in Parliament will look for anything that will support its argument about a given proposal. Typically, however, Parliament will adopt the bill with little debate.

---

[15] We consider this to be one of the more important features of the system, as it removes the government's 'monopoly' on expert legal opinion and makes it impossible for the government to push through legislation without publicly acknowledging constitutional or other problems that might otherwise go unnoticed.

[16] This is the conclusion of B Bengtsson, 'Departementen och Lagrådet' ('The Government Department and the Law Council') SvJT 2009 216–52; and R Lavin, *Lagrådet och den offentliga rätten 1999–2001* ('*The Law Council and Public Law 1999-2001*') (Lund, Juristförlaget, 2001), particularly at 160. Both the authors were professors who became judges and who served on the Law Council.

[17] We should be careful not to be too positive about the competence and actual influence of parliamentary committees. The Swedish Parliament is large in international terms, with 349 MPs for a population of nine million. As there are so many MPs, not all of them can be given an ordinary, or substitute, position in a select committee, which is where the main work of the Riksdag takes place. The ability to reward and punish MPs with places on committees and other (lack of) privileges obviously strengthens the influence of the party offices and one former MP has alleged that ordinary MPs (at least in the Moderate Party) have very little power. See A M Pålsson, *Knapptryckarkompaniet: rapport från Sveriges riksdag* (Stockholm, Atlantis, 2011). We will not go into this issue further in the present work. For a valuable discussion in English of the context of control over EU policy-making, see S Ahlbäck Öbergand and AC Jungar, 'The Influence of the Swedish and Finnish Parliaments over Domestic EU Policies' (2009) 32 *Scandinavian Political Studies* 358.

B. The Special Legislative Procedure for Legislation Limiting Rights

The catalogue of Swedish constitutional rights, as well as the mechanisms for their protection, has come into being in stages, as a result of political compromises, the most recent changes having occurred in 2010.[18] Rights can be divided into three categories; unconditional, 'strong' and 'weak' relative rights. Unconditional rights are the following: freedom of religion, the 'negative' freedom of opinion, thought and conscience, the prohibitions of registration on political grounds, capital punishment, corporal punishment or torture, expulsion of citizens or deprivation of citizenship, retroactive criminal or tax law, retroactive establishment of courts and the right of access to a court to challenge detention[19] as well as the rights set out in the Freedom of the Press and Freedom of Expression Acts. Unconditional rights can be restricted only by constitutional amendment (IG 8:14). However, constitutional amendment is a relatively simple process in Sweden. In general, all that is required is two votes by simple majority in two different parliamentary sessions. There must be an intervening general election and a period of nine months must pass between the first vote and the election. In exceptional, unforeseen cases where constitutional reform is regarded as pressing, the Committee on the Constitution, acting on a 5:1 majority, can waive the nine months requirement, although it is still necessary for there to be an intervening general election.

In 1979, changes were introduced, creating new mechanisms of substantive and procedural protection for a category of 'strong' relative rights. This was a political compromise between the centre/right parties and the Social Democrats. The former wanted both substantive conditions and procedural entrenchment (qualified majority voting) and were broadly in favour of a power of constitutional review for the courts. The latter were strongly against procedural entrenchment and constitutional review.

The strong relative rights are the 'positive' freedoms of opinion—expression, information, assembly, demonstration, association, the prohibition of arbitrary searches and seizures or secret surveillance and other monitoring of personal integrity, the freedom from deprivation of liberty or restrictions in freedom of movement, and the requirement that court proceedings are to be held in public.[20] Strong relative rights can be restricted by statute, but only after satisfying certain substantive conditions. These basically provide that a restriction may only be imposed for a purpose which is acceptable in a democratic society, it may never exceed the bounds of what is necessary with regard to its purpose (proportionality), it may never go so far as to constitute a threat to freedom of opinion, which is a cornerstone of democracy, and it may never be made only on the basis of a political, religious, cultural or similar belief. Additional specific conditions have to be satisfied where the legislator wishes

---

[18] For more details, see I Cameron, 'Protection of Constitutional Rights in Sweden' [1997] *Public Law* 488.

[19] Respectively, IG 2:1 p 6, 2:2, 2:3, para 1, 2:4, 2:5, 2:7, 2:10, 2:11, para 1 and 2:9.

[20] Respectively, IG 2:1, pp 1–5, 2:4, 2:5, 2:6, 2:8, 2:11, para 2. The freedom from deprivations of liberty means that criminal laws providing for custodial sentences must be in statute form (although the government can be authorised to 'fill out' a criminal offence by means of an ordinance in certain circumstances; see IG 8:3) and must satisfy the substantive conditions (proportionality etc).

to restrict the freedoms of expression, information, assembly, demonstration and association.[21] The remaining rights in chapter 2 are 'weak' relative rights which can be limited by a simple statute or, in some cases, even in other ways (usually by government ordinance). In both cases, either less demanding substantive conditions or no substantive conditions apply.

The procedural protection mechanism which was introduced is complicated. The idea of qualified majority voting—which would give a veto to the centre/right parties—was naturally not acceptable to the Social Democrats. The most which they could accept was some form of delay mechanism. Moreover, the Social Democrats did not want any procedural safeguard adopted to apply generally to all rights. Nor did they want it to apply automatically, or unconditionally, as they considered that this would unduly restrict strong government. The issue of which body was to decide on the application of the delay procedure was also the source of disagreement. The centre/right parties wanted it to be the Law Council, whereas the Social Democrats wanted this power to remain with Parliament.

The basic idea behind the procedure, as with the idea of constitutional amendment, is that during the year in which a legislative proposal can be delayed, opposition both within and outside Parliament can be mobilised. The procedure only applies to strong relative rights, and even here certain exceptions are made.[22] Nor does it apply automatically, but only when a group of at least 10 MPs propose it. Should it not be proposed, a bill which restricts strong relative rights can be passed by a simple majority. Even if it is proposed, it does not apply unconditionally: such a proposal can be overruled by a 5:1 majority of the MPs in Parliament. Where there is a simple majority to pass a bill but not a 5:1 majority, the final decision as to whether or not to apply the procedure is a political decision made by the Committee on the Constitution, voting by a simple majority. As the majority in the Committee is formed by the governing party or parties, then, at the end of the day, it is possible for the government to have its way. Nonetheless, the Committee's discretion not to apply the special legislative procedure is restricted, first, by the *travaux préparatoires* to the IG, which specify clearly a number of cases that should be regarded as suitable for the application of the procedure, and, second, by the need to consult the Law Council.

Since it has been introduced, the qualified legislative procedure has only been invoked a few times. This is not to say that it is meaningless: the threat of its invocation encourages political compromises.

[21] IG 2:23 and 2:24.

[22] These are listed in IG 2:22, para 2, namely bills with a duration of a maximum of two years, bills containing a clause providing for a confidentiality requirement on a new category of civil servant, and bills containing a clause providing for a new possibility of engaging in searches and seizures or for a deprivation of liberty for a criminal offence. These exceptions only apply where the provision restricting a constitutional right is in the nature of an appendix to the main body of the bill, and only where the bill in question does not otherwise concern protected constitutional rights, eg, a provision providing for a power of search and seizure as part of a tax bill. These exceptions were made for purely pragmatic reasons. A survey of legislation revealed that these were the most common bills entailing, indirectly, restrictions on constitutional rights. It should be pointed out that, as the procedure applies to all proposed restrictions on freedom of expression and information, it includes proposed amendments to the TF and the YGL. Thus, such constitutional amendments can be subjected to a further period of delay.

C. Some Examples

To illustrate the way in which the process works, or does not work, we give five examples. The first is the prohibition on possession of child pornography. The production or distribution of child pornography has been an offence since 1979; however, before 1999, the mere possession of child pornography was not. One reason for this was the strong protection of freedom of speech and information in the Freedom of the Press and the Freedom of Expression Acts: it was felt to be difficult to 'cut out' this particular—morally repugnant—form of speech/information without damaging the principle that the mere possession of information should not be an offence. However, by the mid-1990s, a consensus had emerged that some form of criminalisation was necessary. Change was spurred on by a case in which a man was prosecuted for distributing child pornography. The principle of openness meant that the evidence in the case—the pornographic pictures—was not covered by available exceptions relating to maintaining secrecy, which in turn meant that it was available to the public on demand. The public outcry about this led to a very speedy change being made in the Secrecy Act. However, the proposal to criminalise simple possession of child pornography required constitutional amendment. As noted above, this normally requires an intervening general election, meaning that, depending on when it is introduced, such a proposal can take between one and four years to carry through. There is an exception, but a minority of MPs in the Committee on the Constitution were reluctant to sanction such a radical change in the law without proper investigation. The issue was thus investigated in detail, the Freedom and the Press and the Freedom of Expression Acts were amended, and criminalisation of possession of child pornography was then introduced in 1999.[23]

A second example concerns the strategic surveillance of telecommunications. The proposal in 2008—prepared by the Ministry of Defence, not the Ministry of Justice—to extend the power of the Defence Radio Establishment (*Försvarets Radio Anstalt* (FRA)) from monitoring only ether-borne communications to also monitoring international telecommunications borne by cable caused a major political controversy in Sweden. The proposal had obtained the political approval of the leaders of the centre/right parties then in government. Even the leaders of the Social Democratic Party had been consulted, informally, and had given their approval. However, the proposal had been prepared very hastily and paid little or no attention to the issue of personal integrity. The Law Council was given only a very brief period in which to scrutinise the proposal. It produced only a short comment on it, noting first that the technicalities made its implications difficult to understand and, second, that the proposal nonetheless did not appear to take proper account of the judgment of the European Court of Human Rights (ECtHR) in *Weber and Saravia v Germany*.[24] The government persisted with its proposal, despite opposition from within the Ministry of Justice. When the implications became clear—through a press campaign—there was a public outcry. A statute providing

---

[23] Prop [Proposition, legislative bill] 1997/98:43, Criminal Code 16:10a.
[24] No 54934/00, 29 June 2006.

for FRA access to cable traffic was nonetheless pushed through Parliament.[25] But the government was forced, by internal opposition and the fact that the Social Democrats were now showing cold feet, to concede that the protections for integrity were inadequate. An all-party political compromise was later reached, adding a complicated battery of safeguards.[26] A Defence Intelligence Court was established (*Försvarsunderrättelsedomstolen* (FUD)) together with an independent control and monitoring body, the Defence Intelligence Inspection (*Statens inspektion för försvarsunderrättelseverksamheten* (SIUN)).[27] This example illustrates how the value of the system of legislative review can be undermined when there is a political agreement to make the change and make it quickly. However, it also shows how the political price for this can be high. The end result was a strong—possibly the strongest in international comparison—system of independent oversight and control of strategic surveillance.

The third example regards the prohibition on wearing of masks in public assemblies. A proposal on such a prohibition was part of the conclusions of the public inquiry on the riots in connection with the international summit meeting in Gothenburg in 2001.[28] This first proposal was taken up and a more concrete criminalisation was proposed which would have forbidden the concealment of identity when participating in public gatherings. This proposal was heavily criticised during the consultation (*remiss*) phase, but was taken to the Law Council anyway. The Law Council found that the proposal was unconstitutional, as it in practice prohibited covering your face (due to cold weather or whatever reason) in such mundane circumstances as in a bus queue. It was obviously disproportionate to its purpose.

The government then withdrew its proposal, redrafted it and came back with a more narrowly tailored statute, introducing additional criteria such as the risk of violence, participation in a public assembly (rather than a simple public gathering) and a criminal intent to cause a disturbance to public order. A possibility to apply for permission by the police authority was also introduced as a way of giving individuals or groups with legitimate reasons for hiding their identity while demonstrating advance notice on how they would be perceived by the police. This proposal was approved by the Law Council and was thereafter adopted as an Act of Parliament.[29] This example highlights the important role of the Law Council, as it most probably was its negative response that made the government reconsider its position. This might be interpreted as if the preceding phase of commentary had no or little impact on the end result, but this would be a misreading of the situation. The negative response by participants in the remiss phase (ie, courts, law faculties and the Bar Council) was in all likelihood instrumental in providing the Law Council with substantive arguments for its conclusion on the issue of constitutionality.

---

[25] SFS 2008:717 om signalspaning i försvarsunderrättelseverksamhet.

[26] Prop 2008/09:201, Förstärkt integritetsskydd vid signalspaning.

[27] See the Security Protection Act 2009:966 and the Security Protection Ordinance 2009:969, the Defence Intelligence Activity Act 2000:130 and the Defence Intelligence Activity Ordinance 2000:131 as amended.

[28] See SOU 2002:122.

[29] Prop 2005/06:11, SFS 2005:900.

As a fourth example, we would like to mention the legislative process on how to handle photographing in places which violates personal integrity. This has connections to several constitutional issues in Sweden, such as the constitutional protection of gathering information and the particular system of protection of mass media that exists in our country, which inter alia provides for the sole responsibility of the editor for anything published in a periodical.[30] After a rather long period of indecision as to whether to do anything at all in the face of challenges that Swedish law is incompatible with Article 8 ECHR on the protection of private life,[31] the government produced a proposal in early 2011.[32] The proposal was to prohibit both photographing people without their implicit or explicit consent, within a dwelling place or in publicly accessible 'private' situations, such as in a shower or changing rooms, where this infringed their personal integrity. It would also have criminalised photographing people outdoors, but then only when the photography would seriously violate their personal integrity. There was a public interest defence. In the *remiss* phase, many institutions (ie, the Parliamentary Ombudsman and the law faculties) as well as representatives of the mass media pointed out that the proposal was difficult to square with the constitutional right of everyone to gather information with the purpose of publishing it.[33] In cases where the photographer claimed to have taken the photos with such a purpose and where such a claim would often be difficult to rebut, the law could not be applied. Thus, if constitutional changes were not made, the law would be an empty gesture with little effect on the protection of personal integrity. The government nevertheless went ahead with its proposal, arguing among other things that the constitutional protection of gathering information with the purpose of publishing it was not affected by the proposal, as the constitutional protection did not extend to obtaining information through the commission of criminal acts (eg, burglary and theft), and this proposal would simply add a new exception to this list, making it a criminal act to take certain kinds of photos.[34] When the Law Council in 2012 scrutinised the proposal, it did not find the government's argument convincing and instead pointed to the very real risk that constitutionally protected behaviour would in fact be criminalised if the law were to be adopted. The government backed down after this, but returned to the issue in late 2012.[35] The law as passed prohibits photography only in certain specific locations (ie, toilets and showers) when the photos are taken covertly. A general exception applies for acts that are justifiable due to the circumstances, serving as a safety valve against disproportionate restrictions on the right to gather information according to the TF/YGL, the IG and the ECHR. It is clear that the lengthy and open legislative procedure contributed to legislation that is much more sensitive to issues on the protection of human rights than would otherwise have been the case.

---

[30] We can also note that, unlike the UK, the usage of CCTV is relatively limited in Sweden.
[31] See the case of *Söderman v Sweden* [GC] No 5786/08, 12 November 2013 (failure to penalise photographing someone in an intimate situation without consent: violation of Article 8).
[32] Ds 2011:1.
[33] See TF 1:1; YGL 1:2.
[34] Ds 2011:1. 22–23.
[35] Proposal sent to the Law Council 20 December, Bill 2012/13:69, SFS 2013:366.

The fifth and final example was in September 2014, when a proposal for a Bill to Parliament was hastily prepared by the new social democratic/green government to restrict patients' possibilities of choosing private health care alternatives. The Law Council found that the proposal had allowed very little time for consultation, and that it was so lacking in substance and analysis of consequences that it did not satisfy the constitutional requirement that legislative proposals be well prepared (7:2 IG). The Law Council stated that it *could* not (not should not) serve as the basis for legislation. The proposal was thereafter withdrawn.

III. DEFERENCE OR DISTRUST—THE COURTS' RESPONSE TO LEGISLATIVE PROTECTION OF HUMAN RIGHTS?

This brings us to the other side of the coin: how does the legislative review of rights in Parliament reflect on the courts' use of human rights in legal procedures and their willingness to accept laws as compatible with human rights standards? Ultimately, this relates to whether the judges are willing to defer to the judgment of Parliament on such issues or if they distrust the political branch of government in such cases.

To begin with, we should note that, unlike the situation in the UK, there is a career judiciary in Sweden. It is very common for law graduates to serve as clerks to district courts upon graduating. Those wishing to become judges or prosecutors serve an additional period as clerks in the courts of appeal and then apply to be accepted as, respectively, prosecutors or judges. What we should especially emphasise here is that an important part of many Swedish judges' professional careers has traditionally been to serve for a number of years within the government, often the Ministry of Justice, but also other ministries. Junior judges serve in departmental and public commissions of inquiry investigating law reform and, under the guidance of their more senior colleagues in the ministries, draft the bills and the *travaux préparatoires* to legislation.[36]

This might seem strange to lawyers more used to the common law tradition of selecting judges mainly from the group of experienced barristers. How can Swedish judges behave with genuine independence if they move back and forth between the bench and the executive branch where in fact they are subordinates in a strict hierarchy? To begin with, we should note that Sweden is hardly unique in this respect: this is actually common in many continental European states. A junior judge never wears two hats simultaneously: either he or she is working in the Ministry or he or she is judging. In both situations, he or she is under the supervision of more senior colleagues—hierarchically superior civil servants and tenured judges respectively— who apply their respective sets of rules and cultural/ethical norms.[37] Second, there

---

[36] These senior civil servants are often individuals who started out as temporarily employed judges in the service of the justice department (or another department), but for one reason or another stayed on even when they could have moved back to the bench. They typically head the different legal sections of the department (criminal law, administrative law, family law etc) and have traditionally often been selected for service in the highest courts in Sweden at later stages of their careers.

[37] For example, under the Code of Judicial Procedure 16:1, when a panel of judges decides cases, less experienced judges must give reasons for their judgment and their vote first (to avoid them being overly influenced by senior judges).

are constitutional blocks on the government influencing the courts (IG 11:3) as well as the already-mentioned block on the government influencing the administration in taking decisions in individual cases (IG 12:2). Backing up these blocks is the professionalism of the civil service and the culture of independence of the judiciary. Naturally, any attempt to influence the courts would be seen as totally unacceptable. But even attempts to influence the administration in taking decisions in individual cases are seen as unacceptable and this would be leaked to the press and investigated by the Committee on the Constitution. Thus, supporting this culture of professionalism is the principle of open access to documentation.

As noted earlier, the Swedish and the British judiciaries differ sharply in terms of the extent to which they refer to the *travaux préparatoires*. Formally speaking, the greatest weight is to be given to the report of the Select Committee. Unlike the position in the UK, this report expresses the opinion of Parliament. Having said this, it usually simply summarises and approves the different positions taken in the bill itself. In Sweden, except for a very few bills which are politically controversial, the drafting of the *travaux préparatoires* to the actual bill is seen as a technical part of the legislative process. Political interest and influence in this part of the process is thus very limited, meaning that the civil servants in the ministries—invariably junior judges—in effect exercise strong influence over what is said in guidance of the courts. Thus, we would say that the Swedish courts' acceptance of *travaux préparatoires* as a vital source of law rests at least partly on the fact that the material content of the will of Parliament has been formulated by judges temporarily working as experts for the government.

Another explanation for the loyalty that judges show the *travaux préparatoires* which at the same time illustrates an important characteristic of Swedish legal culture is that use of the *travaux préparatoires* is very practical. They can solve several problems of legal interpretation with a minimum of effort from the courts' side. Swedish legal culture is more pragmatic than principled, and principles (legal or otherwise) are seldom seen as obstacles to rational and practical arrangements. This might also be changing due to the more principled approach of European law, which of course has its impact on the Swedish legal system, but so far no major change of behaviour can be noted in how Swedish lawyers in general approach legal problems.

CONCLUSION

A number of tentative conclusions can be drawn. Slowness, openness and arenas for compromise characterise the Swedish legislative process. The public inquiry with the participation of politicians from all parties is a very useful tool for political compromise and balancing of interests without full commitment (as no real decision has been taken yet) and without loss of prestige. In Parliament, the use of permanent committees in legislative matters encourage consensus, as you will encounter each other again and again. Institutional mechanisms exist to ensure that the minority is heard and which thus invite compromises. Of course, we should not paint too idealistic a picture about Swedish politicians. Politics is partly about confrontation. Even in Sweden, the ability to respond politically to rational arguments against a proposed legislative solution is not always great. Rational discourse can sometimes only go so far. Still, we would say that a system where multiple voices will be heard in multiple arenas before any final decision is made can be both more rational and more prone to favour legal arguments than a more closed system of legislation.

When it comes to the courts, as already noted, the Swedish courts can be said to have good reasons to trust the outcome of the legislative process. It is both substantially legitimate, in that it involves stakeholders in a reasonably transparent and rational way, and is professionally legitimate, in that the products are actually written by judges in a temporary capacity as civil servants. Somewhat paradoxically perhaps, the Swedish courts' reliance on and trust in legislative decisions is dependent upon those decisions being heavily influenced by experts of various kinds along the way. Although the very first rule expressed in the IG (IG 1:1) is that all public power comes from the people and that Parliament is the representative of the people, as far as the courts, and the administration, are concerned, Parliament is being respected because of its structural ability to take account of and include expert opinion in the political process, not just because it is *Parliament*. We think that this might be a factor of greater importance than is generally realised when discussing the relationship between legislators and courts—it is perhaps more an issue of earned trust than of formal hierarchy in the organisation of the state.

From this perspective, a legislative approach to the protection of human rights might also start a process of communication and learning between Parliament and the courts that in time could result in a situation where the courts usually do not need to involve themselves in issues of human rights unless the issue concerns the practical application of a legislative measure.[38] Such a balanced approach to the protection of human rights would also be beneficial to move the discussion on protection of human rights away from the rather fruitless (and endless) dichotomy of Parliament or the courts to a more structured approach on the system of protection, including other factors as ombudsmen, media, non-governmental organisations (NGOs) and international supervision.[39]

In any case, the main point here is that pitting the courts and legislative assemblies against each other as guarantors of human rights is quite unhelpful and is perhaps even counter-productive. They are both parts of a system of government with different roles to play, but in which those roles do not have clear lines of demarcation. Even in Sweden, where Parliament's constitutional supremacy is dogma and the courts by tradition play a role close to the idea of law as a mechanical technique, the creative element of case law development of statutory law is well established,

---

[38] It should be noted that as a practical issue, human rights in the courts more often concern judging on how legal competences (of the police, migration office, social security authorities, building office etc) are exercised in particular cases, not on whether a law in itself is compatible with humans rights standards. This is an important but sometimes overlooked nuance—in practice, it is the exercise of legal power (the executive power) that is limited by the courts' rulings on human rights rather than the legislative power itself.

[39] The theoretical discussion on judicial review and protection of rights is extensive, but is perhaps not reflective of its practical importance in any given political and legal system. In Friedman's words, it seems to be more of an academic obsession than a practical problem for democracy: B Friedman, 'The Birth of an Academic Obsession: The History of the Countermajoritarian Difficulty, Part V' (2002) 112 *Yale Law Journal* 153.

legitimate and even presupposed by Parliament in many areas where the legislation is 'sketchy' at best. The idea of a shared responsibility is acknowledged in practice in this and many other ways, and now political and legal theory may at last follow suit.

The government, through its access to the expertise of the civil services, is best suited to design systems *and to manage them from day to day.* Parliament has the legitimacy to determine whether or not to accept the proposed design and to decide how to draw the 'big balances' between competing interests in society. It can—at least to some degree and with the help of the media, the courts, the audit authorities etc—re-evaluate previous balances of interests that have turned out to be dysfunctional or otherwise unsatisfactory.

Courts are the 'fine-tuners' of the system, to see if the balancing of Parliament and government works out in practice without unreasonable results. They are always the last institution to confront an issue. They always act (at least in the Swedish system) as the passive receiver of problems and they have little or no power to enforce their views (the least dangerous branch). And because they have a rather limited capacity to actually deal with massive problems of contemporary society, they can almost never do more than scratch the surface of any systematic problem.[40]

The relationship between preview and review comes to the fore yet again. A robust system of preview that is part of the legislative process can diminish the need for any fine-tuning (review) after adoption of legislative acts. In Sweden, this is reinforced by the status of the Law Council as a preliminary opinion of the highest courts.

It is also helpful to remind ourselves of the ever-present overstatement of refusing to apply/striking down legislation by courts, something that happens very rarely in any democracy. Until 2011, the Swedish courts could only refuse to apply legislation which was 'manifestly' in conflict with the constitution. This restriction has now been removed, but constitutional review of legislation resulting in 'striking down the law' is still likely to be very rare in Sweden (fewer than 10 cases in total over the last 50 years). The more practical issue is when the application of a law by some authority is questioned on the grounds of the protection of (constitutional/human) rights. Given the number of cases dealt with at courts, the number of conflicts with 'the will of the legislator' is actually extremely small. And conflicting with the will of the tax inspector (or police inspector) is perhaps not so problematic from a democratic point of view.

In the rare cases of outright conflicts with the legislative will, the actions of the Swedish courts can perhaps be best viewed as 'constitutional flares', warning signals that the legal system is in need of some amendment. For example, the problem can arise of the courts having to review against the standards of the ECHR. While this should be avoided by the good process of preparing legislation, the ECtHR may later change its case law, making the earlier 'Strasbourg proofing' less certain. There is an ongoing debate as to whether it is enough for the Swedish courts to signal such a problem or whether they should go further and refuse to apply the legislation

---

[40] See A Coan, 'Judicial Capacity and the Substance of Constitutional Law' (2012) 122 *Yale Law Journal* 422 for an argument that this last point might be more important than is usually recognised.

which might be in breach of ECtHR case law, thus forcing the government to investigate whether new legislation is necessary.[41]

Finally, it should be noted that the benefits of a structured, open and relatively slow legislative process goes far beyond the issue of protection of human rights. It is of immense importance for any exercise of legislative power in the many areas of law that affect the daily life of citizens, such as welfare, education and health care. Some parts of the Swedish experience are certainly difficult to transfer to any other system, but we are convinced that others can be quite easily adopted. In any case, the role of Parliament in protecting human rights must be viewed within the wider context of the whole legislative system. 'Bad legislation' can violate human rights or have negative effects in other ways. Legislation should be well prepared and well thought-out. It should not unnecessary involve criminalisation or damage legal security. It should achieve, or at least have a good chance of achieving, the purposes for which it is ostensibly passed. It should be an important part of the purpose of the legislative systems to avoid deficient legislation, as that is ultimately a sign of a deficient democracy.

---

[41] See NJA 2013, s 502. For a discussion see I Cameron and T Bull, 'Sweden' in J Gerards and J Fleuren (eds), *Implementation of the European Convention on Human Rights and of the judgments of the ECtHR in national case law, A comparative analysis* (Antwerp, Intersentia, 2014).

14

Guaranteeing International Human Rights Standards in the Netherlands: The Parliamentary Dimension

MARTIN KUIJER*

THE ROLE OF a national parliament with respect to the implementation of international human rights norms is obviously strongly linked with the status of international norms as such in the domestic legal order. In that regard, the Netherlands has a quite unique system. On the one hand, Article 120 of the Constitution of the Netherlands prohibits a judge checking the constitutionality of Acts of Parliament (in line with the doctrine of the supremacy of Parliament). However, at the same time, Articles 93 and 94 of the Constitution provide for direct applicability of international legal norms. Moreover, these norms have a higher standing than domestic legal norms, including the Constitution. So, whereas the Constitution is a relatively weak document, international human rights standards play a vital role in the Dutch domestic legal order and therefore in parliamentary debate. A human rights-related debate in the Netherlands will therefore likely focus on international human rights treaties. Of those international treaties, the European Convention on Human Rights is by far the most relevant for practical purposes, if only because of the detailed case law of the European Court of Human Rights. In this respect, it is important to note that the Dutch judge applies the so-called 'incorporation doctrine', meaning that the norm (ie, a provision of the Convention) is interpreted as it has been interpreted by the Strasbourg Court. It is therefore irrelevant whether the Court judgment was against the Netherlands or against a third country. In practice, Court judgments against third countries have often resulted in changes to Dutch law and parliamentary debate.

* Senior adviser on human rights law to the Minister of Security and Justice and Professor of Human Rights at the VU University Amsterdam. This chapter reflects the author's personal views.

I. RECEPTION OF INTERNATIONAL HUMAN RIGHTS STANDARDS IN (PARLIAMENTARY) PRACTICE[1]

I would like to discern three (roughly delineated) periods in the reception of the international human rights standards laid down in the European Convention on Human Rights and political debate in the Netherlands. The first period runs from 1950 (the coming into existence of the European Convention on Human Rights)[2] to the mid-1970s. This period is characterised by judicial inactivity at the Strasbourg Court (and a lack of Court judgments against the Netherlands in which a violation was found) and a lack of interest in the Court from Dutch politics. The second period runs from the mid-1970s until, approximately, the turn of the century. In this period the Court rendered various judgments (mainly against the Netherlands) that did have substantial implications for the Dutch legal order. As a result of Strasbourg case law, major structural changes were made to the organisation of the Dutch administrative court system (as a result of the *Benthem* case in 1985),[3] substantial amendments to Dutch criminal (procedural) law were made (for example, as a result of the *Brogan v UK* case in 1988,[4] the *Kostovski* case in 1989[5] and the *Lala and Pelladoah* cases in 1994),[6] and a fundamental overhaul of the law concerning psychiatric patients was conducted (as a result of the *Winterwerp* case in 1979).[7] Various areas of law were affected by the Strasbourg case law in this period: criminal (procedural) law, administrative law, immigration law, family law, social security law, civil procedure etc. Because of the Court's judicial activity and its impact, the practical importance of the Court's work became apparent to politicians. The Court (and its case law) became 'mainstream' in Dutch political debate.

---

[1] This section is based on an earlier publication; see M Kuijer, 'The Impact of the Case Law of the European Court of Human Rights on the Political Debate in the Netherlands Concerning the Court', in M van Roosmalen, B Vermeulen, F van Hoof and M Oosting (eds), Fundamental Rights and Principles. Liber Amicorum Pieter van Dijk (Cambridge, Intersentia, 2013) 99–114.

[2] The Convention was signed on 4 November 1950 in Rome and entered into force on 3 September 1953. The Convention was ratified in the Netherlands by law of 28 July 1954. As a result, the various parts of the Kingdom of the Netherlands were bound by the Convention as from 31 August 1954.

[3] *Benthem v The Netherlands* [1985] ECHR 11. The judgment led to the Crown Appeals (Interim Measures) Act (*Tijdelijke wet kroongeschillen*), Official State Gazette (*Staatsblad*), 1987, 317; Parliamentary Documents [*Kamerstukken*] II 1985/86, 19 497). See also N Verheij, 'De toegang tot de rechter in het bestuursrecht' ['Access to Court in Administrative Law'] in RA Lawson and E Myjer (eds), *50 Jaar EVRM* [*50 Years of the ECHR*] (Leiden, NJCM-Boekerij, 2000) 183.

[4] See IM Abels, 'Brogan-wetgeving: herziening van de regeling van de inverzekeringstelling in het Wetboek van Strafvordering' ['Brogan-legislation: Revision of the Rules on Police Custody in the Code of Criminal Procedure'] (1995) *Ars Aequi* 37; E Myjer, 'The Plain Meaning of the Word "Promptly"' in P Mahoney et al (eds), *Protecting Human Rights: The European Perspective* (Cologne, Heymanns, 2000) 975.

[5] *Kostovski v The Netherlands* [1989] ECHR 20.

[6] *Lala and Pelladoah v The Netherlands* [1994] ECHR 31, judgment of 22 September 1994, App Nos 14861/89 and 16737/90.

[7] *Winterwerp v The Netherlands* [1979] ECHR 4, which eventually led to the Psychiatric Hospitals (Compulsory Admissions) Act (*Wet bijzondere opnemingen in psychiatrische ziekenhuizen*), Official State Gazette (*Staatsblad*), 1992, 669. See also G Mintjes, 'De Wet bijzondere opnemingen in psychiatrische ziekenhuizen' ['Psychiatric Hospitals (Compulsory Admissions) Act'] (1993) *Ars Aequi* 114; and M Kuijer, 'Artikel 5 EVRM en de (procedurele) bescherming van de psychiatrische patiënt' ['Article 5 ECHR and the (Procedural) Protection of Psychiatric Patients'] in RA Lawson and E Myjer (eds), *50 Jaar EVRM* [*50 Years of the ECHR*] (Leiden, NJCM-Boekerij, 2000) 61.

The third period covers the most recent years, in which a change of the political attitude towards the Court can be discerned in some quarters. After years of almost unconditional support for the Court's work, one can now distinguish a more critical approach. This coincides with a shift in the subject matter of the cases that are lodged with the Court against the Netherlands. Whilst a decade ago complaints were related to all major areas of domestic law, more recently the overwhelming majority of complaints lodged against the Netherlands relate to asylum and immigration law.

In the first decades of its existence, the Convention resembled a Sleeping Beauty.[8] In itself, and from a theoretical perspective, it was a revolutionary document. For the first time in history, a legally binding document in the politically sensitive field of human rights had been agreed upon. Until then, states regarded human rights issues as a purely domestic matter. Moreover, states had agreed upon an international supervisory mechanism in the field of human rights. And, even more innovatively, public international law directly affected the rights of individuals by granting them an (optional) right of petition. At the time, the only legal entities usually acknowledged by public international law were states. Therefore, there were sufficient reasons to qualify the youthful Convention as a 'Beauty'.

For the first 20 to 25 years of its existence, however, this Beauty was very much asleep. The theoretical importance of the Convention might have been self-evident, but the practical importance of the Convention was fairly non-existent.[9] Lawyers seldom invoked the provisions of the Convention, fearing that the judge would not take their case seriously. One obviously did not have a very strong case if one had to invoke such a vague legal text as the Convention. Since domestic courts were not frequently confronted with provisions of the Convention, they were largely unfamiliar with its requirements. Frequently, courts did not even have a copy of the Convention at their disposal. Legal scholars did not seem too passionate about the Convention either. Eminent Dutch lawyers like Leijten thought that the Convention was drafted in such vague terms that the text would never have any legal impact whatsoever.[10]

The unfamiliarity with the Convention—in the Netherlands as well as in other High Contracting Parties to the Convention—led to inactivity in Strasbourg in these early years. Without any apparent irony, a commentator wrote in 1977: 'The European

---

[8] See also E Myjer, 'Over hoe het EVRM verzeild raakte in de Nederlandse strafrechtspleging en aan wie dat valt toe te rekenen' ['On How the ECHR Ended up in Dutch Criminal Procedure'] in AW Heringa, JGC Schokkenbroek and J van der Velde (eds), *40 Jaar Europees Verdrag voor de Rechten van de Mens [40 Years of the ECHR]* (Leiden, NJCM, 1990) 271.

[9] See also E Bates, *The Evolution of the European Convention on Human Rights* (Oxford, Oxford University Press, 2010).

[10] JCM Leijten, 'Het fluorideringsarrest' ['The Fluoridation Judgment'] in *'t Exempel dwingt [Essays in Honour of Professor Kisch]* (Zwolle, WEJ Tjeenk Willink, 1975) 289, 314: 'The Treaty of Rome is so vague and is so non-committal even within its vagueness, that we ought to be reduced to barbarism before anyone can successfully rely on it. However, once we are barbarians, we will not bother with the Treaty anyway' ('Het Verdrag van Rome tot bescherming van de rechten van de mens is zo vaag en houdt binnen die vaagheid nog zoveel slagen om de arm, dat wij wel volslagen tot barbarij zullen moeten zijn vervallen, voor iemand er—alle directe werking ten spijt—met succes een beroep op kan doen en zijn we eenmaal barbaren geworden, dan trekken we ons zelfs van het Verdrag niets meer aan').

Court of Human Rights enjoyed a busy year in 1976 and delivered judgment in five cases.'[11] The Registry told Wiarda—who had some doubts whether he would be able to combine his function of judge at the Dutch Supreme Court with an appointment as judge at the then part time European Court—that his appointment at the Strasbourg Court would only take two working days per year.[12] This judicial inactivity is also demonstrated by the fact that there are no Court judgments against the Netherlands in this period. The first judgment against the Netherlands was the *Engel* case in 1976 concerning military disciplinary law.[13]

The lack of interest in the Convention by legal practitioners, scholars and courts was also reflected in the level of interest taken by Dutch politicians. Few could imagine that the Convention would have a substantive impact on the Dutch legal order. A Member of the House of Representatives (Second Chamber) described the Convention as 'a clear statement ... against those totalitarian countries in Europe, in which these rights and freedoms unfortunately are not guaranteed'.[14] According to the same parliamentarian, the Dutch legal order obviously fulfilled the minimum safeguards as laid down in the Convention, making the Convention less relevant. The Dutch Government stated in a by now historical passage 'that the aggregate of regulations laid down in Dutch law, whether criminal or other, offers sufficient guarantees so that these principles shall be respected in our country'.[15] On ratification, there was no real political debate about the compatibility of Dutch law with the standards laid down in the Convention. Only some concerns with regard to the Preamble of the Convention were expressed.[16] Many Members of the Dutch Parliament regretted, for example, the fact that the Convention did not explicitly refer to Christianity with regard to European civilisation.

During the 1970s, the theoretical concept of human rights law gradually transformed into a more practical legal instrument. There are probably various reasons why society at large and the legal and parliamentary community in particular became more interested in human rights law. It is dangerous to oversimplify the complex societal changes that took place, but it is safe to say that the renewed interest in human rights law was partly due to the emancipation of society. Society was increasingly characterised by individualism and more empowered citizens. Interference with individual rights or interests by the authorities was being increasingly challenged. Human rights fitted the purposes of this new kind of activism.

---

[11] J Andrews, 'Council of Europe' (1977) *European Law Review* 154.
[12] E Myjer, *Bij een vijftigste verjaardag* [*On the Occasion of a Fiftieth Birthday*] (Nijmegen, Wolf Legal Publishers, 2001) 7 (note 14).
[13] *Engel v The Netherlands* [1976] ECHR 3.
[14] In Dutch: 'een duidelijke uitspraak ... tegenover de totalitaire landen in Europa, waar van de waarborging van deze rechten en vrijheden helaas geen sprake is'.
[15] In Dutch: 'dat het complex regelingen van de Nederlandse wet, zowel van strafrechtelijke als van andere aard, voldoende waarborgen biedt dat deze beginselen in ons land eerbiediging zullen vinden'.
[16] See more elaborately on the Dutch ratification process: YS Klerk and L van Poelgeest, 'Ratificatie à contre-coeur: de reserves van de Nederlandse regering jegens het Europees Verdrag voor de Rechten van de Mens en het individueel klachtrecht' ['Ratification with the Heart Not in it: Reservations of Dutch Government against the European Convention on Human Rights and the Individual Right of Complaint'] (1991) *Rechtsgeleerd Magazijn Themis* 220.

In the Netherlands, the increasing interest in human rights law led to a rise in popularity of the Convention. Having a fairly weak Constitution, the human rights debate focused on the Convention.[17] In the 1970s and 1980s, lawyers slowly started to realise the relevance of the Convention for their legal practice and began to invoke it in domestic proceedings. The first cases against the Netherlands were lodged with the European Court of Human Rights: the case of *Engel* (1976) concerning military disciplinary law, *Winterwerp* (1979) concerning the placement of psychiatric patients, *X and Y* (1985) concerning the need to adopt criminal law sanctions in case of serious (sexual) misconduct, *Benthem* (1985) concerning the organisation of the Dutch administrative court system, *Berrehab* (1988) concerning immigration law and *Kostovski* (1989) concerning the use of anonymous witnesses in criminal proceedings. The fact that the Court found violations in each of these cases illustrated the factual relevance of the Convention for legal practice. Cases could actually be *won* by invoking the Convention. The period of judicial inactivity had ended. Moreover, some of the Court judgments, including cases that were not brought against the Netherlands, had a tremendous impact on the domestic legal order.

The *Van Mechelen* case (1997) can serve as an example.[18] The applicants complained that their criminal conviction had been based essentially on the evidence of police officers whose identity was not disclosed to them and who were not heard either in public or in their presence. The Court concluded that Article 6 of the Convention had been violated. As a result, the then Minister of Justice, Winnie Sorgdrager, released the four applicants almost immediately after the Court's judgment.[19] More importantly, the Code of Criminal Procedure was amended so as to allow requests for revision of final decisions following judgments of the Strasbourg Court. According to Article 457, § 1(3) of the Code of Criminal Procedure, a request for revision can be lodged before the Supreme Court on the ground that a judgment of the European Court of Human Rights has established that the Convention was violated in proceedings that led to the conviction of the applicant or to a conviction on account of the same fact, and based on the same evidence, if revision is necessary in order to provide reparation within the meaning of Article 41 of the Convention.[20]

Judgments of the Court with respect to third countries concerning problems that could also arise in the Netherlands have frequently led to changes in Dutch legislation, case law and/or practice. The 1979 *Marckx* judgment against Belgium, concerning discriminatory treatment of 'illegitimate' children, for example, led to

---

[17] See more elaborately M Kuijer, *Wetgever en constitutie: de betekenis van het Europees Verdrag voor de Rechten van de Mens voor de nationale wetgever* [*Legislator and Constitution: The Meaning of the European Convention on Human Rights for the National Legislator*] (Nijmegen, Wolf Legal Publishers, 2009).

[18] *Van Mechelen and others v The Netherlands*, [1997] ECHR 22.

[19] This led to a parliamentary debate (see Annex Parliamentary Proceedings (*Bijlage Handelingen*) II, 1996-1997, No 1247 and 1254). This proactive attitude following a judgment of the Court was not appreciated by all; the newspaper *De Telegraaf* commented that gangsters had been released because of the European Court ('Gangsters vrij door Euro-Hof'); see *De Telegraaf* (26 April 1997).

[20] See on this issue more elaborately PHPHMC van Kempen, *Heropening van procedures na veroordelingen door het EHRM* [*Reopening of Proceedings after ECtHR Judgments*] (Nijmegen, Wolf Legal Publishers, 2003).

immediate changes in Dutch policy.[21] The 1988 *Brogan* judgment against the UK, concerning pre-trial detention, had a similar impact on Dutch policy.[22] The 1996 *Goodwin* judgment against the UK, concerning a journalistic privilege of non-disclosure, led to an almost immediate change in the case law of the Dutch Supreme Court.[23] And the Belgian *De Cubber* case (1984) led to a lively debate in Dutch law journals about whether the Dutch system of juvenile judges taking pre-trial decisions could be considered compatible with Article 6 of the Convention.[24] Dutch juvenile judges decided after *De Cubber* to stand down as trial judges in case their pre-trial involvement had been substantial.[25]

The increasing body of case law attracted first and foremost the interest of those involved in the administration of justice[26] and academia.[27] Domestic courts were more often confronted with legal arguments based on the Convention. They were asked to rule on the compatibility of domestic laws with the Convention and became more familiar with the Court's case law. The Academy responsible for the (initial and continuous) training of magistrates in the Netherlands (the *Studiecentrum Rechtspleging*) began offering training modules on the Convention and the Court's case law.[28]

Convention standards also became increasingly 'mainstreamed' in the legislative process and the political domain. The Dutch legislator started to check the compatibility of draft legislation with Convention standards more systematically. Human rights concerns about the compatibility of draft legislation with Convention standards

---

[21] The Dutch Court of Cassation quickly responded to the Strasbourg Court's *Marckx* judgment (Court of Cassation, judgment of 18 June 1980, *NJ* 1980, 463) which led to a change in the Dutch Civil Code with retroactive effect (Official State Gazette (*Staatsblad*) 1982, 608).

[22] Following the judgment in *Brogan*, a commission charged with the revision of the Code of Criminal Procedure was requested in January 1989 to examine the consequences of the judgment for the Dutch legal order. Already in March 1989, a report, *De inverzekeringstellingsprocedure in het licht van artikel 5 EVRM* [*The Rules on Police Custody in the Light of Article 5 of the ECHR*], was published, which concluded that Dutch law had to be amended at short notice.

[23] *Goodwin v UK* [1996] ECHR 16.

[24] See the discussion between E Myjer, 'Een nietige rechter-commissaris in kinderstrafzaken' ['An Invalid Examining Magistrate'] (1985) *Trema* 56; G Mannoury, 'De rechter-commissaris: een bevooroordeelde zittingsrechter' ['The Examining Magistrate: A Biased Session Judge'] (1985) *Trema* 61; EP von Brucken Fock, 'De De Cubber-zaak' ['The *De Cubber* Case'] (1985) *Tijdschrift voor Familie- en Jeugdrecht* 65; PAJT van Teeffelen, 'Heeft de De Cubber Case gevolgen voor de strafprocedure in kinderzaken?' ['Does the *De Cubber* Case Affect Criminal Procedure in Children's Cases?'] (1985) *Nederlands Juristenblad* 453; and MLCC de Bruijn-Lückers, 'Het jeugdstrafprocesrecht en de "De Cubber-Case"' ['The Law of Juvenile Criminal Procedure and the *De Cubber* Case'] (1986) *Nederlands Juristenblad* 569.

[25] See E Myjer, *De Vijftig voorbij* [*Over Fifty*] (Nijmegen, Wolf Legal Publishers, 2002) 23.

[26] See P van Dijk, 'De Houding van de Hoge Raad jegens de verdragen inzake de Rechten van de Mens' ['The Attitude of the Court of Cassation Towards Human Rights Treaties'], in *De Hoge Raad der Nederlanden; De plaats van de Hoge Raad in het huidige staatsbestel* [*The Court of Cassation in the Netherlands: Its Position in the Present Constitutional System*] (Zwolle, WEJ Tjeenk Willink, 1988) 173.

[27] The criminal law section of Leiden Law Faculty was one of the first academic institutions in the country to pay attention to the impact of the Convention standards on various parts of criminal (procedural) law, including penitentiary law. Various PhD candidates worked on a Convention-related doctoral thesis. Furthermore, in 1974 the Dutch section of the International Commission of Jurists (*Nederlands Juristen Comité voor de Mensenrechten*) was established.

[28] Likewise, legislative draughtsmen are trained on Convention standards in the Academy for Legislation (*Academie voor Wetgeving*), officials of the Immigration and Naturalisation Service are trained on the requirements of Articles 3 and 8 of the Convention at the Theory of Knowledge Centre of the Immigration and Naturalization Service (*Kennisleercentrum IND*) etc.

became a regular feature in parliamentary debates. One possible explanation for the increased attention to the Convention in politics may be that the main political parties realised that international human rights norms provided a powerful political weapon in parliamentary debate with the Government. Both right-wing and left-wing parties frequently used human rights-related objections to oppose a particular legislative proposal. In that sense, human rights truly became mainstream in Dutch parliamentary debate. The almost unconditional support to the Convention system in the political domain in the Netherlands was striking. The Court could do no wrong, or so it seemed. Governments were severely criticised if there was an impression that Convention standards were not fully implemented. Parliamentary debate focussed on how specific Court judgments needed to be interpreted, on how judgments against third countries could have a similar impact on the Dutch legal order, but not on the Convention standards as such. In short, the Convention mechanism was not seen as intruding on the domestic legal order (or political sovereignty in the national Parliament), but as a welcome addition to the constitutional order of the Kingdom. In various quarters it was argued that a further strengthening of the Constitution was unnecessary in view of the practical role of the Convention.

In more recent years, the overwhelming majority of complaints lodged against the Netherlands have related to asylum and immigration law. Some estimate that roughly 80 per cent of the applications lodged against the Netherlands now relate to the field of asylum and immigration.[29] Note that the reference is deliberately to *complaints* that are lodged at the Court. *Judgments* delivered against the Netherlands are not in similar terms related to asylum or immigration law. In fact, if one looks at the Court judgments against the Netherlands between 2008 and 2014, it even appears that only a minority of cases relate to this topic: there have been 20 judgments,[30] of which six were related to asylum and immigration. In four of these six judgments, the Court actually found a violation. Nevertheless, there is a perception that the Court's case law has an increasing influence on immigration policy.[31]

When one looks at the parliamentary attitude towards the Court in recent years, one does not discern any major change in relation to the reaction to specific substantive judgments of the Court. Following the *Salah Sheekh* judgment[32] concerning expulsions to Somalia, the responsible minister stated that the examination of asylum requests had to be conducted in conformity with the requirements and

---

[29] A Buyse, 'Full swing er tegenaan! Interview met prof. Mr. BEP Myjer' [Full Swing Ahead! Interview with Judge Myjer] in T Barkhuysen, M Kuijer and RA Lawson (eds), *55 Jaar EVRM* (Leiden, NJCM, 2006) 33.

[30] These are judgments on the merits, excluding judgments that are solely related to just satisfaction or judgments in which cases have been struck off the list.

[31] This perception can also be found in other European countries. See, for example, M Bossuyt, 'Judges on Thin Ice: The European Court of Human Rights and the Treatment of Asylum Seekers' (2010) *Inter-American and European Human Rights Journal* 3; M Bossuyt, *Strasbourg et les demandeurs d'asile: des juges sur un terrain glissant* [*Strasbourg and Asylum Seekers: Judges on Thin Ice*] (Brussels, Bruylant, 2010). Bossuyt, the President of the Constitutional Court of Belgium, is very critical of the 'extremist' case law of the Strasbourg Court in the field of asylum-seekers (see the interview at www.vandaag.be).

[32] *Salah Sheekh v The Netherlands* [2007] ECHR 36.

standards laid down in the Court's judgment.[33] The Government therefore took a loyal stance towards the Court, even though some in the political domain criticised the judgment severely.[34] A similar political reaction can be seen in response to the *MSS* judgment[35] concerning the compatibility of Dublin transfers to Greece with the requirements of the Convention. In a letter to Parliament, the Minister for Immigration and Asylum Policy stated: 'Naturally, the Dutch government will respect this judgment.'[36] Likewise, the Court's judgment in the leading case of *Sufi and Elmi* against the UK[37] concerning expulsions to Mogadishu and other parts of Somalia swiftly led to policy amendments in the Netherlands.[38]

However, looking at the Dutch position with regard to the institutional reform of the Court, a certain shift can be discerned. The letter of the Minister of Security and Justice, in association with the Minister of Foreign Affairs, to Parliament of 3 October 2011 is illuminating in this respect.[39] This letter contained the Government's position on the reform of the European Court of Human Rights and on the EU's accession to the Convention. The first substantive topic to be addressed in the letter is 'Embedding the principle of subsidiarity' and the fact that the Court is a subsidiary mechanism that can only supplement the human rights protection provided primarily at a national level. While this is obviously true, the prominent role of the principle in the letter signifies a notable shift in the prevailing general political attitude towards the Court: 'the principle of subsidiarity means that continued vigilance is required on the part of the Court ... in order to do full justice to its subsidiary role ... The Court should also respect the decision of the national (judicial) authority on the facts or the competing interests, unless the decision is manifestly unreasonable'. A few months earlier, the Minister of Foreign Affairs put it like this: 'the Court should not weaken its authority by rendering judgments which are only peripherally related to human rights'.[40] Stef Blok, then Member of Parliament for the Liberal Party, wrote in one of the national newspapers that judges in Strasbourg have become politicians in judicial robes who declare the Convention to be breached even if domestic policy cannot reasonably be considered to be in violation of human rights standards.[41] *C'est le ton qui fait la musique*, and in this instance the tone in the political domain has sharpened.[42]

---

[33] See Parliamentary Documents (*Kamerstukken*) II 2006-2007, 29 344, No 64 (letter of the State Secretary of Justice to Parliament: 'De toetsing van asielaanvragen aan artikel 3 EVRM dient te geschieden met inachtneming van de in deze uitspraak van het Hof opgenomen elementen' ['The Review of Applications for Asylum in the light of Article 3 of the ECHR ought to take into account the elements mentioned in the Court's judgment'].

[34] For example, according to a press release by the Netherlands national news agency (ANP), the then opposition leader Mark Rutte argued that the judgment had to be ignored.

[35] *MSS v Belgium and Greece* [2011] ECHR 108.

[36] Letter of 10 February 2011 (no DDS 5684216/11).

[37] *Sufi and Elmi v UK* [2011] ECHR 1045.

[38] Letter of the Minister for Immigration and Asylum Policy to Parliament of 26 August 2011 (No DDS 5706585/11).

[39] Parliamentary Documents (*Kamerstukken*) II, 2011-2012, 32 735, No 32.

[40] Parliamentary Documents (*Kamerstukken*) II2010-2011, 31 735, No 1.

[41] *Volkskrant* (7 April 2011).

[42] See Donald and Leach, ch 4 in this volume, for consideration of recent challenges to the legitimacy of the European Court of Human Rights in the Netherlands.

II. HUMAN RIGHTS IN THE LEGISLATIVE PROCESS

In accordance with Article 81 of the Constitution, Acts of Parliament are enacted jointly by the Government and the States General, consisting of the House of Representatives and the Senate. Each House has its own permanent Justice Committee and a legal service, both of which place considerable emphasis on compliance with human rights instruments like the Convention when examining draft legislation. However, the Netherlands—like most other Member States of the Council of Europe—does not have a specific parliamentary procedure for the verification of compatibility of draft laws with the Convention.

When drafting legislation, the ministries concerned check the quality of draft legislation and their conformity with the Constitution and relevant provisions of international law. The Convention is of great significance in this process. Drafters assess the legislation in the light of the Convention in the manner laid down in policy on legislative quality and the Instructions on legislation, in particular Instructions 18, 212g and 254. Instruction 18 reads: 'During the drafting of legislation, it must be ascertained which rules of higher law have limited the freedom to regulate in relation to the issue concerned.' Instruction 212g states that the Explanatory Memorandum should contain a justification of the legislation in question. This will include, in any event, the relationship of the Act being drafted to other legislation and to existing and forthcoming international and EU legislation. One of the checks carried out is an investigation by the Legislation Department at the Ministry of Justice in consultation with the Ministry of Foreign Affairs into whether the draft legislation is compatible with obligations arising from international and European law (see Instruction 254). Although the Ministry of Justice bears primary responsibility for monitoring legislation for compliance with the principles of good governance and the rule of law, this does not detract from the responsibility resting on the other ministries to ensure that the legislation they draft is of the highest quality.

In the drafting phase, new statutory measures are submitted to external parties for consultation, including representatives from the legal profession, the judiciary and the independent supervisory body in the area of data protection. In addition, the Dutch section of the International Commission of Jurists (Nederlands Juristen Comité Mensenrechten) frequently renders an opinion on the human rights compatibility of draft legislation. The advice of these individuals and agencies is always dealt with in a substantiated manner in Explanatory Memorandums with legislative proposals. After the Dutch Council of Ministers has given its approval, the proposed regulations are submitted to the Council of State, which advises the Government on legislation and administration. The Council of State applies a policy analysis evaluation, a legal evaluation and a statutory evaluation, and assesses whether a proposed regulation complies with internationally recognised human rights standards. If there is any lack of clarity on this issue, the Council will make a recommendation. The moment that parliamentary debate starts on a certain draft bill, there is therefore already a substantial amount of information available on the issue of compatibility with Convention standards. Parliament is then able to request additional information from the Government in a more focused manner.

In conclusion, the Instructions on legislation which oblige the legislator to include a paragraph in the explanatory memorandum to a bill explaining why the draft legislation is deemed compatible with the requirements of international human rights standards are an essential tool to promote parliamentary debate on the issue. Equally, it is essential for Members of Parliament and their support staff to have access to independent, expert human rights advice, especially if—as in the Netherlands—one does not concentrate the existing expertise within one parliamentary committee like the UK Joint Committee on Human Rights. In addition, evaluation clauses in legislation are useful in case Parliament entertains doubts concerning the human rights compatibility of draft legislation. A substantial number of laws contain an evaluation clause, by means of which the legislation must be evaluated after a number of years. The potential effects in the area of fundamental rights often form a significant part of this evaluation.

III. PARLIAMENT'S SUPERVISORY ROLE CONCERNING THE IMPLEMENTATION OF STRASBOURG JUDGMENTS

Court judgments against the Netherlands in which a violation is found will as a rule lead to parliamentary questions to the Government by one or more political parties. Usually, the questions require the Government to provide information about how it intends to implement the Court judgment and how similar cases may be prevented in future. These parliamentary questions necessitate a speedy reaction by the Government as to what actions are foreseen in the implementation process of a Court judgment. In that manner, Parliament can (and in fact does) play an effective role in the implementation process.

In addition, there is a more general instrument to assist Parliament in its supervisory role. The Government Agent before the ECHR, also on behalf of the Minister of Justice, presents an annual report to Parliament concerning the Court judgments delivered against the Netherlands.[43] These annual reports have been submitted to Parliament since 1996. Following a request from the Senate in 2006, the report also includes information concerning measures adopted to implement adverse Court judgments. Since 2009, the annual report contains where appropriate references to judgments against other States Parties which have had a direct or indirect effect on the Dutch legal system. And since 2010, the annual report also mentions reasoned decisions of the Court in which a complaint has been declared inadmissible or has been struck out of the list of cases. It also provides statistics on pending cases and to which areas of law these cases relate (eg, criminal law and alien law). The annual reporting mechanism may prove a useful tool, facilitating parliamentary debate on Convention-related matters.

---

[43] See Donald and Leach, ch 4 in this volume, for consideration of the Dutch annual report and comparison with the practice in other countries.

CONCLUDING COMMENTS

Involvement of national parliaments is a vital tool in the implementation of international human rights standards. In the Netherlands, both Houses of Parliament play an active role in this field. This is partly due to the fact that the human rights debate in the Netherlands is for the most part a debate on Convention standards. Legal arguments related to Convention standards prove to be a powerful political weapon in parliamentary debates. To assist Parliament in fulfilling its supervisory role, two tools seem to be worth highlighting. In the legislative process, the practice of providing a paragraph of explanation of the human rights compatibility of a draft legislative proposal proves to be extremely useful. Equally, the annual report sent to Parliament on (the implementation of) Strasbourg judgments is considered a useful tool. Having said that, equally essential is for Members of Parliament and their support staff to have access to independent, expert human rights advice and/or training.

Part V

International Initiatives to Increase the Role of Parliaments in Relation to Human Rights

15

The Work of the Parliamentary Assembly of the Council of Europe

ANDREW DRZEMCZEWSKI AND JULIA LOWIS

I. THE PARLIAMENTARY ASSEMBLY OF THE COUNCIL OF EUROPE

THE COUNCIL OF Europe (hereinafter 'the Council' and 'the Organisation'), based in Strasbourg, France, was founded in 1949 with the aim of creating a democratic and legal area throughout the continent, based on the fundamental values of human rights, pluralistic democracy and the rule of law. Founded by 10 countries, the Council now has 47 Member States,[1] with a combined population of some 800 million persons. All of the Organisation's Member States are Parties to the European Convention on Human Rights, compliance with which is primarily supervised by the European Court of Human Rights.[2]

The Parliamentary Assembly of the Council of Europe (hereinafter 'the Assembly') is assigned the function of 'deliberative organ' by the Statute of the Council of Europe.[3] Its important role within the Council is underlined by, in particular, the fact that it elects judges of the Court, the European Commissioner for Human Rights and the Secretary General of the Organisation. The Assembly is comprised of 636 nationally elected parliamentarians (318 Representatives and 318 Substitutes)

---

[1] Nearly all European states have acceded to the Council, with the exception of Belarus. In addition, the Parliaments of Israel, Canada and Mexico have been granted Observer status by the Parliamentary Assembly, and the Parliament of Morocco and the Palestinian National Council enjoy partner for democracy status.

[2] For information generally, see the Council's website, available at: www.coe.int/aboutCoe/index .asp?Lang=en. For information on the European Court of Human Rights, see the Court's website at: www.echr.coe.int/ECHR/homepage_en.

[3] The Assembly, alongside the Committee of Ministers, is one of two statutory organs of the Council and can be seen as linking together the other institutions: 'The Committee of Ministers it holds to account, supplements and supports; the Court it supports whilst respecting the Court's entire independence; with the Congress of local and regional authorities it brings together the other levels of democratic representation and executive responsibilities to join in the common purposes of the strengthening of democracy and upholding the rule of law': Paul Evans and Paul Silk, *The Parliamentary Assembly, Practice and Procedure* (Strasbourg, Council of Europe Publishing, 2012) 38. For more information on the Assembly's role and working methods, see also Members Handbook, Parliamentary Assembly of the Council of Europe, (September 2012), available at: www.assembly.coe.int/AboutUs/APCE_MembersHandbookE .pdf; see also the Assembly's website, available at: www.assembly.coe.int/DefaultE.asp.

from the parliaments of the Member States of the Council,[4] with the balance of political parties within each national delegation reflecting the proportions of the various parties in their national parliaments. The vast majority of members belong to one of the Assembly's five organised political groups: the Group of the European People's Party (EPP), the Socialist Group (SOC), the Alliance of Liberals and Democrats for Europe (ALDE), the European Conservatives Group (EC) (replacing, in July 2014, the European Democrat Group (EDG)) and the Group of the Unified European Left (UEL).

Important powers of the Assembly include proposing multilateral treaties, demanding action from governments represented on the Committee of Ministers (the Organisation's executive organ), 'monitoring' how far states fulfil their promises on democratic standards, proposing sanctions (including recommending the exclusion or suspension of a Member State) and highlighting and/or uncovering new facts about human rights violations. Any member of the Assembly that considers that an issue is relevant for examination and debate by the Assembly may draft a motion for a resolution or a recommendation which, once it has obtained the required number of 20 co-signatories and is approved, will be examined by one of the Assembly's Committees through the appointment of a rapporteur. Motions can also be initiated by a requisite quorum of an Assembly Committee (see below). The rapporteur's draft report will be debated upon and, if ultimately approved, adopted by the plenary Assembly, which meets four times a year in the Palais de l'Europe in Strasbourg.

The substantive work relating to the preparation of reports is carried out by nine permanent committees: the Committee on Political Affairs and Democracy, the Committee on Legal Affairs and Human Rights, the Committee on Social Affairs, Health and Sustainable Development, the Committee on Migration, Refugees and Displaced Persons, the Committee on Culture, Science, Education and Media, the Committee on Equality and Non-discrimination, the Monitoring Committee, the Committee on Rules of Procedure, Immunities and Institutional Affairs and, as of 2015, the committee on the Election of Judges to the European Court of Human Rights.

Mainstream legal and human rights issues are dealt with primarily, but not exclusively, by the Committee on Legal Affairs and Human Rights (hereinafter 'the LAHR Committee').[5] This contribution will therefore be confined to the work of the LAHR Committee, with specific focus on issues relating to compliance with the European Human Rights Convention and the Strasbourg Court's judgments.[6]

---

[4] The number of members allocated to each national delegation is proposed by the Assembly when giving its opinion on the accession of the state to the Council, with the main criteria being population size: see Art 26 of the Statute of the Organisation (which has undergone successive modifications as additional states have become members of the Council), available at: http://assembly.coe.int/nw/xml/RoP/RoP-XML2HTML-EN.asp.

[5] For an overview of the Committee's work and its priorities, see the Assembly's website: www.assembly.coe.int/Mainf.asp?link=/Committee/JUR/role_E.htm.

[6] Other Assembly committees are also involved in supervising the execution of the Strasbourg Court's judgments on a more occasional basis, in particular the Monitoring Committee in its reports on the

II. INCREASING THE ROLE OF PARLIAMENTS

The role played by the Assembly in ensuring respect of Convention standards in States Parties has in recent years been primarily focused on tackling the constantly growing number of applications pending before the Court and the similarly worrying number of non-executed judgments pending before the Committee of Ministers following a finding of violation by the Court.[7] However, the ever-increasing involvement of both the Assembly and national parliaments can also, on a more general level, help to foster a 'human rights culture' within States Parties and can begin to redress what has been termed the 'democratic deficit' in the field of human rights.[8] Thus, the involvement of parliaments is increasingly being recognised as critical to safeguarding the effective operation of the Convention system and ultimately ensuring the long-term viability of the Council of Europe.

The work of the Assembly directed at increasing the role of parliaments in relation to human rights therefore has two distinct, but mutually supportive goals: first, ensuring the rapid and full execution of judgments of the Strasbourg Court; and, second, increasing human rights discourse at the national level,[9] which in turn helps to enhance the democratic legitimacy of human rights. The Brighton Declaration[10] has, at long last,[11] placed renewed emphasis on the parliamentary dimension in the

honouring of obligations and commitments by Member States (see, in this respect, terms of reference of committees: www.assembly.coe.int/Main.asp?link=/Documents/AdoptedText/ta11/ERES1842. htm#PRO, and documents recently issued by the Monitoring Committee: www.assembly.coe.int/Main. asp?link=/CommitteeDocs/ComDocMenuMonEN.htm).

[7] As at 1 December 2014, there were 71,600 applications pending before the Court. At the end of 2014, nearly 11,000 cases were pending before the Committee of Ministers, see 'Supervision of the Execution of Judgments and Decisions of the European Court of Human Rights, Annual Report, 2014' available at: www.coe.int/t/dghl/monitoring/execution/Default_en.asp.

[8] See David Feldman, 'Can and Should Parliament Protect Human Rights?' (2004) 10(4) *European Public Law* 651: 'The main contribution of Parliament to the process of protecting rights and creating a culture of human rights, apart from legislation, consists of using its influence and its scrutiny powers to keep human rights standards at the forefront of the minds of ministers and departments, regulators, and other public authorities. In this way Parliament can influence and encourage (or discourage) developments.'

[9] Increasing national human rights awareness includes introducing formal mechanisms to ensure the systematic verification of all legislation and policies with Convention standards, facilitating debate between parliamentarians, government actors, non-governmental organisations (NGOs) and other human rights institutions, and in particular ensuring parliamentary oversight of actions of the executive.

[10] Adopted at the Third High Level Conference on the Future of the European Court of Human Rights, held at Brighton under the UK Chairmanship of the Committee of Ministers on 19–20 April 2012, available at: https://wcd.coe.int/ViewDoc.jsp?id=1934031.

[11] Although (scant) reference was made to parliaments in the Interlaken Declaration, this was excluded in the subsequent Izmir Declaration. See, in this respect, A Drzemczewski, 'The Parliamentary Assembly's Involvement in the Supervision of the Judgments of the Strasbourg Court' (2010) 28(2) *Netherlands Quarterly of Human Rights* 164, and the critical comments of Mrs Herta Däubler-Gmelin, a former Chairperson of the LAHR: 'The Future of the Strasbourg Court and Enforcement of ECHR Standards: Reflections on the Interlaken Process', Doc AS/Jur (2010) 06 of 21 January 2010, especially §§2–3 and 13; see also Assembly Doc 12811, 'Guaranteeing the Authority and Effectiveness of the European Convention on Human Rights' (Rapporteur

protection of human rights, something that is demonstrated in the following two excerpts:

> The Conference therefore ... expresses the determination of the States Parties to ensure effective implementation of the Convention at national level by taking the following specific measures ... implementing practical measures to ensure that policies and legislation comply fully with the Convention, including by offering to national parliaments information on the compatibility with the Convention of draft primary legislation proposed by the Government.[12]

> Each State Party has undertaken to abide by the final judgments of the Court in any case to which they are a party ... The Committee of Ministers is supervising the execution of an ever-increasing number of judgments. As the Court works through the potentially well-founded applications pending before it, the volume of work for the Committee of Ministers can be expected to increase further ... The Conference therefore ... welcomes the Parliamentary Assembly's regular reports and debates on the execution of judgments.[13]

Despite increasing recognition of the important role which national parliaments and the Assembly play as guarantors of human rights, this, as yet, has not been fully exploited. The ability of parliaments to systematically participate in the implementation of judgments, in addition to verifying all draft legislation for compatibility with the European Convention, presupposes the existence of parliamentary structures, preferably in the form of dedicated human rights committees, which have access to an efficient legal service with specific competence in human rights matters.[14] As yet, very few states possess such structures; for this reason, their establishment in most, if not all, Member States of the Council is currently a primary focus of the LAHR Committee (see further below).

A crucial aspect of the Assembly's working methods is exploiting the dual mandate of its members to support parliamentary involvement at the European level with corresponding involvement at the domestic level.[15] This dual mandate is of fundamental importance in enhancing the subsidiary character of the Convention mechanism, recalling that the primary responsibility to guarantee the rights and freedoms enshrined in the Convention and its protocols falls upon states' national authorities: 'The High Contracting Parties shall secure to everyone within their jurisdiction the rights and freedoms defined in Section I of this Convention'

Ms Marie-Louise Bemelmans-Videc), especially §§ 18 and 55, available at: www.assembly.coe.int/ASP/Doc/XrefViewPDF.asp?FileID=12914&Language=EN.

[12] Brighton Declaration, § A 9 c) ii).

[13] ibid, § F 29 e).

[14] As suggested in Assembly Resolution 1823 (2011) 'National Parliaments: Guarantors of Human Rights in Europe', available at: www.assembly.coe.int/ASP/Doc/XrefViewHTML.asp?FileID=18011&Language=EN.

[15] See statements by Mr Jean-Claude Mignon, President of the Parliamentary Assembly of the Council of Europe, at the Brighton Conference, 19 April 2012, available at: www.assembly.coe.int//Main.asp?link=http://assembly.coe.int/President/Mignon/Discours/2012/19042012_BrightonConferenceE.htm, and the European Conference of Presidents of Parliament, available at: www.assembly.coe.int/Conferences/2012Strasbourg/Background/FutureECHRRoleE.pdf.

(Article 1 of the Convention).[16] It is therefore crucial that parliamentarians' dual role is exploited fully to ensure that standards guaranteed by the Court are effectively protected and implemented domestically without the need for individuals to seek justice in Strasbourg.[17]

The 'subsidiary' nature of the Strasbourg control mechanism has recently—yet again—been emphasised at Brighton.[18] It follows from the principle of subsidiarity that greater involvement of national parliaments in the implementation of the Convention on the domestic plane is logically anterior to parliamentary supervision of the execution of the Court's judgments. However, in order to provide a chronological overview of the progress made in this field, this contribution will consider first, at the European level, the work of the Assembly, before examining the role of national parliaments in both: (i) supervising the implementation of Court judgments; and (ii) scrutinising legislation for human rights compatibility and fostering a human rights culture at the domestic level.

III. THE ROLE OF THE PARLIAMENTARY ASSEMBLY IN SUPERVISING THE COURT'S JUDGMENTS

The main body responsible for supervising the execution of Strasbourg judgments by Member States is the Committee of Ministers, the executive organ of the Council of Europe.[19] Article 46(2) of the Convention provides that: 'The final judgment of the Court shall be transmitted to the Committee of Ministers, which shall supervise its execution.' This has not, however, prevented the Assembly from exercising an increasingly active role in this regard,[20] and the Committee of Ministers itself has acknowledged that the implementation of Strasbourg Court judgments 'has greatly

---

[16] See here P-H Imbert, 'Follow-up to the Committee of Ministers' Recommendations on the Implementation of the Convention at the Domestic Level' in *Reform of the European Human Rights System* (Strasbourg, Council of Europe Publishing, 2004) 33–43.

[17] A key point to be noted is the composition of each Member State's parliamentary delegation: national delegations are always composed in such a way as to ensure fair representation of the political parties or groups in their respective parliaments.

[18] See section B of the Declaration entitled 'Interaction between the Court and National Authorities', in particular § 12 b), which calls for a reference to the principle of subsidiarity and the doctrine of the margin of appreciation to be included in the preamble to the Convention. See now Protocol 15 to the ECHR (not yet in force).

[19] For a recent overview, see *Les mutations de l'activité du Comité des ministres. La surveillance de l'exécution des arrêts de la Cour européenne des droits de l'homme par cet organe du Conseil de l'Europe* (2012, Actes du séminaire de l'Institut international des droits de l'homme René Cassin) passim. See also E Lambert-Abdelgawad, *The Execution of Judgments of the European Court of Human Rights* (Strasbourg, Council of Europe Publishing, 2008) and E Lambert-Abdelgawad, 'The Execution of the Judgments of the European Court of Human Rights: Towards a Non-coercive and Participatory Model of Accountability' (2009) 69 *ZaöRV* 471.

[20] Since, in accordance with Art 46(1) of the Convention, all state organs (the executive, judiciary and legislature) bear a responsibility to ensure compliance with Convention standards, including Court judgments. See here, in particular, A Drzemczewski and J Gaughan, 'Implementing Strasbourg Court Judgments: The Parliamentary Dimension' (2010) *European Yearbook on Human Rights* (edited by W Benedek, W Karl, A Mihr and M Nowak) 247–58; and Drzemczewski (n 11).

benefited in the past and continues to benefit from the Parliamentary Assembly's and national parliaments' greater involvement'.[21] This involvement has taken the form of Resolutions and Recommendations (the latter addressed to the Committee of Ministers) made by the Assembly on the basis of systematic monitoring by the LAHR Committee.

Monitoring the implementation of Strasbourg Court judgments became a key focus of the LAHR Committee's work following the unanimous adoption by the Committee, on 27 June 2000, of the first report on the matter by Mr Erik Jurgens.[22] On the basis of this report, the Assembly adopted Resolution 1226 (2000), highlighting the importance of effective synergy between the Court, the Committee of Ministers and national authorities, and undertaking to play a larger role itself in supervising judgments of the Court.[23] Thereafter, the LAHR Committee was assigned open-ended terms of reference to continue its work in this area: under Resolution 1268 (2002), the Assembly asked it to pursue the exercise, instructing it 'to continue to update the record of the execution of judgments and to report to it when it considers appropriate'. This meant that the Committee was not bound by what is now rule 25.4 of the Assembly's Rules of Procedure, which provides that 'references to committee [to complete a report] shall lapse in two years', enabling the rapporteur[24] to work on the implementation of judgments of the European Court of Human Rights on an open-ended basis, facilitating a sustained dialogue with Member States. However, since 2012, this open-ended arrangement has come to an end. Reports on all topics are now subject to renewal, on a biannual basis, due to a recent streamlining of the Assembly's procedures.[25]

---

[21] Committee of Ministers Reply to Assembly Recommendation 1764 (2006) 'Implementation of the Judgments of the European Court of Human Rights', Doc 11230 of 2 April 2007, §1, available at: http://assembly.coe.int/nw/xml/XRef/X2H-Xref-ViewHTML.asp?FileID=11650&lang=EN.

[22] Assembly Doc 8808 of 12 July 2000 (prepared on the basis of a motion for a resolution on the execution of judgments of the Court and the monitoring of the case law of the European Court and Commission of Human Rights, Doc 7777 of 13 March 1997, presented by Mr Georges Clerfayt and others).

[23] Resolution 1268 (2002) 'Execution of Judgments of the European Court of Human Rights', text adopted on 28 September 2000. See also Recommendation 1477 (2000) and the reply from the Committee of Ministers, Doc 9311 (all texts available on the Assembly's website: www.assembly.coe.int/DefaultE.asp).

[24] To date, there have been three rapporteurs appointed, successively, to work on the implementation of decisions of the European Court of Human Rights: Mr Erik Jurgens (2000–2007), Mr Christos Pourgourides (2007–2012) and Mr Klaas de Vries (2012–).

[25] See Assembly Resolution 1822 (2011) on the Reform of the Parliamentary Assembly, passim, available at: www.assembly.coe.int/ASP/Doc/XrefViewPDF.asp?FileID=18009&Language=EN.

Since 2000, the Assembly has adopted seven reports[26] and resolutions[27] and six recommendations[28] on the subject of the implementation of judgments of the European Court of Human Rights. Between 2006 and 2010, the rapporteurs on this issue (Mr Erik Jurgens and Mr Christos Pourgourides) adopted a proactive approach, conducting in situ visits to States Parties with particularly problematic

[26] Reports on the execution/implementation of judgments of the European Court of Human Rights:
Doc 8808, 'Execution of Judgments of the European Court of Human Rights', available at:
http://assembly.coe.int/nw/xml/XRef/X2H-Xref-ViewHTML.asp?FileID=9013&lang=EN;
Doc 9307, 'Implementation of Decisions of the European Court of Human Rights', available at:
http://assembly.coe.int/nw/xml/XRef/X2H-Xref-ViewHTML.asp?FileID=9585&lang=EN;
Doc 9537, 'Implementation of Decisions of the European Court of Human Rights by Turkey', adopted 5 September 2002, available at:
www.assembly.coe.int/Main.asp?link=/Documents/WorkingDocs/Doc02/EDOC9537.htm;
Doc 10192, 'Implementation of Decisions of the European Court of Human Rights by Turkey', adopted on 1 June 2004, available at:
http://assembly.coe.int/nw/xml/XRef/X2H-Xref-ViewHTML.asp?FileID=10553&lang=EN;
Doc 10351, 'Implementation of Decisions of the European Court of Human Rights', adopted 21 October 2004, available at:
http://assembly.coe.int/nw/xml/XRef/X2H-Xref-ViewHTML.asp?FileID=10712&lang=EN;
Doc 11020, 'Implementation of Judgments of the European Court of Human Rights', adopted on 18 September 2006, available at:
http://assembly.coe.int/nw/xml/XRef/X2H-Xref-ViewHTML.asp?FileID=11344&lang=EN;
Doc 12455, 'Implementation of Judgments of the European Court of Human Rights', adopted on 20 December 2010, available at:
www.assembly.coe.int/ASP/Doc/XrefViewHTML.asp?FileID=12589&Language=EN.
[27] Resolutions on the execution/implementation of judgments of the European Court of Human Rights:
Resolution 1226 (2000), available at:
www.assembly.coe.int/Mainf.asp?link=/Documents/AdoptedText/ta00/ERES1226.htm;
Resolution 1268 (2002), available at:
www.assembly.coe.int/Mainf.asp?link=/Documents/AdoptedText/ta02/ERES1268.htm;
Resolution 1297 (2002), available at:
www.assembly.coe.int/Mainf.asp?link=/Documents/AdoptedText/ta02/ERES1297.htm;
Resolution 1381 (2004), available at:
www.assembly.coe.int/Mainf.asp?link=/Documents/AdoptedText/ta04/ERES1381.htm;
Resolution 1411 (2004) and Resolution 1516 (2006), available at:
www.assembly.coe.int/Mainf.asp?link=/Documents/AdoptedText/ta06/ERES1516.htm and http://assembly.coe.int/Mainf.asp?link=/Documents/AdoptedText/ta06/ERES1516.htm; Resolution 1787 (2011), available at: www.assembly.coe.int/ASP/Doc/XrefViewHTML.asp?FileID=17953&Language=EN.
[28] Recommendations on the execution/implementation of judgments of the European Court of Human Rights:
Recommendation 1477 (2000), available at:
www.assembly.coe.int/Mainf.asp?link=/Documents/AdoptedText/ta00/EREC1477.htm;
Recommendation 1546 (2002), available at:
www.assembly.coe.int/Mainf.asp?link=/Documents/AdoptedText/ta02/EREC1546.htm;
Recommendation 1576 (2002), available at:
www.assembly.coe.int/Mainf.asp?link=/Documents/AdoptedText/ta02/EREC1576.htm;
Recommendation 1684 (2004), available at:
www.assembly.coe.int/Mainf.asp?link=/Documents/AdoptedText/ta04/EREC1684.htm;
Recommendation 1764 (2006), available at:
www.assembly.coe.int/Mainf.asp?link=/Documents/AdoptedText/ta06/EREC1764.htm;
Recommendation 1955 (2011), available at:
www.assembly.coe.int/ASP/Doc/XrefViewHTML.asp?FileID=17954&Language=EN.

instances of non-implementation.[29] During these visits, the rapporteurs discussed the reasons for failure to execute the judgments with members of the national parliaments and government representatives, and underlined the urgent need to find solutions to the problems raised.[30] The aim of the visits was to see how, with the aid of parliamentarians in the relevant countries, the national authorities could be 'encouraged' to speed up the implementation of the reforms and measures needed for the execution of the judgments.

Following the appointment, in January 2012, of Mr Klaas de Vries (the Netherlands, SOC) as the third rapporteur on this subject, as well as consideration of the introductory memorandum on 'Ensuring the Viability of the Strasbourg Court: Structural Deficiencies in States Parties' by Mr Serhii Kivalov (Ukraine, EDG), the LAHR Committee agreed to change its working methods and to hold a series of hearings in Strasbourg with the heads of the 10 parliamentary delegations specifically identified in Mr Pourgourides' report.[31] These are states in which major structural problems have led to repeat violations (Bulgaria, Greece, Italy, the Republic of Moldova, Poland, Romania, the Russian Federation, Turkey and Ukraine), as well as delays in the full implementation of Court judgments (the UK). The final three hearings took place during the January 2013 PACE part-session.[32] During the April 2012 part-session, the LAHR Committee also decided to open these hearings to representatives of civil society. An important goal of these hearings is to provide adequate information to the LAHR Committee in terms of identifying those states which fail to comply with human rights obligations and to bring discussions concerning the (non-)execution of judgments into the public domain, including 'naming and shaming' (a phrase coined by Mr Jurgens) states which can be identified as 'persistent defaulters' in this respect.[33] Such publicity can often, in itself, be a formidable 'arm' at the disposal of parliamentarians.

---

[29] For the sixth report, Mr Jurgens visited five states: Italy, Turkey, Russia, Ukraine and the UK; see Doc 11020 'Implementation of Judgments of the European Court of Human Rights', available at: www.assembly.coe.int/ASP/Doc/XrefViewHTML.asp?FileID=11344&Language=EN; for the seventh report, Mr Pourgourides visited eight states: Bulgaria, Greece, Italy, the Republic of Moldova, Romania, the Russian Federation, Turkey and Ukraine; see Doc 12455 (n 26).

[30] The introduction of in situ visits was based on the conviction that many key points could be resolved through the active involvement of the Assembly in close cooperation with national parliaments, working through their national delegations. Interestingly, the Committee of Ministers has only recently, in an indirect fashion, started to have recourse to in situ supervision of the execution of judgments.

[31] Doc 12455 (n 26).

[32] Hearings were held with the heads of the Italian and Ukrainian delegations during the April 2012 part-session, with the heads of the Bulgarian and Russian delegations during the June 2012 part-session, and with the heads of the Moldovan, Polish and Romanian delegations during the October 2012 part-session. Hearings with the Greek, Turkish and UK delegations took place during the January 2013 part-session. See, in this connection, extracts from all these hearings issued in document AS//Jur (2013) 13 available at / http://www.assembly.coe.int/CommitteeDocs/2013/ajdoc13_2013.pdf

It should be noted, however, that Mr De Vries has now reverted to the system of in situ visits. For further information on this subject consult AS/Jur 'Committee documents and declaration (public)' available at: http://www.assembly.coe.int/Main.asp?link=/CommitteeDocs/ComDocMenuJurNewEN.htm

Mr de Vries intends to have his (8th) report adopted by the AS/Jur in June 2015.

[33] See Conclusions of the Chairperson, Mrs Herta Däubler-Gmelin of the hearing held in Paris on 16 December 2009, Doc AS/Jur (2010) 06 available at: www.assembly.coe.int/CommitteeDocs/2010/20100121_ajdoc06%202010.pdf.

In its Resolution 1787 (2011) on the 'Implementation of the Strasbourg Court's Judgments', the Assembly:

> [C]all[ed] upon the chairpersons of national parliamentary delegations—together, if need be with the competent ministers—of states in which in situ visits were undertaken to present the results achieved in solving substantial problems highlighted in this resolution.[34]

As foreseen by this Resolution, the (then) President of the Assembly, Mr Mevlüt Cavuşoğlu, sent letters to heads of national parliamentary delegations of the above-mentioned countries in April 2011, referring to the need for both the Assembly and national parliaments to take a more active role in supervising the execution of the Strasbourg Court's judgments, and requesting information within six months of the actions taken to implement Resolution 1787 (2011). 'Reminder' letters were sent in December 2011; however replies were received from only five states (Bulgaria, Italy, Poland, Romania and Ukraine).[35]

Subsequently, the present Rapporteur, Mr de Vries, has, with the agreement of the LAHR, pursued in situ visits to certain states which will probably be completed in the Spring of 2015. He then intends to present a draft report, for adoption by the Committee, in June 2015.

The Assembly's human rights work, and especially that of the LAHR Committee, is often undertaken in parallel but not necessarily in coordination with that being undertaken by the Organisation's intergovernmental structures, especially the latter's Steering Committee on Human Rights (the Comité directeur pour les droits de l'Homme (CDDH)). To a certain extent, this is understandable, bearing in mind the totally different nature of the work undertaken by the Assembly, a statutory organ of the Council of Europe, and that carried out by experts on the intergovernmental plane, tasked by the Committee of Ministers to carry out tasks of a technical nature.[36] That said, the Assembly's LAHR Secretariat does try to sit in, as an 'observer' (on behalf of the Assembly), on certain CDDH agenda items, but—due to its heavy workload—this is done sporadically. Parliamentarians (eg, those preparing reports on issues which are also on the CDDH's agenda) tend not to take part in this often cumbersome, highly specialized intergovernmental work. And when this has occurred, the results have not, unfortunately, been very positive, as can be illustrated by a relatively recent example. Regrettably, in its Recommendation (2008) 2 on 'Efficient Domestic Capacity for Rapid Execution of Judgments of the Strasbourg

---

[34] Resolution 1787 (2011) § 10.4, available at: www.assembly.coe.int/ASP/Doc/XrefViewPDF.asp?FileID=17953&Language=EN.

[35] Replies were received from Bulgaria and Italy after the LAHR Committee had held hearings with these two countries in April and June 2012, respectively. The Polish reply was received shortly before the October 2012 hearing. The failure of states to respond (promptly) to requests made by the Assembly has already occurred in the past with respect to the Assembly's involvement in the execution process. Resolution 1268 (2002), 'Implementation of Decisions of the European Court of Human Rights', noted (at § 8) that: 'The Assembly is now able to take stock of one year's experience in reviewing the execution of Court judgments. The situation is varied: five delegations failed to respond to the requests made of them within the deadlines they had been set. Of these five delegations, three replied later and two did not reply'; available at: www.assembly.coe.int/ASP/Doc/XrefViewPDF.asp?FileID=16972&Language=EN.

[36] For detailed information on work undertaken by the CDDH, consult the Steering Committee's portal, available at: www.coe.int/t/dghl/standardsetting/cddh/default_en.asp.

Court',[37] the Committee of Ministers (following the CDDH's proposal) did not heed a 'plea' which LAHR rapporteur Erik Jurgens had made before the CDDH, and recommended—against the strong objections of Mr Jurgens—only that national parliaments be informed 'as appropriate' of measures taken to execute Court judgments, rather than that parliaments be systematically informed of all such measures.[38]

Attitudes may have somewhat evolved in this respect. The recent recognition, in the Brighton Declaration, of the importance of the parliamentary dimension (in, inter alia, scrutinising the effectiveness of states' implementation of Court judgments and the utility of the Assembly's regular reports and debates on this subject) is likely to lead to more frequent interventions by parliamentarians before the Council's intergovernmental structures, be it before the Committee of Ministers (Ministers' Deputies) or the CDDH and vice versa.[39]

IV. ENHANCING THE ROLE OF NATIONAL PARLIAMENTS

> It is indeed important that national parliaments systematically check that draft legislation is compatible with the Convention, that they closely monitor the action taken to execute judgments against their States and that they ensure that changes to national legislation are in line with the measures recommended by the Court.[40]

Greater participation by national parliaments is critical to achieving the dual aims of enhancing the principle of subsidiarity and reducing the pressure on the Court. Such 'upstreaming', both in preventing violations from occurring and assisting the Committee of Ministers (and the Assembly) in supervising the execution of judgments, is a key tool for alleviating the workload of all of the Council institutions and embedding the Convention—and the Court's case law—on the domestic plane.

The recent Assembly Resolution 1823 (2011) on 'National Parliaments: Guarantors of Human Rights in Europe' underlined the key role that parliaments can (and indeed should) play as guarantors of human rights.[41] The Resolution urges

---

[37] CM/Rec (2008) 2, § 9, available at: www.wcd.coe.int/com.instranet.InstraServlet?Index=no&command=com.instranet.CmdBlobGet&InstranetImage=222907&SecMode=1&DocId=1212406&Usage=2.
[38] For background information about this unfortunate episode, see A Drzemczewski 'La nécessité d'impliquer d'avantage l'Assemblée parlementaire dans la surveillance des arrêts de la Cour' in *Les mutations de l'activité du Comité des ministres* (n 19) 144–46.
[39] For a recent overview of follow-up measures taken after the Brighton Conference, see LAHR Secretariat background memorandum, Doc AS/Jur (2012) 42, of 3 December 2012, available at: http://www.assembly.coe.int/CommitteeDocs/2012/ajdoc42_2012.pdf. See also draft report, adopted on 10 December 2014, by the LAHR, entitled 'The effectiveness of the European Convention on Human Rights: the Brighton Declaration and beyond' (rapporteur: Mr Yves Pozzo di Borgo), to be found on the Assembly's website within the 'working documents' rubric. This text is scheduled for discussion and adoption, by the PACE plenary, in April 2015.
[40] Opening Statement by Jean-Claude Mignon, President of the Parliamentary Assembly of the Council of Europe, at the Brighton Conference, 19 April 2012, available at: www.assembly.coe.int//Main.asp?link=http://assembly.coe.int/President/Mignon/Discours/2012/19042012_BrightonConferenceE.htm.
[41] Available at: www.assembly.coe.int/ASP/Doc/XrefViewHTML.asp?FileID=18011&Language=EN. See in particular § 2: '[The potential of national parliaments] needs to be further explored. They are key to the effective implementation of international human rights norms as national level and fulfil their duty to protect human rights through legislating (including the vetting of draft legislation), involvement in the ratification of international human rights treaties, holding the executive to account, liaising with national human rights institutions and fostering the creation of a pervasive human rights culture.'

parliaments to implement a set of basic principles for parliamentary supervision of international human rights standards, including the establishment of dedicated human rights committees whose remits should include, inter alia: (i) the systematic verification of the compatibility of draft legislation with international human rights obligations; (ii) the review of domestic implementation of Court judgments; and (iii) the initiation of legislative proposals and amendments to laws. Further, a key aim of Resolution 1822(2011) on 'Reform of the Parliamentary Assembly'[42] is to reinforce interaction between the Assembly and national parliaments, and to strengthen inter-parliamentary cooperation more generally.

A. The Role of National Parliaments in Supervising Execution of the Court's Judgments

Although, as outlined above, the LAHR Committee has identified for itself a valuable role in supervising the execution of judgments (not least by enhancing the democratic legitimacy of the process),[43] it has become increasingly difficult to monitor the huge volume of cases falling within the rapporteur's mandate[44]—hence the need to reinforce dialogue with national authorities.[45] An enhanced role for national parliaments is particularly appropriate since they may be able in specific instances, more effectively than either the Assembly or the Committee of Ministers, to identify the social or political problems underlying a violation and appreciate exactly what measures are required to prevent the recurrence of similar infringements. In this context, domestic parliamentary involvement, through the passing of remedying legislation, is particularly relevant to the resolution of systemic or structural problems identified by the Court.[46]

---

[42] Available at: assembly.coe.int/ASP/Doc/XrefViewPDF.asp?FileID=18009&Language=EN.

[43] According to Philip Leach: 'The work carried out by PACE in recent years has ensured, to a certain extent, a stronger public and democratic aspect to the [implementation] process'; Philip Leach, 'The Effectiveness of the Committee of Ministers in Supervising the Enforcement of Judgments of the European Court of Human Rights' [2006] *Public Law* 443, 455. See also Philip Leach, 'Opinion on Reform of the European Court of Human Rights' (2009) 6 *European Human Rights Law Review*, 725, 735.

[44] See Christos Pourgourides, 'Implementation of Judgments of the European Court of Human Rights' LAHR document AS/Jur (2009)36, declassified by the Committee on 11 September 2009, especially paras 1 to 7.

[45] See the comments of Mr Jean-Claude Mignon, Conclusions of the President of the Parliamentary Assembly, European Conference of Presidents of Parliament, 20–21 September 2012: 'It is vital for national and legislative bodies to give priority to this issue on their parliamentary agendas, so as to ensure systematic and effective monitoring, within all national parliaments, of the standards guaranteed by the Convention.' Available at: www.assembly.coe.int/Conferences/2012Strasbourg/Background/FutureECHRRoleE.pdf.

[46] As of 1 December 2014, there were 33,781 repetitive cases (identical cases deriving from the same underlying problem) pending before the Court. The issue of 'repetitive' or 'clone' cases is one of the biggest causes of the Court's overload; furthermore, the issue is of particular importance since such cases threaten the effectiveness of the whole Convention system: 'These cases raise issues which go to the effective operation of the rule of law and failure to resolve the underlying problems undermines the Council of Europe's mission of furthering democracy and the rule of law.' See Preliminary Opinion of the Court in preparation for the Brighton Conference, § 35, available at: www.coe.int/t/dgi/brighton-conference/Documents/Court-Preliminary-opinion_en.pdf.

Full and effective implementation at the domestic level can best be achieved through cooperation between all branches of the state (executive, legislature and judiciary),[47] in addition to sharing practices between states. This is particularly so with regard to ensuring the passage of legislation necessary to the implementation of general measures.[48] The need to ensure the active involvement of national parliaments in specific governmental initiatives is often highly desirable, as emphasised in Assembly Recommendation 1764 (2006)[49] and Resolutions 1516 (2006)[50] and 1787 (2011).[51] In this respect, the Committee of Ministers Recommendation (2008) 2 proposes that states designate a national co-coordinator to take overall control and supervision of all issues relating to the execution of judgments, with reference contacts in the relevant national authorities involved in the execution process.[52] In addition to the desirability of national coordinators, particular attention should be paid to the role of parliaments in scrutinising executive practice.[53]

To enable parliaments to effectively supervise the response of governments to an adverse decision of the Strasbourg Court, there must exist a procedure through which a parliament is promptly and systematically informed of such judgments and the measures implemented in the execution thereof. Despite the practical importance of such a mechanism, an assessment conducted by the Secretariat of the LAHR Committee revealed that such a procedure existed in a surprisingly small number of states.[54] In two recent reports, Christos Pourgourides identified the Netherlands, Germany and the UK as providing model mechanisms in

---

[47] See Recommendation 1955 (2011) 'Implementation of Judgments of the European Court of Human Rights', §§ 1.1 and 1.3, available at: www.assembly.coe.int/ASP/Doc/XrefViewPDF .asp?FileID=17954&Language=EN. See also Drzemczewski and Gaughan (n 20) 253, who note particularly that states with strong implementation records are regularly characterised by active involvement of parliamentary actors in the execution process.

[48] See Addendum I to the CDDH report of 12 December 2012, entitled 'CDDH Report on Measures Taken by the Member States to Implement Relevant Parts of the Interlaken and Izmir Declarations' Doc CDDH(2012) R 76, (and Addendum I thereto), available at: www.coe.int/t/dghl/standardsetting/cddh/ CDDH-DOCUMENTS/CDDH(2012)R76_E_final.pdf and www.coe.int/t/dghl/standardsetting/cddh/ CDDH-DOCUMENTS/CDDH(2012)R76_Addendum%20I_EN.pdf.

[49] Recommendation 1764 (2006), § 1.4: '[Recommends that the Committee of Ministers] induce member States to improve and where necessary to set up domestic mechanisms and procedures—both at the level of governments and of parliaments—to secure timely and effective implementation of the Court's judgments through co-ordinated action of all national actors concerned and with the necessary support at the highest political level'.

[50] Resolution 1516 (2006), § 22.2: 'Calls upon the member States to set up, either through legislation or otherwise, domestic mechanisms for the rapid implementation of the Court's judgments, and that a decision-making body at the highest political level within the government take full responsibility for and co-ordinate all aspects of the domestic implementation process'.

[51] Resolution 1787 (2011), §§ 10.1 and 10.2.

[52] CM/Rec (2008) 2 (n 37) § 1.

[53] Parliament's power of maintaining the government, which must regularly come before parliament in order to obtain support for policies, combined with its representative function, dictates that parliament subjects executive practice to substantial scrutiny: see Adam Tomkins, *Public Law* (Oxford, Oxford University Press, 2003) 92. See also Drzemczewski and Gaughan (n 20) 247–58, passim.

[54] See the LAHR Committee Secretariat's 'Background Document: The Role of National Parliaments in Verifying State Obligations to Comply with the European Convention on Human Rights, Including Strasbourg Court Judgments: An Overview' in a selection of texts issued in document AS/Jur (2008) 32 rev, at § 11.

this respect.[55] In the Netherlands and Germany, an annual report is presented to Parliament concerning Strasbourg Court judgments and their domestic implementation. The reports contain an overview of the measures adopted in response to the judgments, and also contain reference to judgments against other States Parties which could have a direct or indirect effect on the Dutch or German legal system (as the case may be).[56] This (relatively new) practice of reporting on judgments against other states is particularly welcome, as it recognises and enforces the interpretative authority (*res interpretata*) of Court judgments. Where states take note of, and react to, Court proceedings to which they are not parties, this can help prevent new human rights violations, which might otherwise have given rise to a large number of new applications to the Court.[57]

---

[55] Doc 12455, § 198; and Assembly Doc 12636, 'National Parliaments: Guarantors of Human Rights', §§ 66–77, available at: www.assembly.coe.int/ASP/Doc/XrefViewPDF.asp?FileID=12866&Language=EN.
See also, in this connection, minutes from a hearing that the LAHR held on Parliamentary Scrutiny of ECHR Standards in Paris on 16 November 2009, Doc AS/Jur (2010) 7 (available on the Committee's website); and Martin Kuijer, 'De betekenis van het Europees verdrag voor de rechten van de mens voor de nationale wetgever' ['The Significance of the ECHR for the National Legislator'], in HR Schouter (ed), *Wetgever en constitutie [The Legislator and the Constitution]*, Proceedings of the Symposium of the Netherlands Association on Legislation and Legislative Policy, 23 April 2009, Nijmegen, 44–86.

[56] In the Netherlands, the report is produced by the Minister of Foreign Affairs, also on behalf of the Minister of Justice. Implementation measures taken in response to adverse judgments have been included since 2006. In Germany, the Ministry of Justice provides annual written reports to Parliament. Implementation measures have been included since 2007, as a direct result of Assembly Resolution 1516 (2006) and Recommendation 1764 (2006). Reports on the Court's case law concerning states other than Germany have been produced since 2010, and are also published on the Ministry of Justice's website. In the UK it is produced by the Ministry of Justice and does not include consideration of case law against other states.

[57] The *res interpretata* authority of the Court results from Arts 1, 19 and 32 of the Convention: it follows from these that whilst Court judgments do not have *erga omnes* effect, national legislators and courts have a duty to take into account the Convention as interpreted by the Court even in judgments concerning violations that have occurred in other countries. The Brighton Declaration calls on States Parties to '[enable and encourage] national courts and tribunals to take into account the relevant principles of the Convention, *having regard to the case law of the Court*' (emphasis added): see Brighton Declaration, § A 9 c) iv). The importance of enforcing the *res interpretata* authority of Court judgments has been emphasised by Mr Pourgourides and Mrs Herta Däubler-Gmelin (see 'The Future of the Strasbourg Court and Enforcement of ECHR Standards: Reflections on the Interlaken Process', Doc AS/Jur (2010) 06, available at: www.assembly.coe.int/CommitteeDocs/2010/20100121_ajdoc06%202010. pdf) and Ms Marie Bemelmans-Videc (see 'Guaranteeing the Authority and Effectiveness of the European Convention on Human Rights', Doc 12811 of 3 January at §§ 34–39, available at: www.assembly.coe. int/ASP/Doc/XrefViewPDF.asp?FileID=12914&Language=EN). In Recommendation 1991 (2012), the Assembly urged the Committee of Ministers 'to address a recommendation to the member States calling on them to reinforce without delay, by legislative, judicial or other means, the interpretative authority (*res interpretata*) of the judgments of the European Court of Human Rights'. However, the Committee of Ministers' Reply was less than forthcoming, citing the responsibility of the States Parties to guarantee the application and implementation of the Convention under the Interlaken Action Plan and stating that 'the Brighton Declaration contains a number of provisions setting out the measures which would enable member States to apply in practice the principle of the interpretative authority of the Court's judgments'. See Assembly Recommendation 1991 (2012) 'Guaranteeing the Authority and Effectiveness of the ECHR', § 2, available at: www.assembly.coe.int/ASP/Doc/XrefViewHTML.asp?FileID=18059&Language=EN. See also CM Reply to Recommendation 1991 (2012), adopted on 12 September 2012, available at: www. wcd.coe.int/ViewDoc.jsp?id=1974685&Site=CM&BackColorInternet=C3C3C3&BackColorIntranet =EDB021&BackColorLogged=F5D383. See also, on this subject, A Drzemczewski, 'Quelques réflexions sur l'autorité de la chose interprétée par la Cour de Strasbourg' in *La conscience des droits. Mélanges en honneur de Jean-Paul Costa* (2011), 243–47.

In respect of the UK, the Joint Committee on Human Rights (JCHR) until 2010 produced regular reports which monitored the Government's response to adverse Strasbourg Court judgments, including a critical assessment of the adequacy of remedial measures taken in terms of their compatibility with the Convention. While the JCHR is currently one of only a handful of parliamentary bodies to have assumed the role of verifying the compatibility of draft legislation with the Convention, this practice should be seen as an essential aspect of parliamentary supervision of implementation of Court judgments, particularly if similar violations are to be prevented in the future.[58]

Developments in this area are still new: enhancing national parliamentary involvement in the implementation of judgments requires amending existing practices and working methods, and greater cooperation between all the institutions involved. Good practice should include governments providing parliaments with regular or annual reports on the implementation of judgments and with copies of action plans which governments are required to submit to the Committee of Ministers,[59] and including the possibility of parliaments being copied-in on all subsequent relevant correspondence with the Committee of Ministers concerning such matters. In addition, a government could be required to inform parliament whenever it intends to intervene as a third party in cases concerning other states (giving reasons for the intervention and providing the substance of its arguments).[60]

Whilst this will inevitably take time, a certain amount of 'pressure' is being placed on members of the Assembly in this respect: Mr Pourgourides has even suggested that 'the Assembly ought to consider suspending the voting rights of national delegations when their parliaments do not seriously exercise parliamentary control over the executive in cases of non-implementation of judgments of the Court'.[61] One of the main goals of the LAHR's current rapporteur, Mr Klaas de Vries, is to help other MPs enhance their national parliaments' role in executing Court judgments, and the hearings held in Strasbourg (referred to above) have identified some promising developments in this respect. In Romania, a sub-committee of the Legal Affairs Committee cooperates with the Government Agent's department in the Ministry of Foreign Affairs, focusing on non-executed Court judgments and the

---

[58] At this juncture, particular emphasis is placed on the verification of draft legislation introduced in response to an adverse finding of the Court. The wider issue of monitoring the compatibility of all domestic law and practice with the Convention is referred to below.

[59] Execution supervision based on action plans with timetables was launched in 2004 and the Committee of Ministers' current working methods are based on states providing such action plans in all cases, at the latest within six months of the date of judgment. The timetable presented in the action plan is normally the starting point for discussions regarding timely execution; see CM/Inf/DH (2012) 41, 'Tools Available to the Committee of Ministers to Supervise the Execution of Judgments and Possible Developments of These'.

[60] See Report of the UK Parliament's Joint Committee on Human Rights 2010, 'Enhancing Parliament's Role in Relation to Human Rights Judgments', available at: www.publications.parliament.uk/pa/jt200910/jtselect/jtrights/85/85.pdf. See also, in this connection, Parliamentary Assembly document PPSD (2014) 22 'The role of parliaments in implementing ECHR standards: overview of existing structures and mechanisms', available at: http://www.assembly.coe.int/CommitteeDocs/2014/E-PPSD14-22%20BackgroundECHRstandards.pdf.

[61] Doc 12455, § 213.

general measures to be taken concerning implementation. This sub-committee is also involved in drafting amendments to existing legislation and has elaborated a draft law on the study of the compatibility of national legal provisions with human rights standards.[62] Italy has a joint permanent committee—of both the legislative and executive branches—responsible for informing Parliament about the requirements of the Convention as interpreted by the Court and advising on the need for the adoption or amendment of specific laws in order to comply with the Court's judgments. In Poland, in February 2014, the Justice and Human Rights and the Foreign Affairs Committee of the Sejm (the lower house) jointly established a permanent Sub-Committee on the execution of judgments of the European Court of Human Rights.[63] Reference should also be made to the Ukrainian draft law 'On the Execution of Judgments and Implementation of Practice of the European Court of Human Rights', sponsored by Mr Holovaty, a former chairperson of the LAHR Committee.[64] This amendment to the Ukrainian Law of 2006 will provide a legal basis for regular and more rigorous parliamentary oversight in line with the Council of Europe's standards; however, it is understood that until now scant, if any, progress has been made regarding this proposal.

Much still remains to be done in order to realise the recommendations made in Resolution 1823 (2011). A point of particular importance to stress is the need for parliaments to possess an efficient 'legal' service—with specific human rights competence—to provide expertise and back-up for busy parliamentarians.[65] In this regard, inspiration can be drawn from the examples of Austria, where the previous head of the Parliament's legal services was a former Government Agent before the Strasbourg Court, and the UK, where the secretariat to the JCHR includes an independent expert (Legal Adviser) in human rights law. Ensuring that parliamentarians have such expertise at their disposal is crucial in enabling them to contribute fully to this process, and furthermore in legitimising this contribution.[66]

---

[62] Law No 29/2011 was adopted by the Romanian Parliament in March 2011. According to the Law, legislative initiatives coming from the Government must be submitted to the Parliament together with a study on the compatibility of the proposed legislation with fundamental rights and freedoms. The law also provides that within three months of the date of an adverse Court judgment, the Government must submit to Parliament the draft law(s) implementing any modifications necessitated by the judgment.

[63] See Assembly document PPSD (2014) 22 (n 60), § 8. See also, in this regard, 'Efficient Enforcement of Judgments of the ECtHR in Poland and in Hungary: A Road Towards Better Institutions and Better Law', A Bodnar and R Uitz, Ernst & Young, *Better Government Programme* Warsaw-Budapest, 2011.

[64] See Donald and Leach, ch 4 in this volume.

[65] The 'Basic Principles for Parliamentary Supervision of International Human Rights Standards' set out in the Resolution include the requirements that human rights training be provided for parliamentarians and their staff, and that human rights committees or analogous structures have access to independent expertise in human rights law.

[66] A number of CDDH members—who are also Government Agents before the Court—have expressed informally to one of the co-authors of this contribution, their reservations as to the utility of affording a greater role to parliaments on the grounds that parliamentarians are likely to be ill-informed, that they can unnecessarily complicate matters (often for short-term politically motivated extraneous reasons), in addition to their having little, if any, experience in the field of human rights and in the implementation of Court judgments. Our answer to this is simple: this criticism in effect reinforces the argument that it is imperative to establish, where they do not exist, appropriate parliamentary structures to cater for this (purported) lack of parliamentary expertise, as can be seen from the experience in Germany, the

In this context, note can be taken of the Assembly's recently created 'Parliamentary Project Support Division' whose role is to increase the visibility and impact of the Assembly's work in national parliaments. In respect of the LAHR Committee, the Support Division has put forward two interrelated priorities: the establishment, in national parliaments, of mechanisms and structures for the supervision of the execution of Strasbourg Court judgments, and improving parliamentary staff's knowledge and understanding of the Convention, as interpreted by the Court. The pursuit of these priorities is now being implemented. The Assembly has held three seminars on this subject for parliamentarians, in co-operation with the Parliament of the United Kingdom in October 2013, the Sejm and the Senate of the Republic of Poland in February 2014 and the Spanish Parliament in Madrid on 31 October 2014. In parallel, capacity building seminars have been organised in Strasbourg for staff of parliaments, one in September 2013 and two in 2014 (January and September) creating a parliamentary network of about 50 lawyers from 26 member states of the Council of Europe.[67] Work on this subject will be pursued in 2015.

B. The Role of National Parliaments in *Ex Ante* Scrutiny and Fostering a Human Rights Culture at the Domestic Level

The work of the Assembly, and of national parliaments, should not be limited to assisting in the supervision of Court judgments: more should be made of the potential of national parliaments to help embed human rights policy at the domestic level, thereby stemming the flow of applications to the Court and enhancing the principle of subsidiarity. The Committee of Ministers has recommended that Member States 'ensure that there are appropriate and effective mechanisms for systematically verifying the compatibility of draft laws with the Convention in the light of the case-law of the Court'.[68] Likewise, Resolution 1726 (2010) of the Assembly:

> [S]tresses the key role national parliaments can play in stemming the flood of applications submerging the Court by, for instance, carefully examining whether (draft) legislation is compatible with the Convention's requirements.[69]

This applies irrespective of whether the bill has been introduced in response to an adverse judgment of the Court: in all circumstances, *ex ante* scrutiny of draft legislation is a principal preventative measure in seeking to avoid unjustified infringement

---

Netherlands and the UK, tied to the need for parliaments to possess an efficient legal service with specific ECHR competence.

[67] For more information on this subject see Parliamentary Assembly document PPSD (2014) 07 rev 4, and Addendum thereto, entitled 'The role of Parliaments in implementing ECHR standards'.

[68] Recommendation Rec (2004) 5 of the Committee of Ministers to Member States on the 'Verification of the Compatibility of Draft Laws, Existing Laws and Administrative Practice with the Standards Laid Down in the European Convention on Human Rights', adopted by the Committee of Ministers on 12 May 2004 at its 114th Session, available at: www.wcd.coe.int/ViewDoc.jsp?id=743297&Site=CM&Bac kColorInternet=C3C3C3&BackColorIntranet=EDB021&BackColorLogged=F5D383.

[69] Assembly Resolution 1726 (2010) 'Effective Implementation of the European Convention on Human Rights: The Interlaken Process', available at: www.assembly.coe.int/ASP/Doc/XrefViewHTML. asp?FileID=17849&Language=EN.

of the Convention guarantees. Here again, it is worth stressing the importance of independent legal expertise to enable parliaments to carry out this task. According to Mr Pougourides, the former Chairperson of the LAHR, 'the UK provides a model mechanism for parliamentary verification of the compliance of draft legislation with the Convention', whereby the government minister responsible for a bill is required to state either that it is compatible with the Convention, or that he or she wishes to proceed with the bill, notwithstanding its incompatibility, and the reasons for that view are then rigorously scrutinised by the JCHR.[70] However, it is worth noting that even where such *ex ante* legislative scrutiny does exist, this mechanism could be further improved by, for example, requiring the minister to state the reasons why the bill is believed to be compatible with Convention standards. Where states engage in *ex ante* scrutiny and make greater efforts to incorporate Convention standards in their domestic systems, this will necessarily enhance the principle of subsidiarity. The importance of doing so should not be understated: it is indeed a key principle which lies at the heart of the Convention system and on which the future of the system may ultimately rest. Recent case law of the Court makes clear that laws which have undergone such scrutiny stand a better chance of withstanding scrutiny by the Court.

V. OVERALL ASSESSMENT

Through the work of the LAHR Committee, the Assembly has carved for itself a prominent role in ensuring the effective implementation of Convention standards within the Council of Europe. The ever-increasing involvement of the Assembly has resulted from two important realisations: first, that reform of the Court alone will not reduce the number of potentially well-founded applications made to it; and, second, that full and prompt compliance with Court judgments can in many instances be achieved through the involvement of both the Committee of Ministers and the Assembly in the follow-up implementation process. As Erik Jurgens has stated:

> [T]he Assembly should continue, and indeed have a more prominent role, in promoting compliance with the Court's judgments. By helping to ensure that member states rapidly comply with judgments, it provides tangible assistance to victims of human rights violations. It also helps the Committee of Ministers to discharge more speedily and effectively its responsibilities in this respect. Lengthy compliance procedures and, still worse, the non-compliance with judgments over long periods of time, affect and undermine the credibility of both the ECHR's system and the Council of Europe. By contrast, rapid compliance with judgments, especially those requiring legislative action, to which the Assembly is best placed to contribute, helps the Strasbourg Court cope with the avalanche of applications by attacking the root causes for repetitive applications.[71]

---

[70] The duty to make this declaration results from s 19 of the Human Rights Act 1998, which has been in force since 2000.

[71] Doc AS/Jur (2005)35, 'Implementation of Judgments of the European Court of Human Rights: Introductory Memorandum' (Rapporteur Mr Erik Jurgens).

However, this contribution has sought to emphasise that the work of the Assembly must go hand in hand with increased parliamentary action on the domestic plane, in respect of which three interrelated issues require further reflection: (i) the need for national parliamentary initiatives; (ii) the establishment of some form of 'general principles' on the role of parliaments in the protection of human rights; and (iii) the importance of an understanding of the wider context in which increased parliamentary involvement is desirable. In regard to the first of these, the dual mandate of members of the Assembly provides a unique opportunity to ensure that standards and practices developed at the European level are put into practice domestically. Developments in national systems should seek to ensure an institutionalisation of parliamentary involvement, primarily through the establishment of formal parliamentary structures tasked with verifying the compatibility of all draft legislation with human rights standards, as well as playing an instrumental role in the implementation of Court judgments. In order to function effectively, such structures must be systematically informed of developments in the human rights sphere (crucially, of judgments rendered against their own and other states) and be supported by an efficient legal service that is able to give expert advice on human rights and related legal questions.

As to the second issue, the 'Draft Principles and Guidelines on the Role of Parliaments in the Protection and Realisation of the Rule of Law and Human Rights'[72] incorporate many of the practices already implemented within the Parliamentary Assembly of the Council of Europe, and it would appear useful to work towards an internationally agreed set of such principles endorsed by parliaments across the globe. It is important to bear in mind, however, that one of the Assembly's main functions with respect to the ECHR—the need to ensure the implementation of Strasbourg Court judgments—is one which is not exercised by other parliamentary bodies. Hence, further reflection would be needed on how the principles, as currently drafted, could be amended so as to accommodate our specific Convention system, in particular the complex relationship between the Court, the Council of Europe's statutory bodies (the Committee of Ministers and the Assembly) and national parliaments.

Finally, it is important to stress that the increased involvement of national parliaments will not only result in a richer application of the principle of subsidiarity, but will also allow democratically elected parliamentarians to play a more prominent role in holding their national executive bodies to account.[73] An outstanding example of this is the initiative taken by the Swiss Parliament in 2010 to 'force' the Swiss Government to notify the UN Security Council that if individuals who had been blacklisted for alleged involvement in terrorist activities by the Security Council were not provided—within a three-year period—adequate fair trial protection

---

[72] See Appendix to this volume.

[73] See David Feldman, 'Can and Should Parliament Protect Human Rights?' (2004) 10(4) *European Public Law* 635, at p 651: 'The main contribution of Parliament to the process of protecting rights and creating a culture of human rights, apart from legislation, consists of using its influence and its scrutiny powers to keep human rights standards at the forefront of the minds of ministers and departments, regulators, and other public authorities. In this way Parliament can influence and encourage (or discourage) developments.'

conforming with Articles 6 and 13 of the Convention, the Swiss authorities should no longer apply the relevant sanctions imposed by the Security Council.[74] This was an initiative spearheaded by a Swiss senator, Dick Marty, a former distinguished member of the Assembly (and former Chairperson of the LAHR).[75] By taking this kind of concrete action in the implementation of their parliamentary mandates, parliaments hold a key role in guaranteeing the *effective* protection of human rights. In so doing, they create an expectation that the government must be held fully accountable for its actions and that any actions taken must be justified from a Convention perspective.

[74] For more details, see LAHR Committee document AS/Jur/Inf (2010) 05, in which information is provided on Mr Marty's unsuccessful request, on behalf of the LAHR, to make a Third Party Intervention before the European Court of Human Rights in the case of *Nada v Switzerland*, available at: www.assembly.coe.int/CommitteeDocs/2010/07122010_blacklists.pdf. See also the Grand Chamber judgment of 12 December 2012 in this case (*Nada v Switzerland* [2012] ECHR 1691), available at: www.coe.echr.int, and in particular the separate opinion of Judge Malinverni.

[75] For an account of the key role played by the Assembly in questioning the fairness of such black-listing by the United Nations Security Council and the European Union, see the LAHR report on this subject (Rapporteur Mr D Marty), Doc 11454) and Addendum, available at: www.assembly.coe.int/ASP/Doc/XrefDocListing_E.asp, and Resolution 1597 (2008) and Recommendation 1824 (2008), both available at: www.assembly.coe.int/Main.asp?link=/Documents/AdoptedText/ta08/ERES1597.htm and www.assembly.coe.int/Main.asp?link=/Documents/AdoptedText/ta08/EREC1824.htm.

16

The Work of the Inter-Parliamentary Union

INGEBORG SCHWARZ

I. FROM 1898 TO 2013: A BRIEF OVERVIEW

AS AN ORGANISATION founded in 1898 by the French and British Members of Parliament (MPs) Frédéric Passy and Randal Cremer to promote peace through the arbitration of conflicts, the Inter-Parliamentary Union (IPU) was bound to engage in promoting and protecting human rights. While questions of democracy and rights issues were from time to time raised in the early years of the organisation, only after the Second World War, the creation of the United Nations (UN), and the development of international human rights norms and standards based on the Universal Declaration of Human Rights did the IPU start to develop first a programme to establish firmly the institution of parliament as such and subsequently a programme to defend and promote human rights.

In particular, it was the painful experience of the military coups in Latin America in the 1970s, the ensuing dissolution of parliaments and the persecution, assassination, torture and forced disappearance of many of their members that led the IPU to establish a human rights programme. It was initially designed to defend the fundamental rights of parliamentarians and took the form of a special body, namely the Committee on the Human Rights of Parliamentarians (CHRP). The Committee started its work in 1976 and gave rise to ever-broadening and intensifying human rights activities of the IPU. Most importantly, its work and the increasing level of human rights awareness of MPs led, in 1992, to the inclusion of human rights in the Statutes of the IPU, which since then state that one of its fundamental objectives shall be to 'contribute to the defence and promotion of human rights, which are universal in scope, and respect for which is an essential factor of parliamentary democracy and development'.

Today, human rights are mainstreamed into all IPU programmes, in particular the programme on the promotion of women in politics, which has a strong human rights component and cooperates closely with the Committee monitoring the Convention on the Elimination of All Forms of Discrimination against Women (see chapter III.B.iii.a). Moreover, long-term projects and campaigns deal with particular human rights issues, namely, violence against women and the fight against AIDS (see also under III.B.v). A three-year project on the fight against child trafficking and labour conducted in the Economic Community of West African States (ECOWAS) region concluded in June 2012 with a commitment of the ECOWAS Parliament to adopt a law to be applied by the states of the region providing for the punishment of child traffickers and for measures to take care of exploited children. Other previous projects relevant to human rights concerned the role of parliaments in reconciliation processes, parliamentary oversight of the security sector, the rights of persons with disabilities and the representation of minorities and indigenous peoples in parliaments.

Apart from the CHRP, human rights are also reflected in the IPU's structure. The IPU has a Standing Committee on Democracy and Human Rights, which prepares reports and resolutions on human rights issues to be debated and adopted at its six-monthly General Assemblies. There is now not a single Assembly without human rights issues on its agenda.

II. THE COMMITTEE ON THE HUMAN RIGHTS OF PARLIAMENTARIANS: ORIGIN OF THE IPU'S HUMAN RIGHTS PROGRAMME

The Committee is to a large extent the backbone of the IPU's Human Rights Programme as its work and experience has inspired and still inspires the general human rights programme of the IPU. It is therefore worth expanding briefly on the functioning and work of this unique body.

As indicated above, the Committee's mandate is to examine cases of human rights violations affecting MPs that are brought to its attention. This has nothing to do with the defence of corporate interests, but everything to do with the fact that if MPs are to promote and protect the human rights of the people they represent, they must in the first place enjoy their own fundamental rights, most particularly freedom of expression. The Committee is composed of ten MPs representing the different geopolitical regions of the world, elected by the IPU's plenary governing body, the Governing Council and serving a five-year term. As of 2013, the Committee meets three times a year (instead of four, which was the case previously). Although its procedure is essentially written, the Committee may conduct on-site missions and hear representatives of all parties to a case, including if possible the alleged victims themselves. On-site missions and hearings enable it to gain considerable insight into how human rights are addressed in the country concerned in general and at the parliamentary level in particular. On the basis of all the information and documents it gathers from the parties concerned and others, in particular human rights non-governmental organisations (NGOs) such as Amnesty International, the Committee drafts a report and adopts decisions. In the decisions, apart from asking case-related questions, it makes recommendations and recalls human rights obligations of the states concerned, in addition to relevant national and supranational jurisprudence, concluding observations of human rights treaty bodies and recommendations of UN special procedures. Through Committee decisions, MPs more often than not become aware of the existence of pronouncements of international and regional human rights mechanisms or supranational courts regarding the human rights situation or a human rights case in their country. The Committee's main means of pressure is the submission of a case to the Governing Council, which opens it up to the general public and the media. This often leads to a satisfactory settlement, such as the release of imprisoned parliamentarians. The Committee examines cases concerning an average of some 150 MPs in some 20 countries worldwide.

The issues confronting the Committee relate most frequently to freedom of expression and association, impunity, arbitrary detention, torture and fair trial concerns. Other problems touch more particularly on specific parliamentary issues, which nevertheless have significant effects on the fundamental rights of the parliamentarian concerned and sometimes also on their electorate, such as loss of the parliamentary mandate, party discipline and parliamentary immunity. The Committee has developed an extensive 'jurisprudence' on these issues and initiated a study on parliamentary immunity and how political parties influence the parliamentary mandates of their members.

III. DEVELOPMENT AND MAIN CONTENT OF THE HUMAN RIGHTS PROGRAMME

A. Finding a Lack of Human Rights Competence in Parliaments

The Committee's experience has revealed that parliamentarians, including parliamentary authorities, very often possess only a vague idea of what human rights are and therefore fail to use their specific powers to promote and protect human rights. In the Committee's early years, it also appeared that human rights were almost non-existent in parliamentary structures. The Committee has furthermore noted that all too often, parliamentarians are unaware of the human rights treaties their parliaments have ratified and still less of the obligations that their states have accepted as parties to those treaties. As a result, they cannot monitor their governments in this respect, are not involved in the various human rights reporting processes, are not included in delegations which report to the treaty-monitoring bodies and, most importantly, are not informed of the concluding observations arising from the reporting process. They are generally also unaware of the Special Procedures and their work.

If one considers that the great majority of states have ratified the International Covenant on Civil and Political Rights (ICCPR) and the International Covenant on Economic, Social and Cultural Rights (ICESCR) in addition to other core human rights treaties and that the majority of concluding observations and recommendations of Special Procedures require parliamentary action, it becomes clear that the absence of parliaments in this process is bound to harm not only the promotion and protection of human rights in the country concerned, but also the effectiveness of the international human rights monitoring mechanisms. The same applies to the regional human rights mechanisms.

The reasons for such parliamentary absence in this process are manifold: on the one hand, such absence is more often than not due to sometimes grave structural and economic problems and to a lack of financial resources, expertise and information; and, on the other hand, it is the lack of political will, the role of political parties, in particular, strict party discipline preventing MPs from criticising their party colleagues in government, thus creating obedient parliamentary majorities, and more generally the lack of independence of parliaments from governments which hinder parliaments in effectively serving as guardians of human rights.

In its Human Rights Programme, the IPU has pledged to pursue the goal of addressing essentially the lack of expertise and information to improve the capacity and competence of parliaments and their members in the field of human rights. To achieve this, it has focused on the parliamentary committee system by promoting the formation of specialised human rights committees, on capacity-building of their members and parliamentarians in general, and the role of parliaments in international and regional human rights mechanisms.

B. Initiatives and Activities to Build and Strengthen Parliamentary Human Rights Capacity and Competence

i. Human Rights in the Structure of Parliament

Building on the CHRP's experience and findings, the IPU decided to first look at the institutional/structural side. How are human rights integrated into the structure and work of parliaments? In particular, is there a specific body to take care of human rights matters? While human rights are a cross-cutting issue and should therefore be taken into consideration by all parliamentary committees, it was felt that the existence of a specialised human rights committee would make human rights visible in the parliamentary structure itself, create a human rights 'competence centre' within parliaments, and facilitate the mainstreaming of human rights into parliamentary work in general. In short, it would facilitate parliamentary ownership of human rights. On the occasion of its 1989 Centenary Conference in London, the IPU therefore encouraged parliaments to set up specific bodies to promote and protect human rights.

The IPU has carried out several activities to follow up on this recommendation. The first was dedicated to establishing the 'state of the art' by gathering data on existing parliamentary human rights bodies. In 1990, the IPU thus published the first World Directory on Parliamentary Human Rights Bodies. The Directory was intended as an information tool for all human rights actors, encouraging them to cooperate with such bodies and create partnerships, and to serve parliamentary human rights committees themselves by facilitating networking among them. The Directory, which is updated at regular intervals, is now available online.[1] In 1990, there were 44 parliamentary bodies with an explicit human rights mandate. By 2004, the number had risen to 164 and, as the latest IPU survey (2012/13) shows, today most parliaments have a committee with human rights in its remit. In addition, the number of committees dealing with specific human rights issues, such as children's rights, minority rights and in particular gender equality, has also risen considerably over the last 10 years.

---

[1] www.ipu.org/parline-e/instanceadvanced.asp.

ii. Strengthening the Human Rights Competence of MPs

When the first edition of the Directory was published, it was suggested that the IPU should organise a meeting to allow members of human rights committees to exchange ideas among themselves and with international human rights experts. The first IPU event bringing together MPs with a particular interest in human rights, but not necessarily members of human rights committees, was a symposium entitled 'Parliament: Guardian of Human Rights', held in 1993 shortly before the Vienna World Conference on Human Rights. It was the first time that a global organisation focused on the subject. The symposium highlighted a number of issues that have since inspired the IPU's Human Rights Programme, in particular concerning the role of parliaments with regard to international human rights mechanisms.[2]

The first capacity-building events for members of parliamentary human rights committees started in 2004. The aim of these events, which were all jointly organised with the Office of the High Commissioner for Human Rights (OHCHR) and other competent organisations, was to familiarise members of such bodies with international human rights standards and to permit an exchange of views with NGOs, human rights experts, members of national human rights institutions and among members themselves, thus facilitating networking. Issues chosen by parliaments were freedom of expression, the right to a fair trial, the human rights aspects of migration and, most recently, on the occasion of the sixtieth anniversary of the Universal Declaration of Human Rights, the major human rights questions marking the final years of the twentieth century.

One of the results of these seminars was the publication of the joint IPU-OHCHR *Human Rights Handbook for Parliamentarians* in 2005. In addition to describing general human rights principles, the international and regional human rights framework and its functioning, and the core content of the human rights enshrined in the Universal Declaration of Human Rights, the Handbook advises parliamentarians on action they can and should take in the field of human rights. An updated edition of the Handbook is being prepared.

Other human rights publications designed for MPs address, among other matters, the issues of children's rights, child labour and child trafficking, the CEDAW Convention and its Optional Protocol, HIV/AIDS, law and human rights and the Convention on the Rights of Persons with Disabilities.[3]

iii. Involving Parliaments in International Human Rights Monitoring Mechanisms

As stated earlier, parliaments are key players in international human rights monitoring processes since they are concerned by between 60 and 70 per cent of the recommendations made by the UN mechanisms, including the Universal Periodic Review (UPR). Their absence from such processes therefore greatly harms the entire human

---

[2] The proceedings of the symposium may be found in 'Parliament: Guardian of Human Rights', Reports and Documents No 21, 1993, available at: www.ipu.org/english/surv95.htm#symposium.
[3] For a full list of handbooks, see: www.ipu.org/english/handbks.htm.

rights monitoring system. The Human Rights Programme has thus increasingly focused on the role and involvement of parliaments in those mechanisms. Activities mainly concern the treaty-monitoring bodies and the UPR process.

a. Treaty Bodies and Parliaments

Aligning legislation and governmental action with international norms, standards and recommendations of monitoring mechanisms has been a longstanding concern of the IPU. A number of resolutions and recommendations adopted by IPU Assemblies or specialised conferences, such as the 1993 Symposium on 'Parliament: Guardian of Human Rights' or the 1998 resolution on 'Strong action by national parliaments in the year of the fiftieth anniversary of the Universal Declaration of Human Rights to ensure the promotion and protection of all human rights in this twenty-first century', stressed the responsibility of parliaments in ensuring the implementation of international and regional human rights treaties and compliance with the recommendations of treaty-monitoring bodies.

Most of the work done in this respect was placed in the context of capacity-building seminars at the international or regional levels with little possibility of intervening in respect of individual parliaments. Thanks to the funding of the UN Democracy Fund, in 2008 the IPU was able to embark on work with individual parliaments and to start a two-year pilot project, the 'Treaty Body Project'. This project targeted parliaments in francophone Africa. In each of the parliaments of the region which consented to participate in the project (Togo, Mauritania, Mali, the Republic of Congo and Gabon), the ratification and reporting status, together with the implementation status of concluding observations, was examined. The parliament then worked out a short-term strategy to address some of the more urgent issues and a medium- to long-term strategy was developed to ensure the future involvement of the parliament concerned in the treaty body process. The project, which was led at the parliamentary level by a group consisting of majority and opposition parliamentarians, parliamentary staff, representatives of national human rights institutions, competent government bodies and NGOs, was quite successful in the sense that concrete results were obtained, such as the release of over 100 detainees in Togo who had been held in long-term preventive detention. The project started off with a regional introductory seminar in Ouagadougou and also concluded with a regional seminar held in Libreville. Parliamentarians present at the latter seminar adopted a Declaration which, inter alia, recommended the continuation of the project and the creation of a human rights observatory in the region. Unfortunately, owing to a shortage of funds, these recommendations have remained a dead letter and no follow-up activity has as yet been possible to determine whether or not the project has had the desired long-term effects.

For the past four years, the IPU has on the occasion of IPU Assemblies been organising one-day workshops devoted to the work of a particular treaty-monitoring body and a specific issue of major concern to it. In addition, following up on decisions taken by the Inter-Parliamentary Council (now the Governing Council) in April 1998 on parliamentary action for national follow-up to international agreements and treaties regarding women, workshops concerning the Committee monitoring the CEDAW have been held regularly in the past 10 years under the IPU's Women's Programme.

The fact that parliaments have been broadly unaware of the work of treaty bodies also has much to do with the fact that treaty bodies themselves largely ignored parliaments. The IPU therefore decided to make every effort to draw the attention of treaty bodies and their members to the decisive role that parliaments play, in particular when it comes to implementing their recommendations. One result of these efforts, which consisted mainly of lobbying treaty body members, was the adoption in 2008 by the CEDAW Committee of a Statement on its relationship with MPs. The Statement provides for the inclusion of a standard paragraph on parliaments in its concluding observations to draw the attention of States Parties to the importance of involving parliaments in the reporting and implementation process. The IPU is further regularly invited to submit to the CEDAW Committee information on women's participation in politics in the state under review. It remains to be seen whether other treaty bodies will follow suit.

The latest IPU survey (2012/13) on the involvement of parliaments in treaty-monitoring bodies and the UPR show that, while parliaments remain largely absent from the process, up to 30 per cent seem to be involved in at least one cycle of the process.[4]

b. The UPR and Parliaments

In line with its efforts to involve parliaments in international human rights monitoring mechanisms, the IPU is increasingly focusing on the UPR process. Parliaments are not mentioned as stakeholders in the General Assembly resolution establishing the UPR,[5] although they are no doubt key players, required as they are to design and oversee the implementation of the legal framework reflecting the human rights obligations binding on the country, to oversee the policies and activities decided on to meet international standards and to allocate sufficient resources to facilitate the implementation of corresponding government programmes. In the IPU's view, parliaments should be involved in drafting the national report, which should be discussed in parliament, parliamentarians should be included in the national delegation to the Human Rights Council when their country's human rights situation is reviewed and, last but not least, the recommendations resulting from the UPR process should be discussed in parliament.

The first IPU initiative with regard to the UPR was designed to draw the attention of parliaments to the UPR and the rightful role of parliament. In a circular letter, the IPU Secretariat told parliaments about the UPR and its functioning, and has kept them abreast of the UPR review schedule and recommendations concerning their countries. Other awareness-raising activities consisted in side events staged during Human Rights Council sessions and, more recently, a seminar held

---

[4] The survey concerned 191 parliaments. Only 68 parliaments responded (36 per cent). The following figures must therefore be viewed with caution: 24 per cent of responding parliaments stated that they took part in preparing national reports, 16 per cent that they were on delegations presenting the report, 27 per cent that debates on recommendations take place and 30 per cent that their parliament participates in the implementation of the recommendations.

[5] In its Art 5(h), the UN General Assembly Resolution 60/251 mentions governments, regional organisations, national human rights institutions and civil society as stakeholders with which the Human Rights Council will work in close cooperation.

in November 2012 together with the Commonwealth Secretariat on 'Strengthening the Role of Parliamentarians in the Implementation of Universal Periodic Review Recommendations'.[6]

A first survey of the involvement of parliaments in the UPR was conducted in 2010 and revealed practically no knowledge of the existence of the UPR process as such. Only a minority of parliaments, such as those of Canada, Germany and the Philippines, had at the time taken the initiative of engaging in the process. The second survey (2012/13) shows a slightly better situation with an increasing number of parliaments being aware of the UPR and participating in at least one step of the process.[7] It is encouraging that more than half of the responding parliaments stated that UPR recommendations were debated in their parliaments and that they took part in implementing them.

Awareness-raising activities by the IPU within the Human Rights Council prompted the Council to organise in late May 2013 a panel discussion on the contribution of parliaments to its work, in particular the UPR.

iv. Children's Rights

The IPU started in 2001 to assist parliaments in their efforts to enhance respect for children's rights. The landmark resolution adopted that year, entitled 'Protecting and Caring for Children, the Driving Force of Future Society', provided the foundation for that work, which was initially part of the IPU's Women's Programme and since 2012 has come under the Human Rights Programme. Since its start in 2001, the IPU has implemented thematic campaigns and has provided capacity-building to parliaments in the area of child trafficking and labour, violence against children, female genital mutilation, and maternal, neonatal and child health. It has also promoted parliamentary involvement in putting into practice the UN Convention on the Rights of the Child and has developed parliamentary information tools (mainly handbooks) on key children's issues. The current strategy aims at supporting parliaments in their efforts to ensure a strong and effective legal framework on children's rights, to build parliamentary structures, such as committees and caucuses, in support of children's rights, to tackle child labour and trafficking, to eliminate malnutrition and to promote birth registration.

v. Specific Action to Combat Violence against Women and Discrimination against Women and AIDS Sufferers

Under its Women's Programme, the IPU has since 2008 been conducting a campaign and a programme of work to support parliaments in their efforts to end violence against women. The activities in this field target three areas, namely building a strong

---

[6] The conclusions of the workshop may be found at: www.ipu.org/splz-e/hr12/conclusions.pdf.

[7] See n 4. The figures on the participation of responding parliaments are as follows: 24 per cent and 15 per cent participate in the drafting and the presentation of the report, respectively. A total of 61 per cent stated that UPR recommendations were debated in parliament and that their parliament took part in implementing them.

and effective legal framework, securing effective implementation of legislation, and reinforcing awareness, sensitisation and visibility of violence against women.[8] In addition, the Women's Programme carries out activities to help parliaments review, repeal or amend laws discriminating against women and to fill legal voids in this respect. Likewise, the IPU's work on AIDS focuses on support for parliaments in reviewing, repealing or amending punitive and discriminatory laws that block effective responses to AIDS and in taking a stronger and more visible stand in speaking out openly about HIV/AIDS and pushing back the forces of stigma.

vi. Partners

Like any other organisation in the field of human rights, the IPU works closely with other international and regional human rights organisations and institutions, in particular with the UN and the Office of its High Commissioner for Human Rights. Regional parliamentary assemblies are major partners, as are other institutions engaging in human rights capacity-building, such as the Westminster Foundation and the Commonwealth. Furthermore, the Human Rights Programme is closely associated with human rights NGOs, in particular Amnesty International.

IV. HUMAN RIGHTS NEED STRONG DEMOCRATIC PARLIAMENTS

Only strong democratic parliaments can truly fulfil their role as guardians of human rights. But what is the meaning of a strong democratic parliament and what are its characteristics? On the basis of a broad parliamentary survey, in 2008 the IPU published a compilation of efforts and good practices of parliaments the world over entitled 'Parliament and Democracy in the Twenty-First Century: A Guide to Good Practice'.[9] The message is that a democratic parliament is one which is representative, transparent, accessible, accountable and effective in its functions. The survey has led to the elaboration of a self-assessment toolkit for parliaments, which is intended to assist parliaments and their members in assessing how their parliaments perform against those widely accepted criteria for democratic parliaments.

The first ever Global Parliamentary Report, published in early 2012 by the IPU and the United Nations Development Programme (UNDP) and devoted to the relationship between parliaments and citizens, shows that parliaments need to reform themselves if they are to be strong, democratic parliaments living up to their human rights responsibilities, because trust in them stands at a very low point all over the world, including in Europe, where massive popular protest against severe austerity measures challenges parliaments having ratified those measures.

It is beyond any doubt that there is an urgent need for parliaments to enhance their human rights capacity and better assume their crucial role as guardians of all human rights, civil and political rights, as well as economic, social and cultural

---

[8] For more information, see: www.ipu.org/wmn-e/vaw/campaign.htm.
[9] The guide is available at: www.ipu.org/english/handbks.htm#democracy.

rights. Will parliamentary human rights committees be able to influence government policies in a manner that is sensitive to human rights? While the proliferation of such bodies in parliaments worldwide is certainly a welcome development, more often than not, as the IPU surveys have shown, they lack the mandate, the powers and the means they would require to achieve precisely that. The Joint Committee on Human Rights of the British Parliament is the exception rather than the rule.

The idea of a set of principles and guidelines on the role of parliaments in the protection and realisation of human rights certainly deserves discussion by parliaments worldwide. As the Paris Principles have shown with regard to national human rights institutions, guidelines can contribute hugely to the effectiveness and hence credibility of national human rights bodies. While it may be preferable and certainly easier to launch the discussion at the regional level first, the IPU, as the only worldwide organisation of parliaments, is no doubt ideally placed to also help launch such a debate at the international level, thus including parliaments in different existing political systems grappling with different human rights implementation problems. Such discussion is a pre-requisite for achieving generally agreed-upon and accepted guidelines for parliamentary human rights committees and, more generally, parliamentary human rights work.

17

The Work of the Westminster Foundation for Democracy

GEORGE KUNNATH AND ANGELA PATRICK[*]

INTRODUCTION

T HE WESTMINSTER FOUNDATION for Democracy (WFD) was established in 1992, following the fall of the Berlin Wall and the collapse of the former Soviet Union. Its work was designed to provide practical support to the fledgling democracies of Eastern Europe. The founding objectives of the WFD were to assist, support and encourage the establishment and development of 'pluralistic democratic practices and political institutions'; to provide advice, guidance and practical assistance in the support of democratic processes; and, finally, to assist in the formation, organisation and management of democratic political parties committed to non-violent policies and programmes.[1] The WFD now works to achieve its objectives globally, working in partnership with parliaments and political parties in emerging democracies in Eastern Europe, Africa and the Middle East.

The WFD is formally a non-departmental public body, sponsored and funded by the Foreign and Commonwealth Office of the UK. It continues to secure its funding principally through UK Government sources, including through the support of the Department for International Development (DFID). However, although the programme is established as a mechanism for bilateral UK support for capacity building, from the outset its priority has been to establish an effective framework for international cooperation and the effective exchange of practical peer-to-peer expertise and hands-on training. This approach is affirmed not only in the strategic goals of the organisation, but is clearly reflected in its governance: six of the members of the Governing Board of the WFD are serving MPs drawn from the Westminster Parliament, with multiple representatives drawn from the main political parties and one nominated to represent the others. This cross-party, non-partisan approach is essential to the work of the WFD, as the success of its individual programmes may depend on building trust and confidence across party lines, bringing opposition and government players together in politically difficult climates.

One of the core tenets of the work of the WFD is an holistic approach to effective parliamentary administration and democratic engagement. In its work, the WFD

---

[*] Angela Patrick is a barrister and Director of Human Rights Policy at JUSTICE. Until 2011, she was Assistant Legal Adviser to the JCHR and acted as an expert trainer for The Westminster Consortium coordinated by The Westminster Foundation for Democracy.

[1] See WFD Annual Report and Accounts, 2013, 5.

has consistently recognised that the effective operation of a parliament engages individuals, bodies and organisations beyond that body corporate and its constituent members. The work of the WFD focuses on the development and operation of individual political parties, on democratic engagement and electoral processes, and on the work of individual parliamentarians and the operation and administration of parliamentary business. Engagement on these issues requires the building of capacity and relationships not only with individual politicians or parliamentary bodies, but also with parliamentary staff and staff engaged directly by parliamentarians or political parties, and with individuals and institutions who engage with parliaments in their work, including civil society organisations. This approach recognises both the central importance of the tripartite parliamentary function—as representative of the views of the people, as legislator and as overseer of all government—but also recognises the important role which others can play in ensuring the effectiveness of that work.

In light of the goals at the heart of the WFD's mission, support for an effective understanding of the rule of law and the importance of constitutional and international protection for human rights standards was perhaps inevitable. The development of the modern democratic process has marched together with the development of international respect for the rule of law and the promulgation of internationally respected human rights standards, as reflected in the United Nations Declaration on Human Rights (UNDHR) and each of the subsequent United Nations (UN) human rights treaties, and in many new constitutions promulgated the world over since the end of the Second World War.

I. THE WESTMINSTER CONSORTIUM

In 2008, the WFD established the Westminster Consortium for Parliaments and Democracy (TWC), a project designed to formalise this international approach to peer-to-peer training on the running of effective parliaments worldwide. The TWC programme 'Strengthening Parliaments' was supported by the DFID's Governance and Transparency Fund on long-term programmes for a five-year period, between September 2008 and 2013.

The TWC aimed to bring together UK organisations and institutions working in democratic engagement, parliamentary development and strengthening and the law, in the development of a multi-disciplinary programme of long-term capacity building for emerging democracies across regions in Eastern Europe, Africa and the Middle East. The Consortium, led by the WFD, consisted of the UK Branch of the Commonwealth Parliamentary Association (CPA-UK), the House of Commons Overseas Office (HOC), the International Bar Association Human Rights Institute (IBAHRI), the National Audit Office (NAO), Thomson Reuters Foundation (TRF) and the University of Essex Institute for Democracy and Conflict Resolution (IDCR). It brought together expertise in parliamentary management, finance and administration, communications, access to information, reporting, the rule of law and human rights both within the UK and in each of the programme partner countries.

The Consortium worked with 22 local partners in six countries (Mozambique, Uganda, Lebanon, Ukraine, Georgia and Morocco). The profiles of the project partners reflect the evolution of the work of the WFD over its last two decades of operation, representing developing parliaments in each of the regions where it has previously worked: in Eastern Europe, Africa and the Middle East. Most of the parliaments involved in the TWC programme are relatively young. The Ugandan Parliament, for example, has only been in existence in its current form for a little over 20 years. In 1986, the National Resistance Movement came to power under the control of now-President Yoweri Museveni, with a single-party system prevailing until 2006. Mozambique made the transition from single-party politics to a multi-party system in 1990 after a tumultuous civil war. Both Ukraine and Georgia are equally young, having declared independence in 1991, following the collapse of the former USSR. Georgia has had a particularly turbulent political youth, following the 'Rose Revolution' in 2003, and Ukraine is now experiencing similar challenges.

The overall goal of the project was to build capacity in each of the regions and to encourage more effective and sustainable regional processes for parliamentary support, training and learning, including through, where appropriate, the establishment of new regional centres for parliamentary study. Its aim was to design and facilitate the delivery of training for both MPs and parliamentary staff through the preparation and delivery of workshops and training materials; to encourage and support international and regional peer-to-peer relationship building and the exchange of information; to support specific projects designed to help integrate the lessons underpinning the programme into the work of the individual partner parliaments; and to encourage the development of sustainable models for future learning across the region.

A. TWC Rule of Law and Human Rights Programme

The TWC programme was the first time that the WFD sought to directly support learning and practice on the importance of the rule of law and human rights for the effective work of its partner parliaments. However, by the start of the programme in 2008, a number of earlier initiatives had identified the importance of parliamentary engagement in the domestic implementation of human rights standards. Notably, the Inter-Parliamentary Union (IPU) published its helpful *Human Rights Handbook for Parliamentarians* in 2005,[2] including useful checklists of the basic functions which parliaments and parliamentarians could perform in the protection and promotion of human rights.[3] Training programmes had been prepared by the World Bank for parliamentary staff,[4] and international bodies, including the Council of

---

[2] Inter-Parliamentary Union et al, *Human Rights Handbook for Parliamentarians*, 2005 www.ipu .org/PDF/publications/hr_guide_en.pdf. For further information on the work of the Inter-Parliamentary Union, see ch 16 in this volume.
[3] ibid, ch 11, 66–80.
[4] World Bank, 'Parliamentary Staff Training Programme on Human Rights'. See www.parliamentarys-trengtheining.org/humanrightsmodule/pdf/humanrightsall.pdf.

Europe Parliamentary Assembly,[5] were increasingly focusing on the importance of effective domestic implementation of international standards and the function of parliamentarians within that role. Launching the IPU *Handbook*, Louise Arbour, the former UN High Commissioner for Human Rights, summarised the important function that parliaments and individual parliamentarians can play in making rights real:

> If human rights are to become a reality for everyone, parliaments must fully play their role and exercise to this effect the specific powers they have, namely legislating, adopting the budget and overseeing the Government.[6]

The TWC Rule of Law and Human Rights programme was developed within the TWC by the IBAHRI working together with local partners and the staff of the Joint Committee on Human Rights (JCHR) at the Westminster Parliament. The IBAHRI has a wealth of experience in providing practical training across the world for lawyers and judges, including in developing countries. This legal expertise on substantive international human rights law and domestic constitutional standards was invaluable in identifying key local partners to work with to design local programming relevant to local parliaments in each of the partner countries. The following organisations provided support throughout the project: in Georgia, the Georgian Young Lawyers' Association (GYLA); in Lebanon, the Faculty of Law at the Lebanese University; in Mozambique, the Centre for Human Rights at the Eduardo Mondlane University; in Uganda, the Foundation for Human Rights Initiative (FHRI); and in Ukraine, the Centre for European Integration (CEI). However, while the IBAHRI brought substantive legal expertise to the project, its training had previously focused on the judiciary and the legal profession. The House of Commons Overseas Office and the legal team of the JCHR were closely involved in the design and delivery of this module of the programme, with a view to bringing a pragmatic, practical and peer-to-peer approach to the project.

Importantly, while the Westminster Parliament may be the 'mother' of all parliaments, its approach to the integration of human rights standards into its work is relatively new, spurred on by the adoption of the Human Rights Act (HRA) in 1998 and the establishment of the JCHR in 2000–01. While relatively new, the JCHR has worked since it was established to build upon existing guidance for parliamentarians, including that developed by the IPU. Its working practices developed against the background of a broad range of domestic and international human rights concerns, including issues arising in the aftermath of the 9/11 and 7/7 terrorist attacks and the fallout from the conflicts in Iraq and Afghanistan, including issues concerning torture, proportionate police powers of pre-trial and other forms of detention, privacy, freedom of expression and the right to protest. Its work was generally accepted regionally and internationally as a source of best practice.

The IBAHRI worked to identify effective and credible local project partners, conscious of the need not only to identify organisations and individuals with expertise

---

in domestic and international human rights standards, but also those who were capable of working effectively with local politicians from different political parties and with parliamentary staff required to maintain their neutrality. An ability to build a rapport without partisan affiliation and to understand the political and resource pressures placed on parliament and on individual parliamentarians was crucial.

When project partners were identified, the project goals for local delivery were identified, with key priorities for development set. The framework for delivery across each of the countries involved one or more international workshops per year, attended by MPs, staff or a combination of both, with further follow-up training and support to be delivered by a combination of both international trainers and local project partners. In addition to these training workshops, and associated materials, it was envisaged that direct contacts between project partners and national parliaments and the WFD would be utilised to identify new methods of working and to support work on individual projects or activities throughout the timeframe of the project. Some of the key project outcomes are identified below, together with further detail on the key challenges and opportunities identified by the TWC.

It was important for the TWC to ensure that this work remained sustainable and relevant to the work of each of the partner parliaments engaged in the programme. The core purpose of the project was long-term learning and the introduction of more effective working methods. The design of each of the parts of the programme focused on a range of issues relevant to the country in question and used case studies and local workshop exercises to highlight tools available to the Westminster Parliament (and, specifically, examples from the work of the JCHR) and locally in order to better enable local parliaments, individual members and specific parliamentary committees to identify existing tools to better promote, protect and respect human rights. For example, in Georgia, one of a number of comparative training exercises focused on the right to protest. At the time, new legislation on policing and the right to public protest was under consideration, which had been subject to detailed consideration by the Venice Commission (the Council of Europe's Commission for Democracy through Law).[7] Participants in the training were invited to consider substantive standards on the right to assembly and freedom of expression in both the International Covenant on Civil and Political Rights and the European Convention on Human Rights. However, they were also invited to consider the application of police powers in hypothetical cases and to consider the tools open to parliamentarians to raise questions about the adequacy of the proposed legislation. Comparative examples were drawn from the work of the JCHR, which had recently conducted a lengthy inquiry on the policing of protest within the UK,[8] and this provided the basis for a constructive engagement with the opportunities for human rights engagement by both Parliaments in Tbilisi and London.

This project was designed to build on existing capacity building measures and to provide pragmatic and practical, tailored support for the parliaments involved.

---

[7] See, eg, Opinion No 547/2009, Law on Assemblage and Manifestations, CDL (2009) 128.
[8] See, eg, Seventh Report of Session 2008–09, *Demonstrating Respect for Rights: A Human Rights Approach to Policing Protest*, HL 47-I/HC 320-I.

The TWC aimed to provide new impetus for each of the partner parliaments to actively consider how they might improve local capacity for work on human rights issues and the resources available for the effective oversight of the implementation of domestic and international human rights guarantees in local legislation, policy and practice.

II. CHALLENGES AND OPPORTUNITIES: WORKING WITH PARLIAMENTS ON HUMAN RIGHTS

The WFD brought to the TWC project decades of experience of working with parliaments and parliamentarians to support learning. With that experience, the WFD recognised that the TWC programme might look very different for each of the partner parliaments in practice. In order to be relevant, the programme would need to be tailored according to the priorities identified for each partner country. Although parliaments share key characteristics and functions of representation, legislation and oversight, not every parliamentary model is the same. Unicameral and bicameral models might adopt very different rules of procedure and approaches to training, for example. More pragmatically, many nominally multi-party systems may yet operate with a significant government majority, which can change the role of parliament and the engagement of its members. Thus, a single approach to parliamentary strengthening is unlikely to yield the same result across different regions and different parliamentary traditions. Some legislatures, particularly in Eastern Europe, have focused historically on the legislative function, with little or no development of the role of parliament in the scrutiny of public policy and executive action. In some systems, few resources have been invested in parliament or its management, with the outcome that staffing levels are low and resources limited, or staffing has been predominantly provided on a partisan basis (either by the individual political parties or drawn from the executive). However, despite the many differences across each of the partner countries working within the TWC programme, there were a number of shared challenges and opportunities which affected the development of the TWC Rule of Law and Human Rights programme, albeit each with different impacts and varying degrees of significance.

A. Finance and Resources

A lack of resources has an obvious and detrimental impact on the operation of a national parliament. It is difficult to engage in any form of effective capacity building without a true understanding of the resources available to parliament in practice. For example, the TWC quickly learnt that in Mozambique, the number of sitting days is often affected by the availability of funds. Similarly, resources might shape the priority given to the establishment of parliamentary committees and their operation. Thus, in Mozambique, a single parliamentary committee deals with all human rights, constitutional and legal issues. In Uganda, until recently, human rights issues were subsumed as a secondary part of the Legal Affairs Committee's mandate. In both countries, establishing an additional committee to look solely at human rights would have significant budgetary implications. During the course of the TWC programme, the Ugandan Parliament decided to take this step, which we consider in some detail below.

However, this lack of investment can be indicative of wider financial problems within the jurisdiction, with limited funds available for effective investment in national programming. Financial limitations or challenges can shape the work of a national parliament for entirely understandable and pragmatic reasons. This in turn will have a significant impact on the interests and priorities for parliamentarians and parliamentary staff. For example, in Lebanon, one of the primary concerns of participants in TWC training, including on human rights, was the long-running and controversial failure to agree a national budget. Equally, anti-corruption measures may be a priority in states where corruption has had a significant impact upon the organisation of national programmes and finances. For example, in May 2010, the national contact of Transparency International in Ukraine reported that 'corruption in Ukraine is a systemic problem existing across the board and at all levels of public administration. Both petty and grand scale corruption are flourishing. Among the institutions which are perceived by the public to be highly corrupt are political parties, legislature, police, public officials and the judiciary'.[9] The impact of corruption on the work of the Ukrainian Parliament Verkhovna Rada and the need to introduce effective anti-corruption measures to improve the operation of domestic institutions was a recurring theme during the operation of the project in Ukraine.

B. Capacity, the Function of Parliament and Effective Oversight

Louise Arbour, in her Foreword to the IPU *Handbook on Human Rights for Parliamentarians*, focused on the ability of parliaments and parliamentarians in each of their functions to have a positive impact on the protection of human rights at a national level. Budgetary control, the promulgation of legislation and the oversight of public administration form the pillars of the function of any effective parliamentary body. Similarly, individual parliamentarians wear multiple hats, performing as legislators, as representatives of their constituents and as party members. These functions can be treated as trite by many in practice, but there is no clear global understanding of how the capacity of national parliaments should be organised and supported to ensure that each of these roles is afforded equal respect in practice. History and the evolution of domestic traditions can mean that a very different balance is struck from one parliament to the next.

A common feature in many developing parliaments is that priority is given to the legislative function and thus significantly more time is spent in passing legislation than conducting oversight of the executive and public agencies. Against this background, parliaments with limited resources often have little time or money for the development of effective and respected structures for the conduct of oversight,

---

[9] See Transparency International Ukraine, Ukraine Report 2011, www.transparency.org/whatwedo/nisarticle/ukraine_2011.

including for compliance with domestic and international human rights standards. The function of individual oversight committees may be little understood, and they may be poorly resourced and not well respected. However, without the rules, procedures, powers, time and resources to conduct effective oversight, a parliament is unable to effectively perform one of its core functions of holding the executive and administration to account. Across all six of the countries that the TWC operated in, there were examples of limitations in the degree of respect afforded to the scrutiny function of parliament and parliamentarians. Even inexpensive tools which were routinely taken for granted by Westminster clerks were often lacking. One example can be found in the distinction between the public and private business of select committees. In some jurisdictions, staff reported that restrictions on private sittings were disruptive; however, in others, an inability to sit in public was similarly limiting the effectiveness of their members' work. The crucial public function of open, accessible and transparent reporting and evidence gathering, balanced with the ability of members to organise their business, deliberate—and argue—in private, was explored in some detail in sessions on the effective operation of scrutiny committees working across party lines.

In a number of the countries where the TWC worked, scrutiny was further inhibited by the wider political landscape in the country. The existence of a significant parliamentary majority for the governing party in a number of the partner countries clearly stifled the opportunities for robust parliamentary scrutiny. For example, the 2011 Transparency International report on Georgia describes the Parliament's weakness to include a 'lack of pluralism, lack of independence from the executive branch, failure to exercise executive oversight and to sufficiently scrutinise the executive branch's legislative proposals'.[10]

Modern parliamentary practice is increasingly focused on the importance of legislative engagement with the effectiveness of legislation in practice, or 'post-legislative scrutiny' as it has come to be known in the UK.[11] However, in countries with younger parliaments, resources are unlikely to be devoted to this function. In practice, limited resources devoted to oversight and scrutiny will often rule out any form of effective post-legislative scrutiny. Each of the six TWC partner parliaments admitted that once legislation has been passed, parliament rarely has time to revisit an issue to see if legislation has been implemented properly or if it has had the desired or intended impact.

C. Understanding and Accessing Parliamentary Tools, Skills and Comparative Experience

Where there are limited resources and oversight is not treated as a priority, it is perhaps unsurprising that in many parliaments there has been little historical

---

[10] Transparency International Georgia, National Integrity System Report, 2011. See www.transparency.ge/nis/2011/conclusion-and-recommendations.

[11] For example, see Law Commission, *Post-legislative Scrutiny* (2006), and the subsequent acceptance of these proposals by the UK Government in 2008.

investment in the practical tools and technical support which are necessary for the conduct of effective and informed parliamentary oversight. Research support for and the direct training of parliamentarians and their staff can be limited and, for example, few scrutiny committees in developing parliaments are equipped with the resources which enable the Westminster Parliament to conduct effective legislative scrutiny, inquiries and other ad hoc investigations. To take one example, while the examination of comparative legislation and jurisprudence from a range of EU countries may be important for Georgia and Ukraine as aspiring candidate countries, in practice, the bulk of comparative legislation is not available in Georgian or Ukrainian translations. While individual staff may bring their own language skills to bear, TWC were told translation services are not routinely available. Similarly, access to independent support staff to support the work of individual parliamentary committees, including independent lawyers with the necessary expertise in human rights law and to high-level training for those staff on relevant international law and practice, was consistently raised during the TWC programme as a significant limitation on the ability of parliament to have a positive impact.

D. Limited Dialogue with Civil Society and Beyond

The work of any parliament relies on effective, albeit arm's-length, working relationships with government, public agencies, academia and international and domestic civil society organisations. These relationships are particularly important where resources are limited. The degree to which parliaments have functioning relationships with government which maintain parliament's independence is generally influenced by the greater political health of the country. The significant degree of distrust with which some parliaments approached other stakeholders, including civil society organisations, including domestic and international non-governmental organisation (NGOs) and academic institutions, was a recurring feature of the work of the TWC during the programme. The informed input of these organisations—whether as a source of research on difficult problems or expertise from work on the ground—can be a valuable resource for parliamentarians if managed appropriately. Yet, in some countries, organisations were instinctively viewed as partisan, whether justifiably so or not, by virtue of their criticism of the government. Unfortunately, this view was often expressed not only by party politicians, but also by parliamentary staff. Staff, acting without political affiliation, could act as an effective filter for the collection of information and input from civil society sources. However, without trust that the information provided is reliable, well-evidenced and impartial, engagement proves extremely difficult.

Each of these challenges has particular implications for parliaments working on human rights issues. The TWC Rule of Law and Human Rights programme was affected to varying degrees in its work by each of the systemic and wider political problems facing developing parliaments. By way of illustration, a few examples follow.

i. Engagement of Civil Society Organisations (CSOs) on Human Rights Issues

In some parliaments, it is perhaps unsurprising that CSOs working on human rights issues and highlighting areas ripe for reform were treated with a significant level of suspicion. Officials in government and in parliament in some of the partner countries expressed a clear, but not necessarily well-founded, perception that most CSOs are unprofessional, emotive and unable to present arguments in a manner that is helpful to parliamentary business. In some cases, these attitudes were grounded in failures by individual organisations and in others were based solely on perceptions fostered over decades. Mutual distrust operated to undermine the efforts of CSOs in their engagement with parliament and parliamentarians, and to perpetuate historical impressions of their work as irrelevant. However, in many cases, this situation operated to discredit legitimate contributions which could be well presented and supported by evidence by individual organisations. Changes to the long-held attitudes of parliamentary staff and national civil society are not simple. Methods of presenting non-partisan, reasoned and accessible information to parliaments in a format which is easily used by non-expert staff and politicians is a skill which many international and domestic organisations strive towards. Development and training in policy, advice and analysis is provided by specialist bodies in many countries. A key skill of politically neutral parliamentary advisers is an ability to disseminate information from a range of sources and to provide information and advice on a non-partisan basis. Relationship management to ensure that parliamentarians are effectively informed and that parliament as a body is accessible to the range of views expressed by informed civil society may be particularly difficult when dealing with human rights concerns, where the issues at hand are likely to be politically sensitive and have impacts on a range of ethical and moral beliefs.

ii. Legislative Scrutiny, Identifying Human Rights Impacts and Setting Priorities

The volume of legislation—and government programming—which is likely to have some impact on human rights in practice is high. In the UK, one of the earliest lessons learnt by the JCHR (and its staff) was that it would be a waste of its limited resources for it to focus on activities, including legislative activities, that were unlikely to cause significant harm to human rights in practice. In most parliaments, identifying those issues which should be scrutinised as a priority is a challenge. In countries with limited capacity and a tradition which focuses on the legislative agenda, prioritisation becomes both more challenging and more important. The identification of some of the most serious human rights implications could in practice be simple. These issues are likely to be subject to significant international and domestic attention, including in the press. However, without clear criteria to prioritise their scrutiny, other political tools are used, in practice, with varying degrees of success, to avoid the debate of some significant issues entirely (for example, pushing controversial issues to the back of the parliamentary timetable, notably the Ugandan Anti-Homosexuality Bill). During the TWC programme, trainers used the

JCHR example as a model to illustrate one means of focusing the resources of both staff and MPs (the JCHR uses a 'filter' model, wherein all legislation is considered and filtered in the first instance for priority by legal staff, subject to review by the committee members).

iii. Expertise and Tools: Signing and Ratifying International Human Rights Treaties

The confluence of the many challenges facing individual parliaments conducting human rights scrutiny is perhaps illustrated best by the difficulties we observed in individual institutions engaging with the first of the important tasks identified by the IPU: engagement with the signing and ratification of international human rights treaties. In most of the partner countries in which we worked, there was considerable frustration at this task. The executive routinely retained responsibility for the negotiation and ratification of international agreements, with no formal mechanism, or little opportunity made, for parliamentary engagement. As recognised by the IPU, this led to a lack of ownership amongst parliamentarians and the parliamentary staff of the international standards in the treaty framework, and, on occasion, a failure to connect those standards to domestic constitutional arrangements (even in those countries with a monist system of law). The TWC tried to illustrate how the UK has similarly struggled to integrate the ratification of international standards into domestic political debate. The role of the JCHR in raising the significance of reservations to the UN Convention on the Rights of the Child (leading, ultimately to the lifting of significant reservations on the treatment of children in the immigration process) and on the ratification of the UN Convention on the Rights of Persons with Disabilities was used to facilitate discussion on how individual parliamentary committees (and individual parliamentarians) might use existing oversight powers to create greater engagement in—and greater responsibility for—the international human rights standards which influence their work.

iv. Expertise and Tools: Access to Independent Legal Advice

An easily illustrated example of the impact of wider limitations on effective human rights scrutiny within parliament is the capacity of individual parliaments to provide access to independent, specialist advice on human rights standards. As is explored elsewhere in this publication, the importance of independent legal advice for effective scrutiny cannot be understated. Yet, if parliamentary resources are scarce, funds for dedicated specialists are likely to be unavailable.

In an environment where there is an active civil society, gaps in provision might be provided by external, objective expertise provided by third-party commentary or ad hoc advice. However, in countries where there is a lack of trust between civil society and parliament, this is unlikely to be a realistic alternative. In some of the countries where the TWC operated, both posed a significant challenge to the objective information available to parliament and to individual parliamentarians.

III. THE TWC RULE OF LAW AND HUMAN RIGHTS PROGRAMME: GOALS AND ACHIEVEMENTS

Taking into account the aims of the TWC project and each of these challenges, the TWC Rule of Law and Human Rights programme focused on a number of shared objectives and specific goals:

a)   Promoting best practice in rules and procedure.
b)   Developing tools and substantive understanding of human rights principles.
c)   Building the capacity of individual Members and Parliamentary staff.
d)   Developing the capacity of Civil Society.
e)   Promoting the establishment of effective human rights committees capable of conducting human rights scrutiny.
f)   Sustaining peer-to-peer learning.

A. Promoting Best Practice in Rules and Procedure

The priority for the TWC, in cooperation with local partners, was helping parliaments to identify how to improve existing rules and procedure to make human rights scrutiny more effective—in particular, rules on the effective functioning and establishment of dedicated, effective committees, and the inclusion of certificates of compliance for new legislation submitted to parliament. To this end, the TWC focused on encouraging individual project participants to reflect on their work and small changes which could create a significant shift in how parliaments view human rights as a core part of their work.

For example, in Ukraine, the workshops and training have resulted in closer cooperation between the committee and the Ombudsman's office (the Ombudsman is a parliamentary appointment, recognised to be the Ukrainian National Human Rights Institution). When the programme began, local partners and programme participants felt that the role of the Ombudsman was marginalised and that its work was viewed with little significance by individual parliamentarians. Ombudsman reports were made and little action taken by the Government or the Verkhovna Rada to address the recommendations made. A new practice has been introduced where an official from the Ombudsman's office is now routinely present at public hearings and evidence sessions of the parliamentary committee tasked with conducting oversight of its work and the human rights performance of the Government, so the Ombudsman is well placed both to inform and to respond speedily to that committee's work.

B. Developing Tools and Substantive Understanding of Human Rights Principles

The TWC project did not seek to replicate existing materials available to staff and MPs on the shared international commitments to human rights. However, during the course of the programme, it became clear that more practical guidance on tools and techniques used by individual parliaments and parliamentarians to increase the effectiveness of their work on human rights was not available.

Midway through the programme, the TWC published *Human Rights and Parliaments: Handbook for Members and Staff*.[12] Developed with local partners in each of the participating countries and with the JCHR staff, this *Handbook* covers the basics of the international human rights framework, key human rights standards and their relationship with domestic constitutional guarantees. However, its primary focus is on parliamentary tools for the protection of human rights, engaging with the role of both parliamentarians and staff. Examples are drawn from global experience, including the work of the JCHR and each of the partner countries, to highlight best practice. It is not designed or intended to be used as an academic text, but instead to trigger the examination of existing practice and to prompt consideration of how individual parliamentary practices might be better used or adapted to protect human rights standards.

The TWC *Handbook* was used to support the last stages of the training provided during the programme and to support the further training beyond its bounds. For example, it has been distributed to members of the East African Legislative Assembly (EALA) and has been used to train staff from the region's parliamentary human rights committees. It has also been translated into Arabic for distribution to staff in the Middle East and North Africa regions during regional training programmes. In Ukraine, a local translation was prepared (supplemented by additional examples drawn from local work) and distributed to both judges and MPs. It has subsequently become an integral tool used in training committee staff and is used as part of induction training for new members of the Verkhovna Rada.

C. Building the Capacity of Individual Members and Parliamentary Staff

The TWC programme prioritised peer-to-peer learning for both MPs and staff, as outlined above. Examples of the work done during the project included the training seminars developed by the TWC; international peer-to-peer exchanges, both regionally and with Westminster; direct support by local partners on individual projects; and encouragement and support for the development of staff forums to support the exchange of information and learning. The ultimate goal of the project was to encourage and to facilitate the development of regional centres for parliamentary learning.

i. Supporting Staff on Individual Projects

The TWC identified—through follow-up work conducted by local partners—individual human rights projects on which they could support individual committees or staff to use the learning garnered as part of the programme. These were, almost routinely, examples of the local academic or NGO partner supporting individual committee staff dealing with a particular piece of legislation with significant human rights impact. This more focused work allowed local partners to help participating staff

---

[12] The TWC *Handbook* is available at: www.ibanet.org/uman_Rights_Institute/About_the_HRI/HRI_Activities/Parliamentary_Strengthening.aspx.

identify existing powers and tools to highlight specific human rights issues during the parliamentary process. For example, with the human trafficking legislation in Ukraine, the TWC local partner, the Center of European Integration (CEI), facilitated constructive engagement between a working group of CSOs engaged in trafficking issues and the Human Rights Committee of the Ukrainian Parliament. They brought together the views of CSOs into a set of recommendations that the Parliament could consider. In Mozambique, committee staff asked for assistance in scrutinising draft agricultural land reform legislation from a human rights perspective. The Committee was 'walked through' the process with support from the TWC's local partners, the Eduardo Mondlane University Centre for Human Rights. This work focused on the right to food, but also explored the challenges facing Parliament in examining legislation which considers limited resources and economic and social rights in practice.

ii. Peer-to-Peer International and Regional Exchanges

Each of the partner parliaments engaged in TWC-supported study exchanges to Westminster, where they were invited to view the work of the JCHR and to discuss its work with individual MPs and staff. However, the TWC also encouraged and supported peer-to-peer regional exchanges between neighbouring parliaments. For example, a visit by Ugandan Committee members to Mozambique involved learning how Mozambique was dealing with discrimination and social and economic rights issues arising in connection with its inheritance laws, which would traditionally advantage male relatives over widows.

Similarly, the Ukrainian Human Rights Committee visited Georgia to study its implementation of the Georgian Criminal Procedure Code (CPC). Georgia had reformed its criminal justice system a few years earlier and a number of concepts incorporated into the new Ukrainian CPC Bill were in place in Georgia at the time of the visit.

iii. Staff Forums

Throughout the training, TWC identified limits in capacity and the risk that human rights issues could be missed or marginalised by an inability of individual members and staff to share information or to support cross-party or cross-committee working (where an issue might easily become 'someone else's problem'). Following one of the TWC training seminars for Human Rights Committee staff in Uganda, the participants realised that several bills with human rights implications had—for this reason—not been considered effectively. They worked to establish a staff-level Human Rights Forum that now meets regularly to discuss any potential issues that exist with new draft legislation being introduced to Parliament, irrespective of the Committee assigned to consider it.

iv. Regional Centres

At the end of the TWC programme, regional centres for parliamentary learning were launched in both Ukraine and Lebanon, with a view to fostering good parliamentary practice across the region, by encouraging shared learning with neighbouring parliaments. At the launch of the new Lebanese Institution for Parliamentary Training and Legislative Studies (see further below), the TWC Rule of Law and Human Rights programme was highlighted, with an Arabic translation of the training materials produced. Reporting from each of the partner countries has identified some increased engagement and activity. While there is clearly much work to be done, the peer-to-peer model has garnered results. One example, sent by local partners in Ukraine, cites an increased willingness of individual committees to examine budgetary allocation for programming with a significant human rights impact. New human trafficking legislation, for example, identified the need to set up 22 regional centres to rehabilitate and reintegrate victims returning to Ukraine. There was a consensus that the legislation passed was positive, but no budget was allocated to support its implementation.

D. Developing the Capacity of Civil Society

A significant proportion of the work of the TWC programme focused on improving the relationship of partner parliaments with local civil society. For example, during each of the study visits to the UK, sessions were arranged with UK CSOs, including JUSTICE and Liberty and local academics working with parliament, to better facilitate an understanding of how constructive engagement could improve the work of parliament and further the work of civil society in practice. This part of the programme also involved engaging directly with local CSO organisations in partner countries to encourage best practice on parliamentary engagement. This work went beyond the Rule of Law and Human Rights programme, but it had a particularly significant impact on the work of civil society on human rights issues. This work followed a broad theme designed to encourage more effective engagement: *Evidence, Advocacy and Access*:

— *Evidence*: without a clear evidence base, easily illustrated and tested, it is easy for politicians and decision makers to dismiss advocacy as unsupported ideological or political rhetoric.
— *Advocacy*: even with an evidence-based understanding of the issue on which individual organisations seek to advocate, good communication skills are needed to understand how to present those ideas effectively to a range of audiences. Non-technical language may be extremely important. Often, avoiding party political bias in the presentation of proposals can be more crucial for those who seek to influence the political process. This can be particularly important in connection with human rights issues, which tend, by their very nature, to raise politically difficult matters.
— *Access*: understanding parliament and building relationships with staff and individual members is a skill fostered by many CSOs in their staff. In many of the partner countries that the TWC worked with, access was possible in theory, but was undermined in practice by distrust on the part of both CSO organisations and parliamentary staff.

The TWC worked to encourage individual CSOs and parliaments to consider each of these challenges domestically. A few examples of its work included the following:

i)   *The importance of freedom of information*: transparency and access to information is often key to the rule of law and to truly effective civil engagement. The TWC has been advising the Parliaments in both Mozambique and Ukraine on freedom of information legislation with international comparisons and study visits to the UK, focusing on the Freedom of Information Act 2000 and its implementation. TWC training for CSOs has centred on domestic freedom of information legislation (relatively new in most of the partner countries). This included working with CSOs to develop the skills to draft effective freedom of information requests to ensure the most effective results within the bounds of domestic law.

ii) *Designing and presenting research to influence Parliament*: the TWC CSO programme, led by the University of Essex, focused on training CSOs to strengthen their research methods. This work was complemented by local CSOs sharing their experience and knowledge with their colleagues in local peer-to-peer learning. For example, in Ukraine, *La Strada*, a CSO focusing on human rights, produces high-quality reports that the Human Rights Committee has found useful, because of the quality of research involved. The Rada and the TWC have supported several workshops where *La Strada* shared its experience with other CSOs, focusing on how to develop useful reports. An example of the impact of this work is the development of a report by a coalition of CSOs led by a CSO from the Crimean Tatar region of Ukraine, following TWC training. They produced research to support education in local ethnic languages (the issue of whether local languages, including Russian, should be recognised was and remains a controversial issue in Ukraine). The presentation of the shadow report by the CSOs helped the Committee on Cultural Issues focusing on this issue understand that the issue of national languages was broader than just the inclusion of Russian and must consider the rights of minority groups.

iii) *Provide training on parliamentary rules and processes*: CSOs need to understand how the legislative, representative and oversight process works in order to prioritise their work and make an impact at the right point in the parliamentary process. Training programmes supported by the TWC in Mozambique and Ukraine have been developed by senior parliamentary staff for local CSOs. These training programmes allow for a frank exchange between parliament and CSOs where each side can present their perspective on the challenges they face working together and how they can be improved.

iv) *Helping CSOs develop effective communications strategies*: working with the Thomson Reuters Foundation (TRF), during the TWC programme, CSOs in partner countries were given training in improving their communications and social media skills. The training focused on how to develop a clear message, hold press conferences, draft and target press releases, and build an online community.

v)   *Fostering better working relationships with Parliament*: the TWC worked to promote more effective relationships between participant CSOs, committee staff and members. The programme saw this as an important step in building credibility and trust between staff and CSOs. Local partner NGOs and participant parliaments have reported that the levels of trust between committee staff and CSOs have improved significantly. This work included, for example, facilitating contact through local WFD staff and arranging meetings to discuss effective joint working as part of international training seminars.

The TWC also encouraged, and supported, partner parliaments to hold CSO 'open days' offering civil society access to Parliament during regular sitting time to meet with MPs and staff within the parliamentary estate. Clerks were encouraged to identify a wide group of CSOs that could attend and to increase the usefulness of these sessions by selecting a theme for the open day. CSOs were provided with space and a table to display the publications and a number of roundtable discussions, and lectures or debates on a set theme were arranged for MPs and their staff to attend. In Mozambique, these themed events became a regular fixture in the parliamentary calendar. After the event, the publications brought by CSOs were donated to the parliamentary library for use by parliamentarians and staff thereafter. During the 2010 Open Day, the library received more than 300 publications. The 2011 Open Day was conducted with the Education for All Network and focused on meeting the Millennium Development Goal (MDG) targets in education.

E. Promoting the Establishment of Effective Human Rights Committees Capable of Conducting Human Rights Scrutiny

There has been an extensive debate about the advantages and disadvantages of the creation of a specific parliamentary committee tasked with conducting human rights scrutiny. This debate is covered elsewhere in this volume. However, it is accepted that there is some substantial benefit in the creation of a dedicated parliamentary mechanism which allocates a clear line of responsibility for the scrutiny of human rights issues and that, in many instances, a single human rights committee may be able to investigate issues which may not be prioritised by committees which were tasked with other political responsibilities. However, of the partner countries participating in the TWC programme, only Georgia's Parliament had a single committee solely dedicated to human rights issues. For example, in Ukraine, the relevant committee's mandate includes human rights, national minorities and international relations. Even in Georgia, local partners reported that the dedicated Human Rights Committee focused primarily on the processing of individual complaints, with limited resources or capacity to examine systemic issues or to undertake wider scrutiny of government policy. So, the TWC programme encouraged each of the partner parliaments to examine the effectiveness of existing mechanisms in conducting human rights scrutiny. It did highlight the benefits of the JCHR single-committee model, including the prioritisation of dedicated, independent legal staff with human rights expertise. However, it also worked to examine whether best practice in other models could be shared.

In Uganda, responsibility for scrutiny of human rights issues tended to be spread across the Legal and Parliamentary Affairs Committee, the Committee on Equal

Opportunities and the Committee on Defence and Internal Affairs. The Legal and Parliamentary Affairs Committee and the Equal Opportunities Committee were allocated a secondary mandate to scrutinise bills passed through Parliament, ensuring compliance with human rights laws. In practice, this often led to bills being passed without thorough scrutiny of human rights issues. During the TWC programme, the TWC and its local partner, the Foundation for Human Rights Initiatives (FHRI), made recommendations to the Ugandan Parliament that a dedicated human rights committee might prove a more effective model. Supporting this proposal, the Director of Legal and Legislative Services in the Parliamentary Commission put a case to the Speaker and, following the February 2011 elections, the Parliament moved to establish the new Human Rights Committee. The Committee was established, but not without opposition. A concession was made, which allowed the majority party to hold the Chair. However, the Speaker, Rebecca Kadaga, took a strong stand against resistance from members who claimed that minority groups, including those campaigning for equal protection for lesbian women and gay men, would use the Committee to promote an overtly political 'agenda'.

F. Sustaining Peer-to-Peer Learning

At the heart of the TWC programme was the sharing of international and regional best practice between parliaments working on human rights issues. In 2009, the TWC programme brought together parliamentary staff and CSOs from the six participating countries to share their challenges on human rights training within parliament, ways of improving the impact of training and identifying indicators of success. The TWC encouraged each of the partner parliaments to work to identify indicators that parliaments can use to measure their effectiveness in dealing with human rights issues. These included identifying more references to international human rights standards in their work, in committees and during floor debates; higher levels of press coverage for the work of parliament where it relates to these issues; the number of new human issues being raised in reports of the human rights committees; the volume of new legislation and private members' bills initiated on human rights issues; the number of CSO reports and government reports to the UN bodies scrutinised by the human rights committees; examples of changes in the rules of parliament designed to address human rights concerns; referrals of legislation to the Venice Commission by national parliaments; and the number of parliamentary inquiries initiated to address specific rights issues.

Throughout the programme, the TWC fostered regional learning on best practice, for example, focusing in 2010 on the use of the newly published handbook in the regions participating in the programme. In 2011, this work led to a supported roundtable discussion at the East African Legislative Assembly (EALA) on the role of Parliament in upholding the rule of law. This regional discussion focused on the dissemination of best practices for parliaments on human rights and fostering strategic links between the EALA and civil society groups including the East Africa Law Society (EALS) and East Africa Civil Society Organisations Forum (EACSOF). In 2012, this initiative was followed up by training for all East African Congress human rights parliamentary committees (including South Sudan) in Uganda. Roundtable discussion considered regional challenges for members and the variance in the implementation of human rights standards regionally. Issues considered included the lack of a clear coordinating mechanism on human rights in every member state to follow up the implementation of recommendations and reports from human rights bodies; limited capacity (in terms of information and skills) to scrutinise and perform oversight functions on issues related to human rights (including the availability of dedicated, specialist legal advice for parliaments); the enforcement of parliamentary resolutions and recommendations on human rights issues; and a lack of appreciation and awareness of the role that the regional organisations should and can play in the protection and promotion of human rights in the region.

The TWC also supported the Lebanese Parliament and the Arab Inter-Parliamentary Union (AIPU) to establish the Institute for Parliamentary Training and Legislative Studies (AIPTLS). The Institute, which was launched in November 2011, is designed as a sustainable development vehicle that can access 22 Arab Parliaments to disseminate good practice and promote learning across the region. The WFD is planning to work with the AIPTLS to continue providing regional training on human rights to committee staff.

Concrete examples of the best practice shared are highlighted in the TWC *Handbook*. One significant example includes the adoption by the Head of Legislative Services at the Ugandan Parliament, together with the Speaker, of a commitment to a new model of scrutiny triggered by learning about the work of the JCHR around section 19 of the UK HRA 1998. The HRA model is designed to preserve the central role of Parliament and section 19 requires that each piece of legislation placed before Parliament is to be certified by a minister as to its compatibility with the human rights protected by the Act. During TWC training, JCHR staff shared how this model ensured that the executive must take ownership of the human rights issues arising in legislation and, as such, had allowed the JCHR to put pressure on sequential administrations to publish increasingly comprehensive explanations of their view that particular measures were compatible with domestic and international human rights standards. The Ugandan participants—following discussion with TWC trainers—worked to put together a model for Ugandan scrutiny based on government certification of all draft government bills as compatible with Part 4 of the Ugandan Constitution. This certification model might increase the prominence of human rights issues in legislative debate, if used effectively. However, the engagement of senior staff and officials in the debate alone has highlighted to individual parliamentarians and to government the important role which parliament plays in ensuring that the rights of individuals guaranteed by the constitution and international human rights law should be at the heart of good government.

IV. LESSONS AND OPPORTUNITIES YET TO COME

There is much work yet to be done, but the TWC programme illustrates the value of long-term commitment to peer-to-peer learning and a practical approach to increasing the responsibility of parliaments—through the work of individual MPs and parliamentary staff—for the protection and promotion of domestic and international human rights standards. Throughout the progress of the TWC programme, the WFD and its partners in the UK and in programme participating countries have identified a number of important lessons for future global engagement designed to support the understanding of individual parliaments of the rule of law and their effective work on human rights issues. None of these are straightforward and most reflect the myriad of challenges which parliaments face in emerging democracies. However, together with the challenges outlined above, those involved in the TWC project believe that these lessons can help inform the opportunities for improvement yet to come.

A. Human Rights, the Rule of Law and Development

CSOs, academics and donor organisations should keep the important relationship between development, human rights and the rule of law at the forefront of their work in emerging democracies. As outlined above, improvements to human rights protection are closely aligned with achievements in development more widely. Without investment in the democratic infrastructure of government more broadly, the task of parliaments taking responsibility for human rights protection will be fundamentally restricted. Equally, in countries with a priority focus on implementing the MDGs (in the TWC programme, Mozambique and Uganda), the link between the MDGs and the wider international human rights framework can often be lost. The MDGs are grounded in human rights principles and they dovetail neatly with the international human rights framework. Training provided by the TWC on how individual parliamentary control of budgets for the implementation of health, education and agriculture programming, placed in the wider context of the International Covenant on Economic and Social Rights, domestic constitutional commitments and the MDGs was particularly welcomed. Both international donors and partners, and individual parliaments should consider this connection more clearly, particularly when working on the achievement of economic and social rights.

Importantly, the TWC team met some practical resistance focusing on human rights scrutiny and parliamentary engagement over other perceived development priorities. Over five years of engagement—across political and administrative functions, staff and individual MPs—this project gave the lie to this initial scepticism, as participants increasingly came to recognise that many of the key issues raised by the programme were often high-profile and politically sensitive ones at the heart of the function of any democratic parliament. As a few key figures in each of the project partner countries began to embrace the pragmatic basis for the project, they began to identify individual improvements, some incremental, others more fundamental, which could both better equip parliament to protect human rights and improve the better functioning of the parliamentary process (see, for example, the Uganda certification example discussed above).

B. Corruption and Human Rights

No programme on the rule of law and human rights in emerging democracies can work effectively without recognising the devastating effect of corruption, not only on the rule of law and the effectiveness of government, but also on the effective protection of human rights. In countries grappling with serious issues of corruption, the implementation of regional and international anti-corruption standards should be a priority. Political challenges notwithstanding, engaged individual parliamentarians and parliaments can play a crucial role.

C. Engaging with Civil Society

Projects which engage with both parliaments and local civil society are likely to be most sustainable. In emerging democracies without a long history of civil society engagement, distrust of external influence can fundamentally stifle the development of constructive civil debate and the proper oversight of national institutions. Investment in both parliamentary learning and training for CSOs, and in mutual recognition, may contribute significantly to the building of more effective engagement on human rights issues across the spectrum.

D. Regional and International Engagement on Human Rights Issues

Whether through the IPU, supported by regional bodies or through further donor investment, there is a need for further investment in ongoing peer-to-peer learning and support on the practical challenges which parliaments face in meeting their responsibility for the protection of human rights standards in practice. Local and regional contacts might be best supported to foster regular dialogue on specific shared challenges. However, there is a continuing need for guidance based on shared practice at an international level. The little guidance thus far provided by the UN on the role of parliamentarians is helpful, but limited. Reinvestment in guidelines and support for parliamentarians at the inter-governmental level would significantly focus attention on the development and democratic issues associated with the engagement of individual parliamentarians and national parliaments in the protection of domestic and international human rights standards.

E. Human Rights and Good Government

In its early work, the TWC found that human rights 'issues' could be dismissed by many politicians and officials as 'legalistic' and thus 'for the lawyers', or marginalised as political backbiting driven by the opposition. Yet, the important function of parliamentarians—most particularly as representatives of the people—in holding government to account is uniquely served by domestic constitutional standards and the international human rights framework. The message that those standards are largely designed to protect the individual against poor government decision-making is a particularly powerful one for training individuals involved in the activities of parliament. Work on human rights protection by national parliaments presents not only a responsibility for individual parliamentarians, but also an opportunity to improve their effectiveness. By holding government and public agencies to those standards, individual parliamentarians work to create a practical framework which places people (and their competing rights) at the heart of government decision-making. That this work makes both parliament and government more effective is trite. Individual parliamentarians might prefer to see human rights as granting them both a shield and a sword; to help them protect their constituents from unlawful and unfair government action and to arm them with the tools to challenge government when they get it wrong. For all democratically elected individuals, including those in emerging democracies, this analogy should be a powerful one.

Part VI

The Implications for Legislative Human Rights Review for Courts

18

The Use of Parliamentary Materials by Courts in Proportionality Judgments

HAYLEY J HOOPER*

THIS CHAPTER BEGAN its life as an empirical enquiry into the use of Joint Committee on Human Rights (JCHR) reports by courts in judicial review pursuant to the Human Rights Act 1998.[1] Judicial consideration of parliamentary materials in proportionality judgments accounts for a very small numerical subset of two larger areas: (1) proportionality adjudication generally; and (2) cases which engage the debate about parliamentary privilege and the appropriate relationship between courts and Parliament. So, although the use of JCHR reports in proportionality review accounted for an extremely small number of judgments, it soon became clear that their use raised questions about the proper scope of the law of parliamentary privilege in relation not only to their specific use, but to all parliamentary materials at all levels in human rights adjudication. Although courts are apparently 'mindful of the importance of refraining from trespassing upon the province of Parliament or, so far as possible, even appearing to do so',[2] the argument made here is that the evaluation of parliamentary materials in proportionality judicial review goes beyond the mere 'use' of parliamentary materials and actually *questions* parliamentary proceedings in terms of the validity of legislative choices.

One of the tasks of the law of parliamentary privilege is to insulate proceedings in Parliament from outside scrutiny. Due to this, normative evaluations of parliamentary debates by the courts are still considered by some to be prima facie a 'constitutional anathema' in the UK.[3] However, in a series of cases which postdate the enactment of the Human Rights Act 1998, the Speaker of the House of Commons has intervened in litigation on a variety of subject matters to argue that the use of Select Committee reports and Hansard in general runs contrary to

* Thanks to Alison L Young, Nick Barber, Paul P Craig, Murray Hunt, Se-Shauna Wheatle and Aileen McHarg for helpful and instructive comments. I would also like to acknowledge financial support from the Carnegie Trust for the Universities of Scotland. All errors and omissions are mine alone.

[1] M Hunt, H Hooper and P Yowell, 'Parliaments and Human Rights: Redressing the Democratic Deficit' AHRC Public Policy Series (No 5) (April 2012) ch 3, available at: www.ahrc.ac.uk/News-and-Events/Publications/Documents/Parliaments-and-Human-Rights.pdf.

[2] *R (on the application of HS2 Action Alliance Ltd) v Secretary of State for Trade and Industry* [2014] UKSC 3 [95].

[3] S Briant, 'Dialogue, Diplomacy and Defiance: Prisoners' Voting Rights at Home and in Strasbourg' (2011) 3 *European Human Rights Law Review* 243, 248.

Article 9 of the Bill of Rights. In short, due to 'the incorporation into domestic law of the requirements of the European Convention on Human Rights, the boundary between that which is protected by Article 9 and that which is not has become less clear'.[4] This chapter considers the legitimacy of the use of parliamentary materials generally by courts during proportionality review in accordance with human rights standards.

Although the use of parliamentary material in proportionality review is most likely to remain no more than an interesting niche feature of adjudication, it is a practice that has under-explored implications for British constitutional law—[5]so much so that the aforethought 'obvious' rules in this area found in *Pepper v Hart*[6] and *British Railways Board v Pickin*,[7] concerning, respectively, the use of *travaux préparatoires* and the general duty upon courts to refrain from scrutinising the process by which an Act of Parliament is enacted respectively, are no longer clear-cut (that is, if they ever were). However, when these rules are checked against the practice of citing parliamentary materials in proportionality review, they are nothing short of ambiguous.

What further complicates this enquiry—and perhaps even compels it—is the fact that the engagement with parliamentary materials by courts does not follow any form of pattern, whether real or imagined.[8] In fact, this unsystematic treatment is the core of potential problems. Aside from a handful of interventions by the Speaker of the House of Commons and the Clerk of Parliament regarding the use of Select Committee reports in litigation, there has been no attempt by any court or by parliamentarians to reach a constitutional settlement about the proper scope of this practice.

This chapter argues that current practices in this area are potentially capable of generating results which are undesirable. The argument proceeds in three stages. First, it will be shown that the existing case law on parliamentary privilege is not apt to cope with the emerging practices in judicial reasoning in the wake of the Human Rights Act 1998. Second, it will review the decisions which engage with judicial scrutiny of parliamentary materials to demonstrate that they contain no consistent rules. Finally, specific examples of judicial reference to parliamentary materials will be considered in order to explain the problems caused by this practice in the absence of a principled framework. In July 2013, the Joint Committee on Parliamentary Privilege concluded that 'recent instances of judicial questioning of proceedings in Parliament are best "treated as ... mistakes", rather than a challenge to Parliament. [S]uch mistakes may have serious consequences: ... their frequency in judicial review

---

[4] R Gordon QC and A Street, 'Select Committees and Coercive Powers—Clarity or Confusion?' (2012), 18, available at: www.consoc.org.uk/wp-content/uploads/2012/06/Select-Committees-and-Coercive-Powers-Clarity-or-Confusion.pdf.

[5] The practice has been considered briefly in PA Joseph, 'Parliament's Attenuated Privilege of Freedom of Speech' (2010) 126 *Law Quarterly Review* 568, 589–91 and in-depth more recently in A Kavanagh, 'Judges, Parliament and Proportionality: Exploring Some Forbidden Territory' (2014) 34(3) *Oxford Journal of Legal Studies* 443-479.

[6] *Pepper (Inspector of Taxes) v Hart* [1993] AC 593.

[7] *British Railways Board v Pickin* [1974] AC 765.

[8] Hunt, Hooper and Yowell (n 1) 50.

cases risks having a chilling effect upon parliamentary free speech.'[9] However, this chapter is not a plea to end the practice of reference to parliamentary materials in proportionality judgments; this would be both naïve and unrealistic. Instead, it aims to alert both constitutional actors and scholars to the need for self-reflection and occasionally caution in this exercise.

I. PARLIAMENTARY PRIVILEGE

There is debate as to the proper purpose, function and of course scope of the rules on parliamentary privilege. Parliamentary privilege is primarily an aspect of the separation of powers, which was historically a separation between the Crown and Parliament,[10] but has developed into the separation between the legislature, executive and judiciary that is a widely recognised feature of many contemporary democratic constitutional orders. In its simplest terms, parliamentary privilege is thought to have two distinct but related aspects: (i) the promotion of free speech and, in turn, democratic good governance; and (ii) the right of 'exclusive cognisance' held by Parliament, ie, 'the right of each House of Parliament to regulate its own proceedings and internal affairs without interference from any outside body'.[11]

In recent times, the courts have expressed the view that it is their prerogative to define the proper scope of parliamentary privilege, including the meaning and scope of Article 9.[12] According to the former Attorney-General Baroness Scotland, 'the respective roles of the courts and Parliament in relation to privilege are now well settled'.[13] However, the Government Green Paper of April 2012 was of the view that privilege 'protects Parliament's internal affairs from interference from the courts'.[14] Clearly, then, there is debate as to which institution has the 'last word' on the scope and nature of privilege. *Edinburgh and Dalkeith Railway v Wauchope* remains authority for the proposition that a court cannot assess the propriety of the process used to pass an Act of Parliament, but is limited to looking only at the parliamentary roll.[15] But as we shall see, the rules of parliamentary privilege have been relaxed or modified to permit what is simply seen as the 'use' of parliamentary materials to assist judicial decision-making. This section explains the origins, ambiguities and limitations of these rules. Their shortcomings become particularly clear with respect to proportionality review of legislation, which is examined below.

---

[9] Joint Committee on Parliamentary Privilege, *Parliamentary Privilege* (HC 2013–14, 100/HL 2014–14 30) para 135.

[10] A Tomkins, *Public Law* (Oxford, Clarendon Press, 2003) 39–43.

[11] HM Government, *Green Paper on Parliamentary Privilege* (Cm 8318, 2012) 9, para 7.

[12] *R (Chaytor and others) (Rev 2)* [2011] 1 AC 684 [16].

[13] Committee on an Issue of Privilege, *Police Searches on the Parliamentary Estate (First Report)* (HC 2009–10, 62) Evidence, para 1.30.

[14] HM Government, *Green Paper on Parliamentary Privilege* (Cm 8318, 2012) 8, para 1.

[15] *Edinburgh and Dalkeith Railway v Wauchope* (1842) 8 Cl & Fin 723, HL cited in D Oliver and G Drewry, 'The Law and Parliament' in D Oliver and G Drewry (eds), *The Law and Parliament* (London, Butterworths, 1998) 4.

A. Freedom of Speech in Parliament

Article 9 of the Bill of Rights of 1689 declares that 'freedom of speech and debates or proceedings in Parliament ought not to be impeached or questioned in any court or place out of Parliament'. The Bill of Rights was enacted in the wake of the 'Glorious Revolution' of 1688–89 for the purpose of curbing arbitrary abuse of power by the monarch and to establish the rights of Parliament in relation to the Crown.[16] It fits the mould of neither a 'modern Bill of Rights' as ordinarily understood, nor a written constitution for the UK.[17] Nevertheless, Article 9 is considered to be 'a fundamental constitutional principle that arguably has a stronger claim than Magna Carta to be regarded as a foundation of our parliamentary democracy'.[18] The intention of Article 9 when it was adopted was to insulate speech by parliamentarians from civil or criminal liability for statements made in Parliament so as to promote freedom of expression, and in turn democracy, to the maximum possible extent.

The free speech clause in the Bill of Rights has been a privilege jealously guarded by Parliament. Nonetheless, the law in this area has developed considerably over time. Until 1840, even the reporting of parliamentary activity in newspapers was prohibited.[19] In *Stockdale v Hansard*[20] (which led to the passing of the Parliamentary Papers Act 1840), the High Court held that parliamentary privilege protected documents printed by order of the House for its own members' exclusive use, but that such protection did not extend to papers made available outside the House to members of the public.[21] Broadcasting of parliamentary proceedings from both the Chambers and the Select Committees on television or radio was prohibited until as recently as 1988.[22] There is some evidence to suggest that the freedom of speech of parliamentarians has been judicially regarded as more important than the right of ordinary citizens to free expression because of the nature of the constitutional function that parliamentarians perform.[23]

Two decisions regarding the limits upon curial enquiry into the legislative process are well known to students of constitutional law: *British Railways Board v Pickin*[24]

---

[16] Tomkins (n 10) ch 2.

[17] L Maer and O Gay, 'The Bill of Rights 1689', House of Commons Library (SN/PC/0293: 5 October 2009) para 1. See also O Gay and H Tomlinson, 'Privilege and Freedom of Speech' in A Horne, G Drewry and D Oliver (eds), *Parliament and the Law (Hart Studies in Constitutional Law)* (Oxford, Hart Publishing, 2013).

[18] AW Bradley, 'The Damian Green Affair—All's Well That Ends Well?' [2012] *Public Law* 396, 397.

[19] Parliamentary Papers Act 1840, s 1. See also Joint Select Committee on Parliamentary Privilege, *First Report* (1998–99, HL 43-I / HC 214-I) ch 8, para 341.

[20] *Stockdale v Hansard* [1839] EWHC (QB) J21.

[21] See also Joint Select Committee on Parliamentary Privilege (n 19) ch 8, para 340.

[22] PM Leopold, 'Parliamentary Privilege and the Broadcasting of Parliament' (1989) 9(1) *Legal Studies* 53.

[23] See, eg, *Lord Carlile and others v Home Secretary* [2012] EWHC 617 (Admin) [26]. However, in the Court of Appeal in *R (Lord Carlile and others) v Home Secretary* [2013] EWCA Civ 199, McCombe LJ suggested that there was no reason to 'to afford a higher value, from the outset, to the rights of politicians (under Article 10) over and above other citizens' (at [107]). For a developed discussion of parliamentary privilege and media reporting rights, see A Geddis, 'What We Cannot Talk About We Must Pass over in Silence: Judicial Orders and Reporting Parliamentary Speech' [2010] *Public Law* 443.

[24] *British Railways Board v Pickin* (n 7).

and *Pepper v Hart*.[25] In *Pickin*, the House of Lords held that the courts are not empowered to declare an Act of Parliament invalid by investigating the legislative process and declaring it to be somehow defective. To that end:

> [It] must be for Parliament to decide whether it is satisfied that an Act should be passed in the form and with the wording set out in the Act. It must be for Parliament to decide what documentary material or testimony it requires and the extent to which Parliamentary privilege should attach.[26]

The *ratio* of *Pickin* is that when Parliament is legislating, it is for *Parliament alone* to decide on the scope of its own process, including which evidence it shall hear in debate and the range of factors it shall consider, or decline to consider, when enacting legislation. The specific issue before the Court in *Pickin* was whether it could consider if British Railways had deliberately concealed information from Parliament so that the British Railways Act 1968 was passed. Thus, as Oliver and Drewry point out, prior to the enactment of the Human Rights Act 1998, it was a rule of both the common law and parliamentary privilege that Parliament was entirely responsible for its own processes.[27]

Almost two decades after *Pickin*, the House of Lords ruled in *Pepper v Hart* that parliamentary privilege did not preclude a court from consulting *travaux préparatoires*, such as speeches by a minister proposing a bill, to determine the meaning of a statute where a literal interpretation of the ordinary language would lead to an absurd or unclear result. However, the rule in *Pepper v Hart* laid down an important restriction regarding the type of material a court could use to make such an interpretive enquiry. When determining Parliament's intention in a legislative provision, the court could only consider statements made by the relevant minister or another promoter of the bill. This meant that other materials, such as excerpts from debates on the floor of either House, could not be considered. However, Krishnaprasad observes that parliamentary reports, such as Select Committee reports, were admissible even before the House of Lords decided *Pepper v Hart*. This fact was acknowledged in *Pepper v Hart* by Lord Browne-Wilkinson, who stated that courts already resorted to 'white papers, reports of official committees and Law Commission reports' in order to determine the 'mischief' at which legislation is directed.[28] Moreover, it is considered permissible to have regard to ministerial statements in the course of an ordinary judicial review action.[29] The Joint Committee on Parliamentary Privilege, reporting in the 1998–99 session, considered that such reference to ministerial statements and committee reports in judicial review cases had become an 'established practice' and that 'Parliament should welcome this recent development'.[30]

---

[25] *Pepper (Inspector of Taxes) v Hart* (n 6).

[26] *British Railways Board v Pickin* (n 7), Lord Morris of Borth-y-Gest, 10.

[27] Oliver and Drewry (n 15) 4.

[28] KV Krishnaprasad, '*Pepper v Hart*: Its Continuing Implications in the United Kingdom and India' (2011) 32(3) *Statute Law Review* 227, 229; *Pepper (Inspector of Taxes) v Hart* (n 6), Lord Browne-Wilkinson, 23.

[29] *R v Secretary of State for the Home Department ex p Brind* [1991] 1 AC 696.

[30] Joint Committee on Parliamentary Privilege (n 19) ch 2, paras 49–50.

B. Parliamentary Privilege as 'Exclusive Cognisance'

The other aspect of parliamentary privilege is 'exclusive cognisance', which in recent times has been called 'a reflection of parliamentary sovereignty'.[31] Accordingly, courts cannot 'strike down Parliament's decisions by challenging the procedures used to reach the decisions, nor may they suspend someone as a member of either House'.[32] The 2012 Green Paper on *Parliamentary Privilege* also recognised that Parliament can limit its 'exclusive cognisance' by statute. Prior to the publication of this Green Paper, the UK Supreme Court discussed 'exclusive cognisance' in *R v Chaytor*.[33] Their Lordships held that parliamentary privilege could not insulate members of either House from the consequences of a criminal investigation in respect of allegedly fraudulent expenses claims. Interestingly, there was only one attempt made to connect the principle of 'exclusive cognisance' in *Chaytor* with broader debates concerning parliamentary sovereignty, which was directly quoted from the 1999 *Joint Committee on Parliamentary Privilege Report*.[34]

According to Lord Phillips in *Chaytor*, 'exclusive cognisance' refers to the right of Parliament and also to the right of each individual House to 'manage its own affairs without interference from the other [House] or from outside Parliament'.[35] The Supreme Court also ruled that exclusive cognisance had additional aspects. Lord Clarke viewed exclusive cognisance as the privilege of Parliament as a whole, not of individual parliamentarians. The second characteristic, which flowed from the first, was that Parliament as a whole could relinquish its 'exclusive cognisance' and had clearly done so in the case of 'ordinary crime' because the Theft Act 1968 applied throughout England and Wales.[36] Although there were various references to examples of Parliament waiving its right to 'exclusive cognisance' either through primary legislation or administrative practice, the Court was not invited to determine a test for when 'exclusive cognisance' was waived. This of course means that it remains unclear whether the Human Rights Act 1998 touches upon the 'exclusive cognisance' of Parliament.

The fact that parliamentary privilege has two aspects, then, potentially creates a dilemma. If the most important aspect of privilege is that it exists to promote freedom of speech, democracy and the separation of powers, as appears to be the case in Article 9, then there may be some room for citation of parliamentary materials. However, if we approach Article 9 as merely being a subset of 'exclusive cognisance', then it becomes much more difficult to view the citation of parliamentary

---

[31] HM Government, *Green Paper on Parliamentary Privilege* (Cm 8318, 2012) para 26.
[32] ibid, para 27.
[33] *R (Chaytor and others) (Rev 2)* (n 12).
[34] Joint Committee on Parliamentary Privilege (n 19). The quotation is from para 247: 'The dividing line between privileged and non-privileged activities of each House is not easy to define. Perhaps the nearest approach to a definition is that the areas in which the courts ought not to intervene extend beyond proceedings in Parliament, but the privileged areas must be so closely and directly connected with proceedings in Parliament that intervention by the courts would be inconsistent with Parliament's sovereignty as a legislative and deliberative assembly.'
[35] *R (Chaytor and others) (Rev 2)* (n 12) [63].
[36] *Wellesley v Duke of Beaufort* (1831) 2 Russ & M 639, 655, Lord Brougham LC; *R (Chaytor and others) (Rev 2)* (n 12) [99].

materials in judgments regarding the proportionality of legislation as permissible. This is because, as we shall see, in reviewing proportionality of legislation, the court may be invited to take a position on how well Parliament has balanced competing considerations during the legislative process. But nothing in either *Chaytor* or the 2012 Green Paper on privilege suggests that freedom of speech should be seen as an inferior sub-category of privilege to 'exclusive cognisance'. If that were the case, there may be some cause for arguing that parliamentary materials were entirely inadmissible in court proceedings. However, as argued below, relevant case law has touched only on the relationship between free speech in Parliament and the citation of parliamentary materials. Therefore, the argument herein assumes that Article 9 is a stand-alone facet of parliamentary privilege which is not subordinate to exclusive cognisance or parliamentary sovereignty. In view of this, thinking critically about the relationship between proportionality review and the citation of parliamentary materials is all the more important.

II. PROPORTIONALITY REVIEW UNDER THE HUMAN RIGHTS ACT 1998

The doctrine of proportionality is a concept adapted from German administrative law[37] which aims to ensure that legislative and administrative restrictions on human rights can be justified as legitimate and necessary.[38] Proportionality review is the general standard of judicial review in Human Rights Act cases.[39] Articles 8, 9, 10 and 11 of the European Convention on Human Rights (ECHR) have 'in-built' limitation clauses which assist in proportionality-led reasoning. Judicial review of the proportionality of a legislative measure under the Human Rights Act involves the application of a four-stage judicial test for deciding whether an interference with a right is proportionate. This was clearly elucidated in *Huang*[40] and subsequently confirmed in *Quila*: (i) is the legislative objective sufficiently important to justify limiting a fundamental right?; (ii) are the measures which have been designed to meet it rationally connected to it?; (iii) are they no more than are necessary to accomplish it?; and finally (iv) do they strike a fair balance between the rights of the individual and the interests of the community?[41]

Proportionality review has been seen as potentially providing a more stringent form of review than traditional *Wednesbury* 'reasonableness' review, although it is generally accepted that both forms of review involve some judicial scrutiny of a decision's 'merits'.[42] In proportionality review, the task of the court is to assess

---

[37] DM Beatty, *The Ultimate Rule of Law* (New York, Oxford University Press, 2004) ch 5; D Grimm, 'Proportionality in Canada and German Jurisprudence' (2007) 57 *University of Toronto Law Journal* 383. According to Lord Reed, the concept has 'origins in German administrative law, where it forms the basis of a rigorously structured analysis of the validity of legislative and administrative acts': *Bank Mellat v HM Treasury (No 2)* [2013] UKSC 39; [2013] 4 All ER 533 [68], Lord Reed.

[38] J Rivers, 'Proportionality and Variable Intensity of Review' (2006) 65(1) *Cambridge Law Journal* 174.

[39] *R (Daly) v Home Secretary* [2001] 2 AC 532 HL [26], Lord Steyn.

[40] *Huang v Secretary of State for the Home Department* [2007] 2 AC 167 [19], Lord Bingham.

[41] *R (Quila) v Secretary of State for the Home Department* [2012] 1 AC 621 [45].

[42] PP Craig, 'Proportionality, Rationality and Review' (2010) *New Zealand Law Review* 265.

'whether a fair balance was struck between the demands of the general interest of the community and the requirements of the protection of the individual's fundamental rights'.[43] By contrast, the starkest formulation of *Wednesbury* unreasonableness is that a decision may be found to be unreasonable if it is 'so unreasonable that no reasonable authority could ever have come to it'.[44] In short, reasonableness review allows for limited constraint on the exercise of administrative discretion. In direct contrast, proportionality mandates a penetrating enquiry into a legislative or administrative measure which necessitates that the court conducts its own explicit interest balancing exercise.

There has been vociferous opposition to the idea of proportionality review *in general terms* from some academic commentators who view it as a judicial seizure of democratic power caused by the intrusion of adjudication into the realm of democratic legislative policy.[45] In fact, Griffith famously commented that the proportionality clause in Article 10 of the ECHR, which guarantees freedom of expression, appeared to be a 'statement of a political conflict pretending to be a resolution of it'.[46] However, defenders of such review assert that when Parliament enacted the Human Rights Act 1998, it willingly made proportionality review a feature of British constitutional life.[47] Therefore, if the consultation of parliamentary materials in proportionality review of legislation is to be properly considered more controversial than such review in general, then the process of judicial consideration of parliamentary materials must *go beyond* so-called ordinary proportionality review in some way, or at least risk inhibiting its optimal operation in some broader sense. It must, in some sense, risk compromising the independence of the judiciary, or the independence of parliamentary process broadly conceived. If the use of parliamentary materials in proportionality adjudication is worthy of attention, then it must satisfy two criteria. First, the use of such reports in adjudication must speak to a feature of adjudication not present in so-called ordinary statutory interpretation. Second, interpretation of this type must somehow go beyond the acceptable limits of the rule on recourse to parliamentary materials permitted in *Pepper v Hart*. Therefore, the citation of parliamentary materials in proportionality judgments must threaten the 'constitutional goods' of free speech, democracy and the separation of powers more acutely than other forms of adjudication.

In other words, the question which underpins this enquiry is: does proportionality adjudication involving a question of the compatibility of legislation under the Human Rights Act 1998 involve something more than 'simply interpretation of statutory words as enacted'? Must it be more controversial because it involves 'interpretation of statutory words with a view to making them, as far as possible, compatible

---

[43] *Sporrong and Lönnroth v Sweden* (1982) 5 EHRR 35 [69].

[44] *Associated Provincal Picture Houses Ltd v Wednesbury Corporation* [1947] 2 All ER 680, Master of the Rolls.

[45] See generally JAG Griffith, 'The Political Constitution' (1979) 42 *Modern Law Review* 1; A Tomkins, *Our Republican Constitution* (Oxford, Hart Publishing, 2005); R Hirschl, *Towards Juristocracy: The Origins and Consequences of the New Constitutionalism* (Cambridge MA, Harvard University Press, 2004); and J Morgan, 'Law's British Empire' (2002) 22 *Oxford Journal of Legal Studies* 729.

[46] Griffith (n 45) 14.

[47] AL Young, *Parliamentary Sovereignty and the Human Rights Act* (Oxford, Hart Publishing, 2008).

with an external standard'?[48] Although Lord Browne-Wilkinson admitted that prior to *Pepper v Hart*, judges would privately consult *Hansard* in their chambers to uncover the intention of Parliament,[49] the answer to both of these questions is affirmative, and the first one obviously so. Proportionality review is qualitatively different from statutory interpretation, even in cases where statutory interpretation requires a complex departure from the literal wording of the text with justification based upon external sources. It is more controversial than this simply because of the nature of the interest balancing exercise which *must* take place. That is not to say that there may not be instances in the general law of statutory interpretation which require interest balancing. However, in proportionality adjudication courts must undertake an independent, rational evaluation of competing claims upon which there could be a range of reasonable answers, or 'reasonable disagreement'.[50]

This chapter highlights that it is at least possible for proportionality review which makes use of parliamentary materials to be controversial in a manner that goes beyond the general criticism of proportionality review made by judicial review 'sceptics'.[51] Three particularly controversial aspects of the practice are discussed here. First, the 'guiding principles' of law which regulate the use of parliamentary materials in judgments conflict with the rule in *Pepper v Hart*. Second, the current flexibility with which parliamentary materials are used in legal argument actually risks compromising judicial independence in proportionality judgments. Finally, the approach taken by the courts when using parliamentary materials to evaluate the proportionality of legislation may lead judges to constrain and misunderstand the proper institutional functions of Parliament. None of this is to suggest that further controversies could not be outlined, nor does it suggest that the practice of citing parliamentary materials in judgments cannot pass without incident. Equally, the consideration of parliamentary materials might be subject to the same pitfalls as any other 'social science' evidence used in judgments.[52]

III. JUDICIAL USE OF PARLIAMENTARY MATERIALS: THE CASE LAW

Blackburn was correct in declaring that the Human Rights Act 'promises to be a major readjustment in our legal and parliamentary traditions'.[53] Given the torrid historical backdrop which preceded the creation of the immutable right to freedom of expression in Parliament, it is perhaps understandable that the parliamentary authorities treat any perceived encroachment into privileged territory with suspicion.

---

[48] Krishnaprasad (n 28) 233.

[49] PA Joseph, 'Parliament's Attenuated Privilege of Freedom of Speech' (2010) 126 *Law Quarterly Review* 568, 590.

[50] R Bellamy, *Political Constitutionalism: A Republican Defence of the Constitutionality of Democracy* (Cambridge, Cambridge University Press, 2007) 246.

[51] T Campbell, KD Ewing and A Tomkins (eds), *The Legal Protection of Human Rights: Sceptical Essays* (Oxford, Oxford University Press, 2011).

[52] J King, 'Constitutional Rights and Social Welfare: A Comment on the Canadian *Chaoulli* Health Care Decision' (2006) 69 *Modern Law Review* 631–43.

[53] R Blackburn, 'Parliament and Human Rights' in Oliver and Drewry (eds) (n 15) 175.

As discussed above, perceived attempts by the British courts to evaluate parliamentary proceedings are treated with hostility.[54] However, it is not entirely clear that courts avoid such evaluation of parliamentary activity in the context of human rights adjudication.

The issue in the specific context of the Human Rights Act 1998 came before the House of Lords in *Wilson*,[55] when the Speaker of the House of Commons objected to the use of *Hansard* to determine the intended meaning of various provisions of the Consumer Credit Act 1974. The Secretary of State for Trade and Industry opposed a decision of a lower court in Mrs Wilson's favour, which stated that the exclusion of a judicial remedy in section 127(3) of the Consumer Credit Act 1974 amounted to a disproportionate method of securing a legislative policy objective and so interfered with Mrs Wilson's Convention rights under Article 6(1) and Article 1 of Protocol 1 ECHR.

Their Lordships rejected the Speaker's argument that the use of *Hansard* in Human Rights Act 1998 compatibility review violated parliamentary privilege. In doing so, the Court justified this departure from the 'straightforward' identification of legislative intent permitted in *Pepper v Hart* by classifying review of the proportionality of a legislative measure as a *fundamentally different adjudicative task* which Parliament had consciously conferred upon the courts. Lord Nicholls pointed out that unlike the usual situation of legislative interpretation envisaged by the rule in *Pepper v Hart*, compatibility review was concerned with 'practicalities',[56] and such review of practicalities involved the making of a 'value judgement'[57] on the part of the court. Although conducting such review would normally mean that 'the facts will often speak for themselves',[58] recourse to debates on the floor of either House and to other parliamentary materials was both permissible and necessary because for courts to refuse to do so would be to '[fail] in the due discharge of the new role assigned to them by Parliament'.[59] According to the House of Lords in *Wilson*, this new role did not amount to 'questioning Parliament' in any way. Consideration of parliamentary materials was better understood as part of a requirement upon the court to perform its constitutional duty by better positioning itself to 'understand the legislation'.[60] Lord Nicholls emphasised that it was still the view of the House of Lords that 'the court is called upon to evaluate the proportionality of the legislation, not the adequacy of the minister's exploration of the policy options or his explanations to Parliament'.[61]

The deliberate inability of the courts to invalidate primary legislation under the Human Rights Act 1998 lends credibility to the suggestion in *Wilson* that parliamentary privilege is not threatened by the use of such materials. After all, the

---

[54] S Briant, 'Dialogue, Diplomacy and Defiance: Prisoners' Voting Rights at Home and in Strasbourg' (2011) 3 *European Human Rights Law Review* 243, 248.
[55] *Wilson v Secretary for Trade and Industry* [2004] 1 AC 816.
[56] ibid [61], Lord Nicholls.
[57] ibid.
[58] ibid.
[59] ibid [64], Lord Nicholls.
[60] ibid.
[61] ibid [67], Lord Nicholls.

rules in sections 3 and 4 of the Act mean that a court cannot invalidate legislation during judicial review at all, let alone because Parliament's legislative process was inadequate, ie, because it did not take account of some body of evidence when interfering with a particular human right. In this respect, the common law rule that parliamentary procedures are the prerogative of Parliament seems to survive intact regardless of the innovation in *Wilson*.

Despite this, Joseph's argument that: 'A policy justification [from *Hansard*] that was palpably deficient would be highly probative in applying the proportionality test' remains persuasive. Consider the facts of *Animal Defenders International*.[62] The Government had issued a section 19(1)(b) of the Human Rights Act 1998 statement in Parliament in respect of the Communications Bill, asserting that it wished to proceed with a blanket ban on 'political advertising'. The Secretary of State was of the view that using section 19(1)(b) was the appropriate course of action because although the Government was of the view that the ban was compatible with Article 10 ECHR, the decision of Strasbourg in *VgT Verein v Switzerland*[63] rendered the law unclear. The reason for this blanket ban was that constructing a legislative measure to reflect nuanced situations would prove an insurmountable task. The political organisation Animal Defenders International unsuccessfully challenged section 321(2) of the Communications Act 2003 as being incompatible with Article 10 ECHR before the House of Lords.

In the leading speech, Lord Bingham acknowledged that the Government had proceeded under section 19(1)(b) even though, in the Lords' view, the ban was not incompatible with Article 10 ECHR. Consideration of parliamentary materials was extensive and Lord Bingham noted that:

> [D]espite an express request by the Joint Human Rights Committee to consider compromise solutions, the government judged that no fair and workable compromise solution could be found which would address the problem, a judgment which Parliament accepted. I see no reason to challenge that judgment.[64]

The House of Lords concluded that Parliament's solution was appropriate, but only after a searching inquiry. By the same token, then, it could be inferred that the Court at the apex of the domestic judicial system would have had no qualms about consulting parliamentary materials to conclude a legislative measure was a *disproportionate* interference with a Convention right if the parliamentary treatment had been somehow inadequate. In other words, Joseph's concerns about courts using *Hansard* to determine the inadequacy of a legislative measure certainly carry weight in light of *Animal Defenders International*.[65]

---

[62] *R (Animal Defenders International) v Secretary of State for Culture, Media and Sport* [2008] AC 1312.

[63] *VgT Verein v Switzerland* (2001) 34 EHRR 159.

[64] *R (Animal Defenders International) v Secretary of State for Culture, Media, and Sport* (n 62) [32], Lord Bingham.

[65] The Grand Chamber of the ECtHR also upheld the proportionality of the ban, albeit by a narrow split of 9:8. The majority view was based on extensive examination of the Westminster Parliament's approach: *Animal Defenders International v UK* [2013] ECHR 362. For a cogent discussion, see J King, 'Deference, Dialogue and Animal Defenders International' United Kingdom Constitutional Law Blog (25 April 2013), available at: www.ukconstitutionallaw.org.

All is not as clear as it once seemed. Moreover, there exists a strain of judicial reasoning from the lower courts which relates to consultation of parliamentary materials in situations other than proportionality review considered by the House of Lords in *Wilson*. Some four years after *Wilson*, in a case called *Bradley*,[66] the Administrative Court concluded that an attempt by the claimants to rely upon evidence given by the Ombudsman to a Select Committee in judicial review proceedings was precluded by Article 9 of the Bill of Rights 1689. This conclusion was in the context of a partially successful judicial review claim concerning the Government's rejection of the findings of the Parliamentary Commissioner for Administration (hereinafter the 'Ombudsman'). In the same case, it was also held that reliance upon a *finalised report* of the Ombudsman did not contravene the rule in Article 9. So, according to Bean J in *Bradley*, a literal reading of section 16(3) of the Parliamentary Privileges Act 1987 would be, in his view, absurd because it would in effect 'prohibit reliance on reports of the Joint Committee on Human Rights, which ... have been cited in a number of appellate cases in this jurisdiction'.[67]

Bean J considered that the two types of parliamentary proceeding (the evidence given to Parliament and the finalised report of the Ombudsman or Committee) could reasonably be distinguished. The distinction was drawn in the following terms: the Report of the Select Committee represented a finalised view of the majority of its members, and as a result it was unlikely that future citation in legal proceedings would mean that 'a Committee would be inhibited from expressing its view, whether critical or supportive of the actions of government'.[68] In other words, citation of Select Committee reports would not have a 'chilling effect' on parliamentary speech.

By contrast, referring to Select Committee evidence resembled questioning the content of a parliamentary debate, because unlike a published Select Committee or Ombudsman report, citation of such evidence in a judicial evaluation would amount to an evaluation of the *quality of the speech and reasoning processes* in Parliament and would therefore amount to the contravention of parliamentary privilege. The core of the distinction seems to be, then, that finalised reports can be equated with clear statements of parliamentary intention (like those by bill sponsors and ministers, as permitted by *Pepper v Hart*), whereas evidence to committees is equivalent to general debate on the floor of either House, the content of which is prohibited from judicial examination by the rule in Article 9 of the Bill of Rights. But Bean J's classification is obviously wider than the rule in *Pepper v Hart*, which purports to restrict courts to looking at statements of sponsoring ministers or other supporters of a bill.

Although the above distinction applies to a wider category of materials than *Pepper v Hart*, it would remain somewhat reassuring to those concerned about the possible 'chilling effect' of curial enquiry into parliamentary speech. However, the tentative distinction drawn by Bean J in *Bradley* appears to be subtly undermined by the dicta in *R (Wheeler) v Prime Minister*.[69] Wheeler unsuccessfully challenged

---

[66] *R (Bradley) v Secretary for Work and Pensions* [2007] EWHC 242 (Admin).
[67] ibid [32], Bean J.
[68] Ibid [35], Bean J.
[69] *R (Wheeler) v Prime Minister and Foreign Secretary* [2008] EWHC 1409 (Admin).

an alleged failure to adhere to a purported legitimate expectation in the form of a promise by the Government to hold a referendum relating to the ratification of the (then) proposed European Union Constitution. When the Treaty which aimed to establish a Constitution for the European Union was abandoned in favour of a conventional treaty amending the existing legal framework (the Lisbon Treaty), the Government decided that such a measure no longer required a referendum. In the course of the explication of the facts of the case before the Administrative Court, various parliamentary materials were cited without objection because their status as purely explanatory aides was agreed upon by all sides. In the course of the elucidation of the facts, various 'promises'—in the ordinary sense of the term—to hold a referendum were recounted from *Hansard*.[70]

Wheeler sought an order from the court requiring the executive to introduce a bill into Parliament or, pursuant to section 101(4) of the Political Parties, Elections and Referendums Act 2000, to lay an Order for a referendum before Parliament. The Court concluded that none of the materials relied upon by the claimant amounted to a promise giving rise to a legitimate expectation in administrative law that a referendum would be held. However, it concluded that even if the materials relied upon had been enough to prima facie give rise to such a legitimate expectation, it would not be enforceable because 'a promise of this kind place[s] it in the realm of politics, not of the courts'.[71] The reason given was that a decision of this type fell firmly within 'the macro-political field'—the realm of politics that is driven by broad public interest considerations which are by their very nature multi-layered and entail wide-ranging general considerations of policy.[72]

In respect of general considerations of parliamentary privilege raised by the claim, the Court, relying on dicta from *ex parte Smedley*, made general comments to the effect that it would be contrary to constitutional convention for a court to make comments on the merits of proposed legislation.[73] Moreover, it was held that the claimant's request that the Court should compel the introduction of an Order into Parliament, if granted, would amount to the Court compelling Parliament to legislate. The introduction of a bill into Parliament 'forms part of the proceedings of Parliament' and it was accordingly beyond the competence of the court to compel Parliament to act in such a way—in fact, for a court to do so would be 'to trespass impermissibly on the province of Parliament'.[74]

Regarding the more specific issue of relying upon the work of parliamentary committees in legal proceedings, the court in *Wheeler* laid down two legal propositions. The first was that 'the *opinion* expressed by a Parliamentary committee is generally irrelevant to the issue of *fact* to be decided by the court'. The second point was that reliance on such an opinion by one party risks the situation where the other

---

[70] ibid [5]–[9].

[71] ibid [41].

[72] *R v Secretary of State for Education and Employment ex p Begbie* [2000] 1 WLR 1115 [1130F]–[1131D].

[73] *R v Her Majesty's Treasury ex p Smedley* [1985] QB 657 as discussed in *R (Wheeler) v Prime Minister and Foreign Secretary* (n 69) [47].

[74] *R (Wheeler) v Prime Minister and Foreign Secretary* (n 69) [49] and *Prebble v Television New Zealand Ltd* [1995] 1 AC 321.

party contends the opinion is wrong. Activity of this sort in a court amounts to 'the questioning of proceedings in Parliament, in breach of Parliamentary privilege'.[75] The legitimacy of judicial consideration of opinions of parliamentary committees was not afforded the same degree of scrutiny in *Animal Defenders International*. Moreover, in *Wheeler*, the court was of the opinion that the claimant's use of parliamentary materials to serve factual ends created problems in both respects. This consequence did not seem to be considered at all in *Bradley*.

Clearly, the law of parliamentary privilege in Article 9, which has the dual aims of protecting free speech in Parliament and preserving the separation of powers, requires clarification both in general terms and specifically with respect to the citation of parliamentary materials. There is a tension in the case law regarding the propriety of the use of parliamentary materials to illuminate issues of fact, insofar as we think of facts as being contestable facts. The dicta in *Wheeler* regarding the status of parliamentary materials places the distinction between so-called 'completed' works of Parliament, such as the final reports of committees and the Ombudsman, and 'works in progress', such as evidence to committees and contributions made on the floor of each House (other than ministerial statements), in jeopardy. The justification for the relaxation of the rules of parliamentary privilege in *Wilson* is based upon their Lordships' conclusion that Parliament consciously altered the doctrine of parliamentary sovereignty when enacting the Human Rights Act 1998 to permit proportionality review thereunder. This is, apparently, what allows judicial evaluation of parliamentary materials as a guide to parliamentary action in the 'macro-political field'. Whether this distinction is either one of sustainable principle or reasonable practice compels further enquiry.

The distinction between ministerial statements and completed works, as opposed to 'works in progress', was blurred further in *R (Age UK) v Secretary of State for Business, Innovation and Skills*.[76] The issue in the case was whether or not the Employment Equality Age Regulations[77] constituted a proportionate interference with the principle of non-discrimination in EU law. In this case, decided in 2009, the Attorney-General submitted that it was constitutionally improper—on grounds of parliamentary privilege—for a court 'to receive in these proceedings the record of evidence given by a witness to a Parliamentary Committee, and the views of the Committee itself'.[78] Blake J rejected this submission and ruled that there was no constitutional impediment to 'the court receiving the material that the parties … place before it for the purpose of informing itself as to the statutory history … relevant considerations that led to the formation of policy … the aim of the policy [and] the existence of factors that might be relevant to the assessment of whether the Regulations were proportionate'.[79] In Blake J's view, there were three relevant

---

[75] *R (Wheeler) v Prime Minister and Foreign Secretary* (n 69) [54].
[76] *R (Age UK) v Secretary of State for Business, Innovation and Skills, the Equality and Human Rights Commission and HM Attorney-General* [2009] EWHC 2336 (Admin).
[77] Employment Equality Age Regulations 2006 (SI 1031/2006).
[78] *R (Age UK) v Secretary of State for Business, Innovation and Skills, the Equality and Human Rights Commission and HM Attorney General* (n 76) [44].
[79] Ibid [50], Blake J.

aspects of the preceding case law in *Prebble*,[80] *Al Fayed*,[81] *Bradley*[82] and *OGC*.[83] First, the Court 'must ... ensure that it does not directly or indirectly impugn or question any proceedings in Parliament'. Second, the definition of 'impugn or question' in practice means that a court cannot 'receive evidence of what is said in Parliament for the purpose of agreeing or disagreeing with it'. Finally, the court must reach its *own conclusions* as to the legality and proportionality of legislation or administrative decision-making. In short, a court cannot reach such conclusions by 'agreeing or disagreeing with the expressions of opinion that may have occurred inside Parliament, however eminent or well qualified may be the people expressing those opinions'.[84]

It may be that Blake J was attempting to rationalise existing practice with respect to proportionality judgments. However, it has not proved easy to draw principled boundaries for the acceptable judicial consideration of parliamentary materials. The bright line envisaged in *Age UK* between agreement and disagreement with parliamentary opinion on the one hand and guidance as to 'statutory history [and] relevant considerations that led to the formation of policy' on the other, which would not imperil independent judicial conclusions, is not readily visible. The best illustration of this dilemma comes by way of example. In *R (N) v Health Secretary and Nottingham Healthcare NHS Trust*,[85] a residential patient in a mental health facility challenged the ban on smoking in the workplace[86] as a disproportionate interference with his Article 8 ECHR rights. The patient, N, also considered that the ban constituted discrimination in contravention of Article 14 ECHR in respect of his 'other status' as a residential mental patient. The Court of Appeal ruled against N, holding that the workplace ban on smoking constituted a proportionate and non-discriminatory interference with his human rights in pursuit of the broader policy goal of protecting public health in the workplace. In doing so, the Court made reference to a report of the JCHR[87] quoting in particular the Committee's conclusion that:

> [T]he fact that [the ban] does not extend to a person's home, and that provision is made to exempt places which are peoples' de facto homes, the interference with the private life of smokers is in our view likely to be upheld as being proportionate.[88]

It would of course be both impossible as a matter of fact and improper as a matter of assumption to suggest that the Court of Appeal abdicated independent judgment in favour of adopting the reasoning of a parliamentary committee. At the same time,

---

[80] *Prebble v Television New Zealand Ltd* (n 74).

[81] *Hamilton v Al Fayed* [2001] 1 AC 395.

[82] *R (Bradley and others) v Secretary of State for Work and Pensions* [2007] EWHC 242 (Admin).

[83] *Office of Government Commerce (OGC) v Information Commissioner, HM Attorney-General and Speaker of the House of Commons* [2008] EWHC 737 (Admin).

[84] *R (Age UK) v Secretary of State for Business, Innovation and Skills, the Equality and Human Rights Commission and HM Attorney-General* (n 76) [51], Blake J.

[85] *R (N) v Health Secretary and Nottingham Healthcare NHS Trust* [2009] EWCA Civ 795.

[86] Smoke-free (Exemption & Vehicles) Regulations 2007 (SI 2007/765), reg 10(3).

[87] Joint Committee on Human Rights, *Legislative Scrutiny: Third Progress Report (6th Report)* (2005–06, HL 96, HC 787).

[88] ibid, para 1.37 cited in *R (N) v Health Secretary and Nottingham Healthcare NHS Trust* (n 85) [19].

it cannot be readily disputed that the Court of Appeal agreed with the conclusions of the JCHR, contra the formulation of Blake J in the lower Administrative Court. Whether the Court of Appeal effectively 'agreed' with the conclusion of the JCHR that the regulations were proportionate by accident, grand design or as part of a much more complex evidence-based judgment in which the JCHR report formed only a small consideration is impossible to tell. Who knows? In effect, then, the use of parliamentary materials in their completed form (let alone specific evidence or proceedings) always carries with it the attendant risk that courts will implicitly endorse or disagree with the content of proceedings in Parliament. Obviously, whether or not this has any adverse consequences for the quality or scope of parliamentary proceedings is a matter of fact outside the scope of enquiry of this chapter. What is important for this enquiry is that *R (N) v Health Secretary* aptly illustrates that no principled judicial formulation of the appropriate interaction with parliamentary materials functions in practice.

IV. JUDICIAL USE OF PARLIAMENTARY MATERIALS: SOME DIFFICULT EXAMPLES

The distinction drawn in *Wheeler* between ministerial statements to Parliament and completed or 'published' Select Committee reports, as opposed to other forms of debate, collapsed in *Age UK*. Moreover, as we can see above, it is not always certain that such a distinction is adhered to in practice. In spite of this, it does not follow directly that the freeform use of parliamentary materials in judgments is a cause for concern in and of itself. Therefore, the purpose of this section is to illustrate that despite the generally benign deployment of parliamentary materials in proportionality review, there are instances where this practice could be considered undesirable. To do this, we must consider judicial engagement with the parliamentary process a little more widely. The reason for doing so is that although judicial consideration of the use of parliamentary materials in 'straightforward' proportionality judgments under the Human Rights Act 1998 alone reflects the type of naïve approach taken in *Wilson*: this type of judicial reasoning is not hermetically sealed. Second, as discussed at the outset, engagement with parliamentary materials in proportionality adjudication forms a small part of two larger considerations: (1) proportionality adjudication generally; and (2) debates about parliamentary privilege and the appropriate relationship between the courts and Parliament.

A. Implications for Judicial and Parliamentary Independence

It is worth reversing the conundrum discussed above to illustrate that it is not always courts which seek to engage problematically with Parliament. In short, the traffic is capable of two-way flow. Blake J was correct to caution against the judicial practice of adopting parliamentary proceedings as reasons for considering a particular decision or legislative measure to be proportionate. But recent changes to government policy regarding the deportation of foreign criminals and the scope of Article 8 ECHR rights provides an example of how adopting a particular view of parliamentary processes can be used as an attempt to compel a particular outcome before a court. The purpose of the change in immigration policy was to provide the courts with parliamentary approved guidance on how the Home Office viewed the relationship between Article 8 ECHR and the deportation of foreign criminals after their release from prison.

The Home Secretary amended certain immigration rules using the 'negative resolution procedure', under which debate on statutory instruments on the floor of either House does not routinely take place. However, the rule change was preceded by a debate on 'Family Migration'.[89] There was then a further debate in the House of Commons on 19 June 2012,[90] whilst the House of Lords proceeded with the conventional negative resolution procedure. A number of judgments regarding the compatibility of decisions to deport foreign criminals with Article 8 ECHR followed the debate and the introduction of the rule changes.[91] Beginning with *MF (Nigeria)*, the Upper Tribunal held that although immigration rules generally have the force of law,[92] the new guidelines on Article 8 ECHR and foreign criminals could not:

[R]eplace the law that is binding upon us. Our duties under primary legislation are no less than they were before. We are still required by s.6 of the HRA not to act contrary to a person's Convention rights and by s.2 to take account of Strasbourg jurisprudence. We are still bound to reach decisions on specific human rights grounds of appeal under s.84 of the 2002 Act and s.33 of the UK Borders Act 2007.[93]

Although counsel for the deportee in *MF (Nigeria)*, drawing inspiration from the dicta of Lord Bingham in *Huang*,[94] argued that debates under the negative resolution procedure could not be equated with the fuller debates undertaken to approve primary legislation, the Upper Tribunal refused to adjudicate upon this point.[95] By contrast, in *Izuazu*, a case on the same point of law, the Upper Tribunal did reach a position on this question. It concluded that although the Immigration Rules in question were subject to the negative resolution procedure, insofar as the House of Commons actually discussed the rules at length, this did not amount to or equate with a debate in *Parliament* because Parliament comprised both the House of Commons and the House of Lords. This meant that the Tribunal was still bound to conduct its own independent evaluation of the proportionality of any deportation in relation to Article 8 ECHR with reference to relevant jurisprudence as per section 2 of the Human Rights Act 1998. The Upper Tribunal reached this decision for a number of compelling reasons. First, the Immigration Rules are 'not the product of active debate in Parliament where non-nationals seeking leave to remain are in any

---

[89] Debate on 'Family Migration' HC Deb 11 June 2012, vol 546, col 48.
[90] Debate on 'European Convention on Human Rights' HC Deb 19 June 2012, vol 546, col 760.
[91] *MF (Article 8—New Rules)* [2012] UKUT 393 (IAC); *R (Wankuama) v Home Secretary* [2012] EWHC 3526 (Admin); *Izuazu (Article 8—New Rules) Nigeria* [2013] UKUT 45 (IAC); *Ogundimi (Article 8—New Rules) Nigeria* [2013] UKUT 60 (IAC).
[92] *Odelola v Secretary of State for the Home Department* [2009] UKHL 25 [6], Lord Hoffmann and [27], Lord Brown.
[93] *MF (Article 8—New Rules)* (n 91) [32].
[94] *Huang v Secretary of State for the Home Department* (n 40) [17], Lord Bingham.
[95] *MF (Article 8—New Rules)* (n 91) [47].

event represented' and this amounted to a 'weak form' of parliamentary scrutiny.[96] Second, despite the presence of a more 'active debate of the new rules in the House of Commons than is often the case under the negative procedure resolution', the House of Commons alone *did not constitute Parliament*.[97]

The political reaction was a forceful one. Writing in the *Mail on Sunday*, Home Secretary Theresa May MP expressed the view that the changes to the Immigration Rules meant that it was 'clear that I would introduce primary legislation should the Commons' acceptance of my amendments not be sufficient to persuade judges to change the way they interpreted Article Eight [ECHR]. But I hoped that the outcome of the debate would be enough'. The Home Secretary continued by stating that 'some judges evidently do not regard a debate in Parliament on new immigration rules, followed by the unanimous adoption of those rules, as evidence that Parliament actually wants to see those new rules implemented'.[98] It is clear from her newspaper article that the Home Secretary was of the view that a debate in the House of Commons should have been sufficient to 'send a signal' to the courts that immigration cases regarding the deportation of foreign criminals should produce certain outcomes. In other words, the Home Secretary appeared to be of the view that any parliamentary debate on the outcomes that the Immigration Rules—no matter how incomplete those rules may be or how insufficient debate may be— should require the courts to defer to the Government's position, because the position had already been 'legitimised' by Parliament. The concern, in my view, raised by this episode is that it is not only courts that can risk compromising Parliament with the use of parliamentary materials, but the Government—by instituting a debate in one House of Parliament—can attempt to influence the independence of adjudication in proportionality cases. If those eager to protect parliamentary privilege before the courts are concerned about the 'chilling effect' upon parliamentary speech, then episodes such as this are surely the other side of the coin and should attract equal concern.[99]

[96] *Izuazu (Article 8—New Rules) Nigeria* (n 91) [49], applying *R (Stellato) v Home Secretary* [2007] 2 AC 70.

[97] ibid.

[98] Theresa May MP, 'It's MY Job to Deport Foreigners Who Commit Serious Crime, and I'll Fight Any Judge Who Stands in My Way' *Mail on Sunday* (17 February 2013), available at: www.dailymail.co.uk/debate/article-2279828/Its-MY-job-deport-foreigners-commit-crime--Ill-fight-judge-stands-way-says-Home-Secretary.html.

[99] Parliament subsequently enacted the Immigration Act 2014, which contained s 19: 'Article 8 of the ECHR: Public Interest Considerations'. In this section the legislation set out in detail Parliament's understanding of the requirements of Article 8 ECHR in the immigration context. In its first report on the Bill, the JCHR declared that it was 'uneasy about a statutory provision which purports to tell courts and tribunals that "little weight" should be given to a particular consideration in such a judicial balancing exercise. That appears to us to be a significant legislative trespass into the judicial function'. Joint Committee on Human Rights, *Legislative Scrutiny: Immigration Bill (8th Report)* (2013–14, HC 935, HL 102) para 60. In its second report on the Bill, the JCHR repeated this concern and suggested amendments to remedy the perceived trespass into the judicial function. These amendments were not adopted. Joint Committee on Human Rights, *Legislative Scrutiny: Immigration Bill (Second Report) (12th Report)* (2013–14, HC 1120, HL 142) para 111.

B. Prisoner Voting: Misconceptions about the Role of Parliament?

The tentative distinction between ministerial statements and completed reports on the one hand, and evidence to committees and debate in Parliament or either House on the other is of course a doctrine of the domestic courts, so it is no surprise that the European Court of Human Rights (ECtHR) does not consider it to be relevant. As Barber points out, section 6(3)(b) of the domestic Human Rights Act 1998 is a jurisdictional bar which prevents domestic courts from reviewing the conduct of either House of Parliament for conformity with Convention rights. But the same bar does not exist for the Strasbourg Court.[100] This led to the ECtHR finding that parliamentary speech involving criminal allegations could in principle violate Article 6 ECHR in *A v UK*.[101] The majority applied a proportionality test and concluded that the aims of absolute parliamentary privilege—protecting free speech and maintaining the separation of powers—justified interference with the applicant's Article 6 ECHR rights.

This is not to suggest that scholars should remain unconcerned with the treatment of parliamentary materials in supranational courts. The case law on prisoner voting in respect of section 3 of the Representation of the People Act 1983 provides another concerning example. The saga of litigation against the UK Government with respect to its 'blanket ban' on prisoner voting is well known. However, for those interested in the relationship between courts and parliamentary privilege, some aspects merit revisiting.

The ECtHR has consistently held that section 3 of the 1983 Act was incompatible with Article 3 of Protocol 1 of the ECHR. This protocol mandates that States Parties 'undertake to hold free elections at reasonable intervals by secret ballot, under conditions which will ensure the free expression of the opinion of the people in the choice of the legislature'. Since the Victorian Forfeiture Act of 1870, UK law has never taken the view that 'the people' in this context has included serving prisoners. Two decisions against the UK government—*Hirst v UK (No 2)*[102] and *Greens and MT v UK*[103]—found that the British commitment to the 'civic death' of prisoners violated Article 3 of Protocol 1 because the Westminster Parliament had neither considered any legislative revisions regarding prisoners' right to vote for some time, nor had acted upon recent reports on the topic by the JCHR.

This chapter does not take issue with the decision reached by the ECtHR concerning prisoners' right to vote. Instead, the argument here is that the treatment of parliamentary material, particularly in *Hirst (No 2)*, represents a mischaracterisation of the institutional role of the Westminster Parliament which may not be generalisable to all parliaments in Council of Europe states. It is important to note that the proportionality dilemma in the British prisoner voting cases is slightly more nuanced than the 'standard' proportionality dispute. In a 'standard' dispute, the Court is charged with deciding whether a particular legislative provision or administrative decision

---

[100] N Barber, 'Parliamentary Immunity and Human Rights' (2003) 119 *Law Quarterly Review* 557, 559.

[101] *A v UK* (2003) 36 EHRR 51 (ECHR) [74]–[77].

[102] *Hirst v UK (No 2)* [2004] ECHR 122.

[103] *Greens and MT v UK* [2011] ECHR 686.

interferes with an ECHR right with a 'built-in' proportionality clause, such as Article 10(2) ECHR, in which the text of the Convention outlines legitimate reasons for limiting the scope of the right to freedom of expression. Article 3 of the First Protocol has no such clause. In the prisoner voting cases, the Strasbourg Court was tasked with evaluating two things. The first was whether or not the British Government was entitled to have its law upheld under the 'margin of appreciation' doctrine. The jurisprudence of the Court acknowledged that the text of Article 3 of Protocol 1 did not indicate the presence of an absolute right. The Court used the margin of appreciation to acknowledge that, subject to some constraints, the implementation of legislation giving effect to Convention rights will vary between Member States. The second consideration—which directly affected whether or not relief was to be granted under the margin of appreciation doctrine—was the operation of proportionality. The Court had to decide whether or not the ban in section 3 of the 1983 Act was a proportionate restriction on the franchise as defined by Article 3 of Protocol 1, but was not given specific guidance on limiting factors by the text of the Convention.

In *Hirst (No 2)*, the fourth section of the ECtHR found that the ban on prisoner voting in section 3 of the 1983 Act constituted a ban which was disproportionate because it stripped a large number of convicted prisoners (approximately 70,000) of their right to vote in a manner which was indiscriminate. The ECtHR reiterated this conclusion in *Greens and MT*. When denying the British Government the benefit of the margin of appreciation in *Hirst (No 2)*, the Court concluded that:

> The Court would observe that there is no evidence that the legislature in the United Kingdom has ever sought to weigh the competing interests or to assess the proportionality of the ban as it affects convicted prisoners.[104]

The Grand Chamber endorsed this criticism.[105] In *Greens and MT*, specific reference was made to a report of the JCHR.[106] The Court focused upon the Committee's 'overriding disappointment [at] the lack of progress in this case. [The] Government has not yet published the outcome of its second consultation, which closed almost 6 months ago, in September 2009. This appears to show a lack of commitment on the part of the government to proposing a solution for Parliament to consider'.[107]

On 10 February 2011, a backbench debate was held on prisoner voting. The debate was one 'of conscience', ie, without a party whip.[108] Nicol considered that whilst the 'over-representation of the Conservative Party is significant',[109] the debate featured 'considerations of constitutional principle' to a greater degree 'than caricatures ... suggest'.[110] But the Strasbourg Court remained dissatisfied with the British position.

---

[104] *Hirst v UK (No 2)* (n 102) [51].
[105] ibid [78]–[79].
[106] Joint Committee on Human Rights, *Enhancing Parliament's Role in Relation to Human Rights Judgments (15th Report)* (2009–10, HL 85, HC 455).
[107] ibid, para 1.08.
[108] Debate on 'Voting by Prisoners' HC Deb 19 February 2011, vol 523, col 493.
[109] D Nicol, 'Legitimacy of the Commons Debate on Prisoner Voting' [2011] *Public Law* 681, 662.
[110] ibid, 681.

If we return to the text of the ECtHR judgments in *Hirst (No 2)* and *Greens and MT*, we can observe just how little attention was paid to the workings of the Westminster Parliament as an institution. This is the real cause for concern. Although the Court noted the diversity in responses to prisoner voting throughout the Council of Europe—'some 18 countries imposed no restriction, 13 prohibited all prisoners from voting, with some restrictions imposable in another 12'[111]—it based its consideration to refuse the benefit of the margin of appreciation on an extremely limited understanding of the legislative agenda, and in turn overlooked in many respects what Parliament does in a wider constitutional sense. It is not solely an institution charged with the protection of human rights. This must have had some impact on the overall conclusions as to proportionality. In reality, the Court's consideration of the British efforts regarding prisoner voting amounted to one sentence at paragraph 51 of *Hirst (No 2)* and an extremely short extract from one report of one parliamentary committee (the JCHR) in *Greens and MT*. Of course, this argument acknowledges that Westminster has a commitment to human rights in legal and moral terms. The riposte would be simply that the franchise is legitimately restricted in a number of ways (age, legal capacity, citizenship etc) and that the Court's conclusion on proportionality was one which could be the subject of 'reasonable disagreement'. This is certainly the case when we look to the text of Article 3 of Protocol 1: there is no reference to acceptable definitions of the franchise beyond 'the people'. In the previous example on immigration (above), the core of the possible problem was that a court was being asked by the Government to compromise its independence on the basis of a partial codification of human rights obligations allegedly 'legitimised' by a debate in the House of Commons. The danger inherent in the prisoner voting example is the other side of that coin. Here a court is effectively compelling the Government, and in turn Parliament, to alter its legislative agenda which has been legitimised by the democratic process.

The European Court noted that no discussion of or legislation concerning the entitlement of prisoners to the vote had been put before Parliament in recent memory, and that the disenfranchisement of prisoners could be traced to a Victorian ideal.[112] Both observations are undoubtedly correct. Yet, the European Court was happy to engage with a highly limited spectrum of parliamentary material without evidence that it had even considered the vast array of activities that Parliament as a whole and individual parliamentarians engage in as part of the democratic mandate. In the simplest terms, the fact that prisoner voting had been ignored by both chambers of Parliament since the 1983 Act overlooked that it was simply not an electoral issue. Parliamentarians— even those on the JCHR—are elected (or appointed) to serve a multitude of interests. Whilst many constituents care about human rights, they have many other concerns to which elected members and peers have a constitutional duty to attend.

For example, in one day of parliamentary business randomly selected by the author (14 February 2013), the House of Commons debated 26 subjects indexed in *Hansard*, including the Equality and Human Rights Commission, but covering

---

[111] *Hirst v UK (No 2)* (n 102) [32].
[112] ibid [17].

topics as diverse as sport, mobile telephone coverage, sexual violence and library closures. On the same day in the House of Lords, there were 44 separate subjects in *Hansard*, including (but not limited to) migration, food prices, the Bank of England, taxation, cats (yes, cats) and terrorism. This suggests that the legislature's work and commitments cannot be accurately pictured in either one sentence or by considering a small aspect of the work of one parliamentary committee. Therefore, the use of parliamentary materials in the Strasbourg prisoner voting judgments is an aspect of this practice that is of questionable legitimacy. Obviously, a court cannot be expected to survey the entire history and function of a parliament. This is precisely my point. An accurate determination of how an institution such as the Westminster Parliament should divide its time on any one issue would no doubt require many economists, mathematicians, ethicists and possibly even lawyers. This group would doubtless dispute the appropriate methodology, let alone reach the right answer. As such, caution must be exercised by courts, especially supranational courts from which there is no appeal, in their approach to judging the activities of parliaments for conformity with external standards on issues to which there can reasonably be a plurality of views.

CONCLUSION

Despite the reticence expressed throughout this chapter regarding judicial use of parliamentary materials, it seems counter-intuitive that any hard-and-fast rule should preclude either counsel from citing or courts from considering the work of a parliamentary committee expert in human rights or any other committee whose subject-matter area may reasonably impinge upon a proportionality decision. Although this chapter has pointed out two 'hard' examples as an illustration of when the practice can become problematic and has argued that it is relatively unconstrained by settled legal rules either in UK law or under the European Convention, this shouldn't be interpreted as a plea to call time on the practice. Instead, it is a plea for caution to be exercised by all constitutional actors—the courts, government and Parliament.

The case law from the British courts has failed to find a principled distinction between the types of parliamentary materials with which the courts can engage, and the relationship with the better-known legal rules on parliamentary privilege remains an ambiguous one. Moreover, it is not argued here that such a distinction could be possible, let alone workable. After all, there is much debate as to whether parliamentary intention can even be discovered through interpretation of primary legislation,[113] let alone the individualised statements by ministers, debates on the floor of either House, or the final reports of committees whose authorship is attributable to a small number of parliamentarians. Under the doctrine of proportionality, the courts are obliged to conduct their own independent stage-by-stage evaluation of legislative and administrative measures and to reach their own conclusion as to the appropriate balance to be struck between conflicting legitimate interests. As such, they should exercise due caution when considering parliamentary materials during this exercise so as both to preserve their own independence and to respect the independence of Parliament.

---

[113] R Ekins, 'The Intention of Parliament' [2010] *Public Law* 709.

19

Judicial Review and Parliamentary Debate: Enriching the Doctrine of Due Deference

LIORA LAZARUS AND NATASHA SIMONSEN

P ARLIAMENTARY SOVEREIGNTY IS often conceptualised as the opposite of judicial supremacy, and the struggle for democratic legitimacy with respect to human rights as a perennial tug of war.[1] Some of the contributions in this volume, however, argue that the relationship between courts and the legislature need not be a zero-sum game, as these institutions can work together to protect human rights. This chapter makes some bold propositions on how to develop that partnership and enrich the doctrine of due deference. Our argument is that rigorous and respectful judicial examination of democratic processes enhances constitutional dialogue, increases the opportunities for judicial deference, heightens the transparency with which deference is exercised and therefore makes it more likely that deference will be accorded where it has been shown to be justified. This proposal challenges established constitutional orthodoxy in the UK. Our argument is not confined to the UK, but in any event constitutional orthodoxy is an evolving phenomenon that has adapted to changing constitutional landscapes and is increasingly receptive to shifting global trends.

This chapter is divided into two sections. Section I outlines the doctrine of due deference and its relationship to judicial review, making a case for courts to consider the quality of legislative debate when deciding whether and how to defer. Section II proposes a set of criteria that we think judges ought to take into account when exercising deference.

The discussion that follows is premised on a particular set of assumptions. We assume a high level of institutional functioning and competence of parliament, the executive and the courts. We assume further that each of these institutions is

---

[1] See, eg, R Ekins, 'Judicial Supremacy and the Rule of Law' (2003) 119 *Law Quarterly Review* 127; PA Joseph, 'Parliament, the Courts, and the Collaborative Enterprise' (2004) 15 *King's College Law Journal* 321; R Ekins, 'The Authority of Parliament: A Reply to Professor Joseph' (2005) 16 *King's College Law Journal* 51. For a criticism of this dichotomous understanding of parliamentary and judicial supremacy, see M Hunt, 'Reshaping Constitutionalism' in J Morison, K McEvoy and G Anthony (eds), *Judges, Transition and Human Rights* (Oxford, Oxford University Press, 2007) 467–77. See also R Ekins, *The Nature of Legislative Intent* (Oxford, Oxford University Press, 2012).

committed both to protecting human rights and to fostering a constructive constitutional dialogue. With these parameters in place, there is a case that domestic and supranational courts should consider the quality of democratic deliberation in their decisions about when and how to defer to the judgment of the elected branches regarding the justification for interfering with a right.

I. DUE DEFERENCE AND JUDICIAL REVIEW

Opponents of judicial review of legislation argue that it diverts and undermines democracy.[2] The judiciary's common response to this criticism is to exercise self-restraint and defer to the legislature when evaluating the human rights compatibility of legislation.[3] But the relationship between the three branches of government with respect to human rights is now evolving towards a 'modern constitutionalism which rejects the old dichotomy between political and legal constitutionalism' and embraces the shared responsibility of 'all branches of the State, the Government, the Parliament and the Courts … to uphold the rule of law'.[4] This dialogic model of constitutionalism views the judiciary and the legislature as partners in a common enterprise[5] rather than adversaries in a perpetual contest for supremacy. It calls on the one hand to strengthen democratic oversight of human rights and on the other hand to find creative ways for courts to complement these participatory processes.

The constitutional dialogue model has developed in the UK and elsewhere[6] against the backdrop of a changing human rights landscape. These changes include the creation of parliamentary select committees to strengthen the role of parliaments in protecting and promoting human rights, and to improve the quality of legislative

---

[2] See generally J Waldron, 'Judicial Review and the Conditions of Democracy' (1998) 6 *Journal of Political Philosophy* 335; J Waldron, 'Moral Truth and Judicial Review' (1998) 43 *American Journal of Jurisprudence* 75; J Waldron, *The Dignity of Legislation* (Cambridge, Cambridge University Press, 1999); M Tushnet, *Taking the Constitution Away from the Courts* (Princeton, Princeton University Press, 1999); Ekins, 'Judicial Supremacy and the Rule of Law' (n 1); LD Kramer, *The People Themselves: Popular Constitutionalism and Judicial Review* (Oxford, Oxford University Press, 2004); J Waldron, 'The Core of the Case against Judicial Review' (2005) 115 *Yale Law Journal* 1346.

[3] See, eg, RA Edwards, 'Judicial Deference under the Human Rights Act' (2002) 65 *Modern Law Review* 859; A Kavanagh, 'Participation and Judicial Review: A Reply to Jeremy Waldron' (2003) 22 *Law and Philosophy* 451.

[4] M Hunt, 'The Joint Committee on Human Rights' in A Horne, D Oliver and G Drewry (eds), *Parliament and the Law* (Oxford, Hart Publishing, 2013).

[5] A Barak, *The Judge in a Democracy* (Princeton, Princeton University Press, 2006) 15–19; A Barak, *Purposive Interpretation in Law* (Princeton, Princeton University Press, 2007) 250. See also B McLachlin, 'Charter Myths' (1999) 33 *University of British Columbia Law Review* 23, 34–36, describing the 'symbiotic' relationship between courts and the legislature in realising the rights in the Canadian Charter. See further Joseph (n 1) 322–23, describing the 'constitutional relationship of interdependence and reciprocity' between parliament and the courts, in which each branch 'is engaged in a collaborative enterprise … committed to the same ends and ideals, albeit in different, task-specific ways'. This relationship of 'institutional *interdependence*' should be distinguished from their 'operational *independence*' (at 335, emphasis in original).

[6] These features are common to other developed countries with constitutional democratic models of government such as Canada, Germany, South Africa, Israel, Australia and New Zealand.

deliberation on rights.[7] At the same time, there has been growth and strengthening of independent human rights institutions, equality bodies, non-governmental organisations and other civil society groups,[8] leading to a broader human rights 'bricolage'.[9] These developments support stronger institutional oversight and have resulted in an improved array of mechanisms for resolving conflicts with respect to human rights. These changes are important steps towards creating and maintaining a culture of justification, whereby citizens can reasonably expect that every exercise of power will be justified, and 'the leadership given by government rests on the cogency of the case offered in defence of its decisions, not the fear inspired by force at its command'.[10]

However, the human rights landscape is also characterised by significant challenges. These include the increasing pressure on courts through expanding demand for judicial review on human rights grounds,[11] leading to parallel efforts to restrict access to relief.[12] The mounting pressure on judicial processes is augmented by calls for special measures and exceptions on national security grounds, leading to

---

[7] See, eg, C Evans and S Evans, 'Legislative Scrutiny Committees and Parliamentary Conceptions of Human Rights' [2006] *Public Law* 785; M Hunt, 'The Impact of the Human Rights Act on the Legislature: A Diminution of Democracy or a New Voice for Parliament?' (2010) 6 *European Human Rights Law Review* 601.

[8] There is a growing body of literature on this trend and its implications: see, eg, R Murray, 'The Relationship between Parliaments and National Human Rights Institutions' in Morison, McEvoy and Anthony (n 1) 357–76; T Pegram, 'Diffusion across Political Systems: The Global Spread of National Human Rights Institutions' (2010) 32 *Human Rights Quarterly* 729; R Carver, 'A New Answer to an Old Question: National Human Rights Institutions and the Domestication of International Law' (2010) 10 *Human Rights Law Review* 1; R Carver, 'One NHRI or Many? How Many Institutions Does it Take to Protect Human Rights?—Lessons from the European Experience' (2011) 3 *Journal of Human Rights Practice* 1; B de Witte, 'New Institutions for Promoting Equality in Europe: Legal Transfers, National Bricolage and European Governance' (2012) 60 *American Journal of Comparative Law* 49.

[9] De Witte (n 8).

[10] E Mureinik, 'A Bridge to Where—Introducing the Interim Bill of Rights' (1994) 10 *South African Journal on Human Rights* 31, 32. See also D Dyzenhaus, 'Law as Justification: Etienne Mureinik's Conception of Legal Culture' (1998) 14 *South African Journal on Human Rights* 11; and L Lazarus, 'Conceptions of Liberty Deprivation' (2006) 69 *Modern Law Review* 738. See also Dyzenhaus, ch 21 in this volume.

[11] For a brief analysis of the increasing number of judicial review applications in the UK, see R Rogers, 'Judicial Review Statistics: How Many Cases are There and What are They About?' *The Guardian Datablog* (19 November 2012), available at: www.guardian.co.uk/news/datablog/2012/nov/19/judicial-review-statistics. The raw data is available at: www.gov.uk/government/publications/judicial-and-court-statistics-annual. See also, as regards Strasbourg, www.echr.coe.int/echr/en/header/reports+and+statistics/reports/annual+reports. For discussion of the implications of that increase, see the report of the Joint Committee on Human Rights, 'Enhancing Parliament's Role with Respect to Human Rights Judgments', *15th Report of Session 2009–10* (26 March 2010, HL 85/HC 455). See also N Simonsen, 'The Strasbourg Court, the 'Exhaustion of Domestic Remedies' Rule, and the Principle of Subsidiarity: Between a Rock and a Hard Place?' *Oxford Human Rights Hub* (18 March 2013), available at: http://ohrh.law.ox.ac.uk/the-strasbourg-court-the-exhaustion-of-domestic-remedies-rule-and-the-principle-of-subsidiarity-between-a-rock-and-a-hard-place/.

[12] See, in the UK, the proposals to restrict access to judicial review in Pt 4 of the Criminal Justice and Courts Bill currently before Parliament. Reduced funding and access restrictions to legal aid as a result of the Government's legal aid reforms will also have the effect of limiting access to judicial review in the UK. In the European Court of Human Rights context, see the Interlaken Declaration and Action Plan (19 February 2010), aiming to improve implementation of European Court of Human Rights judgments at the national level.

the development of new regimes for secret evidence and special advocates, and the development of preventative models to supplement the criminal law.[13]

The recent changes in the human rights landscape and the challenges they bring necessitate a shift in the institutional pattern of human rights protection. In particular, we think these developments present new possibilities for courts to exercise restraint where it is appropriate, and to be more transparent about their reasons for doing so. But these developments also raise some important and difficult questions. To what extent should courts consider the quality of democratic debate? What considerations should guide courts in considering legislative materials? Our view is that courts should consider the quality of democratic debate in deciding whether and how to defer to the legislature when reviewing human rights. If parliament has done its job well, its decisions should invite a high degree of deference from the courts. Thus, our model positions parliaments squarely in the centre of the frame.

Supranational courts too should pay close attention to democratic debates in Member States to bolster the principle of subsidiarity.[14] The Strasbourg Court has followed this approach when applying the margin of appreciation in the recent cases of *Hirst (No 2)*,[15] *Animal Defenders International*[16] and *Shindler.*[17] In each of these cases, the Strasbourg Court assessed the quality of the democratic debate that had preceded the passage of rights-restricting measures to determine to what extent the margin of appreciation applied. This is a welcome development in the Court's case law, offering a useful departure point for extension by domestic courts.

Given their proximity to domestic legislative processes, domestic courts should defer as often as they justifiably can to preserve the legitimacy of judicial review. Presently, this objective is hampered by the absence of a clear and principled answer to the question of how and when English courts should defer.[18] Aside from the question-begging proposition that some matters fall within the competence of the legislature or executive while others lie within the competence of the courts,[19] attempts

---

[13] For a discussion of these aspects, see L Lazarus, B Goold and C Goss, 'Control without Punishment: Understanding Coercion' in J Simon, and R Sparks (eds), *The SAGE Handbook of Punishment and Society* (London, SAGE Publications, 2012) 463–92.

[14] See Hunt, ch 1 in this volume.

[15] *Hirst v UK (No 2)* (2006) 42 EHRR 41. See in particular [21]–[24], [78] and [79].

[16] *Animal Defenders International v UK* App No 48876/08, 22 April 2013 (GC). See in particular [42]–[55], [108], [110] and [114].

[17] *Shindler v UK* App No 19840/09, 7 May 2013. See in particular [22]–[28], [102] and [117].

[18] See, inter alia, C Gearty, 'Reconciling Parliamentary Democracy and Human Rights' (2002) 118 *Law Quarterly Review* 248, 249, describing the engagement of the senior judiciary with the Human Rights Act 1998 as 'rather ad hoc and unprincipled'. See also J Jowell, 'Judicial Deference: Servility, Civility or Institutional Capacity?' [2003] *Public Law* 592, arguing that: 'It is becoming clearer by the day that the most difficult question for the courts in the interpretation of the Human Rights Act 1998 is the extent to which they should defer to Parliament and other institutions of government on matters relating to the public interest'; and R Clayton, 'Judicial Deference and "Democratic Dialogue": The Legitimacy of Judicial Intervention under the Human Rights Act 1998' [2004] *Public Law* 33, observing that: 'English courts have yet to articulate a developed approach towards judicial deference when considering human rights claims.'

[19] See the opinion of Hoffmann LJ in *R (Prolife Alliance) v BBC* [2003] UKHL 23; [2004] 1 AC 185. Jowell summarises this proposition as the 'dichotomy … between principle (involving moral rights against the state—a matter for judges to determine) and policy (involving utilitarian calculations of the public good—a matter for the legislature or its agents to determine)': ibid, 593, citing R Dworkin, *Taking Rights Seriously* (Cambridge, MA, Harvard University Press, 1978). Hunt's description of this 'spatial

to structure analysis of deference have met with limited success. Notwithstanding Laws LJ's more rigorous exposition in *Roth*,[20] many cases continue to follow the opaque approach to deference in *R v Lichniak*.[21] There, Lord Bingham (with whom Lord Steyn agreed) asserted without substantiation that '*a degree of deference* [was] due to the judgment of a democratic assembly on how a particular social problem is best tackled'.[22] The critical questions that the case left unanswered, and which subsequent cases also skirt around, are what degree of deference is due, when is it justified, and how are courts to determine the degree of deference that is due in any particular case?

Our view is that, in a culture of justification, deference should be *earned* by the legislature.[23] Rather than simply noting, as Lord Bingham did in *Lichniak*, that 'there have been numerous occasions on which Parliament could have amended [the section] had it wished',[24] courts should consider whether parliament 'meaningfully engaged' with the rights considerations in play.[25] Concretely, this means they should consider whether parliament rigorously debated the measure; what kind of scrutiny it was subjected to, both in committee and in parliament as a whole; the nature of the right that the measure impugns; and the extent of the restriction on the right.[26] Structuring the assessment of deference according to such criteria will not only increase the transparency with which deference is exercised, but will also lead to new opportunities for deference where parliament is doing its job well.

In contrast, if courts are free to ignore the deliberations of the democratically elected branches, and if they fail to defer as a consequence, they will likely face a crisis of legitimacy at some point, regardless of their constitutional mandate. In the tension between majoritarian democratic processes and protecting fundamental rights, judicial review is justified as a corrective or complement to democracy. Even if, like Ely, we see judicial review merely as self-correction where majoritarianism fails to protect the interests of the unrepresented or the minority, then it follows that judicial review must always examine whether the legislature has applied its mind to the rights considerations in question and act where those processes have fallen

---

language of areas or margins of discretion' is apt: see M Hunt, 'Sovereignty's Blight: Why Contemporary Public Law Needs the Concept of "Due Deference"' in N Bamforth, and P Leyland (eds), *Public Law in a Multi-layered Constitution* (Oxford, Hart Publishing, 2003) 339.

[20] *International Transport Roth GmbH and others v Secretary of State for the Home Department* [2002] EWCA Civ 158; [2003] QB 728, per Laws LJ dissenting.

[21] *R v Lichniak* [2002] UKHL 47; [2003] 1 AC 903.

[22] ibid, 912, per Bingham LJ, citations omitted, emphasis added.

[23] Hunt (n 19) 340, footnote omitted, emphasis in original.

[24] *R v Lichniak* (n 21) 911, per Bingham LJ.

[25] The concept of 'meaningful engagement' is transplanted here from South African jurisprudence, including, inter alia, *Occupiers of 51 Olivia Road Berea Township and 197 Main Street Johannesburg v City of Johannesburg and others* [2008] ZACC 1 (CC); *Residents of Joe Slovo Community, Western Cape v Thubelisha Homes and others* [2009] ZACC 16 (CC); *City of Johannesburg Metropolitan Municipality v Blue Moonlight Properties 39 (Pty) Ltd and another* [2011] ZACC 33 (CC); *City of Johannesburg v Changing Tides 74 (Pty) Ltd and 97 others* [2012] ZASCA 116 (CC). In the South African context 'meaningful engagement' has been used as an interim remedy to prompt the parties to come to a deliberative solution without the court's intervention. While the context is different, the standards applied in the assessment of meaningful engagement may well offer guidance in terms of how courts can assess the quality of democratic deliberation.

[26] These criteria are developed in section II below.

short.[27] It is hard to see how judicial review can be justified if it ignores legislative deliberation altogether.

The same arguments apply with equal if not greater force to international courts, where the principle of subsidiarity 'underpins the obligation on State Parties to ensure Convention rights are secured at the national level'.[28] The further international courts are from the democratic deliberations of signatory states, the more strained the international order will become.[29] The Strasbourg Court has acknowledged that 'the national authorities have direct democratic legitimation and are, as the Court has held on many occasions, in principle better placed than an international court to evaluate local needs and conditions'.[30] The recently concluded Protocol 15 to the European Convention will add a reference to the preamble 'affirming' that States Parties 'in accordance with the principle of subsidiarity, have the primary responsibility to secure the rights and freedoms defined in this Convention ... and that in doing so they enjoy a margin of appreciation'.[31]

In the Strasbourg context, assessing the quality of legislative debate in deciding whether a particular measure falls within the margin of appreciation allows the principle of subsidiarity to operate to its fullest effect. Until recently, the European Court was criticised for its failure to develop clear criteria or principles as to when a measure falls within the margin of appreciation.[32] However, in *Animal Defenders International*, the Strasbourg Court built on its earlier decision in *Hirst (No 2)*, developing an approach that bears directly on the performance of parliament in its deliberative process. The Grand Chamber said that a determination of the proportionality of a general measure demands an assessment of 'the legislative choices underlying it', including the 'quality of the parliamentary and judicial review of the necessity of the measure'.[33] It went on to analyse the legislative history of the prohibition on political advertising on broadcast television in detail.[34] This included a review of the provision by a parliamentary committee in 1998; the publication of a White Paper in 2001 which included discussion of relevant Strasbourg case law; consultation with specialist bodies such as the Electoral Commission; scrutiny by the Joint Committee on Human Rights; and the bipartisan support which the

[27] JH Ely, *Democracy and Distrust: A Theory of Judicial Review* (Cambridge, MA, Harvard University Press, 1980); see also A Nolan, *Children's Socio-economic Rights, Democracy and the Courts* (Oxford, Hart Publishing, 2011).
[28] L Lazarus, C Costello, N Ghanea and K Ziegler, 'The Evolution of Fundamental Rights Charters and Case Law', European Parliament Directorate-General for Internal Policies (1 February 2011) 75, available at: www.ssrn.com/abstract=2210448.
[29] This presumably explains why the European Court appears to have softened its position in the face of public outcry over the prisoner voting debate in the UK in *Scoppola v Italy* (2013) 56 EHRR 19.
[30] *Hatton v UK* [2002] 34 EHRR 1 [97].
[31] Article 1, Protocol 15 amending the Convention for the Protection of Human Rights and Fundamental Freedoms, open for signature 24 May 2013 (not yet in force). See Hunt, ch 1 in this volume.
[32] See, eg, E Brems, 'Margin of Appreciation Doctrine in the Case-law of the European Court of Human Rights' (1996) 56 *Zeitschrift Fur Auslandisches Offentliches Recht und Volkerrecht* 240; HC Yourow, *The Margin of Appreciation Doctrine in the Dynamics of European Human Rights Jurisprudence* (Leiden, Martinus Nijhoff, 1996); Y Arai-Takahashi, *The Margin of Appreciation Doctrine and the Principle of Proportionality in the Jurisprudence of the ECHR* (Cambridge, Intersentia, 2002).
[33] *Animal Defenders International v UK* (n 16) [108]. The quality of the legislative and judicial review of the measure was later described as 'of central importance' to the outcome (at [113]).
[34] ibid [42]–[55].

passage of the Communications Act 2003 had attracted.[35] The Grand Chamber thus described the impugned measure as 'the culmination of an exceptional examination by parliamentary bodies of the cultural, political and legal aspects of the prohibition'[36] and confirmed that this justified the degree of deference that domestic courts had afforded to parliament in judicial review.[37] It also justified the UK Parliament being afforded a wide margin of appreciation in deciding how best to implement the Article 10 right to freedom of expression.

We broadly support the Strasbourg Court's approach to the margin of appreciation in *Animal Defenders International*. In what follows, we propose a set of criteria to further structure its analysis of parliamentary debate and apply it across other cases, as well as to help domestic courts in the UK and elsewhere to develop a more principled doctrine of due deference. The level of scrutiny that courts apply in assessing legislative debate will no doubt differ depending on the court's mandate and the legal culture.[38] In some countries, judicial scrutiny of democratic processes follows from an obligation to enforce constitutional norms of democratic procedure. For example, the South African Constitution obliges Parliament to facilitate public participation in its decision-making processes.[39] In the *Doctors for Life* case, the South African Constitutional Court held that all branches of government have an interest in the courts making sure that Parliament fulfils its constitutional obligations and in correcting democratic procedures if required.[40] This is a strong mandate to confer upon a constitutional court, but even in countries such as Israel, where the courts lack that explicit mandate, they are often asked to scrutinise parliamentary debates.[41] Even English courts are not unfamiliar with questions of the relevance and weight to be attached to parliamentary materials.[42] Our proposal builds upon this experience, as well as the example set by the Strasbourg Court in recent decisions.

[35] ibid [114].
[36] ibid.
[37] ibid [115]. For a summary of the domestic proceedings, see the judgment of the House of Lords in *R (on the application of Animal Defenders International) v Secretary of State for Culture, Media and Sport* [2008] UKHL 15; [2008] 1 AC 1312.
[38] See, eg, M Hunt, 'The Human Rights Act and Legal Culture: The Judiciary and the Legal Profession' (1999) 26 *Journal of Law and Society* 86.
[39] See Constitution of the Republic of South Africa 1996, ss 59 and 72. See further ss 73–82, which oblige 'public debate' on proposed constitutional amendments (s 74(5)(c)) and allow members of the National Assembly to apply to the Constitutional Court for a determination of the constitutionality of a proposed bill.
[40] *Doctors for Life International v Speaker of the National Assembly and others* (2006) 6 SA 416 (CC) (17 August 2006).
[41] The Israeli Supreme Court—with no express constitutional mandate to do so—has considered matters such as, inter alia: whether the Prime Minister of Israel had correctly exercised his discretion with respect to removal of a Minister from office (HCJ 3094/93 *Movement for Quality Government v State of Israel* 47(5) PD 404); and whether an outgoing executive acted lawfully in entering peace negotiations with the Palestinians, in circumstances where it lacked the confidence of the Parliament (HCJ 5167/00, *Weiss v Prime Minister of Israel* 55(2) PD 455); and decisions of the Speaker of the Knesset with respect to tabling matters in Parliament and the length of time for debate (HC 9070/00 *Livnat v Chairman of Constitution, Law & Justice Committee* 55(4) PD 800, 813). For discussion of these and other cases, see Barak (n 5); and D Barak-Erez, 'Broadening the Scope of Judicial Review in Israel: Between Activism and Restraint' (2009) 3 *Indian Journal of Constitutional Law* 118.
[42] See Hooper, ch 18 in this volume.

These propositions may encounter resistance based on practical grounds, such as the potential lengthening of court proceedings and/or the complexity of judgments;[43] the limited capacity and expertise of parliamentarians with respect to human rights;[44] or fears that judicial scrutiny might have a 'chilling' effect on parliamentary speech.[45] But the gains of enhancing democratic dialogue and improving the transparency with which deference is exercised weigh strongly against such pragmatic considerations. In any event, a clear discussion of due deference at the outset of judicial rights analysis offers the potential to shorten rather than lengthen court proceedings. In our view, objections grounded in constitutional orthodoxy are no more insurmountable than these pragmatic objections. The prospect of courts taking a view on the quality of democratic debate arguably raises no greater constitutional danger than would the prospect of courts ignoring those debates altogether. As Simon Brown LJ said in *Roth*, 'constitutional dangers exist no less in too little judicial activism as in too much'.[46] The politics of assessing a democratic debate are no less fraught than the politics of rights interpretation and judicial override of legislation.

We believe that the debate on the legitimacy of judicial review has reached an impasse and objections grounded in constitutional orthodoxy ought to be re-evaluated. This contribution is given in the spirit of moving this debate on from the question of whether courts should exercise judicial review of legislation to the question of how best such review can be conducted in light of an overriding commitment to parliamentary democracy. If we shift the debate to these terms, the critical issue becomes how that analysis should be structured.

II. CRITERIA FOR EVALUATING LEGISLATIVE DEBATE

We propose a set of specific criteria to give structure to the overarching question, given the quality of the deliberative process, of how weighty are the justifications which have been offered for interfering with the right or rights in question? Our approach suggests that certain institutional questions ought to be resolved before the proportionality analysis takes place.[47] If the quality of legislative debate has been strong, then the court should approach the rights-limiting measure with a presumption of deference that may be rebutted only by very weighty rights considerations.

[43] See, eg, the criticisms in J Steyn, '*Pepper v Hart*: A Re-examination' (2001) 21 *Oxford Journal of Legal Studies* 59.
[44] See, eg, the factors pointed out by Evans and Evans which 'make it difficult for parliamentarians adequately to analyse human rights issues in parliamentary debate', such as the 'crowded parliamentary agenda, combined with bills of ever greater complexity' and the fact that 'many, perhaps most, members of parliaments lack the expertise that would allow them to make an assessment of the human rights implications of legislation, even if they had the time or interest to do so': Evans and Evans (n 7) 785–86, citation omitted.
[45] See, eg, the discussion in Hooper, ch 18 in this volume.
[46] *Roth* (n 20) 754, per Simon Brown J.
[47] *Cf* the discussion of deference in the interstices of proportionality analysis in Hooper, ch 18 in this volume and Roach, ch 20 in this volume. *Cf* also J Rivers, 'Proportionality and Variable Intensity of Review' (2006) 65 *Cambridge Law Journal* 174.

Legislative debate that engaged meaningfully with rights considerations was evident in the passage of rights-restricting measures in *Animal Defenders International*[48] and in *Shindler*,[49] and in both cases the quality of the debate was invoked to support the Court's conclusion that the measures fell within the state's margin of appreciation. In *Animal Defenders International*, a majority of the Grand Chamber endorsed the parliamentary debate in the context of its analysis of the proportionality of the measure, attaching 'considerable weight' to the view of the legislature that the measure was 'necessary in a democratic society'.[50] In *Shindler*, the Court considered the parliamentary debate and select committee proceedings as evidence that 'Parliament has sought to weigh the competing interests and to assess the proportionality of the [rule]'.[51]

Conversely, where the legislative debate invites little deference, the courts should be exacting in their scrutiny. This more exacting approach was evident in *Hirst (No 2)*, where the Grand Chamber observed that there was 'no evidence that Parliament [had] ever sought to weigh the competing interests or assess the proportionality of a blanket ban on the right of a convicted prisoner to vote' and, further, that there had been no 'substantive debate by members of the legislature' in light of human rights standards.[52] We support the general approach adopted by the Strasbourg Court in these cases. But our analysis goes further. We would require courts to make a prior assessment of the quality of deliberative debate according to certain key criteria. Once this analysis is concluded, it will form one consideration in the proportionality analysis. This contrasts with the ad hoc invocation of the quality of legislative debate in the interstices of the proportionality analysis.

In all of this, transparency is key. Just as courts should develop clear criteria in their application of the proportionality analysis, so they should be transparent in their evaluation of the democratic deliberative process. The clearer the criteria and the better the reasoning used by courts when taking a view on the democratic deliberative process, the greater the potential for focused democratic dialogue between the arms of the state.

While the Strasbourg Court has taken the lead in this area, it is also worth noting that domestic courts have developed analytical tools to govern their analysis of legislative materials in other judicial proceedings. Domestic and international courts commonly refer to deliberative processes to clarify the ordinary meaning of the words in a statute or to resolve ambiguities in the text.[53] The construct

---

[48] The legislative background to the Communications Bill 2002 (UK), which prohibited political advertising on broadcast television, is outlined in *Animal Defenders International* (n 16) [35]–[64].

[49] The legislative background to the measure, which prohibited British citizens who had been living abroad for more than 15 years from voting, is described in *Shindler* (n 17) [15]–[28].

[50] *Animal Defenders International* (n 16) [116].

[51] *Shindler* (n 17) [117].

[52] *Hirst v UK (No 2)* (n 15) [79]. The Court echoed this phrase in respect of Hungary's restriction of the franchise for persons under guardianship in *Alajos Kiss v Hungary* App No 38832/06 (20 May 2010) [41].

[53] See, in the UK, *Pepper (Inspector of Taxes) v Hart* [1993] AC 593. In Australia, see *Saeed v Minister for Immigration* [2010] HCA 23. Internationally, see the 1969 Vienna Convention on the Law of Treaties, arts 31–32. But *cf* J Waldron, 'Legislators' Intentions and Unintentional Legislation' in *Law and Disagreement* (Oxford, Oxford University Press, 1999), arguing that there is no such thing as

of 'legislative intention' pervades statutory interpretation and judicial review.[54] There is, no doubt, room for improvement in the way that the English courts have approached these questions,[55] but our point is that reference to legislative debate does not always invite charges of constitutional heresy. In Australia, which is not renowned for its unorthodox constitutionalism, the Acts Interpretation Act allows courts to consider 'any relevant material ... in any official record of debates in the Parliament'.[56] In Sweden, the intention of Parliament, discerned through the drafting debates and the *travaux préparatoires* to the legislation, is the most important interpretive tool available to courts.[57] Further, much of the criticism in England of courts' engagement with legislative material could be mitigated if courts were more transparent in their analysis of legislative debate and deployed consistent criteria across cases.[58]

In the discussion that follows, we propose a set of criteria to guide courts in the slightly different context of judicial review of the human rights compatibility of legislation. These criteria give substance and structure to the courts' assessment of the degree of deference due to democratic deliberation. They aim to help courts resolve whether the justification offered for the rights restriction is adequate in a democracy.

A. The Representative Conditions in Which Legislative Debate Takes Place

Supporters of judicial review of legislation frequently argue that unfettered majoritarian process leads to an unfair override of the interests of the silent minority. In such conditions, Ely, for example, would argue that human rights review plays a crucial democratic role.[59] The first question a court should ask itself is therefore whether parliament can demonstrate engagement with the otherwise unrepresented voices of the minority. Was the democratic debate on human rights, or limitations on rights, inclusive of representatives of those whose rights would be affected? For example, did anyone in the deliberative process represent the interests of

---

collective legislative intention: 'Legislators will come to the chamber from different communities, with different ideologies, and different perspectives on what counts as a good reason or a valid consideration in political argument. The only thing they have in common, in their diversity and in the welter of rhetoric and mutual misunderstanding that counts for modern political debate, is the given text of the measure currently under consideration' (at 145).

[54] See above nn 40–42 and accompanying text.

[55] See, eg, the criticisms of R Munday, 'In the Wake of "Good Governance": Impact Assessments and the Politicisation of Statutory Interpretation' (2008) 78 *Modern Law Review* 385, arguing that English courts have, on occasion, incorrectly invoked Regulatory Impact Assessments (reports produced by the executive branch) to try to discern the intentions of the legislature in the course of statutory interpretation (at 392).

[56] Acts Interpretation Act 1901 (Cth), s 15AB(2)(h). Statutes in each state broadly echo the federal provision. See, eg, Interpretation Act 1987 (NSW), s 34; Interpretation of Legislation Act 1984 (Vic), s 35.

[57] See Bull and Cameron, ch 13 in this volume. See also I Cameron, 'The Swedish Experience of the European Convention on Human Rights since Incorporation' (1999) 48 *International and Comparative Law Quarterly* 20.

[58] See, eg, Steyn (n 43), emphasising the importance of delineating between statements that are indicative of *executive* as distinct from *legislative* intention.

[59] See Ely (n 27).

asylum-seekers, the Roma or Muslim minorities? Did this debate engage with their democratically represented views, or was the consultative process instead character-ised by 'legislative or executive indifference and inertia'?[60] Was there a balance of views or empathy with rights-bearers, given the democratic conditions surrounding the particular question at hand? This question is not concerned with 'the substantive merits of the political choice' made by parliament,[61] but rather with the degree of participation and the quality of the representation involved in the process.

No doubt it can be argued that participation of representatives of the affected minority is important for instrumental reasons, since it may lead to better legislative outcomes. The *Doctors for Life* case shows that when courts scrutinise democratic processes, it can improve the quality of the legislation that is ultimately adopted.[62] But we think that participation in public debate is itself a substantive good. Shue argues that participation is a fundamental constituent of the basic right to liberty.[63] Waldron describes participation as the 'right of rights'[64] and argues persuasively that 'there is a certain dignity in participation, and an element of insult and dishon-our in exclusion, that transcends issues of outcome'.[65] These insights are often mar-shalled in support of parliament rather than judges being cast as the final arbiters on rights, since it is the institution with the widest participation.[66] Some theorists deploy these arguments to discredit judicial review of legislation, on the grounds of its lack of democratic legitimacy.[67] But this relies on an underlying premise that all the relevant interests were represented in the deliberative process, and thus the choice favoured by the majority should prevail. This premise does not always hold. Many rights-bearers are totally 'excluded from majority decision procedures', such as children, prisoners and asylum-seekers.[68] Other rights-bearers, while formally enfranchised, may be excluded or marginalised in majoritarian processes in more subtle and complex ways.[69] If the relevant interests have not been represented 'at the point of substantive decision', then the majoritarian premise does not hold.[70]

Constitutional democracy is about more than simple majoritarianism; it is about 'democratic conditions', namely 'equal status for all citizens'.[71] Dworkin argues that majoritarian institutions must themselves 'provide and respect the democratic conditions'.[72] Our proposition goes slightly further, namely that it is only when those democratic conditions are provided and respected that parliaments can be

---

[60] Nolan (n 27) xxvii.
[61] Ely (n 27) 181.
[62] *Doctors for Life* (n 40).
[63] H Shue, *Basic Rights: Subsistence, Affluence, and US Foreign Policy* (2nd edn, Princeton, Princeton University Press, 1996) 71–78.
[64] J Waldron, 'Participation: The Right of Rights' in Waldron, *Law and Disagreement* (n 53) 232–54.
[65] J Waldron, 'A Right-Based Critique of Constitutional Rights' (1993) 13 *Oxford Journal of Legal Studies* 18, 40.
[66] See ibid.
[67] See, inter alia, ibid; Ekins (n 1).
[68] Nolan (n 27) 118.
[69] Ely (n 27).
[70] ibid, 121.
[71] R Dworkin, *Freedom's Law: The Moral Reading of the American Constitution* (Oxford, Oxford University Press, 1996) 17.
[72] ibid.

taken to have *earned* the deference of the courts. Consequently, courts should 'keep the machinery of democratic government running as it should; [making] sure the channels of political participation and communication are kept open'.[73] In this way, courts can enforce the democratic conditions that they themselves are accused of undermining.[74]

Courts' consideration of the 'representative conditions of democratic debate' might also engage questions of the shape and make-up of the particular democratic legislature. Is it constituted by a first-past-the-post majority? Do minorities get a higher level of representation through proportional representation? Are elected representatives 'beholden to an effective majority [who] are systematically disad-vantaging some minority out of a simple hostility'?[75] Is there an upper house with 'teeth'? Are there other mechanisms in the human rights bricolage[76] for representing minority views, such as in select committee proceedings or in public consultations and reviews? Does the parliament really work as a deliberative institution—or is there a continuous one-party majority? Is there a pervasive culture of political cor-ruption? The representative conditions of democratic debate form one important consideration in deciding whether deference is due.

B. The Quality of the Consideration Given to the Views of Rights-Bearers

Criterion two follows as a logical consequence of criterion one and relies on the same justifications. While the first criterion considers the structural question of rep-resentation, criterion two asks courts to assess the quality of the legislative attention given to the concerns of the affected rights-bearers. In other words, where criterion one asks whether the minority voices were represented, criterion two asks whether parliament *meaningfully engaged* with these minority voices. Were their views taken into account and considered in good faith? Were the relevant interests given weight or were they simply heard and ignored? To what extent were the recommendations of parliamentary select committees, national human rights institutions or equality bodies weighed up in the legislative debate? As with criterion one, criterion two rec-ognises that 'the duty of representation which lies at the core of our system requires more than a voice and a vote'.[77]

The approach we advocate here draws in some ways on the concept of 'meaning-ful engagement' that has been developed by the South African Constitutional Court. This interim remedy requires government and public bodies to consider the implica-tions of policy measures for affected groups and individuals, and to enter into good faith discussions with those people in an attempt to secure a mutually advantageous outcome. The concept derives from the 2008 *Occupiers of 51 Olivia Road* case, in which more than 400 people who had been squatting in unsafe buildings in

---

[73] ibid, 123, paraphrasing Ely (n 27) 76.
[74] See Fredman, ch 22 in this volume.
[75] Ely (n 27) 103.
[76] De Witte (n 8).
[77] Ely (n 27) 135.

inner-city Johannesburg challenged a council eviction order.[78] Rather than directly resolving the question of whether the eviction order breached the applicants' constitutional rights,[79] the Constitutional Court ordered the parties to 'meaningfully engage' with each other to find an appropriate solution.[80] While developed from earlier cases,[81] meaningful engagement was also grounded in the constitutional rights to life and dignity.[82] The obligation to meaningfully engage is one of process rather than outcome: a municipality seeking to evict people need not necessarily succeed in its negotiations with the occupiers, but 'it is the duty of a court to take into account whether ... at least, the municipality has made reasonable efforts towards meaningful engagement', and the absence of any engagement at all would be a persuasive factor weighing against the municipality.[83] This approach adopted by South Africa's Constitutional Court has much to offer beyond housing rights, and indeed beyond South African borders. One commentator has observed that 'at its best, engagement [may] avoid the need for court involvement altogether'.[84] 'Meaningful engagement' exists as an interim remedy in the South African context. However, it might also offer substantive guidance in framing the Court's assessment of parliamentary engagement with the views of affected minority rights-bearers. In this way, it offers a benchmark against which to evaluate when deference might be exercised by the court.

C. Was There Evidence Presented to the Legislature of the Necessity of the Measure that Restricts or Violates Rights?

Criterion three demands an assessment of the reasons for introducing the rights-restricting measure. It relates to the manner in which the legislation was introduced into parliament and the justifications that were offered in its defence. How necessary is the restriction or violation? What is the public interest that it aims to serve? Did the legislature consider other alternatives or was the solution adopted the only one proposed? Was there a meaningful attempt to engage with a broader policy problem? Were the reasons for the adoption of the measure discussed by parliamentarians? Was there a discussion of the relationship between the means chosen and

---

[78] *Occupiers of 51 Olivia Road Berea Township* (n 24).

[79] Section 26(3) of the South African Constitution provides that: 'No one may be evicted from their home, or have their home demolished, without an order of a court made after considering all the relevant circumstances. No legislation may permit arbitrary evictions.'

[80] *Occupiers of 51 Olivia Road Berea Township* (n 24) [6]–[23], Yacoob J.

[81] The court order was grounded in two earlier cases: in *Grootboom*, the Constitutional Court ordered the city to take reasonable measures to realise the respondents' right to housing (*Government of the Republic of South Africa v Grootboom* 2000 (11) BCLR 1169 (CC)). In *Port Elizabeth Municipality*, the Court resolved to 'encourage and require the parties to engage with each other in a proactive and honest endeavour to find mutually acceptable solutions (*Port Elizabeth Municipality v Various Occupiers* 2005 1 SA 217 (CC) [39]).

[82] South African Constitution, ss 10 and 11; quoted in *Occupiers of 51 Olivia Road Berea Township* (n 24) [16], Yacoob J.

[83] ibid [21].

[84] B Ray, '*Occupiers of 51 Olivia Road v City of Johannesburg*: Enforcing the Right to Adequate Housing through "Engagement"' (2008) 8 *Human Rights Law Review* 703, 709.

the ends pursued? Was there plausible evidence presented to parliament for why the rights restriction was necessary or desirable to pursue?

The Strasbourg Court considered this criterion in *Animal Defenders International*, observing that the UK Parliament had considered the measure to be necessary by reference to the need to 'prevent the distortion of crucial public interest debates and, thereby, the undermining of the democratic process'.[85] The applicants argued that less restrictive measures were available to achieve the same objective, such as banning political broadcasts only during election periods. However, the Grand Chamber noted that those alternatives had been thoroughly discussed during the deliberative process in Parliament, and there were 'reasonable' and 'rational' grounds for preferring the broader measure that was ultimately adopted.[86] *Animal Defenders International* lends weight to criterion three. It establishes that where there is plausible evidence presented to the legislature for the necessity of the measure and alternatives to it are meaningfully discussed in parliament, a greater degree of deference or a broader margin of appreciation is due.

In conducting this assessment, courts should also recognise that moral arguments about rights or their limitations may be present even where the language of rights is not explicit. Bearing in mind that 'one of the strengths of parliaments as protectors of human rights is said to be precisely that capacity to move beyond legalistic definitions of rights',[87] courts should recognise rights-talk even when it appears in unfamiliar guises. The prisoners' voting rights debate in the UK House of Commons, for example, was dominated by concerns about the legitimacy of the European Court of Human Rights rather than any extensive engagement with the nature of the right to vote.[88] Nevertheless, submerged within that rhetoric was an underlying 'forfeiture of rights' argument: 'if you break the law you can't make the law'. Courts should thus be alive to the possibility that moral arguments about rights can take varied forms, but they should also be sceptical of empty rhetoric.

D. The Courts' Democratic Mandate, Institutional Role and Place in Constitutional Culture

This criterion acknowledges that constitutional cultures and mandates vary significantly and that courts' perceptions of their own role in a constitutional democracy will affect the level of scrutiny applied. For example, the constitutional mandate could be very broad, but the court could be self-limiting where democratic deliberation and executive review or regulation in the light of human rights is exceptionally strong. Alternatively, courts may feel that it is legitimate to extend their mandate or to push the boundaries of popular understandings of their mandate where the quality of democratic deliberation or executive deliberation is particularly weak.

---

[85] *Animal Defenders International* (n 16) [116].
[86] ibid [122].
[87] Evans and Evans (n 7) 806.
[88] HC Deb 10 February 2011, col 493, considered in detail by Fredman in ch 22 in this volume.

By constitutional culture, we mean the 'legal norms and principles that form fundamental underlying precepts for our polity',[89] the 'institutional values of the legal system'[90] or, as Laws LJ said in *Roth*, 'our judgment as to the deference owed to the democratic powers will reflect the culture and conditions of the British state'.[91] For example, Germany has a 'highly articulated rights culture' and as such public confidence in the judiciary may support a more interventionist position by the courts,[92] whereas in countries such as the UK, where the place of justiciable rights within the constitutional culture is matter of continuous dispute,[93] a greater degree of deference to more representative institutions may be warranted.[94]

Judicial intervention can enhance democratic deliberation by introducing considerations that can be taken into account in legislative debate. In a dialogic model, the courts may be called upon to define the parameters of the rights that are implicated by a proposed legislative measure and the permissibility of restrictions, if any. A good practical example was the institutional dialogue following the decisions of the Victorian Supreme Court and the High Court of Australia in a case concerning the compatibility of reverse burdens of proof with the presumption of innocence.[95] Ideally, parliament or the executive should take judicial remedial action in good faith and embark on a discussion of the substantive issues articulated by the court.[96] In Clayton's words, 'the judicial decision causes a public debate in which the ... values play a more prominent role than they would if there was no judicial decision'.[97] Ideally, the response from the legislature will be respectful of the values identified by the court, but will achieve the same or similar objectives.[98]

When thinking about the court's mandate, it is important to distinguish between its constitutional deliberative position and its remedial power. For example, in

[89] WN Eskridge, 'Public Values in Statutory Interpretation' (1989) 137 *University of Pennsylvania Law Review* 1007, 1008. Eskridge cites the principle of non-discrimination as one example of a 'public value' in the US. *Cf* Sunstein's conception of 'background norms' in C Sunstein, 'Interpreting Statutes in the Regulatory State' (1989) 103 *Harvard Law Review* 405.

[90] Joseph (n 1) 338.

[91] *Roth* (n 20) 765, per Laws LJ, dissenting.

[92] L Lazarus, *Contrasting Prisoner's Rights* (Oxford, Oxford University Press, 2004) 3.

[93] See, eg, B Goold, L Lazarus, R Desai and Q Rasheed, 'The Relationship between Rights and Responsibilities', *Ministry of Justice Research Paper No 18/09*, 1 December 2009, available at: www.papers.ssrn.com/sol3/papers.cfm?abstract_id=2022270.

[94] For a discussion of the emerging human rights culture in the UK, see, eg, M Hunt, 'The Human Rights Act and Legal Culture: The Judiciary and the Legal Profession' (1999) 26 *Journal of Law and Society* 86; AL Bendor and Z Segal, 'Constitutionalism and Trust in Britain: An Ancient Constitutional Culture, a New Judicial Review Model' (2001) 17 *American University International Law Review* 683; Hunt (n 7) 601.

[95] See *R v Momcilovic* [2010] VSCA 50 and *Momcilovic v The Queen* [2011] HCA 34. Following that decision, the Victorian Parliament's Scrutiny of Acts and Regulations Committee recommended that the Government consider repealing the provisions of the Victorian Charter of Human Rights related to courts and tribunals. However, the Government rejected this submission and issued a detailed response, declaring that it was 'strongly committed to the principles of human rights and considers that legislative protection for those rights provides a tangible benefit to the Victorian community': Victorian Government Response to the Review of the Charter of Human Rights and Responsibilities Act 2006 (14 March 2012), available at: www.parliament.vic.gov.au.

[96] *Cf* the poor quality of the parliamentary debate in *Hirst v UK (No 2)* (n 15) 79 and in *Alajos Kiss v Hungary* (n 52).

[97] Clayton (n 18) 42; *cf* Roach, ch 20 in this volume.

[98] Clayton (n 18).

'weak' models of judicial review, the court has the power to issue declarations of incompatibility as distinct from 'strong' judicial review offering legislative strike-down of legislation.[99] The more anti-democratic the remedy, the greater the caution with which it should be used. Courts may have a greater impact on the democratic process by adopting a weak remedy but a strong criticism. In a dialogic model, judicial analysis of the strengths and weaknesses in a particular parliamentary debate may enrich subsequent debate in legislative chambers. This may occur, for example, when a matter is returned to parliament following a declaration of incompatibility by the courts.[100] In that circumstance, judicial intervention can contribute to a more constructive dialogue in parliament when the assembly considers the matter the second time around. Kent Roach's contribution in this volume discusses how judicial invalidation of old laws can enhance democracy by demanding that parliamentarians revisit the issue, often leading to better-tailored legislative outcomes.[101] But even short of judicial strike-down, judicial interventions through declarations of incompatibility can lead to productive parliamentary debate.[102] A good example of this process working well was in the debate in the UK over preventative detention of foreign terrorist suspects post-9/11. When Parliament passed a law permitting the detention of foreign terrorist suspects on the say-so of the Home Secretary, the House of Lords remitted the matter to Parliament for reconsideration, and the regime of administrative detention was ultimately replaced by control orders.[103] Judicial intervention enhanced the quality of the subsequent deliberative debate, and the UK Parliament responded with a less rights-restricting measure.

Hence, we might view a court's criticism of parliamentary debate as an interim measure, in much the same way as the 'meaningful engagement' measure works in the South African context. By prompting democratic reconsideration of rights-limiting legislation, the court enriches the deliberative process. It also avoids the question of which institution has the final say—a perennial question in constitutional debate which in many ways distracts from the rights issues in play.

E. The Nature of the Right

Courts, as the 'guardians of rights',[104] must be prepared to disagree with the legislature notwithstanding the quality of democratic debate. Recall that the over-arching question that these criteria seek to answer is how weighty are the rights

---

[99] Waldron, 'The Core of the Case against Judicial Review' (n 2) 1354.

[100] See, eg, PW Hogg, and AA Bushell, 'The Charter Dialogue between Courts and Legislatures (or Perhaps the Charter of Rights isn't Such a Bad Thing after All)' (1997) 35 *Osgoode Hall Law Journal* 75; for a discussion of the dialogue model in New Zealand and the UK, see Joseph (n 1). See generally Clayton (n 18).

[101] See Roach, ch 20 in this volume. See also K Roach, *The Supreme Court on Trial: Judicial Activism or Democratic Dialogue* (Toronto, Irwin Law, 2001).

[102] For a comparative assessment of the success of different models of judicial review in different jurisdictions, see S Gardbaum, *The New Commonwealth Model of Constitutionalism: Theory and Practice* (Cambridge, Cambridge University Press, 2013).

[103] See *A v Secretary of State for the Home Department (No 2)* [2005] UKHL 71.

[104] Rivers (n 47) 205.

considerations, given the countervailing quality of democratic deliberations? By this stage of the analysis, the court will have answered a series of institutional questions encompassed by criteria one to four. This puts it in a stronger position to evaluate the deference questions that now arise in the interstices of the rights analysis. This includes, first, the interpretive determination of whether the right is engaged and, second, as regards qualified rights, the conduct of the proportionality analysis.

The permissibility of rights-restrictions is inextricably bound up with the nature of the right in question. Rights 'may be limited to pursue a wide range of public and private interests', but 'that range is not unlimited, and the limits vary according to the rights in question'.[105] The importance of the right and the gravity of the limitations will ideally be reflected in the democratic deliberations.

But even so, in exceptional circumstances, courts must be prepared to declare certain measures incompatible with human rights, notwithstanding the most robust and rigorous debate. As the Strasbourg Court observed in *Shindler*:

> This is not to say that because a legislature debates, possibly even repeatedly, an issue and reaches a particular conclusion thereon, that conclusion is necessarily Convention compliant. It simply means that the review is taken into consideration by the Court for the purpose of deciding whether a fair balance has been struck between competing interests.[106]

In *Shindler*, the Court agreed with the legislature that the restrictions were Convention compliant. However, the Court observed correctly that a strong deliberative process cannot 'neutralise' a clear rights violation. For example, if a legislature votes to torture terrorist suspects, no matter how strong the deliberative process, there is no role for deference to play. *Jus cogens* norms are one category into which legislative intrusions—even with the best possible parliamentary debate—may be clearly excluded.

CONCLUSION

Asking courts to evaluate the quality of democratic deliberation is, on its face, a bold proposal. But we make this proposal in the context of the shift towards a form of constitutionalism in which responsibility for upholding human rights is shared across all branches of government, together with a changing landscape of human rights institutions. In this context, it is imperative to ensure the integrity of the framework as a whole. In our view, this proposal will strengthen the partnership between courts and parliaments in furthering human rights. This proposal invites courts to set the parameters of the debate, while parliament determines where and how to strike the balance in all but the most exceptional cases. Rather than undermining democratic politics, this approach has the potential to strongly enhance that democratic engagement. In a constitutional democracy premised on human rights

---

[105] ibid, 195.
[106] *Shindler* (n 17) 117.

and fundamental freedoms, it is no longer appropriate to 'equate "democratic principle" with "majority approval"'.[107]

The concepts of due deference in the domestic context and the margin of appreciation in the Strasbourg context are in urgent need of further substantiation. Lord Irvine, writing extra-judicially, rightly observed that 'we cannot simply recite the need for "deference" or "self-restraint". Rather, we must, where appropriate, argue the case for it carefully and persuasively'.[108] In this chapter, we have made a case for a set of criteria that should inform the courts in this endeavour. This is not an invitation to judicial activism; nor is strengthening deference tantamount to promoting the 'abdication of judicial responsibility'.[109] This is a proposal to deepen the rigour with which deference is exercised, and an invitation to parliament to stand at the centre of rights deliberation.

---

[107] Jowell (n 18) 597.

[108] D Irvine, 'The Impact of the Human Rights Act: Parliament, the Courts and the Executive' [2003] *Public Law* 308, 316.

[109] TRS Allan, 'Human Rights and Judicial Review: A Critique of Due Deference' (2006) 65 *Cambridge Law Journal* 671, 675.

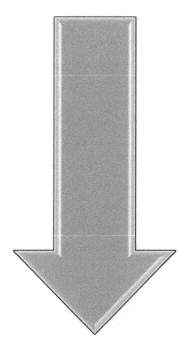

Criteria for evaluating democratic deliberation about rights

- The representative conditions of democratic debate

- The extent to which Parliament meaningfully engaged with the views and interests of minority rights bearers

- The representative make up of Parliament

- The power and make up of a second chamber

- The existence of a a long standing one party democracy

- The existence of political corruption

- The quality of legislative scrutiny

- The extent to which recommendations of parliamentary bodies charged with rights based scrutiny are taken into account

- The quality of the evidence for the rights limitations presented to the legislative assembly

- The Courts' own constitutional mandate

- Quality of moral and political reasoning about rights

The nature of the right

- How weighty are the rights considerations, given the countervailing quality of democratic deliberations?

- Is the right absolute and subject to deference at all?

- Does the right—by definition or by factual application—protect minority interests?

- Does the right engage questions of political representation or exchange?

- Does the right engage majority and redistributive interests?

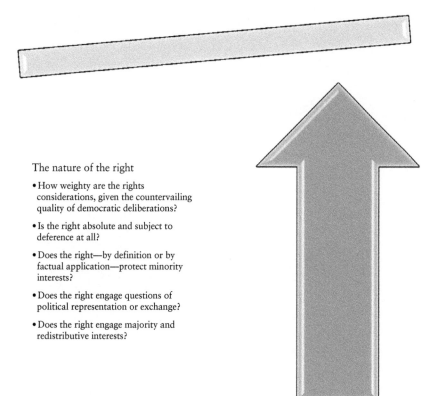

Figure 19.1: How much deference is due to democratic deliberation?

20

The Varied Roles of Courts and Legislatures in Rights Protection

KENT ROACH*

T HERE HAS BEEN an unfortunate tendency in scholarly and political debates about judicial review to view both courts and legislatures as monolithic institutions. This approach to institutional performance has too often reduced debate about judicial review to a binary choice that pits courts against legislatures. Those who champion a legislative role allegedly have the people on their side as well as the dubious historical performance of the courts. Those who champion the courts have the alleged importance of principle on their side as well as the dubious historical role of legislatures in enacting harsh measures against minorities. The debate has, quite frankly, grown old and tired. There is a need for fresh approaches that examine the different role that courts and legislatures can play both in defining and protecting human rights, and justifying reasonable and legislatively prescribed limits on such rights.

The empirical tone of this collection is promising in moving the debate beyond polarised questions of whether one stands with the judges or the legislators. In the first section of this chapter, I will attempt to disaggregate and make more complex the category of 'legislature' and 'courts'. Defenders of judicial review, including myself, have tended to think about legislatures as a monolithic and majoritarian institution. The study that prompted this book, however, helpfully demonstrates that legislatures are complex and nuanced.[1] There are upper and lower houses, with the former either not being elected or tied to a different electoral cycle than the latter. Debate in the Houses of Parliament often has a very different tone from debate in a legislative committee where civil society representatives and others can be heard. Committees such as the Joint Committee on Human Rights have a potential to raise concerns about rights in the legislative process that might otherwise be neglected. Critics of legislatures would be well-advised not to generalise and to specify what part of the legislative process concerns them.

If defenders of judicial review have oversimplified the legislative process as simply based on majoritarianism, defenders of legislative review have romanticised the

* I thank Aileen Kavanagh for helpful comments on an earlier draft of this chapter.
1 Murray Hunt, Hayley J Hooper and Paul Yowell, *Parliaments and Human Rights: Redressing the Democratic Deficit (No 5 Public Policy Series)* (Swindon, Arts and Humanities Research Council, 2012).

legislative process as one based on reasonable disagreements about rights and public regarding reasons. A key concept here is a distinction that Andrew Dismore, a former Chair of the Joint Committee on Human Rights, drew between consideration of the rights of 'vulnerable persons in the mainstream' and the rights of those 'on the fringes of the society for whom public sympathy is low or non-existent'.[2] To his credit, Mr Dismore has argued that the Joint Committee is concerned with both the former category—women, children and the elderly—and the latter category of 'less popular, often demonized groups, who do not have the ear of the media or general public sympathy',[3] such as those accused of crime and non-citizens. Nevertheless, the fact that this distinction was made both by him and in the study of Parliament and Human Rights is telling. We cannot afford to ignore the reality of politics that can demonise the truly unpopular including those accused of crime and non-citizens.

In light of the attempts to disaggregate and complicate the simplistic contrasts between legislative and judicial decision-making in the first section of this chapter, the second section of the chapter will survey how legislative deliberation about rights should influence the courts. Here again, there has been a tendency to lump together issues and to focus on the bottom line. Critics of judicial review love to focus on evenly divided court decisions that reach problematic decisions. Much of the debate has focused on whether courts should have a monopoly on the interpretation of rights and the competing claims that judges and legislators have to interpret rights. This is an important albeit well-worn debate that will be addressed in this chapter, but this chapter will also attempt to move beyond this debate to focus on the role that legislatures and courts should play in the various parts of proportionality tests that are so frequently used in judicial review. We should examine the strengths and weaknesses of courts and legislatures at each stage of proportionality analysis rather than engage in the tired and polarised debate of courts versus legislatures.

I. BEYOND A POLARISED DEBATE ABOUT THE ROLE OF COURTS AND LEGISLATURES

A. Disaggregating the Legislature and its Treatment of Rights

The last generation of constitutional scholarship at least in North America often assumed a Jim Crow legislative process pitted against the Warren Court. Ronald Dworkin's[4] and especially John Hart Ely's views of the legislative process were largely forged in the reality of the Warren Court's struggles against the segregated South of the US in the 1950s as well as the internment of Japanese Americans during the Second World War.[5] Defenders of the legislative process can rightly complain that such negative views of the legislative process are not merited today.[6] Minorities

---

[2] HC Deb 13 March 2008, vol 473, col 115WH (Andrew Dismore) as quoted in ibid at 34.
[3] HC Deb 19 February 2007, vol 457, col 82 (Andrew Dismore) as quoted in ibid at 35.
[4] Ronald Dworkin, *Taking Rights Seriously* (Cambridge, MA, Harvard University Press, 1977).
[5] John Hart, *Democracy and Distrust* (Cambridge, MA, Harvard University Press, 1980).
[6] Jeremy Waldron, *Law and Disagreement* (Oxford, Oxford University Press, 1999).

such as gays and lesbians have not received everything they wanted from the legislative process, but they have not been entirely shut out from it either. The treatment of those suspected of terrorism and Muslims post-9/11 has been problematic, but legislatures to their credit have not authorised internment on racial or religious grounds. Even Professor Ely recognised that divisive questions such as access to abortion did not have the same dynamic as the treatment of the classic discrete and insular minorities.[7] Bruce Ackerman has even made the provocative argument that the discreteness of some minorities may give them an edge in the political process, at least as compared to diffuse and unorganised groups.[8] To borrow Andrew Dismore's evocative phrase, we can no longer assume that the legislature will discriminate against minorities 'in the mainstream'.

Although the politics of today should not be denigrated as crudely majoritarian, its dangers should not be ignored. As the welfare state has shrunk and the economy has lurched from global crisis to global crisis, criminal justice and immigration policies have become the site of symbolic, expressive and at times utterly irrational and cruel politics. The harsh and emotional politics of 'governing through crime'[9] has been attractive to governments of all political stripes. New Labour in the UK and the Democrats in the US have not hesitated to play the 'crime card'. Progressive parties throughout the world are increasingly unwilling to risk votes by appearing to be 'soft' on crime or other security issues such as terrorism. The legislative process has the potential to place checks on a government's mobilisation of crime and other hot button issues, but only to the extent that legislators in opposition are prepared to take political risks. Although it is unfair of defenders of judicial review to posit a Jim Crow legislative process, it is also unfair of defenders of legislatures to posit a politics that is simply a calm environment for reasoned discussion and disagreement about rights.[10] There is a need for careful evaluation of legislative policy-making to reveal who are most vulnerable in the legislative process. A starting hypothesis would be that while minorities 'in the mainstream' may often be able to protect themselves in the legislative process, truly unpopular groups such as those accused of crime and non-citizens may be particularly vulnerable.

As suggested above, the legislative process needs to be disaggregated. There is growing evidence that the unelected upper houses in the UK and Canada may be more receptive to rights claims than elected lower houses.[11]These findings are intriguing because they are consistent with institutionalist approaches which stress that the prospect of standing for frequent re-election may make legislators less willing to take unpopular stands.

---

[7] John Hart Ely, 'The Wages of Crying Wolf' (1973) 83 *Yale Law Journal* 920.

[8] Bruce Ackerman, 'Beyond Carolene Products' (1985) 85 *Harvard Law Review* 713.

[9] Jonathan Simon, *Governing through Crime* (New York, Oxford University Press, 2007). For my related discussion of the 'criminalisation of politics', see Kent Roach, *Due Process and Victims' Rights: The New Law and Politics of Criminal Justice* (Toronto, University of Toronto Press, 1999).

[10] Gregoire Webber, *The Negotiable Constitution* (Cambridge, Cambridge University Press, 2009).

[11] Danny Nicol, 'The Human Rights Act and the Politicians' (2004) 24 *Legal Studies* 451; Janet Hiebert, 'Parliament and the Human Rights Act' (2006) 4 *International Journal of Constitutional Law* 1; Kent Roach, 'The Role and Capacities of Courts and Legislatures in Reviewing Canadian Anti-terrorism Law' (2008) 24 *Windsor Review of Legal and Social Issues* 5.

The legislative process also should be disaggregated to include the work of committees. Parliamentary committees in Canada are much less well staffed than those in the UK and there is no equivalent of the Joint Committee on Human Rights. This, combined with the failure of the Minister of Justice to ever report on an inconsistency of proposed legislation with the Charter,[12] may help explain why Canadian courts have frequently resorted to invalidating legislation. At the same time, the scholarly reports of the Joint Committee on Human Rights or even reference to those reports in legislative debates should not be taken as ends in themselves. The ultimate question should be the degree to which parliamentary committees can persuade governments to amend bills to make them more rights-friendly. Such influence cannot be captured in quantitative studies of reference to human rights in legislative debates. It will require more detailed case studies of a variety of policy measures. These studies should include both rights claims by minorities in the mainstream and the truly unpopular. One danger of such studies is that the choice of case studies will inevitably be partial. Those with polarised views in favour of either the courts or legislatures will dismiss studies as based on an inadequate data set. An empirical move in the scholarship is desirable, but past polarised battles over judicial review will not easily be left behind.

II. DISAGGREGATING THE JUDICIARY AND ITS TREATMENT OF RIGHTS

If defenders of judicial review have unfairly focused on the most unappealing aspects of the legislative process, so too have critics of judicial review often focused on the most problematic features of courts. They frequently ignored the fact that much judicial review pits the unelected judges against officials in the executive and not against an elected legislature. Courts that invalidate executive behaviour may play an important role in encouraging the legislative process to consider and monitor what might otherwise be low-visibility administration. Courts and legislatures may have a common interest in forcing the executive to be more transparent and to respect the demands of legality.

Just as there has been an unfortunate tendency to downplay actors in the legislative process who may be concerned with rights, there has been a tendency to downplay actors in the judicial process that may have concerns about democratic politics. The government's appointment power will help keep most of the judiciary within the mainstream. The judiciary is a reactive institution and both governments and civil society help determine the strength of support structures that are necessary to bring cases to courts.[13] Courts often have to rely on data that is controlled by government. For example, the Newton Committee report played an important role in the House of Lords' decision in the *Belmarsh* case.[14] Governmental decisions to collect (or not collect) statistics can be critical in determining the fate of legislation

---

[12] Kent Roach, 'Not Just the Government's Lawyer: The Attorney General as the Defender of the Rule of Law' (2006) 31 *Queen's Law Journal* 598.
[13] Charles Epp, *The Rights Revolution* (Chicago, University of Chicago Press, 1998).
[14] *A v Secretary of State for the Home Department (No 1)* [2004] UKHL 56.

that is challenged in the courts. Decisions by 'the Court' are not simply those of an unrepresentative judiciary: they are decisions of 'the Court and company', and the 'company' often has roots in the political system or civil society.

It would also be naïve to think that even independent courts are oblivious to the political effects of their rulings. In Canada and South Africa, courts can suspend declarations of invalidity in order to give legislatures an opportunity to displace the blunt remedy of a declaration of invalidity. This can reduce the gap that is sometimes stressed between the Canadian Charter of Rights and Freedoms as a bill of rights that gives courts 'strike-down' powers and other bills of rights that withhold such powers.

It is also important to distinguish between judicial review of recent legislative policies that may command a majority in Parliament and older policies that may simply be a result of inertia. Judicial criticism or invalidation of an old law may be a way to increase democracy by requiring legislators to take a fresh look. In Canada, the invalidation of an old vagrancy law in a case involving a suspected paedophile actually encouraged Parliament to enact a law that was more fit for purpose in protecting children against sexual predators in the internet age. Similarly, the invalidation of a 1982 rape shield provision that restricted the admissibility of complainants' prior sexual history resulted in a 1992 law that incorporated feminist criticisms of other parts of sexual assault law.[15]

Detailed empirical studies of the actual performance of courts and legislatures on questions of rights protection are a promising means to escape the dead end of polarised debate about judicial review. An important part of such empirical studies should be an attempt to disaggregate both courts and legislatures to make clear that each process has strengths and weaknesses in different contexts and at various pressure points. An empirical turn in the literature may result in more light and less heat being thrown at the tired and polarised courts versus legislature debate.

III. THE ROLE OF LEGISLATURES AND COURTS IN DELIBERATING ABOUT RIGHTS AND JUSTIFIED LIMITS ON RIGHTS

A. The Debate about Interpreting Rights: Who is the Primary Decision-Maker?

Mark Tushnet and Larry Kramer have defended the ability of legislatures and the executive to interpret the constitution and to act on such interpretations even when the interpretations differ from the courts.[16] They draw on a long American tradition of coordinate construction. Thomas Jefferson defended the ability of the elected branches of government to act on their own interpretation of the Constitution. Although coordinate construction has been used for regressive ends in the US by Andrew Jackson in opposition to Aboriginal rights and by the Deep South in

---

[15] These episodes of interaction or dialogue between courts and legislatures are discussed in K Roach, *The Supreme Court on Trial: Democratic Dialogue or Judicial Activism* (Toronto, Irwin Law, 2001) ch 14.

[16] Mark Tushnet, *Taking the Constitution Away from the Courts* (Princeton, Princeton University Press, 1999); Larry D Kramer, *The People Themselves* (New York, Oxford University Press, 2004).

defence of Jim Crow laws, it also has a progressive pedigree. Abraham Lincoln defied the courts on a number of issues, including slavery and habeas corpus, and both Franklin Delano Roosevelt and Barack Obama hinted that they might act on their interpretation of the Constitution had the US Supreme Court overturned the New Deal and health-care reform respectively. Jeremy Waldron has likewise stressed the ability of legislatures to deliberate about rights. He suggests that there are many reasonable disagreements about rights and there is no reason to prefer the interpretation of rights by unelected judges over those selected by the majority of elected representatives.[17]

At some risk of reverting to familiar debates about judicial review, I still maintain the reservations that I have previously expressed[18] about legislative interpretation of rights. In my view, judicial deference to legislative interpretation of rights has the potential to undermine the anti-majoritarian role of courts and judicial review. As elected institutions, legislatures will have an incentive to minimise the rights of the truly unpopular, most notably those accused of crime. Given the respect that our polity has for rights, legislators may have an incentive to deny that rights are at stake. They may attempt to dismiss rights claims by emotive forms of contextualisation. For example, claims that prisoners should have the vote or claims based on privacy may be dismissed on the basis that criminals should not enjoy such rights. Such an approach is not based on a reasonable disagreement about rights, but a denial of the existence of rights.

The issue of whether courts should defer to legislative interpretations of rights is particularly pressing under the American Bill of Rights and with respect to the unqualified rights protected under the European Convention on Human Rights and the Human Rights Act 1998. Aileen Kavanagh has made an interesting argument that there is a role for judicial deference even with respect to rights.[19] Mark Tushnet has similarly argued that it is a mistake to think that the unqualified rights in the American Bill of Rights admit of no qualification.[20] Both of these claims seem right, but I still think it will be useful to distinguish the questions of judicial deference owed to legislative interpretation of rights and the judicial deference owed to legislative justification of limits on rights.

Kavanagh argues that judges should be deferential and only interfere with unreasonable laws because the legislature remains the primary decision-maker. This view makes sense because legislatures are the experts about the legislative objectives for limiting rights. Conversely, however, and borrowing from Kavanagh's helpful terminology, I would argue that courts should be the primary decision-maker about the scope of rights. Countries that enact bills of rights generally expect that judges will determine whether rights are in play even if they specifically contemplate a legislative role in limiting or overriding rights. In determining whether to accept a limit on

[17] Waldron (n 6).
[18] Roach (n 15).
[19] Aileen Kavanagh, *Constitutional Review under the UK Human Rights Act* (Cambridge, Cambridge University Press, 2011).
[20] Mark Tushnet, 'Judicial Activism or Restraint in a Section 33 World' (2003) 52 *University of Toronto Law Journal* 89.

unqualified rights, courts should attempt to distinguish legislative reasoning about the scope of the right from legislative reasoning about whether a limit on a right is justified. Courts should review legislative interpretations of rights on something closer to a correctness standard in recognition that they are a primary decision-maker about the scope of rights. This is particularly important when we are speaking of rights claims made by the truly unpopular which the legislature will have strong incentives to deny. Such an approach to rights should also encourage legislatures to recognise that rights are at play and to compile the best case for their limitation.

A judicial lead in defining rights leaves much room for the legislature. Legislatures will lead with respect to the reasons for limiting rights. They will be able to articulate their objectives, the alternatives that they considered and the evidence upon which they acted. Following Kavanagh's suggestions, courts can recognise that the legislature remains the primary decision-maker on these issues.

I have also never rejected the possibility that, in extraordinary situations where the legislature is convinced that the court's interpretation of rights is wrong, legislatures should be able to act on an interpretation of rights that differs from the judiciary's interpretation. Such actions should, however, be extraordinary and they should be clearly signalled to the populace and defended by the government. In Canada, I have suggested that Parliament should use the section 33 override of rights which allows a law to stand for a renewable five years notwithstanding the court's interpretation of rights. The British analogy might be a reasoned parliamentary decision not to act in the face of a declaration of incompatibility under section 4 of the Human Rights Act or perhaps to enact laws in the absence of a ministerial statement of compatibility. The fact that legislatures rarely act in this manner may be taken by some as a sign of judicial supremacy. This argument, however, discounts the primary role of legislatures in justifying limitations on rights and their secondary role in interpreting rights. The reluctance of legislatures to stand up for interpretations of rights that differ from judicial interpretation may simply reflect the fact that legislatures and governments are not particularly well-suited to engage in the interpretation of rights.[21] The judiciary, not the legislature, is the primary decision-maker about rights. If this is accepted, the fact that legislatures have rarely contested judicial interpretations of rights by overriding them or ignoring judicial declarations of rights may seem less extraordinary. At the same time, the absence of such legislative engagement on these issues should not result in hyperbolic claims about judicial supremacy or government by unelected judges. The legislature remains the primary and dominant decision-maker about limitations on rights. The rest of the chapter will focus on this latter topic.

B. The Debate about Legislative Objectives: What Objectives are Legitimate?

Limitation clauses such as those found in the Canadian Charter, the New Zealand Bill of Rights and the South African Constitution are open-ended with respect to

---

[21] Alexander Bickel, *The Least Dangerous Branch* (2nd edn, New Haven, Yale University Press, 1986).

the types of legislative objectives that can limit rights. This can be contrasted with the European Convention, which circumscribes what type of legislative objectives can justify limits on particular rights. The open-ended approach is generally to be preferred because it allows legislatures to be candid about their reasons for limiting rights. For example, fiscal constraint has been recognised in Canada as a legislative objective that can limit all Charter rights, whereas 'the economic well being of the country' is only recognised as a legitimate objective for limiting privacy rights, but not other rights such as freedom of association under the European Convention. I do not doubt that the legislative objectives can be creatively fitted into circumscribed categories, but this can result in the inflation of both objective and rights. For example, economic restraint matters could be ratcheted up to be matters of national security. Crime control concerns could be elevated to the need to protect the rights and freedoms of others.

My colleague David Beatty has argued that courts should be willing to accept the broadest array of legislative objectives as legitimate and that such an open-ended approach helps establish the legitimacy of judicial review.[22] His approach reflects the more open-ended Canadian approach over the more circumscribed European approach, but it should not be forgotten that the Canadian approach is not completely open-ended. Legislative objectives that are simply objections or refusals to recognise the right are not, even in Canada, legitimate legislative objectives for limiting rights. For example, Parliament's desire to enforce observance of the Christian Sabbath was not a legitimate objective for limiting freedom of religion[23] and the Supreme Court has found that governments could not articulate any legitimate legislative objective for not protecting gays and lesbians from discrimination or for excluding same-sex couples from benefits for heterosexual couples.[24] These latter judgments are similar to those made by the House of Lords in *Ghaidan v Godin-Mendoza*,[25] which could find no objective for excluding same-sex couples from legislation to protect couples who rent. Legislatures should generally be free to pick and define the objective for limiting rights, but the denial of the existence of a right or the expression of prejudice against a group is not a legitimate objective to limit a right.

In the vast majority of cases, the Canadian courts accept the Government's objective for limiting rights.[26] Nevertheless, the rise of emotional and symbolic politics based on the expression of animus towards criminals, non-citizens and others who are truly unpopular may force courts to reject some legislative objectives for limiting rights. Jeremy Waldron has cited Lord Devlin's interventions in legislative debates as a 'provocative model' of how judges can participate in a dialogue as a citizen and without having the power to bang a gavel and make authoritative decisions.[27] There is, however, a dark side to Waldron's evocation of Devlin. Although Waldron

---

[22] David Beatty, *The Ultimate Rule of Law* (Oxford, Oxford University Press, 2005).
[23] *R v Big M Drug Mart* [1985] 1 SCR 295.
[24] *Vriend v Alberta* [1998] 1 SCR 493; *Canada v Hislop* [2007] 1 SCR 429,
[25] *Ghaidan v Godin-Mendoza* [2004] UKHL 30.
[26] Leon Trakman et al, 'R v Oakes 1986–1997' (1998) 36 *Osgoode Hall Law Journal* 83, 95.
[27] Jeremy Waldron, 'Some Models of Dialogue between Judges and Legislators' (2004) 23 SCLR 2d7, 23.

maintains that each side in the famous Hart–Devlin debate 'listened to the other and responded in an intellectually rigorous and respectable way', we should not confuse the debates of public intellectuals with the actual basis for legislating that Devlin defended. Devlin argued that the community was justified in enacting criminal laws in order to express 'a real feeling of reprobation. No society can do without intolerance, indignation and disgust'.[28] Devlin's and society's sense of disgust has evolved. Devlin eventually abandoned his opposition to the criminalisation of adult consensual sex between two men as gays became minorities in the mainstream. But the sense of emotional disgust that he defended as a legitimate basis for legislation is unfortunately alive and well today. Today it is often directed at those accused of or imprisoned for crime or non-citizens associated with crime, terrorism or illegal migration. Waldron and his many followers often fail to confront this ugly side of contemporary politics.

Emotional and disgust-based objectives of the type associated with Lord Devlin pose a serious challenge to proportionality analysis. They are not so much attempts to obtain outcomes in society that can be rationally evaluated, but moral or symbolic statements that are ends in themselves. If they are accepted in proportionality analysis as a legitimate basis for limiting rights, such acceptance may short circuit the other components of the proportionality analysis. In other words, it is difficult to see how the expression of a particular vision of disgust or morality is not rationally connected to that very objective. Moreover, it is difficult to evaluate less rights-invasive alternatives, especially if one accepts Lord Devlin's view that criminal law has a unique function in expressing a community's values. Such legislative objectives defy proportionality analysis because they are self-executing. This perhaps explains why the Supreme Court could find no objective for Alberta's decision not to protect gays and lesbians against private sector discrimination. As Justice Iacobucci explained, a legislative objective for the purpose of proportionality analysis should be 'a goal ... which makes plain that which is not immediately obvious'[29] from a reading of the law enacted. The expression of disgust is not a rational goal that can be achieved by more or less proportionate means: it is an end in itself.

The inability of courts to subject legislative objectives that are purely expressive of morality or emotions to proportionality analysis suggests that there may be an intractable conflict between judges and legislators if the former remain committed to proportionality analysis and the latter remain committed to expressive and symbolic politics. The UK Prime Minister David Cameron revealed much when he stated in Parliament no less that 'it makes me physically ill even to contemplate having to give the vote to anyone who is in prison. Frankly, when people commit a crime and go to prison, they should lose their rights, including the right to vote'.[30] His Devlin-like sense of disgust was also reflected in a bipartisan manner by David

---

[28] Patrick Devlin, *The Enforcement of Morals* (Oxford, Oxford University Press, 1965) 17.

[29] *Vriend v Alberta* [1998] 1 SCR 493 [114].

[30] HC Deb 3 November 2010, vol 517, col 921 (David Cameron) See also Tim Whitehead, 'Prisoners Could Get Vote Within Six Months if UK Loses Last Legal Battle in Europe' *Daily Telegraph*, (22 May 2012) available at: www.telegraph.co.uk/news/politics/9282231/Prisoners-could-get-vote-within-six-months-if-UK-loses-last-legal-battle-in-Europe.html.

Davis and Jack Straw, who argued that 'those who break the law cannot make the law'. They interpreted the underlying right differently from the European Court of Human Rights and pronounced that no rights were at stake. The issue was, they claim, a 'minor social policy issue'[31] on which Parliament must prevail. The bipartisan support of this position suggests that we are not dealing here with a Waldron-like reasonable disagreement about rights, but a denial of rights on the basis of emotional animus if not outright disgust and disregard for prisoners.

The conflict that is emerging between courts and legislatures over expressive legislative objectives is reflected by conflicts emerging throughout the globe over prisoner voting. In Canada, the Supreme Court of Canada in 2002 struck down a law restricting prisoner voting in a controversial 5:4 decision. The majority of the Court very reluctantly accepted that the Government's objectives for denying the vote to prisoners serving two years or more in prison—promoting respect for civic responsibility and the rule of law—were important enough to limit the Charter right to vote. Chief Justice McLachlin, however, expressed concerns that because such objectives were 'vague and symbolic', it was impossible to subject them to proportionality analysis:

> Who can argue that respect for the law is not pressing? Who can argue that proper sentences are not important? Who can argue that either of these goals, taken at face value, contradicts democratic principles? However, precisely because they leave so little room for argument, vague and symbolic objectives make the justification analysis more difficult. Their terms carry many meanings, yet tell us little about why the limitation on the right is necessary, and what it is expected to achieve in concrete terms ... The rhetorical nature of the government objectives advanced in this case renders them suspect. The first objective, enhancing civic responsibility and respect for the law, could be asserted of virtually every criminal law and many non-criminal measures ... To establish justification, one needs to know what problem the government is targeting, and why it is so pressing and important that it warrants limiting a *Charter* right. Without this, it is difficult if not impossible to weigh whether the infringement of the right is justifiable or proportionate.[32]

---

[31] David Davis and Jack Straw, 'We Must Defy Strasbourg on Prisoner Votes' *Daily Telegraph* (24 May 2012), available at: www.telegraph.co.uk/news/uknews/law-and-order/9287633/We-must-defy-Strasbourg-on-prisoner-votes.html.

[32] *Sauve v Canada (Attorney-General)* [2002] 3 SCR 519 [22] and [24]. I disclose that I represented Aboriginal Legal Services of Toronto (ALST), which intervened in this case. These are the written submissions we made to the Court with respect to s 1: 'ALST submits that this is one of the rare cases where the objectives advanced by the government are not pressing and substantial enough to justify a violation of *Charter* rights ... The objectives advanced by the Respondents—the idea that disenfranchisement may supplement the criminal sanction and the enhancement of civic responsibility and the rule of law—may be valid explanations for the politics behind the enactment of s 51(e), but they cannot constitute pressing and substantial objectives important enough to justify the violation of the *Charter*. The Respondents' submissions, at paragraph 3 of their factum, that "Canada has never embraced lawlessness as a tradition to be tolerated or respected" and at paragraph 43 that "it is surely always a pressing and substantial objective to foster and enhance civic responsibility and law-abidingness in a democracy" reveal the emptiness behind the government's objectives once the political rhetoric about allowing Clifford Olson [a notorious mass murderer] to vote has been rightly discarded. Objectives that really amount to objections to the very idea that all citizens are given the right to vote in s 3 of the *Charter* do not amount to pressing and substantial objectives ... Another reason for not accepting the Respondents' claimed objectives is that they are so vague and amorphous as to make subsequent s 1 analysis redundant. As explanations, as opposed to goals, the ideas of affirming law-abidingness and supplementing the criminal sanction are self-fulfilling or, as the Respondents assert at paragraph 71 of their factum, 'fully met' merely by judicial acceptance of

In this passage, the majority of the Court came very close to dismissing the objectives of promoting civic responsibility and the rule of law as legitimate objectives for limiting the right of prisoners to vote.

In the end, however, the Canadian court, like the European Court of Human Rights,[33] accepted the legitimacy of the vague and symbolic objectives of promoting civic responsibility and respect for the rule of law as legitimate objectives for limiting prisoner voting rights. Chief Justice McLachlin then applied the various steps of the proportionality analysis before concluding that the Government had not justified denying the vote to all prisoners serving sentences of two years imprisonment or more. Nevertheless, it may have been better for the Court simply to have concluded that the objectives offered by the Government were not a legitimate basis for denying a right. The Court's discussion of the subsequent steps in the proportionality analysis in fact came back to the inability of the 'rhetorical' 'vague' and 'symbolic' objectives to justify a violation of a right. As suggested above, such objectives are self-actualising and it is not really possible to determine whether they are rationally connected to achieving some social outcome or whether less rights-invasive means would achieve that goal. Courts would be more candid if they simply evaluated whether such objectives are legitimate in a constitutional democracy committed to rights, even at the likely cost of being seen as undemocratic for rejecting some legislative objectives. This insight suggests that debates with the UK Parliament prompted in part by the Grand Chamber's judgment in *Scoppola v Italy (No 3)* about whether the legislative cut-off of four years' imprisonment or less for prisoners' right to vote is appropriate may be somewhat beside the point. The real issue should be the legitimacy of Parliament's objective in limiting prisoners' rights to vote. In my view, the legislative objective of expressing disgust or distaste of prisoners even when dressed up in vague language about promoting civil responsibility and respect for the rule of law or crime prevention should not be a legitimate objective for limiting rights.

One possible argument against this approach is that it is too rationalistic. It does not leave much room for the use of legislation to express emotions including what Lord Devlin would have called societal disgust at certain social practices. The rationalist demands of proportionality analysis may exclude purely symbolic and expressive legislative objectives. If this is true, it is a significant restraint on legislative deliberation about rights, especially given the centrality of proportionality analysis to modern constitutionalism and the tendency of politicians to appeal to the strong

them as sufficiently important to justify a *Charter* violation and without further exploration of whether the violation is a rational and proportionate way to advance such objectives. The majority of the Court of Appeal also erred by applying such a tautological or circular approach that short circuits well established s 1 analysis when it stated that to conclude that the measures were not proportional "would be to challenge Parliament's right to utilize the law to enhance civic responsibility and to establish consequences which express Canada's abhorrence of serious crime" ... The Court should not accept such vague and inherently self-fulfilling objectives that makes s 1 analysis a one stage process that simply depends on the objectives of the impugned legislation. Factum of Aboriginal Legal Services of Toronto, 24 July 2001, paras 55–59 available at: www.aboriginallegal.ca/docs/sauve.factum.final.htm.

[33] *Hirst v UK* [2005] 42 EHRR 41 [75]; *Frodl v Austria* [2011] 52 EHRR 5 [30]; *Scoppola v Italy (No 3)* [2013] 56 EHRR 19 [92].

emotions of their supporters. Should democrats be concerned about such a possibility? Perhaps, but we need to remember that courts do not apply proportionality analysis to every piece of legislation—only those that violate rights. Elected officials still have a bully pulpit to express their ideas, including their views of morality and disgust. There is plenty of room for the use of symbols and emotions in politics, just not in legislation that infringes rights.

C. The Debate about Rational Connection and Overall Balance: Courts and Legislatures in a Common Democratic Cause?

As suggested above, traditional debates about judicial review that pit the courts against the legislature ignore the important role of the executive. The executive often possesses information that it may wish to keep secret but if released could improve both legislative and judicial deliberations. The prospect of judicial review may help pry information out of an increasingly secret executive. In particular, governments may have to reveal the evidence (or lack of evidence) that they have to support legislation that places limits on rights. In particular, the government should reveal in consultations, Parliament and in committee information about the extent of the harms it is trying to prevent or reduce and explain why a law that limits rights will achieve these ends. The overall balance stage of proportionality analysis may also encourage governments to invest in research about the effectiveness of laws Again, however, governments will have an incentive not to disclose unfavourable data. It is especially important for democracy that courts insist that governments have the burden to introduce evidence that is necessary to justify the proportionality of limitation on rights. As Aharon Barak notes, 'proportionality is an analytical and legal tool. It is fed by extrinsic data'.[34] The government bears the burden to justify limits on rights and in this sense it must produce data that can then be subject to challenge not only in courts but in Parliament and other public venues for debate. Proportionality analysis in the courts can be democracy enhancing by requiring governments to place more of their thinking process and the information on which they act in the public domain. Of course, governments can remain silent and hide behind doctrines such as solicitor–client privilege and Cabinet confidences. The courts cannot force governments to be candid. As will be seen, however, they can draw adverse inferences from the government's silence.

Both Aharon Barak and Dieter Grimm express the view that rational connection analysis will only eliminate a small amount of 'run away cases'.[35] This may be true if we assume a healthy and rational legislative process. Nevertheless, rational connection requirements can be an important check on Lord Devlin-type legislation meant to express disgust at unpopular groups and solidarity with popular ones. Judges should ask the government for evidence about how prisoner disenfranchisement will deter crime or promote greater political participation by others. The inability

---

[34] Aharon Barak, *Proportionality* (Cambridge, Cambridge University Press, 2012) 467.
[35] ibid; Dieter Grimm, 'Proportionality in Canada and German Jurisprudence' (2007) 57 *University of Toronto Law Journal* 383.

of governments to produce evidence on these matters should reveal that the real objectives of such laws are not the legitimate goals of reducing crime or encouraging people to vote, but rather the less laudable objectives of expressing disgust and antipathy towards prisoners. As argued above, these latter objectives should not be considered by the courts to be legitimate legislative objectives for limiting rights.

Judicial proportionality analysis can be a check on excessive governmental secrecy. It provides an incentive for governments to put more information into the public domain about the evidence they used to legislate and why they rejected less rights-restrictive alternatives. Janet Hiebert has criticised the majority of the Supreme Court of Canada for engaging in policy analysis 'for which legal training provides virtually no guidance' in a controversial decision that struck down a complete ban on tobacco adverting. She argued that Parliament should not have to share the Court's 'pre-occupation'[36] with whether the legitimate objectives of curbing tobacco use could be attained through less rights-invasive measures. This analysis, however, discounts how the majority of the Court was particularly concerned that a study that the Government had commissioned on the very topic of the adequacy of less rights-invasive alternatives was not put before the Court. The Court drew an adverse inference from the Government's claim of Cabinet privilege.[37] In short, it thought the Government was hiding evidence in a manner usually associated with the tobacco companies. Chief Justice McLachlin was not impressed that 'the Attorney General contented himself with the bland statement that a complete ban is justified because Parliament "had to balance competing interests" somehow. Its response to the minimal impairment argument is not evidence, but a simple assertion that Parliament has the right to set such limits as it chooses'.[38] As in the prisoner voting rights case, Chief Justice McLachlin had little time for raw assertions of government power that refused to engage with the various steps of proportionality analysis.

D. Courts, Legislatures and Least-Restrictive Alternatives

Courts are most comfortable in striking down legislation on the basis that there are other less rights-invasive means to pursue the governmental objective. This avoids having to pronounce on the more controversial issues of the legitimacy of the legislative objective or the overall balance. Legislatures can make important contributions by deliberating about why less rights-invasive alternatives will not satisfy the relevant legislative objective(s). Some may criticise such approaches by suggesting that it legalises politics or makes them accept the court's preoccupation with proportionality. Such criticisms, however, discount the diversity and flexibility of the legislative process. Addressing the hard proportionality questions in committee and in the seventh and eighth paragraphs of the minister's speech on second reading should not fetter the ability of elected members to make other forms of argument.

[36] Janet Hiebert, *Charter Conflicts* (Montreal, McGill-Queen's University Press, 2002) 83–84.
[37] *RJR-MacDonald Inc v Canada (Attorney-General)* [1995] 3 SCR 19 [166].
[38] ibid [167].

Judges may rightly ignore much parliamentary debate, but they should listen to those parts of the debate that address the relevant questions posed by proportionality analysis. Legislators may not like having to address the difficult questions posed by proportionality analysis, but they ignore them at the peril of subsequent adverse judicial decisions.

In the 1994 *Daviault* case,[39] the Supreme Court made the unprecedented decision that extreme intoxication that produced involuntary behaviour could be a defence to sexual assault. The Court stressed that the defence should be rare, but that it was required under section 7 of the Canadian Charter. The decision outraged the public and Parliament. Within a year and with all-party approval, Parliament enacted a law that reversed the decision with respect to violent offences such as manslaughter, assault and sexual assault. I have argued elsewhere that Parliament should have used the override to justify such an 'in your face' reply to the Court's interpretation of the Constitution and that the Canadian court should reject such legislative defiance, much as the US Supreme Court dismissed Congress' attempt to overrule *Miranda* as part of President Nixon's 1968 war on crime.[40] I suggested at the time that the existence of the override option demonstrated that the Charter avoided the judicial supremacy of the American experience.

Nevertheless, the override is not the only option. The more recent trend in the Canadian cases is for lower courts to hold that Parliament's reply legislation still violates rights under the Charter for the reasons given by the majority of the Court in *Daviault*, but nevertheless is justified as a reasonable limit under section 1 of the Charter.[41] This allows courts to uphold what many have criticised as an interpretative monopoly on rights (but which I believe makes sense, given the anti-majoritarian nature of rights and the dangers that elected officials will understandably conclude that rapists and other accused do not have rights), while at the same time allowing the government an opportunity to justify limits on rights. One problem with this approach, however, is that the Supreme Court has never held that any violation of Canada's due process clause under section 7 has been justified under section 1 as a proportionate and reasonable limit on the rights. Indeed, the Court has even suggested that violation of section 7 could only be limited under section 1 in emergency situations. Elsewhere, I have criticised this special preference for the section 7 right as inconsistent with the overall dialogic structure of the Charter.[42]

Although the Canadian Parliament was well aware that its legislative reply to *Daviault* would be subject to future judicial scrutiny, it could have done a better job in justifying the law as a proportionate limit on rights. In particular, Parliament could have better explained why a less rights-invasive alternative that the Supreme Court had almost pre-approved in its proportionality analysis in *Daviault* would not be as effective as the new law in responding to the serious social problem of

---

[39] *R v Daviault* [1994] 3 SCR 63.

[40] Kent Roach, 'Dialogue or Defiance?" Legislative Reversals of Supreme Court Decisions in Canada and the United States' (2006) 4 *International Journal of Constitutional Law* 347.

[41] *R v SN* 2012 NUCJ 2; *R v Dow* 2010 QCSC 4276.

[42] Kent Roach, 'Mind the Gap: Canada's Different Criminal and Constitutional Standards of Fault' (2011) 61 *University of Toronto Law Journal* 545.

intoxicated violence against women and children. In *Daviault*, the Court had indicated that the creation of a new intoxication-based offence that would apply to those who committed assaults or sexual assaults while extremely intoxicated was a less rights-invasive alternative than simply denying the accused any intoxication defence. In the consultations that led to the legislative reply, women's groups and rape crisis centres made strong arguments that a new intoxication-based offence would not be effective because it would suggest that sexual violence was less serious if the accused was intoxicated and would encourage plea bargains to the new offence. Unfortunately, these arguments are not reflected in the preamble to the legislation restricting the *Daviault* defence. They were also not well presented in legislative committee proceedings, which focused more on scientific evidence that refuted the Court's premise that extreme intoxication could produce involuntary behaviour and were cut short because of parliamentary scheduling. The constitutionality of the new law has still not been decided by the Supreme Court, but Parliament could have done a better job in educating the Court about why its preferred alternative of a new intoxication-based offence would not be as effective as the law that Parliament enacted.

As part of the judicial obligation to justify their conclusions about the disproportionality of rights-infringing legislation, courts may have to discuss less restrictive alternatives. Nevertheless, they should be careful not to rule on the constitutionality of such future alternatives. The issue of whether there is a more proportionate alternative depends on the evidence that is placed before the court when that alternative is actually enacted and challenged. This is a live issue in Canada because when invalidating the use of secret evidence for the purposes of immigration detention, the Supreme Court mentioned the British special advocates as a less rights-restrictive alternative and the Government seized on this in enacting reply legislation.[43] The Supreme Court subsequently upheld the constitutionality of the new legislation. It appropriately did not defer to its prior and abstract holding that special advocates respected rights more than secret hearings but rather examined the second look case with fresh eyes on the basis of the evidence before it. It concluded that the process was fair not only because of special advocates but because of new requirements that ensured that non-citizens were informed of the gist of the case against them and by provisions that allowed judges to authorise special advocates to communicate with others on a case-by-case basis after they had seen the secret evidence.[44]

Legislatures that explain why they did not pursue a less rights-restrictive option may rightly be rewarded with judicial decisions that accept the law as a justified, proportional and reasonable limits on rights. This is not because of any ex ante posture of judicial deference, but simply because the legislature will have attempted to answer the hard questions posed by proportionality analysis. In turn, legislatures that ignore such questions do so at their peril. Judicial deference is not a matter of

---

[43] *Charkaoui v Canada* [2007] 1 SCR 350. See Kent Roach, 'Charkaoui and Bill C-3: Some Implications for Anti-terrorism Policy and Dialogue between Courts and Legislatures' (2008) 42 *Supreme Court Law Review (2nd)* 281.
[44] *Canada (Minister of Citizenship) v Harkat* 2014 SCC 37.

automatic respect or submission.[45] It has to be earned through rational justification and concrete evidence.

CONCLUSION

Debate about judicial review has become bogged down and polarised by competing abstract claims about the virtues of courts and legislatures. A fresher approach may be to disaggregate the many different roles that legislatures and courts play in rights protection. Empirical studies that attempt to measure actual legislative performance on rights issues may be helpful. They should also bear in mind that legislative concern and respect for the rights of minorities in the mainstream may not necessarily result in such respect for the rights of the truly unpopular. A person facing re-election may find it easier to accept or defend the rights of young people, gays and lesbians or the elderly as compared to the rights of the accused, non-citizens or transsexuals.

The legislature is not equally equipped to contribute to all issues involved in the protection of rights. This chapter has suggested that legislatures are ill-suited to interpreting rights, especially the rights of the truly unpopular. Elected politicians may often be inclined to deny that rights of the accused or prisoners are at stake rather than engage in a Waldron-like reasonable disagreement about rights based on public regarding reasons. In extraordinary circumstances, legislatures can act on an interpretation of rights that differs from that of the courts, but legislatures should be forced to justify and reconsider such interpretations. The special signals and sunsets under the section 33 override in the Canadian Charter are especially useful in this regard. In the UK, a failure to respond to a declaration of incompatibility under section 4 of the Human Rights Act or a willingness to adopt a law in the absence of a ministerial statement of compatibility might play a similar role in alerting the populace to a disagreement between the courts and Parliament about the nature or existence of rights. In any event, courts should be the primary decision-maker about the existence and scope of rights.

If legislatures are not well-suited to interpret rights, they are much better positioned to justify limitations on rights for a range of important social objectives. Legislatures should be prepared to take the lead in this justification process. In general, they should be able to employ a broad and dynamic range of legislative objectives in order to limit rights. That said, not every legislative objective is acceptable. Those designed to convey emotions such as Lord Devlin's sense of disgust or even more friendly emotions such as solidarity may defy rational proportionality analysis. Even though ultimately accepted by the Supreme Court of Canada and the European Court of Human Rights in prisoner voting rights case as legitimate, vague and symbolic legislative objectives such as promoting civic responsibility and respect for the rule of law do not really provide a sound basis for proportionality analysis. Courts might be more candid if they simply dismissed the legitimacy of

---

[45] Aileen Kavanagh, 'Defending Deference?' (2010) 126 *Law Quarterly Review* 222.

such objectives as a reason for limiting prisoner voting rights. It can be argued that such an approach unduly legalises and rationalises politics. The dangers of a court-centred debate can, however, be overstated. The courts will still accept the legitimacy of the vast majority of legislative objectives. They will only reject the objective in extraordinary circumstances when the lack of evidence of a rational connection between a legitimate objective and the impugned measure or the government's admitted aims suggest that the legislature is simply expressing emotional disgust or rejecting the very premise of the right. Legislatures will remain the primary decision-maker about most objectives for limiting rights and on questions of rational connection and least restrictive means. Legislatures need not be preoccupied with the proportionality of every law. They can engage in populist and emotional politics when not limiting rights. Nevertheless, they ignore the difficult and rational questions posed by proportionality analysis at the peril of judicial intervention when they legislate in a way that limits rights as interpreted by the courts.

Part VII

A Democratic Culture of Justification

21

What is a 'Democratic Culture of Justification'?

DAVID DYZENHAUS*

T HE TERM 'CULTURE of justification' was coined by Etienne Mureinik, a South African public lawyer, to describe what he took to be the ambition of South Africa's Interim Constitution:

If the new Constitution is a bridge away from a culture of authority, it is clear what it must be a bridge to. It must lead to a culture of justification—a culture in which every exercise of power is expected to be justified; in which leadership given by government rests on the cogency of the case offered in defence of its decisions, not the fear inspired by the force at its command. The new order must be a community built on persuasion, not coercion.[1]

Mureinik clearly thought that the political order of democracy thrives when a culture of justification prevails. As a lawyer, he was most concerned with the legal aspects of such a culture, with the kind of order that we should design if we are concerned to give *legal* effect to two fundamental political commitments: democracy and human rights.

In describing the culture of authority that had to be left behind, he pointed out that the legal basis of apartheid was the doctrine of parliamentary sovereignty: 'Universally, that doctrine teaches that what Parliament says is law, without the need to offer justification to the courts.'[2] In addition, because South Africa was undemocratic, there was no justification offered to the people. A bill of rights, he thought, 'is a compendium of values empowering citizens affected by laws or decisions to demand justification'.[3]

Hence, in Mureinik's picture, a culture of justification is not only one in which parliamentarians offer political justifications to the electorate for their laws, but is also one in which they offer legal justifications in terms of the values set out in the bill of rights. That is a kind of political justification. But it is more than a

* I thank the participants at the conference for which the original version of this chapter was prepared for discussion, as well as those who attended a seminar on the same topic in the University of Glasgow, School of Law, especially Adam Tomkins. Finally, I thank Marcelo Rodriguez Ferrere for excellent research assistance.
1 Etienne Mureinik, 'A Bridge to Where?: Introducing the Interim Bill of Rights' (1994) 10(1) *South African Journal on Human Rights* 31, 32.
2 ibid.
3 ibid.

justification of why one policy is better than another since it is also a justification of why the policy is consistent with the legally protected rights of those it affects. Moreover, it is a justification not only to citizens but also to the courts, a feature inherent in the structure of a bill of rights that permits rights to be limited.

Mureinik set out the structure of such a justification in his discussion of the guarantee of administrative justice in the Interim Constitution. This guarantee, he said, would deal a 'mortal blow' to the doctrine of 'deep deference' to executive decisions that prevailed under apartheid, one which required that a decision be '"grossly unreasonable to so striking a degree" as to warrant the appropriate inference'. In contrast, courts would be required to develop a theory of what makes a decision justifiable.

A good starting point would be to recognise that the justifiability of an administrative decision is a matter not of second-guessing the policy choices that it entails, which is the prerogative of the decision-maker, but rather of the soundness of the process of deciding which went into its making. It is suggested that an administrative decision cannot be taken to be justifiable unless: (a) the decision-maker has considered all the serious objections to the decision taken and has answers which plausibly meet them; (b) the decision-maker has considered all the serious alternatives to the decision taken and has discarded them for plausible reasons; and (c) there is a rational connection between premises and conclusion—between the information (evidence and argument) before the decision-maker and the decision taken. A decision-maker who is conscious while deliberating as to what decision to give that a court may eventually scrutinise his or her decision under these criteria is under serious pressure to deploy a thorough and disciplined decision-making process; one likely to yield wise decisions.[4]

It is clear from the general argument that Mureinik thought both that the justification of legislative policy objective must follow the same basic structure and that, despite the point about not second-guessing policy choices, the structure might on occasion rule out an objective as illegitimate. For example, he argued that non-emergency political detention was ruled out because no law that sought to put such a regime in place could survive the process of justification, and he suggested that the same would be true of torture and slavery.[5]

In this chapter, I examine the right to vote, which, like the rights against certain kinds of detention, slavery and torture, has a claim on a special place in the rights pantheon. My inquiry is into the structure of justification appropriate when Parliament decides to deprive one class of citizens, prison inmates, of that right. The right is of special importance to 'political constitutionalists', one of the main positions in contemporary debate about the appropriate relationship between Parliament and the judiciary in a society committed to human rights. As Richard Bellamy, a leading proponent, says of their position, it 'is grounded in at least one

---

[4] ibid 38.
[5] ibid 35–38.

right— ... "the right of rights"—that of participating as an equal claimer of rights in collective decision making'.[6]

Political constitutionalists are opposed to judicial review of the 'legal constitutionalist' sort Mureinik advocated because they insist that democratically elected legislatures and not judges are best placed to interpret a bill of rights. Part of their case against judicial review is that they suppose that judicialised or legalist reasoning distorts and cramps the attention that important moral issues deserve. They say that the interpretation of rights is a quintessentially political exercise and so should be carried out by Parliament—the body with the legitimacy and expertise to do so. However, because for them the right to vote is the most fundamental of a society's human rights commitments, any attempt by the demos to limit the right must raise special problems.

I will argue that these problems indicate that the debate should be focused not on who should ultimately decide questions such as prisoners' right to vote, but on achieving an institutional structure that makes possible appropriate processes of justification. With this focus in place, political constitutionalists will have to accept that there is no longer any real distance between their position and that of legal constitutionalism. However, this is not so much a victory for legal constitutionalism as an indication of the need to move beyond both positions.

I. POLITICAL VERSUS LEGAL CONSTITUTIONALISM

In the past, the camps in this debate divided starkly because 'Benthamite legal positivists', the forebears of contemporary political constitutionalism, regarded rights-talk as politically dangerous, especially when given legal effect, because such talk undermines democracy. In particular, such talk gives to judges the authority to review both legislation and executive implementation of the legislation on the basis of their subjective interpretations of the rights. It thus elevated the dog law with which Bentham equated the common law, the arbitrary opinions of judge and co, into an undemocratic check on democratically produced statutes.

Judges were enabled by such talk to superimpose their subjective judgments about the public good on the statutes that were the instruments of the content determined in the deliberations about overall utility in the legislative assembly. In other words, on this position, positive law delivers the content of normative judgments determined outwith the legal order, and opportunities to adulterate that content must be avoided.

Notice that on the Benthamite position, a bill of rights enforced by judges is illegitimate whether it is entrenched by the legislature in a constitution or is contained in an ordinary statute, repealable or amendable by simple majority, just as it would be illegitimate for the legislature to cede its sovereignty to another body or person. Indeed, the enactment of a bill of rights, entrenched or not, is a partial cession of

---

[6] Richard Bellamy, 'Political Constitutionalism and the Human Rights Act' (2011) 9(1) *International Journal of Constitutional Law* 86, 93, citing Jeremy Waldron, *Law and Disagreement* (Oxford, Oxford University Press, 1999) ch 11.

sovereignty and thus is to be resisted despite any apparent democratic provenance. The legal positivist aspect of this position is that its proponents suppose that if law is to transmit the content of the legislature's judgments back to the people who elect their representatives in order to make such judgments, the content of the particular laws must be determinable as far as possible by tests that discern the content that those representatives intended the laws to have. In other words, since indeterminate or ambiguous laws provide occasions for judges to fill in the gaps with their subjective views as to what the law ought to be, the fewer such occasions, the better.

In contrast, legal constitutionalists suppose that government according to law entails moral commitments, including to certain human rights, that legitimise judges in interpreting statutes in light of these commitments. Put differently, even where there is no bill of rights, there is a constitutional morality implicit in legal order upon which judges should rely in order to determine what the law requires. A bill of rights, whether contained in an entrenched constitution or a statute such as the Human Rights Act 1998 (HRA), formalises this role and both adds rights and makes more precise the structure of rights-based adjudication. But it does not represent either a radical change in judicial role or a subversion of democracy, since a democratic government is not only one in which the legislature makes law, but also one that governs according to law, and thus according to the constitutional morality implicit in legal order. The position is anti-positivist in the sense that the content of the law is considered in part determinable by moral/legal tests that seek to show how particular laws comply with or further constitutional morality.

The issue between these camps was likely intractable. But at least the lines of controversy were clearly drawn because of the stark contrast between, on the one hand, the Benthamite legal positivists with their hostility to both legalised human rights and judicial review, and, on the other, the legal constitutionalists who usually regarded a bill of rights as no more than a significant updating of the content of constitutional morality and of the role of judges in upholding it. Matters have become more complex but perhaps more tractable with recent important interventions by Jeremy Waldron and Richard Bellamy in the debate.[7]

Matters are more complex because both Waldron and Bellamy advocate political constitutionalism, but are no longer hardline critics of human rights. All they oppose is judicial review in the sense of judges having the last word about whether a statute is unconstitutional and hence lacking in legal force because of its failure to comply with legally protected rights. Indeed, in his major article on judicial review, Waldron sets up his 'core case' against such review on the basis of four assumptions, including 'a commitment on the part of most members of the society and most of its officials to the idea of individual and minority rights', as expressed in a bill of rights.[8]

Waldron argues, however, that the society in question 'ought to settle the disagreements about rights that its members have using its legislative institutions'—'there is no need for decisions about rights made by legislatures to be second-guessed by

---

[7] Jeremy Waldron, 'The Core of the Case against Judicial Review' (2006) 115(6) *Yale Law Journal* 1346.

[8] ibid 1359.

courts'.[9] Similarly, Bellamy argues that a bill of rights such as the HRA is fully consistent with political constitutionalism, which he equates with parliamentary sovereignty, which he understands following Waldron as Parliament having the last word about questions of the interpretations of rights. He also adduces 'the deliberative qualities of legislatures, as compared with courts, and the accountability of legislators to citizens'.[10]

Hence, the disagreement between political and legal constitutionalists seems to boil down to whether judges or legislatures should have the last word when it comes to the interpretation of human rights. Waldron has even suggested that it might be a positive advantage to have judges issuing the kind of declaration of incompatibility between a statute and a right that is contemplated by the HRA because that conclusion 'while not dispositive from the point of view of the legislative-style process, may serve as a useful warning to the effect that the legislative process might have missed something important'.[11] Bellamy agrees[12] and sees a similar role for the Joint Committee on Human Rights (JCHR) that in the UK gives advice to both Houses of Parliament on human rights issues, because its reports have 'ensured that rights considerations are raised in parliamentary debates and are often referred to in that context'.[13]

In sum, since political constitutionalists no longer object to bills of rights, as long as legislatures retain the last word—indeed, think that such bills with court-produced legal effects can be productive—the distance between the legal constitutionalists and at least one offshoot of Benthamite legal positivism has narrowed. And that makes the issue between the camps potentially more tractable.

One can attempt to decide this debate empirically, for example, by comparing within a jurisdiction the relative contributions made by the judiciary and Parliament to the securing of rights over a defined period.[14] This method is, however, suspect in that in a jurisdiction in which Parliament is supreme, to the extent it enacts statutes that serve the cause of human rights, it will clearly do better than the judiciary, especially when many of the judiciary's significant failures that get thrown into the mix are failures of resistance in the face of statutes that sought explicitly to limit or to undermine rights.

The alternative is a normative argument. For example, Waldron has argued that legislatures are able to reason on moral issues in a more all-things-considered way, and so the very thing that is supposed to allay fears of judicial arbitrariness—the fact that judges are constrained by legal texts and precedent—favours Parliament as a moral reasoner when it comes to rights interpretation. Waldron has cited in this regard a couple of times the UK Bill proposing to liberalise abortion law that occasioned a debate that is 'as fine an example of a political institution grappling

[9] ibid 1346.
[10] Bellamy (n 6) 92.
[11] Jeremy Waldron, 'Judges as Moral Reasoners' (2009) 7(1) *International Journal of Constitutional Law* 2, 23–24.
[12] Bellamy (n 6) 111.
[13] ibid 99–100.
[14] See, eg, KD Ewing and CA Gearty, *The Struggle for Civil Liberties: Political Freedom and the Rule of Law in Britain, 1914–1945* (Oxford, Oxford University Press, 2000).

with moral issues as you could hope to find'.[15] He contrasts this with the US Supreme Court's 50-page opinion in *Roe v Wade*, in which there are 'but a couple of paragraphs dealing with the moral importance of reproductive rights in relation to privacy, and the few paragraphs addressed to the other moral issue at stake—the rights status of the foetus—are mostly taken up with showing the diversity of opinions on the issue. A lot of the fifty pages is either a review of case law and doctrine or a review of the history of the issue'.[16]

In a similar vein, Bellamy objects to the fact that 'legal advisers play a crucial role in the JCHR's deliberations' and their advice 'consists largely of second-guessing the likely judgments of the courts', since that might lead to the UK Parliament feeling 'constrained by legalistic reasoning in its rights deliberations', thus reducing the deliberative advantage of political over legal constitutionalism.[17] In addition, he worries about Parliament's ability to 'control the judicial process'. Too much seems to turn 'on how deferential the courts are—or can be made to be—to what Parliament decides on the rights question'.[18]

I will suggest that the dichotomy on which political constitutionalism trades—Parliament or the judges as final interpreters—is a false one. I will rely mainly, as does Waldron, on a normative argument in relation to just one set of debates, in my case study in Canada,[19] though it is a debate that has taken place in several other jurisdictions, for example, the UK, South Africa and New Zealand, that represent different points on the continuum Waldron depicts as stretching from strong to weak judicial review.[20]

At the strongest end, courts have the authority to strike down legislation as well as the authority to interpret a statute to make it more rights-compliant. At the weakest end, courts are confined to an authority to attempt to interpret statutes to make them human rights-compliant.[21] Hence, New Zealand is at this end, while the UK is further along the continuum because there the courts have both that interpretive authority and the authority to issue a declaration of incompatibility if the statute cannot be interpreted in such a way as to render it human rights-compliant. But this is still weak judicial review because the declaration does not affect the validity of the statute, though it potentially triggers a process of amendment, either by the responsible minister, who would not have that authority but for the declaration, or by Parliament itself. Canada has a somewhat problematic place on the continuum because, Waldron says,

[15] Waldron (n 7) 1346.

[16] Waldron (n 11) 20.

[17] Bellamy (n 6)100.

[18] ibid.

[19] See Sandra Fredman, 'From Dialogue to Deliberation: Human Rights Adjudication and Prisoners' Rights to Vote' [2013] *Public Law* 292–311 and ch 23 below, an illuminating comparison of the South African and UK debates on deprivations of prisoners' right to vote. These debates have the same dismal structure as the Canadian one I describe below. Fredman argues convincingly that this structure shows the need to develop a model of deliberative democracy in which judges participate and thus make an essential contribution to a culture of justification. Our arguments are, in my view, completely complementary and mine differs from hers only in that it proceeds mainly by exploring tensions within the political constitutionalist position that require the development of an alternative model such as the one she develops.

[20] Waldron (n 7) 1354–57.

[21] New Zealand is the example.

section 33 of the Charter allows Canadian legislatures 'to legislate "notwithstanding" the rights in the Charter'. However, because section 33 is 'rarely invoked', he counts the Canadian arrangement as a strong form of judicial review.[22]

Before I embark on my analysis of the deprivation of the right to vote in Canada, it is important to note one inaccuracy and one omission in Waldron's depiction. The inaccuracy is that Waldron fails to note that section 33 applies only to some of the rights protected by the Charter, and that the rights that cannot be overridden are the rights in the section headed 'Democratic Rights', including section 3, which says: 'Every citizen of Canada has the right to vote in an election of members of the House of Commons or of a legislative assembly and to be qualified for membership therein.'[23] The omission is that in distinguishing forms of strong and weak judicial review, Waldron does not count as a criterion whether the bill of rights permits, as in section 1 of the Charter, rights to be limited by the legislature as long as the limit can be shown to be proportionate.[24]

This kind of limitation is for many legal constitutionalists an important formal recognition of what is sometimes called the 'coordinate' role of democratically elected parliaments in interpreting the bill of rights. Parliament's authority to interpret the bill of rights is fully recognised, so that courts will defer to their parliament's interpretation as long as the interpretation is appropriately justified.

That Waldron ignores the place of proportionality in his most elaborate argument against strong judicial review might indicate a view among political constitutionalists, perhaps inherited from Benthamite legal positivism, that interpretive devices such as proportionality are just more or less elaborate disguises of the fact that judges are dispensing dog law. But this view is in some tension with their claim that the legal discipline to which judicial reasoning is subject marks it as inferior to Parliament's all-things-considered interpretation of bills of rights, since that claim is about the stringency, not the laxness of the discipline to which judges are subject. This tension arises because political constitutionalists pose the question in terms of a contest of interpretations. They thus pose the question as one about who is best placed to interpret and hence should have final authority to interpret, rather than and more appropriately as an issue about justification.

II. PRISONERS' RIGHT TO VOTE IN CANADA

A. Act I

Section 51(e) of the Canada Elections Act, RSC 1985, c E-2, disqualified all prison inmates from voting. This matter was one of several topics considered by the

---

[22] Waldron (n 7) 1345–46.

[23] Canadian Charter of Rights and Freedoms, s 3, pt I of the Constitution Act, 1982, being sched B to the Canada Act 1982 (UK), 1982, c 11.

[24] Section 1 of the Canadian Charter of Rights and Freedoms guarantees the rights and freedoms set out in it subject only to such reasonable limits prescribed by law as can be demonstrably justified in a free and democratic society.

Royal Commission on Electoral Reform and Party Financing in 1989 (the 'Lortie Commission'), which released its findings in 1992. A research report was produced for the Commission that traced the deprivation of the right to vote to the idea that convicted persons suffer a 'civil death' that amounts to a complete forfeiture of rights.[25] It concluded that preserving this relict of civil death is incompatible with the extension of the franchise and with the turn to rehabilitation in penal philosophy, as well as with Canada's sense of self as 'one of the front runners among democratic countries when it comes to legal and political equality'.[26] It also noted that depriving inmates of the right to vote is a measure that applies disproportionately to aboriginal people, to the poor and to the disadvantaged,[27] and it is relevant that Richard Sauvé, the author of both constitutional challenges described below, is an aboriginal Canadian.[28]

The Commission itself thought there was only one valid objection to prisoner voting: 'that prisoners have violated the law and thus have demonstrated that they are unwilling to abide by the norms of responsible citizenship'.[29] However, it pointed out that the relationship in the statute was in fact not between law-breaking and disqualification from voting, but between incarceration and the disqualification.[30] Therefore, it found that the blanket prohibition was too broad, that allowing prisoners to vote might serve the goal of rehabilitation and that extending the punishment of confinement to include disenfranchisement is a 'limitation on democratic rights that is clearly a legacy of the past'.[31]

However, the Commission then leapt to the conclusion that those convicted of the most serious violations could nevertheless be deprived of the right to vote. This deprivation is, it claimed, 'rationally connected to the specific limitation on an individual's right to vote, because persons convicted of these crimes have offended the very foundations of a civilized political community. In so doing, they have declared themselves unwilling to participate in civil society in ways that respect the most fundamental rights of others or the basic character of the political system'. In addition, the Commission claimed that this disqualification is a minimal impairment of the right since it is 'limited to the period of incarceration'. Finally, 'and most important', it said, is that such a 'disqualification is proportional in terms of its purpose and effect. It removes the vote only from those persons whose criminal behaviour has seriously violated the fundamental criteria of democratic citizenship ... those convicted of treason or of the most serious offences against individuals'. Thus, the Commission recommended that 'persons convicted of an offence punishable by a

[25] Pierre Landreville and Lucie Lemonde, 'Voting Rights for Prison Inmates' in Michael Cassidy (ed), *Democratic Rights and Electoral Reform in Canada* (Ottawa, Royal Commission on Electoral Reform and Party Financing and Canada Communications Group-Publishing, Supply and Services Canada, 1991) 29, 68.
[26] ibid 88.
[27] ibid 89.
[28] See Kent Roach, *The Supreme Court on Trial: Judicial Activism or Democratic Dialogue* (Toronto, Irwin Law, 2001) 187–89.
[29] *Reforming Electoral Democracy: Final Report, Vol 1* (Ottawa, The Commission, 1991), 42.
[30] ibid 43.
[31] ibid 45.

maximum of life imprisonment and sentenced for 10 years or more be disqualified from voting during the time they are in prison'.[32]

B. Act II

Legal challenges to the statutory deprivation of the right to vote had begun prior to Commission of Inquiry. In the same year as it produced its findings, but prior to the release of the Commission's Report, in *Sauvé v Canada (Attorney-General)*, the Ontario Court of Appeal struck down the deprivation of the right to vote.[33] Arbour JA for the Court rejected the Government's argument that there is a 'need for a liberal democracy to rely on a "decent and responsible citizenry"'. She said that a 'symbolic' objective did not pass muster as a 'justification for the violation of a constitutionally protected right' and added that she doubted that such a justification was feasible in the wake of the constitutional entrenchment of the right in Canada because 'the slow movement toward universal suffrage in Western democracies took an irreversible step forward in Canada in 1982 by the enactment of s. 3 of the Charter'.[34] She also expressed her concern that the deprivation for the right to vote looked like a punishment for being imprisoned 'rather than for the commission of an offence'.[35] Thus, she concluded that if 'the objective of s. 51(e) is to punish offenders, that objective is missed altogether by a provision that punishes inmates and that is therefore both over- and under-inclusive. Whether this is viewed as a question of proportionality or objective, the result remains that it fails as a constitutional justification'.[36]

Arbour JA's decision turned on her view that the provision failed as a legitimate objective and therefore had to fail as a matter of proportionality. Hence, she did not proceed to the stage of deciding whether the limit on rights was proportionate. Her stance in this regard seems driven by the fact that, whilst she recognised that there is no hierarchy of constitutional rights in the Charter and so 'no scale for permissible infringement', she also thought that 'some rights will attract fewer acceptable limitations under s. 1'.[37] Here she quoted with approval an extract from the Federal Court of Appeal in *Belczowski v Canada*, which had also invalidated the deprivation in 1992:

> [T]he right to vote, going as it does to the very foundations and legitimacy of a free and democratic society, is, if anything, even more in need of constitutional protection than most of the other guaranteed rights and freedoms, no matter how important the latter may be.[38]

And, as we have seen, this is a fact recognised by the Charter, since the right to vote is one of the rights not subject to the section 33 override.

---

[32] ibid.
[33] *Sauvé v Canada (Attorney-General)* (1992) 89 DLR (4th) 644 (Ont CA) Arbour JA.
[34] ibid [20].
[35] ibid [22].
[36] ibid [23].
[37] ibid [12].
[38] *Belczowski v Canada* (1992) 90 DLR (4th) 330 (FCA) Hugessen J.

C. Act III

In the wake of these decisions, a parliamentary committee, the Special Committee on Electoral Reform, discussed the Lortie Commision's Report. The core consideration of members was not the legitimacy of the disenfranchisement, but instead the vulnerability of it to challenge under the Charter. Its minutes show little evidence of debate informed by the questions of principle canvassed by the courts and by the Commission. Rather, the members seemed torn, on the one hand, between the thought that the only policy that would not be challenged before the courts was one that did not limit the right at all, and that any limit was arbitrary and thus likely to fall before a Charter challenge, and, on the other hand, that the Government would not accept no limit. Therefore, a limit of seven years was discussed, with members offering in support that: the number seven has some biblical significance; two years on the basis that a two-year term in Canada leads to incarceration in a federal penitentiary rather than a provincial one and thus marks a degree of seriousness; and that the Government seemed to favour seven years. In addition, some suggested five years, either on the basis that it is between two or seven years or that it would cover the life of at least one government.[39] In the end, the Committee recommended disenfranchisement of all prisoners sentenced to two years' imprisonment or more, a time period that marked the difference between imprisonment in a federal and a provincial penitentiary.

D. Act IV

In the actual parliamentary debate in 1993, Peter Milliken, a member of the opposition Liberal Party, moved two amendments, both of which failed: the first would have removed the restriction altogether, while the other would have imposed it on prison inmates 'sentenced to five years or more in a correctional institution'.[40] He clearly regarded the first as the principled measure and the second as a compromise that would appeal more to the majority Conservative Party. His argument was that the Charter gives all citizens the right to vote, and that punishment and the criminal law are not intended to deprive an inmate of citizenship.[41] In contrast, Conservative backbenchers took the view that commission of a crime is an affront to society, a consequence of which is that prisoners lose their rights, including the right to vote.[42] Several members of opposition parties stressed the importance of rehabilitation, but, other than Milliken's opening statement, it was, to adapt some of Waldron's language describing the abortion debate in the UK Parliament, about as dismal 'an example of a political institution grappling ... with moral issues as you could hope to find'.[43]

---

[39] Special Committee on Electoral Reform, *Minutes of Proceedings and Evidence of the Special Committee on Electoral Reform*, (February–March 1993) 12.18–12.23 (Chair: Jim Hawkes).
[40] *House of Commons Debates*, 34th Parl, 3rd Sess, No 14 (2 April 1993) 18011–13 (Peter Milliken).
[41] ibid.
[42] ibid 18016–17.
[43] Waldron (n 11) 19–20.

E. Act V

The decisions of the Ontario Court of Appeal and of the Federal Court of Appeal went on appeal to the Supreme Court of Canada, where, in what must be one of the shortest judgments on record, the Court held:

> The Attorney General of Canada has properly conceded that s. 51(e) of the *Canada Elections Act*, R.S.C., 1985, c. E-2, contravenes s. 3 of the *Canadian Charter of Rights and Freedoms* but submits that s. 51(e) is saved under s. 1 of the *Charter*. We do not agree. In our view, s. 51(e) is drawn too broadly and fails to meet the proportionality test, particularly the minimal impairment component of the test, as expressed in the s. 1 jurisprudence of the Court.[44]

Despite the extreme brevity of this judgment, it is important to see that it takes a rather more nuanced approach than did the Ontario Court of Appeal, for the Supreme Court seemed to invite a parliamentary response that would be rights-compliant because it would be a minimal impairment, rather than a negation, of the right, and hence that Parliament could in principle cure the problem. In reaction to this decision and following the debates outlined in Act IV above, Parliament replaced the total deprivation of the right to vote with a new section 51(e) (SC 1993, c 19, s 23), which denied the right to vote to all inmates serving sentences of two years or more.

F. Act VI

Sauvé brought a second challenge, which was upheld by the Federal Court, Trial Division, but was rejected by 2:1 in the Federal Court of Appeal. The Supreme Court upheld the challenge 5:4. I will not go much into the substance of each judgment because I want to focus on the issue of judicial deference to parliamentary interpretations of human rights. However, I do want to note that in contrast to Waldron's description of *Roe v Wade* as containing 'but a couple of paragraphs dealing with the moral importance of reproductive rights',[45] these judgments all address the moral issues at length and with great seriousness.

Of the three courts that dealt with the matter, Wetston J in the Trial Division gave the debates sketched in Act IV the most attention. He found it difficult to identify an explicit objective for disenfranchisement in the actual debates in the Special Committee or in Parliament.[46] However, he thought that he could find an implied objective—denouncing criminal conduct through the use of a voting disqualification—that he considered legitimate, despite the fact that there was no empirical evidence to suggest that the 'disenfranchisement of prisoners reduces crime, or serves a morally educative function, or could operate as an effective punitive sanction'.[47]

---

[44] *Sauvé v Canada (Attorney-General)* [1993] 2 SCR 438 [2].
[45] ibid [20].
[46] *Sauvé v Canada* [1996] 1 FC 857 [41]–[43].
[47] ibid [86] (see Wetston J's implication of the objective at [42]).

Nevertheless, he found that the measure was a disproportionate response since punishment had to be tailored by a judge to fit the crime. In this regard, he found that the debates hardly considered disenfranchisement as a sentencing tool and were instead concerned with preventing judicial consideration of the issue. Wetston J's own view was that disenfranchisement had a legitimate use in the sentencing process, to be used as a specific punishment on a case-by-case basis.[48]

Linden JA for a majority of the Federal Court of Appeal (Isaac CJ concurring) overruled Wetston J's decision. He started his judgment by describing the case as continuing the 'dialogue' between the judiciary and legislature on the issue of disenfranchisement, thus picking up a theme that had begun in an influential article and was then adopted by Canada's Supreme Court to describe the relationship between the legislature and the judiciary in Canada.[49] According to the dialogue metaphor, judicial review in Canada should not be seen as a kind of debate stopper, because section 33, the override section, allows the legislature to have the last word on many issues and section 1, the limitation section, allows it to respond to judicial invalidations of particular statutory provisions by designing a more proportionate legal regime, that is, one that limits rights less intrusively.[50]

In Linden JA's view, the 1993 amendment thus showed that 'Parliament responded to this *judicial advice* by enacting legislation aimed at accomplishing part of its objectives while complying with the Charter'.[51] In contrast to the finding of Wetston J in the Court below, he found that enhancement of civic responsibility and respect for the rule of law and enhancement of the penal sanction were the objectives which motivated Parliament.[52] He said that he had reviewed the parliamentary debate and that he noted 'with interest that Parliament, both in general session and in Committee, debated this measure vigorously'.[53] Parliament conducted the debates in full consideration of the previous judicial views on disenfranchisement and its compliance with the Charter. The enactment was in response to the unconstitutionality of the prior version of the legislation and thus promoted objectives 'which were less "symbolic" and which pursued what Parliament believed to be sound penal and electoral policy'.[54]

Linden JA also held that it was important to be sensitive to Parliament's views on penal and electoral policy, and that the vigorous debate was seeking to respond to judicial concerns, which, after all, never ruled out disenfranchisement altogether, and thus left the option of narrower disenfranchisement possible.[55] He accordingly held that section 51(e) was a proportionate response as an alternative to longer terms of imprisonment for serious crime and that: '*To conclude otherwise would be*

---

[48] ibid [99].

[49] Peter Hogg and Alison Bushell, 'The Charter Dialogue between Courts and Legislatures (or Perhaps the Charter of Rights isn't Such a Bad Thing after All)' (1997) 35(1) *Osgoode Hall Law Journal* 75; *Vriend v Alberta* [1998] 1 SCR 493.

[50] See Kent Roach, 'Dialogue or Defiance: Legislative Reversals of Supreme Court Decisions in Canada and the United States' (2006) 4(2) *International Journal of Constitutional Law* 347.

[51] *Sauvé v Canada* (1999) 180 DLR (4th) 385 [1] (FCA) Linden J, emphasis added.

[52] ibid [45].

[53] ibid [41].

[54] ibid [42].

[55] ibid [61].

to challenge Parliament's right to utilize the law to enhance civic responsibility and to establish consequences which express Canada's abhorrence of serious crime.'[56] The disenfranchisement was thus a reasonable and demonstrably justified limit.

The Supreme Court disagreed and allowed Sauvé's appeal against the Federal Court of Appeal's decision. In his dissent, Gonthier J, like Linden, argued that the essence of dialogue theory 'is that neither the courts nor Parliament hold a monopoly on the determination of values'.[57] If Parliament has justified its reasonable limit on a right, the dialogue ends; the Court does not have the last word and cannot substitute Parliament's reasonably held policy choices for its own.[58]

Gonthier also claimed, despite the fact that Wetston had found considerable difficulty in discerning anything explicit from the legislative debates, that they:

[D]emonstrate that there was a view that disenfranchisement would have an 'educative effect' ... Further, the debates emphasize the view that the prisoners actually disenfranchised themselves by their engaging in criminal conduct.[59]

Gonthier adopted in full Linden's description of the debates in Parliament and before the Commission, arriving at the same conclusion that Parliament had enacted reasonable and sufficiently justified legislation.[60]

In contrast, McLachlin CJ for the majority reasoned that dialogue theory did not amount to legislative reconsideration of rights-infringing legislation compelling judicial deference if the revised legislation still does not conform to the Constitution:

The healthy and important promotion of a dialogue between the legislature and the courts should not be debased to a rule of 'if at first you don't succeed, try, try again'.[61]

She and Gonthier also disagreed on the characterisation of the issue. Gonthier suggested that it boiled down to a clash of political and social philosophies, both of them reasonable, so that Parliament was entitled to choose between the two, and the courts were under a duty to defer to that choice. McLachlin held that if the issue concerns a 'core democratic' right, it does not fall 'within a "range of acceptable alternatives" among which Parliament may pick and choose at its discretion'.[62] She argued that the right to vote is one of these core democratic rights and its denial is not simply a question of 'competing social philosophies', nor does legislative debate make it so. For her, the mere presence of legislative or public debate should not by itself warrant judicial deference to the outcome of the debate: the courts must retain their ability to scrutinise that outcome and safeguard core democratic rights.[63]

It is, McLachlin thus argued, 'precisely when legislative choices threaten to undermine the foundations of the participatory democracy guaranteed by the *Charter* that courts must be vigilant in fulfilling their constitutional duty to protect the integrity

---

[56] ibid [96], emphasis added.
[57] *Sauvé v Canada* 2002 SCC 68 [104], 218 DLR (4th) 577.
[58] ibid.
[59] ibid [165].
[60] ibid [188].
[61] ibid [17].
[62] ibid [13].
[63] ibid.

of this system'.[64] Accordingly, the legislature was under a duty to properly justify its decision to infringe Charter rights by clearly identifying the objective it wants to achieve and why the infringement is necessary to achieve it: 'people should not be left guessing about why their Charter rights have been infringed'.[65] Otherwise, if the legislature were able to offer symbolic or abstract reasons for infringing rights, 'judicial review either becomes vacuously constrained or reduces to a contest of "our symbols are better than your symbols"':[66]

> At the end of the day, people should not be left guessing about why their Charter rights have been infringed. Demonstrable justification requires that the objective clearly reveal the harm that the government hopes to remedy, and that this objective remain constant throughout the justification process ... If Parliament can infringe a crucial right such as the right to vote simply by offering symbolic and abstract reasons, judicial review either becomes vacuously constrained or reduces to a contest of 'our symbols are better than your symbols'. Neither outcome is compatible with the vigorous justification analysis required by the Charter.[67]

Both the majority judgment and the dissent are problematic. On the one hand, McLachlin seems undecided between the proposition that no limit on the right to vote of inmates could be justified and the proposition that Parliament and/or the Government's lawyers had failed to show that this particular limit was justified. On the other hand, Gonthier attributed to Parliament a justification that was not presented in the debates and that justification was not one that went to showing why the limit was proportional; indeed, it was less a justification than a repeat of the visceral reaction that one finds in parliamentary debates on the issue of the right of prisoners to vote: that inmates should suffer civil death. As Steve Coughlan commented in an incisive annotation to the decision: 'Although pre-Charter there might have been equally reasonable competing theories of social and political philosophy, Canada picked one of those policies when the Charter was enacted, and it cannot be argued now that all the competing philosophies are still on the same footing.'[68]

Naturally, this point raises the question whether it would ever be possible to justify a limit on the right of rights. But we can note that some limits are not only justifiable but also easy to justify—for example, a limit on the age at which one is eligible to vote. That justifications for other limits seem very hard to conceive is not a problem confined to the right of rights. As we saw Mureinik suggest, if the bill of rights does not outright prohibit torture or political detentions in normal times, this opens up a space for Parliament to attempt to justify a limit. But, as I take Coughlan to indicate, this space screens out certain kinds of justifications—those that were considered acceptable in the days before the bill of rights and which went not to a justification of a limit on a right, but to the denial that there was such a right.

---

[64] ibid [15].
[65] ibid [23].
[66] ibid.
[67] ibid.
[68] Steve Coughlan, 'Justification in the Face of Competing Social and Political Philosophies' Annotation, (2003) 5 CR (6th) 208.

Coughlan also pointed out why the majority judgment and the dissent share a common problem in framing the issue as one about dialogue, Dialogue, he said, 'is a metaphor, not an interpretive technique'.[69] He continued:

> Courts ought not to question whether they are doing the dialogue process correctly, or whether their process is adequately 'dialogic'. Courts are simply engaged in the process of seeing whether legislation violates some particular Charter right and if so whether it can be justified under s. 1 … [T]he simple fact that Parliament has had a second kick at the can should not sway a court to save the legislation. The metaphor is simply an attempt to describe what was already occurring: it is letting the tail wag the dog for courts to try to change their behaviour to suit the metaphor. If the new law meets Charter scrutiny, it should be upheld; if it does not, it should be struck down.[70]

As I will now argue, the metaphor does make an important point, though it characterises this point inaccurately. It is that the issue of who has final authority, Parliament or the judiciary, might be a distraction from what should be our main concern, namely, justification. It might even be the case that talking of the issue as one about interpretation, that is, who is better placed to interpret human rights, misses the main concern in the same way as casting the issue as one about final authority. For the main concern is not how to interpret the core of the right, but the appropriate process for testing whether a limit on the right has been justified.

III. DEFERENCE AND JUSTIFICATION

Christopher Manfredi, a Canadian political scientist who falls into the political constitutionalist camp and who also appeared as an expert witness for the government in *Sauvé* in Act VI, commented on this saga in a paper entitled 'The Day the Dialogue Died'.[71] On his description, the invocation of dialogue by Linden in the Federal Court of Appeal in *Sauvé* had issued a 'challenge to the Supreme Court: Either let the legislation stand or rule definitively that Parliament may not, for any reason or by any means, disenfranchise inmates'.[72] He concluded that the majority in the Supreme Court had 'decided that the time had come to end the conversation about criminal disenfranchisement. In this instance, the Court decided to have the last word, and it had at its disposal the means to do so'.[73] Manfredi clearly regarded the decision as judicial supremacist in nature and as evidence that in Canada there is 'automatic deference to the meaning offered by a single institution', instead of what he took to be appropriate: a recognition by the courts of the coordinate role of Parliament in interpreting human rights, a role that he took to be explicitly recognised in the notwithstanding provision, that is, the override in section 33.

---

[69] ibid.
[70] ibid.
[71] Christopher P Manfredi, 'The Day the Dialogue Died: A Comment on *Sauvé v Canada*' (2007) 45(1) *Osgoode Hall Law Journal* 105.
[72] ibid 110.
[73] ibid 122.

However, a dialogue stops by definition when the authority that has the last word speaks, and the Supreme Court had final authority in regard to section 3 only because the right to vote is one of the core democratic rights protected from section 33. So the complaint should not be that the dialogue stopped, but that the Court was wrong not to defer to Parliament's interpretation. In addition, that Parliament has a coordinate role in interpretation does not depend on section 33. Such a role is already explicitly recognised in section 1, since section 1 permits Parliament to limit rights if it can provide a sufficient justification for such a limit, and section 1 clearly applies to section 3. Finally, there is a case for deference to Parliament's interpretation only when Parliament takes heed of the rights in an appropriate fashion—and there are several complex issues here.

One such issue is well identified by Manfredi when he points out that it is 'relatively easy … for courts to move from "did not give reasons' to "did not give *good* reasons" to "did not give *good enough* reasons"'. Thus, Manfredi claims that the 'distinction between "good enough reasons" and "good enough policy" breaks down'.[74] However, if deference is not to be automatic, the court has to decide whether reasons were offered of a sort that could justify the limit. If there is no middle ground between that exercise and the court simply legislating the policy it prefers, then the answer is to forget about ideas such as dialogue or coordinate interpretative authority and to make Parliament both the first and the last interpreter of human rights, which is to say that its first word should also count as its last. On this view, courts should 'automatically' defer just because Parliament has pronounced on an issue and its pronouncement happens to limit a right. An implication would be that any statutory provision enacted prior to the adoption of the bill of rights and that limits a right must be regarded by the courts as a justified limit because it follows that when Parliament limits a right after deliberating about what policy to enact by definition, it has interpreted the right.

This absurd implication exposes an important faultline in political constitutionalism. Political constitutionalists do not insist that Parliament's first word should also be the last; rather, they insist that Parliament should have the last word, and so they concede that the interventions of courts and other institutions can improve the quality of that last word. However, only the first position is consistent with their argument as to why Parliament is best placed to interpret human rights. If the judiciary adds no special value to the process—indeed, if its style of reasoning cramps and distorts the issues—why consult judges at all?

Consider that in Canada, the statutory section that deprived prisoners of the franchise was enacted prior to the Charter. Section 51 of the 1985 Act, the provision that was litigated in *Sauvé* and was thus enacted three years after the advent of the Charter, simply took over section 14 of a 1970 statute without any parliamentary debate. In turn, section 14 of the 1970 Act was simply a carryover from the earlier section 14(2)(e) of the Canada Elections Act 1960. Moreover, in 1970 a member of the opposition proposed an amendment that would have removed the clause that

---

[74] ibid 115, citing Martin Shapiro, 'The Giving Reasons Requirement' in Martin Shapiro and Alec Stone Sweet (eds), *On Law, Politics and Judicialization* (Oxford, Oxford University Press, 2002) 228.

deprived all inmates of the vote and, in contrast to the 1992 parliamentary debate, there is in this debate a full and serious discussion of a range of issues, as least on the part of those who supported the amendment. They argued that it was inappropriate to preserve a relic of civil death into an era where not only had there been an ever-widening franchise but also in which the purpose of punishment has come to be seen increasingly as rehabilitative.[75]

In contrast, those who supported the deprivation offered the usual visceral response that deprivation is by stipulation a fitting punishment for those who have transgressed society's laws, especially those who have committed more serious transgressions.[76] Lawbreakers were likened to those who seek to 'destroy' their country: 'If we give prisoners the franchise, we must give it to saboteurs and traitors too.'[77] And the parliamentarians who opposed the amendment had no qualms about the idea that a prison inmate experiences a total loss of his civic rights until his re-entry to society.

With some nuances, with considerably less sophistication and with the exception of Milliken's intervention, the 1970 debate is, as we saw, almost exactly the debate that gets played out in 1992 in the wake of a successful Charter challenge and the report of a Royal Commission. For the parliamentarians who were in 1992 opposed to doing away with the deprivation altogether were not concerned with justifying a limit on a right protected by the Charter, but with finding a limit that might count as a politically acceptable compromise between total deprivation and no deprivation. To adapt language from a UK Court of Appeal judgment which overruled the decision of a school in a matter on religious dress and the school's uniform code, none of them 'started from the premise' that the inmates had a right that is recognised by Canadian law and the onus lay on the parliamentarians to justify their 'interference with that right'.[78]

Notice that this description was true of both sides in the 1970 debate, because even those who supported the amendment seemed to see their interventions as justifying an extension of the right to vote and not as a question of whether the deprivation was a justified limit on a right. Hence, in principle, the advent of the Charter in 1982 made a huge difference in that section 3 both made it the case that Canadians had a legally protected right to vote and, because section 3 is one of the democratic rights immunised against parliamentary override, gave the right to vote enhanced protection subject only to limitation in accordance with section 1. I say 'in principle' because, as we have seen, this fact did not make a normative difference

---

[75] See, eg, *House of Commons Debates*, 28th Parl, 2nd Sess, No 8 (22 June 1970) at 8460–62 (Mr Howard), 8466–67 (Mr Goyer) and 8471–72 (Mr Benjamin). Perhaps the most telling bit of reasoning in the debates is this 'parallel' drawn by Mr Howard at 8461: 'They used to say that the people who were excluded from the vote were people in mental hospitals, those in jail, and Indians. A few years ago we took the Indians off the proscribed list and everyone ... will agree that since then political parties and candidates have paid more attention to Indian people and Indian affairs, even when that has not been done for political reasons ... The point is that candidates and parties began to be more interested in Indian affairs. I think something similar would happen to inmates of penitentiaries.'

[76] See, eg, ibid at 8468–69 (Mr Fortin), 8469–70 (Mr Mongrain) and 8470–71 (Mr Bigg).

[77] ibid 8466 (Mr Laprise); *cf* ibid 8468–69 (Mr Fortin).

[78] *R (on the application of SB) v Headteacher and Governors of Denbigh High School* [2005] EWCA Civ 199 [76].

to the parliamentarians opposed to Milliken's amendments, only a prudential one, that is, to what they thought they could get away with in the face of an inevitable Charter challenge.

A second major complexity is directly tied to the idea that the right to vote is the right of rights. Support for the disenfranchisement of prisoners has trouble distancing itself from the kind of visceral sentiment that approves of the idea of civil death for prisoners because they have declared themselves to be enemies of civilised society. Consider that in New Zealand, the Electoral Act of 1993 changed the legal situation of prisoners from one of total disenfranchisement to disenfranchisement of prisoners serving sentences of three years' imprisonment or longer.[79] However, the Electoral (Disqualification of Sentenced Prisoners) Amendment Act 2010 returned to the pre-1993 state of disenfranchising all prisoners, regardless of the length of sentence. This legislation was sponsored by a backbench Member of Parliament of the governing National Party, who received his Party's support on the basis that a crime, because it is an affront to society, leads to the loss of rights, should the community so decide.[80]

Prior to the passage of the legislation, the Attorney-General advised Parliament to no avail that the blanket disenfranchisement of prisoners appeared to be inconsistent with section 12 of the Bill of Rights Act and that it could not be justified under section 5 of that Act.[81] Hence, Andrew Geddis has argued that the 'perfunctory' debate on this important issue not only calls into question the moral basis of the prohibition, but also undermines 'the very basis for the claim that Parliament ought to be the final lawmaking institution for society'.[82] In the context of this chapter, it is noteworthy that Geddis, after setting out a sympathetic account of Waldron's case for parliamentary interpretation of human rights, points out that Waldron himself has said prior to this episode that legislative deliberation in New Zealand had started to fall short of the standard required to justify legislative supremacy. Geddis comments that Parliament's 'behaviour when making law risks placing New Zealand outside those "core cases" in which [Waldron's] defence of legislative supremacy applies'.[83]

We see here that Waldron recognises that actual practice in New Zealand puts pressure on some of the assumptions in his argument against judicial review. For his argument assumes not only, as we have seen, that there is 'a commitment on the part of most members of the society and most of its officials to the idea of individual and minority rights', but also that there is 'persisting, substantial, and good

[79] Andrew Geddis, 'Prisoner Voting and Rights Deliberation: How New Zealand's Parliament Failed' [2011] *New Zealand Law Review* 443, 446.
[80] ibid 447.
[81] New Zealand, 'Report of the Attorney-General under the New Zealand Bill of Rights Act 1990 on the Electoral (Disqualification of Convicted Prisoners) Amendment Bill', March 2010, J4.
[82] Geddis (n 79) 462.
[83] ibid 462, citing Jeremy Waldron, 'Compared to What? Judicial Activism and New Zealand's Parliament' [2005] *New Zealand Law Journal* 441; Jeremy Waldron, *Parliamentary Recklessness: Why We Need to Legislate More Carefully* (Auckland, Maxim Institute, 2008) 30: 'That's what New Zealand's Parliament has become: a place where preordained positions are stated, with hopefully as little fuss and as little public expense as possible. Parliament—the one forum supposedly dedicated to public debate—is becoming the one place where public debate is perfunctory, a simple matter of political posturing.'

faith disagreement about rights (i.e., about what the commitment to rights actually amounts to and what its implications are) among the members of the society who are committed to the idea of rights'.[84]

Now while the statutory bill of rights in New Zealand expresses a deep commitment to rights, the second assumption seems in light of this episode naïve. For it surely shows that one reason why we need institutions that are given a role as guardians of human rights is because the commitment to minority rights is often lacking. We want *legal* commitments to human rights because they are there to guard against the 'pervasive prejudice' that Waldron has said has the result that his 'core argument against judicial review ... cannot be sustained'.[85]

The New Zealand episode is particularly illuminating for two reasons. The first is the ignored advice of the Attorney-General. The second and most important is that the New Zealand bill of rights authorises only rights-compliant interpretations if possible, but not a judicial declaration of incompatibility when such interpretation is not in fact possible. In this second situation there is no formal avenue open to challenge the statute, and thus judges are disabled from insisting that Parliament engage in the process of justification that should attend an explicit statutory limitation or deprivation of a right.

The legal materials are not then, as Waldron sometimes seems to imply, diversions or distractions from the all-things-considered moral reasoning in which legislatures are able to engage in a fashion not open to judges. Rather, the materials are the stuff of a special kind of disciplined moral reasoning, one which enables both judges and legislatures to work within the framework of the human rights values that have attracted a broad consensus at a high level, and thus to decide on the basis of principle as well as policy.[86] But for that to happen, the work has to be done in a way that is framed by the principles at stake.

As I have suggested elsewhere,[87] more important in provoking the kind of moral debate Waldron extols than the choice of which institution should have the last word is the creation of an institutional structure in which judicial decisions can call into question whether a statute is compatible with constitutional commitments. My suggestion is not that judges are the only agents of promoting such debate. Parliamentary committees such as the JCHR that are given the role of requiring that Parliament engage in such debate might be even more effective if they are given the right kind of institutional teeth, especially if they operate in a political culture of justification in which politicians are willing to take the committees seriously. But even if it is right that such committees might be more effective than judges, the issue is not an either/or one. If judges are an essential element in sustaining the culture, the point is to work out how best these institutions should interact.

[84] Waldron (n 7) 1360.
[85] ibid 1404.
[86] See Fredman (n 19).
[87] See David Dyzenhaus, 'Are Legislatures Good at Morality? Or Better at it than Courts?' (2009) 7(1) *International Journal of Constitutional Law* 46, 51–52.

In my view, the New Zealand interlude indicates that the institutional structure of such a culture is inadequate when judges are not given the formal authorisation to make a declaration of incompatibility, because that deficiency precludes the possibility of a legal challenge to a Parliament that has failed dismally in its role of furthering human rights to which it purports to be committed. And so I would tentatively conclude that a legal order in which the structure exists requires that judges have either the authority to declare the incompatibility of a statute with the bill of rights or to declare its invalidity.

If that conclusion is right, it follows that the issue of whether legislatures or judges should have final authority is something of a distraction. Even if it is the case that in legal orders at the strongest end of the continuum of judicial review, for example, the US, there is more judicial deference on occasion, this deference will not manifest itself appropriately. By this I mean that in such orders it will be the case that the relationship between the legislature and the judiciary has to be negotiated by the two institutions in terms of which got the interpretation of the right correct. When the judges disagree with the legislature, but find it politically inexpedient to overrule it, they will not so much defer as pretend that they think that the legislature was correct. In other words, deference properly so called becomes possible only when we move away from conceiving of the issue as one in which there is a contest of interpretations and see it rather as an issue of how to ensure that there is an appropriate and public process of justification. Hence, at the strongest end of the continuum, part of the problem is that justification does not occur in a democratically appropriate manner.[88]

And with this point in place, we can see why a culture of justification is necessary to a democracy, at least for those who start with Waldron's third assumption: 'a commitment on the part of most members of the society and most of its officials to the idea of individual and minority rights'. For this assumption marks a sea change in the traditional debate about judicial review and narrows the gap between legal and political constitutionalists to the point where the debate is about quite tractable issues of institutional design.

Moreover, I suspect that the gap becomes even narrower when one notices that questions about appropriate institutional design are heavily context-dependent; for example, the fact that the tradition is one of parliamentary supremacy rather than the mixed constitution associated with a presidential system must influence the relationship between the legislature and judges, even after that jurisdiction takes the decision to entrench a bill of rights. In other words, since important considerations of design such as who should have the last word may depend on factors extraneous to that debate, its scope might turn out to be minute, to say the least.

This result, as I suggested above, has come about because of the way that political constitutionalists have moved away from their Benthamite positivist roots. It is no longer the case on their position that the normative content of the law is determined outwith the legal order, so that law is understood as the mere instrument of politically determined content. Rather, this content must be determined in a way that is

---

[88] See Roach (n 50).

respectful of human rights, in part, I suspect, because it is difficult to find anyone today who would claim that a legal order can be considered democratic if it is not committed to serving the human rights of those who are subject to its law. Once the implications of taking that step are properly understood, we can move away from what has become a rather sterile debate and concentrate on the important issue of how to reform our legal orders so that they best live up to the ideal of a culture of justification.

22

From Dialogue to Deliberation: Human Rights Adjudication and Prisoners' Rights to Vote

SANDRA FREDMAN[*]

INTRODUCTION

T HE BASIC DILEMMA of human rights adjudication is easily stated. Unconstrained decision-making by elected representatives may invade the basic human rights of individuals and minorities. Majority voting may even be used to disenfranchise individuals or groups. It is precisely for this reason that the need arises for constitutional constraints on the elected body, including bills of rights. However, the interpretation of human rights inevitably requires value judgments and, even more so, the justifiable limits. And here the democratic dilemma seems at its most acute. If the power of interpretation and limitation of human rights is left to elected legislators on the basis of majority voting, perpetual minorities may be perpetually subordinated. But leaving judges to make the final decision flies in the face of the basic principle that all fundamental decisions in society should be taken by the people themselves. Prisoners' voting rights throw the dilemma into particularly sharp relief. Should an elected legislature have the final say on removing the fundamental right to vote from a section of the population, particularly one which is deeply unpopular and which politicians have no natural interest in defending? This is a question which has confronted courts in a range of jurisdictions.

The most promising way out of this dilemma is to move away from a polarisation between courts and legislatures, and instead regard both as contributing to a democratic resolution of human rights disputes. An increasingly influential stream of thought characterises the relationship as one of dialogue. Rather than courts having the final say, judicial decisions provoke a response from the legislature. In this chapter, I aim to go beyond a dialogic model and propose one based on deliberative democracy. I take as a starting point the principle that the primary role

[*] This chapter is a slightly modified and updated version of an article which appeared in [2013] *Public Law* 292. I am grateful to Professor David Dyzenhaus, Justice Kate O'Regan and Professor Kent Roach for their valuable comments on earlier drafts of this and to Chris McConnachie for his excellent research assistance.

in determining the meaning and limits of human rights belongs with the elected legislature. However, democracy should mean more than majoritarianism. Drawing on the distinction between interest bargaining and value-based or deliberative decisions, I argue that human rights can only be properly addressed within a democracy through deliberative means. In other words, the power of the principle should constitute the reason for adopting it, rather than the power of those whose interests it serves. Otherwise, those without political power risk perpetual subordination, undermining the raison d'etre of human rights protection. It is here that the courts are in a position to make a unique contribution to the democratic resolution of human rights issues. I argue that the courts should ensure that human rights decisions are indeed taken deliberatively within the constraints set by the human rights themselves.

This chapter begins by evaluating dialogic theories of human rights adjudication. It then sets out a deliberative alternative and sketches its application in a human rights context. I call this a 'bounded deliberative' approach. The third section applies these principles to prisoners' voting rights cases. South Africa and the UK are chosen because, while the decision in the South African case of *NICRO*[1] exemplifies the deliberative approach, the UK position is more complex. The decision of the European Court of Human Rights (ECtHR) in *Hirst*[2] might have set the court on a path towards a deliberative approach, but the deference manifested in the most recent case of *Scoppola*[3] is disappointing, particularly in its failure to follow the South African model of insisting on proper evidential or principled support before a state's limitation on the fundamental right to vote should be regarded as justifiable.[4]

I. THE DIALOGIC APPROACH

The dialogic approach originated in a highly influential article by Hogg and Bushell,[5] which argued that the record of decisions under the Canadian Charter demonstrated that judges did not in fact have the last word on the matter. Instead, the legislature was generally able to respond to judicial invalidation of legislation in ways that preserved the basic legislative objective. 'While the Charter would often influence the design of legislation that encroached on a guaranteed right', legislatures 'would usually be able to accomplish what they wanted to do while respecting the requirements of the Charter'.[6] Having examined the aftermath of every case in which a law had been declared contrary to the Charter by the Supreme

---

[1] *Minister of Home Affairs v National Institute for Crime Prevention and the Re-integration of Offenders (NICRO)* Case CCT 03/04 [2004] ZACC 10 (South African Constitutional Court).

[2] *Hirst v UK (No 2)* (2006) 42 EHRR 41 (ECtHR Grand Chamber).

[3] *Scoppola v Italy (No 3)* (Application No 126/05) 22 May 2012.

[4] For an excellent account of the Canadian and New Zealand parallels, see Dyzenhaus, ch 21 in this volume. See also *Roach v Electoral Commissioner* [2007] HCA 43 (Australia).

[5] P Hogg and A Bushell, 'The Charter Dialogue Between Courts and Legislatures (or Perhaps the Charter of Rights isn't Such a Bad Thing After All)' (1997) 35 *Osgoode Hall Law Journal* 75.

[6] P Hogg, A Thornton and W Wright, 'Charter Dialogue Revisited: Or Much Ado about Metaphors' (2007) 45 *Osgoode Hall Law Journal* 1, 3.

Court of Canada, they found that, out of 66 cases, all but 13 had elicited some response from the legislature. In seven cases, the legislation was simply repealed, but in the remaining 46, a new law was substituted for the old one. Although the legislature re-enacted the same law in two cases (in effect defying the court), in all the other cases the legislature 'respected the judicial decision by adding some civil libertarian safeguards in the new version of the law, but maintained the legislative purpose'.[7] The result was that, in the Canadian context, judicial review did not mean that judges had the last word. Although these claims were primarily empirical, they quickly formed the basis for normative arguments in favour of a dialogic model. Thus, Iacobucci J enthusiastically embraced the dialogic model in *Vriend v Alberta*.[8] It has also seemed apt to describe the UK Human Rights Act 1998, which gives courts the power to issue a declaration of incompatibility, but not to strike down legislation.

The dialogic model is an attractive one. Rather than taking the side of either unadulterated parliamentary sovereignty or a robust judicial supremacy, it characterises the process of decision-making as collaborative. However, a closer look reveals a deep ambiguity as to the role of the judiciary. Can judges ultimately make authoritative decisions on the meaning of human rights or should they defer the authoritative decision to the legislature? The dialogic approach is compatible with either. Tushnet takes the view that the task of the court should be 'to bring constitutional values ... into focus in the legislative forum', but leave the final decision to the legislature.[9] Similarly, for Roach, the courts' expertise in interpreting rights justifies their drawing 'the attention of the legislature to fundamental values that are likely to be ignored or finessed in the legislative process', but not in their attempting to 'end the conversation or conduct a monologue in which [their] ... Charter rulings are the final word'.[10] By contrast, Hogg, Thornton and Wright argue that the 'final authority for interpreting the Charter rests properly with the judiciary'.[11] Similarly, Hickman's preferred 'strong form' dialogue reflects a belief that 'courts have a vital constitutional role in protecting fundamental principles from the sway of popular sentiment'.[12] Courts should not simply impose these principles, but should work with the executive and legislature in 'evolving them and in fostering their acceptance'. In doing so, courts should have the capacity for compromise in the interests of expediency, while at the same time 'insulating fundamental principles even in the face of such compromises'.[13]

The deliberative model goes beyond dialogue by focusing not simply on the final decision, whether legislative or judicial, but also on the quality of the deliberation in both arenas (and potential in relation to civil society too). It is through the

---

[7] ibid 4.

[8] *Vriend v Alberta* [1998] 1 SCR 493 (Supreme Court of Canada).

[9] M Tushnet, 'Dialogic Judicial Review' (2009) 61 *Arkansas Law Review* 205, 212.

[10] K Roach, *The Supreme Court on Trial: Judicial Activism or Democratic Dialogue* (Toronto, Irwin Law Books, 2001) 530–31.

[11] Hogg, Thornton and Wright (n 6) 31.

[12] T Hickman, 'Constitutional Dialogue, Constitutional Theories and the Human Rights Act 1998' [2005] *Public Law* 306, 316.

[13] ibid.

requirement that a human rights determination be justified in a deliberative manner that democratic resolution of human rights disputes can take place. It is to this model that I now turn.

II. THE DELIBERATIVE MODEL

The deliberative model aims to find a role for courts in human rights adjudication which enhances rather than undermines democratic participation.[14] To do so, it draws on Habermas' distinction between two kinds of coordination: 'interest-governed' and 'value-oriented' coordination.[15] Interest-governed coordination presupposes that each party comes to the bargaining table with fixed interests, the aim being to induce the other party to accept its claim. There is no challenge to the validity of those interests. Success depends on factual power, be it economic, political or collective, rather than the power of reasons. Correspondingly, resolution lies in victory, surrender or compromise, but not a change in the parties' perceptions of their own interests. This contrasts with value-oriented or deliberative coordination. Here the parties do not come to the table with fixed interests; they enter the process aiming to justify their positions by appeal to reasons that all parties can accept, while at the same time being open to persuasion.[16] Thus, instead of taking preferences as given, deliberative democracy is capable of influencing preference formation itself.[17]

Deliberative procedures will always coexist alongside interest bargaining. Habermas concedes that in complex societies, it is often the case that interests are sufficiently diverse that consensus is not possible.[18] In such cases, resort must be had either to majority voting or to bargaining between success-oriented parties who are willing to cooperate. Similarly, Sunstein describes the legislative process as a continuum, at one pole of which interest group pressures are determinative, while at the other end, legislators engage in deliberation in which interest group pressures play little or no role. Along the continuum, outcomes depend on an amalgam of pressure, deliberation and other factors.[19] Even for those decisions in which interest bargaining is unavoidable, deliberative procedures are necessary to ensure that all interested parties are provided with equal opportunities to influence one another.[20]

While interest-based bargaining is an inevitable and often an appropriate component of democracy, the possibility of deliberation stands out as an alternative which can transcend inequalities in bargaining power. Most importantly, human rights should not be addressed on the basis of interest bargaining. If they were, those with superior numerical, political or financial power might always trump the rights of those without power. As Rawls noted, even when blatant exclusionary practices

---

[14] For an expanded version of this section, see S Fredman, *Human Rights Transformed: Positive Rights and Positive Duties* (Oxford, Oxford University Press, 2008) ch 4.
[15] J Habermas, *Between Facts and Norms* (Cambridge, Polity Press, 1997) 139–41.
[16] ibid 25–26.
[17] ibid.
[18] ibid 166.
[19] CR Sunstein, 'Interest Groups in American Public Law' (1985) 38 *Stanford Law Review* 29, 48–49.
[20] Habermas (n 15) 166.

are not in place, social and economic inequalities in a modern democratic state are so large that those with greater wealth and position usually control political life and enact legislation and social policies that advance their interests.[21] Human rights should therefore only be addressed within a democracy through deliberative means. The power of the principle must itself be the reason for adopting it, rather than the numbers of those who back it. It is here that courts can potentially fulfil a democratic role. When human rights are at issue, courts should augment democratic participation by steering decision-making away from interest bargaining towards value-oriented deliberation or, indeed, by functioning as a forum for deliberation. Importantly, however, these should not act as a substitute for parliamentary mechanisms such as cross-party select committees, which are also capable of conducting rights-based debates in a deliberative manner. The UK Joint Committee on Human Rights (JCHR) is a particularly good example of such a mechanism.

III. ADJUDICATING HUMAN RIGHTS: BOUNDED DELIBERATION

To what extent, then, can courts contribute to a deliberative resolution of human rights issues? At first sight, they are an unlikely option. Adversarial litigation appears to be a paradigm interest bargaining framework. Litigation is arguably bipolar, retrospective and sufficiently expensive to serve only elites. However, on closer inspection, it is clear that judicial decision-making is essentially deliberative. It is not the parties' political, numerical or economic strength that persuades courts, but the strength of their reasoning. Judges are required to come to the process open to the possibility of being persuaded by one side or the other, and the outcome is often a synthesis of the arguments of both sides. Thus, while the primary responsibility for articulating and delivering human rights responsibilities lies with Parliament, decision-makers must be in a position to justify their decisions in a deliberative sense. This builds on Mureinik's influential conception of a 'culture of justification'.[22] Judges are often referred to as 'unelected and unaccountable'. However, accountability means more than removing representatives from power when they fall out of favour with a majority of the electorate. Accountability also means that both elected representatives and judges have the duty to explain and justify their decisions in ways which are capable of convincing others. Courts should not prescribe to elected representatives exactly what decisions should be taken, but should instead require them to justify why those decisions have been made in the light of other competing principles. Dyzenhaus argues that this role is inherently democratic: 'What justifies all public power is the ability of its incumbents to offer

---

[21] J Rawls, *Justice as Fairness* (Cambridge, MA, Harvard University Press, 2001) 148–50.
[22] E Mureinik, 'A Bridge to Where?: Introducing the Interim Bill of Rights' (1994) 10 *South African Journal on Human Rights* 31, 32; see also D Dyzenhaus, 'Law as Justification: Etienne Mureinik's Conception of Legal Culture' (1998) 14 *South African Journal on Human Rights* 11.

adequate reasons for the decisions which affect those subject to them ... The courts' special role is as an ultimate enforcement mechanism for such justification.'[23]

Courts are therefore in a position to augment deliberative democracy in human rights adjudication in two complementary ways. First, the court functions as a deliberative forum in its own right. This might require important adaptations; indeed, in public law cases, the adversarial structure is increasingly moderated by wider standing and interventions. Moreover, the arguments of the parties, as well as both majority and dissenting judgments, feed into the wider deliberative process. Second, courts can steer legislative and executive decision-making away from interest bargaining and towards deliberation. They do this by insisting that decision-makers justify their decisions on the interpretation or limitation of human rights in a deliberative manner. By requiring decision-makers to lay out and substantiate their reasons, with evidence where appropriate, courts can constitute an incentive for decision-makers to make decisions in a deliberative way even outside of the courtroom.

It could be argued, however, that a deliberative approach is incompatible with the very essence of human rights adjudication. Deliberative models assume an open-ended approach, allowing the process to produce a solution with no preconditions. Thus, Cohen argues that, apart from sharing a commitment to deliberative democracy itself, participants need not share a conception of the good.[24] Human rights, by contrast, require a prior commitment to the observation of human rights. Moreover, court proceedings themselves suggest closure, precluding the possibility of further deliberation. This is precisely why many might oppose judicial intervention.

However, the issue is more complex than this. Human rights pose particularly difficult challenges because they are neither fully determined nor open to thoroughgoing deliberative solutions. If they were fully determined, then both courts and legislatures could simply apply formulaic responses. Both institutions would be bound by the same mandatory norms and neither would be superior. However, human rights are open to a range of interpretations in particular contexts. Similarly, the question of whether human rights have justifiably been limited inevitably requires a judgment. On the other hand, human rights are not simply open moral questions; they are based on a consensus which has developed over time and is universally accepted as to what the fundamentals of being human in a political society require. It is within the framework set by this prior deliberative consensus that current decision-making must take place. Thus, human rights place real constraints on both judicial and legislative decision-making, while at the same time being open to interpretation.

It is in this interpretative space that the deliberative approach functions. Human rights decisions should be taken in a deliberative rather than an interest-based mode, and the primary deliberative role belongs with the legislature. However, one cannot assume, as Waldron does, that there is necessarily a commitment on the part

---

[23] D Dyzenhaus, 'The Politics of Deference: Judicial Review and Democracy' in M Taggart (ed), *The Province of Administrative Law* (Oxford, Hart Publishing, 1997) 305.

[24] J Cohen, 'Deliberation and Democratic Legitimacy' in A Hamlin and P Pettit (eds), *The Good Polity* (Oxford, Blackwell, 1989) 23.

of most members of the society to the idea of individual and minority rights.[25] There may be a very high-level commitment, for example, in the simple fact of having a bill of rights. But it is hard to maintain that all human rights disputes are about good faith disagreements about the meaning of rights, as will be seen below in relation to prisoners' voting rights. It is here that courts can make a unique contribution to the democratic resolution of human rights disputes. Courts should enhance the democratic accountability of decision-makers by insisting on a deliberative justification for the interpretation or limitation of rights. Although ideally this should trigger deliberative justification in the legislature itself, whether on the floor of the house or in select committees, courts can also function as a forum of accountability. This is particularly true for decisions taken which affect groups without the political power to influence the decision.

At the same time, courts are not entitled to impose their views on open-ended moral grounds. The deliberative approach is bounded in that it operates within the constraints of human rights, which are themselves a product of prior deliberative consensus. The role of the court is not to exercise a conclusive veto or to prescribe an authoritative interpretation, but nor is justification measured against an open-ended standard of rationality or reasonableness, as in administrative law. Decision-makers must be in a position to persuade the court that they have fulfilled their human rights obligations, account being taken both of the pre-existing deliberative consensus and of the fact that there is room for reasonable disagreement. The model I propose is therefore not one of pure deliberative democracy, but of 'bounded deliberation'.

Waldron regards the fact that courts do not have a mandate to reason in an open-ended moral manner, but are bound by a pre-existing legal framework as a reason why they are unsuitable for human rights adjudication: the institutional setting in which judges act and the role they adopt 'require them to address questions about rights in a particular legalistic way—indeed, in a way that, sometimes, makes it harder rather than easier for essential moral questions to be identified and addressed'. He contrasts this with 'legislative approaches, which proceed by identifying all the issues and all the opinions that might be relevant to a decision, rather than artificially limiting them in the way that courts do'.[26] As the debates on prisoners' voting rights show, this idealises legislative decision-making. Indeed, much relevant evidence and opinion is frequently omitted from legislative consideration. More importantly, it is paradoxical to valorise the output of legislative deliberation while at the same time regarding legal materials as irrelevant to judicial decision-making. A bill of rights makes judges more rather than less accountable, because they too have to justify their own decisions against a background of values reached by a process of prior consensus. In this way, a bill of rights acts as a mechanism for accountability for both the legislature and the judiciary.

It may be asked how the deliberative model can be reconciled with the need to reach a binding decision in a particular case. Human rights deliberation and

[25] J Waldron, 'The Core of the Case against Judicial Review' (2006) 115 *Yale Law Journal* 1346, 1359
[26] J Waldron, 'Judges as Moral Reasoners' (2009) 7 *International Journal of Constitutional Studies* 2.

development should not be fossilised by non-revisable decisions. However, as Habermas argues, there is a need to reach a point of closure under pressure of time, both for the parties before the court and in creating settled expectations by which others, including state bodies, can organise their decisions and actions.[27] In practice, while decisions might be binding on the parties before them, they remain revisable in the longer term through the dynamic forum of deliberative democracy, just as the common law can be revised by statute. This can be achieved through a change in the moral consensus, or changed justifications, and can be reflected in the nature of the remedy, through declaratory remedies, suspended strike down remedies and so on.

IV. PRISONERS' RIGHT TO VOTE

In the remainder of this chapter, I consider how a deliberative model might be used in relation to prisoners' rights to vote, comparing and contrasting South Africa and the UK. Disenfranchisement of citizens is a paradigm case in which interest-based reasoning by elected representatives is inappropriate. Since those who are disenfranchised are unable to influence the outcome through the normal electoral processes, it is hard to see how the role of courts can be gainsaid. This is especially true for prisoners: politicians taking an interest- based approach are unlikely to stand up for them, as the debates below show. Indeed, removing the vote from prisoners is often seen as an easy vote-catcher. Nor can courts be accused of simply serving the interests of elites; they are the only forum in which prisoners' voices can be heard.

What role, then, should the courts play? The familiar spectrum sees courts either deferring to any solution that is not wholly arbitrary (a deference approach) or having the power to provide the 'right' answer (a correctness approach). The deliberative model is more nuanced. It does not give the judges the final say, nor does it require courts to defer. Instead, courts demand a deliberative explanation for the legislature's chosen solution, within the boundaries of the pre-existing deliberative consensus on the right. In the context of prisoners' voting rights, this debate takes place, not about the interpretation of the right to vote, which is uncontested, but about its appropriate limits. The deliberative model requires, as a start, that any justification be supported by evidence of its necessity and efficacy. It is not enough simply to put forward the Government's opinion as to the need for a limitation. The state must also be capable of convincing the court that, on the substance, the impugned policy is consistent with the background value in the right itself, including that all should treated with equal concern and respect, and that all should have a right to participate in political decision-making. At the same time, the court should not dictate the result. There are several possible solutions to the question of whether and how the right should be limited, more than one of which might satisfy the requirements of bounded deliberation. What is required is that any solution be supported by evidence (where factual claims are made) and principled reasons (for policy). For example, a justification based on deterrence should be supported by

---

[27] Habermas (n 15) 178.

evidence that withdrawal of the vote has a deterrent function. Purely interest-based reasoning should not be capable of supporting a justification. This approach is not simply an insistence on proportionality. Proportionality is an elastic principle, which can be applied with varying degrees of intensity. Rather than focusing on the balancing process per se, the deliberative model assesses the quality of the reasoning which lies behind the application of the proportionality principle, in the light of the background values intrinsic in the right.

Both South Africa and the UK have instituted prohibitions on prisoners' right to vote, and both have faced judicial challenge. They differ in several respects. The South African Constitution gives judges the power to invalidate legislation, whereas the UK Human Rights Act can yield, at most, a declaration of incompatibility. The role of the ECtHR, as a supranational court, is inevitably different from a domestic constitutional court. Arguably too, the text of the South African Constitution is more expressly value based than the ECHR. In the following analysis, these differences must be kept in mind. Nevertheless, the interplay between the legislative and judicial processes is remarkably similar.

A. South Africa

i. Bounded Deliberation and the Role of the Court

There have been two major Constitutional Court cases in South Africa concerning prisoners' right to vote. In the first, *August*,[28] prisoners challenged the failure of the Electoral Commission to put in place mechanisms for prisoners to vote. The Court held that, since there was no express provision barring prisoners from voting, it should be assumed that such a right existed. Section 19 of the Constitution, which guarantees the right to vote, had therefore been breached. This left open the possibility that statutory provision might be made to limit or negate prisoners' rights to vote. Just five months before the April 2004 elections, the Electoral Act was amended to expressly remove the right to vote from all convicted prisoners except those who were in prison because they were unable to pay a fine.[29] Prisoners were also deprived of the right to register as voters. In the *NICRO* case, the Constitutional Court was called on to decide the constitutionality of this measure.[30] It struck down the provision by a majority of 10:2, with Madala and Ngcobo JJ dissenting.

These two cases could be seen as a form of dialogue. The legislature responded to *August* with express legislation. *NICRO* constituted a 'second look'. What is more interesting, however, is the basis on which the judicial decisions were made. The first level of analysis requires the court to set the framework within which bounded deliberation should operate, drawing on pre-existing deliberative sources. For this, the Court was able to draw on the Constitution's express statement of the guiding values of the new democratic order, constituting a framework of reference to

[28] *August v Electoral Commission* (CCT8/99) [1999] ZACC 3 (South African Constitutional Court).
[29] Electoral Laws Amendment Act 34 of 2003 amending the Electoral Act 73 of 1998.
[30] *Minister of Home Affairs v NICRO* (n 1).

which both courts and legislature are accountable. Not surprisingly, in the context of a history of disenfranchisement and degradation, universal adult suffrage is one of the values on which the Republic of South Africa is founded.[31] It is against this fundamental value that any attempt to limit the right to vote must be judged. Thus, in *August*, Sachs J stated: 'Universal adult suffrage on a common voters roll is one of the foundational values of our entire constitutional order … The vote of each and every citizen is a badge of dignity and of personhood. Quite literally, it says that everybody counts.'[32] Sachs J was also able to draw on a pre-existing deliberative consensus for the 'well-established principle of common law … that prisoners are entitled to all their personal rights and personal dignity not temporarily taken away by law or necessarily inconsistent with the circumstances in which they have been place'.[33] In addition, he looked to international consensus to reinforce the deliberative force of this contention.[34]

Once the deliberative boundaries have been set, the next question concerns the extent to which a court insists on a deliberative solution. Did the court take on itself the task of providing an authoritative resolution of the problem (a 'correctness' approach)? Did it defer to any non-arbitrary justification (a 'deference' approach)? Or can the court be seen to be performing a deliberative role in the bounded context described above (a 'deliberative' approach)?

As we have seen, *August* left space for deliberative dialogue. The Court deferred to the expertise of the Electoral Commission in relation to the precise details of implementing prisoners' voting rights.[35] In addition, Sachs J emphasised that the judgment 'should not be read as suggesting that Parliament is prevented from disenfranchising certain categories of prisoners'. But the Court was not required to assess the quality of the deliberation within these boundaries. This task was left to the *NICRO* case. Here too, the Court began by stressing the deliberative space left to the legislature. Thus, Chaskalson CJ, for the majority, rejected the argument that the right to vote in the South African context was not subject to any limitation. Indeed, since the minister had conceded that the voting rights of prisoners had been limited, the case hinged on whether the limitation could be justified. At the same time, Chaskalson CJ stressed the bounded nature of the deliberation. Any limitation must be informed by the foundational values in section 1 of the Constitution. Moreover, section 3 of the Constitution, which gives all citizens the right to vote, provides that all citizens are equally subject to the duties and responsibilities of citizenship. This includes an obligation to respect the rights of others and to obey the law. Most importantly, any limitation must fulfil the requirements of the general limitation clause in section 36(1) of the Constitution. Far from being a tangential legal document, as Waldron suggests, this section structures the deliberation in a way which makes it difficult for interest-based reasoning to dominate. Thus, section 36(1) provides: '(1) The rights in the Bill of Rights may be limited only in terms of law of general application to

---

[31]   1996 Constitution, s 1(d).
[32]   *August v Electoral Commission* (n 28) [17]. See also *Haig v Canada* 105 DLR 4th 577 SCR, 613.
[33]   ibid *August v Electoral Commission* p [18].
[34]   *O'Brien v Skinner* 414 US 524 (1973) (US Supreme Court).
[35]   *August v Electoral Commission* (n 28) [38]–[39].

the extent that the limitation is reasonable and justifiable in an open and democratic society based on human dignity, equality and freedom, taking into account all relevant factors, including—(a) the nature of the right; (b) the importance of the purpose of the legislation; (c) the nature and extent of the limitation; (d) the relation between the limitation and its purpose; and (e) less restrictive means to achieve that purpose.'

Chaskalson CJ paid careful attention to the nature of the deliberative process. In particular, he insisted on a high standard of accountability. While recognising that facts and policy are often intertwined in a justification enquiry, he made it clear that the party relying on justification should place sufficient information before the court. This is necessary both to establish the facts on which the justification depends and, as to the policy that is being furthered, the reasons for that policy, and why it is considered reasonable to limit a constitutional right in pursuit of that policy.[36] 'That is important, for if this is not done the court may be unable to discern what the policy is, and the party making the constitutional challenge does not have the opportunity of rebutting the contention through countervailing factual material or expert opinion.'[37] He accepted that there may be cases where a court can uphold a claim of justification based on common sense and judicial knowledge, despite the absence of such information on the record. But in the final resort, 'context is all important and sufficient material should always be placed before a court dealing with such matters to enable it to weigh up and evaluate the competing values and interests in their proper context'.[38] The key point, taken from Canadian Chief Justice McLachlan, was that: 'At the end of the day, people should not be left guessing about why their Charter rights have been infringed.'[39]

Within this framework, the Court was careful to espouse a deliberative approach. Rather than asking whether the Government's contentions were right or wrong, Chaskalson CJ asked whether they were convincing, in the light of the fundamental right to vote. Particularly important is the rejection of interest-based arguments. Three arguments were put forward. First, the Government contended, to make special provision for prisoners to vote would be costly. This is precisely the type of interest-based argument that can be flushed out under deliberative scrutiny. While resource-based arguments may enter into value-based reasoning, courts should not accept such arguments merely on the basis of assertion, but should insist on proper evidence. Thus, Chaskalson CJ accepted that resources could not be ignored when assessing whether reasonable arrangements had been made for enabling citizens to vote. However, the Government did not place any information before the court on costs and logistics, and did not suggest that arrangements could not be made. Indeed, arrangements were made at all prisons to accommodate unsentenced prisoners and those who were imprisoned because they could not pay their fines.[40]

---

[36] *Minister of Home Affairs v NICRO* (n 1) [36].
[37] ibid.
[38] ibid [37].
[39] *Sauvé v Canada (Chief Electoral Officer)* [2002] 3 SCR 519 (Supreme Court of Canada) [23]. See also [21]: 'The Parliamentary debates offer more fulmination than illumination.'
[40] *Minister of Home Affairs v NICRO* (n 1) [49].

Ultimately, 'the right to vote is foundational to democracy … a precious right which must be vigilantly respected'.[41]

The second argument could be addressed in more deliberative terms. The Government argued that the resources used to provide special arrangements for prisoners to enable them to register and vote would divert resources from others, such as pregnant women, who might find it difficult to access polling stations. The Court did not find this convincing: 'The mere fact that it may be reasonable not to make special arrangements for particular categories of persons who are unable to reach or attend polling stations on election day does not mean that it is reasonable to disenfranchise prisoners.'[42]

The final argument most explicitly drew on interest-based arguments. Allowing prisoners to vote would send a message to the public that the Government was soft on crime. Chaskalson CJ gave short shrift to this argument:

> A fear that the public may misunderstand the government's true attitude to crime and criminals provides no basis for depriving prisoners of fundamental rights that they retain despite their incarceration. It could hardly be suggested that the government is entitled to disenfranchise prisoners in order to enhance its image; nor could it reasonably be argued that the government is entitled to deprive convicted prisoners of valuable rights that they retain in order to correct a public misconception as to its true attitude to crime and criminals.[43]

Chaskalson CJ made it clear that a policy denouncing crime and communicating to the public that citizens' rights are related to their duties would be legitimate and consistent with the Constitution. But the Government had not placed sufficient evidence before the Court to enable it to assess whether depriving prisoners of the vote was an appropriate way to achieve this.

Thus, the Court left open the space for Parliament to address the question in a deliberative way and to provide the Court with the kind of reasons that might convince it of the need to limit prisoners' rights. It is true that the particular dispute was resolved in favour of the prisoners; in fact, prisoners were hurriedly added to a special register and given the right to vote in the 2004 elections with apparently no ill effects. This may appear to close off debate rather than inviting further deliberation. However, as was argued above, a deliberative approach is not inconsistent with closure in a particular case, although further deliberation will need to take place with the reality of the living experiment in mind.

The dissenting judges were less insistent on accountability and more willing to decide the case in terms of their own view of the correctness of the arguments. Thus, although both Ngcobo and Madala JJ agreed that a proper foundation should be provided for a justification defence, the absence of such a justification should not prevent the court from disposing of the case on the basis of its own common sense. Nevertheless, their disagreement with the majority was not based on deference, but on substantive principle. For Madala J, this was that 'the temporary removal of the

[41] ibid [47].
[42] ibid [53].
[43] ibid [56].

vote and its restoration upon the release of the prisoner is salutary to the development and inculcation of a caring and responsible society'. This principle was derived
not from the Government's case, which he conceded was imperfectly formulated,
but from the dissenting judgment of Gonthier J in the Canadian *Sauvé* case.[44] For
Ngcobo J, the 'policy that is being pursued here is one of denouncing crime and sending a message to criminals that the rights citizens have are related to their duties and
obligations as citizens ... It requires no reasons to understand the need to pursue the
policy of denouncing crime'. Moreover, the means were appropriate: 'This limited
limitation of the right to vote sends an unmistakable message to the prisoner ... That
message is a necessary effort to fight crime.'[45]

ii. The Legislative Debate

The majority's insistence on a deliberative approach in *NICRO* is an excellent
demonstration of the arguments made above in favour of bounded deliberation.
Contrary to Waldron's assumption of a good faith effort on the part of the legislature to provide its own interpretation of the meaning of the right to vote, there
was little or no genuine discussion of the issue during the South African legislative
process.[46] The provisions on prisoners' voting rights in the Electoral Amendment
Bill, which was certified in September 2003, were clearly drafted hastily.[47] The
only semblance of discussion on the provision occurred in the Portfolio Committee
on Home Affairs, and here too the debate was perfunctory, particularly in light of
the fact that only three weeks remained to deal with the Bill. (The composition of
Portfolio Committees in the South African National Assembly, which are mandated
to shadow the work of national government departments, reflects the numerical
strengths of the parties represented in the Assembly.)

Of the six occasions on which the Committee considered the Bill,[48] there was some
mention of prisoners' voting rights in only two.[49] One concern was to ensure that
the proposed clause was constitutional, as required by the *August* decision, but the
Committee seemed to regard this as requiring that voting limitations be the same as
constitutional restrictions on individuals standing as candidates for the legislature.
Other points raised in support of the proposal were vague and general. This can
be seen in relation to the relevance of public perceptions of crime. Although it was
made clear that no study had been made of public perception, the Chair declared
that it was important not to be seen to be supporting murderers and rapists. More
deliberative were concerns about consistency, such as the contrast between white-
collar criminals, who might be sentenced to large fines but not imprisonment and
would therefore retain the vote, and those who were in prison because they were

[44] *Sauvé v Canada (Chief Electoral Officer)* (n 39).
[45] *Minister of Home Affairs v NICRO* (n 1) [147]: he did find it disproportionate that prisoners awaiting an appeal were disenfranchised.
[46] I am indebted to Chris McConnachie for his excellent research into the parliamentary debates on
this issue.
[47] Amendment Bill Gazetted (GG No 25422 of 1 September 2003).
[48] 2, 9, 10, 11 16 and 17 September 2003
[49] 9 and 17 September 2003.

too poor to pay a fine. In fact, the Bill was amended to exclude those in prison for failure to pay a fine. Some helpful deliberative input came from submissions to the Committee from outside organisations, the Human Rights Commission and the Southern African Catholic Bishops' Conference. However, the debate on these contributions was perfunctory at best, and the State Law Adviser confessed on two occasions that 'we have not been furnished with any reason for the limitation or why the limitation is important'.[50]

When the Bill reached the National Assembly, the debate focused on the issue of voters abroad being deprived of their rights. Prisoners were only referred to as a counterpoint to these arguments. Thus, it was stated as totally unacceptable that certain prisoners should be allowed to vote while law-abiding citizens who were temporarily overseas should be denied the right to vote.[51] The only speaker to object to the exclusion of prisoners was the AZAPO MP, but this was based on an interest-oriented rather than a deliberative position. As such, he protested that some prisoners should vote, including members of the Azanian People's Liberation Army, the constituency of his own party.

The issue of prisoners' voting rights has attracted almost no further attention since the *NICRO* case. Although the offending provision has not been formally removed from the Electoral Act 1998, a concerted drive was carried out to allow prisoners to register for the 2009 election, including a voter education campaign. As a result, over 17,000 prisoners in about 194 correctional facilities took the opportunity to register.[52]

B. The UK

Prisoners in the UK have been deprived of the right to vote by a succession of measures dating back at least as far as 1870. It was this general and automatic disenfranchisement of convicted prisoners that came before the ECtHR in *Hirst*.[53] Like the South African Court, the Grand Chamber emphasised that while the right to vote was foundational to democracies, it could be justifiably limited.[54] The question was therefore what would constitute an acceptable limitation. The Court held that Contracting States had a wide margin of appreciation in determining appropriate limitations. However, in this case, it had been exceeded. The prohibition 'applies automatically to all [convicted] prisoners, irrespective of the length of their sentence and irrespective of the nature or gravity of their offence and their individual circumstances. Such a general, automatic and indiscriminate restriction on a vitally important Convention right must be seen as falling outside any acceptable margin of appreciation, however wide that margin might be'.[55]

---

[50] 17 September 2003, paras 20 and 23.
[51] 26 September 2003.
[52] Electoral Commission for South Africa Annual Report 2009, 37.
[53] *Hirst v UK (No 2)* (n 2) [68]. See art 3, Protocol 1 ECHR.
[54] *Hirst v UK (No 2)* (n 2) [60].
[55] ibid [82].

Two main issues are addressed here. First, can the bounded deliberative model be discerned within the shifting boundaries of the ECtHR's doctrine of margin of appreciation, or does it slide into deference on the one hand or correctness on the other? Second, within the boundaries, how should the quality of deliberation be assessed?

i. Bounded Deliberation and the Margin of Appreciation

The debate about prisoners' voting rights takes place against a background of much deliberation at both the European and international levels. In this sense, the court operates within a framework of bounded deliberation. At the international level, it has been made clear that the period of suspension of the right to vote should be proportionate to the offence and the sentence.[56] At the European level, the guidelines are more specific. Suspension of political rights may only be made on grounds of mental incapacity or a criminal conviction for a serious offence and, even then, it must be provided for by law and subject to the proportionality principle. Moreover, withdrawal of political rights should only be carried out by express decision of a court of law.[57] The ECHR in *Hirst* expressly drew on these prior deliberative principles in setting its own framework for deliberation.[58] Voting was a right and not a privilege, and prisoners continued to enjoy all the Convention rights except for liberty.[59] Any conditions imposed 'must not thwart the free expression of the people in the choice of the legislature'.[60] In addition, any conditions must pursue a legitimate aim by proportionate means. Within these bounds, however, it was for each Contracting State to mould its own democratic vision.[61]

To what extent, then, can the margin of appreciation be seen as functioning to both facilitate and contain deliberation? The UK Government argued that the prohibition aimed to confer an additional punishment, to prevent crime and to enhance civic responsibility. Despite its rejection of the notion that imprisonment involves the forfeiture of rights beyond liberty, the Court accepted that the prohibition on prisoners' voting rights might be regarded as pursuing these aims, whatever doubts there may be as to the efficacy of achieving these aims through a bar on voting.[62] So far as the aims were concerned, then, the Court's use of the margin could be regarded as deferent rather than deliberative. In relation to the means, however, the Court was unequivocal. Such an indiscriminate restriction fell outside any acceptable margin of appreciation.[63] Nevertheless, it did not drift into a 'correctness'

---

[56] General Comment No 25 adopted by the Human Rights Committee under the International Covenant on Civil and Political Rights (ICCPR) 1996, para 14.

[57] European Commission for Democracy through Law (the Venice Commission) Code of Good Conduct on Elections 51st Opinion 190/2002 para 1.1(d)(i)—(v). See also more generally the European Prison Rules (Recommendation No R (87) 3 of the Committee of Ministers of the Council of Europe), para 64.

[58] *Hirst v UK (No 2)* (n 2) [71].

[59] ibid [69].

[60] ibid [62].

[61] ibid [60]–[61].

[62] ibid [74]–[75].

[63] ibid [82]

approach; indeed, it refused to accede to the UK Government's demand for guidance as to what restrictions, if any, would be compatible with the Convention. Instead, it reiterated that its function is to rule in principle on the compatibility of existing measures, leaving it to the state to choose the means to discharge its obligations.

This leaves open the question of how the Court would assess deliberation within the boundaries of the margin of appreciation. As a start, legislative debate is essential. The Court regarded it as of central significance that the impugned provision, section 3 of the Representation of the People Act 1983, had never been debated in Parliament. Instead, in 1983, Parliament 're-enacted without debate section 4 of the Representation of the People Act 1969, the substance of which dated back to the Forfeiture Act 1870 of the previous century, which in turn reflected earlier rules of law relating to the forfeiture of certain rights by a convicted "felon" (the so-called "civic death" of the times of King Edward III)'.[64] Since debate had not taken place, the Court was not called on to assess its deliberative quality. However, it did give some pointers. Like the South African Court, it stated emphatically that there was no place under the Convention system 'for automatic disenfranchisement based purely on what might offend public opinion'.[65] To this extent, it rejected interest-based reasoning. It was more equivocal than the South African Court on the role of evidence. The applicants argued that no evidence had been produced to substantiate the claims that deprivation of the vote furthered the articulated aims of preventing crime and enhancing civic responsibilities.[66] The Court did not react directly to this beyond stating that 'the principle of proportionality requires a discernible and sufficient link between the sanction and the conduct and circumstances of the individual concerned'. The only evidence it referred to was that criminal courts in England and Wales made no reference to disenfranchisement and that there was no direct link between the facts of any individual case and the removal of the right to vote.

It was this last point which led the Chamber, in later cases, to move in the direction of requiring a strong deliberative basis, at least at the level of individual sentencing decisions. Thus, in *Frodl*, the Court held that it was an essential element 'that the decision on disenfranchisement should be taken by a judge' and should be accompanied by specific reasoning 'explaining why in the circumstances of the specific case disenfranchisement was necessary'.[67] Similarly, in *Scoppola*,[68] the Chamber held that the Italian ban was in breach of the Convention, in part because of the lack 'of any examination by the trial court of the nature and gravity of the offence'. Likewise, other human rights adjudicators have taken up the baton and have insisted on proper reasoned support for a ban on prisoners' rights to vote.[69]

However, the sparks of a deliberative approach in *Hirst* appear to have been extinguished by the Grand Chamber in *Scoppola*. At one level, there are strong signs of bounded deliberation. Indeed, courts and adjudicative bodies are now

---

[64] ibid [22].
[65] ibid [70].
[66] ibid [44].
[67] *Frodl v Austria* (no 20201/04, 8 April 2010).
[68] *Scoppola v Italy (No 3)* (n 3) (Chamber) [48]–[49].
[69] See Human Rights Committee in *Yevdokimov and Rezanov v Russian Federation* (No 1410/2005, 21 March 2011) [7.5].

cross-referring to each other across a range of jurisdictions to derive the deliberative consensus from which to draw their background values. It was this consensus which the Court used in *Scoppola* to reject the UK's contention that *Hirst* should be overturned. Indeed, 'analysis of the relevant international and European documents and comparative-law information reveals the opposite trend, if anything—towards fewer restrictions on convicted prisoners' voting rights'.[70] To this extent, it reaffirmed the principle that an automatic and indiscriminate disenfranchisement irrespective of the length of sentence or gravity of the offence and their individual circumstances constituted a breach of the Convention.

Nevertheless, the Court upheld the Italian ban, which appeared more lenient in that it kicked in at three years rather than two, but was harsher in that it lasted for five years for those sentenced to three to five years, and for life to those sentenced to five years or more,[71] subject to rehabilitation.[72] Particularly disappointing was the rejection of the principle that each deprival of the vote should be justified deliberatively at the time of sentence.[73] Indeed, the Court required no justification at all as to why the prohibition on voting rights served the stated aims.[74] As the lone dissenting opinion argued, no evidence had been provided that either of the stated aims was fulfilled by a voting ban. He argued that the first aim, prevention of crime, can only be justified on an individual basis, ruling out all automatic disenfranchisement. The second, namely that disenfranchisement may contribute to the proper functioning of the democratic process, in his view, is even more difficult to assume without clear and full justification. Indeed, disenfranchisement may have the opposite effect.[75] Rather than arguing the ban was wrong as such, however, he dissented on the basis that no sufficient assessment of proportionality had been made either by the legislature or by the courts to justify the deprivation of voting rights.[76] The Court therefore moved ineluctably away from a deliberative towards a deferent approach.

ii. The Role of Legislative Debate

The emphasis attached to legislative debate in *Hirst* prompted a private members' motion endorsing the prohibition, which was extensively debated in Parliament.[77] The prohibition was upheld by an overwhelming majority. Arguably, therefore, the deliberative model is working at its best: the Court's decision triggered debate at the national level. Indeed in *Scoppola*,[78] the UK Government intervened to argue that *Hirst* should be overturned in the light of this debate.

---

[70] *Scoppola v Italy (No 3)* (n 3) (GC) [95].
[71] Section 2 of Decree 223/1967.
[72] Italian Criminal Code, arts 178 and 179.
[73] This is one example where, for particular crimes and if other parts of the sentence are adjusted, there might conceivably be a deliberative justification for an individualised deprivation of the vote for a specified time.
[74] *Scoppola v Italy (No 3)* (n 3) [90]–[91].
[75] ibid, Dissenting Opinion of Judge David Thór Björgvinsson.
[76] ibid.
[77] Hansard 10 February 2011, col 493.
[78] *Scoppola v Italy (No 3)* (Application No 126/05), heard by the Grand Chamber on 2 November 2011.

464   *Sandra Fredman*

However, the deliberative model demands more than a debate; it requires deliberative rather than interest-based coordination. Can the parliamentary debate be described as deliberative? Space precludes an analysis of the full 99 pages of the debate. Instead, the speech of MP David Davis, who proposed the motion, and the accompanying interventions, give a representative flavour of the debate.[79]

By far the most pervasive themes were dislike of prisoners and dislike of the ECHR in equal measure. Thus, Mr Davis referred to 'Hirst the axe-killer;' to the '28,000 people convicted of serious violent crimes, sex crimes and crimes against children [who] would be incorporated' and to the thousands of people who 'will have committed serious crimes from which we would recoil'.[80] Similarly, distaste of the ECtHR manifested in various and often contradictory assertions. ECtHR judges were criticised both because they belonged to 'unelected European institutions that wish to bypass our established laws'[81] and because they were 'politically appointed ... Indeed, some of them have no experience in court, even in their own countries, let alone ours'.[82] Moreover, they should not adjudicate on UK issues because they 'come from authoritarian regimes'.[83]

Although less emotive, much of the rest of Mr Davis' argument was based on assertion, with little reasoned or evidential proof. Frequently repeated in one form or the other was the statement that: 'When someone commits a crime that is sufficiently serious to put them in prison, they sacrifice many important rights: not only their liberty, of course, but their ... right to vote.'[84] This flies in the face of international consensus and therefore is necessarily outside of bounded deliberation. Another is the 'simple and straightforward' concept: 'If you break the law, you cannot make the law.'[85] This is clearly too wide, encompassing as it does many non-imprisonable offences. Mr Davis also argued that deprivation of the vote was justified because only very serious crimes attracted prison sentences. A challenge by an opposing MP, based on a specific example of a young woman given a sentence of imprisonment for stealing a pair of jeans, was rejected as a 'hard case which makes bad law',[86] but no specific evidence was given in either direction. Mr Davis further disputed the ECtHR's contention that the blanket ban was disproportionate, arguing that the proportionality lay in the fact that disenfranchisement only lasted the length of the sentence: 'If the sentence reflects the crime, the denial of the vote also reflects the crime.'[87] No evidence was brought to support the presumption that judges or magistrates factor disenfranchisement into their sentencing decisions; as we have seen, the ECtHR found the opposite.

A different approach was to assert that that there has never been any demand by prisoners themselves for the right to vote. According to one intervener, Bernard

[79] Hansard 10 February 2011, cols 493–96.
[80] ibid, cols 495–96.
[81] ibid, col 495.
[82] ibid.
[83] ibid, col 496.
[84] ibid, col 493.
[85] ibid.
[86] ibid, col 494.
[87] ibid, col 495.

Jenkin MP, it is only because 'lawyers got hold of it' that it became an issue. He cited his own experience as a member of the Prisons Task Force as proof.[88] It is hard to believe that all the cases brought to court were entirely on the instigation of lawyers. There have been a string of judicial review cases in the UK,[89] a further successful application to the ECtHR in 2012[90] and another 2,500 applications to the ECtHR, around 1,500 of which are awaiting a decision (ironically considerably aggravating the backlog in the court's caseload).[91] In any event, whether or not prisoners demand the right to vote is irrelevant to the question of whether they should be entitled to vote. Anyone can choose not to exercise their rights, but choosing not to exercise a right is quite different from being deprived of that right.

A third argument was that the right to vote would not be effective in cutting crime: 'Indeed, if there were an argument that giving prisoners the vote would cut recidivism, cut re-offending rates and help the public in that way, I would consider the matter, but giving prisoners the vote would not stop one crime in this country, and that is after all the point of the justice system in the first place.'[92] No evidence was produced for this argument. More importantly, this mistakes the purpose of the right, which is not (directly at least) to reduce crime. Other recognised rights, such as the right not to be subjected to inhuman or degrading treatment while in prison, are rightly not conditional on proof of their instrumental value in reducing crime. A fourth argument was that automatic disenfranchisement was a means of ensuring consistency: 'What the Court calls a blanket rule, I call uniform justice.'[93] Of course, consistency on its own is not sufficient to justify deprivation of the vote: a uniform rule giving all prisoners the right would be equally consistent.

A closer look at even this snippet of the debate reveals that it was conducted in highly emotive terms, with little supporting evidence or justification for many of the assertions made. Although the Court can be credited for stimulating a debate that would not otherwise have occurred, it is difficult to consider the parliamentary proceedings as having sufficiently deliberative credentials. While not all parliamentary debates should be required to be deliberative, this standard is crucial in a case in which an elected majority is attempting to use its legislative power to deprive a part of the population of its very ability to voice its concerns through the political process. It is in this situation that the Court can function as a legitimate forum to give appropriate voice to those potentially excluded.

It is not only the Court that can provide deliberative space. An alternative model of a potentially deliberative approach can be found in the proceedings of the Parliamentary Joint Committee, appointed by Parliament in May 2013 in order to scrutinise a draft Government bill setting out various options for introducing

---

[88] ibid, col 494.
[89] *Smith v Scott* 2007 SLT 137 (Registration Appeal Court (Scotland)); *Traynor and another v Secretary of State for Scotland* [2007] CSOH 78 (Court of Session); *R v Secretary of State, ex p Toner and Walsh* [2007] NIQB 18 (Queen's Bench (Northern Ireland)); *Chester v Secretary of State for Justice* [2009] EWHC 2923 (Admin) (High Court).
[90] *Greens and MT v UK* (2011) 53 EHRR 21 (ECtHR).
[91] ibid [111].
[92] Hansard 10 February 2011, col 494.
[93] ibid.

a limited right to vote for prisoners.[94] The Committee, which was a cross-party committee comprising six MPs and six peers, took oral and written evidence and made recommendations in a report to both Houses.[95] The proceedings before the Committee demonstrate well the power of a deliberative approach. It is not so much that Committee members had the opportunity to interrogate the experts who give evidence before them—it is that the opinions of Committee members needed to be justified in the light of that evidence. Where evidence was given by other members of Parliament, this worked in both directions.

This can be seen by examining the way the Joint Committee dealt with some of the points raised in the parliamentary debates.[96]As will be recalled, one of the main arguments put forward by David Davis MP in the parliamentary debate was that those who break the law should not make the law. The Joint Committee proceedings gave members the opportunity to require Mr Davis to justify his position. Lord Norton suggested to him that 'the problem with that, of course, is that not everyone who breaks the law goes to prison. Why does the cut-off apply the moment someone is sent to prison?' Mr Davis conceded: 'This is rough and ready and there is no theoretical basis for it, but it is an easy way to do it.' Pressing it further, Lord Norton asked: 'Logically under your argument, we could go even further back and say that they lose the franchise the moment they break the law?' David Davis' response was simply to reassert: 'It is very simple. A custodial sentence is imposed for a serious crime and that is enough to justify taking away the vote, full stop.' But the deliberative process does not allow such an assertion to go without further justification. For Lord Norton, the point was 'one of principle. You have said that if someone breaks the law, they should lose the right. You are now saying that some people who break the law should not lose the right. It is about the point at which it kicks in, and therefore there is no basic principle here'.[97]

Also central to Mr Davis' position in the parliamentary debates was the assertion that 'when someone commits a crime that is sufficiently serious to put them in prison, they sacrifice many important rights: not only their liberty, of course, but their ... right to vote'. Similarly, he stated: 'If the sentence reflects the crime, the denial of the vote also reflects the crime.'[98] This issue was dealt with in a far more deliberative manner in the Joint Committee. As one of the experts put it: 'We do not punish prisoners other than by taking their liberty away, so why should we take this particular right away as well? ... We do not say that people who have got life sentences have to have worse prison conditions than others ... We do not say that prisoners should not be able to get married and so on and so forth.'[99]

---

[94]   Committee of the House of Lords and House of Commons on the Draft Voting Eligibility (Prisoners) Bill, www.parliament.uk/business/committees/committees-a-z/joint-select/draft-voting-eligibility-prisoners-bill.

[95]   See *Report of the Joint Committee on the Draft Voting Eligibility (Prisoners) Bill*, Session 2013–14, HL Paper 103/HC 924 (18 December 2013).

[96]   Corrected Transcript of Oral Evidence Session 4 (QQ 69–92) Taken Before the Joint Committee on the Draft Voting Eligibility (Prisoners) Bill, Wednesday 10 July 2013

[97]   Corrected Transcript of Oral Evidence Session 5 (QQ 93–109) Taken Before the Joint Committee on the Draft Voting Eligibility (Prisoners) Bill, 23–24.

[98]   Hansard 10 February 2011, col 495.

[99]   Corrected Transcript of Oral Evidence Session 4 (QQ 69–92) Taken Before the Joint Committee on the Draft Voting Eligibility (Prisoners) Bill, Wednesday 10 July 2013, 13.

As will be recalled, a central theme in Mr Davis' speech was to assert that many of those who might be potentially enfranchised 'will have committed serious crimes from which we would recoil'. Put in less emotive terms, this argument is about a sense of 'fair play'. As the Chair of the Committee put it, 'the reason why public opinion does not want 60,000 or 70,000 prisoners to have the vote is ... based on the sense of fair play and a sense of distaste if people serving out their sentences were to be given the vote while in custody'.[100] This argument is particularly difficult to sustain under deliberative scrutiny. As one of the experts stated: 'Speaking to German colleagues about this question, they are somewhat bemused by the problem. When I have described to them what Parliament is worried about—there seems to be a sentiment that it is not fair play for prisoners to vote—they just looked puzzled. There are a lot of bad people in society and some of them are in prison. It is not a prison issue, it is an offence issue.'

Under a deliberative spotlight, therefore, this argument quickly turns into the more principled question of whether the punishment fits the crime. Here the debate canvassed different options: whether deprivation of the right to vote should be confined to specific offences, such as electoral fraud, or whether it should be an ancillary sentence applied by judges in individual sentencing cases, and so on. Illustrating the power of the deliberative approach, one of the members of the Committee, Lorely Burt, having listened to the discussion, stated: 'I am absolutely fascinated by this discussion. I am very taken with the argument put forward that, if you were focusing on punishment, it is very difficult to justify logically why you would take away the right to vote in the vast majority of circumstances.'

A further argument floated in the parliamentary debate was that the right to vote would not be effective in cutting crime. No evidence was given to support this. However, in the Select Committee, important alternatives were put forward. For example, part of the expert evidence was to point out that 'in German law, German prison legislation places a positive duty on all prison officials to encourage prisoners to vote. It is simply seen as part of the rehabilitative function of the prison'.[101]

It was also argued strenuously on the floor of the House that prisoners did not want to vote. Jack Straw reiterated this before the Committee. His evidence was anecdotal: 'In all the conversations I have had with prisoners never once, not once, did a prisoner of his own volition raise the issue of his loss of the right to vote.' The Joint Committee, however, had sought out evidence itself. As the Chair reported: 'As a Committee, last week we visited HMP High Down and HMP Downview. It was really unanimous among the prisoners we met that they should have the vote. All of them said that.'[102]

The proceedings of the Committee were nevertheless constrained. First, its terms of reference were confined to the three options presented to it: namely, restating the

[100] Corrected Transcript of Oral Evidence Session 4 (QQ 69–92) Taken Before the Joint Committee on the Draft Voting Eligibility (Prisoners) Bill, Wednesday 10 July 2013.
[101] Corrected Transcript of Oral Evidence Session 4 (QQ 69–92) Taken Before the Joint Committee on the Draft Voting Eligibility (Prisoners) Bill, Wednesday 10 July 2013, p 12.
[102] Corrected Transcript of Oral Evidence Session 4 (QQ 69–92) Taken Before the Joint Committee on the Draft Voting Eligibility (Prisoners) Bill, Wednesday 10 July 2013, 13.

blanket ban, applying the ban only to prisoners serving sentences of over four years, or only enfranchising prisoners with sentences of less than six months. Second, its power was one of recommendation only. At the same time, the Committee was frequently reminded that the margin of appreciation given by the ECtHR was dependent on a reasoned justification, which would not apply to a simple blanket ban. It is this which maintains the deliberative space.

CONCLUSION

The deliberative model discussed here leaves open a number of questions. Should deliberation take place within the legislature or is it sufficient for the Government to put forward deliberative justifications for the purposes of the litigation? Is an ex post facto deliberative justification sufficient? Conversely, is real deliberation stultified if it takes place expressly with a view to conforming with judicial prescriptions?

The examination of the prisoners' voting cases suggests some tentative answers. While a deliberative debate in the legislature is the ideal, debate in the legislature should not be seen as exhausting all possibilities for deliberation. Deliberation can also be facilitated by insisting that the state presents a fully deliberative argument in support of its position in court. Judgments by courts would need to take a similarly deliberative stance, particularly in relation to individual sentencing decisions. Nor should the spectre of the 'judge over your shoulder' be regarded as neutralising the value of legislative deliberation. If the court sets out the parameters for good decision-making, as in *NICRO*, rather than imposing its view, then bounded deliberation is facilitated, not negated.

This chapter has attempted to sketch out an approach to adjudication of human rights which reinforces rather than undermines democracy. The South African jurisprudence is a good illustration of such an approach. There remain some important questions which need further examination. However, once we move beyond a rigid dichotomy between courts and legislatures towards more collaborative approaches, the solutions are not nearly as intractable as might be thought.

23

Enhancing Parliaments' Role in the Protection and Realisation of Human Rights

MURRAY HUNT

T HE INTRODUCTION TO this volume sought to define the nature of the democratic deficit for the purposes of this collection and argued for a reorientation of the debate around the concept of a democratic culture of justification. Many of the contributions to this volume have considered the extent to which the concerns which animate the democratic critique of human rights can be accommodated within the existing legal and institutional framework for their protection, especially if it is reconceptualised in the way suggested in chapter one. This concluding chapter considers what scope there is to assuage the concerns which lie behind the democratic critique by increasing and enhancing the role of parliaments within the existing human rights framework, including the European Convention on Human Rights (ECHR) and the United Nations (UN) system, and how that might be done. It also suggests some priorities for future thinking, research and action in this area.

I. INCREASING THE ROLE OF PARLIAMENTS IN THE ECHR SYSTEM: SUBSIDIARITY, THE MARGIN OF APPRECIATION AND NATIONAL IMPLEMENTATION

The ECHR is widely recognised as probably the most successful regional system for the protection of human rights in the world, yet it is only relatively recently that the role of national parliaments in this system has become the subject of serious consideration. As Andrew Drzemczewski and Julia Lowis demonstrate in their contribution, this has largely been due to the work of the Parliamentary Assembly of the Council of Europe and in particular the Assembly's Committee on Legal Affairs and Human Rights, which has worked assiduously to draw attention generally to the importance of the parliamentary dimension of human rights protection and promotion and, specifically, to increase the role of national parliaments in relation to the ECHR.[1] The most significant initiatives have been designed to encourage

---

[1] Chapter 15 in this volume.

national parliaments to take a more active role in supervising the implementation of judgments of the European Court of Human Rights,[2] but they have also sought to encourage national parliaments to scrutinise systematically all draft legislation to ensure that it is compatible with the ECHR.

Progress towards recognising the importance of the role of national parliaments in the Convention system has been slow, however. It should never be forgotten that stewardship of the Convention system rests with an essentially intergovernmental process, and governments are not always the best champions of national parliaments, which can sometimes obstruct or slow down the implementation of a government's will. Until recently, parliaments have generally not been mentioned in the outcome documents of the high-level conferences held to consider the future of the ECHR system. In the Brighton Declaration, however, which marked the end of the UK's chairmanship of the Council of Europe in 2012, the Council of Europe States agreed to take a number of practical measures designed to achieve better national implementation of the Convention, including by providing national parliaments with information about the compatibility with the Convention of draft legislation, which should facilitate better parliamentary scrutiny of laws for ECHR compatibility.

The main impetus for this recent breakthrough in recognising the role of national parliaments has come from the growing realisation that better national implementation of the Convention is the key to its long-term survival. The urgent need to take effective action to reduce the huge backlog of cases awaiting determination by the European Court has led to renewed attention to ways of preventing so many cases from reaching it. At the same time, there has been growing concern in some states, including but not confined to the UK,[3] that the Court has exceeded its jurisdiction in some decisions, interfering excessively with the democratic decisions of national authorities.

The confluence of these concerns about effectiveness and legitimacy has brought about a renewed interest in the concepts of subsidiarity and the margin of appreciation, culminating in the agreement of an amending Protocol to the Convention which will add to its Preamble a reference to both.[4] The new recital at the end of the Preamble will affirm that the states, 'in accordance with the principle of subsidiarity, have the primary responsibility to secure the rights and freedoms defined in this Convention and the Protocols thereto, and that in doing so they enjoy a margin of appreciation, subject to the supervisory jurisdiction of the European Court of Human Rights'. However, the precise implications of this development for the role of national parliaments in the Convention system requires careful consideration, because experience shows that the concepts of subsidiarity and the margin of appreciation are apt to be misunderstood, especially in the heat forged by passionate arguments about democratic legitimacy. The place of parliaments in the European system of rights protection depends on a clear understanding of the key concept

---

[2] See Donald and Leach, ch 4 in this volume, and their forthcoming book, *Parliaments and the European Court of Human Rights* (Oxford, Oxford University Press, forthcoming 2015).
[3] See ibid for other examples of similar concerns in some other Council of Europe states.
[4] Protocol 15 ECHR, considered further below.

of subsidiarity in the particular context of the ECHR, and the subtle interrelationship between that concept, national implementation of the Convention and the Strasbourg Court's doctrine of the margin of appreciation.

In debates about the legitimacy of the European Court of Human Rights or particular decisions, it is not uncommon to hear both the principle of subsidiarity and the margin of appreciation invoked in support of arguments that the Court should not interfere with national laws or policies. For example, 'subsidiarity' is said to be about 'which cases get decided at home and which in Strasbourg'[5] or about identifying 'the things that really matter' that should be dealt with in Strasbourg, leaving everything else to national authorities.[6] The margin of appreciation is similarly described as being a doctrine about the Court leaving certain types of decision alone. The Policy Exchange paper 'Bringing Rights Back Home', for example, argues that the Court should extend 'an absolute margin of appreciation' to states on the prioritisation of rights which come into conflict, such as privacy and freedom of expression. In short, the principle of subsidiarity and the doctrine of the margin of appreciation are often invoked in the national sphere as if they were synonymous with the primacy of national law over Convention law: the Court is often asserted to be 'subsidiary' to national authorities, and the margin of appreciation is claimed for states as if it were a doctrine of exclusive competence.

Such arguments are premised on a conception of subsidiarity which is about competing supremacies and delimiting the boundaries of the respective spheres of the national authorities and the Court. They are based on a spatial metaphor, in which 'areas' are defined for national authorities on the one hand and the Court on the other, as if the purpose of the concepts is to police boundaries in a jurisdictional way, concerning respective remits. Subsidiarity in the ECHR is a quite different creature, reflecting the particular nature of the supranational machinery, flowing from the obligation in Article 1 of the Convention to secure the Convention rights. In other words, it is not a 'hands-off' doctrine, but imposes an obligation on the national authorities to do something to implement the Convention rights. The role of the Court itself is defined in a way which reflects this premise.[7] Significantly, the obligation in Article 1 is on the state: all branches, not just the courts, and therefore including parliament. The Convention system is therefore subsidiary in the sense that primary responsibility for protecting human rights lies with the states at the national level. The principle of subsidiarity therefore imposes a duty on states to make sure that the Convention has been properly implemented in their national law.[8]

---

[5] Rt Hon Michael Howard MP, former Conservative Home Secretary, 'Parliament Must Redefine Human Rights' *Daily Telegraph* (23 November 2011)

[6] David Cameron, Speech on the European Court of Human Rights' (25 January 2012), www.gov.uk/government/speeches/speech-on-the-european-court-of-human-rights.

[7] See art 19 ECHR, where the Court's role is defined as being 'to ensure the observance of the engagements undertaken by' the signatory states.

[8] As the President of the Court, Mr Dean Spielmann explains, the Convention regime is subsidiary to the national systems safeguarding human rights, not to the political will or policy of the national authorities: 'Allowing the Right Margin: the European Court of Human Rights and the National Margin of Appreciation Doctrine: Waiver or Subsidiarity of European Review?', Speech to Max Planck Institute for Comparative Public Law and International Law, Heidelberg, 13 December 2013. See also 'Whither the Margin of Appreciation?', Current Legal Problems Lecture, UCL, 20 March 2014.

The margin of appreciation doctrine must be understood in the light of this underlying conception of subsidiarity. The Attorney-General, intervening for the UK in the prisoner voting case of *Scoppola v Italy*, argued that the question of whether prisoners should be allowed to vote:

[I]s, and should be, a political question, by which I mean a question for democratically elected representatives to resolve, against the background of the circumstances and political culture of their own particular state. The view that sensitive issues of social policy of this kind should be decided by national Parliaments is, we say, entirely *consistent* with the jurisprudence of the Court. It is reflected in the Court's doctrine of the margin of appreciation.[9]

However, a state's margin of appreciation is not an area of decision-making within which states can adopt whatever laws or policies they like, untouched by the Convention. It cannot be invoked to argue that the Court does not have the power even to enter into the adjudication of an issue which is deemed to be within the remit of the national authorities. The margin of appreciation, properly understood, is the degree of deference which states are entitled to expect from the Court to the extent that they can demonstrate that the particular law, policy or judgment being challenged is the product of a national process which operates in such a way as to ensure the effective protection of Convention rights. It is, in short, a 'due deference' doctrine. As in the rest of modern public law, deference from the European Court of Human Rights cannot be expected as an entitlement derived from a mere assertion of national sovereignty, but can be *earned* by states demonstrating that the national law under challenge was the product of a deliberative process which conscientiously engaged with all the relevant human rights issues and reached a decision which, in substance, is defensible in a democracy. And a pre-requisite to earning that respect is that there has been proper democratic deliberation about the issue in parliament.

A number of cases show what happens when there is no consideration by either the Government or Parliament of the proportionality of an interference with Convention rights.[10] That lack of consideration makes it more difficult for the Government to invoke the margin of appreciation. But it is now becoming increasingly apparent in the Court's case law that this works both ways, so that a law is more likely to be found to be within the state's margin of appreciation if it is demonstrated to the Court's satisfaction that there has been such consideration of proportionality by the Government and Parliament.[11]

The relevance of parliamentary scrutiny at the national level to the Court's proportionality assessment can be demonstrated by comparing two challenges to limitations on the right to vote in the UK. In the well-known prisoner voting case *Hirst v UK*, the Government invoked the margin of appreciation to defend the ban

---

[9] See the argument of the Attorney-General to the Grand Chamber in *Scoppola v Italy (No 3)* [2011] ECHR 2417. See also D Grieve, 'European Convention on Human Rights: Current Challenges' (Lincoln's Inn, London 24 October 2011), https://www.gov.uk/government/speeches/european-convention-on-human-rights-current-challenges.

[10] *Hirst v UK (No 2)* (2005) 42 EHRR 849 and *Dickson v UK* (2007) 46 EHRR 927; and see also *Alajos Kiss v Hungary* (Application No 38832/06) 10 May 2010, [41].

[11] See Lazarus and Simonsen, ch 19 in this volume, for consideration of the implications of these cases for judicial consideration of the quality of democratic deliberation.

on prisoner voting, arguing that where Parliament has considered the matter and there is no clear international consensus, it must be within the range of possible approaches to remove the right to vote from any person whose conduct was so serious as to merit imprisonment. However, the Court did not consider that much weight should be attached to the position adopted by the legislature as 'there is no evidence that Parliament has ever sought to weight the competing interests or to assess the proportionality of a blanket ban … it cannot be said that there was any substantive debate by members of the legislature on the continued justification in light of modern-day penal policy and of current human rights standards for maintaining such a general restriction on the rights of prisoners to vote'.[12]

In *Shindler v UK*, on the other hand, the question of restrictions on the right of British citizens to vote in parliamentary elections when they are resident overseas had been extensively considered and debated in Parliament in recent years before the current law was arrived at.[13] The Court, explaining its general approach to deciding whether restrictions on the right to vote are justified, said that 'whether the impugned measure has been subjected to parliamentary scrutiny is also relevant, albeit not necessarily decisive, to the Court's proportionality assessment'.[14] In reaching its conclusion that the UK rule permitting British citizens to continue to vote in parliamentary elections for 15 years after they had ceased to be resident struck a fair balance between the competing interests, the Court noted that there was 'extensive evidence … to demonstrate that Parliament has sought to weigh the competing interests and to assess the proportionality of the fifteen year rule'. The question of non-residents' voting rights had been examined and reported on by parliamentary select committees and debated in Parliament on several occasions in recent years, and the extent of this parliamentary consideration clearly influenced the Court's conclusion that the restriction on the right to vote was within the margin of appreciation available to the domestic legislature in regulating parliamentary elections. Significantly, however, the Court in *Shindler* made clear that the mere fact that Parliament has debated an issue cannot be determinative of the proportionality question:

[T]his is not to say that because a legislature debates, possibly even repeatedly, an issue and reaches a particular conclusion thereon, that conclusion is necessarily Convention compliant. It simply means that that review is taken into consideration by the Court for the purpose of deciding whether a fair balance has been struck between competing interests.[15]

[12] *Hirst v UK (No 2)* [2005] ECHR 681 [78]–[79].
[13] *Shindler v UK* (Application No 19840/09) (7 May 2013).
[14] ibid [102].
[15] ibid [117]. See also, to similar effect, *Animal Defenders International v UK* (Application No 48876/08) (22 April 2013) [35]–[55], [106]–[111] and [116], and the Concurring Opinion of Judge Bratza at [12]; *SH v Austria* (2011) 52 EHRR 6; *Friend v UK* (2010) 50 EHRR SE6; *RMT v UK* (especially the reference at [86] to 'in particular the democratically elected parliaments' when explaining the wide margin of appreciation that the Court usually affords to national authorities when deciding what is in the public interest on social and economic grounds).

Protocol 15, when it comes into force,[16] will provide an opportunity to embed these recent development in the Court's case law[17] into the Registry and Court's general practices, in order to signal a real change of approach by the Court in response to the calls to pay more attention to national parliaments. In cases where a challenge is made to the Convention compatibility of a law passed by parliament or pursuant to a law passed by parliament, for example, the Registry could routinely ask the Government to provide it with all relevant evidence of parliamentary consideration of the human rights compatibility of the law in question. Where relevant, the Court in its judgments could more regularly include in the 'Relevant domestic law and practice' section of its judgments a section summarising the relevant parliamentary consideration of the human rights issues, as well as a more explicit explanation of the role played by that parliamentary consideration (or lack of it) in the Court's judgment as to whether the law is within the state's margin of appreciation.

National actors would then be clearer that the Court is more prepared to accord due respect to national decision-makers on difficult Convention balancing questions where those decision-makers can demonstrate a serious and conscientious engagement with the Convention issues. By the same token, it would be clearer that such respect is not warranted where such engagement cannot be demonstrated. In other words, over time, it will become much clearer that the onus is on the Government to demonstrate such national engagement if it wants to invoke the margin of appreciation. This would give Member States more of an incentive to develop proper systems of national implementation such as proper ECHR impact assessment in policy-making, reasoned statements of compatibility accompanying legislation, parliamentary human rights committees or other parliamentary mechanisms for systematic scrutiny of the Government's explanations, and robust systems for the swift and full implementation of judgments by involving parliaments closely in the scrutiny of remedial legislation. In the long run, the Court will be seen to be paying closer attention to parliaments, and it will become clearer to national governments that laws and policies have a greater chance of withstanding scrutiny in the European Court of Human Rights where a state has proper processes in place in its legislature to test properly the compatibility of laws and policies with the ECHR.

Another so far little explored way of increasing the involvement of national parliaments in the ECHR system would be for each of the 47 Judges of the Court to appear before the relevant committee of their national parliament. In 2012, the President of the European Court of Human Rights, Sir Nicolas Bratza, and the

---

[16] The UK signed the Protocol on the day it was opened for signature (24 June 2013), and laid it before Parliament, with a view to its ratification, on 28 October 2014. The JCHR welcomed the amendment to the Preamble of the ECHR as an important signifier of a new emphasis on the primary responsibility of the Member States to secure the rights and freedoms set out in the Convention and looked to the Court to ensure that the amendment leads to even closer attention being paid to the reasoned assessment of Convention compatibility by the national authorities: *Protocol 15 to the European Convention on Human Rights*, Fourth Report of Session 2014–15, HL Paper 71/HC 837, paras 3.17–3.19.

[17] As Robert Spano, a judge of the European Court of Human Rights, has suggested, the Court in these recent cases has demonstrated its willingness to defer to the reasoned and thoughtful assessment by national authorities of their Convention obligations, and so begun to develop a more 'qualitative, democracy-enhancing' approach to its supervisory function: see 'Universality or Diversity of Human Rights? Strasbourg in the Age of Subsidiarity' (2014) *Human Rights Law Review* 1.

Registrar, Erik Freiberg, appeared before the Joint Committee on Human Rights (JCHR) of the UK Parliament.[18] This was the first time that the President of the Court, and possibly any serving member of the Court, had appeared at a hearing before a committee of a national parliament. The President indicated that he hoped that other national judges would follow his example. For serving judges of the European Court of Human Rights to appear before their national parliaments clearly raises some sensitive issues about the purpose of such appearances, and there would need to be absolute clarity that the purpose is not to hold the national judge to account for his or her judicial decisions as that would undermine the independence of the Court's judges. However, it should be possible to draw up a memorandum of understanding between the Court and the national parliaments which would make explicit the purpose of such appearances and should ensure that the considerable benefits of such appearances are secured whilst avoiding the worst pitfalls and, above all, any compromise of the judges' independence, whether actual or perceived. The Lord Chief Justice of England and Wales appears annually before the House of Lords Constitution Committee, and the experience gained in these sessions could help to inform any memorandum of understanding between the Court and national parliaments.

II. INCREASING THE ROLE OF PARLIAMENTS IN THE UN HUMAN RIGHTS SYSTEM

The renewed focus on national implementation of the ECHR and in particular on the role of parliaments as key agents of such implementation is a regional manifestation of a wider trend in the international system for the protection of human rights. In recent years, there has been growing concern about the so-called 'implementation gap' which afflicts international human rights law:[19] a sense that the priority is no longer standard-setting, devising adequate mechanisms for monitoring states' performance against those standards, or gathering the necessary evidence and information, but finding ways to ensure that states give effect to those norms at the national level. There is now no shortage of detailed norms and standards on human rights which states have committed themselves in international law to observe. There are well-developed monitoring mechanisms which keep states' compliance with those norms under constant review and, with the advent of the Universal Periodic Review (UPR) by the Human Rights Council, there is now a much higher-profile review mechanism to which States attach much more political significance. Nor, as a result of the work of those monitoring mechanisms, is there a lack of reliable and detailed

---

[18] Joint Committee on Human Rights, 'Uncorrected Transcript of Oral Evidence: Human Rights Judgments' (13 March 2012, HC 873-iii), http://www.parliament.uk/documents/joint-committees/human-rights/JCHR_Transcript_13_March_2012_UNCORRECTED.pdf.

[19] See, eg, *From Judgment to Justice: Implementing International and Regional Human Rights Decisions* (Open Society Justice Initiative, 2010), drawing attention to the 'implementation crisis' afflicting the regional and international system for the protection and promotion of human rights due to serious shortcomings in the systems, both national and international, for ensuring that human rights decisions are implemented by states.

information about precisely how States are failing to live up to these commitments. The real challenge lies in finding the most effective levers in the national system for securing the necessary changes in law, policy or practice which would give practical effect to these commitments.

The UN and its human rights machinery has therefore been looking for partners in the national systems which can help overcome the pressing problem of implementation. For many years, these efforts were focused on the development of 'national human rights institutions' (NHRIs), independent bodies with a special role in the promotion and protection of human rights at the national level. Thanks to the concerted efforts of the Office of the High Commissioner for Human Rights (OHCHR), considerable progress has been made in the establishment of NHRIs, and there has long been an internationally agreed set of principles (the Paris Principles), which set out certain minimum requirements that the competence and responsibilities of NHRIs are expected to meet in order to gain recognition by the UN as NHRIs.[20]

It is only very recently, however, that the UN bodies have begun to think about how to make more of the potential that national parliaments have to offer, not only as engines for effective national implementation, but as the legitimators of norms which are often the product of processes perceived to lack democratic credentials. As the limitations of national human rights institutions have gradually become apparent, so the possibilities offered by parliaments have begun to be explored by the UN machinery. Ingeborg Schwarz's chapter describes the history of efforts by the Inter-Parliamentary Union (IPU)[21] to increase the role of parliaments in relation to human rights and to encourage greater interaction and cooperation between UN processes, national parliaments and the IPU itself.[22] As she observes, there was for many years very little involvement of parliaments or parliamentarians in the international human rights machinery, and parliamentarians often knew little about the internationally legally binding human rights obligations that their countries had voluntarily undertaken, or the mechanisms that exist to monitor their implementation. With the exception of the CEDAW Committee, which has been unusually far-sighted in its engagement with national parliaments, the UN treaty bodies did little to explore the potential for national parliaments to contribute to their monitoring. The UPR process treated parliaments as just another 'stakeholder', on a par with non-governmental organisations (NGOs) and NHRIs, with no particular role specified in any of the resolutions of the Human Rights Council establishing the process.[23] An evaluation by the IPU of the first UPR cycle, which took place between 2008 and 2011, found 'the almost complete absence of parliamentary participation'.[24]

---

[20] *Principles relating to the Status of National Institutions for the Promotion and Protection of Human Rights (the Paris Principles)*, adopted by General Assembly Resolution 48/134 of 20 December 1993.

[21] The IPU is the global organisation of parliaments, with a membership of 164 national parliaments.

[22] Schwarz, ch 16 in this volume.

[23] See, eg, *The Role of Parliaments in the Universal Periodic Review* (Geneva, Friedrich Ebert Stiftung Foundation, April 2009) http://library.fes.de/pdf-files/bueros/genf/06264.pdf.

[24] *Strengthening the Role of Parliamentarians in the Implementation of Universal Periodic Review Recommendations: Conclusions* (outcome document of a workshop organised jointly by the IPU and the Commonwealth Secretariat in Geneva, November 2012).

That has certainly been true to date of the UK's first and second UPRs by the Human Rights Council, which took place in 2008 and 2012 respectively. The first review in 2008 passed Parliament by entirely. There is no record of any parliamentary consideration of the UK's review or its outcome, and even Parliament's human rights committee, the JCHR, did not engage with the process. The Government kept the JCHR closely informed about the UK's second review, in 2012, sending it copies of the UK's national report to the Human Rights Council after it had been submitted to the UN, of the Working Group's Report (including the recommendations made to the UK) and of the UK's response to the UPR recommendations, again after it had been presented to the Human Rights Council. Although Parliament's human rights committee was kept closely informed in this way and was proactively notified by the Government about the timetable of the review and the Government's preparations, there was a notable difference of approach towards Parliament compared to the devolved administrations, national human rights institutions and civil society organisations. The latter were actively involved in and consulted by the Government at all stages of the process, including in the drawing up of the UK's national report, considering how to respond to the recommendations and monitoring their implementation. They were also actively involved in the conduct of the actual review itself at hearings in Geneva. It was left to Parliament, however, to initiate any more active participation in the process, and in the absence of such initiative, there was no parliamentary consideration of or debate about the national report, the Council's recommendations or the Government's response to them, and no parliamentary involvement in the review itself conducted by the Human Rights Council. Apart from a couple of written parliamentary questions in April and May 2012 about who would be representing the Government at the review and what issues the Government was proposing to raise,[25] and the JCHR's brief consideration of the UK's national report and the Working Group's recommendations, there was no other parliamentary activity concerning the UK's second periodic review by the Human Rights Council.

However, the efforts of the IPU, the OHCHR and others to increase the role of parliaments in UN processes in general and in relation to human rights in particular have recently begun to bear fruit. In December 2010, the UN General Assembly decided to take a more systematic approach to integrating a parliamentary contribution to major UN deliberative processes and to its review of states' international commitments.[26] In May 2012, in what the UN Secretary-General described as a signal of 'a new beginning to this evolving partnership',[27] the UN General Assembly adopted a resolution which addressed the role of parliaments at the UN for the first time.[28] The resolution recognises the unique role of national parliaments in relation

---

[25] HC Deb 25 April 2012, col 937W and HC Deb 1 May 2012, cols 1445–46W. The Government simply replied that the UK had submitted its national report to the Human Rights Council on 5 March 2012 and held consultation events with civil society organisations before doing so.

[26] A/65/123 (13 December 2010).

[27] A/68/827, Report of the Secretary-General, *Interaction between the United Nations, National Parliaments and the Inter-Parliamentary Union* (2 April 2014).

[28] GA Res 66/261, *Interaction between the United Nations, National Parliaments and the Inter-Parliamentary Union* (29 May 2012). See also GA Res 65/123 (13 December 2010).

to the work of the UN in various fields, including the rule of law and human rights, and encourages the IPU to provide a parliamentary contribution to the UN human rights treaty body system and to the Human Rights Council, building on the practice developed in relation to the Convention on the Elimination of all Forms of Discrimination against Women (CEDAW).

There have followed the beginnings of some attempts to strengthen the role of parliamentarians in the UPR process. A number of recommendations emerged from an international workshop on the subject organised by the IPU and the Commonwealth Secretariat, including the need for parliaments to develop mechanisms for enhancing their contribution to the preparation of the national report to the Human Rights Council, to be represented during the presentation of the national report and its examination by the Human Rights Council, and, above all, to be closely involved in monitoring the implementation of the recommendations which come out of the review.[29] In the UK, the JCHR has sought to follow up recommendations of the last UPR, with a view to there being more parliamentary involvement in the UK's Mid-Term Report to the Human Rights Council which was submitted to the UN in August 2014.

In 2013 the Human Rights Council itself held its first discussion of the contribution of parliaments to the work of the Council and its periodic review.[30] The objectives of the discussion in the Human Rights Council included the promotion of a better understanding of the role of national parliaments in the promotion and protection of human rights, enhanced awareness and understanding of the work and functioning of the Human Rights Council in national parliaments, and an exploration of practical ways of bringing about an increased parliamentary contribution to the work of the Human Rights Council, especially its UPR and Special Procedures. The discussion was intended to be two-way, considering how parliaments can provide assistance to the Human Rights Council and how the Council in turn can provide input into the work of parliaments and the IPU. The discussion revealed unanimity about the desirability of increasing the role of parliaments in the promotion and protection of human rights, but little in the way of concrete detail as to how that universally desired aim could be achieved. The discussion demonstrates the urgent need for some better way of sharing best practices between national parliaments.[31] In the meantime, recommendations for action are steadily proliferating. The Open Society Justice Initiative, in its recent report on structures and strategies for implementing international human rights decisions, rightly recognises that the national implementation of international human rights norms, including decisions of courts and recommendations of treaty bodies, is a complex political process in which the important role of parliaments has been historically overlooked, and it makes a number of detailed recommendations aimed at strengthening that role.[32]

---

[29] *Strengthening the Role of Parliamentarians in the Implementation of UPR Recommendations* (n 22).

[30] Panel on the contribution of parliaments to the work of the Human Rights Council and its Universal Periodic Review, 29 May 2013.

[31] See the discussion below of the scope for internationally agreed Principles and Guidelines on the Role of Parliaments in Promoting and Protecting the Rule of Law and Human Rights.

[32] *From Rights to Remedies: Structures and Strategies for Implementing International Human Rights Decisions* (Open Society Justice Initiative, 2013) 18–19 and ch III.

In May 2014 the UN General Assembly adopted a further resolution recognising the need for greater interaction between the UN and national parliaments and calling for stronger cooperation between the two.[33] It is clear from the supporting documentation and the speeches in the Assembly that the motivation behind these initiatives at the international level include not only instrumental concerns about effectiveness, but democratic concerns about the legitimacy of the international system for the protection of human rights. The UN Secretary-General, for example, said not only that it was clear today that it is only by involving other actors such as national parliaments, as well as governments, that the UN can hope to achieve its goals, but that mobilising parliaments at the national level promotes greater transparency, accountability and participation at the global level, which 'goes a long way to establishing a more democratic international order'.[34] Indeed, the resolution itself refers to the need to 'continue efforts to bridge the democracy gap in international relations'. Enhancing the role played by national parliaments serves the goal of effective implementation, because it is Parliament that adopts the necessary legislation to take international commitments forward, adopts the budget to provide the resources to make it possible and hold governments to account for their commitments at the UN. But it also serves the goal of legitimation, because the representative function of parliaments means they are best placed to ensure that what is decided at the UN makes sense to citizens at large, and reflects their views and aspirations. The aim is to make sure that parliaments are fully aware of what is taking place at the UN 'before the deal is sealed' and that they debate what is being proposed at the UN level, both amongst themselves and with the government, 'so that, at the end of the day, there is full national ownership of the process'.[35]

While some progress has begun to be made towards greater parliamentary involvement in the UPR process and the work of the treaty-monitoring bodies, there is a great deal more to do as far as the UN's Special Procedures are concerned. The work of the UN's Special Rapporteurs is not well known or understood in national parliaments and there appear to be few examples of them engaging directly with parliaments or parliamentarians. The general unfamiliarity of parliamentarians with the work of the UN's Special Procedures or their place in the international human rights machinery contributes to a political climate in which their legitimacy is sometimes openly called into question.[36] In an attempt to raise their profile and increase understanding of their work, the JCHR in the UK Parliament has recently taken evidence from two UN Special Rapporteurs at public hearings, the Special Rapporteur on promoting and protecting human rights while countering terrorism[37] in connection with the Committee's ongoing work on counter-terrorism and human

[33] A/RES/68/272, *Interaction between the United Nations, National Parliaments and the Inter-Parliamentary Union* (19 May 2014).
[34] Report of the Secretary-General (n 27) paras 1–5.
[35] Statement by the President of the IPU, Hon Abdelwahad Radi, to the General Assembly, 19 May 2014 http://www.ipu.org/Un-e/sp-unga190514.pdf.
[36] See, eg, the recent visits to the UK by the UN Special Rapporteurs on Housing and on Violence against Women and Girls.
[37] Ben Emmerson QC (26 March 2014) http://www.parliament.uk/documents/joint-committees/human-rights/JCHR_HC_1202_TRANSCRIPT_Anderson_Emmerson_260314.pdf.

rights, and the Special Rapporteur on violence against women[38] at the outset of the Committee's inquiry into that subject.

III. FUTURE PRIORITIES

From the themes which are explored in this collection, there emerge a number of priority areas for future thinking, research and action concerning parliaments and human rights. One priority must be for more work to be done at the national level in those jurisdictions where legislative human rights review has taken root in order to attempt to assess its strengths and weaknesses.[39] In the UK, it would be a small start in this direction, for example, if an assessment could be made of the quality of parliamentary debate on human rights in the 2010–15 Parliament and a comparison made with the quality of debate in the 2001–05 and 2005–10 Parliaments, applying the methodology developed in the editors' 2012 Arts and Humanities Research Council project. Another very worthwhile research project would be to apply or adapt the methodology already developed by the UCL project on select committee effectiveness[40] to the JCHR in order to arrive at some sort of assessment of the take-up of the recommendations it makes in its reports, including a comprehensive analysis of the fate of amendments to bills recommended by the JCHR.

More useful still would be an in-depth and theoretically informed account of the various ways in which Parliament has sought to increase its role in relation to human rights since the passage of the Human Rights Act in 1998, looking in detail at particular case studies of legislation, responses to court judgments about human rights, and particular human rights treaties with a view to identifying good and bad examples of each area of work and coming up with some feasible recommendations for improving Parliament's engagement with human rights. A key issue to be addressed by such a study would be whether there is a need to mainstream human rights in Parliament rather than leaving them to the work of a single specialised committee and, if so, how best to integrate the rule of law and human rights into the work of Parliament across the board. Parliament does not have the resources to conduct such research projects itself and is dependent on members of the academy to take a sufficient interest, and on the research-funding bodies to be satisfied that such research has a sufficiently significant impact on the development of public policy to warrant the investment of increasingly scarce public funds.

Equally urgent is the need for more thinking and research about the role of parliaments in relation to the many positive obligations that human rights law imposes on states. This is an area that remains both under-theorised and under-developed in practice. Even in the contributions to this collection, there is a notable concentration

---

[38] Rashida Manjoo (2 April 2014) http://data.parliament.uk/writtenevidence/committeeevidence.svc/evidencedocument/human-rights-committee/violence-against-women-and-girls/oral/9574.html.

[39] For example, in the Commonwealth, New Zealand, Australia and the UK and, more recently, some of the African Commonwealth countries such as Uganda; in Europe, Germany, the Netherlands, Poland, Ukraine and Romania.

[40] M Russell and M Benton, 'Selective Influence: The Policy Impact of House of Commons Select Committees' (Constitution Unit, 2011).

of attention on the role of parliaments in constraining governments and enforcing compliance with the restraints imposed by human rights law, and a corresponding neglect of the role of parliaments in taking positive steps to fulfil or realise human rights, both by legislating to enhance human rights and by holding the government to account for their record of implementing such laws. There are many examples of the JCHR in the UK Parliament encouraging Parliament to fulfil this important role, but these are little discussed in the literature. There may be some interesting lessons to be learnt from some of the devolved jurisdictions in this respect. In Wales, for example, less partisan disagreement about human rights and a stronger consensus about the existing institutional arrangements for their protection[41] appears to have led to the Welsh Assembly focusing on the promotion of certain human rights where the relevant substantive areas of law making are within the Assembly's competence, and to the adoption of an explicitly human rights-based approach to policy rather than a focus on negative compliance. This has led, for example, to a groundbreaking measure imposing a duty on the Welsh Ministers to have due regard to the require-ments of the United Nations Convention on the Rights of the Child (UNCRC) when exercising any of their functions.[42]

Another priority should be to increase the amount of comparative work being undertaken in this area. There is a lot of interesting academic work already being done on these questions, in a number of jurisdictions and across a number of dif-ferent disciplines, but there is surely scope to bring some of these projects together across both disciplinary and international boundaries. A more ambitious research project would be to establish an international team of researchers to undertake comparative research on the existing capacity of parliaments worldwide, building on the surveys already undertaken by the IPU,[43] to arrive at a reliable picture of the current state of development of legislative rights review globally and to coordinate national teams applying a common research methodology in those states where leg-islative rights review is well established, to identify examples of good practice from across the world, and to begin to change the terms of the debate globally about the respective roles of courts and parliaments in relation to human rights.

The product of any future research should be directed at achieving a step-change in parliamentary involvement in human rights across the world. As is apparent from Part IV of this collection, a variety of bodies, including the IPU, the Office of the High Commissioner for Human Rights, the UN Development Programme, the Parliamentary Assembly of the Council of Europe and the Westminster Foundation for Democracy,[44] continue to be engaged in a number of projects designed to build the capacity of parliaments around the world to hold their governments to their human rights commitments. Many of these admirable initiatives focus on training

[41] As Sherlock points out, the Commission on a Bill of Rights found much less public antipathy or hostility towards the European Court of Human Rights and the ECHR in Wales than in England.

[42] Rights of Children and Young Persons (Wales) Measure 2011.

[43] Since the early 1990s, the IPU has been compiling information on the role, structure, function-ing and contact details of parliamentary human rights committees, published until 2004 in its *World Directory of Parliamentary Human Rights Bodies,* and now accessible online as an integral part of the IPU's PARLINE database: www.ipu.org/parline-e/Instance-hr.asp.

[44] See Kunnath and Patrick, ch 17 in this volume.

of both members and parliamentary staff, and they have brought into being some excellent training materials.[45] Human rights training of parliamentarians, however, requires a political commitment from both national governments and parliaments, which is not always forthcoming. Busy parliamentarians have many demands on their time that leave very little opportunities for training. Elections provide a periodic opportunity, since all new members must receive some form of induction, but there is much else to compete for their attention at what is always a very busy time for a newly elected member of parliament.

There are many others practical ways of enhancing the role of national parliaments which are worth considering. There already exists a small, informal network of relevant lawyers who advise national or sub-national parliaments on rule of law and human rights issues, and of academic lawyers with an interest in the same, but there may be scope for a more formal network of such lawyers, properly resourced to facilitate the exchange of relevant information and to provide a forum for sharing best practice. There may also be scope for the international human rights machinery to appoint dedicated rapporteurs whose sole task it is to increase meaningful parliamentary involvement in human rights issues. There could be, for example, a UN Special Rapporteur on increasing the role of parliaments in relation to human rights, and regional equivalents, with specific mandates to assist national parliaments to find ways of mainstreaming international and regional human rights standards into the full range of their activities, and with a clear responsibility for demonstrating improvements.

Perhaps the most effective way to bring about a step-change, however, would be to develop an internationally agreed set of principles and guidelines on the role of parliaments in the protection and realisation of the rule of law and human rights. There is a striking gap here which is testament to how recently the international human rights machinery has begun to appreciate the importance of the role of parliaments in the protection and realisation of human rights and the rule of law. Internationally agreed principles relating to the Status of National Human Rights Institutions (hereinafter 'the Paris Principles') have existed since 1991.[46] In February 2012, a set of principles on the Relationship between National Human Rights Institutions and Parliaments (hereinafter 'the Belgrade Principles') were also agreed. To date, however, there is no internationally agreed set of principles and guidelines on the role of parliaments in the protection and realisation of the rule of law and human rights, despite the steadily growing interest in the subject, as documented in this volume and reflected in the large number of texts and materials which have been generated on the subject since 1993.[47] Notwithstanding the increasing amount

---

[45] Eg, the series of very helpful and informative IPU Handbooks on human rights for parliamentarians, such as *Human Rights—Handbook for Parliamentarians* (2005) and the Westminster Consortium's excellent *Human Rights and Parliament: Handbook for Members and Staff* (2011).

[46] See UN Fact Sheet No 19, *National Institutions for the Promotion and Protection of Human Rights* for an account of the emergence of national human rights institutions in the last few decades in response to the growing recognition that the problem of effective implementation of human rights at the national level calls for the establishment of national infrastructures for their protection and promotion.

[47] A selection of the most important of these materials is collected in the Annex to the Draft Principles and Guidelines in the Appendix to this volume.

of interest and discussion, and the steadily accumulating experience of legislative rights review in some jurisdictions, there has been no attempt to date to distil from those discussions and from best practice around the world a set of principles or guidelines that might assist parliaments everywhere to devise the appropriate structures, mechanisms and practices which are required in order for them to discharge their important obligations and responsibilities in relation to human rights. The time has come to initiate a discussion about the desirability of such an agreed set of principles and guidelines, and what they might cover in order to be of real practical benefit to parliaments and parliamentarians everywhere.

A draft set of principles and guidelines was discussed at the AHRC conference in 2012 and is included as an Appendix to this volume. The purpose of the draft is merely to demonstrate the practical feasibility of such an exercise and to stimulate initial discussion about what such a set of internationally agreed principles and guidelines might look like. Its content has been distilled from the various sources collected in the Annex and from practices in different parliaments which are publicly known. Inevitably there will be many other examples of good practice not yet in the public domain, and these can be reflected in future drafts.

Any such set of principles and guidelines could have a number of purposes. They could be intended to include a small set of minimum core standards which should apply to any parliament and any parliamentary human rights body. They could also contain guidance to parliaments about how they can increase their capacity to protect and realise human rights and the rule of law, including examples of best practice drawn from around the world. The aim could be both to prescribe some minimum requirements if parliaments are to be able to fulfil their responsibility to protect and promote human rights and the rule of law, and to provide some helpful suggestions about ways in which parliaments can increase their capacity to do so, if they so wish.

Any such set of principles and guidelines intended for international discussion and eventual agreement faces the very real difficulty that the institutional arrangements which underpin democracy, human rights and the rule of law vary enormously from country to country. But this diversity of practice ought not to deter us from seeking to identify some principles and guidelines which are capable of being relevant to every country. Of course, there can be no 'one size fits all' set of institutional arrangements: human rights and rule of law machinery must always be developed with great sensitivity to local cultural, legal and political traditions. Indeed, this is the approach which has been taken, over a number of decades now, to building and strengthening both national parliaments and national human rights institutions. Inevitably, not all of the principles and guidelines will be relevant to every country, and some will be more relevant than others for particular countries. But this fact does not render the exercise redundant, as the proven value of the Paris Principles has demonstrated. The universal commitment to human rights, democracy and the rule of law requires us to take seriously the responsibility to devise arrangements in every country which make it more likely that those abstract ideals can be made into a concrete reality for every one of the world's seven billion people.

Appendix

Draft Principles and Guidelines on the Role of Parliaments in the Protection and Realisation of the Rule of Law and Human Rights

Parliaments have a special role in the protection and realisation of the rule of law, including human rights. As the pre-eminent representative institution of the State, Parliaments enjoy particular democratic legitimacy. In their capacity as representatives of the people, parliamentarians are key actors in the protection and realisation of human rights and in building a society imbued with the values of democracy, human rights and the rule of law. Parliaments should seek to use their democratic legitimacy to build a culture of respect for and fulfilment of both human rights and the rule of law, founded as far as possible on a national consensus.

Reasonable people can sometimes disagree about the scope of a particular human right, the priority to be given to one right over another where rights conflict and the strength of justifications for interfering with human rights. Such disagreement about human rights is legitimate and Parliament, as the representative institution, is a legitimate forum for such disagreement. One of Parliament's most important functions is to represent people's views in the policy-making process. Disagreement about human rights should always take place within the framework of the State's commitments to human rights in both national law (constitutional or otherwise) and international law (including obligations assumed under international human rights treaties).

As an organ of the State, Parliaments share with the Executive and the Judiciary the obligation to respect, protect and fulfil the human rights which are recognised in national law and in international treaties by which the State has agreed to be bound. International and regional mechanisms for protecting human rights are subsidiary to the national machinery. Primary responsibility for securing in national law the rights and freedoms recognised in international treaties, and for ensuring the availability at national level of an effective remedy if those rights or freedoms are violated, rests with the State. Parliaments share that responsibility with the Executive and the Judiciary.

Because of the nature of their functions, and in particular their role in making law, Parliaments are the national authorities which are particularly well-placed to ensure that effective measures are taken to prevent violations, and to ensure that national law provides practical and effective means by which remedies may be sought for alleged violations of rights and freedoms. Their other important function, oversight of the Executive, also makes them well-placed to monitor the Executive's performance of its own responsibilities to protect and realise human rights and to comply with the rule of law.

These Principles and Guidelines are intended to assist parliaments and parliamentarians everywhere to fulfil their important role in the protection and realisation of human rights in a democracy committed to the rule of law. References to human rights in these Principles and Guidelines are to human rights recognised in both national and international law. References to the "rule of law" are the principles identified in the Report on the Rule of Law by the Venice Commission for Democracy through law.

I. PARLIAMENTARY STRUCTURES

Parliaments should have adequate internal structures to enable them to fulfil their responsibility to protect and realise human rights and uphold the rule of law.

These internal parliamentary structures should ensure rigorous, regular and systematic monitoring of the government's performance of its responsibilities to secure the rights and freedoms recognised in national law and in the State's international obligations.

A. Specialised Human Rights Committee

Parliaments should identify or establish a specialised parliamentary Human Rights Committee.

The specialised parliamentary Human Rights Committee could be a committee dedicated solely to human rights. Parliaments could, however, identify or establish a relevant parliamentary committee which expressly includes human rights as part of its remit. In these Principles and Guidelines, either type of committee is referred to as 'the Human Rights Committee'.

B. Mainstreaming Human Rights and the Rule of Law across Parliament

In addition to establishing a specialised Human Rights Committee, Parliaments should take active steps to mainstream human rights and the rule of law across the entire range of Parliament's activities and functions.

Parliaments should ensure that expert advice on human rights and the rule of law, including but not confined to legal advice, is available to all parliamentary committees and to all parliamentary officials.

All parliamentary committees should identify which human rights and rule of law principles are most relevant to their work. They should proactively seek expert advice, including legal advice, about the relevant human rights and the rule of law principles whenever their work engages a human right or the rule of law.

The parliamentary legal service should include lawyers with expertise in human rights law.

Parliaments should ensure that the necessary institutional safeguards are in place to guarantee the independence of Parliament's legal advisers, including written procedures for dealing with improper pressure from members of Parliament or other parliamentary staff.

The parliamentary legal service should proactively deploy its expertise in human rights law to ensure that Parliament and all parliamentary committees receive expert advice about relevant human rights law across the full range of their functions and activities, and to assist them to identify when their work engages human rights or the rule of law.

Parliaments should put in place the necessary systems to ensure that the Speaker of the Parliament (or equivalent) is always informed in advance, and if necessary advised, when a parliamentary proceeding engages Parliament's responsibility to protect and/or realise human rights and the rule of law.

Parliaments should ensure that any relevant reports of the specialised parliamentary human rights committee are both drawn to the attention of and made available to members before any parliamentary proceeding which will include consideration of human rights and rule of law issues.

Parliaments should ensure that any relevant reports of the National Human Rights Institution are both drawn to the attention of and made available to members before any parliamentary proceeding which will include consideration of human rights or rule of law issues.

C. Budgets

Parliaments have a special role in the determination of budgetary allocations and should seek to use all appropriate opportunities to ensure that due priority is given in the setting of national budgets to the fulfilment of the State's human rights and rule of law obligations.

II. THE SPECIALISED PARLIAMENTARY HUMAN RIGHTS COMMITTEE

A. Establishment

The specialised parliamentary Human Rights Committee must be established by Parliament, not the Executive, and its permanent existence should be enshrined in Parliament's Standing Orders.

B. Remit

The remit of the specialised parliamentary Human Rights Committee should be broadly defined. It should concern human rights in the State in question and should reflect the fact that Parliament has the obligation both to protect and to realise human rights in that State.

It need not be part of the Human Rights Committee's remit to consider individual complaints, other than as examples of a more general human rights issue.

The remit of the specialised Human Rights Committee should be defined in such a way as to enable the committee to take into account all relevant sources of human rights standards in both national and international law.

C. Composition and Guarantees of Independence and Pluralism

The independence of the parliamentary Human Rights Committee from both the Government and non-state actors, including NGOs, is vital to its credibility.

The composition of the Human Rights Committee should be defined in such a way as to ensure that there can be no Government majority on the Committee.

The composition of the Human Rights Committee should be as inclusive as possible of all the parties represented in the Parliament and should reflect the principles of pluralism and gender balance.

Bicameral parliaments should consider whether the Human Rights Committee should be a Joint Committee of both Houses where possible.

Members of the Human Rights Committee should be appointed by a transparent process which commands public trust and confidence in the independence of the Committee.

Parliaments should ensure that mechanisms exist for any possible conflicts of interest to be declared by members of the Human Rights Committee.

Members of the Human Rights Committee should have a proven expertise and interest in human rights.

Members of the Government should be ineligible to be members of the Human Rights Committee. A member of the Human Rights Committee who is appointed to the Government should immediately resign from the Committee.

The Chair of the Human Rights Committee should be elected by members of Parliament and should be a senior parliamentarian of proven independence.

D. Powers

The Human Rights Committee should have the power

— to initiate inquiries of its own choosing
— to compel witnesses to attend, including Government ministers
— to compel the production of papers
— to hold oral evidence hearings
— to conduct visits, including visits abroad

— to access places of detention without notice
— to report to Parliament
— to make recommendations to the Government.

Where possible, the Human Rights Committee could have various powers of initiative, including the power:

— to initiate parliamentary debates on its reports or on subjects of its choosing
— to propose amendments to legislation
— to introduce bills into Parliament concerning matters within its remit.

E. Staff

The Human Rights Committee should be supported by specialised staff with expertise in human rights law and policy.

In order to ensure the independence of the Human Rights Committee, including the appearance of independence, the staff of the Committee should not be on secondment either from Government or from NGOs.

III. FUNCTIONS OF THE HUMAN RIGHTS COMMITTEE

The principal function of the specialised Human Rights Committee should be to inform parliamentary debate about human rights by:

— Advising Parliament about the human rights which are relevant to any issue being considered by Parliament
— Identifying the relevant factual questions which must be answered if Parliament is to be satisfied that it is acting compatibly with human rights
— Obtaining information from the Government about the justification for actions or inaction which affect human rights
— Advising Parliament about the human rights framework in which human rights issues should be considered by Parliament.

A. Core Functions

(1) Legislative Scrutiny

The Human Rights Committee could systematically scrutinise all Government Bills for their compatibility with human rights.

To facilitate such legislative scrutiny, the Human Rights Committee could ask the Executive to report systematically to Parliament on the compatibility of draft legislation with human rights in the form of a human rights memorandum in relation to every Bill.

The Human Rights Committee could seek to identify opportunities for Parliament to legislate to give effect or better effect to human rights obligations, including the implementation of treaty obligations, recommendations of the treaty bodies and judgments of Courts (national or international) concerning human rights.

(2) *Scrutiny of Executive Response to Human Rights Judgments of Courts*

The Human Rights Committee could systematically scrutinise the Executive's response to court judgments against the Government concerning human rights, including the judgments of international courts, with a view to reporting to Parliament on the promptness and adequacy of the Executive's response.

To facilitate such scrutiny, the Human Rights Committee could ask the Executive to report at least annually to Parliament on its responses to human rights judgments.

The Human Rights Committee could monitor relevant developments in human rights law, including judgments of international courts in cases against other States, with a view to identifying possible implications for national law, policy or practice.

(3) *Scrutiny of Compliance with and Implementation of International Human Rights Obligations*

The Human Rights Committee could monitor the State's compliance with and implementation of its international human rights obligations.

(a) Scrutiny of State's Compliance with Existing International Human Rights Treaties

The Human Rights Committee could scrutinise the State's reports to the UN treaty bodies, and any other compliance reports provided by the Executive to any other international mechanism concerning human rights.

The Human Rights Committee could consider sending any relevant report it has published directly to the monitoring bodies, and in appropriate cases sending a representative of the Committee to attend any relevant hearing before the monitoring bodies.

The Human Rights Committee could monitor the Executive's response to the Concluding Observations of the UN treaty bodies and seek opportunities to follow up the most significant of the recommendations contained in those Observations.

(b) Scrutiny of International Treaties Prior to Ratification

The Human Rights Committee could scrutinise proposed human rights treaties, and other international treaties with implications for human rights, and report to Parliament thereon, prior to their ratification.

Pre-ratification scrutiny of treaties could include scrutiny of the Government's justification for any proposed reservations or interpretative declarations to the treaty.

(c) Scrutiny of State of Accessions/Ratifications

The Human Rights Committee could ascertain and keep under review the Government's reasons for not acceding to or ratifying existing international human rights treaties.

(4) Inquiries into Topical Human Rights Issues

The Human Rights Committee could hold inquiries into topical issues concerning human rights, particularly in areas where there is concern about the country's compliance with its human rights commitments whether national or international.

The Human Rights Committee could develop a rigorous methodology for ensuring that it only conducts such inquiries where it is satisfied that it is uniquely placed, as a specialised parliamentary committee, to make a significant contribution to public understanding of the issue in question, over and above that made by other bodies, including national human rights institutions, or other parliamentary committees.

(5) Scrutiny of Government Policy Generally for Human Rights Compatibility

The Human Rights Committee may choose not to confine itself to scrutiny of legislation but could also scrutinise Government policy generally where it has significant human rights implications, in order to assist Parliament perform its function of oversight of the Executive.

(6) Monitoring the Adequacy of the National System for the Protection of Human Rights

The Human Rights Committee could keep the practical effectiveness of national mechanisms for the protection and realisation of human rights under review, including in particular:

— The adequacy of legal remedies
— Access to legal remedies
— The availability of effective alternatives to legal remedies.

B. Other Functions

The Human Rights Committee could also develop the following functions.

(1) Pre-legislative Scrutiny

The Human Rights Committee could also scrutinise Government policy proposals raising significant human rights issues which are likely to become legislative proposals.

(2) Post-legislative Scrutiny

The Human Rights Committee could also conduct post-legislative scrutiny of legislation with significant human rights implications on which it reported during the legislation's passage through Parliament.

(3) *Scrutiny of Secondary Legislation*

If resources permit, the Human Rights Committee could also scrutinise secondary legislation for human rights compatibility. Parliaments should ensure that mechanisms exist for identifying significant human rights issues raised by secondary legislation.

IV. WORKING METHODS OF THE HUMAN RIGHTS COMMITTEE

The Human Rights Committee should publish a statement of its working practices. It should keep its working practices under regular review in the light of practical experience.

A. Priority Policy and Work Programme

The parliamentary Human Right Committee should, after public consultation and discussion with, amongst others, NHRIs, publish an explicit priority policy indicating the human rights issues it proposes to prioritise in its work programme, and the criteria according to which it will assess the significance of a human rights issue when deciding on its priorities.

B. Decision by Consensus

The Human Rights Committee should strive to reach consensus on the issues on which it reports, so far as it is possible to do so.

C. Transparency

The Human Rights Committee should maintain an up-to-date website, on which all relevant documents are publicly accessible.

All correspondence with the Human Rights Committee shall be published on the Committee's website as soon as possible after it has been sent or received.

In order to maintain public trust and confidence the Human Rights Committee should, so far as possible, avoid considering confidential material when it is carrying out its functions.

D. Civil Society

The Human Rights Committee should conduct its work in such a way as to provide opportunities for civil society to have a direct input into parliamentary consideration of human rights issues.

E. Reporting

The Human Rights Committee should report regularly to Parliament on its activities in the performance of its functions.

The Human Rights Committee should report annually to Parliament on its activities during the year and on the outcome of every review of its working practices.

The Human Rights Committee should expect the Executive to respond within a reasonable time to recommendations it makes in its reports.

F. Follow up

The Human Rights Committee should seek to follow up its reports and recommendations, including by seeking opportunities for parliamentary debate or Executive action.

V. KEY RELATIONSHIPS

Parliaments and the parliamentary Human Rights Committee should develop and maintain consistent and effective working relationships with a range of key interlocutors. Such relationships should be established and maintained at the level of both members and officials.

A. Relationship with the Executive

Parliaments and the Human Rights Committee should help the Executive to understand how Parliament will fulfil its responsibilities to protect and realise human rights by developing, in close consultation with the Executive, detailed guidance for the Executive in respect of each of the functions identified above.

B. Relationship with Courts

Parliaments should seek to ensure that mechanisms are in place, which are consistent with the important principle of the separation of powers, for representative judicial views to be made available to Parliament to assist it in its scrutiny of laws or policies which affect the exercise of the judicial function or otherwise have significant implications for the rule of law.

Where a court wishes to consider what parliamentary consideration there has been of any human rights issue the court has to determine, Parliaments should facilitate such judicial consideration.

C. Relationship with NHRIs

Parliaments and the Human Rights Committee shall establish an effective co-operation with National Human Rights Institutions, and in doing so shall have particular regard to the Belgrade Principles on the Relationship between National Human Rights Institutions and Parliaments.

D. Relationship with Other Parts of National Human Rights Machinery

The Human Rights Committee shall develop working relationships with other parts of the national human rights machinery, including Ombudsmen, relevant commissioners, and independent reviewers, with a view to ensuring the coherence and co-ordination of that machinery, and its optimal use of resources for the protection and realisation of human rights.

E. Relationship with Civil Society

Parliament and the Human Rights Committee should be well connected with relevant civil society networks.

F. Relationship with International Human Rights Machinery

The Human Rights Committee should establish and maintain a close relationship with all parts of the relevant regional and international human rights machinery, including the UN treaty bodies and Special Procedures.

G. Relationship with Other Parliamentary Committees

The Human Rights Committee shall establish effective working relationships with other parliamentary committees with a view to ensuring that opportunities for Parliament to fulfil its obligations to protect and realise human rights are not missed.

H. Relationship with the Media

Parliaments and their Human Rights Committee should maintain close relations with the media, and be particularly vigilant about the importance of free and independent media to the protection of human rights in a democracy.

I. Relationship with Academic Institutions

Parliaments and the Human Rights Committee should maintain close relations with academic institutions, including human rights research institutes, so that relevant academic research about human rights informs scrutiny of policy and legislation, and research agendas in universities are informed about the human rights issues which are of pressing practical concern.

J. Relationship with the Legal Profession

Parliaments and the Human Rights Committee should maintain close relations with the legal profession and its representative bodies, and in particular with practitioners in relevant fields including human rights and constitutional law.

VI. TRAINING AND RESEARCH SERVICES

A. Training

Parliaments could provide or arrange appropriate induction training in human rights and the rule of law for all new members of Parliament and staff, and at regular intervals thereafter.

Parliaments should ensure that every member of Parliament is provided with a copy of the IPU's Handbook on Human Rights for Parliamentarians and other relevant materials about the role of Parliament in relation to human rights.

Parliaments should avail themselves of appropriate technical assistance available from international organisations to assist them to build their capacity to fulfil their role in the protection and realisation of human rights and the rule of law.

B. Research Support

Parliaments should ensure that their libraries and on-line resources provide access to the most relevant human rights materials required by parliamentarians to fulfil their role in the protection and realisation of human rights and the rule of law.

Parliaments should ensure that their research services include appropriate expertise in human rights and proactively provide regular updates to all members of parliament on significant human rights issues, in anticipation of the human rights issues likely to be most relevant to parliamentary business.

VII. EFFECTIVENESS

Parliaments should develop a methodology for assessing their effectiveness in the protection and realisation of human rights.

Annex to Draft Principles and Guidelines

Parliaments, the Rule of Law and Human Rights

COLLECTION OF RELEVANT TEXTS AND MATERIALS 1993–2014

Report of the Committee on Legal Affairs and Human Rights, *The effectiveness of the European Convention on Human Rights: the Brighton Declaration and beyond* (Rapporteur: Mr Yves Pozzo di Borgo) (10 December 2014) http://website-pace.net/documents/19838/1041670/20141210-BeyondBrighton-EN. pdf/9b39d1d4-e9b2-44ea-baaa-901ced892426

Effective Parliamentary Oversight of Human Rights: A Framework for Designing and Determining Effectiveness (June 2014) www.kcl.ac.uk/law/research/parliamentshr/assets/ Outcome-Document---Advance-Copy-5-June-2014.pdf

UN General Assembly Resolution A/RES/68/272, *Interaction between the United Nations, national parliaments and the Inter-Parliamentary Union* (19 May 2014) www.un.org/en/ ga/search/view_doc.asp?symbol=A/RES/68/272

Report of the Secretary-General A/68/827, *Interaction between the United Nations, National Parliaments and the Inter-Parliamentary Union* (2 April 2014) www.ipu.org/ Un-e/a-68-827.pdf

From Rights to Remedies: Structures and Strategies for Implementing International Human Rights Decisions (Open Society Justice Initiative, 2013) 18–19 and ch III www. opensocietyfoundations.org/reports/rights-remedies-structures-and-strategies-implementing-international-human-rights-decisions

Panel discussion on the contribution of parliaments to the work of the Human Rights Council and its Universal Periodic Review (29 May 2013) www.ohchr.org/EN/NewsEvents/Pages/ DisplayNews.aspx?NewsID=13375&LangID=E

PACE Resolution 1914 (2013), *Ensuring the Viability of the Strasbourg Court: Structural Deficiencies in States Parties* (22 January 2013) http://assembly.coe.int/ASP/XRef/X2H-DW-XSL.asp?fileid=19396&lang=en

Strengthening the Role of Parliamentarians in the Implementation of Universal Periodic Review Recommendations: Conclusions (outcome document of a workshop organised jointly by the IPU and the Commonwealth Secretariat, Geneva) (November 2012) www. ipu.org/splz-e/hr12/conclusions.pdf

Belgrade Principles on the Relationship between National Human Rights Institutions and Parliaments (23 February 2012) www.ohchr.org/EN/NewsEvents/Pages/ ParliamentsAndNHRIs.aspx

PACE Resolution 1856(2012), *Guaranteeing the Authority and Effectiveness of the European Convention on Human Rights* (24 January 2012) http://assembly.coe.int/Main.asp?link=/ Documents/AdoptedText/ta12/ERES1856.htm

PACE Recommendation 1991(2012), *Guaranteeing the Authority and Effectiveness of the European Convention on Human Rights* (24 January 2012) http://assembly.coe.int/Main. asp?link=/Documents/AdoptedText/ta12/EREC1991.htm

Report of the Committee on Legal Affairs and Human Rights, *Guaranteeing the Authority and Effectiveness of the European Convention on Human Rights* (Rapporteur: Mrs Bemelmans-Videc), Parliamentary Assembly Doc 12811 (3 January 2012) http://assembly. coe.int/ASP/Doc/XrefViewHTML.asp?FileId=12914&Language=en

PACE Resolution 1823(2011), *National Parliaments: Guarantors of Human Rights in Europe* (23 June 2011) http://assembly.coe.int/ASP/Doc/ATListingDetails_E.asp?ATID=11349

Report of the Committee on Legal Affairs and Human Rights, *National Parliaments: Guarantors of Human Rights in Europe* (Rapporteur: Mr Christos Pourgourides), Parliamentary Assembly Doc 12636 (6 June 2011) http://assembly.coe.int/ASP/Doc/ XrefViewPDF.asp?FileID=12866&Language=EN

Report on the Rule of Law adopted by the European Commission for Democracy through Law (Venice Commission) (25–26 March 2011) http://www.venice.coe.int/webforms/ documents/CDL-AD(2011)003rev-e.aspx

Human Rights and Parliaments: Handbook for Members and Staff, the Westminster Consortium/International Bar Association (March 2011) www.ibanet.org/Human_Rights_ Institute/About_the_HRI/HRI_Activities/Parliamentary_Strengthening.aspx

PACE Resolution 1787 (2011), *Implementation of Judgments of the European Court of Human Rights* (26 January 2011) http://assembly.coe.int/Main.asp?link=/Documents/ AdoptedText/ta11/ERES1787.htm

PACE Recommendation 1955 (2011), *Implementation of Judgments of the European Court of Human Rights* (26 January 2011) http://assembly.coe.int/Main.asp?link=/Documents/ AdoptedText/ta11/EREC1955.htm

Report of the Committee on Legal Affairs and Human Rights, *Implementation of Judgments of the European Court of Human Rights* (Rapporteur: Mr Christos Pourgourides), Parliamentary Assembly Doc 12455 (20 December 2010) http://assembly.coe.int/ASP/ XRef/X2H-DW-XSL.asp?fileid=12589&lang=en

Seminar Report, OSCE Regional Seminar for Parliamentary Staffers on Parliamentary Oversight and Independent Institutions, Tirana, Albania (20–21 December 2010) www. osce.org/odihr/78844

Seminar Report, OHCHR Sub-regional Seminar for Parliamentarians on the Role of Parliament in the Promotion and Protection of Human Rights, Monrovia (22–24 November 2010)

Summary of Recommendations, *Improving Implementation and Follow-up: Treaty Bodies, Special Procedures, Universal Periodic Review*, Open Society Justice Initiative, the Brookings Institution and UPR-Watch (Geneva) (22–23 November 2010) www2.ohchr. org/english/bodies/HRTD/docs/ReportConference.pdf

Strengthening Subsidiarity: Integrating the Strasbourg Court's Case-Law into National Law and Judicial Practice, Presentation of Mr Christos Pourgourides, Chairperson of the Committee on Legal Affairs and Human Rights, Parliamentary Assembly of the Council of Europe, to the Conference on the Principle of Subsidiarity, AS/Jur/Inf (2010) 04, Skopje (1–2 October 2010) http://assembly.coe.int/CommitteeDocs/2010/20101125_skopje.pdf

PACE Resolution 1726, *Effective Implementation of the European Convention on Human Rights: The Interlaken Process* (29 April 2010) http://assembly.coe.int/Main.asp?link=/ Documents/AdoptedText/ta10/ERES1726.htm

Report of the Committee on Legal Affairs and Human Rights, *Effective Implementation of the European Convention on Human Rights: The Interlaken Process* (Rapporteur: Mrs Bemelmans-Videc), Parliamentary Assembly Doc 12221 (27 April 2010) http://assembly. coe.int/ASP/Doc/XrefViewHTML.asp?FileId=12418&Language=en

Enhancing Parliament's Role in relation to Human Rights Judgments, Joint Committee on Human Rights, Fifteenth Report of Session 2009-10, HL Paper 85/HC 455 (9 March 2010) www.publications.parliament.uk/pa/jt200910/jtselect/jtrights/85/8502.htm

International Co-ordinating Committee of National Human Rights Institutions for the Promotion and Protection of Human Rights (ICC) Sub-committee on Accreditation, *General Observations* (June 2009) www.ihrc.ie/download/pdf/genera_observations_sca.pdf

JURISTRAS Project, *Why Do States Implement Differently the European Court of Human Rights Judgments? The Case Law on Civil Liberties and the Rights of Minorities* (April 2009) http://archive-gr.com/page/1278501/2013-01-31/http://www.juristras.eliamep.gr/?p=301

Viewpoint of the Council of Europe Commissioner for Human Rights, Thomas Hammarberg, *National Parliaments Can Do More to Promote Human Rights* (16 February 2009)

Primer on Parliaments and Human Rights, UN Development Programme (11 October 2008) www.undp.org/content/dam/aplaws/publication/en/publications/democratic-governance/dg-publications-for-website/parliaments-and-human-rights-a-primer/HR_Pub_Parlts&HR.pdf

Towards Stronger Implementation of the European Convention on Human Rights at National Level, colloquy organised under the Swedish Chairmanship of the Committee of Ministers, Stockholm (9–10 June 2008) www.coe.int/t/dghl/standardsetting/cddh/Publications/Stockholm_Proceedings.pdf

Enhanced Regional Parliamentary Co-operation with Human Rights Treaty Bodies (March 2008) www.ipu.org/splz-e/libreville09.htm

Committee of Ministers' Recommendation CM/Rec(2008)2 to members states on efficient domestic capacity for rapid execution of judgments of the European Court of Human Rights (6 February 2008) https://wcd.coe.int/ViewDoc.jsp?id=1246081&Site=CM

Conclusions of the Seminar on the Role of Parliaments in the Implementation of International and Regional Human Rights Instruments, Ouagadougou (1–3 October 2007) www.ipu.org/splz-e/ouaga07/conclusions.pdf

World Bank Institute Professional Development Program for Parliamentarians and Parliamentary Staff, Human Rights module (August 2007) www.parliamentary-strengthening.org/humanrightsmodule/pdf/humanrightsall.pdf

PACE Resolution 1516 (2006), *Implementation of Judgments of the European Court of Human Rights* (2 October 2006) http://assembly.coe.int/Main.asp?link=/Documents/AdoptedText/ta06/ERES1516.htm

Report of the Committee on Legal Affairs and Human Rights, *Implementation of Judgments of the European Court of Human Rights* (Rapporteur: Mr Erik Jurgens), Parliamentary Assembly Doc 11020 (18 September 2006) http://assembly.coe.int/ASP/Doc/XrefViewHTML.asp?FileID=11344&Language=EN

Human Rights: A Handbook for Parliamentarians (IPU/OHCHR) (2005) (new edition forthcoming) www.ipu.org/PDF/publications/hr_guide_en.pdf

Report of the Second Expert Seminar, *Democracy and the Rule of Law* E/CN.4/2005/58 (18 March 2005) www2.ohchr.org/english/issues/rule_of_law/democracy.htm

National Democratic Institute for International Affairs, *Parliamentary Human Rights Committees* (2004) www.accessdemocracy.org/files/1905_gov_parlhrscommittees_080105.pdf

The Abuja Guidelines on the Relationship between Parliaments, Parliamentarians and Commonwealth National Human Rights Institutions (Abuja, Nigeria) (23–26 March 2004) www.britishcouncil.org/governance-national-human-rights-institutions-and-legislatures.doc

Report of the International Workshop on 'National Human Rights Institutions and Legislatures: Building an Effective Relationship' (Abuja, Nigeria) (23–25 March 2004)

Strengthening Parliament as a Guardian of Human Rights: The Role of Parliamentary Human Rights Bodies, Reports and Documents of a Seminar for Chairpersons and Members of Parliamentary Human Rights Bodies organised by the Inter-Parliamentary Union (IPU) and the United Nations Development Programme (UNDP) with the support of the Office of the United Nations High Commissioner for Human Rights (OHCHR), Geneva (15–17 March 2004) www.ipu.org/pdf/publications/hr04_en.pdf

Resolution adopted by the 108th Conference of the Inter-Parliamentary Union, *Parliaments' Role in Strengthening Democratic Institutions and Human Development in a Fragmented World* (Santiago de Chile) (11 April 2003) www.ipu.org/conf-e/108-1.htm

Report of the High Commissioner for Human Rights, *Continuing Dialogue on Measures to Promote and Consolidate Democracy*, E/CN.4/2003/59 (27 January 2003) www2.ohchr.org/english/issues/rule_of_law/democracy.htm

Resolution adopted by the 100th Inter-Parliamentary Conference, *Strong Action by National Parliaments in the Year of the 50th Anniversary of the Universal Declaration of Human Rights to Ensure the Promotion and Protection of all Human Rights in the 21st Century* (Moscow) (11 September 1998) www.ipu.org/conf-e/100-1.htm

Inter-Parliamentary Union Symposium, *Parliament: Guardian of Human Rights*, Budapest (19–22 May 1993) www.ipu.org/splz-e/budapest.htm

The Paris Principles Relating to the Status of National Institutions for the Promotion and Protection of Human Rights, defined at the first International Workshop on national Institutions for the Promotion and Protection of Human Rights (Paris) (7–9 October 1991) http://www.ohchr.org/EN/ProfessionalInterest/Pages/StatusOfNationalInstitutions.aspx

Select Bibliography

BOOKS

Alston, P, *Promoting Human Rights Through Bills of Rights: Comparative Perspectives* (Oxford, Oxford University Press, 1999)

Baker, D, *Not Quite Supreme: The Courts and Coordinate Constitutional Interpretation* (Kingston, McGill-Queen's University Press, 2010)

Bauman, R and Kahana, T, *The Least Examined Branch: The Role of Legislatures in the Constitutional State* (Cambridge, Cambridge University Press, 2006)

Bellamy, R, *Political Constitutionalism: A Republican Defence of the Constitutionalism of Democracy* (Cambridge, Cambridge University Press, 2007)

Bickel, A, *The Least Dangerous Branch: The Supreme Court at the Bar of Politics* (New Haven, Yale University Press, 1986)

Bingham, T, *The Rule of Law* (London, Penguin, 2010)

Blackburn, R and Plant, R, *Constitutional Reform Now* (London, Blackstone Press, 1998)

Brazier, A, Katlikowski, S and Rosenblatt, G, *Law in the Making* (London, Hansard Society, 2007)

Bynoe, I and Spencer, S, *Mainstreaming Human Rights: In Whitehall and Westminster* (London, Institute for Public Policy Research, 1999)

Campbell, T, *Human Rights: From Philosophy to Practice* (Aldershot, Dartmouth, 2001)

Campbell, T, Ewing, K and Tomkins, A, *The Legal Protection of Human Rights: Sceptical Essays* (Oxford, Oxford University Press, 2011)

Campbell, T, Goldsworthy, J and Stone, A, *Protecting Human Rights: Instruments and Institutions* (Oxford, Oxford University Press, 2003)

Canovan, M, *The People* (Cambridge, Polity Press, 2005)

Dembour, M, *Who Believes in Human Rights? Reflections on the European Convention* (Cambridge, Cambridge University Press, 2006)

Devins, N and Douglas, D, *Redefining Equality* (Oxford, Oxford University Press, 1998)

Devins, N and Fisher, L, *The Democratic Constitution* (Oxford, Oxford University Press, 2004)

Devins, N and Whittington, K, *Congress and the Constitution* (Durham, NC, Duke University Press, 2005)

Dyzenhaus, D, *The Constitution of Law: Legality in a Time of Emergency* (Cambridge, Cambridge University Press, 2006)

Eisgruber, C, *Constitutional Self-government* (Cambridge, MA, Harvard University Press, 2001)

Ekins, R, *The Nature of Legislative Intent* (Oxford, Oxford University Press, 2012)

Ely, J, *Democracy and Distrust: A Theory of Judicial Review* (Cambridge, MA, Harvard University Press, 1980)

Epp, C, *Making Rights Real: Activists, Bureaucrats, and the Creation of the Legalistic State* (Chicago, University of Chicago Press, 2010)

Erdos, D, *Delegating Rights Protection: The Rise of Bills of Rights in the Westminster World* (Oxford, Oxford University Press, 2010)

Evans, C and Evans, S, *Australian Bills of Rights: The Law of the Victorian Charter and ACT Human Rights Act* (London, Butterworths, 2008).

Ewing, K, *Bonfire of the Liberties: New Labour, Human Rights, and the Rule of Law* (Oxford, Oxford University Press, 2010)

Flinders, M, *Democratic Drift: Majoritarian Modification and Democratic Anomie in the United Kingdom* (Oxford, Oxford University Press, 2010)

Goldsworthy, J, *Parliamentary Sovereignty: Contemporary Debates* (Cambridge, Cambridge University Press, 2010)

Griffin, J, *On Human Rights* (Oxford, Oxford University Press, 2008)

Griffith, J, *Parliamentary Scrutiny of Government Bills* (London, Allen & Unwin, 1974)

Hickman, T, *Public Law after the Human Rights Act* (Oxford, Hart Publishing, 2010)

Hiebert, J, *Charter Conflicts: What is Parliament's Role?* (Kingston, McGill-Queen's University Press, 2002)

Hirschl, R, *Towards Juristocracy: The Origins and Consequences of the New Constitutionalism* (Cambridge, MA, Harvard University Press, 2007)

Hoffman, D, *The Impact of the UK Human Rights Act on Private Law* (Harlow, Pearson Education, 2011)

Horne, A, Drewry, G and Oliver, D (eds), *Parliament and the Law* (Oxford, Hart Publishing, 2013)

Huscroft, G, *Expounding the Constitution: Essays in Constitutional Theory* (Cambridge, Cambridge University Press, 2008)

Kavanagh, A, *Constitutional Review under the UK Human Rights Act* (Oxford, Oxford University Press, 2009)

Kelly, J, *Governing with the Charter: Legislative and Judicial Activism and Framer's Intent* (Vancouver, University of British Columbia Press, 2005)

Kinley, D, *The European Convention on Human Rights: Compliance without Incorporation* (Aldershot, Dartmouth, 1993)

Komesar, N, *Imperfect Alternatives: Choosing Institutions in Law, Economics, and Public Policy* (Chicago, University of Chicago Press, 1997)

Koopmans, T, *Courts and Political Institutions: A Comparative View* (Cambridge, Cambridge University Press, 2003)

Kuile, GT, *Of Bills and Rights: Human Rights Proofing Legislation: Comparing the United Kingdom and the Netherlands* (Cambridge, Intersentia Ltd, 2013)

McCorquodale, R, *The Rule of Law in International and Comparative Perspective* (London, BIICL, 2010)

McKay, WR and Johnson, C, *Parliament and Congress: Representation and Scrutiny in the Twenty-First Century* (Oxford, Oxford University Press, 2010)

Oliver, D, *The Changing Constitution* (Oxford, Oxford University Press, 2007)

Oliver, D and Drewry, G, *The Law and Parliament* (London, Butterworths, 1998)

Raz, J, *Between Authority and Interpretation: On the Theory of Law and Practical Reason* (Oxford, Oxford University Press, 2009)

Roach, K, *The Supreme Court on Trial: Judicial Activism or Democratic Dialogue* (Toronto, Irwin Law, 2001)

Rosenberg, G, *The Hollow Hope: Can Courts Bring about Social Change?* (Chicago, University of Chicago Press, 1991)

Russell, M, *The Contemporary House of Lords: Westminster Bicameralism Revived* (Oxford, Oxford University Press, 2013)

Smith, N, *The, Human Rights Legislation* (London, Constitution Unit, 1996)

Sunstein, C, *Designing Democracy: What Constitutions Do* (Oxford, Oxford University Press, 2001)

Tomkins, A, *Our Republican Constitution* (Oxford, Hart Publishing, 2005)

Tushnet, M, *Taking the Constitution Away from the Courts* (Princeton, Princeton University Press, 1999)
—— *Bills of Rights (International Library of Essays on Rights)* (Aldershot, Ashgate, 2007)
—— *Weak Courts, Strong Rights: Judicial Review and Social Welfare Rights in Comparative Constitutional* Law (Princeton NJ, Princeton University Press, 2009)
Vermeule, A, *Law and the Limits of Reason* (Oxford, Oxford University Press, 2009)
Waldron, J, *Law and Disagreement* (Oxford, Oxford University Press, 1999)
—— *The Dignity of Legislation* (Oxford, Oxford University Press, 1999)
Webber, GCN, *The Negotiable Constitution: On the Limitations of Rights* (Cambridge, Cambridge University Press, 2009)
Whittington, K Kelemen, R and Caldeira, G, *The Oxford Handbook of Law and Politics* (Oxford, Oxford University Press, 2008)
Ziegler, K, Baranger, D and Bradley, A (eds), *Constitutionalism and the Role of Parliaments* (Oxford, Hart Publishing, 2007)
Zurn, C, *Deliberative Democracy and the Institutions of Judicial Review* (Cambridge, Cambridge University Press, 2007)

JOURNAL ARTICLES

Aleinikoff, T, 'Constitutional Law in the Age of Balancing' (1986) 96 *Yale Law Journal* 943
Arden, Dame M, 'The Changing Judicial Role: Human Rights, Community Law and the Intention of Parliament' (2008) 67(3) *Cambridge Law Journal* 487
Barber, NW, 'Prelude to the Separation of Powers' (2001) 60 *Cambridge Law Journal* 59
Bellamy, R, 'Political Constitutionalism and the Human Rights Act' (2011) 9 *International Journal of Constitutional Law* 86
Blackburn, R, 'A Human Rights Committee for the UK Parliament—The Options' [1998] *European Human Rights Law Review* 534
Black-Branch, JL, 'Parliamentary Supremacy or Political Expediency?: The Constitutional Position of the Human Rights Act under British Law' (2002) 23(1) *Statute Law Review* 59
Boumans, E and Norbart, M, 'The European Parliament and Human Rights' (1989) 7 *Netherlands Human Rights Quarterly* 36
Davis, KC, 'Facts in Lawmaking' (1980) 80 *Columbia Law Review* 931
De Londras, F, 'Controlling the Executive in Times of Terrorism: Competing Perspectives on Effective Oversight Mechanisms' (2010) 30 *Oxford Journal of Legal Studies* 19
Drzemczewski, A, 'Recent Parliamentary Initiatives to Ensure Compliance with Strasbourg Court Judgments' in Drzemczewski, A, *L'Homme et le Droit: en homage au Professeur Jean-Francois Flauss* (Paris, Editions Pedone, 2014)
Dyzenhaus, D, 'Are Legislatures Good at morality? Or Better at it than the Courts?' (2009) 7 *International Journal of Constitutional Law* 46
Ek, VMC, 'Fedralismo Judical en Mexico. Concepciones, Evolucion, Y Perspectivas' (2013) 17 *Revista d'estudis autonòmics i federals* 107
Evans, C and Evans, S, 'Evaluating the Human Rights Performance of Legislatures' (2006) 6 *Human Rights Law Review* 545
Evans, C and Evans, S, 'Legislative Scrutiny Committees and Parliamentary Conceptions of Human Rights' [2006] *Public Law* 785
—— 'Parliamentary Scrutiny of Legislation and Human Rights' [2002] *Public Law* 323
Feldman, D, 'Can and Should Parliament Protect Human Rights?' (2004) 10(4) *European Public Law* 635

—— 'The Impact of Human Rights on the UK Legislative Process' (2004) 25 *Statute Law Review* 91

—— 'Injecting Law into Politics and Politics into Law: Legislative and Judicial Perspectives on Constitutional Human Rights' (2005) 34 *Common Law World Review* 103

Finnis, J, 'A Bill of Rights for Britain? The Moral of Contemporary Jurisprudence' (1985) 71 *Proceedings of the British Academy* 303

—— 'Reassessing the New Commonwealth Model of Constitutionalism' (2010) 8 *International Journal of Constitutional Law* 167

Gardbaum, S, 'How Successful and Distinctive is the Human Rights Act-An Expatriate Comparatist's Assessment' (2011) 74(2) *Modern Law Review* 195

Gearty, C, 'Reconciling Parliamentary Democracy and Human Rights' (2002) 118 *Law Quarterly Review* 248

Geddis, A, 'Parliamentary Privilege: Quis Custodiet Ipsos Custodes?' [2005] *Public Law* 696

Goldoni, M, 'Constitutional Reasoning According to Political Constitutionalism: Comment on Richard Bellamy' (2013) 14(8) *German Law Journal* 1053

Goldsmith, P, 'Parliament for Lawyers: An Overview of the Legislative Process' (2002) 4 *European Journal of Law Reform* 511

Goldsworthy, J, 'Homogenizing Constitutions' (2003) 23 *Oxford Journal of Legal Studies* 483

Griffith, JAG, 'The Political Constitution' (1979) 42 *Modern Law Review* 1

Hazell, R, 'Who is the Guardian of Legal Values in the Legislative Process: Parliament or the Executive?' [2004] *Public Law* 495

Hickman, T, 'In Defence of the Legal Constitution' (2005) 55 *University of Toronto Law Journal* 981

Hiebert, JL, 'A Hybrid-Approach to Protect Rights—An Argument in Favour of Supplementing Canadian Judicial Review with Australia's Model of Parliamentary Scrutiny' (1998) 26 *Federal Law Review* 115

—— 'New Constitutional Ideas: Can New Parliamentary Models Resist Judicial Dominance When Interpreting Rights' (2003) 82 *Texas Law Review* 1963

—— 'Interpreting a Bill of Rights: The Importance of Legislative Rights Review' (2005) 35 *British Journal of Political Science* 235

—— 'Parliament and the Human Rights Act: Can the JCHR Help Facilitate a Culture of Rights?' (2006) 4 *International Journal of Constitutional Law* 1

—— 'Parliamentary Bills of Rights: An Alternative Model?' (2006) 69 *Modern Law Review* 7

—— 'Compromise and the Notwithstanding Clause: Why the Dominant Narrative Distorts Our Understanding' in JB Kelly and C Manfredi (eds), *Contested Constitutionalism: Reflections on the Canadian Charter of Rights and Freedoms (Law and Society Series)* (Vancouver, University of British Columbia Press, 2010)

—— 'Governing under the Human Rights Act: The Limitations of Wishful Thinking' [2012] *Public Law* 27

Hogg, PW and Bushell, AA, 'The Chater Dialogue between Courts and Legislatures. (or Perhaps the Charter of Rights isn't Such a Bad Thing after all) (1997) 35 *Osgoode Hall Law Journal* 75

Hunt, M, 'Enhancing Parliament's Role in Relation to Economic and Social Rights' (2010) 6 *European Human Rights Law Review* 242

—— 'The Impact of the Human Rights Act on the Legislature: A Diminution of Democracy or a New Voice for Parliament?' (2010) *European Human Rights Law Review* 601

Lord Irvine, 'The Impact of the Human Rights Act: Parliament, the Courts and the Executive' [2003] *Public Law*) 308

Rt Hon Lord Hoffmann, 'Human Rights and the House of Lords' (1999) 62(2) *Modern Law Review* 159

King, J, 'Institutional Approaches to Judicial Restraint' (2008) 28 *Oxford Journal of Legal Studies* 409

Kinley, D, 'Human Rights Scrutiny in Parliament: Westminster Set to Leap Ahead' (1999) 10 *Public Law Review* 252

—— 'Exile on Main Street: Australia's Legislative Agenda for Human Rights' (2012) 1 *European Human Rights Law Review* 58

Kitterman, CM, 'The United Kingdom's Human Rights Act of 1998: Will the Parliament Relinquish its Sovereignty to Ensure Human Rights Protection in Domestic Courts?' (2000–01) 583(7) *ILSA Journal of International and Comparative Law* 583

Klug, F, 'Breaking New Ground: The Joint Committee on Human Rights and the Role of Parliament in Human Rights Compliance' (2007) 3 *European Human Rights Law Review* 231

Lester, A, 'Parliamentary Scrutiny of Legislation under the Human Rights Act 1998' (2002) 4 *European Human Rights Law Review* 432

—— 'The Human Rights Act 1998: Five Years on' (2004) 3 *European Human Rights Law Review* 258

Magnarella, PJ, 'The Legal, Political and Cultural Structures of Human Rights Protection and Abuses in Turkey' (1994) 3 *Journal of International Law and Practice* 439

McCorkindale, C and McKerrell, M, 'Assessing the Relationship between Legislative and Judicial Supremacy in the UK: Parliament and the Rule of Law after *Jackson*; (2012) 101(4) *The Round Table: The Commonwealth Journal of International Affairs* 341

McQueen, H, 'Parliamentary Business: A Critical Review of Parliament's Role in New Zealand's Law-Making Process' (2010) 16 *Auckland University Law Review* 1

Mureinik, E, 'A Bridge to Where? Introducing the Interim Bill of Rights' (1994) 10 *South African Journal on Human Rights* 31

Nicol, D, 'The Human Rights Act and the Politicians' (2004) 24 *Legal Studies* 451

Nolan, CJ, 'The Influence of Parliament on Human Rights in Canadian Foreign Policy' (1985) 7 *Human Rights Quarterly* 373

O'Brien, N and Thompson, B, 'Human Rights Accountability in the UK: Deliberative Democracy and the Role of the Ombudsman' (2010) 5 *European Human Rights Law Review* 504

Oliver, D, 'Improving Scrutiny Standards: The Case for Standards and Checklists' [2006] *Public Law* 219

Reidy, A, 'A Human Rights Committee for Westminster' (July 1999) Constitution Unit

Roach, K, 'The Role and Capacities of Courts and Legislatures in Reviewing Canada's Anti-Terrorism Law' (2008) 24 *Windsor Review of Legal and Social Issues* 5

Ryle, M, 'Pre-legislative Scrutiny: A Prophylactic Approach to Protection of Human Rights' [1994] *Public Law* 192

Suchkova, M, 'An Analysis of the Institutional Arrangements within the Council of Europe and within Certain Member States for Securing the Enforcement of Judgments' (2011) *European Human Rights Law Review* 448

Sunstein, CR and Vermeule, A, 'Interpretation and Institutions' (2003) 101 *Michigan Law Review* 885

Tierney, S, 'Determining the State of Exception: What Role for Parliament and the Courts?' (2005) 68(4) *Modern Law Review* 668

Tolley, M, 'Parliamentary Scrutiny of Legislation under the Human Rights Act 1998' (2009) 44 *Australian Journal of Political Science* 41

Tomkins, A, 'The Role of the Courts in the Political Constitution' (2010) 60 *University of Toronto Law Journal* 1

Versteeg, M, 'Unpopular Constitutionalism' (2014) 89 *Indiana Law Journal* 1133

Waldron, J, 'Legislating with Integrity' (2003) 72 *Fordham Law Review* 373

—— 'The Core of the Case against Judicial Review' (2005) 115 *Yale Law Journal* 1346

—— 'Judges as Moral Reasoners' (2009) 7 *International Journal of Constitutional Law* 2

—— 'Representative Lawmaking' (2009) 89 *Boston University Law Review* 335

—— 'Refining the Question about Judges' Moral Capacity' (2009) 7 *International Journal of Constitutional Studies* 69

Walker, K, 'Who's the Boss? The Judiciary, the Executive, the Parliament and the Protection of Human Rights' (1995) 25 *University of Western Australia Law Review* 238

Watchirs, H and McKinnon, G, 'Five Years' Experience of the Human Rights Act 2004 (ACT): Insights for Human Rights Protection in Australia' (2010) 33 *University of New South Wales Law Journal* 136

Webber, GCN, 'The Unfulfilled Potential of the Court and Legislature Dialogue' (2009) 42 *Canadian Journal of Political Science/Revue canadienne de science politique* 443

Whittington, K, 'In Defense of Legislatures' (2000) 28 *Political Theory* 690

Williams, G and Burton, L, 'Australia's Exclusive Parliamentary Model of Rights Protection' (2013) 34 (1) *Statute Law Review* 58

Young, A, 'Is Dialogue Working under the Human Rights Act 1998?' [2011] *Public Law* 773

REPORTS AND OFFICIAL PUBLICATIONS

Beetham, D, *Parliament and Democracy in the Twenty-First Century: A Guide to Good Practice* (Geneva, Inter-Parliamentary Union, 2006)

Byrnes, A, 'The Protection of Human Rights in NSW through the Parliamentary Process—A Review of the Recent Performance of the NSW Parliament's Legislation Review Committee' (2009) University of New South Wales Faculty of Law Research Series

Cali, B, Koch, A and Bruch, N, 'The Legitimacy of the European Court of Human Rights: The View from the Ground' (2011), The Project Report: www.ecthproject.files.wordpress.com/2011/04/ecthrlegitimacyreport.pdf

De Vos, C, 'From Rights to Remedies: Structures and Strategies for Implementing International Human Rights Decisions' (Open Society Justice Initiative, New York, 2013)

Fox, R and Korris, M, *Making Better Law: Reform of the Legislative Process from Policy to Act* (London, Hansard Society, 2009)

Hammarberg, T, 'National Parliaments Can Do More to Promote Human Rights' (Strasbourg Commissioner for Human Rights for the Council of Europe, 16 February 2009)

Hansard Society, *Representative Democracy: Briefing Paper 1: House of Commons Reform* (London, Hansard Society, 2009)

Inter-Parliamentary Union, *Parliament: Guardian of Human Rights* (1993)

JUSTICE, 'Auditing for Rights: Developing Scrutiny Systems for Human Rights Compliance' (JUSTICE, 2001)

National Democratic Institute for International Affairs, *Parliamentary Human Rights Committees* (2004)

New Labour, *Bringing Rights Home: Labour's Plans to Incorporate the European Convention on Human Rights into UK Law* (Cm 3782, 1997)

Nowak, M, *Human Rights: A Handbook for Parliamentarians* (Geneva, IPU/UNHCHR, 2005) 'Scrutiny of Legislation for Consistency with Obligations under the European Convention on Human Rights', memorandum by Lords Irvine, Simon, Alexander and Lester (1994)

Strengthening Parliament as a Guardian of Human Rights: The Role of Parliamentary Human Rights Bodies, Reports and Documents of a Seminar for Chairpersons and Members of Parliamentary Human Rights Bodies organised by the Inter-Parliamentary

Union (IPU) and the United Nations Development Programme (UNDP) with the support of the Office of the United Nations High Commissioner for Human Rights (OHCHR), Geneva, 15–17 March 2004

UNDP Primer on Parliaments and Human Rights (United Nations Development Program, New York, 2004)

The Westminster Consortium/International Bar Association, Human Rights and Parliaments: Handbook for Members and Staff (2011)

World Bank Parliamentary Staff Training Program, *Human Rights* (Washington DC, World Bank Institute, 2009)

Wright Committee, *Rebuilding the House* (2009)

Index